**English Grammar And Analysis, By W.
Davidson And J.c. Alcock. [with] Key**

# Davidson and Alcock's
# EDUCATIONAL WORKS.

1. **A First English Grammar and Analysis.**
   32 pages, price 2d.

2. **An Intermediate English Grammar and Analysis.**
   80 pages, price 6d.

3. **English Grammar and Analysis,** with copious Exercises and Examination Papers. 256 pages, strongly bound, price 2s.

4. **Complete Manual of Parsing.**
   New edition. 204 pages, strongly bound, price 1s. 6d.

5. **Complete Manual of Analysis and Paraphrasing.**
   232 pages, price 2s.

6. **Key to English Grammar and Analysis.**
   Strongly bound, price 5s.

*Just published, price 1s. each.*

**Allman's Parsing Copy Book,** with Full Instructions for Use.

**Allman's Copy Book of Grammatical Analysis,** with Full Instructions for Use.

LONDON:
T. J. ALLMAN, 463, OXFORD STREET.

# KEY

TO

# ENGLISH GRAMMAR AND ANALYSIS.

BY

WILLIAM DAVIDSON, B.A. (Lond.),

AND

JOSEPH CROSBY ALCOCK,

AUTHORS OF
"THE COMPLETE MANUAL OF PARSING," "ENGLISH GRAMMAR AND ANALYSIS,"
"FIRST ENGLISH GRAMMAR AND ANALYSIS," "INTERMEDIATE
ENGLISH GRAMMAR AND ANALYSIS," AND "COMPLETE
MANUAL OF ANALYSIS AND PARAPHRASING."

LONDON:
T. J. ALLMAN, 463, OXFORD STREET.

# ABBREVIATIONS.

| | | | |
|---|---|---|---|
| Abs. | Abstract. | Jg. | Joining. |
| Act. | Active. | Lim. | Limiting. |
| Add. | Address. | M. | Mood. |
| Adj. | Adjective. | Man. | Manner. |
| Adv. | Adverb. | Mas. | Masculine. |
| Aff. | Affirmation. | Mea. | Measure. |
| Agr. | Agreeing. | Mod. | Modifying. |
| Ant. | Antecedent. | N. | Noun. |
| App. | Apposition. | Neg. | Negation. |
| Bet. | Between. | Neu. | Neuter. |
| C. | Case. | Nom. | Nominative. |
| Card. | Cardinal. | Nu. | Numeral. |
| Col. | Collective. | Num. | Number. |
| Com. | Common. | Obj. | Objective. |
| Comp. | Comparative. | Ord. | Ordinal. |
| Compd. | Compound. | P. | Plural. |
| Compl. | Complementary. | Pass. | Passive. |
| Conj. | Conjunction. | Per. | Person. |
| Co-ord. | Co-ordinate. | Perf. | Perfect. |
| Cop. | Copulative. | Pers. | Personal. |
| Cor. | Correlative. | Pl. | Participle. |
| Def. | Definite. | Pluperf. | Pluperfect. |
| Defec. | Defective. | Pos. | Positive. |
| Deg. | Degree. | Poss. | Possessive. |
| Dir. | Direct. | Pot. | Potential. |
| Dis. | Distinguishing. | Prep. | Preposition. |
| Disj. | Disjunctive. | Pres. | Present. |
| Dist. | Distributive. | Prog. | Progressive. |
| Emph. | Emphatic. | Pron. | Pronoun. |
| Equiv. | Equivalent. | Prop. | Proper. |
| Fem. | Feminine. | Qual. | Qualifying. |
| Fut. | Future. | Ref. | Referring. |
| Gen. | Gender. | Reg. | Regular. |
| Ger. | Gerund. | Rel. | Relative. |
| Gov. | Governed. | Rn. | Relation. |
| Imper. | Imperative. | S. | Singular. |
| Imperf. | Imperfect. | Sent. | Sentence. |
| Incl. | Included. | Sents. | Sentences. |
| Indef. | Indefinite. | Sh. | Showing. |
| Indg. | Indicating. | Subj. | Subjunctive. |
| Indic. | Indicative. | Superl. | Superlative. |
| Indir. | Indirect. | T. | Tense. |
| Infin. | Infinitive. | Tr. | Transitive. |
| Interj. | Interjection. | Und. | Understood. |
| Interrog. | Interrogative. | V. | Verb. |
| Intr. | Intransitive. | Vo. | Voice. |
| Irreg. | Irregular. | | |

# KEY
## TO
# ENGLISH GRAMMAR AND ANALYSIS.

N.B.—Where an alternative method of parsing may be used, it is either supplied in the "Key," or a reference is given to the "Complete Manual of Parsing."

### Exercise 1.

1. *In the school-room:*  Desk, map, book, slate, form, &c.
2. *In the house:*  Chair, table, knife, fork, plate, &c.
3. *In the country:*  Field, hedge, farm, bird, tree, &c.
4. *In the town:*  House, street, shop, market, &c.
5. *In a joiner's shop:*  Plane, chisel, hammer, plank, &c.
6. *In a railway station:*  Engine, carriage, rails, platform, &c.

### Exercise 2.

1. *Six persons:*  Thomas, James, Margaret, Nelson, Rupert, Stephen.
2. *Six places:*  Newcastle, London, Dublin, Paris, Constantinople, Bristol.
3. *Six animals:*  Cow, stag, horse, pig, dog, cat.
4. *Six rivers:*  Thames, Danube, Amazon, Nile, Tyne, Severn.
5. *Six mountains:*  Snowdon, Skiddaw, Ben Nevis, Plinlimmon, Helvellyn, Cross Fell.
6. *Six flowers:*  Rose, lily, tulip, daisy, cowslip, violet.

### Exercise 3.

1. Bird, tree. 2. Bee, honey, flowers. 3. George, apple. 4. Mary, stockings, brother. 5. Fox, crow. 6. Rats, ship. 7. Lamb, mountain. 8. Sparrow, cage, window. 9. Napoleon, Waterloo. 10. Children, table. 11. Bells.

### Exercise 4.

1. Barks. 2. Screams. 3. Twitters. 4. Sings. 5. Laughs. 6. Flows. 7. Build. 8. Soars. 9. Runs. 10. Shines. 11. Loves. 12. Roared. 13. Brought. 14. Reads. 15. Crossed. 16. Tends.

## Exercise 5.

1. The *sun* shines. 2. The maiden *sings*. 3. The dog *barks*. 4. The knife *cuts*. 5. The printer *works*. 6. The weaver *sits*. 7. The sister *knits*. 8. The heart *beats*. 9. The needle *breaks*. 10. The crow *flies*. 11. The nail *rusts*. 12. The kite *rises*. 13. The mole *eats*. 14. The snake *bites*. 15. The rain *falls*. 16. The gate *opens*. 17. The sea *foams*. 18. The night *approaches*. 19. The plant *grows*. 20. The farmer *sows*. 21. The blacksmith *strikes*. 22. The hen *cackles*. 23. The eagle *soars*. 24. The lamb *bleats*. 25. The wasp *stings*. 26. The worm *moves*. 27. The scholar *learns*. 28. The crowd *departs*. 29. The butterfly *flutters*. 30. The miller *grinds*.

## Exercise 6.

1. *Cork* floats. 2. The *swallow* skims. 3. The *child* creeps. 4. The *bird* flies. 5. *Mary* dances. 6. The *sun* sets. 7. The *wind* blows. 8. The *king* dies. 9. The *dyer* dyes. 10. The *girl* smiles. 11. The *boy* trembled. 12. The *cat* mews. 13. The *artist* paints. 14. The *lion* roars. 15. The *corn* grows. 16. The *farmer* sows. 17. The *miller* grinds. 18. The *scholar* is praised. 19. The *key* was lost. 20. *Fire* burns. 21. The *ox* was bought. 22. The *widow* mourns. 23. The *mouse* nibbles. 24. The *lady* walks. 25. The *sluggard* is blamed. 26. The *postman* knocks. 27. The *bugle* sounded. 28. The *mason* builds. 29. The *messenger* watched. 30. The *scythe* cuts. 31. The *Nile* overflows.

## Exercise 7.

*The Adjectives are in Italics, and the words qualified or limited follow.*

1. *The* king, *powerful* king. 2. *The* night, *long* night, *cold* night. 3. *A* scene, *frightful* scene. 4. *Many* trees, *large* trees, *orange* trees, *the* ground. 5. *Great* throne, *the* throne. 6. *The* streets, *empty* streets. 7. *Rough* shelves, *the* books. 8. *A* suit, *black* velvet. 9. *Drowsy* tinklings, *the* folds, *distant* folds. 10. *The* birds, *wild* birds, *warbling* tale. 11. *The* winds, *soft* winds, *low* winds. 12. *Noisy* groups, *the* house-doors, *the* sun, *cheerful* sun.

NOTE.—In such examples as 3 and 4 where more than one adjective precedes a noun, it would, perhaps, in parsing the first adjective, be more correct to regard the noun and intervening adjective or adjectives as forming a compound, qualified or limited by the first adjective. It is, however, more convenient to parse each adjective as qualifying the noun only.

## Exercise 8.

1. *A large* oak. 2. *The blue* sky. 3. *Sweet* honey. 4. *Good* bread. 5. *A dark* eye. 6. *An immense* desert. 7. *An iron* ship. 8. *Brown* sand. 9. *A clever* surgeon. 10. *A long* chain. 11. *A hard* pencil. 12. *The open* window. 13. *A ripe* cherry. 14. *A white* hand. 15. *Numerous* herds. 16. *Powerful* wings. 17. *A strong* current. 18. *A wise* man. 19. *A dull* day. 20. *A bright* colour. 21. *Fine* dust. 22. *A little* fly. 23. *A straw* hive. 24. *A pretty* village. 25. *A clear* lake. 26. *A short* tail. 27. *An old* tortoise. 28. *A rapid* stream. 29. *A fertile* meadow. 30. *A beautiful* rainbow.

### Exercise 9.

1. A huge *mountain*. 2. An open *door*. 3. A wonderful *story*. 4. Sixty *men*. 5. A rosy *cheek*. 6. A lame *boy*. 7. A low *house*. 8. A little *dog*. 9. A great *king*. 10. A busy *woman*. 11. A poor *child*. 12. A glittering *sea*. 13. The painted *door*. 14. A blue *dress*. 15. A round *table*. 16. A snowy *day*. 17. A golden *cloud*. 18. A distant *country*. 19. A sweet *plum*. 20. A soft *cushion*. 21. An old *barn*. 22. A warm *fire*. 23. A wooden *bowl*. 24. A young *mouse*. 25. A happy *girl*. 26. A loud *cry*. 27. A green *field*. 28. A wild *ass*. 29. A withered *leaf*. 30. A yellow *rose*.

### Exercise 10.

1. Over *the* (adj.) *joyous* (adj.) *feast* (n.) *the* (adj.) *sudden* (adj.) *darkness* (n.) *descended* (v.). 2. *The* (adj.) *old* (adj.) *man* (n.) *lay* (v.) down on *the* (adj.) *bare* (adj.) *ground* (n.). 3. *Philip* (n.) *saw* (v.) *the* (adj.) *bright* (adj.) *loving* (adj.) *smile* (n.). 4. *The* (adj.) *dark* (adj.) *walls* (n.) of *the* (adj.) *castle* (n.) *frowned* (v.) against *the* (adj.) *soft* (adj.) *blue* (adj.) *sky* (n.). 5. She *reached* (v.) *the* (adj.) *narrow* (adj.) *porch* (n.) and *the* (adj.) *tall* (adj.) *door* (n.). 6. *The* (adj.) *leafless* (adj.) *tree* (n.) *waves* (v.) in *the* (adj.) *raging* (adj.) *storm* (n.). 7. *Rank* (adj.) *weeds* (n.) and *grasses* (n.) *careless* (adj.) and *nodding* (adj.) *grew* (v.) where *Romans* (n.) *trembled* (v.). 8. I *hear* (v.) *the* (adj.) *merry* (adj.) *sound* (n.) of *tinkling* (adj.) *bells* (n.). 9. *A* (adj.) *few* (adj.) *dry* (adj.) *sticks* (n.) *gave* (v.) us *a* (adj.) *cheerful* (adj.) *blaze* (n.) in *the* (adj.) *open* (adj.) *air* (n.). 10. With *a* (adj.) *small* (adj.) *knife* (n.) *the* (adj.) *traveller* (n.) *cut* (v.) off *a* (adj.) *large* (adj.) *cluster* (n.) of *ripe* (adj.) *grapes* (n.).

### Exercise 11.

1. He. 2. We, it. 3. Me, you, that. 4. I, my. 5. Us. 6. We, him, his. 7. Its. 8. It. 9. They. 10. She, her, her.

### Exercise 12.

1. Hedgehogs rob orchards and carry away apples sticking to *their* spines in order that *they* may hoard *them* up for the winter. 2. The cowslips hold up *their* heads. 3. The hen sits upon *her* nest. 4. The king sat on *his* throne : *it* was made of gold. 5. The lark builds *her* nest amongst the grass, and *she* feeds *her* young ones daily.

### Exercise 13.

1. *I* (pron.) once *stopped* (v.) *a* (adj.) *deaf* (adj.) and *dumb* (adj.) *boy* (n.). 2. *He* (pron.) *wages* (v.) *perpetual* (adj.) *war* (n.) on *the* (adj.) *seal* (n.) and *walrus* (n.). 3. *They* (pron.) *say* (v.) *it* (pron.) *stirs* (v.) *the* (adj.) *sluggish* (adj.) *blood* (n.). 4. *They* (pron.) *are shooting* (v.) *the* (adj.) *poor* (adj.) *birds* (n.). 5. *We* (pron.) *gather* (v.) *ripe* (adj.) *apples* (n.). 6. *I* (pron.) *saw* (v.) *many* (adj.) *flowering* (adj.) *limes* (n.) and *weeping* (adj.) *willows* (n.). 7. *He* (pron.) *has given* (v.) *him* (pron.) *a* (adj.) *large* (adj.) *penknife* (n.). 8. *She* (pron.) *opened* (v.) *her* (pron.) *door* (n.) to *the* (adj.) *weary* (adj.) *woman* (n.).

### Exercise 14.

*The Adverbs are in Italics and the modified words follow.*

1. *Brightly* shone. 2. *Softly* slept. 3. *Silently* went, *sadly* went; *back* went, *again* went. 4. *To-morrow* will write. 5. *Softly* step, *low* speak. 6. *Again* came. 7. *Here* will arrive, *to-day* will arrive. 8. *Too* rich. 9. *Very* badly, *badly* reads. 10. *Extremely* fast, *fast* runs. 11. *Very* loudly, *loudly* roars. 12. *Exceedingly* deep.

### Exercise 15.

I. 1. The horse trots *quickly*. 2. The dog barks *furiously*. 3. The moon shines *brightly*. 4. The serpent hisses *angrily*. 5. The lightning flashes *incessantly*. 6. The bird flies *swiftly*.
II. 1. The day is *rather* cool. 2. The sea is *exceedingly* smooth. 3. The leaves are *very* green. 4. The boy is *remarkably* diligent. 5. The wall is *excessively* high. 6. The well is *extremely* deep.
III. 1. John writes *very* ill. 2. The gardener works *exceedingly* hard. 3. The river runs *too* slowly. 4. He came *quite* recently. 5. The swallow flies *very* swiftly. 6. The mother treads *very* softly.

### Exercise 16.

1. *The* (adj.) *gardens* (n.) *were fringed* (v.) *usually* (adv.) with *nettles* (n.). 2. *I* (pron.) *see* (v.) *my* (pron.) *sister* (n.) *there* (adv.) *again* (adv.). 3. *He* (pron.) *walked* (v.) *cheerfully* (adv.) *onward* (adv.) through *the* (adj.) *green* (adj.) *fields* (n.). 4. *My* (pron.) *father* (n.) *always* (adv.) *rose* (v.) at *dawn* (n.). 5. *She* (pron.) *drank* (v.) *very* (adv.) *weak* (adj.) *tea* (n.) from *an* (adj.) *extremely* (adv.) *large* (adj.) *cup* (n.). 6. *I* (pron.) *know* (v.) *it* (pron.) *too* (adv.) *well* (adv.). 7. *They* (pron.) *sleep* (v.) *soundly* (adv.) upon *their* (pron.) *downy* (adj.) *beds* (n.). 8. *The* (adj.) *new* (adj.) *servant* (n.) *presently* (adv.) *brought* (v.) *the* (adj.) *breakfast* (n.) into *the* (adj.) *cheerful* (adj.) *room* (n.).

### Exercise 17.

*Each Preposition is placed between the words it relates.*

1. Riders *on* asses, hurry *along* river-side. 2. Flowed *at* distance, distance *from* them. 3. Flutter *from* bush, flutter *to* bush. 4. Careth *for* sheep, bringeth *to* fold. 5. Knell *of* day. 6. Walked *with* pace. 7. Flew *over* summit, summit *of* mountain. 8. Beat *against* panes. 9. Was followed *by* dog. 10. Lay *along* foot, foot *of* hills.

### Exercise 18.

1. *Brave* (adj.) *Urien* (n.) *sleeps* (v.) *upon* (prep.) *his* (pron.) *craggy* (adj.) *bed* (n.). 2. *The* (adj.) *way* (n.) *to* (prep.) *London* (n.) *is* (v.) *long* (adj.) *and* (conj.) *difficult* (adj.). 3. *Blue* (adj.) *wreaths* (n.) *of* (prep.) *smoke* (n.) *ascend* (v.) *through* (prep.) *the* (adj.) *trees* (n.). 4. *The* (adj.) *vessel* (n.) *rose* (v.) *upon* (prep.) *its* (pron.) *prow* (n.). 5. *They* (pron.) *travelled* (v.) *by* (prep.) *land* (n.). 6. *The* (adj.) *road* (n.) *wound* (v.) *at* (prep.) *times* (n.) *through* (prep.) *dreary* (adj.) *woods* (n.). 7. *He* (pron.) *immediately* (adv.) *dropped* (v.) *on* (prep.) *his* (pron.) *knees* (n.). 8. *We* (pron.) *found* (v.) *him* (pron.) *in* (prep.) *an* (adj.) *open* (adj.) *place* (n.) *in*

(prep.) *the* (adj.) *wood* (n.). 9. *In* (prep.) *a* (adj.) *dream* (n.) *of* (prep.) *the* (adj.) *night* (n.) *I* (pron.) *was wafted* (v.) *away* (adv.). 10. *Afar* (adv.) *in* (prep.) *the* (adj.) *desert* (n.) *I* (pron.) *love* (v.) *to ride* (v.). 11. *They* (pron.) *are flashing* (v.) *down* (adv.) *from* (prep.) *the* (adj.) *mountain-brows* (n.).

### Exercise 19.

*Each Conjunction is placed, in Italics, between the sentences it joins.*

1. The sun had set, *but* still the visitor tarried. 2. She bowed her head *and* [she] departed. 3. You see *that* he deceives you. 4. He came, *yet* I saw him not. 5. What is sweeter *than* honey [is sweet]? 6. *Neither** music [pleased him] *nor* painting pleased him. 7. He came *because* his master required him.

* The conjunction *neither* introduces the sentence " music pleased him."

### Exercise 20.

1. *Lend* (v.) *thy* (pron.) *power* (n.), *and* (conj.) *lend* (v.) *thine* (pron.) *ear* (n.). 2. *He* (pron.) *trembled* (v.) *when* (conj.) *the* (adj.) *crowd* (n.) *gazed* (v.) *upon* (prep.) *him* (pron.). 3. *He* (pron.) *went* (v.) *to* (prep.) *London* (n.), *but* (conj.) *on* (prep.) *his* (pron.) *return* (n.) *he* (pron.) *died* (v.). 4. *He* (pron.) *brings* (v.) *them* (pron.) *where·* (conj.) *the* (adj.) *quiet* (adj.) *waters* (n.) *glide* (v.). 5. *They* (pron.) *separated* (v.) *before* (conj.) *their* (pron.) *father* (n.) *arrived* (v.). 6. *The* (adj.) *king* (n.) *either* (conj.) *governed* (v.) *badly* (adv.) *or* (conj.) *his* (pron.) *ministers* (n.) *failed* (v.) *in* (prep.) *their* (pron.) *duty* (n.). 7. *The* (adj.) *simple* (adj.) *peasant* (n.) *obeyed* (v.) *his* (pron.) *master* (n.) *cheerfully* (adv.) *because* (conj.) *he* (pron.) *loved* (v.) *him* (pron.). 8. *My* (pron.) *heart* (n.) *leaps* (v.) *up* (adv.) *when* (conj.) *I* (pron.) *behold* (v.) *a* (adj.) *rainbow* (n.) *in* (prep.) *the* (adj.) *sky* (n.).

### Exercise 21.

1. O! 2. Lo! 3. Hark! 4. Hurrah! 5. Hush! 6. Bravo! 7. Oh! 8. Behold! 9. Ho! 10. Hail!

### Exercise 22.

1. *Oh !* (interj.) *speak* (v.) *again* (adv.) *bright* (adj.) *angel* (n.). 2. *O* (interj.) *father !* (n.) *I* (pron.) *hear* (v.) *the* (adj.) *sound* (n.) *of* (prep.) *guns* (n.). 3. *Hark !* (interj.) *what* (adj.) *murmurs* (n.) *arise* (v.) *from* (prep.) *the* (adj.) *heart* (n.) *of* (prep.) *those* (adj.) *mountainous* (adj.) *deserts* (n.). 4. *Ah !* (interj.) *no* (adv.) *longer* (adv.) *wizard* (adj.) *fancy* (n.) *builds* (v.) *its* (pron.) *castles* (n.) *in* (prep.) *the* (adj.) *air* (n.). 5. *Indeed !* (interj.) *you* (pron.) *greatly* (adv.) *surprise* (v.) *me* (pron.), *for* (conj.) *the* (adj.) *soldier* (n.) *never* (adv.) *mentioned* (v.) *it* (pron.). 6. *Hurrah !* (interj.) *the* (adj.) *fight* (n.) *begins* (v.) *and* (conj.) *the* (adj.) *enemy* (n.) *wavers* (v.) 7. *Merrily* (adv.), *O* (interj.) *merrily* (adv.), *chime* (v.) *the* (adj.) *bells* (n.) *from* (prep.) *the* (adj.) *old* (adj.) *church* (adj.) *tower* (n.).

### Exercise 23.

| 1. Suddenly | An adv., | because it modifies the v. " uttered." |
| the | An adj., | ,, limits the n. " animal." |
| poor | An adj., | ,, qualifies the n. " animal." |

| | | | |
|---|---|---|---|
| animal | A n., | because | it is a name. |
| uttered | A v., | ,, | says what the animal did. |
| a | An adj., | ,, | limits the n. "howl." |
| shrill | An adj., | ,, | qualifies the n. "howl." |
| howl | A n., | ,, | is a name. |
| and | A conj., | ,, | joins the sents. "Suddenly the poor animal uttered a shrill howl" and "*the poor animal* threw himself into the water." |
| threw | A v., | because | it says what the animal did. |
| himself | A pron., | ,, | is used instead of the n. "animal." |
| into | A prep., | ,, | shows the rn. bet. "threw" and "water." |
| the | An adj., | ,, | limits the n. "water." |
| water. | A n., | ,, | is a name. |
| 2. It | A pron., | ,, | is used instead of the n. "*river.*" |
| flows | A v., | ,, | says what it does. |
| with | A prep., | ,, | shows the rn. bet. "flows" and "stream." |
| a | An adj., | ,, | limits the n. "stream." |
| gentle | An adj., | ,, | qualifies the n. "stream." |
| stream | A n., | ,, | is a name. |
| through | A prep., | ,, | shows the rn. bet. "flows" and "country." |
| the | An adj., | ,, | limits the n. "country." |
| flat | An adj., | ,, | qualifies the n. "country." |
| country. | A n., | ,, | is a name. |
| 3. Laziness | A n., | ,, | is a name. |
| travels | A v., | ,, | says what laziness does. |
| so | An adv., | ,, | modifies the adv. "slowly." |
| slowly | An adv., | ,, | modifies the v. "travels." |
| that | A conj., | ,, | joins the sents. "Laziness travels so slowly" and "poverty soon overtakes it." |
| poverty | A n., | because | it is a name. |
| soon | An adv., | ,, | modifies the v. "overtakes." |
| overtakes | A v., | ,, | says what poverty does. |
| it. | A pron., | ,, | is used instead of the n. "Laziness." |
| 4. The | An adj., | ,, | limits the n. "lobsters." |
| young | An adj., | ,, | qualifies the n. "lobsters." |
| lobsters | A n., | ,, | is a name. |
| leave | A v., | ,, | says what lobsters do. |
| the | An adj., | ,, | limits the n. "parent." |
| parent | A n., | ,, | is a name. |
| and | A conj., | ,, | joins the sents. "The young lobsters leave the parent" and "*the young lobsters* immediately seek for refuge in the smallest clefts of rocks." |
| immediately | An adv., | because | it modifies the v. "seek." |
| seek | A v., | ,, | says what the lobsters do. |
| for | A prep., | ,, | shows the rn. bet. "seek" and "refuge." |
| refuge | A n., | ,, | is a name. |
| in | A prep., | ,, | shows the rn. bet. "seek" and "refuge." |
| the | An adj., | ,, | limits the n. "clefts." |
| smallest | An adj., | ,, | qualifies the n. "clefts." |
| clefts | A n., | ,, | is a name. |
| of | A prep., | ,, | shows the rn. bet. "clefts" and "rocks." |
| rocks | A n., | ,, | is a name. |
| and | A conj., | ,, | joins the sents. "*the young lobsters* immediately seek for refuge in the smallest clefts of rocks" and "*the young lobsters immediately seek for refuge* in crevices at the bottom of the sea." |
| in | A prep., | because | it shows the rn. bet. "seek" and "crevices." |
| crevices | A n., | ,, | is a name. |
| at | A prep., | ,, | shows the rn. bet. "crevices" and "bottom." |
| the | An adj., | ,, | limits the n. "bottom." |
| bottom | A n., | ,, | is a name. |
| of | A prep., | ,, | shows the rn. bet. "bottom" and "sea." |
| the | An adj., | ,, | limits the n. "sea." |
| sea. | A n., | ,, | is a name. |
| 5. The | An adj., | ,, | limits the n. "boy." |
| boy | A n., | ,, | is a name. |
| stood | A v., | ,, | says what the boy did. |
| on | A prep., | ,, | shows the rn. bet. "stood" and "deck." |

ENGLISH GRAMMAR AND ANALYSIS. 15

| | | | |
|---|---|---|---|
| the | An adj., | because it | limits the n. "deck." |
| burning | An adj., | ,, | qualifies the n. "deck." |
| deck. | A n., | ,, | is a name. |
| 6. We | A pron., | ,, | is used instead of a name. |
| buried | A v., | ,, | says what we did. |
| him | A pron., | ,, | is used instead of the n. "Sir John Moore." |
| darkly | An adv., | ,, | modifies the v. "buried." |
| at | A prep., | ,, | shows the rn. bet. "buried" and "dead." |
| dead | A n., | ,, | is a name. |
| of | A prep., | ,, | shows the rn. bet. "dead" and "night." |
| night. | A n., | ,, | is a name. |
| 7. Slowly | An adv., | ,, | modifies the verb *laid*. |
| and | A conj., | ,, | joins the sents. "Slowly *we laid him down*" and "*sadly we laid him down*." |
| sadly | An adv., | because it | modifies the verb "laid." |
| we | A pron., | ,, | is used instead of a name. |
| laid | A v., | ,, | says what we did. |
| him | A pron., | ,, | is used instead of the n. "Sir John Moore." |
| down. | An adv., | ,, | modifies the v. "laid." |
| 8. His | A pron., | ,, | is used instead of a name. |
| horsemen | A n., | ,, | is a name. |
| hard | An adv., | ,, | modifies the v. "ride." |
| behind | A prep., | ,, | shows the rn. bet. "ride" and "us." |
| us | A pron., | ,, | is used instead of a name. |
| ride. | A v., | ,, | says what the horsemen do. |
| 9. The | An adj., | ,, | limits the n. "trumpets." |
| trumpets | A n., | ,, | is a name. |
| sound | A v., | ,, | says what the trumpets do. |
| the | An adj., | ,, | limits the n. "charge." |
| charge | A n., | ,, | is a name. |
| and | A conj., | ,, | joins the sents. "The trumpets sound the charge" and "*the trumpets sound* the retreat." |
| the | An adj., | because it | limits the n. "retreat." |
| retreat. | A n., | ,, | is a name. |
| 10. Then | An adv., | ,, | modifies the v. "tracked." |
| downwards | An adv., | ,, | modifies the v. "tracked." |
| from | A prep., | ,, | shows the rn. bet. "tracked" and "edge." |
| the | An adj., | ,, | limits the n. "hill's." |
| steep | An adj., | ,, | qualifies the n. "hill's." |
| hill's | A n., | ,, | is a name. |
| edge | A n., | ,, | is a name. |
| They | A pron., | ,, | is used instead of a name. |
| tracked | A v., | ,, | says what they did. |
| the | An adj., | ,, | limits the n. "footmarks." |
| footmarks | A n., | ,, | is a name. |
| small | An adj., | ,, | qualifies the n. "footmarks." |
| And | A conj., | ,, | joins the sents. "Then downwards from the steep hill's edge They tracked the footmarks small" and "*they tracked the footmarks small* through the broken hawthorn hedge." |
| through | A prep., | because it | shows the rn. bet. "*tracked*" and "hedge." |
| the | An adj., | ,, | limits the n. "hedge." |
| broken | An adj., | ,, | qualifies the n. "hedge." |
| hawthorn | An adj., | ,, | qualifies the n. "hedge." |
| hedge | A n., | ,, | is a name. |
| And | A conj., | ,, | joins the sents. "*They tracked the footmarks small* through the broken hawthorn hedge" and "*they tracked the footmarks small* by the long stone wall." |
| by | A prep., | because it | shows the rn. bet. "*tracked*" and "wall." |
| the | An adj., | ,, | limits the n. "wall." |
| long | An adj., | ,, | qualifies the n, "wall." |
| stone | An adj., | ,, | qualifies the n. "wall." |
| wall. | A n., | ,, | is a name. |

### Exercise 24.

| | | | |
|---|---|---|---|
| 1. Her | A pron., | because it | is used instead of a name. |
| thunders | A n., | ,, | is a name. |

| | | | |
|---|---|---|---|
| shook | A v., | because | it says what the thunders did. |
| the | An adj., | ,, | limits the n. "deep." |
| mighty | An adj., | ,, | qualifies the n. "deep." |
| deep. | A n., | ,, | is a name. |
| 2. The | An adj., | ,, | limits the n. "harpies." |
| harpies | A n., | ,, | is a name. |
| of | A prep., | ,, | shows the rn. bet. "harpies" and "shore." |
| the | An adj., | ,, | limits the n. "shore." |
| shore | A n., | ,, | is a name. |
| shall pluck | A v., | ,, | says what the harpies shall do. |
| the | An adj., | ,, | limits the n. "eagle." |
| eagle | A n., | ,, | is a name. |
| of | A prep., | ,, | shows the rn. bet. "eagle" and "sea." |
| the | An adj., | ,, | limits the n. "sea." |
| sea. | A n., | ,, | is a name. |
| 3. I | A pron., | ,, | is used instead of a name. |
| wandered | A v., | ,, | says what I did. |
| far | An adv., | ,, | modifies the v. "wandered." |
| into | A prep., | ,, | shows the rn. bet. "wandered" and "prairie." |
| the | An adj., | ,, | limits the n. "prairie." |
| bare | An adj., | ,, | qualifies the n. "prairie." |
| prairie. | A n., | ,, | is a name. |
| 4. He | A pron., | ,, | is used instead of a name. |
| sometimes | An adv., | ,, | modifies the v. "contemplated." |
| contemplated | A v., | ,, | says what he did. |
| the | An adj., | ,, | limits the n. "height." |
| towering | An adj., | ,, | qualifies the n. "height." |
| height | A n., | ,, | is a name. |
| of | A prep., | ,, | shows the rn. bet. "height" and "oak." |
| the | An adj., | ,, | limits the n. "oak." |
| oak. | A n., | ,, | is a name. |
| 5. Her | A pron., | ,, | is used instead of a name. |
| tears | A n., | ,, | is a name. |
| fell | A v., | ,, | says what tears did. |
| with | A prep., | ,, | shows the rn. bet. "fell" and "dews." |
| the | An adj., | ,, | limits the n. "dews." |
| dews | A n., | ,, | is a name. |
| at | A prep., | ,, | shows the rn. bet. "fell" and "even." |
| even. | A n., | ,, | is a name. |
| 6. Day | A n., | ,, | is a name. |
| and | A conj., | ,, | joins the sents. "*the fountain calls to the billow during the* day" and "the fountain calls to the billow *during the* night." |
| night | A n., | because | it is a name. |
| to | A prep., | ,, | shows the rn. bet. "calls" and "billow." |
| the | An adj., | ,, | limits the n. "billow." |
| billow | A n., | ,, | is a name. |
| the | An adj., | ,, | limits the n. "fountain." |
| fountain | A n., | ,, | is a name. |
| calls. | A v., | ,, | says what the fountain does. |
| 7. Mariner | A n., | ,, | is a name. |
| mariner | A n., | ,, | is a name. |
| furl | A v., | ,, | says what the mariner is to do. |
| your | A pron., | ,, | is used instead of the n. "mariner's." |
| sails. | A n., | ,, | is a name. |
| 8. The | An adj., | ,, | limits the n. "wind." |
| wind | A n., | ,, | is a name. |
| blows | A v., | ,, | says what the wind does. |
| softly | An adv., | ,, | modifies the v. "blows." |
| round | A prep., | ,, | shows the rn. bet. "blows" and "wold." |
| the | An adj., | ,, | limits the n. "wold." |
| open | An adj., | ,, | qualifies the n. "wold." |
| wold. | A n., | ,, | is a name. |
| 9. The | An adj., | ,, | limits the n. "light." |
| light | A n., | ,, | is a name. |
| of | A prep., | ,, | shows the rn. bet. "light" and "candles." |
| candles | A n., | ,, | is a name. |
| is | A v., | ,, | asserts. |

| | | | |
|---|---|---|---|
| dim | An adj., | because it qualifies the n. "light." | |
| unwholesome | An adj., | ,, | qualifies the n. "light." |
| hurtful | An adj., | ,, | qualifies the n. "light." |
| to | A prep., | ,, | shows the rn. bet. "hurtful" and "eyes." |
| the | An adj., | ,, | limits the n. "eyes." |
| eyes | A n., | ,, | is a name. |
| and | A conj., | ,, | joins the sents. "*the light of candles is* hurtful to the eyes" and "*the light of candles is* expensive." |
| expensive | An adj., | because it qualifies the n. "light." | |
| the | An adj., | ,, | limits the n. "light." |
| light | A n., | ,, | is a name. |
| of | A prep., | ,, | shows the rn. bet. "light" and "sun." |
| the | An adj., | ,, | limits the n. "sun." |
| sun | A n., | ,, | is a name. |
| is | A v., | ,, | asserts. |
| strong | An adj., | ,, | qualifies the n. "light." |
| pleasant | An adj., | ,, | qualifies the n. "light." |
| wholesome | An adj., | ,, | qualifies the n. "light." |
| and | A conj., | ,, | joins the sents. "*the light of the sun is* wholesome" and "*it costs nothing.*" |
| it | A pron., | because it is used instead of the n. "light." | |
| costs | A v., | ,, | asserts. |
| nothing. | A n., | ,, | is a name. |
| 10. The | An adj., | ,, | limits the n. "grandee." |
| proud | An adj., | ,, | qualifies the n. "grandee." |
| grandee | A n., | ,, | is a name. |
| still | An adv., | ,, | modifies the v. "lingers." |
| lingers | A v., | ,, | says what the grandee does. |
| in | A prep., | ,, | shows the rn. bet. "lingers" and "saloons." |
| his | A pron., | ,, | is used instead of the n. "grandee's." |
| perfumed | An adj., | ,, | qualifies the n. "saloons." |
| saloons | A n., | ,, | is a name. |
| or | A conj., | ,, | joins the sents. "The proud grandee still lingers in his perfumed saloons" and "*the proud grandee* reposes within damask curtains." |
| reposes | A v., | because it says what the grandee does. | |
| within | A prep., | ,, | shows the rn. bet. "reposes" and "curtains." |
| damask | An adj., | ,, | qualifies the n. "curtains." |
| curtains. | A n., | ,, | is a name. |
| 11. He | A pron., | ,, | is used instead of a name. |
| springs | A v., | ,, | says what he does. |
| from | A prep., | ,, | shows the rn. bet. "springs" and "hammock." |
| the | An adj., | because it limits the n. "hammock." | |
| hammock | A n., | ,, | is a name. |
| he | A pron., | ,, | is used instead of a name. |
| flies | A v., | ,, | says what he does. |
| to | A prep., | ,, | shows the rn. bet. "flies" and "deck." |
| the | An adj., | ,, | limits the n. "deck." |
| deck | A n., | ,, | is a name. |
| Amazement | A n., | ,, | is a name. |
| confronts | A v., | ,, | says what amazement does. |
| him | A pron., | ,, | is used instead of a name. |
| with | A prep., | ,, | shows the rn. bet. "confronts" and "images." |
| images | A n., | ,, | is a name. |
| dire | An adj., | ,, | qualifies the n. "images." |
| Wild | An adj., | ,, | qualifies the n. "winds." |
| winds | A n., | ,, | is a name. |
| and | A conj., | ,; | joins the sents. "Wild winds *drive the vessel a wreck*" and "mad waves drive the vessel a wreck." |
| mad | An adj., | because it qualifies the n. "waves." | |
| waves | A n., | ,, | is a name. |
| drive | A v., | ,, | says what waves do. |
| the | An adj., | ,, | limits the n. "vessel." |
| vessel | A n., | ,, | is a name. |
| a | An adj., | ,, | limits the n. "wreck." |
| wreck | A n., | ,, | is a name. |
| The | An adj., | ,, | limits the n. "masts." |

| | | | |
|---|---|---|---|
| masts | A n., | ,, | because it is a name. |
| fly | A v., | ,, | says what the masts do. |
| in | A prep., | ,, | shows the rn. bet. "fly" and "splinters." |
| splinters | A n., | ,, | is a name. |
| the | An adj., | ,, | limits the n. "shrouds." |
| shrouds | A n., | ,, | is a name. |
| are | A v., | ,, | asserts. |
| on | A prep., | ,, | shows the rn. bet. "are" and "fire." |
| fire. | A n., | ,, | is a name. |
| 12. I | A pron., | ,, | is used instead of a name. |
| have danced | A v., | ,, | says what I have done. |
| upon | A prep., | ,, | shows the rn. bet. "have danced" and "wave." |
| the | An adj., | | because it limits the n. "wave." |
| trackless | An adj., | ,, | qualifies the n. "wave." |
| ocean | An adj., | ,, | qualifies the n. "wave." |
| wave | A n., | ,, | is a name. |
| When | A conj., | ,, | joins the sents. "I've danced on the trackless ocean wave" and "wild winds held unfettered revelry." |
| wild | An adj., | | because it qualifies the n. "winds." |
| winds | A n., | ,, | is a name. |
| held | A v., | ,, | says what the winds did. |
| unfettered | An adj., | ,, | qualifies the n. "revelry." |
| revelry. | A n., | ,, | is a name. |

## Exercise 25.

**I. Proper Nouns**: Cadwallo's, Goldsmith, Ireland, Toby, Columbus, America.

**II. Common Nouns**: Tongue, buds, cheek, rose, fish, heart, lake, uncle, knife, fork.

**III. Common Nouns (Abstract)**: Protection, law, spring, summer, persecution, fury, eve, composure, resignation, morning.

## Exercise 26.

*The Abstract Nouns are in Italics.*

**1. Sun**: Bright, *brightness;* hot, *heat;* warm, *warmth;* brilliant, *brilliance.*

**2. Paper**: White, *whiteness;* smooth, *smoothness;* useful, *usefulness.*

**3. Rose**: Sweet, *sweetness;* fragrant, *fragrance;* lovely, *loveliness.*

**4. Knife**: Sharp, *sharpness;* useful, *usefulness;* hard, *hardness;* brittle, *brittleness;* cold, *coldness;* flat, *flatness.*

**5. Lion**: Brave, *bravery;* fierce, *fierceness;* strong, *strength;* bold, *boldness.*

**6. Robber**: Wicked, *wickedness;* cruel, *cruelty;* crafty, *craftiness.*

**7. Window**: Transparent, *transparency;* clear, *clearness;* high, *height.*

**8. Oak**: Strong, *strength;* tough, *toughness;* firm, *firmness;* durable, *durability;* thick, *thickness.*

**9. Lark**: Flying, *flight;* merry, *mirth;* blithe, *blitheness.*

**10. Honey**: Sweet, *sweetness;* soft, *softness.*

**11. King**: Proud, *pride;* brave, *bravery;* majestic, *majesty;* haughty, *haughtiness.*

**12. Water**: Pure, *purity;* clear, *clearness;* transparent, *transparency;* abounding, *abundance.*

### Exercise 27.

**Proper Nouns:** London, Moscow, Australia, Canada, Ceylon, Paris.
    **Common Nouns:** Gate, bread, street, house, island, river.
    **Abstract Nouns:** Season, idleness, singing, envy, philosophy, health.

### Exercise 28.

**1. Masculine:** John, boar, colt, Joseph, victor, peacock, hero, actor, porter, hunter, shepherd.
    **2. Feminine:** Mary, vixen, lass, witch, cow, sultana, donna, moorhen, queen, governess, slut, duck, bride.
    **3. Neuter:** Regiment,* beech, stone, flower.
    **4. Common:** Witness, parent, pig, guardian, cousin, neighbour, scholar, child, teacher, ass, friend.

\* See *Gr.* § 37, *Obs.* 2.

### Exercise 29.

Horse, *mare;* husband, *wife;* sultan, *sultana;* czar, *czarina;* uncle, *aunt;* bull, *cow;* monk, *nun;* tiger, *tigress;* landgrave, *landgravine;* son, *daughter;* giant, *giantess;* brother, *sister;* heir, *heiress;* stag, *hind;* Jew, *Jewess;* lad, *lass;* earl, *countess;* friar, *nun;* peer, *peeress;* shepherd, *shepherdess;* lord, *lady;* marquis, *marchioness;* duke, *duchess;* beau, *belle;* host, *hostess;* buck, *doe;* hart, *roe;* priest, *priestess;* margrave, *margravine;* bachelor, *maid* or *spinster;* spinner, *spinster;* don, *donna;* administrator, *administratrix;* fox, *vixen;* emperor, *empress;* father, *mother;* nephew, *niece;* gander, *goose;* votary, *votress;* wizard, *witch;* he-ass, *she-ass;* bridegroom, *bride;* viscount, *viscountess;* widower, *widow;* gentleman, *lady.*

### Exercise 30.

Analysis, *analyses;* church, *churches;* fish, *fishes* (number), *fish* (quantity); loaf, *loaves;* hoof, *hoofs;* hiss, *hisses;* donkey, *donkeys;* knife, *knives;* grotto, *grottos;* lady, *ladies;* fife, *fifes;* penny, *pennies* (separate coins), *pence* (a sum); brother, *brothers* (sons of the same parent), *brethren* (members of the same society or church); boy, *boys;* potato, *potatoes;* knight-errant, *knights-errant;* man, *men;* staff, *staves;* tooth, *teeth;* cloth, *cloths* (pieces or kinds of cloth), *clothes* (garments); ox, *oxen;* genius, *geniuses* (men of talent), *genii* (fabulous spirits); bandit, *banditti;* index, *indices* (algebraic exponents), *indexes* (tables of contents); hat, *hats;* goose, *geese;* desk, *desks;* alkali, *alkalies;* glory, *glories;* chimney, *chimneys;* cow, *cows;* half, *halves;* mason, *masons;* colloquy, *colloquies;* brush, *brushes;* deer, *deer;* fox, *foxes;* apparatus, *apparatus;* suffix, *suffixes;* pea, *peas* (number), *pease* (quantity); crutch, *crutches;* beau, *beaux;* kiss, *kisses;* cherub, *cherubs* (English), *cherubim* (Hebrew); oasis, *oases;* apex, *apices;* day, *days;* mouse, *mice;* beauty, *beauties;* focus, *foci;* story, *stories;* topaz, *topazes;* cargo, *cargoes;* die, *dies* (stamps for coining), *dice* (small cubes used in games); datum, *data;* seraph, *seraphs* (English), *seraphim* (Hebrew); life, *lives;* genus, *genera;* animalculum, *animalcula.*

## Exercise 31.

Wharfs, *wharf*; phenomena, *phenomenon*; monkeys, *monkey*; footmen, *footman*; calves, *calf*; mice, *mouse*; classes, *class*; men, *man*; skiffs, *skiff*; appendices, *appendix*; tyros, *tyro*; hypotheses, *hypothesis*; leaves, *leaf*; stories, *story*; bases, *basis*; dicta, *dictum*; storeys, *storey*; teeth, *tooth*; woes, *wo*; radii, *radius*; beaux, *beau*; horses, *horse*; halves, *half*; cherubim, *cherub*; nebulæ, *nebula*; chimneys, *chimney*; gipsies, *gipsy*; automata, *automaton*; houses, *house*; genera, *genus*; foxes, *fox*; genii, *genius*; grasses, *grass*; oxen, *ox*; axes, *axis*; women, *woman*; media, *medium*; nuncios, *nuncio*; knives, *knife*; staves, *staff*; kine, *cow*; mottoes, *motto*.

## Exercise 32.

**Singular:** 1. Side; 2. Agitation, Great Britain; 3. Loch Lomond, Scotland, water; 4. Cloth; 5. Wonder, admiration; 6. Fleet; 7. Mother; 8. Direction; 9. Field.

**Plural:** 1. Waves; 2. Lakes, rivers, springs; 3. Banks; 4. Chairs; 5. People, trains; 6. Captains, officers; 7. Kine; 8. Bowmen, shafts; 9. Bands, foemen; 10. Cavaliers, sanctuaries.

## Exercise 33.

1. Snow, *third*; ground, *third*. 2. Men, *first*; legs, *third*. 3. Soldiers, *second*; arms, *third*. 4. Henry Thompson, *first*; truth, *third*. 5. Sun, *third*; valley, *third*. 6. Pine, *third*; mountain, *third*. 7. Father, *second*. 8. Boy, *third*; pony, *third*. 9. Man, *third*; ladder, *third*. 10. Stranger, *second*; grove, *third*.

## Exercise 34.

|      | Sing.       | Plu.         | Sing.      | Plu.       | Sing.      | Plu.       |
|------|-------------|--------------|------------|------------|------------|------------|
| Nom. | Lady,       | Ladies.      | Breeze,    | Breezes.   | Father,    | Fathers.   |
| Poss.| Lady's,     | Ladies'.     | Breeze's,  | Breezes'.  | Father's,  | Fathers'.  |
| Obj. | Lady,       | Ladies.      | Breeze,    | Breezes.   | Father,    | Fathers.   |

|      | Sing.         | Plu.           | Sing.      | Plu.       | Sing.       | Plu.       |
|------|---------------|----------------|------------|------------|-------------|------------|
| Nom. | Conscience,   | Consciences.   | Forest,    | Forests.   | Woman,      | Women.     |
| Poss.| Conscience',  | Consciences'.  | Forest's,  | Forests'.  | Woman's,    | Women's.   |
| Obj. | Conscience,   | Consciences.   | Forest,    | Forests.   | Woman,      | Women.     |

|      | Sing.     | Plu. | Sing.   | Plu.    |
|------|-----------|------|---------|---------|
| Nom. | Cadmus,   | ———  | Tooth,  | Teeth.  |
| Poss.| Cadmus',  | ———  | Tooth's,| Teeth's.|
| Obj. | Cadmus,   | ———  | Tooth,  | Teeth.  |

## Exercise 35.

Goodness', oak's, doctor's, thrush's, Socrates', James's, convenience', butler's, church's, knight's, guide's, queen's, cherub's, gentleman's.

## Exercise 36.

Children's, fathers', clowns', geese's, beauties', servants', **corporals'**, nuncios', stairs', sheep's, pennies' or pence', hunters', roses', **candles'**.

## Exercise 37.

1. Dews, *nom.*; night, *obj.* 2. Sounds, *nom.*; life, *obj.* 3. Maids, *nom.*; flowers, *obj.*; Sarah's, *poss.*; grave, *obj.* 4. Lord's, *poss.*; son, *nom.* 5. Master, *nom.*; robber's, *poss.*; footsteps, *obj.* 6. Widow, *nom.*; town, *obj.*; north, *obj.*; England, *obj.*; stall, *obj.*; apples, *obj.*; sweetmeats, *obj.* 7. Dinner, *obj.*; Stephen's, *poss.*; father, *nom.*; room, *obj.* 8. Husband's, *poss.*; eyes, *nom.*; pleasure, *obj.*; cheerfulness, *obj.*; countenance, *obj.* 9. Report, *nom.*; Tom's, *poss.*; heart, *obj.*; mouth, *obj.* 10. Breakfast, *nom.*; tea, *obj.*; woman, *obj.*; water, *obj.*; Amur, *obj.*

## Exercise 38.

1. Fortunatus — A prop. n., mas. gen., s. num., 3rd per., nom. c. to the v. "had."
had — A v.
a — An adj.
wishing — An adj.
hat. — A com. n., neu. gen., s. num., 3rd per., obj. c., gov. by the tr., v. "had."

2. Man's — A com. n., mas. gen., s. num., 3rd per., poss. c., gov. by the n. "unhappiness."
unhappiness — An abs. n., neu. gen., s. num., 3rd per., nom. c. to the v. "comes."
comes — A v.
of — A prep.
his — A pron.
greatness. — An abs. n., neu. gen., s. num., 3rd per., obj. c., gov. by the prep. "of."

3. The — An adj.
spell — An abs. n., neu. gen., s. num., 3rd per., nom. c., to the v. "was broken."
was broken — A v.
by — A prep.
a — An adj.
sound — An abs. n., neu. gen., s. num., 3rd per., obj. c., gov. by the prep. "by."
of — A prep.
carriage-wheels. — A comp. com. n., neu. gen., p. num., 3rd per., obj. c., gov. by the prep. "of."

4. I — A pron.
have roasted — A v.
wild — An adj.
eggs — A com. n., neu. gen., p. num., 3rd per., obj. c., gov. by the tr. v. "have roasted."
in — A prep.
the — An adj.
sand — A com. n., neu. gen., s. num., 3rd per., obj. c., gov. by the prep. "in."
of — A prep.
Sahara. — A prop. n., neu. gen., s. num., 3rd per., obj. c., gov. by the prep. "of."

5. The — An adj.
little — An adj.
woman — A com. n., fem. gen., s. num., 3rd per., nom. c. to the v. "shook."
shook — A v.
her — A pron.
head. — A com. n., neu. gen., s. num., 3rd per., obj. c., gov. by the tr. v. "shook."

6. John's — A prop. n., mas. gen., s. num., 3rd per., poss. c., gov. by the n. "tramp."
heavy — An adj.
tramp — An abs. n., neu. gen., s. num., 3rd per., nom. c. to the v. "was heard."
was heard — A v.
upon — A prep.
the — An adj.

|   |   |
|---|---|
| staircase. | A com. n., neu. gen., s. num., 3rd per., obj. c., gov. by the prep. "upon." |
| 7. The | An adj. |
| surgeons | A com. n., mas. gen., p. num., 3rd per., nom. c. to the v. "dressed." |
| dressed | A v. |
| his | A pron. |
| wounds. | A com. n., neu. gen., p. num., 3rd per., obj. c., gov. by the tr. v. "dressed." |
| 8. The | An adj. |
| news | An abs. n., neu. gen., s. num., 3rd per., nom. c. to the v. "produced." |
| of | A prep. |
| Hampden's | A prop. n., mas. gen., s. num., 3rd per., poss. c., gov. by the n. "death." |
| death | An abs. n., neu. gen., s. num., 3rd per., obj. c., gov. by the prep. "of." |
| produced | A v. |
| great | An adj. |
| consternation | An abs. n., neu. gen., s. num., 3rd por., obj. c., gov. by the tr. v. "produced." |
| in | A prep. |
| his | A pron. |
| party. | A com. col. n., neu. gen., s. num., 3rd per., obj. c., gov. by the prep. "in." |
| 9. The | An adj. |
| mute | An adj. |
| herd | A com. col. n., com. gen., p. num., 3rd per., nom. c. to the v. "snuff." |
| snuff | A v. |
| the | An adj. |
| shivering | An adj. |
| gale. | A com. n., neu. gen., s. num., 3rd per., obj. c., gov. by the tr. v. "snuff." |
| 10. Lead | A com. n., neu. gen., s. num., 3rd per., nom. c. to the v. "was fetching." |
| was fetching | A v. |
| a | An adj. |
| high | An adj. |
| price | An abs. n., neu. gen., s. num., 3rd per., obj. c., gov. by the tr. v. "was fetching." |
| in | A prep. |
| Antwerp. | A prop. n., neu. gen., s. num., 3rd per., obj. c., gov. by the prep. "in." |
| 11. The | An adj. |
| people | A com. n., com. gen., p. num., 3rd per., nom. c. to the v. "rang." |
| rang | A v. |
| the | An adj. |
| bells | A com. n., neu. gen., p. num., 3rd per., obj. c., gov. by the tr. v. "rang." |
| for | A prep. |
| joy. | An abs. n., neu. gen., s. num., 3rd per., obj. c., gov. by the prep. "for." |
| 12. I | A pron. |
| bind | A v. |
| the | An adj. |
| sun's | A com. n., neu. gen., s. num., 3rd per., poss. c., gov. by the n. "throne." |
| throne | A com. n., neu. gen., s. num., 3rd per., obj. c., gov. by the tr. v. "bind." |
| with | A prep. |
| a | An adj. |
| burning | An adj. |
| zone | A com. n., neu. gen., s. num., 3rd per., obj. c., gov. by the prep. "with." |
| And | A conj. |
| the | An adj. |
| moon's | A com. n., neu. gen., s. num., 3rd per., poss. c., gov. by the n. *throne* und. |

| | |
|---|---|
| with | A prep. |
| a | An adj. |
| girdle | A com. n., neu. gen., s. num., 3rd per., obj. c., gov. by the prep "with." |
| of | A prep. |
| pearl | A com. n., neu. gen., s. num., 3rd per., obj. c., gov. by the prep "of." |
| The | An adj. |
| volcanoes | A com. n., neu. gen., p. num., 3rd per., nom. c. to the v. "are." |
| are | A v. |
| dim | An adj. |
| and | A conj. |
| the | An adj. |
| stars | A com. n., neu. gen., p. num., 3rd per., nom. c. to the v. "reel." |
| reel | A v. |
| and | A conj. |
| swim | A v. |
| When | A conj. |
| the | An adj. |
| whirlwinds | A com. n., neu. gen., p. num., 3rd per., nom. c. to the v. "unfurl." |
| my | A pron. |
| banner | A com. n., neu. gen., s. num., 3rd per., obj. c., gov. by the tr. v. "unfurl." |
| unfurl. | A v. |

### Exercise 39.

1. Few, *quantity*; this, *dis.*; more, *quantity*. 2. A, *dis.*; black, *quality*. 3. A, *dis.*; transient, *quality*. 4. The, *dis.*; golden, *quality*. 5. All, *quantity*; those, *dis.* 6. Four, *quantity*. 7. The, *dis.*; wild, *quality*; dear, *quality*; native, *quality*. 8. The, *dis.*; little, *quality*; red, *quality*; the, *dis.*; the, *dis.* 9. High, *quality*; black, *quality*; the, *dis.* 10. More, *quantity*; golden, *quality*; the, *dis.*; little, *quality*; parlour, *quality*. 11. Each, *quantity*; two, *quantity*. 12. Every, *quantity*; several, *quantity*. 13. The, *dis.*; windy, *quality*; wet, *quality*. 14. The, *dis.*; low, *quality*; damp, *quality*; hard, *quality*. 15. The, *dis.*; last, *quality*; cold, *quality*; feeble, *quality*. 16. The, *dis.*; flashing, *quality*; feathery, *quality*; the, *dis.*; stormy, *quality*; a, *dis.*

### Exercise 40.

1. Many, *indef. nu.* 2. Any, *bulk or mass.* 3. Some, *bulk or mass.* 4. Some, *indef. nu.* 5. No, *bulk or mass.* 6. All, *indef. nu.* 7. All, *bulk or mass.* 8. Every, *dist. nu.* 9. Neither, *dist. nu.* 10. Two, *def. card. nu.* 11. Several, *indef. nu.* 12. Second, *def. ord. nu.*

### Exercise 41.

*A* stranger, *a* house, *an* honour, *a* harp, *an* ostrich, *a* mountain, *an* eagle, *a* palace, *an* hour, *a* hill, *a* sunbeam, *an* egg, *a* bush, *a* queen, *a* bird, *an* ox, *an* ounce, *a* glass, *a* tree, *an* apple, *an* orange, *a* temple, *a* blossom, *an* apricot, *a* voice, *an* owl, *a* metal, *an* oven, *a* town, *a* home.

### Exercise 42.

| Pos. | Comp. | Superl. | Pos. | Comp. | Superl. |
|---|---|---|---|---|---|
| Hollow, | hollower, | hollowest. | Weary, | wearier, | weariest. |
| Melancholy, | more melancholy, | most melancholy. | Yellow, | yellower, | yellowest. |
| | | | Dim, | dimmer, | dimmest. |
| Distant, | more distant, | most distant. | Coarse, | coarser, | coarsest. |
| Costly, | costlier, | costliest. | Rich, | richer, | richest. |
| Wild, | wilder, | wildest. | Calm, | calmer, | calmest. |
| Busy, | busier, | busiest. | Little, | less, | least. |

| Pos. | Comp. | Superl. | Pos. | Comp. | Superl. |
|---|---|---|---|---|---|
| Dry, | drier, | driest. | Horrible, | more horrible, | most horrible. |
| Clean, | cleaner, | cleanest. | Fair, | fairer, | fairest. |
| Harmless, | more harmless, | most harmless. | Fragrant, | more fragrant, | most fragrant. |
| Old, | older, elder, | oldest, eldest. | Pure, | purer, | purest. |
| Wonderful, | more wonderful, | most wonderful. | Pretty, | prettier, | prettiest. |
| Good, | better, | best. | Agreeable, | more agreeable, | most agreeable. |
| Lovely, | lovelier, | loveliest. | Great, | greater, | greatest. |
| Sweet, | sweeter, | sweetest. | Giddy, | giddier, | giddiest. |
| Dangerous, | more dangerous, | most dangerous. | Nigh, | nigher, | nighest, next. |
| Far, | farther, | farthest. | Bad, | worse, | worst. |
| Beautiful, | more beautiful, | most beautiful. | Fierce, | fiercer, | fiercest. |
| Glad, | gladder, | gladdest. | Clear, | clearer, | clearest. |
| Brave, | braver, | bravest. | Marvellous, | more marvellous, | most marvellous. |
| Gallant, | more gallant, | most gallant. | Observant, | more observant, | most observant. |

## Exercise 43.

1. Adown — A prep.
   the — A dis. adj., lim. the n. "glen."
   glen — A com. n., neu. gen., sing. num., 3rd per., obj. c., gov. by the prep. "adown."
   rode — A v.
   armed — An adj. of quality, qual. the n. "men."
   men — A com. n., mas. gen., p. num., 3rd per., nom. c. to the v. "rode."
2. Martin — A prop. n., mas. gen., s. num., 3rd per., nom. c. to the v. "had dealt."
   had dealt — A v.
   a — A dis. adj., lim. the n. "stroke."
   heavier — An adj. of quality, comp. deg., qual. the n. "stroke."
   stroke — An abs. n., neu. gen., s. num., 3rd per., obj. c., gov. by the tr. v. "had dealt."
   than — A conj.
   he — A pron.
   intended — A v.
3. Caius — A prop. n., mas. gen., s. num., 2nd per., nom. c. of add.
   of — A prep.
   all — An indef. nu. adj. of quantity, qual. the n. "Romans."
   the — A dis. adj., lim. the n. "Romans."
   Romans — A prop. n., com. gen., p. num., 3rd per., obj. c., gov. by the prep. "of."
   thou — A pron.
   hast — A v.
   the — A dis. adj., lim. the n. "sight."
   keenest — An adj. of quality, superl. deg., qual. the n. "sight."
   sight — An abs. n., neu. gen., s. num., 3rd per., obj. c., gov. by the tr. v. "hast."
4. His — A pron.
   steady — An adj. of quality, pos. deg., qual. the n. "hand."
   hand — A com. n., neu. gen., s. num., 3rd per., nom. c. to the v. "made."
   made — A v.
   the — A dis. adj., lim. the n. "furrow."
   straightest — An adj. of quality, superl. deg., qual. the n. "furrow."
   furrow — A com. n., neu. gen., s. num., 3rd per., obj. c., gov. by the tr. v. "made."
5. Towards — A prep.
   evening — An abs. n., neu. gen., s. num., 3rd per., obj. c., gov. by the prep. "towards."
   they — A pron.
   reached — A v.
   a — A dis. adj., lim. the n. "village."
   little — An adj. of quality, pos. deg., qual. the n. "village."
   secluded — An adj. of quality, pos. deg., qual. the n. "village."

| | |
|---|---|
| village | A com. n., neu. gen., s. num., 3rd per., obj. c., gov. by the tr. v. "reached." |
| amid | A prep. |
| the | A dis. adj., lim. the n. "hills." |
| Surrey | A prop. n., used as an adj. of quality, qual. the n. "hills." |
| hills | A com. n., neu. gen., p. num., 3rd per., obj. c., gov. by the prep. "amid." |
| ivy-clad | A compd. adj. of quality, qual. the n. "village." |
| and | A conj. |
| topped | An adj. of quality, qual. the n. village." |
| by | A prep. |
| a | A dis. adj., lim. the n. "spire." |
| golden | An adj. of quality, qual. the n. "spire." |
| spire. | A com. n., neu. gen., s. num., 3rd per., obj. c., gov. by the prep. "by." |
| 6. The | A dis. adj, lim. the n. "boat." |
| boat | A com. n., neu. gen., s. num., 3rd per., nom. c. to the v. "has left." |
| has left | A v. |
| a | A dis. adj., lim. the n. "land." |
| stormy | An adj. of quality, pos. deg., qual. the n. "land." |
| land. | A com. n., neu. gen., s. num., 3rd per., obj. c., gov. by the tr. v. "has left." |
| 7. More | An adj. of quantity (bulk or mass), comp. deg., qual. the n. "good." |
| good | An abs. n., neu. gen., s. num., 3rd per., nom. c. to the v. "was." |
| was | A v. |
| everywhere. | An adv. |
| 8. I | A pron. |
| received | A v. |
| no | A def. card. nu. adj. of quantity, qual. the n. "hurt." |
| other | An indef. nu. adj. of quantity, qual. the n. "hurt." |
| hurt | An abs. n., neu. gen., s. num., 3rd per., obj. c., gov. by the tr. v. "received." |
| and | A conj. |
| the | A dis. adj., lim. the n. "dwarf." |
| dwarf | A com. n., com. gen., s. num., 3rd per., nom. c. to the v. "was pardoned." |
| was pardoned | A v. |
| at | A prep. |
| my | A pron. |
| desire. | An abs. n., neu. gen., s. num., 3rd per., obj. c., gov. by the prep. "at." |
| 9. He | A pron. |
| gently | An adv. |
| took | A v. |
| me | A pron. |
| up | An adv. |
| in | A prep. |
| both | A def. card. nu. adj. of quantity, qual. the n. "hands." |
| his | A pron. |
| hands. | A com. n., neu. gen., p. num., 3rd per., obj. c., gov. by the prep. "in." |
| 10. I | A pron. |
| took | A v. |
| a | A dis. adj., lim. the n. "cudgel." |
| thick | An adj. of quality, pos. deg., qual. the n. "cudgel." |
| cudgel | A com. n., neu. gen., s. num., 3rd per., obj. c., gov. by the tr. v. "took. |
| and | A conj. |
| threw | A v. |
| it | A pron. |
| with | A prep. |
| all | An adj. of quantity (bulk or mass), qual. the n. "strength." |
| my | A pron. |
| strength. | An abs. n., neu. gen., s. num., 3rd per., obj. c., gov. by the prep. "with." |
| 11. He | A pron. |

| | |
|---|---|
| bowed | A v. |
| to | A prep. |
| several | An indef. nu. adj. of quantity, qual. the n. "persons." |
| well-dressed | A compd. adj. of quality, qual. the n. "persons." |
| persons. | A com. n., com. gen., p. num., 3rd per., obj. c., gov. by the prep. "to." |
| 12. A | A dis. adj., lim. the n. "event." |
| most wonderful | An adj. of quality, superl. deg., qual. the n. "event." |
| event | An abs. n., neu. gen., s. num., 3rd per., nom. c. to the v. "occurred." |
| occurred. | A v. |
| 13. London | A prop. n., neu. gen., s. num., 3rd per., nom. c. to the v. "is." |
| is | A v. |
| larger | An adj. of quality, comp. deg., qual. the n. "London." |
| than | A conj. |
| Paris. | A prop. n., neu. gen., s. num., 3rd per., nom. c. to the v. is und. |
| 14. The | A dis. adj., lim. the n. "letter." |
| letter | A com. n., neu. gen., s. num., 3rd per., nom. c. to the v. "was written." |
| was written | A v. |
| in | A prep. |
| the | A dis. adj., lim. the n. "language." |
| simplest | An adj. of quality, superl. deg., qual. the n. "language." |
| language. | A com. n., neu. gen., s. num., 3rd per., obj. c., gov. by the prep. "in." |
| 15 Soft | An adj. of quality, pos. deg., qual. the n. "beam." |
| and | A conj. |
| pale | An adj. of quality, pos. deg., qual. the n. "beam." |
| is | A v. |
| the | A dis. adj., lim. the n. "beam." |
| moony | An adj. of quality, qual. the n. "beam." |
| beam | A com. n., neu. gen., s. num., 3rd per., nom. c. to the verb "is." |
| Moveless | An adj. of quality, qual. the n. "stream." |
| still | An adv. |
| the | A dis. adj., lim. the n. "stream." |
| glassy | An adj. of quality, qual. the n. "stream." |
| stream | A com. n., neu. gen., s. num., 3rd per., nom. c. to the v. is und. |
| The | A dis. adj., lim. the n. "wave." |
| wave | A com. n., neu. gen., s. num., 3rd per., nom. c. to the v. "is." |
| is | A v. |
| clear | An adj. of quality, pos. deg., qual. the n. "wave." |
| the | A dis. adj., lim. the n. "beach." |
| beach | A com. n., neu. gen., s. num., 3rd per., nom. c. to the v. "is." |
| is | A v. |
| bright | An adj. of quality, pos. deg., qual. the n. "beach." |
| With | A prep. |
| snowy | An adj. of quality, qual. the n. "shell." |
| shell | A com. n., neu. gen., s. num., 3rd per., obj. c., gov. by the prep. "with." |
| and | A conj. |
| sparkling | An adj. of quality, pos. deg., qual. the n. "stones." |
| stones | A com. n., neu. gen., p. num., 3rd per., obj. c., gov. by the prep. *with* und. |
| The | A dis. adj., lim. the n. "shore-surge." |
| shore-surge | A compd. com. n., neu. gen., s. num., 3rd per., nom. c. to the v. "comes." |
| comes | A v. |
| in | A prep. |
| ripples | A com. n., neu. gen., p. num., 3rd per., obj. c., gov. by the prep. "in." |
| light | An adj. of quality, pos. deg., qual. the n. "ripples." |
| In | A prep. |
| murmurings | An abs. n., neu. gen., p. num., 3rd per., obj. c., gov. by the prep. "in." |
| faint | An adj. of quality, pos. deg., qual. the n. "murmurings." |
| and | A conj. |
| distant | An adj. of quality, pos. deg., qual. the n. "moans." |

means. An abs. n., neu. gen., p. num., 3rd per., obj. c., gov. by the prep. *in* und.

N.B.—In subsequent parsing exercises, the parsing of the articles *a* or *an* and *the* will be omitted.

## Exercise 44.

1. I, *pers.* 2. He, *pers.*; himself, *compd. pers.* 3. She, *pers.* 4. It, *pers.* 5. His own, *compd. pers.*; him, *pers.* 6. What, *interrog.*; thou, *pers.* 7. Ye, *pers.*; ye, *pers.* 8. Herself, *compd. pers.* 9. He, *pers.* 10. He, *pers.*; which, *rel.* 11. I, *pers.*; myself, *compd. pers.* 12. Who, *rel.*; it, *pers.* 13. That, *rel.* 14. Whoever, *compd. rel.* 15. I, *pers.*; you, *pers.*; what, *compd. rel.*; he, *pers.*

## Exercise 45.

**Note on the Gender of Pronouns.**—Whenever the noun for which any pronoun (except *it* or *its*) stands cannot be easily ascertained, the pronoun may be parsed as of common gender: this is generally done in the following pages. If, however, the context is known, the proper gender (masculine or feminine, as the case may be,) of the pronoun should be given and an explanatory note added.

| | | |
|---|---|---|
| 1. | he | A pers. pron., mas. gen., s. num., 3rd per., nom. c. to the v. "falls." |
| 2. | us | A pers. pron., com. gen., p. num., 1st per., obj. c., gov. by the tr. v. "let." |
| | them | A pers. pron., com. gen., p. num., 3rd per., obj. c., gov. by the prep. "of." |
| | that | A rel. pron., com. gen., p. num., 3rd per., agr. with its ant. "them," nom. c. to the v. "sleep." |
| | thy | A pers. pron., com. gen. by personification, s. num., 2nd per., poss. c., gov. by the n. "deep." |
| 3. | His | A pers. pron., mas. gen., s. num., 3rd per., poss. c., gov. by the n. "hour-glass." |
| | he | A pers. pron., mas. gen., s. num., 3rd per., nom. c. to the v. "spoke." |
| 4. | I | A pers. pron., com. gen., s. num., 1st per., nom. c. to the v. "can recover." |
| 5. | Your | A pers. pron., com. gen., p. num., (or s. num., p. form), 2nd per., poss. c., gov. by the n. "years." |
| 6. | what | An interrog. pron., neu. gen., s. num., 3rd per., obj. c., gov. by the prep. "to." |
| | I | A pers. pron., com. gen., s. num., 1st per., nom. c. to the v. "can liken." |
| | her | A pers. pron., fem. gen., s. num., 3rd per., poss. c., gov. by the n. "smile." |
| 7. | She | A pers. pron., fem. gen., s. num., 3rd per., nom. c. to the v. "had been." |
| | us | A pers. pron., com. gen., p. num., 1st per., obj. c., gov. by the prep. "with." |
| 8. | my | A pers. pron., com. gen., s. num., 1st per., poss. c., gov. by the n. "daughter." |
| 9. | They | A pers. pron., com. gen., p. num., 3rd per., nom. c. to the v. "left." |
| | her | A pers. pron., fem. gen., s. num., 3rd per., poss. c., gov. by the n. "stead." |
| 10. | I | A pers. pron., com. gen., s. num., 1st per., nom. c. to the v. "saw." |
| | which | A rel. pron., neu. gen., s. num., 3rd per., agr. with its ant. "doom," nom. c. to the v. "had been prepared." |
| | me | A pers. pron., com. gen., s. num., 1st per., obj. c., gov. by the prep. "for." |
| | myself | A compd. pers. pron., com. gen., s. num., 1st per., obj. c., gov. by the tr. v. "congratulated." |
| | which | A rel. pron., neu. gen., s. num., 3rd per., agr. with its ant. "accident," obj. c., gov. by the prep. "by." |

| | | |
|---|---|---|
| I | A pers. pron., com. gen., s. num., 1st per., nom. c. to the v. "had escaped." | |
| 11. itself | A compd. pers. pron., neu. gen., s. num., 3rd per., obj. c., gov. by the tr. v. "forced." | |
| my | A pers. pron., com. gen., s. num., 1st per., poss. c., gov. by the n. "nostrils." | |
| 12. It | A pers. pron., neu. gen., s. num., 3rd per., nom. c. to the v. "had." | |
| who | A rel. pron., fem. gen., s. num., 3rd per., agr. with its ant. "Olivia," nom. c. to the v. "mistook." | |
| it | A pers. pron., neu. gen., s. num., 3rd per., obj. c., gov. by the tr. v. "mistook." | |

## Exercise 46.

| | |
|---|---|
| 1. You | A pers. pron., com. gen., p. num. (or s. num., p. form), 2nd per., nom. c. to the v. "keep." |
| still | An adv. |
| keep | A v. |
| your | A pers. pron., com. gen., p. num. (or s. num., p. form), 2nd per., poss. c., gov. by the n. "eyes." |
| eyes. | A com. n., neu. gen., p. num., 3rd per., obj. c., gov. by the tr. v. "keep." |
| 2. Who | An interrog. pron., com. gen., s. num., 3rd per., nom. c. to the v. "clothed." |
| clothed | A v. |
| you. | A pers. pron., com. gen., p. num. (or s. num., p. form), 2nd per., obj. c., gov. by the tr. v. "clothed." |
| 3. I | A pers. pron., com. gen., s. num., 1st per., nom. c. to the v. "owe." |
| owe | A v. |
| all | An adj. of quantity (bulk or mass), qual. the n. *good* und. |
| this | A dis. adj., lim. the n. *good* und. |
| to | A prep. |
| your | A pers. pron., fem. gen., s. num., p. form, 2nd per., poss. c., gov. by the n. "goodness." |
| goodness | An abs. n., neu. gen., s. num., 3rd per., obj. c., gov. by the prep. "to." |
| madam | A com. n., fem. gen., s. num., 2nd per., nom. c. of add. |
| for | A prep. |
| it | A pers. pron., neu. gen., s. num., 3rd per., obj. c., gov. by the prep. "for." |
| you | A pers. pron., fem. gen., s. num., p. form, 2nd per., nom. c. to the v. "have." |
| have | A v. |
| my | A pers. pron., com. gen., s. num., 1st per., poss. c., gov. by the n. "prayers." |
| prayers. | An abs. n., neu. gen., p. num., 3rd per., obj. c., gov. by the tr. v. "have." |
| 4. We | A pers. pron., com. gen., p. num., 1st per., nom. c. to the v. "ran." |
| ran | A v. |
| directly | An adv. |
| to | A prep. |
| my | A pers. pron., com. gen., s. num., 1st per., poss. c., gov. by the n. "colleague's." |
| colleague's | A com. n., com. gen., s. num., 3rd per., poss. c., gov. by the n. "house." |
| house | A com. n., neu. gen., s. num., 3rd per., obj. c., gov. by the prep. "to." |
| and | A conj. |
| left | A v. |
| our | A pers. pron., forming with the adj. "own" a compd. pers. pron. |
| own | An intensive adj. of quality, qual. the n. "house." |
| our own | A compd. pers. pron., com. gen., p. num., 1st per., poss. c., gov. by the n. "house." |
| house | A com. n., neu. gen., s. num., 3rd per., obj. c., gov. by the tr. v. "left." |

| | | |
|---|---|---|
| | open. | An adj. of quality, pos. deg., qual. the n. "house." |
| 5. | At | A prep. |
| | Malsio's | A prop. n., mas. gen., s. num., 3rd per., poss. c., gov. by the n. "house." |
| | house | A com. n., neu. gen., s. num., 3rd per., obj. c., gov. by the prep. "at." |
| | we | A pers. pron., com. gen., p. num., 1st per., nom. c. to the v. "found." |
| | found | A v. |
| | many | An indef. nu. adj. of quantity, qual. the n. "people." |
| | people | A com. n., com. gen., p. num., 3rd per., obj. c., gov. by the tr. v. "found." |
| | who | A rel. pron., com. gen., p. num., 3rd per., agr. with its ant. "people," nom. c. to the v. "had fled." |
| | had fled | A v. |
| | to | A prep. |
| | him | A pers. pron., mas. gen., s. num., 3rd per., obj. c., gov. by the prep. "to." |
| | in | A prep. |
| | great | An adj. of quality, pos. deg., qual. the n. "perplexity." |
| | perplexity. | An abs. n., neu. gen., s. num., 3rd per., obj. c., gov. by the prep. "in." |
| 6. | What | An interrog. pron., neu. gen., s. num., 3rd per., obj. c., gov. by the tr. v. "are doing." |
| | are doing | A v. |
| | you. | A pers. pron., com. gen., p. num. (or s. num., p. form), 2nd per., nom. c. to the v. "are doing." |
| 7. | My | A pers. pron., com. gen., s. num., 1st per., poss. c., gov. by the n. "companion." |
| | companion | A com. n., mas. gen., s. num., 3rd per., nom. c. to the v. "laid." |
| | laid | A v. |
| | himself | A compd. pers. pron., mas. gen., s. num., 3rd per., obj. c. gov. by the tr. v. "laid." |
| | down | An adv. |
| | with | A prep. |
| | his | A pers. pron., mas. gen., s. num., 3rd per., poss. c., gov. by the n. "head." |
| | head | A com. n., neu. gen., s. num., 3rd per., obj. c., gov. by the prep. "with." |
| | upon | A prep. |
| | precious | An adj. of quality, pos. deg., qual. the n. "portmanteau." |
| | portmanteau. | A com. n., neu. gen., s. num., 3rd per., obj. c., gov. by the prep. "upon." |
| 8. | redbreast | A com. n., com. gen., s. num., 3rd per., nom. c. to the v. "sings." |
| | sings | A v. |
| | from | A prep. |
| | tall | An adj. of quality, pos. deg., qual. the n. "larch." |
| | larch | A com. n., neu. gen., s. num., 3rd per., obj. c., gov. by the prep. "from." |
| | that | A rel. pron., neu. gen., s. num., 3rd per., agr. with its ant. "larch," nom. c. to the v. "stands." |
| | stands | A v. |
| | beside | A prep. |
| | our | A pers. pron., com. gen., p. num., 1st per., poss. c., gov. by the n. "door." |
| | door. | A com. n., neu. gen., s. num., 3rd per., obj. c., gov. by the prep. "beside." |
| 9. | Thou | A pers. pron., com. gen. by personification, s. num., 2nd per., nom. c. to the v. "art." |
| | art | A v. |
| | welcome | An adj. of quality, pos. deg., qual. the n. "month." |
| | month | An abs. n., com. gen. by personification, s. num., 3rd per., nom. c. after the v. "art." |
| | | A prep. |
| | me. | A pers. pron., com. gen., s. num., 1st per., obj. c., gov. by the prep. "to." |
| 10. | I | A pers. pron., com. gen., s. num., 1st per., nom. c. to the v. "had." |
| | had | A v. |

| | |
|---|---|
| little | An adj. of quality, pos. deg., qual. the n. "daughter." |
| daughter | A com. n., fem. gen., s. num., 3rd per., obj. c., gov. by the tr. v. "had." |
| And | A conj. |
| she | A pers. pron., fem. gen., s. num., 3rd per., nom. c. to the v. "was given." |
| was given | A v. |
| to | A prep. |
| me | A pers. pron., com. gen., s. num., 1st per., obj. c., gov. by the prep. "to." |
| To lead | A v. |
| me | A pers. pron., com. gen., s. num., 1st per., obj. c., gov. by the tr. v. "to lead." |
| gently | An adv. |
| backward | An adv. |
| To | A prep. |
| Heavenly | An adj. of quality, qual. the n. "Father's." |
| Father's | A prop. n., mas. gen., s. num., 3rd per., poss. c., gov. by the n. "knee." |
| knee. | A com. n., neu. gen., s. num., 3rd per., obj. c., gov. by the prep. "to." |

## Exercise 47.

1. Served, *tr.* 2. Loved, *tr.* 3. Fell, *intr.* 4. Shook, *tr.* 5. Spoke, *intr.* 6. Expired, *intr.* 7. Started, *intr.* 8. Rushed, *intr.* 9. Began, *intr.* 10. Talked, *intr.* 11. Went, *intr.* 12. Crossed, *tr.* 13. Found, *tr.* 14. Reaps, *tr.* 15. Ended, *intr.* 16. Bloom, *intr.* 17. Loved, *tr.* 18. Contained, *tr.* 19. Drowned, *tr.* 20. Gazed, *intr.;* kissed, *tr.;* was, *intr.;* bound, *tr.*

## Exercise 48.

1. Was crowded, *pass.* 2. Were destroyed, *pass.* 3. Was thanked, *pass.* 4. Attacked, *act.* 5. Made, *act.* 6. Watched, *act.* 7. Was swung, *pass.* 8. Brought, *act.* 9. Were sketched, *pass.* 10. Are ended, *pass.*

## Exercise 49.

1. His name *was demanded* by the earl. 2. The servants *are called* by their names by him. 3. The goodness of the master *is seen* by you even in his old house-dog. 4. A warrant *was directed* to Sir James Tyrrel by the king. 5. A beggar *is sued* by no man. 6. My eyes *were fixed* on a thousand different objects. 7. A welcoming *is proclaimed* by our streams. 8. His crook *has been thrown* aside by him. 9. The flies and gnats *are followed* by swallows. 10. The heaviest gale *is enjoyed* by the little petrel.

## Exercise 50.

1. They *brought* Perkin into the king's court. 2. Spectators *thronged* the streets. 3. The nobles *drew* their swords. 4. In the winter they *left* him without a fire. 5. They *placed* benches below the platform. 6. People *lined* the road. 7. They *tear* up and *trample* down the greensward. 8. They *established* a general peace. 9. A sleep *rounds* our little life. 10. For a time the parents *feed* their young on the wing.

### Exercise 51.

1. Fly, *imper.*  2. Can choose, *pot.*  3. Watch, *indic.*; to break, *infin.*  4. Could avail, *pot.*  5. Could leave, *pot.*  6. Come, *imper.*  7. Entered, *indic.*  8. Marched, *indic.*  9. Was, *indic.*; to drink, *infin.*  10. May beg, *pot.*; to ask, *infin.*  11. Renounce, *imper.*; cries, *indic.*  12. Toll, *imper.*  13. Fly, *imper.*; intercept, *subj.*  14. Must change, *pot.*  15. Needs, *indic.*  16. Will slacken, *indic.*; stir, *subj.*  17. Consider, *subj.*; had, *indic.*  18. May repose, *pot.*  19. Be lost, *subj.*  20. To disenthrone, *infin.*; war, *indic.*; be, *subj.*; to regain, *infin.*

### Exercise 52.

*The Noun or Pronoun to which the Participle refers is in Italics.*

1. Singing *skylark*.  2. Crying *I*; roaring *I*; been *whipped boy*; whipped *boy*.  3. Being *injured Spaniard*; injured *Spaniard*.  4. Impelled *stone*.  5. Driven *saw-mill*.  6. Mingled *regret*.  7. Unsheathing *he*.  8. Blazing *piece*.  9. Kicking *man*; putting *man*.

### Exercise 53.

1. Entering, *verbal n.*  2. Filling, *pl.*  3. Having gained, *verbal n.*  4. Finishing, *verbal n.*; commencing, *verbal n.*  5. Blessing, *pl.*; adoring, *pl.*  6. Muttering, *pl.*  7. Having declared, *verbal n.*  8. Escaping, *verbal n.*; breaking, *verbal n.*  9. Fighting, *pl.*  10. Advancing, *pl.*  11. Setting, *verbal n.*  12. Winning, *verbal n.*

### Exercise 54.

1. Has had, *perf.*  2. Will carry, *fut.*  3. Shut, *past.*  4. Has wov'n, *perf.*  5. Boweth, *pres.*  6. Hath spent, *perf.*  7. Pervades, *pres.*  8. Will have faded, *fut. perf.*; come, *pres.*  9. Shalt seek, *fut.*  10. Shall be strewed, *fut.*  11. Stood, *past.*  12. Had opened, *pluperf.*  13. Are lost, *pres.*; have been preserved, *perf.*  14. Has passed, *perf.*; crosses, *pres.*

### Exercise 55.

1. Were disappointed, *p.*  2. Sounded, *s.*  3. Come, *s.*  4. Was laced, *s.*  5. Are, *p.*  6. Replied, *s.*  7. Look, *p.*; are fed, *p.*  8. Please, *p.*  9. Was veiled, *s.*  10. Take, *p.*  11. Blow, *p.*  12. Is, *s.*

### Exercise 56.

1. Waked, *first*; fled, *third*; brought, *third*.  2. Supports, *third*; dost ask, *second*.  3. Abound, *third*.  4. Fly, *first*.  5. Comfort, *second*.  6. Can teach, *third*.  7. Shall catch, *first*.  8. Shall go, *first*; have said, *first*.  9. Lost, *first*; came, *first*.  10. Appear, *third*.

### Exercise 57.

1. *Was*, indg. pass. vo., past t.  2. *Can*, indg. pot. m., pres. t.  3. *Was*, indg. past t., prog. form.  4. *Must*, indg. pot. m., pres. t.; *be*, indg. pass. vo.  5. *Was*, indg. past t., prog. form.  6. *Do*, indg. pres. t., and completing the interrog. form of the v.  7. *Could*, indg. pot. m., past t.  8. *Had*, indg. pluperf. t.; *been*, indg. prog. form.  9. *Did*, indg. past. t., emph. form.  10. *Hast*, indg. perf. t.  11. *Must*, indg. pot. m.,

pres. t. 12. *Was*, indg. past t., prog. form. 13. *May*, indg, pot. m., pres. t. 14. *Have*, indg. perf. t. 15. *Should*, indg. pot. m., past t. 16. *Could*, indg. pot. m., past t. 17. *Might*, indg. pot. m.; *have*, together with "might," indg. pluperf. t. 18. *Shall*, indg. fut. t. 19. *Will*, indg. fut. t. 20. *Must*, indg. pot. m., pres. t.; *canst*, indg. pot. m., pres. t.

### Exercises 58—63.

In conjugating the verbs (Exercise 58) *save, praise, receive, desire, conquer, defend;* (Exercise 59) *frighten, want, release, turn, carry, persuade;* (Exercise 60) *puzzle, search, finish, consider, fear, reward;* (Exercise 61) *ask, pray, support, demand, mention, try;* (Exercise 62) *disturb, save, chase, betray, turn, regard;* (Exercise 63) *convince, call, visit, raise, pity, frighten;* for **love, lovest, loves, loved, lovedst,** and **loving** in the corresponding conjugation of the verb **love** substitute respectively the words which are here placed under them.

### Exercise 58.

| *Love.* | *Lovest.* | *Loves.* | *Loved.* | *Lovedst.* | *Loving.* |
|---|---|---|---|---|---|
| Save | Savest | Saves | Saved | Savedst | Saving. |
| Praise | Praisest | Praises | Praised | Praisedst | Praising. |
| Receive | Receivest | Receives | Received | Receivedst | Receiving. |
| Desire | Desirest | Desires | Desired | Desiredst | Desiring. |
| Conquer | Conquerest | Conquers | Conquered | Conqueredst | Conquering. |
| Defend | Defendest | Defends | Defended | Defendedst | Defending. |

### Exercise 59.

| *Love.* | *Lovest.* | *Loves.* | *Loved.* | *Lovedst.* | *Loving.* |
|---|---|---|---|---|---|
| Frighten | Frightenest | Frightens | Frightened | Frightenedst | Frightening. |
| Want | Wantest | Wants | Wanted | Wantedst | Wanting. |
| Release | Releasest | Releases | Released | Releasedst | Releasing. |
| Turn | Turnest | Turns | Turned | Turnedst | Turning. |
| Carry | Carriest | Carries | Carried | Carriedst | Carrying. |
| Persuade | Persuadest | Persuades | Persuaded | Persuadedst | Persuading. |

### Exercise 60.

| *Love.* | *Lovest.* | *Loves.* | *Loved.* | *Lovedst.* | *Loving.* |
|---|---|---|---|---|---|
| Puzzle | Puzzlest | Puzzles | Puzzled | Puzzledst | Puzzling. |
| Search | Searchest | Searches | Searched | Searchedst | Searching. |
| Finish | Finishest | Finishes | Finished | Finishedst | Finishing. |
| Consider | Considerest | Considers | Considered | Consideredst | Considering. |
| Fear | Fearest | Fears | Feared | Fearedst | Fearing. |
| Reward | Rewardest | Rewards | Rewarded | Rewardedst | Rewarding. |

### Exercise 61.

| *Love.* | *Lovest.* | *Loves.* | *Loved.* | *Lovedst.* | *Loving.* |
|---|---|---|---|---|---|
| Ask | Askest | Asks | Asked | Askedst | Asking. |
| Pray | Prayest | Prays | Prayed | Prayedst | Praying. |
| Support | Supportest | Supports | Supported | Supportedst | Supporting. |
| Demand | Demandest | Demands | Demanded | Demandedst | Demanding. |
| Mention | Mentionest | Mentions | Mentioned | Mentionedst | Mentioning. |
| Try | Triest | Tries | Tried | Triedst | Trying. |

### Exercise 62.

| *Love.* | *Lovest.* | *Loves.* | *Loved.* | *Lovedst.* | *Loving.* |
|---|---|---|---|---|---|
| Disturb | Disturbest | Disturbs | Disturbed | Disturbedst | Disturbing. |
| Save | Savest | Saves | Saved | Savedst | Saving. |
| Chase | Chasest | Chases | Chased | Chasedst | Chasing. |
| Betray | Betrayest | Betrays | Betrayed | Betrayedst | Betraying. |

| *Love.* | *Lovest.* | *Loves.* | *Loved.* | *Lovedst.* | *Loving.* |
|---|---|---|---|---|---|
| Turn | Turnest | Turns | Turned | Turnedst | Turning. |
| Regard | Regardest | Regards | Regarded | Regardedst | Regarding. |

## Exercise 63.

| *Love.* | *Lovest.* | *Loves.* | *Loved.* | *Lovedst.* | *Loving.* |
|---|---|---|---|---|---|
| Convince | Convincest | Convinces | Convinced | Convincedst | Convincing. |
| Call | Callest | Calls | Called | Calledst | Calling. |
| Visit | Visitest | Visits | Visited | Visitedst | Visiting. |
| Raise | Raisest | Raises | Raised | Raisedst | Raising. |
| Pity | Pitiest | Pities | Pitied | Pitiedst | Pitying. |
| Frighten | Frightenest | Frightens | Frightened | Frightenedst | Frightening. |

## Exercise 64.

| *Present.* | *Past.* | *Past or Complete Participle.* | *Present.* | *Past.* | *Past or Complete Participle.* |
|---|---|---|---|---|---|
| Abide, | Abode, | Abode. | Lead, | Led, | Led. |
| Beseech, | Besought, | Besought. | Gild, | Gilded, gilt, | Gilded, gilt. |
| Cast, | Cast, | Cast. | Hear, | Heard, | Heard. |
| Dare (to venture), | Durst, | Dared. | Arise, | Arose, | Arisen. |
| | | | Awake, | Awaked, awoke, | Awaked. |
| Dare (to challenge), | Dared, | Dared. | Chide, | Chode, chid, | Chidden, chid. |
| Fall, | Fell, | Fallen. | | | |
| Take, | Took, | Taken. | Dig, | Dug, digged, | Dug, digged. |
| Swear, | Swore, | Sworn. | Shred, | Shred, | Shred. |
| Stand, | Stood, | Stood. | Wed, | Wedded, wed, | Wedded, wed. |
| Speak, | Spoke, | Spoken. | Split, | Split, | Split. |
| Hang (intrans.), | Hung, | Hung. | Keep, | Kept, | Kept. |
| | | | Hit, | Hit, | Hit. |
| Hang (trans.), | Hanged, | Hanged. | Shrink, | Shrank, | Shrunk. |
| Lade, | Laded, | Laden. | Tear, | Tore, | Torn. |
| Quit, | Quitted, quit, | Quitted, quit. | Sweat, | Sweated, sweat, | Sweated, sweat. |
| Saw, | Sawed, | Sawed, sawn. | | | |
| Shoe, | Shod, | Shod. | Leap, | Leaped, leapt, | Leaped, leapt. |
| Shoot, | Shot, | Shot. | Feel, | Felt, | Felt. |
| Say, | Said, | Said. | Seek, | Sought, | Sought. |
| Read, | Read, | Read. | Learn, | Learned, learnt, | Learnt. |
| Grow, | Grew, | Grown. | | | |
| Lay, | Laid, | Laid. | Help, | Helped, | Helped, holpen. |
| Have, | Had, | Had. | | | |
| Get, | Got, | Gotten. | Give, | Gave, | Given. |
| Am, | Was, | Been. | Speed, | Sped, | Sped. |
| Set, | Set, | Set. | Tell, | Told, | Told. |
| Catch, | Caught, | Caught. | Work, | Work, wrought, | Worked, wrought. |
| Deal, | Dealt, | Dealt. | | | |
| Feed, | Fed, | Fed. | Do, | Did, | Done. |
| Show, | Showed, | Shown. | Choose, | Chose, | Chosen. |
| See, | Saw, | Seen. | Eat, | Ate, | Eaten. |
| Bind, | Bound, | Bound. | Draw, | Drew, | Drawn. |
| Weave, | Wove, | Woven. | Spell, | Spelled, spelt, | Spelled, spelt |
| Teach, | Taught, | Taught. | | | |

N.B.—In conjugating any irregular verb, as *smite, catch, weave, see,* for **love, lovest, loves, loved** (past tense), **lovedst, loving, loved** (complete participle) in the corresponding conjugation of the verb **love**, substitute respectively the words which are here placed under them.

| **Love.** | **Lovest.** | **Loves.** | **Loved** (past t.). | **Lovedst.** | **Loving.** | **Loved** (past or complete pl.). |
|---|---|---|---|---|---|---|
| Smite | Smitest | Smites | Smote | Smotest | Smiting | Smitten. |
| Catch | Catchest | Catches | Caught | Caughtest | Catching | Caught. |
| Weave | Weavest | Weaves | Wove | Wovest | Weaving | Woven. |
| See | Seest | Sees | Saw | Sawest | Seeing | Seen. |

*Obs.* 1. In any tense, except the past tense, where **loved** occurs, the past or com-

# 34 KEY TO

plete participle of the irregular verb must be substituted for it, as **loved** is, in all such cases, a past or complete participle. Thus, in conjugating the above verbs, instead of **loved** we should, in the cases mentioned, use *smitten, caught, woven,* and *seen.*

*Obs.* 2. In the passive voice, **loved** is always a past or complete participle, and consequently the past or complete participle of the irregular verb conjugated must be used in its place.

## Exercise 65.

1. Go, *irreg.*, (also *defec.*, Gr. § 163, *Obs.* 1); climb, *reg.* 2. Rambled, *reg.* 3. Began, *irreg.;* to look, *reg.* 4. Raged, *reg.* 5. Bid, *irreg.;* meet, *irreg.* 6. Weigh, *reg.* 7. Foregoes, *defec.* 8. Must, *defec.;* come, *irreg.;* dare, *irreg.;* come, *irreg.* 9. Look, *reg.;* tell, *irreg.* 10. Ought, *defec.;* to go, *irreg.*, (also *defec.*, Gr. § 163, *Obs.* 1). 11. Came, *irreg.;* quoth, *defec.* 12. Worth, *defec.* 13. March, *reg.* 14. Advised, *reg.;* to enter, *reg.* 15. Soared, *reg.* 16. Thank, *reg.;* taught, *irreg.* 17. Lays, *irreg.* 18. Hear, *irreg.;* mutter, *reg.* 19. Come, *irreg.* 20. Had, *irreg.;* brought, *irreg.*

## Exercise 66.

1. Methought. 2. Rained. 3. Methinketh. 4. Rained. 5. Freezes. 6. Has rained, [has] hailed, [has] snowed, [has] thundered. 7. Methought. 8. Thawed.

## Exercise 67.

| | |
|---|---|
| 1. rain | A com. n., neu. gen., s. num., 3rd per., nom. c. to the v. "continued." |
| still | An adv. |
| continued | A reg. intr. v., indic. m., past t., s. num., 3rd per., agr. with its nom. "rain." |
| to | A particle, indg. infin. m. |
| to fall | An irreg. intr. v., infin. m., pres. t., gov. by the v. "continued." |
| incessantly. | An adv. |
| 2. Suddenly | An adv. |
| sharp | An adj. of quality, pos. deg., qual. the n. "flash." |
| flash | A com. n., neu. gen., s. num., 3rd per., nom. c. to the v. "lighted." |
| of | A prep. |
| lightning | A com. n., neu. gen., s. num., 3rd per., obj. c., gov. by the prep. "of." |
| followed | A past pl. from the tr. v. "to follow," ref. to the n. "flash." |
| by | A prep. |
| instantaneous | An adj. of quality, qual. the n. "thunder-peal." |
| thunder-peal | A compd. com. n., neu. gen., s. num., 3rd per., obj. c., gov. by the prep. "by." |
| lighted | A reg. tr. v., act. vo., indic. m., past t., s. num., 3rd per., agr. with its nom. "flash." |
| up | An adv. |
| all | An adj. of quantity (bulk or mass), qual. the n. "forest." |
| forest. | A com. n., neu. gen., s. num., 3rd per., obj. c., gov. by the tr. v. "lighted." |
| 3. demand | An abs. n., neu. gen., s. num., 3rd per., nom. c. to the v. "had been increasing." |
| for | A prep. |
| amusement | An abs. n., neu. gen., s. num., 3rd per., obj. c., gov. by the prep. "for." |
| and | A conj. |
| instruction | An abs. n., neu. gen., s. num., 3rd per., obj. c., gov. by the prep. *for* und. |
| had | An aux. v. to "been increasing," indg. pluperf. t. |
| during | A prep. |
| course | An abs. n., neu. gen., s. num., 3rd per., obj. c., gov. by the prep. "during." |
| of | A prep. |

| | |
|---|---|
| twenty | A def. card. nu. adj. of quantity, qual. the n. "years." |
| years | An abs. n., neu. gen., p. num., 3rd per., obj. c., gov. by the prep. "of." |
| been | A past pl. from the intr. v. "to be," ref. to "increasing demand," and aux. to "increasing," indg. prog. form. |
| gradually | An adv. |
| increasing | A pres. pl. from the intr. v. "to increase," ref. to "demand." |
| had been increasing. | A reg. intr. v., indic. m., pluperf. t., prog. form, s. num., 3rd per., agr. with its nom. "demand." |
| 4. On | A prep. |
| passage | An abs. n., neu. gen., s. num., 3rd per., obj. c., gov. by the prep. "on." |
| boat | A com. n., neu. gen., s. num., 3rd per., nom. c. to the v. "was driven." |
| was | An aux. v. to "driven," indg. pass. vo., past t. |
| driven | A past pl. from the tr. v. "to drive," ref. to "boat." |
| was driven | An irreg. tr. v., pass. vo., indic. m., past t., s. num., 3rd per., agr. with its nom. "boat." |
| by | A prep. |
| midnight | An abs. n. used as an adj. of quality, qual. the n. "storm." |
| storm | A com. n., neu. gen., s. num., 3rd per., obj. c., gov. by the prep. "by." |
| on | A prep. |
| rocks. | A com. n., neu. gen., p. num., 3rd per., obj. c., gov. by the prep. "on." |
| 5. Why | An adv. |
| do | An aux. v. to "treat," indg. pres. t., and completing the interrog. form of the v. |
| I | A pers. pron., com. gen., s. num., 1st per., nom. c. to the v. "do treat." |
| (to) treat | A reg. tr. v., act. vo., infin. m., pres. t., gov. by the v. "do." |
| do treat | A reg. tr. v., act. vo., indic. m., pres. t., s. num., 1st per., agr. with its nom. "I." |
| thee | A pers. pron., com. gen., s. num., 2nd per., obj. c., gov. by the tr. v. "do treat." |
| thus. | An adv. |
| 6. Though | A conj. |
| enemies | A com. n., com. gen., p. num., 3rd per., nom. c. to the v. "surround." |
| surround | A reg. tr. v., act. vo., subj. m., pres. t., p. num., 3rd per., agr. with its nom. "enemies." |
| me | A pers. pron., com. gen., s. num., 1st per., obj. c., gov. by the tr. v. "surround." |
| yet | A conj. |
| other | An indef. nu. adj. of quantity, qual. the n. "men." |
| men | A com. n., mas. gen., p. num., 3rd per., nom. c. to the v. *shall hear* und. (Other men *shall hear* and other times shall hear.) |
| and | A conj. |
| other | An indef. nu. adj. of quantity, qual. the n. "times." |
| times | An abs. n., neu. gen., p. num., 3rd per., nom. c. to the v. "shall hear." |
| shall | An aux. v. to "hear," indg. fut. t., emph. form, expressing "certainty." |
| (to) hear | An irreg. intr. v., infin. m., pres. t., gov. by the v. "shall." |
| shall hear. | An irreg. intr. v., indic. m., fut. t., emph. form, p. num., 3rd per., agr. with its nom. "times." |
| 7. experiment | An abs. n., neu. gen., s. num., 3rd per., nom. c. absolute. |
| having | A pres. pl. from the tr. v. "to have," ref. to "experiment," aux. to "failed," indg. perf. t. |
| thus | An adv. |
| failed | A past pl. from the intr. v. "to fail," ref. to "experiment." |
| having failed | A perf. pl. from the intr. v. "to fail," ref. to "experiment." |
| Cæsar | A prop. n., mas. gen., s. num., 3rd per., nom. c. to the v. "rose." |
| rose | An irreg. intr. v., indic. m., past t., s. num., 3rd per., agr. with its nom. "Cæsar." |
| and | A conj. |
| ordered | A reg. tr. v., act. vo., indic. m., past t., s. num., 3rd per., agr. with its nom. *Cæsar* und. |

| | |
|---|---|
| crown | A com. n., neu. gen., s. num., 3rd per., obj. c., gov. by the tr. v. "ordered." |
| to | A particle, indg. infin. m. |
| be | An aux. v. to "carried," indg. pass. vo. |
| carried | A past pl. from the tr. v. "to carry," ref. to "crown." |
| to be carried | A reg. tr. v., pass. vo., infin. m., pres. t., gov. by the v. "ordered." |
| to | A prep. |
| Capitol. | A prop. n., neu. gen., s. num., 3rd per., obj. c., gov. by the prep. "to." |

8. I — A pers. pron., com. gen., s. num., 1st per., nom. c. to the v. "love."

| | |
|---|---|
| love | A reg. tr. v., act vo., indic. m., pres. t., s. num., 1st per., agr. with its nom. "I." |
| you | A pers. pron., com. gen., p. num. (or s. num., p. form), 2nd per., obj. c., gov. by the tr. v. "love." |
| for | A prep. |
| lulling | A ger. from the tr. v. "to lull," neu. gen., s. num., 3rd per., obj. c., gov. by the prep. "for." (See also *Gr.* § 124, *Obs.* 4; *Man. of Parsing*, pp. 11, 73.) |
| me | A pers. pron., com. gen., s. num., 1st per., obj. c., gov. by the tr. ger. "lulling." |
| back | An adv. |
| into | A prep. |
| dreams | An abs. n., neu. gen., p. num., 3rd per., obj. c., gov. by the prep. "into." |
| Of | A prep. |
| blue | An adj. of quality, pos. deg., qual. the n. "mountains." |
| Highland | A prop. adj. of quality, qual. the n. "mountains." |
| mountains | A com. n., neu. gen., p. num., 3rd per, obj. c., gov. by the prep. "of." |
| and | A conj. |
| echoing | A pres. pl. used as an adj. of quality, qual. the n. "streams." |
| streams | A com. n., neu. gen., p. num., 3rd per., obj. c., gov. by the prep. *of* und. |
| And | A conj. |
| of | A prep. |
| birchen | An adj. of quality, qual. the n. "glades." |
| glades | A com. n., neu. gen., p. num., 3rd per., obj. c., gov. by the prep. "of." |
| breathing | A pres. pl. from the tr. v. "to breathe," ref. to "glades." |
| their | A pers. pron., neu. gen., p. num., 3rd per., poss. c., gov. by the n. "balm." |
| balm | A com. n., neu. gen., s. num., 3rd per., obj. c., gov. by the tr. pl. "breathing." |
| While | A conj. |
| deer | A com. n., com. gen., s. num., 3rd per., nom. c. to the v. "was seen." |
| was | An aux. v. to "seen," indg. pass. vo., past t. |
| seen | A past pl. from the tr. v. "to see," ref. to "deer." |
| was seen | An irreg. tr. v., pass. vo., indic. m., past t., s. num., 3rd per., agr. with its nom. "deer." |
| glancing | A pres. pl. from the intr. v. "to glance," ref. to "deer." |
| in | A prep. |
| sunshine | An abs. n., neu. gen., s. num., 3rd per., obj. c., gov. by the prep. "in." |
| remote | An adj. of quality, pos. deg., qual. the n. "sunshine." |
| And | A conj. |
| deep | An adj. of quality, pos. deg., qual. the n. "crush." |
| mellow | An adj. of quality, pos. deg., qual. the n. "crush." |
| crush | An abs. n., neu. gen., s. num., 3rd per., nom. c. to the v. "made." |
| of | A prep. |
| wood-pigeon's | A compd. com. n., com. gen., s. num., 3rd. per., poss. c., gov. by the n. "note." |
| note | An abs. n., neu. gen., s. num., 3rd per., obj. c., gov. by the prep. "of." |
| Made | An irreg. tr. v., act. vo., indic. m., past t., s. num., 3rd per., agr. with its nom. "crush." |

ENGLISH GRAMMAR AND ANALYSIS.    37

| | |
|---|---|
| music | An abs. n., neu. gen., s. num., 3rd per., obj. c., gov. by the tr. v. "made." |
| that | A rel. pron., neu. gen., s. num., 3rd per., agr. with its ant. "music," nom. c. to the v. "sweeten'd." |
| sweeten'd | A reg. tr. v., act. vo., indic. m., past t., s. num., 3rd per., agr. with its nom. "that." |
| calm. | An abs. n., neu. gen., s. num., 3rd per., obj. c., gov. by the tr. v. "sweeten'd." |
| 9. Men | A com. n., mas. gen., p. num., 3rd per., nom. c. to the v. "must work." |
| must | An aux. v. to "work," indg. pot. m., pres. t. |
| (to) work | An irreg. intr. v., infin. m., pres. t., gov. by the v. "must." |
| must work | An irreg. intr. v., pot. m., pres. t., p. num., 3rd per., agr. with its nom. "men." |
| and | A conj. |
| women | A com. n., fem. gen., p. num., 3rd per., nom. c. to the v. "must weep." |
| must | An aux. v. to "weep," indg. pot. m., pres. t. |
| (to) weep | An irreg. intr. v., infin. m., pres. t., gov. by the v. "must." |
| must weep | An irreg. intr. v., pot. m., pres. t., p. num., 3rd per., agr. with its nom. "women." |
| Though | A conj. |
| storms | A com. n., neu. gen., p. num., 3rd per., nom. c. to the v. "be." |
| be | An irreg. intr. v., subj. m., pres. t., p. num., 3rd per., agr. with its nom. "storms." |
| sudden | An adj. of quality, pos. deg., qual. the n. "storms." |
| and | A conj. |
| waters | A com. n., neu. gen., p. num., 3rd per., nom. c. to the v. be und. |
| deep | An adj. of quality, pos. deg., qual. the n. "waters." |
| And | A conj. |
| harbour | A com. n. used as an adj. of quality, qual. the n. "bar." |
| bar | A com. n., neu. gen., s. num., 3rd per., nom. c. to the v. "be moaning." |
| be | An aux. v. to "moaning," indg. pres. t., prog. form. |
| moaning | A pres. pl. from the intr. v. "to moan," ref. to "bar." |
| be moaning. | A reg. intr. v., subj. m., pres. t., s. num., 3rd per., agr. with its nom. "bar." |
| 10. soul's | A com. n., neu. gen., s. num., 3rd per., poss. c., gov. by the n. "cottage." |
| dark | An adj. of quality, pos. deg., qual. the n. "cottage." |
| cottage | A com. n., neu. gen., s. num., 3rd per., nom. c. to the v. "lets." |
| battered | A past pl. from the tr. v. "to batter," used as an adj. of quality, qual. the n. "cottage." |
| and | A conj. |
| decayed | An adj. of quality, qual. the n. *cottage* und. |
| Lets | An irreg. tr. v., act. vo., indic. m., pres. t., s. num., 3rd per., agr. with its nom. "cottage." |
| in | An adv. |
| new | An adj. of quality, pos. deg., qual. the n. "light." |
| light | A com. n., neu. gen., s. num., 3rd per., obj. c., gov. by the tr. v. "lets." |
| through | A prep. |
| chinks | A com. n., neu. gen., p. num., 3rd per., obj. c., gov. by the prep. "through." |
| that | A rel. pron., neu. gen., p. num., 3rd per., agr. with its ant. "chinks," obj. c., gov. by the tr. v. "has made." |
| time | An abs. n., neu. gen., s. num., 3rd per., nom. c. to the v. "has made." |
| has | An aux. v. to "made," indg. perf. t. |
| made | A past pl. from the tr. v. "to make," ref. to "that." |
| has made. | An irreg. tr. v., act. vo., indic. m., perf. t., s. num., 3rd per., agr. with its nom. "time." |
| 11. Speeding | A pres. pl. from the intr. v. "to speed," ref. to "train." |
| on | An adv. |
| with | A prep. |
| might | An abs. n., neu. gen., s. num., 3rd per., obj. c., gov. by the prep. "with." |
| and | A conj. |

| | |
|---|---|
| main | An abs. n., neu. gen., s. num., 3rd per., obj. c., gov. by the prep. *with* und. |
| Hitherward | An adv. |
| rides | An irreg. intr. v., indic. m., pres. t., s. num., 3rd per., agr. with its nom. "train." |
| gallant | An adj. of quality, pos. deg., qual. the n. "train." |
| train. | A com. col. n., neu. gen., s. num., 3rd per., nom. c. to the v. "rides." |
| 12. barking | A pres. pl. from the intr. v. "to bark," used as an adj. of quality, qual. the n. "sound." |
| sound | An abs. n., neu. gen., s. num., 3rd per., obj. c., gov. by the tr. v. "hears." |
| shepherd | A com. n., mas. gen., s. num., 3rd per., nom. c. to the v. "hears." |
| hears | An irreg. tr. v., act vo., indic. m., pres. t., s. num., 3rd per., agr. with its nom. "shepherd." |
| cry | An abs. n., neu. gen., s. num., 3rd per., obj. c., in app. with "sound." |
| as | A conj. |
| of | A prep. |
| dog | A com. n., com. gen., s. num. 3rd per., obj. c., gov. by the prep. "of." |
| or | A conj. |
| fox | A com. n., com. gen., s. num., 3rd per., obj. c., gov. by the prep. *of* und. |
| He | A pers. pron., mas. gen., s. num., 3rd per., nom. c. to the v. "halts." |
| halts | A reg. intr. v., indic. m., pres. t., s. num., 3rd per., agr. with its nom. "he." |
| and | A conj. |
| searches | A reg. intr. v., indic. m., pres. t., s. num., 3rd per., agr. with its nom. *he* und. |
| with | A prep. |
| his | A pers. pron., mas. gen., s. num., 3rd per., poss. c., gov. by the n. "eyes." |
| eyes | A com. n., neu. gen., p. num., 3rd per., obj. c., gov. by the prep. "with." |
| Among | A prep. |
| scattered | A past pl. from the tr. v. "to scatter," used as an adj. of quality, qual. the n. "rocks." |
| rocks | A com. n., neu. gen., p. num., 3rd per., obj. c., gov. by the prep. "among." |
| And | A conj. |
| now | An adv. |
| at | A prep. |
| distance | An abs. n., neu. gen., s. num., 3rd per., obj. c., gov. by the prep. "at." |
| can | An aux. v. to "discern," indg. pot. m., pres. t. |
| (to) discern | A reg. tr. v., act. vo., infin. m., pres. t., gov. by the v. "can." |
| can discern | A reg. tr. v., act. vo., pot. m., pres. t., s. num., 3rd per., agr. with its nom. *he* und. |
| stirring | A verbal or abs. n., neu. gen., s. num., 3rd per., obj. c., gov. by the tr. v. "can discern." |
| in | A prep. |
| brake | A com. n., neu. gen., s. num., 3rd per., obj. c., gov. by the prep. "in." |
| of | A prep. |
| fern | A com. n., neu. gen., s. num., 3rd per., obj. c., gov. by the prep. "of." |
| And | A conj. |
| instantly | An adv. |
| dog | A com. n., com. gen., s. num., 3rd per., nom. c. to the v. "is seen." |
| is | An aux. v. to "seen." indg. pass. vo., pres. t. |
| seen | A past pl. from the tr. v. "to see," ref. to "dog." |
| is seen | An irreg. tr. v., pass. vo., indic. m., pres. t., s. num., 3rd per., agr. with its nom. "dog." |
| Glancing | A pres. pl. from the intr. v. "to glance," ref. to "dog." |
| through | A prep. |

| | |
|---|---|
| that | A dis. adj., lim. the n. "covert.' |
| covert | A com. n., neu. gen., s. num., 3rd per., obj. c., gov. by the prep. "through." |
| green. | An adj. of quality, pos. deg., qual. the n. "covert." |

### Exercise 68.

1. Also, *deg.* 2. Low, *man.* 3. Here, *place.* 4. Too, *deg.*; at last, *time.* 5. Anon, *time.* 6. So, *man.* 7. Now, *time.* 8. Yes, *m.* (*aff.*). 9. Still, *deg.*; more, *deg.* 10. Not, *m.* (*neg.*). 11. Upward, *place.* 12. Afield, *place.* 13. To and fro, *compd. adv. or advl. phrase, place.* 14. Sometimes, *time;* near, *place.* 15. Never, *time;* elsewhere, *place;* so, *deg.* 16. Perchance, *m.* (*probability and doubt*). 17. Together, *man.;* gently, *man.;* carefully, *man.;* about, *place.* 18. Here, *place;* very, *deg.;* much, *mea.*

### Exercise 69.

1. Wherefore. 2. Where. 3. Why. 4. How. 5. Whither. 6. Whence. 7. Wherewith. 8. Where. 9. Wherewithal. 10. Whereby. 11. Wherein. 12. When.

### Exercise 70.

Yet, *time;* once, *num. and order;* heretofore, *time;* well, *man.;* gently, *man.;* now, *time;* still, (1) *time,* (2) *deg.;* how, (1) *man.,* (2) *deg.;* oft, *time;* perhaps, *m.* (*probability and doubt*); fast, *man.;* ever, *time;* not, *m.* (*neg.*); so, (1) *man.* (2) *deg.;* bravely, *man.;* more, (1) *deg.,* (2) *time;* when, *time;* then, *time;* no, *m.* (*neg.*); hither, *place;* already, *time;* where, *place;* only, *deg.;* dearly, *man.;* soon, *time;* within, *place;* certainly, *m.* (*aff.*); here, *place;* almost, *deg.;* really, *m.* (*aff.*).

### Exercise 71.

1. They speak *angrily.* 2. He treated his brother *kindly.* 3. *Vainly* doth valour bleed, while avarice and rapine share the land. 4. Act *humbly.* 5. How marvellous are thy works! *wisely* hast thou made them all. 6. The knight spoke *sincerely.* 7. They came *eagerly,* and departed *reluctantly.* 8. His successor was received *joyfully* and *gladly.* 9. They cultivated *more successfully* the sublime science of astronomy. 10. They worked *industriously.*

### Exercise 72.

Dear, *dearly;* weary, *wearily;* noble, *nobly;* generous, *generously;* brave, *bravely;* dark, *darkly;* gay, *gaily;* distinct, *distinctly;* cheerful, *cheerfully;* glad, *gladly;* bright, *brightly;* glorious, *gloriously;* sweet, *sweetly;* soft, *softly;* wild, *wildly;* sad, *sadly;* right, *rightly;* large, *largely;* graceful, *gracefully;* near, *nearly;* gallant, *gallantly;* wide, *widely;* bold, *boldly;* sure, *surely;* hearty, *heartily;* happy, *happily;* fierce, *fiercely;* warm, *warmly;* exquisite, *exquisitely;* real, *really.*

### Exercise 73.

1. They *now* regarded us with suspicion. 2. He lived *securely* in a strong castle. 3. The widow was *very* poor. 4. My father was *away* from home. 5. Summer has come *again.* 6. *There* they lay weltering

in their blood. 7. We heard the news *yesterday*. 8. The old man could *scarcely* walk. 9. The work was *well* done. 10. I *often* travelled through that forest. 11. They would *not* listen to me. 12. The men were ordered to march *forward*.

N.B.—Any sentence containing one of the adverbs will suffice.

## Exercise 74.

| Pos. | Comp. | Superl. | Pos. | Comp. | Superl. |
|---|---|---|---|---|---|
| Much, | More, | Most. | Little, | Less, | Least. |
| Gladly, | More gladly, | Most gladly. | Hard, | Harder, | Hardest. |
| Near, | Nearer, | Nearest, next. | Loud, | Louder, | Loudest. |
| Soon, | Sooner, | Soonest. | Forth, | Further, | Furthest. |
| Badly | Worse, | Worst. | Long, | Longer, | Longest. |
| Sumptuously, | More sumptuously, | Most sumptuously. | Civilly, | More civilly, | Most civilly. |
| Far, | Farther, | Farthest. | Early, | Earlier, | Earliest. |
| Seldom, | Seldomer, | Seldomest. | Happily, | More happily, | Most happily. |
| Late, | Later, | Last. | Merrily, | More merrily, | Most merrily. |
| Often, | Oftener, | Oftenest. | Nigh, | Nigher, | Nighest, next. |
| Ill, | Worse, | Worst. | Evilly, | Worse, | Worst. |
| Vigorously, | More vigorously, | Most vigorously. | Rapidly, | More rapidly, | Most rapidly. |

## Exercise 75.

1. Seldom, *pos.*; here.* 2. More exactly, *comp.* 3. Closest, *superl.*; most, *superl.* 4. Fast, *pos.*; fast, *pos.* 5. Better, *comp.* 6. Most divinely, *superl.* 7. Better, *comp.* 8. Most bitterly, *superl.* 9. Loud, *pos.*; louder, *comp.* 10. Never;* more deep [ly], *comp.*

* Not compared.

## Exercise 76.

| | | |
|---|---|---|
| 1. I | | A pers. pron., com. gen., s. num., 1st per., nom. c. to the v. "am." |
| | am | An irreg. intr. v., indic. m., pres. t., s. num., 1st per., agr. with its nom. "I." |
| | for | A prep. |
| | managing | A ger. from the tr. v. "to manage," neu. gen., s. num., 3rd per., obj. c., gov. by the prep. "for." (See *Gr.* § 124, *Obs.* 4; *Man. of Parsing*, pp. 71—74.) |
| | it | A pers. pron., neu. gen., s. num., 3rd per., obj. c., gov. by the tr. ger. "managing." |
| | rationally. | An adv. of man., mod. the ger. "managing." |
| 2. Weeks | | An abs. n., neu. gen., p. num., 3rd per., nom. c. to the v. "went." |
| | went | An irreg. intr. v., indic. m., past t., p. num., 3rd per., agr. with its nom. "weeks." |
| | by. | An adv. of place, mod. the v. "went." |
| 3. Adam | | A prop. n., mas. gen., s. num., 3rd per., nom. c. to the v. "saw." |
| | immediately | An adv. of time, mod. the v. "saw." |
| | saw | An irreg. tr. v., act. vo., indic. m., past t., s. num., 3rd per., agr. with its nom. "Adam." |
| | in | A prep. |
| | his | A pers. pron., mas. gen., s. num., 3rd per., poss. c., gov. by the n. "mind." |
| | mind | A com. n., neu. gen., s. num., 3rd per., obj. c., gov. by the prep. "in." |
| | plan | A com. n., neu. gen., s. num., 3rd per., obj. c., gov. by the tr. v. "saw." |
| | for | A prep. |
| | building | A ger. from the tr. v. "to build," neu. gen., s. num., 3rd per., obj. c., gov. by the prep. "for." |
| | it | A pers. pron., neu. gen., s. num., 3rd per., obj. c., gov. by the tr. ger. "building." |

| | |
|---|---|
| up | An adv. of man., mod. the ger. "building." |
| again. | An adv. of time, mod. the ger. "building." |
| 4. Giving | A pres. pl. from the tr. v. "to give," ref. to "I." |
| up | An adv. of man., mod. the pl. "giving." |
| argument | An abs. n., neu. gen., s. num., 3rd per., obj. c., gov. by the tr. pl. "giving." |
| I | A pers. pron., com. gen., s. num., 1st per., nom. c. to the v. "went." |
| went | An irreg. intr. v., indic. m., past t., s. num., 1st per., agr. with its nom. "I." |
| straight | An adv. of man, mod. the v. "went." |
| to | A prep. |
| my | A pers. pron., com. gen., s. num., 1st per., poss. c., gov. by the n. "lodgings." |
| lodgings. | A com. n., neu. gen., p. num., 3rd per., obj. c., gov. by the prep. "to." |
| 5. Harness | A reg. tr. v., act. vo., imper. m., pres. t., p. num. (or s. num., p. form), 2nd per., agr. with its nom. *you* und. |
| me | A pers. pron., com. gen., s. num., 1st per., obj. c., gov. by the tr. v. "harness." |
| down | An adv. of place, mod. the v. "harness." |
| with | A prep. |
| your | A pers. pron., com. gen., p. num. (or s. num., p. form), 2nd per., poss. c., gov. by the n. "bands." |
| iron | A com. n., used as an adj. of quality, qual. the n. "bands." |
| bands. | A com. n., neu. gen., p. num., 3rd per., obj. c., gov. by the prep. "with." |
| 6. Show | An irreg. tr. v., act. vo., imper. m., pres. t., s. or p. num., 2nd per., agr. with its nom. *thou* or *you* und. |
| him | A pers. pron., mas. gen., s. num., 3rd per., obj. c., gov. by the tr. v. "show." |
| in. | An adv. of place, mod. the v. "show." |
| 7. I | A pers. pron., com. gen., s. num., 1st per., nom. c. to the v. "did wonder." |
| did | An aux. v. to "wonder," indg. past t., and completing the neg. form of the v. |
| not | An adv. of m. (neg.) mod. the v. "did wonder." |
| (to) wonder | A reg. intr. v., infin. m., pres. t., gov. by the v. "did." |
| did wonder. | A reg. intr. v., indic. m., past t., s. num., 1st per., agr. with its nom. "I." |
| 8. He | A pers. pron., mas. gen., s. num., 3rd per., nom. c. to the v. "enquired." |
| then | An adv. of time, mod. the v. "enquired." |
| enquired | A reg. intr. v., indic. m., past t., s. num., 3rd per., agr. with its nom. "he." |
| after | A prep. |
| ghost. | A com. n., com. gen., s. num., 3rd per., obj. c., gov. by the prep. "after." |
| 9. I | A pers. pron., com. gen., s. num., 1st per., nom. c. to the v. "am." |
| am | An irreg. intr. v., indic. m., pres. t., s. num., 1st per., agr. with its nom. "I." |
| to | A particle, indg. infin. m. |
| to desire | A reg. tr. v., act. vo., infin. m., pres. t., gov. by the v. "am." |
| that | A conj. |
| you | A pers. pron., com. gen., s. num., p. form., 2nd per., nom. c. to the v. "would give." |
| would | An aux. v. to "give," indg. pot. m., past t. |
| now | An adv. of time, mod. the v. "would give." |
| and | A conj. |
| then | An adv. of time, mod. the v. "would give." |
| (to) give | An irreg. tr. v., act. vo., infin. m., pres. t., gov. by the v. "would." |
| would give | An irreg. tr. v., act. vo., pot. m., past t., s. num., p. form., 2nd per., agr. with its nom. "you." |
| us | A pers. pron., com. gen., p. num., 1st per., obj. c., gov. by the prep. *to* und. |
| lesson | An abs. n., neu. gen., s. num., 3rd per., obj. c., gov. by the tr. v. "would give." |

| | |
|---|---|
| on | A prep. |
| good | An adj. of quality, pos. deg., qual. the n. "humour." |
| humour. | An abs. n., neu. gen., s. num., 3rd per., obj. c., gov. by the prep. "on." |
| 10. Partridge | A prop. n., mas. gen., s. num., 3rd per., nom. c. to the v. "declared." |
| immediately | An adv. of time, mod. the v. "declared." |
| declared | A reg. tr. v., act. vo., indic. m., past t., s. num., 3rd per., agr. with its nom. "Partridge." |
| it | A pers. pron., neu. gen., s. num., 3rd per., nom. c. to the v. "was." |
| was | An irreg. intr. v., indic. m., past t., s. num., 3rd per., agr. with its nom. "it." |
| finest | An adj. of quality, superl. deg., qual. the n. "place." |
| place | A com. n., neu. gen., s. num., 3rd per., nom. c. after the v. "was." |
| he | A pers. pron., mas. gen., s. num., 3rd per., nom. c. to the v. "had been." |
| had | An aux. v. to "been," indg. pluperf. t. |
| ever | An adv. of time, mod. the v. "had been." |
| been | A past pl. from the intr. v. "to be," ref. to "he." |
| had been | An irreg. intr. v., indic. m., pluperf. t., s. num., 3rd per., agr. with its nom. "he." |
| in. | A prep. (In *which* he had ever been.) |
| 11. Deep | An adv. of man., mod. the v. "mourns." |
| mourns | A reg. intr. v., indic. m., pres. t., s. num., 3rd per., agr. with its nom. "turtle." |
| turtle | A com. n., com. gen., s. num., 3rd per., nom. c. to the v. "mourns." |
| in | A prep. |
| sequestered | An adj. of quality, pos. deg., qual. the n. "bower." |
| bower. | A com. n., neu. gen., s. num., 3rd per., obj. c. gov. by the prep. "in." |
| 12. Oft | An adv. of time, mod. the v. "shall lift." |
| shall | An aux. v. to "lift," indg. fut. t., emph. form, expressing "certainty." |
| pilgrim | A com. n., com. gen., s. num., 3rd per., nom. c. to the v. "shall lift." |
| (to) lift | A reg. tr. v., act. vo., infin. m., pres. t., gov. by the v. "shall." |
| shall lift | A reg. tr. v., act. v., indic. m., fut. t., emph. form, s. num., 3rd per., agr. with its nom. "pilgrim." |
| latch. | A com. n., neu. gen., s. num., 3rd per., obj. c., gov. by the tr. v. "shall lift." |
| 13. I | A pers. pron., com. gen., s. num., 1st per., nom. c. to the v. "can listen." |
| can | An aux. v. to "listen," indg. pot. m., pres. t. |
| (to) listen | A reg. intr. v., infin. m., pres. t., gov. by the v. "can." |
| can listen | A reg. intr. v., pot. m., pres. t., s. num., 1st per., agr. with its nom. "I." |
| to | A prep. |
| thee | A pers. pron., com. gen., s. num., 2nd per., obj. c., gov. by the prep. "to." |
| yet. | An adv. of time, mod. the v. "can listen." |
| 14. Down | An adv. of place, mod. the v. "throws." |
| he | A pers. pron., mas. gen., s. num., 3rd per., nom. c. to the v. "throws." |
| throws | An irreg. tr. v., act. vo., indic. m., pres. t., s. num., 3rd per., agr. with its nom. "he." |
| his | A pers. pron., mas. gen., s. num., 3rd per., poss. c., gov. by the n. "flowers." |
| flowers. | A com. n., neu. gen., p. num., 3rd per., obj. c., gov. by the tr. v. "throws." |
| 15. Beneath | A prep. |
| these | A dis. adj., lim. the n. "boughs." |
| fruit-tree | A compd. com. n. used as an adj. of quality, qual. the n. "boughs." |
| boughs | A com. n., neu. gen., p. num., 3rd per., obj. c., gov. by the prep. "beneath." |

| | |
|---|---|
| that | A rel. pron., neu. gen., p. num., 3rd per., agr. with its ant. "boughs," nom. c. to the v. "shed." |
| shed | An irreg. tr. v., act. vo., indic. m., pres. t., p. num., 3rd per., agr. with its nom. "that." |
| Their | A pers. pron., neu. gen., p. num., 3rd per., poss. c., gov. by the n. "blossoms." |
| snow-white | A compd. adj. of quality, qual. the n. "blossoms." |
| blossoms | A com. n., neu. gen., p. num., 3rd per., obj. c., gov. by the tr. v. "shed." |
| on | A prep. |
| my | A pers. pron., com. gen., s. num., 1st per., poss. c., gov. by the n. "head." |
| head | A com. n., neu. gen., s. num., 3rd per., obj. c., gov. by the prep. "on." |
| With | A prep. |
| brightest | An adj. of quality, superl. deg., qual. the n. "sunshine." |
| sunshine | A com. n., neu. gen., s. num., 3rd per., obj. c., gov. by the prep. "with." |
| round | A prep. |
| me | A pers. pron., com. gen., s. num., 1st per., obj. c., gov. by the prep. "round." |
| spread | A past pl. from the tr. v. "to spread," ref. to "sunshine." |
| Of | A prep. |
| Spring's | An abs. n. used as a prop. n., neu. gen., s. num., 3rd per., poss. c., gov. by the n. "weather." |
| unclouded | An adj. of quality, qual. the n. "weather." |
| weather | An abs. n., neu. gen., s. num., 3rd per., obj. c., gov. by the prep. "of." |
| In | A prep. |
| this | A dis. adj., lim. the n. "nook." |
| sequestered | An adj. of quality, pos. deg., qual. the n. "nook." |
| nook | A com. n., neu. gen., s. num., 3rd per., obj. c., gov. by the prep. "in." |
| how | An adv. of deg., mod. the adj. "sweet." |
| sweet | An adj. of quality, pos. deg., qual. "to sit." |
| To | A particle, indg. infin. m. |
| To sit | An irreg. intr. v., infin. m., pres. t., used as an abs. n., neu. gen., s. num., 3rd per., nom. c. to the verb *is* und. |
| upon | A prep. |
| my | A pers. pron., com. gen., s. num., 1st per., poss. c., gov. by the n. "orchard-seat." |
| orchard-seat | A compd. com. n., neu. gen., s. num., 3rd per., obj. c., gov. by the prep. "upon." |
| And | A conj. |
| birds | A com. n., com. gen., p. num., 3rd per., obj. c., gov. by the tr. v. "to greet." |
| and | A conj. |
| flowers | A com. n., neu. gen., p. num., 3rd per., obj. c., gov. by the tr. v. "to greet." |
| once | An adv. of num., mod. the v. "to greet." |
| more | An adv. of time, mod. the v. "to greet." |
| to | A particle, indg. infin. m. |
| to greet | A reg. tr. v., act. vo., infin. m., pres. t., used as an abs. n., neu. gen., s. num., 3rd per., nom. c. to the v. *is* und. (*How sweet to greet is.*) |
| My | A pers. pron., com. gen., s. num., 1st per., poss. c., gov. by the n. "friends." |
| last | An adj. of quality, superl. deg., qual. the n. "year's." |
| year's | An abs. n., neu. gen., s. num., 3rd per., poss. c., gov. by the n. "friends." |
| friends | A com. n., com. and neu. gen., p. num., 3rd per., obj. c., in app. with "birds and flowers." |
| together. | An adv. of man., mod. the v. "to greet." |

## Exercise 77.

1. Robin *on* spray. 2. To be executed *with* despatch. 3. Busied *with* sketching. 4. Sat *on* block; sat *with* head; resting *on* planing-table. 5. Was *on* point; point *of* setting. 6. Hurried *across* Chase; stalking *along* paths; paths *between* fern. 7. Have looked *for* which; have looked [*on*] nights; have looked [*on*] mornings. 8. Ripe *for* rising. 9. Zealous *for* inquiry. 10. Were *in* afternoon; were *in* barge; games *on* river. 11. Wore *in* day; shirt *of* mail; wore *under* robes; slept *with* guard; guard *of* men. 12. Lives *in* Washington; world *of* care.

## Exercise 78.

1. Was acquainted-with. 2. Dream-of. 3. Talked-of. 4. Prate-of. 5. Beware-of. 6. Will speak-to. 7. Is harping-on. 8. Had heard-of. 9. Thought-of. 10. Laugh-at. 11. Beware-of. 12. Smiling-at. 13. Stand-by. 14. Made-for. 15. Met-with. 16. Wondered-at. 17. Did come-by. 18. Play-at.

## Exercise 79.

1. It — A pers. pron., neu. gen., s. num., 3rd per., nom. c. to the v. "was."
was — An irreg. intr. v., indic. m., past. t., s. num., 3rd per., agr. with its nom. "it."
nigh — A prep., sh. the rn. bet. "was" and "hour."
hour — An abs. n., neu. gen., s. num., 3rd per., obj. c., gov. by the prep. "nigh."
of — A prep., sh. the rn. bet. "hour" and "prayer."
evening — An abs. n. used as an adj. of quality, qual. the n. "prayer."
prayer. — An abs. n., neu. gen., s. num., 3rd per., obj. c., gov. by the prep. "of."

2. From — A prep., sh. the rn. bet. "had received," and "nature."
nature — An abs. n., neu. gen., s. num., 3rd per., obj. c., gov. by the prep. "from."
he — A pers. pron., mas. gen., s. num., 3rd per., nom. c. to the v. "had received."
had — An aux. v. to "received," indg. pluperf. t.
received — A past pl. from the tr. v. "to receive," ref. to "figure."
had received — A reg. tr. v., act. vo., indic. m., pluperf. t., s. num., 3rd per., agr. with its nom. "he."
uncouth — An adj. of quality, pos. deg., qual. the n. "figure."
figure. — A com. n., neu. gen., s. num., 3rd per., obj. c., gov. by the tr. v. "had received."

3. On — A prep., sh. the rn. bet. "takes" and "Areopagus."
Areopagus — A prop. n., neu. gen., s. num., 3rd per., obj. c., gov. by the prep. "on."
Christian — A prop. adj. of quality, qual. the n. "leader."
leader — A com. n., mas. gen., s. num., 3rd per., nom. c. to the v. "takes."
takes — An irreg. tr. v., act. vo., indic. m., pres. t., s. num., 3rd per., agr. with its nom. "leader."
his — A pers. pron., mas. gen., s. num., 3rd per., poss. c., gov. by the n. "stand."
stand. — A com. n., neu. gen., s. num., 3rd per., obj. c., gov. by the tr. v. "takes."

4. This — A dis. adj., lim. the n. "tale."
tale — An abs. n., neu. gen., s. num., 3rd per., nom. c. to the v. "awakened."
awakened — A reg. tr. v., act. vo., indic. m., past t., s. num., 3rd per., agr. with its nom. "tale."
pity — An abs. n., neu. gen., s. num., 3rd per., obj. c., gov. by the tr. v. "awakened."
of — A prep., sh. the rn. bet. "pity" and "auditors."

| | |
|---|---|
| auditors. | A com. n., com. gen., p. num., 3rd per., obj. c., gov. by the prep. "of." |
| 5. They | A pers. pron., com. gen., p. num., 3rd per., nom. c. to the v. "went." |
| went | An irreg. intr. v., indic. m., past t., p. num., 3rd per., agr. with its nom. "they." |
| into | A prep., sh. the rn. bet. "went" and "Leicestershire." |
| Leicestershire | A prop. n., neu. gen., s. num., 3rd per., obj. c., gov. by the prep. "into." |
| and | A conj. |
| came | An irreg. intr. v., indic. m., past t., p. num., 3rd per., agr. with its nom. *they* and. |
| to | A prep., sh. the rn. bet. "came" and "Bosworth Field." |
| Bosworth Field. | A compd. prop. n., neu. gen., s. num., 3rd per., obj. c. gov. by the prep. "to." |
| 6. senate | A com. col. n., neu. gen., s. num., 3rd per., nom. c. to the v. "awarded." |
| awarded | A reg. tr. v., act. vo., indic. m., past t., s. num., 3rd per., agr. with its nom. "senate." |
| prize | A com. n., neu. gen., s. num., 3rd per., obj. c., gov. by the tr. v. "awarded." |
| of | A prep., sh. the rn. bet. "prize" and "eloquence." |
| eloquence | An abs. n., neu. gen., s. num., 3rd per., obj. c., gov. by the prep. "of." |
| to | A prep., sh. the rn. bet. "awarded" and "Tiberius." |
| Tiberius. | A prop. n., mas. gen., s. num., 3rd per., obj. c., gov. by the prep. "to." |
| 7. Augustus | A prop. n., mas. gen., s. num., 3rd per., nom. c. to the v. "wrote." |
| wrote | An irreg. tr. v., act. vo., indic. m., past t., s. num., 3rd per., agr. with its nom. "Augustus." |
| verses | A com. n., neu. gen., p. num., 3rd per., obj. c., gov. by the tr. v. "wrote." |
| against | A prep., sh. the rn. bet. "wrote" and "Asinius." |
| Asinius. | A prop. n., mas. gen., s. num., 3rd per., obj. c., gov. by the prep. "against." |
| 8. allegory | A com. n., neu. gen., s. num., 3rd per., nom. c. to the v. "has been read." |
| of | A prep., sh. the rn. bet. "allegory" and "Bunyan." |
| Bunyan | A prop. n., mas. gen., s. num., 3rd per., obj. c., gov. by the prep. "of." |
| has | An aux. v. to "been read," indg. perf. t. |
| been | A past pl. from the intr. v. "to be," ref. to "read allegory," and aux. to "read," indg. pass. vo. |
| read | A past pl. from the tr. v. "to read," ref. to "allegory." |
| has been read | An irreg. tr. v., pass. vo., indic. m., perf. t., s. num., 3rd per., agr. with its nom. "allegory." |
| by | A prep., sh. the rn. bet. "has been read" and "thousands." |
| many | An indef. nu. adj. of quantity, qual. the n. "thousands." |
| thousands | A com. n., com. gen., p. num., 3rd per., obj. c., gov. by the prep. "by." |
| with | A prep., sh. the rn. bet. "has been read" and "tears." |
| tears. | A com. n., neu. gen., p. num., 3rd per., obj. c., gov. by the prep. "with." |
| 9. At | A prep., sh. the rn. bet. "passes" and "end." |
| end | A com. n., neu. gen., s. num., 3rd per., obj. c., gov. by the prep. "at." |
| of | A prep., sh. the rn. bet. "end" and "valley." |
| long | An adj. of quality, pos. deg., qual. the n. "valley." |
| dark | An adj. of quality, pos. deg., qual. the n. "valley." |
| valley | A com. n., neu. gen., s. num., 3rd per., obj. c., gov. by the prep. "of." |
| he | A pers. pron., mas. gen., s. num., 3rd per., nom. c. to the v. "passes." |
| passes | A reg. tr. v., act. vo., indic. m., pres. t., s. num., 3rd per., agr. with its nom. "he." |
| dens | A com. n., neu. gen., p. num., 3rd per., obj. c., gov. by the tr. v. "passes." |

| | |
|---|---|
| in | A prep., sh. the rn. bet. "dwell" and "which." |
| which | A rel. pron., neu. gen., p. num., 3rd per., agr. with its ant. "dens," obj. c., gov. by the prep. "in." |
| old | An adj. of quality, pos. deg., qual. the n. "giants." |
| giants | A com. n., mas. gen., p. num., 3rd per., nom. c. to the v. "dwell." |
| dwell. | An irreg. intr. v., indic. m., pres. t., p. num., 3rd per., agr. with its nom. "giants." |
| 10. His | A pers. pron., mas. gen., s. num., 3rd per., poss. c., gov. by the n. "cry." |
| last | An adj. of quality, superl. deg., qual. the n. "cry." |
| cry | An abs. n., neu. gen., s. num., 3rd per., nom. c. to the v. "comes." |
| of | A prep., sh. the rn. bet. "cry" and "anger." |
| anger | An abs. n., neu. gen., s. num., 3rd per., obj. c., gov. by the prep. "of." |
| comes | An irreg. intr. v., indic. m., pres. t., s. num., 3rd per., agr. with its nom. "cry." |
| back | An adv. of place, mod. the v. "comes." |
| from | A prep., sh. the rn. bet. "comes" and "skies." |
| skies. | A com. n., neu. gen., p. num., 3rd per., obj. c., gov. by the prep. "from." |
| 11 He | A pers. pron., mas. gen., s. num., 3rd per., nom. c. to the v. "told." |
| told | An irreg. tr. v., act. vo., indic. m., past. t., s. num., 3rd per., agr. with its nom. "he." |
| how | A conj. |
| murderers | A com. n., com. gen., p. num., 3rd per., nom. c. to the v. "walked." |
| walked | A reg. intr. v., indic. m., past. t., p. num., 3rd per., agr. with its nom. "murderers." |
| earth | A com. n., neu. gen., s. num., 3rd per., obj. c., gov. by the prep. *upon* und. |
| Beneath | A prep., sh. the rn. bet. "walked" and "curse." |
| curse | An abs. n., neu. gen., s. num., 3rd per., obj. c., gov. by the prep. "beneath." |
| of | A prep., sh. the rn. bet. "curse" and "Cain. |
| Cain | A prop. n., mas. gen., s. num., 3rd per., obj. c., gov. by the prep. "of." |
| With | A prep., sh. the rn. bet. "walked" and "clouds." |
| crimson | An adj. of quality, qual. the n. "clouds." |
| clouds | A com. n., neu. gen., p. num., 3rd per., obj. c., gov. by the prep. "with." |
| before | A prep., sh. the rn. bet. "clouds" and "eyes." |
| their | A pers. pron., com. gen., p. num., 3rd per., poss. c., gov. by the n. "eyes." |
| eyes | A com. n., neu. gen., p. num., 3rd per., obj. c., gov. by the prep. "before." |
| And | A conj. |
| flames | A com. n., neu. gen., p. num., 3rd per., obj. c., gov. by the prep. *with* und. |
| about | A prep., sh. the rn. bet. "flames" and "brain." |
| their | A pers. pron., com. gen., p. num., 3rd per., poss. c., gov. by the n. "brain." |
| brain. | A com. n., neu. gen., s. num., 3rd per., obj. c., gov. by the prep. "about." |
| 12. He | A pers. pron., mas. gen., s. num., 3rd per., nom. c. to the v. "sat." |
| sat | An irreg. intr. v., indic. m., past. t., s. num., 3rd per., agr. with its nom. "he." |
| upon | A prep., sh. the rn. bet. "sat" and "shore." |
| wave-washed | A compd. adj. of quality, qual. the n. "shore." |
| shore | A com. n., neu. gen., s. num., 3rd per., obj. c., gov. by the prep. "upon." |
| With | A prep., sh. the rn. bet. "sat" and "madness." |
| madness | An abs. n., neu. gen., s. num., 3rd per., obj c., gov. by the prep. "with." |
| in | A prep., sh. the rn. bet. "madness" and "eye." |

| | |
|---|---|
| his | A pers. pron., mas. gen., s. num., 3rd per., poss. c., gov. by the n. "eye." |
| eye. | A com. n., neu. gen., s. num., 3rd per., obj. c., gov. by the prep. "in." |

## Exercise 80.

N.B.—A conjunction joins two sentences. When a conjunction appears to join words, two sentences are, in reality, implied. It is, however, sometimes difficult to resolve satisfactorily a construction of this kind into two sentences. In such cases it will be sufficient to consider the conjunction as joining words and to take the words so joined as a compound form. (*Parsing*, pp. 84, 85.)

*The Conjunctions are placed between the Sentences they join.*

1. I pressed my shivering children to my bosom, *but* I could not speak. 2. Daisy *and*\* buttercup. 3. The winter was long *and* [the winter was] dreary; [the winter was] dreary *but* it is all over now. 4. Every avenue to escape was closed, *for* the entrance to the square was choked up. 5. It was not long before sunset *when* the van of the royal procession entered the gates of the city. 6. You can correct it *if* what you have written should turn out imperfect. 7. The little birds will cover us with leaves *as* they did [cover] the babes in the wood. 8. I never knew *how* ill she was; I never knew *till* the fever came upon her. 9. I am never alarmed *except*† [it be]; [it be] *when* I am informed; I am informed *that* the sovereigns want treasure. 10. You are more active *than* I [am active].

## Exercise 81.

1. Neither...nor. 2. Such...that. 3. Such...as. 4. Where...there. 5. Nor...nor. 6. Though...yet. 7. Whether...or. 8. Both...and. 9. So...that. 10. Nor...nor...nor. 11. Either...or. 12. When...then. 13. As...so. 14. Rather...than. 15. Since...therefore.

## Exercise 82.

| | |
|---|---|
| 1. He | A pers. pron., mas. gen., s. num., 3rd per., nom. c. to the v. "was." |
| was | An irreg. intr. v., indic. m., past t., s. num., 3rd per., agr. with its nom. "he." |
| gallant | An adj. of quality, pos. deg., qual. the pron. "he." |
| and‡ | A cop. conj., jg. the sents. "He was gallant" and "*he was* free." |
| free. | An adj. of quality, pos. deg., qual. the pron. *he* und. |
| 2. He | A pers. pron., mas. gen., s. num., 3rd per., nom. c. to the v. "darted." |
| darted | A reg. intr. v., indic. m., past t., s. num., 3rd per., agr. with its nom. "he." |
| to | A prep., sh. the rn., bet. "darted" and "conclusion." |
| conclusion | An abs. n., neu. gen., s. num., 3rd per., obj. c., gov. by the prep. "to." |
| rather | An adv. of deg., mod. the v. "darted." |
| by | A prep., sh. the rn. bet. "darted" and "intuition." |
| intuition | An abs. n., neu. gen., s. num., 3rd per., obj. c., gov. by the prep. "by." |
| than | A disj. conj., cor. to adv. "rather," jg. the sents. "He darted ... intuition" and "*he darted to a conclusion* by reasoning." |

\* It is more convenient to make the conj. "and" join "daisy" and "buttercup." The sentences implied, however, are "The daisy is nodding courteously" and "the buttercup is nodding courteously."

† *Except when* may also be taken together as a compd. conj.

‡ *And* may also be parsed as joining the words *gallant* and *free.*

## 48 KEY TO

| | |
|---|---|
| by | A prep., sh. the rn. bet. *darted* und. and "reasoning." |
| reasoning. | An abs. n., neu. gen., s. num., 3rd per., obj. c., gov. by the prep. "by." |
| 3. If | A cop. conj., jg. the sents. "I should have dropped" and "I had looked a moment longer," and indg. subj. m. |
| I | A pers. pron., com. gen., s. num., 1st per., nom. c. to the v. "had looked." |
| had | An aux. v. to "looked," indg. pluperf. t. |
| looked | A past pl. from the intr. v. "to look," ref. to "I." |
| had looked | A reg. intr. v., subj. m., pluperf. t., s. num., 1st per., agr. with its nom. "I." |
| moment | An abs. n., neu. gen., s. num., 3rd per., obj. c., gov. by the prep. *for* und. |
| longer | An adv. of time, comp. deg., mod. the v. "had looked." |
| I | A pers. pron., com. gen., s. num., 1st per., nom. c. to the v. "should have dropped." |
| should | An aux. v. to "have dropped," indg. pot. m. |
| have | An aux. v. to "dropped," and, together with "should," indg. pluperf. t. |
| dropped | A past pl. from the intr. v. "to drop," ref. to "I." |
| should have dropped. | A reg. intr. v., pot. m., pluperf. t., s. num., 1st per., agr. with its nom. "I." |
| 4. He | A pers. pron., mas. gen., s. num., 3rd per., nom. c. to the v. "suffered." |
| suffered | A reg. intr. v., indic. m., past t., s. num., 3rd per., agr. with its nom. "he." |
| but | A disj. conj., jg. the sents. "He suffered" and "his pangs are o'er." |
| his | A pers. pron., mas. gen., s. num., 3rd per., poss. c., gov. by the n. "pangs." |
| pangs | An abs. n., neu. gen., p. num., 3rd per., nom. c. to the v. "are." |
| are | An irreg. intr. v., indic. m., pres. t., p. num., 3rd per., agr. with its nom. "pangs." |
| o'er. | An adv. of time, mod. the v. "are." |
| 5. Out | An adv. of man., mod. the v. "went." |
| went | An irreg. intr. v., indic. m., past t., s. num., 3rd per., agr. with its nom. "taper." |
| taper | A com. n., neu. gen., s. num., 3rd per., nom. c. to the v. "went." |
| as | A cop. conj., jg. the sents. "Out went the taper" and "she hurried in." |
| she | A pers. pron., fem. gen., s. num., 3rd per., nom. c. to the v. "hurried." |
| hurried | A reg. intr. v., indic. m., past t., s. num., 3rd per., agr. with its nom. "she." |
| in. | An adv. of place, mod. the v. "hurried." |
| 6. He | A pers. pron., mas. gen., s. num., 3rd per., nom. c. to the v. "swam." |
| swam | An irreg. intr. v., indic. m., past t., s. num., 3rd per., agr. with its nom. "he." |
| Esk | A prop. n., neu. gen., s. num., 3rd per., obj. c., in app. with "river." |
| river | A com. n., neu. gen., s. num., 3rd per., obj. c., gov. by the prep. *across* und. |
| where | A cop. conj., jg. the sents. "He swam the Esk river" and "ford there was none." |
| ford | A com. n., neu. gen., s. num., 3rd per., nom. c. to the v. "was." |
| there | An adv. of place, mod. the v. "was." |
| was | An irreg. intr. v., indic. m., past t., s. num., 3rd per., agr. with its nom. "ford." |
| none. | A def. card. nu. adj. of quantity, qual. the n. "ford." |
| 7. Ere | A cop. conj., jg. the sents. "The bride had consented" "and he alighted at Netherby gate." |
| he | A pers. pron., mas. gen., s. num., 3rd per., nom. c. to the v. "alighted." |
| alighted | A reg. intr. v., indic. m., past t., s. num., 3rd per., agr. with its nom. "he." |
| at | A prep., sh. the rn. bet. "alighted" and "gate." |
| Netherby | A prop. adj. of quality, qual. the n. "gate." |

ENGLISH GRAMMAR AND ANALYSIS. 49

| | |
|---|---|
| gate | A com. n., neu. gen., s. num., 3rd per., obj. c., gov. by the prep. "at." |
| bride | A com. n., fem. gen., s. num., 3rd per., nom. c. to the v. "had consented." |
| had | An aux. v. to "consented," indg. pluperf. t. |
| consented | A past pl. from the intr. v. "to consent," ref. to "bride." |
| had consented. | A reg. intr. v., indic. m., pluperf. t., s. num., 3rd per., agr. with its nom. "bride." |
| 8. Let | An irreg. tr. v., act. vo., imper. m., pres. t., s. or p. num., 2nd per., agr. with its nom. *thou* or *you* und. |
| not | An adv. of m. (neg.), mod. the v. "let." |
| man | A com. n., mas. gen., s. num., 3rd per., obj. c., gov. by the tr. v. "let." |
| (to) move | A reg. intr. v., infin. m., pres. t., gov. by the v. "let." |
| from | A prep., sh. the rn. bet. "move" and "rank." |
| his | A pers. pron., mas. gen., s. num., 3rd per., poss. c., gov. by the n. "rank." |
| rank | A com. n., neu. gen., s. num., 3rd per., obj. c., gov. by the prep. "from." |
| before | A cop. conj., jg. the sents. "Let not ... rank" and "I give the sign," and indg. subj. m. |
| I | A pers. pron., com. gen., s. num., 1st per., nom. c. to the v. "give." |
| give | An irreg. tr. v., act. vo., subj. m., pres. t., s. num., 1st per., agr. with its nom. "I." |
| sign. | An abs. n., neu. gen., s. num., 3rd per., obj. c., gov. by the tr. v. "give." |
| 9. When | A cop. conj., jg. the sents. "I am ashamed" and "I receive your long letters." |
| I | A pers. pron., com. gen., s. num., 1st per., nom. c. to the v. "receive." |
| receive | A reg. tr. v., act. vo., indic. m., pres. t., s. num., 1st per., agr. with its nom. "I." |
| your | A pers. pron., com. gen., s. num., p. form, 2nd per., poss. c., gov. by the n. "letters." |
| long | An adj. of quality, pos. deg., qual. the n. "letters." |
| letters | A com. n., neu. gen., p. num., 3rd per., obj. c., gov. by the tr. v. "receive." |
| I | A pers. pron., com. gen., s. num., 1st per., nom. c. to the v. "am." |
| am | An irreg. intr. v., indic. m., pres. t., s. num., 1st per., agr. with its nom. "I." |
| ashamed. | An adj. of quality, pos. deg., qual. the pron. "I." |
| 10. king | A com. n., mas. gen., s. num., 3rd per., nom. c. to the v. "sat." |
| sat | An irreg. intr. v., indic. m., past t., s. num., 3rd per., agr. with its nom. "king." |
| on | A prep., sh. the rn. bet. "sat" and "brow." |
| rocky | An adj. of quality, pos. deg., qual. the n. "brow." |
| brow | A com. n., neu. gen., s. num., 3rd per., obj. c., gov. by the prep. "on." |
| Which | A rel. pron., neu. gen., s. num., 3rd per., agr. with its ant. "brow," nom. c. to the v. "looks." |
| looks | A reg. intr. v., indic. m., pres. t., s. num., 3rd per., agr. with its nom. "which." |
| o'er | A prep., sh. the rn. bet. "looks" and "Salamis." |
| sea-born | A compd. adj. of quality, qual. the n. "Salamis." |
| Salamis | A prop. n., neu. gen., s. num., 3rd per., obj. c., gov. by the prep. "o'er." |
| And | A cop. conj., jg. the sents. "A king sat .. brow" and "ships .. below." |
| ships | A com. n., neu. gen., p. num., 3rd per., nom. c. to the v. "lay." |
| in | A prep., sh. the rn. bet. "lay" and "thousands." |
| thousands | A com. n., neu. gen., p. num., 3rd per., obj. c., gov. by the prep. "in." |
| lay | An irreg. intr. v., indic. m., past t., p. num., 3rd per., agr. with its nom. "ships." |
| below | An adv. of place, mod. the v. "lay." |
| And | A cop. conj., jg. the sents. "ships..below" and "men were in nations *below*." |

4

| | |
|---|---|
| men | A com. n., mas. gen., p. num., 3rd per., nom. c. to the v. *were* und. |
| in | A prep., sh. the rn. bet. *were* und. and "nations." |
| nations | A com. n., neu. gen., p. num., 3rd per., obj. c., gov. by the prep. "in." |
| all | An indef. nu. adj. of quantity, qual. the nouns *ships* and *men* und. |
| were | An irreg. intr. v., indic. m., past t., p. num., 3rd per., agr. with its nom. *ships* and *men* und. |
| his | A pers. pron., mas. gen., s. num., 3rd per., poss. c., gov. by the nouns *ships* and *men* und. |
| He | A pers. pron., mas. gen., s. num., 3rd per., nom. c. to the v. "counted." |
| counted | A reg. tr. v., act. vo., indic. m., past t., s. num., 3rd per., agr. with its nom. "he." |
| them | A pers. pron., neu. and mas. gen., p. num., 3rd per., obj. c., gov. by the tr. v. "counted." |
| at | A prep., sh. the rn. bet. "counted" and "break." |
| break | An abs. n., neu. gen., s. num., 3rd per., obj. c., gov. by the prep. "at." |
| of | A prep., sh. the rn. bet. "break" and "day." |
| day | An abs. n., neu. gen., s. num., 3rd per., obj. c., gov. by the prep. "of." |
| And | A cop. conj., jg. the sents. "He counted .. day" and "where were they?" |
| when | A cop. conj., jg. the sents. "where were they?" and "the sun set." |
| sun | A com. n., neu. gen., s. num., 3rd per., nom. c. to the v. "set." |
| set | An irreg. intr. v., indic. m., past t., s. num., 3rd per., agr. with its nom. "sun." |
| where | An interrog. adv. of place, mod. the v. "were." |
| were | An irreg. intr. v., indic. m., past t., p. num., 3rd per., agr. with its nom. "they." |
| they? | A pers. pron., neu. and mas. gen., p. num., 3rd per., nom. c. to the v. "were." |

## Exercise 83.

| | |
|---|---|
| 1. Alas | An interj. |
| we | A pers. pron., com. gen., p. num., 1st per., nom. c. to the v. "turn." |
| turn | A reg. intr. v., indic. m., pres. t., p. num., 1st per., agr. with its nom. "we." |
| to | A particle, indg. infin. m. |
| to brave | A reg. tr. v., act. vo., infin. m., pres. t., gov. by the v. "turn." |
| billows | A com. n., neu. gen., p num., 3rd per., obj. c., gov. by the tr. v. "to brave." |
| of | A prep., sh. the rn. bet. "billows" and "sway." |
| world's | A com. n., neu. gen., s. num., 3rd per., poss. c., gov. by the n. "sway." |
| tempestuous | An adj. of quality, pos. deg., qual. the n. "sway." |
| sway. | An abs. n., neu. gen., s. num., 3rd per., obj. c., gov. by the prep. "of." |
| 2. Ah | An interj. |
| forgive | An irreg. tr. v., act. vo., imper. m., pres. t., s. or p. num., 2nd per., agr. with its nom. *thou* or *you* und. |
| stranger | A com. n., com. gen., s. num., 3rd per., obj. c., gov. by the tr. v. "forgive." |
| rude. | An adj. of quality, pos. deg., qual. the n. "stranger." |
| 3. Ha | An interj. |
| what | An interrog. pron., neu. gen., s. num., 3rd per., obj. c., gov. by the tr. v. "seest." |
| seest | An irreg. tr. v., act. vo., indic. m., pres. t., s. num., 2nd per., agr. with its nom. "thou." |
| thou | A pers. pron., com. gen., s. num., 2nd per., nom. c. to the v. "seest." |
| there. | An adv. of place, mod. the v. "seest." |
| 4. Oh | An interj. |
| sing | An irreg. intr. v., imper. m., pres. t., s. or p. num., 2nd per., agr. with its nom. *thou* or *you* und. |

## ENGLISH GRAMMAR AND ANALYSIS. 51

| | |
|---|---|
| unto | A prep., sh. the rn. bet. "sing" and "roundelay." |
| my | A pers. pron., fem. gen., s. num., 1st per., poss. c., gov. by the n. "roundelay." |
| roundelay | A com. n., neu. gen., s. num., 3rd per., obj. c., gov. by the prep. "unto." |
| Oh | An interj. |
| drop | A reg. tr. v., act. vo., imper. m., pres. t., s. or p. num., 2nd per., agr. with its nom. *thou* or *you* und. |
| briny | An adj. of quality, pos. deg., qual. the n. "tear." |
| tear | A com. n., neu. gen., s. num., 3rd per., obj. c., gov. by the tr. v. "drop." |
| with | A prep., sh. the rn. bet. "drop" and "me." |
| me | A pers. pron., fem. gen., s. num., 1st per., obj. c., gov. by the prep. "with." |
| Dance | A reg. intr. v., imper. m., pres. t., s. or p. num., 2nd per., agr. with its nom. *thou* or *you* und. |
| no | An adv. of m. (neg.), mod. the adv. "more." |
| more | An adv. of time, mod. the v. "dance." |
| at | A prep., sh. the rn. bet. "dance" and "holiday." |
| holiday | An abs. n., neu. gen., s. num., 3rd per., obj. c., gov. by the prep. "at." |
| Like | An adj. of quality, pos. deg., qual. the pron. *thou* or *you* und. |
| running | A pres. pl., used as an adj. of quality, qual. the n. "river." |
| river | A com. n., neu. gen., s. num., 3rd per., obj. c., gov. by the prep. *to* und. |
| be | An irreg. intr. v., imper. m., pres. t., s. or p. num., 2nd per., agr. with its nom. *thou* or *you* und. |
| My | A pers. pron., fem. gen., s. num., 1st per., poss. c., gov. by the n. "love." |
| love | A com. n., mas. gen., s. num., 3rd per., nom. c. to the v. "is." |
| is | An irreg. intr. v., indic. m., pres. t., s. num., 3rd per., agr. with its nom. "love." |
| dead. | An adj. of quality, qual. the n. "love." |
| Gone | A past pl. from the intr. v. "to go," ref. to "love." |
| to | A prep., sh. the rn. bet. "gone" and "death-bed." |
| his | A pers. pron., mas. gen., s. num., 3rd per., pos. c., gov. by the n. "death-bed." |
| death-bed | A compd. com. n., neu. gen., s. num., 3rd per., obj. c., gov. by the prep. "to." |
| All (= quite) | An adv. of deg., mod. the phrase "under the willow-tree." |
| under | A prep., sh. the rn. bet. "death-bed" and "willow-tree." |
| willow-tree. | A compd. com. n., neu. gen., s. num., 3rd per., obj. c., gov. by by the prep. "under." |
| 5. Oh | An interj. |
| could | An aux. v. to "fly," indg. pot. m., past t. |
| I | A pers. pron., com. gen., s. num., 1st per., nom. c. to the v. "could fly." |
| (to) fly | An irreg. intr. v., infin. m., pres. t., gov. by the v. "could." |
| could fly | An irreg. intr. v., pot. m., conditional form, past. t., s. num., 1st per., agr. with its nom. "I." (*If* I could fly.) |
| I | A pers. pron., com. gen., s. num., 1st per., nom. c. to the v. "would fly." |
| 'd = would | An aux. v. to "fly," indg. pot. m., past. t. |
| (to) fly | An irreg. intr. v., infin. m., pres. t., gov. by the v. "would." |
| would fly | An irreg. intr. v., pot. m., past. t., s. num., 1st per., agr. with its nom. "I." |
| with | A prep., sh. the rn. bet. "would fly" and "thee." |
| thee | A pers. pron., com. gen., s. num., 2nd per., obj. c., gov. by the prep. "with." |
| We | A pers. pron., com. gen., p. num., 1st per., nom. c. to the v. "would make." |
| 'd = would | An aux. v. to "make," indg. pot. m., past t. |
| (to) make | An irreg. tr. v., act. vo., infin. m., pres. t., gov. by the v. "would." |
| would make | An irreg. tr. v., act. vo., pot. m., past t., p. num., 1st per., agr. with its nom. "we." |
| with | A prep. sh. the rn. bet. "would make" and "wing." |
| joyful | An adj. of quality, pos. deg., qual. the n. "wing." |

4—2

| | |
|---|---|
| wing | A com. n., neu. gen., s. num., 3rd per., obj. c., gov. by the prep. "with." |
| Our | A pers. pron., com. gen., p. num., 1st per., poss. c., gov. by the n. "visit." |
| annual | An adj. of quality, qual. the n. "visit." |
| visit | An abs. n., neu. gen., s. num., 3rd per., obj. c., gov. by the tr. v. "would make." |
| o'er | A prep., sh. the rn. bet. "would make" and "globe." |
| globe | A com. n., neu. gen., s. num., 3rd per., obj. c., gov. by the prep. "o'er." |
| Companions | A com. n., com. gen., p. num., 1st per., nom. c., in app. with "we." |
| of | A prep., sh. the rn. bet. "companions" and "spring." |
| Spring. | An abs. n., neu. gen., s. num., 3rd per., obj. c., gov. by the prep. "of." |
| 6. O | An interj. |
| that | A cop. conj., jg. the sents. "*I wish*" and "those lips had language," and indg. subj. m. |
| those | A dis. adj., lim. the n. "lips." |
| lips | A com. n., neu. gen., p. num., 3rd per., nom. c. to the v. "had." |
| had | An irreg. tr. v., act. vo., subj. m., past t., p. num., 3rd per., agr. with its nom. "lips." |
| language | A com. n., neu. gen., s. num., 3rd per., obj. c., gov. by the tr. v. "had." |
| Life | An abs. n., neu. gen., s. num., 3rd per., nom. c, to the v. "has passed." |
| has | An aux. v. to "passed," indg. perf. t. |
| passed | A past pl. from the intr. v. "to pass," ref. to "life." |
| has passed | A reg. intr. v., indic. m., perf. t., s. num., 3rd per., agr. with its nom. "life." |
| With | A prep., sh. the rn. bet. "passed" and "me." |
| me | A pers. pron., mas. gen., s. num., 1st per., obj. c., gov. by the prep. "with." (Me, *i.e.* Cowper.) |
| but | An adv. of deg., mod. the adv. "roughly." |
| roughly | An adv. of man., mod. the v. "has passed." |
| since | A cop. conj., jg. the sents. "Life has passed..roughly" and "I heard thee last." |
| I | A pers. pron., mas. gen., s. num., 1st per., nom. c. to the v. "heard." |
| heard | An irreg. tr. v., act. vo., indic. m., past t., s. num., 1st per., agr. with its nom. "I." |
| thee | A pers. pron., fem. gen., s. num., 2nd per., obj. c., gov. by the tr. v. "heard." (Thee, *i.e.* Cowper's mother.) |
| last | An adv. of time, mod. the v. "heard." |
| Those | A dis. adj., lim. the n. "lips." |
| lips | A com. n., neu. gen., p. num., 3rd per., nom. c. to the v. "are." |
| are | An irreg. intr. v., indic. m., pres. t., p. num., 3rd per., agr. with its nom. "lips." |
| thine | A pers. pron., fem. gen., s. num., 2nd per., poss. c., gov. by the n. "lips." |
| thy | A pers. pron., forming with the adj. "own," a compd. pers. pron. |
| own | An intensive adj. of quality, qual. the n. "smiles." |
| thy own | A compd. pers. pron., fem. gen., s. num., 2nd per., poss. c., gov. by the n. "smiles." |
| sweet | An adj. of quality, pos. deg., qual. the n. "smiles." |
| smiles | An abs. n., neu. gen., p. num., 3rd per., obj. c., gov. by the tr. v. "see." |
| I | A pers. pron., mas. gen., s. num., 1st per., nom. c. to the v. "see." |
| see | An irreg. tr. v., act. vo., indic. m., pres. t., s. num., 1st per., agr. with its nom. "I." |
| same | A dis. adj., lim. the n. *smiles* und. |
| that | A rel. pron., neu. gen., p. num., 3rd per., agr. with its ant. *smiles* und., nom. c. to the v. "solaced." |
| oft | An adv. of time, mod. the v. "solaced." |
| in | A prep., sh. the rn. bet. "solaced" and "childhood." |
| childhood | An abs. n., neu. gen., s. num., 3rd per., obj. c., gov. by the prep. "in." |

ENGLISH GRAMMAR AND ANALYSIS.

solaced     A reg. tr. v., act. vo., indic. m., past t., p. num., 3rd per., agr. with its nom. "that."
me.     A pers. pron., mas. gen., s. num., 1st per., obj. c., gov. by the tr. v. "solaced."

### Exercise 84.

1. That, *dis. adj.*; all, *adj. of quantity (bulk or mass)*. 2. Yet, *adv. of time*. 3. But, *adv. of deg*. 4. That, *dis. adj*. 5. All (=everything). *n*. 6. Little, *adj. of quantity (bulk or mass)*. 7. What, *compd. rel. pron.*; other, *indef. nu. adj. of quantity*. 8. Few, *indef. nu. adj. of quantity*; since, *adv. of time*. 9. Much, *adv. of mea.*; for, *prep*. 10. After, *prep.*; most, *n.*; that, *rel. pron*. 11. Little, *adj. of quality*; half, *adj. of deg.*; others, *n.*; but, *disj. conj*.. 12. But, *prep*. 13. Most, *n.*, (or, *adj.*, qual. *endeavour* und.). 14. Eke, *adv. of deg.*; that, *dis. adj*. 15. More, *indef. nu. adj. of quantity*. 16. But, *prep*.

### Exercise 85.

| Prim. word. | Deriv. | Prim. word. | Deriv. | Prim. word. | Deriv. |
|---|---|---|---|---|---|
| Bear, | Bier. | Knit, | Knot, net. | Lie, | Lay. |
| Say, | Saw (a saying). | Bite, | Bit. | Flit, | Fleet. |
| Heat, | Hot. | Tell, | Tale. | Hold, | Hilt. |
| Thief, | Thieve. | Dig, | Ditch. | Lose, | Loss. |
| Hook, | Hitch. | Melt, | Smelt. | Wake, | Watch. |
| Rob, | Crib. | Dog, | Dodge. | Feed, | Food. |
| Wing, | Swing. | Gold, | Gild. | Pride, | Proud. |
| Grass, | Graze. | Fall, | Fell. | Break, | Breach, breech. |
| Cool, | Chill. | | | | |

### Exercise 86.

| Deriv. | Prim. word. | Deriv. | Prim. word. | Deriv. | Prim. word. |
|---|---|---|---|---|---|
| Ditch, | Dig. | Wrench, | Wring. | Sheen, | Shine. |
| Woof, | Weave. | Twirl, | Whirl. | Band, | Bind. |
| Stumble, | Tumble. | Breach, | Break. | Brood, | Breed. |
| Shock, | Shake. | Choice, | Choose. | Raise, | Rise. |
| Bliss, | Bless. | Strife, | Strive. | Reel, | Roll. |
| Seat, | Sit. | Lot, | Let. | Milch, | Milk. |
| Gap, | Gape. | Full, | Fill. | Doom, | Deem. |
| Splash, | Plash. | Snake, | Sneak. | Clock, | Click. |
| Strong, | String. | | | | |

### Exercise 87.

| Prefix in Italics. | Meaning of Prefix. | Prefix in Italics. | Meaning of Prefix. |
|---|---|---|---|
| *With*-hold. | From. | *For*-lorn. | Through=throughly, completely. |
| *To*-morrow. | This. | | |
| *Un*-happy. | Not. | *Fore*-shew. | Before. |
| *Mis*-lead. | Amiss. | *Be*-night. | Over (To *overtake* by night). |
| *In*-step. | In. | *Be*-side. | Near. |
| *N*-ever. | Not. | *A*-board. | On. |
| *Out*-do. | Beyond. | *To*-gether. | To, at (implying addition). |
| *Over*-throw. | Above. | *Un*-loose. | Reversal. |
| *Up*-roar. | Upwards. | *Under*-hand. | Beneath. |
| *En*-able. | To make. | *Be*-dizen. | Over=all over. |
| | | *Mid*-shipman. | Middle. |

### Exercise 88.

| Prefix in Italics. | Meaning of Prefix. | Prefix in Italics. | Meaning of Prefix. |
|---|---|---|---|
| *Ante*-cedent. | Before. | *Ad*-duce. | To. |
| *Post*-pone. | After. | *Per*-cussion. | Through. |
| *Re*-trieve. | Back. | *Circum*-ference. | Round. |
| *Retro*-grade. | Backward. | *Semi*-tone. | Half. |
| *Sub*-mit. | Under. | *Trans*-mit. | Across. |

| Prefix in Italics. | Meaning of Prefix. | Prefix in Italics. | Meaning of Prefix. |
|---|---|---|---|
| Extra-vagant. | Beyond. | Inter-jection. | Between, among. |
| Con-struct. | Together. | Contra-vene. | Against. |
| Equi-lateral. | Equally. | Bene-diction. | Well. |
| Pre-face. | Before (præ). | Dis-solve. | Asunder. |
| Preter-natural. | Beside, contrary to (præter). | In-fuse. | Into. |
|  |  | In-clement. | Not. |
| Ultra-montane. | Beyond. | Intro-mit. | Within. |
| Sim-ple. | Without (sine). | Bi-sect. | Twice (bis). |
| Pro-gress. | Before. | Ob-struct. | Against. |
| Sub-terranean. | Under. | Amb-ient. | Round (am). |
| Sup-press. | Under (sub). | Ab-dicate. | From. |
| Ex-plore. | Out of. |  |  |

## Exercise 89.

| Prefix in Italics. | Meaning of Prefix. | Prefix in Italics. | Meaning of Prefix. |
|---|---|---|---|
| Syn-thesis. | With. | Cata-strophe. | Down. |
| Amphi-theatre. | Both. | Dys-entery. | Ill. |
| Hypo-crite. | Under. | Anti-podes. | Against. |
| Meta-morphosis. | Change. | Em-phasis. | In (en). |
| Philo-logy. | Loving. | En-thusiasm. | In. |
| Poly-gon. | Many. | Hemi-stich. | Half. |
| Mono-gram. | Alone. | Eu-logy. | Well. |
| A-nomaly. | Not. | Hetero-dox. | Different. |
| Pan-theist. | All. | Pros-elyte. | Towards. |
| Pro-logue. | Before. | Pseudo-apostle. | False. |
| Apo-logy. | From. | Peri-od. | Around. |
| Dia-gram. | Through. | Para-dox. | Beside. |
| Auto-crat. | Self. | Meta-physics. | Change. |
| Ana-tomy. | Up. | Hypo-critical. | Under. |
| Arch-i-tect. | Head. | Homo-logous. | The same. |

## Exercise 90.

| Prefix in Italics. | Meaning of Prefix. | Language. | Prefix in Italics. | Meaning of Prefix. | Language. |
|---|---|---|---|---|---|
| Of-fal. | Away (off fall). | E. | With-draw. | Back, from. | E. |
| Peri-patetic. | Around. | Gr. | Ir-regular. | Not (in). | L. |
| Ev-angelist. | Well (eu). | Gr. | El-lipsis. | In (en). | Gr. |
| Ultra-liberal. | Beyond. | L. | Dia-meter. | Through. | Gr. |
| A-wake. | From. | E. | Sus-tain. | Under (sub). | L. |
| Ex-tract. | Out of. | L. | Sur-pass. | Over. | Fr. |
| Ex-odus. | Out of. | Gr. | For-swear. | Against. | E. |
| Ant-arctic. | Against (anti). | Gr. | Fore-tell. | Before. | E. |
| Arch-bishop. | Head. | Gr. | Male-factor. | Ill. | L. |
| Mis-lead. | Amiss. | E. | Non-sense. | Not. | L. |
| Semi-tone. | Half. | L. | Pur-vey. | For. | Fr. |
| De-part. | Down, from. | L. | A-d-vance.* | From. | L. |
| Al-most. | All. | E. | Be-neath. | Near. | E. |
| Un-wise. | Not. | E. | Dif-fer. | Asunder (dis). | L. |
| Par-ody. | Beside (para). | Gr. | Auto-maton. | Self. | Gr. |
| Super-structure. | Over. | L. | Tra-verse. | Across (trans.). | L. |
| Dis-honour. | Asunder. | L. | Counter-feit. | Against. | Fr. |
| Over-bear. | Above. | E. |  |  |  |

## Exercise 91.

| Suffix in Italics. | Meaning of Suffix. | Suffix in Italics. | Meaning of Suffix. |
|---|---|---|---|
| Nap-kin. | Little. | Hatch-et. | Little. |
| Dark-ness. | State or condition. | Ring-let. | Little. |
| Sail-or. | One who. | Bloo-m. | That which (blows). |
| Song-ster. | One who. | Gird-le. | That with which. |
| Wis-dom. | Quality or state. | Helm-s-man. | The man who (steers). |
| Wid-th. | Quality. | Lord-ship. | State. |
| Sigh-t. | That which (is seen). | Slug-g-ard. | One who (is slow). |
| Wild-ing. | Little. | Mock-ery. | Action. |
| Chick-en. | Little. | Hat-red. | State. |

\* *Advance* is a corruption of Latin *ab ante* (from before) through French *avancer*.

| Suffix in Italics. | Meaning of Suffix. | Suffix in Italics. | Meaning of Suffix. |
|---|---|---|---|
| Walk-ing. | Action. | Pan-try. | Place (for bread). |
| Fir-kin. | Little (fourth). | Know-ledge. | State (of knowing). |
| Wed-lock. | State. | Steal-th. | Action (of stealing). |
| Hill-ock. | Little. | | |

## Exercise 92.

| Suffix in Italics. | Meaning of Suffix. | Suffix in Italics. | Meaning of Suffix. |
|---|---|---|---|
| God-like. | Like. | House-less. | Void of. |
| East-erly. | Direction. | Boot-ed. | Furnished with (boots). |
| Ten-th. | Number, forming ordinal. | Ford-able. | May or can be (forded). |
| | | Ten-fold. | Times involved. |
| Up-ward. | Having direction. | Silver-n. | Made of (silver). |
| Dew-y. | Pertaining to. | Silver-y. | Pertaining to. |
| Cloud-compelling. | Having quality forming participial adj. act. | Stead-fast. | Fast, firm. |
| | | Wood-en. | Made of. |
| Frolic-some. | Partaking of. | Tear-ful. | Full of. |
| Love-ly. | Like. | Hill-y. | Pertaining to. |
| Fif-ty. | Ten. | Win-some. | Partaking of. |
| Six-teen. | Ten. | Fro-ward. | Having direction. |
| Truth-ful. | Full (of truth). | Nine-ty. | Ten. |
| Black-ish. | Rather (black). | | |

## Exercise 93.

| Suffix in Italics. | Meaning of Suffix | Suffix in Italics. | Meaning of Suffix. |
|---|---|---|---|
| Dib-b-le. | Often (repetition, occupation). | Wor-r-y (Fr. wear). | To make. |
| | | Clean-se. | To make. |
| Knee-l. | " " | Weak-en. | To make. |
| Fal-t-er (Fr. fail). | " " | Beck-on. | Often (repetition). |
| Shiv-er. | " " | Wand-er. | " " |
| Glea-m. | " " | Tal-k. | " " |

## Exercise 94.

| Suffix in Italics. | Meaning of Suffix. | Suffix in Italics. | Meaning of Suffix. |
|---|---|---|---|
| Bad-ly. | Like. | Side-long. | Manner. |
| Seld-om. | Time. | Beside-s. | Manner. |
| Hi-ther. | To (this place). | Whe-re. | At or in what place). |
| Straight-way. | Manner. | On-ce. | Time. |
| No-wise. | Manner. | Whil-st. | Time. |
| Hither-ward. | Towards (place). | He-nce. | From (this place). |

## Exercise 95.

| Suffix in Italics. | Meaning of Suffix. | Suffix in Italics. | Meaning of Suffix. |
|---|---|---|---|
| Cour-age. | State. | Secre-cy. | State. |
| Endur-ance. | State or condition. | Plaint-iff. | Person. |
| Occa-sion. | State of. | Mortgag-ee. | Person acted upon. |
| Matri-mony. | State. | Spons-or. | One who (answers). |
| Vehi-cle. | Instrument. | Administra-trix. | She who (administers). |
| Part-icle. | Little. | Dign-ity. | State. |
| Glob-ule. | Little. | Lab-our. | State. |
| Grand-eur. | State. | Discre-tion. | State or act. |
| Scep-tre. | Instrument. | Opin-ion. | State. |
| Cult-ure. | State. | Chap-el. | Small. |

## Exercise 96.

| Suffix in Italics. | Meaning of Suffix. | Suffix in Italics. | Meaning of Suffix. |
|---|---|---|---|
| Ramp-ant. | Having quality. | Pictur-esque. | Like. |
| Equ-al. | Belonging to. | Serv-ile. | Belonging to. |
| Honor-ary. | Belonging to. | Glori-ous. | Full of. |
| Desol-ate. | Belonging to. | Sim-ple. | Fold (plex). |
| Favour-able. | May or can be. | Joc-ose. | Full of. |

KEY TO

| Suffix in Italics. | Meaning of Suffix. | Suffix in Italics. | Meaning of Suffix. |
|---|---|---|---|
| Christ-ian. | Belonging to. | Mori-bund. | Making. |
| Extre-me. | Most. | Flu-ent. | Having quality. |
| Turb-ulent. | Full of. | Un-ique. | Belonging to. |
| Tim-id. | Having quality. | Cur-sory. | Having quality. |
| Sol-ar. | Belonging to. | Sal-ine. | Made of. |

### Exercise 97.

| Suffix in Italics. | Meaning of Suffix. | Suffix in Italics. | Meaning of Suffix. |
|---|---|---|---|
| Alien-ate. | To make. | Horri-fy. | To make. |
| Simpli-fy. | To make. | Ed-it. | To make. |
| Termin-ate. | To make. | Coal-esce. | To become more and more. |
| Facilit-ate. | To make. | Lim-it. | To make. |
| Exped-ite. | To make. | | |
| Cred-it. | To make. | | |

### Exercise 98.

| Suffix in Italics. | Meaning of Suffix. | Suffix in Italics. | Meaning of Suffix. |
|---|---|---|---|
| Mus-ic. | Science of. | Tri-ad. | An embodiment of. |
| Magnet-ism. | Science of. | Diora-ma. | Thing. |
| Monarch-y. | Abstract idea. | Dynam-ics. | Science of. |
| Basil-isk. | Small. | Athle-te. | One who. |
| Analys-t. | One who. | Politi-cian. | One who. |
| Monas-tery. | Place. | Etymolog-y. | Science. |

### Exercise 99.

| Suffix in Italics. | Meaning of Suffix. | Suffix in Italics. | Meaning of Suffix. |
|---|---|---|---|
| Harmon-ic. | Belonging to. | Prac-tical. | Belonging to. |
| Man-iac. | Having quality. | Petr-ine. | Made of. |
| Cycl-oidal. | Resembling the form of. | Didac-tic. | Having quality. |
| Ela-stic. | Having quality. | Oligarch-ical. | Belonging to. |
| Mim-ic. | Belonging to. | Rhomb-oidal. | Resembling the form of. |

### Exercise 100.

| Suffix in Italics. | Meaning of Suffix. | Language. | Suffix in Italics. | Meaning of Suffix. | Language. |
|---|---|---|---|---|---|
| Botan-ize. | To make. | Gr. | Secret-ary. | One who. | L. |
| Perambul-ate. | To make. | L. | Clean-se. | To make. | E. |
| Ling-er. | To repeat. | E. | Crea-tion. | State. | L. |
| Magni-fy. | To make. | L. | Labora-tory. | Place for. | L. |
| Drunk-ard. | One who. | E. | Sul-l-y. | To make. | E. |
| Argill-aceous. | Of the nature of. | L. | Destruc-tive. | Having quality. | L. |
| Arithme-tical. | Belonging to. | Gr. | Analy-sis. | Process. | Gr. |
| Lign-eous. | Made of. | L. | Delica-cy. | State. | L. |
| Rag-g-ed. | Having quality. | E. | Fine-ry. | Collection of. | E. |
| Verb-ose. | Full of. | L. | Bond-age. | State. | E. |
| Agit-ate. | To make. | L. | Bishop-ric. | Dominion. | E. |
| Angel-ic. | Belonging to. | Gr. | Ora-tion. | Act of. | L. |
| Tri-ad. | An embodiment of. | Gr. | Panora-ma. | Thing. | Gr. |
| | | | Pesti-ferous. | Bearing. | L. |
| Sancti-mony. | Condition. | L. | Leg-ible. | May or can be. | L. |
| Trust-ee. | Person to whom. | L. | Aneur-ism. | State. | Gr. |
| Laugh-ter. | State. | E. | Weal-th. | State. | E. |
| Obel-isk. | Little. | Gr. | Floo-d. | State. | E. |
| Lass-ie. | Little. | E. | Lamb-kin. | Little. | E. |
| Brew-ster. | One who. | E. | Rub-escent. | Growing. | L. |
| Anatom-y. | Science. | Gr. | Pyram-idal. | Resembling the form of. | Gr. |
| Hat-red. | State. | E. | Fut-ile. | Having quality. | L. |
| Politi-cian. | One who. | Gr. | Live-ly. | Like. | E. |
| Barri-ster. | One who. | E. | South-ward. | Direction. | E. |
| Soph-ist. | One who. | Gr. | Glim-m-er. | To make. | E. |
| Shepherd-ess. | She who. | E. | | | |

| Suffix in Italics. | Meaning of Suffix. | Language. | Suffix in Italics. | Meaning of Suffix. | Language. |
|---|---|---|---|---|---|
| Can-*ine*. | Belonging to. | L. | Pati-*ent*. | Having quality. | L. |
| Cedr-*ine*. | Made of. | Gr. | Low-*er* (verb). | To make. | E. |
| Mar-*ine*. | Belonging to. | L. | Consola-*tory*. | Having quality. | L. |
| Ferv-*id*. | Having quality. | L. | Val-*our*. | Quality. | L. |
| Wood-*en*. | Made of. | E. | Duck-*ling*. | Little. | E. |

## Exercise 101.

| | | |
|---|---|---|
| *Farm* | A n. | } farm-yard = a yard belonging to a farm. |
| *Yard* | A n. | |
| *Book* | A n. | } book-stand = a stand for books. |
| *Stand* | A n. | |
| *Bread* | A n. | } bread-basket = a basket for holding bread. |
| *Basket* | A n. | |
| *Free* | An adj. | } freeman = a man who is free. |
| *Man* | A n. | |
| *Spend* | A v. | } spendthrift = one who spends the savings of thrift. |
| *Thrift* | A n. | |
| *Break* | A v. | } breakfast = the meal which breaks one's fast. |
| *Fast* | A n. | |
| *Fore* | An adv. | } foresight = the act of seeing beforehand. |
| *Sight* | A n. | |
| *By* | An adv. | } by-lane = a side lane. |
| *Lane* | A n. | |
| *Well*[1] | An adv. | } welcome = a kindly reception. |
| *Come* | A v. | |
| *Hold* | A v. | } holdfast = that which holds fast. |
| *Fast* | An adv. | |
| *Errand* | A n. | } errand-boy = a boy who goes on errands. |
| *Boy* | A n. | |
| *Race* | A n. | } racehorse = a horse bred for racing. |
| *Horse* | A n. | |
| *Thorough* | An adv. | } thoroughfare = a fare or passage for going through. |
| *Fare* | A n. | |
| *Riding* | A ger. | } riding-whip = a whip used when riding. |
| *Whip* | A n. | |
| *After* | An adv. | } afterthought = a thought after an action or event. |
| *Thought* | A n. | |
| *Stop* | A v. | } stopgap = that which stops a gap or opening. |
| *Gap* | A n. | |
| *Blue* | An adj. | } bluebeard = a man whose beard is blue. |
| *Beard* | A n. | |
| *Quick* | An adj. | } quicksilver = a fluid metal like liquid silver, which moves as if quick or living. |
| *Silver* | A n. | |
| *Out* | An adv. | } outlet = the way or means by which anything is let out. |
| *Let* | A v. | |
| *Cousin* | A n. | } cousin-german = a first cousin. |
| *German* | An adj. | |

## Exercise 102.

| | | |
|---|---|---|
| *Sky* | A n. | } sky-blue = blue like the sky. |
| *Blue* | An adj. | |
| *Fair* | An adj. | } fair-haired = having fair or light-coloured hair. |
| *Hair* | A n. | |
| *Ed* | Suffix. | |
| *Heart* | A n. | } heart-rending = rending or breaking the heart. |
| *Rending* | An incomp. pl. | |
| *All* | An adv. | } all-powerful = having power to do all things. |
| *Powerful* | An adj. | |
| *Full* | An adv. | } full-blown = blown to its full extent. |
| *Blown* | A complete pl. | |
| *Ell* | A n. | } ell-long = having the length of an ell. |
| *Long* | An adj. | |
| *Close* | An adj. | } close-grained = having its grain close. |
| *Grain* | A n. | |
| *Ed* | Suffix. | |

58  KEY TO

| | | |
|---|---|---|
| Under | An adv. | |
| Done | A complete pl. | underdone = done under the mark. |
| Home | A n. | |
| Bound | A complete pl. | homebound = bound for home. |
| Full | An adj. | |
| Ear | A n. | full-eared = having the ears full. |
| Ed | Suffix. | |
| Long | An adj. | |
| Neck | A n. | long-necked = having a long neck. |
| Ed | Suffix. | |
| Grass | A n. | |
| Green | An adj. | grass-green = green like grass. |
| Well | An adv. | |
| Built | A complete pl. | well-built = built well, *i.e.*, in an excellent manner. |

### Exercise 103.

| | | | | | |
|---|---|---|---|---|---|
| Himself | { Him / Self | | Thyself | { Thy / Self | |
| Her own | { Her / Own | | One's own | { One's / Own | |
| Whatsoever | { What / So-ever | | Themselves | { Them / Selves | |
| Whoso | { Who / So | | Whichever | { Which / Ever | |
| Their own | { Their / Own | | Whoever | { Who / Ever | |

### Exercise 104.

| | | |
|---|---|---|
| Over | An adv. | |
| Lap | A v. | overlap = to lap or fold over the top of. |
| Back | A n. | |
| Bite | A v. | backbite = to speak evil behind the back. |
| White | An adj. | |
| Wash | A v. | whitewash = to wash white. |
| Under | An adv. | |
| State | A v. | understate = to state under the mark. |
| Way | A n. | |
| Lay | A v. | waylay = to lie in the way for. |
| Fore | An adv. | |
| Tell | A v. | foretell = to tell beforehand. |

### Exercise 105.

| | | |
|---|---|---|
| Al[l] | An adj. | |
| Ways | A n. | always = through all ways, continually. |
| Some | An adj. | |
| Times | A n. | sometimes = at some times. |
| Mean | An adj. | |
| While | A n. | meanwhile = in the mean while, *i.e.*, in the intervening time. |
| Down | A prep. | |
| Stairs | A n. | downstairs = down or below stairs. |
| Hence | An adv. | |
| Forward | An adv. | henceforward = from this time forward. |
| Hereto | An adv. | |
| Fore | An adv. | heretofore = before this time, formerly. |
| Length | A n. | |
| Ways | A n. | lengthways = in the way or manner of the length. |
| There | An adv. | |
| Upon | A prep. | thereupon = upon that. |
| No | An adj. | |
| Where | An adv. | nowhere = in no place. |
| Here | An adv. | |
| By | A prep. | hereby = by means of this. |

## Exercise 106.

| | | | | | |
|---|---|---|---|---|---|
| Inside | { In | An adv. | Without | { With | A prep. |
| | Side | A n. | | Out | An adv. |
| Into | { In | A prep. | Owing to | { Owing | An incomplete pl. |
| | To | A prep. | | To | A prep. |
| Underneath | { Under | A prep. | Upon | { Up | A prep. |
| | Neath | A prep. | | On | A prep. |
| Throughout | { Through | A prep. | Within | { With | A prep. |
| | Out | An adv. | | In | A prep. |

## Exercise 107.

| | | | | | |
|---|---|---|---|---|---|
| Furthermore | { Further | An adv. | Howbeit | { How | An adv. |
| | More | An adv. | | Be | A v. |
| Whereupon | { Where | An adv. | | It | A pron. |
| | Upon | A prep. | Nevertheless | { Never | An adv. |
| Likewise | { Like | An adj. | | The | An adv. |
| | Wise | A n. | | Less | An adv. |
| Wherein | { Where | An adv. | However | { How | An adv. |
| | In | A prep. | | Ever | An adv. |
| Moreover | { More | An adv. | | Al [1]=although, a conj. | |
| | Over | An adv. | Albeit | { Be | A v. |
| Wherewith | { Where | An adv. | | It | A pron. |
| | With | A prep. | | | |

## Exercise 108.

N.B.—In Exercises 108—207, words which illustrate rules and observations are in black type.

1. **squirrel**  A com. n., com. gen., s. num., 3rd per., nom. c. to the v. "ascends."
    ascends  A reg. tr. v., act. vo., indic. m., pres. t., s. num., 3rd per., agr. with its nom. "squirrel."
    neighbouring  An adj. of quality, qual. the n. "beech."
    beech.  A com. n., neu. gen., s. num., 3rd per., obj. c., gov. by the tr. v. "ascends."
2. bold  An adj. of quality, pos. deg., qual. the n. "bird."
    **bird**  A com. n., com. gen., s. num., 3rd per., nom. c. to the v. "alights."
    of  A prep., sh. the rn. bet. "bird" and "prey."
    prey  A com. n., neu. gen., s. num., 3rd per., obj. c., gov. by the prep. "of."
    alights.  A reg. intr. v., indic. m., pres. t., s. num., 3rd per., agr. with its nom. "bird."
3. **He**  A pers. pron., mas. gen., s. num., 3rd per., nom. c. to the v. "sees."
    sees  An irreg. tr. v., act. vo., indic. m., pres. t., s. num., 3rd per., agr. with its nom. "he."
    me.  A pers. pron., com. gen., s. num., 1st per., obj. c., gov. by the tr. v. "sees."
4. cottage  A com. n. used as an adj. of quality, qual. the n. "curs."
    **curs**  A com. n., com. gen., p. num., 3rd per., nom. c. to the v. "bark."
    at  A prep., sh. the rn. bet. "bark" and "pilgrims."
    early  An adj. of quality, pos. deg., qual. the n. "pilgrims."
    pilgrims  A com. n., com. gen., p. num., 3rd per., obj. c., gov. by the prep. "at."
    bark.  A reg. intr. v., indic. m., pres. t., p. num., 3rd per., agr. with its nom. "curs."
5. Down  A prep., sh. the rn. bet. "rings" and "slope."
    rough  An adj. of quality, pos. deg., qual. the n. "slope."
    slope  A com. n., neu. gen., s. num., 3rd per., obj. c., gov. by the prep. "down."
    ponderous  An adj. of quality, pos. deg., qual. the n. "waggon."
    **waggon**  A com. n., neu. gen., s. num., 3rd per., nom. c. to the v. "rings."
    rings.  An irreg. intr. v., indic. m., pres. t., s. num., 3rd per., agr. with its nom. "waggon."

## KEY TO

| | |
|---|---|
| 6. **maid** | A com. n., fem. gen., s. num., 3rd per., nom. c. to the v. "had." |
| of | A prep., sh. the rn. bet. "maid" and "honour." |
| honour | An abs. n., neu. gen., s. num., 3rd per., obj. c., gov. by the prep. "of." |
| had | An irreg. tr. v., act. vo., indic. m., past t., s. num., 3rd per., agr. with its nom. "maid." |
| her | A pers. pron., forming with the adj. "own" a compd. pers. pron. |
| own | An intensive adj. of quality, qual. the n. "equipage." |
| her own | A compd. pers. pron., fem. gen., s. num., 3rd per., poss. c., gov. by the n. "equipage." |
| equipage. | A com. n., neu. gen., s. num., 3rd per., obj. c., gov. by the tr. v. "had." |
| 7. **prophet** | A com. n., mas. gen., s. num., 3rd per., nom. c. to the v. "hath." |
| hath | An irreg. tr. v., act. vo., indic. m., pres. t., s. num., 3rd per., agr. with its nom. "prophet." |
| no | An adj. of quantity (bulk or mass), qual. the n. "honour." |
| honour | An abs. n., neu. gen., s. num., 3rd per., obj. c., gov. by the tr. v. "hath." |
| in | A prep., sh. the rn. bet. "hath" and "country." |
| his | A pers. pron., forming with the adj. "own" a compd. pers. pron. |
| own | An intensive adj. of quality, qual. the n. "country." |
| his own | A compd. pers. pron., mas. gen., s. num., 3rd per., poss. c., gov. by the n. "country." |
| country. | A com. n., neu. gen., s. num., 3rd per., obj. c., gov. by the prep. "in." |
| 8. **wrinkle** | A com. n., neu. gen., s. num., 3rd per., nom. c. to the v. "may be." |
| on | A prep., sh. the rn. bet. "wrinkle" and "cheek." |
| cheek | A com. n., neu. gen., s. num., 3rd per., obj. c., gov. by the prep. "on." |
| may | An aux. v. to "be," indg. pot. m., pres. t. |
| (to) be | An irreg. intr. v., infin. m., pres. t., gov. by the v. "may." |
| may be | An irreg. intr. v., pot. m., pres. t., s. num., 3rd per., agr. with its nom. "wrinkle." |
| course | A com. n., neu. gen., s. num., 3rd per., nom. c. after the v. "may be." |
| of | A prep., sh. the rn. bet. "course" and "tears." |
| secret | An adj. of quality, pos. deg., qual. the n. "tears." |
| tears. | A com. n., neu. gen., p. num., 3rd per., obj. c., gov. by the prep. "of." |
| 9. **experience** | An abs. n., neu. gen., s. num., 3rd per., nom. c. to the v. "was." |
| of | A prep., sh. the rn. bet. "experience" and "trapper." |
| trapper | A com. n., mas. gen., s. num., 3rd per., obj. c., gov. by the prep. "of." |
| was | An irreg. intr. v., indic. m., past t., s. num., 3rd per., agr. with its nom. "experience." |
| in | A prep., sh. the rn. bet. "was" and "right." |
| right. | An abs. n., neu. gen., s. num., 3rd per., obj. c., gov. by the prep. "in." |
| 10. wise | An adj. of quality, pos. deg., qual. the n. "caution." |
| **caution** | An abs. n., neu. gen., s. num., 3rd per., nom. c. to the v. "was observed." |
| was | An aux. v. to "observed," indg. pass. vo., past t. |
| observed | A past pl. from the tr. v. "to observe," ref. to "caution." |
| was observed | A reg. tr. v., pass. vo., indic. m., past t., s. num., 3rd per., agr. with its nom. "caution." |
| in | A prep., sh. the rn. bet. "was observed" and "respect." |
| this | A dis. adj., lim. the n. "respect." |
| respect | An abs. n., neu. gen., s. num., 3rd per., obj. c., gov. by the prep. "in." |
| for | A cop. conj., jg. the sents. "A wise caution..respect" and "the treachery..expedition." |
| **treachery** | An abs. n., neu. gen., s. num., 3rd per., nom. c. to the v. "might have imperilled." |
| of | A prep., sh. the rn. bet. "treachery" and "deserter." |
| single | An adj. of quality, qual. the n. "deserter." |
| deserter | A com. n., mas. gen., s. num., 3rd per., obj. c., gov. by the prep. "of." |

| | |
|---|---|
| might | An aux. v. to "have imperilled," indg. pot. m. |
| have | An aux. v. to "imperilled," and, together with "might," indg. pluperf. t. |
| imperilled | A past pl. from the tr. v. "to imperil," ref. to "success." |
| might have imperilled | } A reg. tr. v., act. vo., pot. m., pluperf. t., s. num., 3rd per., agr. with its nom. "treachery." |
| success | An abs. n., neu. gen., s. num., 3rd per., obj. c., gov. by the tr. v. "might have imperilled." |
| of | A prep., sh. the rn. bet. "success" and "expedition." |
| expedition | An abs. n., neu. gen., s. num., 3rd per., obj. c., gov. by the prep. "of." |
| had | An aux. v. to "been known," indg. pluperf. t. |
| its | A pers. pron., neu. gen., s. num., 3rd per., poss. c., gov. by the n. "object." |
| exact | An adj. of quality, qual. the n. "object." |
| **object** | An abs. n., neu. gen., s. num., 3rd per., nom. c. to the v. "had been known." |
| been | A past pl. from the intr. v. "to be," ref. to "known object," and aux. to "known," indg. pass. vo. |
| known | A past pl. from the tr. v. "to know," ref. to "object." |
| had been known. | An irreg. tr. v., pass. vo., subj. m., pluperf. t., s. num., 3rd per., agr. with its nom. "object." (*If* its exact object had been known.) |

## Exercise 109.

| | |
|---|---|
| 1. It | A pers. pron., neu. gen., s. num., 3rd per., nom. c. to the v. "was." |
| was | An irreg. intr. v., indic. m., past t., s. num., 3rd per., agr. with its nom. "it." |
| **friar** | A com. n., mas. gen., s. num., 3rd per., nom. c. after the v. "was." |
| of | A prep., sh. the rn. bet. "friar" and "orders." |
| orders | An abs. n., neu. gen., p. num., 3rd per., obj. c., gov. by the prep. "of." |
| gray. | An adj. of quality, pos. deg., qual. the n. "orders." |
| 2. To | A prep., sh. the rn. bet. "was" and "peasants." |
| peasants | A com. n., com. gen., p. num., 3rd per., obj. c., gov. by the prep. "to." |
| of | A prep., sh. the rn. bet. "peasants" and "times." |
| old | An adj. of quality, pos. deg., qual. the n. "times." |
| times | An abs. n., neu. gen., p. num., 3rd per., obj. c., gov. by the prep. "of." |
| world | A com. n., neu. gen., s. num., 3rd per., nom. c. to the v. "was." |
| outside | A prep, sh. the rn. bet. "world" and "experience." |
| their | A pers. pron., forming with the adj. "own" a compd. pers. pron. |
| own | An intensive adj. of quality, qual. the n. "experience." |
| their own | A compd. pers. pron., com. gen., p. num., 3rd per., poss. c., gov. by the n. "experience." |
| direct | An adj. of quality, pos. deg., qual. the n. "experience." |
| experience | An abs. n., neu. gen., s. num., 3rd per., obj. c., gov. by the prep. "outside." |
| was | An irreg. intr. v., indic. m., past t., s. num., 3rd per., agr. with its nom. "world." |
| **region** | A com. n., neu. gen., s. num., 3rd per., nom. c. after the v. "was." |
| of | A prep., sh. the rn. bet. "region" and "vagueness." |
| vagueness | An abs. n., neu. gen., s. num., 3rd per., obj. c., gov. by the prep. "of." |
| and | A cop. conj., jg. the senta. "To the peasants..vagueness" and "*to the peasants of old times the world outside their own direct experience was a region of* mystery." |
| mystery. | An abs. n., neu. gen., s. num., 3rd per., obj. c., gov. by the prep. *of* und. |
| 3. Their | A pers. pron., com. gen., p. num., 3rd per., poss. c., gov. by the n. "priests." |
| priests | A com. n., mas. gen., p. num., 3rd per., nom. c. to the v. "were called." |

| | |
|---|---|
| were | An aux. v. to "called," indg. pass. vo., past t. |
| called | A past pl. from the tr. v. "to call," ref. to "priests." |
| were called | A reg. tr. v., pass. vo., indic. m., past t., p. num., 3rd per., agr. with its nom. "priests." |
| **Druids.** | A prop. n., mas. gen., p. num., 3rd per., nom. c. after the v. "were called." |
| 4. Mary | A prop. n., fem. gen., s. num., 3rd per., nom. c. to the v. "would cease." |
| would | An aux. v. to "cease," indg. pot. m., past t. |
| soon | An adv. of time, mod. the v. "would cease." |
| (to) cease | A reg. intr. v., infin. m., pres. t., gov. by the v. "would." |
| would cease | A reg. intr. v., pot. m., past t., s. num., 3rd per., agr. with its nom. "Mary." |
| to | A particle, indg. infin. m. |
| to be | An irreg. intr. v., infin. m., pres. t., gov. by the v. "would cease." |
| **difficulty.** | An abs. n., neu. gen., s. num., 3rd per., nom. c. after the v. "to be." |
| 5. I | A pers. pron., mas. gen., s. num., 1st per., nom. c. to the v. "would be." |
| would | An aux. v. to "be," indg. pot. m., past t. |
| (to) be | An irreg. intr. v., infin. m., pres. t., gov. by the v. "would." |
| would be | An irreg. intr. v., pot. m., past t., s. num., 1st per., agr. with its nom. "I." |
| **merman** | A com. n., mas. gen., s. num., 3rd per., nom. c. after the v. "would be." |
| bold. | An adj. of quality, pos. deg., qual. the n. "merman." |
| 6. All | An adj. of quantity (bulk or mass), qual. the n. "world." |
| world | A com. n., neu. gen., s. num., 3rd per., nom. c. to the v. "is." |
| is | An irreg. intr. v., indic. m., pres. t., s. num., 3rd per., agr. with its nom. "world." |
| **stage.** | A com. n., neu. gen., s. num., 3rd per., nom. c. after the v. "is." |
| 7. My | A pers. pron., com. gen., s. num., 1st per., poss. c., gov. by the n. "son." |
| eldest | An adj. of quality, superl. deg., qual. the n. "son." |
| son | A com. n., mas. gen., s. num., 3rd per., nom. c. to the v. "was bred." |
| was | An aux. v. to "bred," indg. pass. vo., past t. |
| bred | A past pl. from the tr. v. "to breed," ref. to "son." |
| was bred | An irreg. tr. v., pass. vo., indic. m., past t., s. num., 3rd per., agr. with its nom. "son." |
| **scholar.** | A com. n., mas. gen., s. num., 3rd per., nom. c. after the v. "was bred." |
| 8. He | A pers. pron., mas. gen., s. num., 3rd per., nom. c. to the v. "was born." |
| was | An aux. v. to "born," indg. pass. vo., past t. |
| born | A past pl. from the tr. v. "to bear," ref. to "he." |
| was born | An irreg. tr. v., pass. vo., indic. m., past t., s. num., 3rd per., agr. with its nom. "he." |
| **heir** | A com. n., mas. gen., s. num., 3rd per., nom. c. after the v. "was born." |
| to | A prep., sh. the rn. bet. "heir" and "estate." |
| large | An adj. of quality, pos. deg., qual. the n. "estate." |
| estate. | A com. n., neu. gen., s. num., 3rd per., obj. c., gov. by the prep. "to." |
| 9. Elizabeth | A prop. n., fem. gen., s. num., 3rd per., nom. c. to the v. "was proclaimed." |
| was | An aux. v. to "proclaimed," indg. pass. vo., past t. |
| proclaimed | A past pl. from the tr. v. "to proclaim," ref. to "Elizabeth." |
| was proclaimed | A reg. tr. v., pass. vo., indic. m., past t., s. num., 3rd per., agr. with its nom. "Elizabeth." |
| **queen.** | A com. n., fem. gen., s. num., 3rd per., nom. c. after the v. "was proclaimed." |
| 10. He | A pers. pron., mas. gen., s. num., 3rd per., nom. c. to the v. "returned." |
| returned | A reg. intr. v., indic. m., past t., s. num., 3rd per., agr. with its nom. "he." |
| to | A prep., sh. the rn. bet. "returned" and "country." |

| | |
|---|---|
| his | A pers. pron., forming with the adj. "own" a compd. pers. pron. |
| own | An intensive adj. of quality, qual. the n. "country." |
| his own | A compd. pers. pron., mas. gen., s. num., 3rd per., poss. c., gov. by the n. "country." |
| country | A com. n., neu. gen., s. num., 3rd per., obj. c., gov. by the prep. "to." |
| **millionaire.** | A com. n., mas. gen., s. num., 3rd per., nom. c. after the v. "returned." |

## Exercise 110.

| | |
|---|---|
| 1. My | A pers. pron., mas. gen., s. num., 1st per., poss. c., gov. by the n. "wife." |
| wife | A com. n., fem. gen., s. num., 3rd per., nom. c. to the v. "insisted." |
| insisted | A reg. intr. v., indic. m., past t., s. num., 3rd per., agr. with its nom. "wife." |
| upon | A prep., sh. the rn. bet. "insisted" and "being called." |
| her | A pers. pron., fem. gen., s. num., 3rd per., poss. c., gov. by the ger. "being called." |
| being called | A compd. ger. from the tr. v. "to call," neu. gen., s. num., 3rd per., obj. c., gov. by the prep. "upon." (See also *Parsing*, pp. 71-74.) |
| **Olivia.** | A prop. n., fem. gen., s. num., 3rd per., nom. c. after the ger. "being called." |
| 2. I | A pers. pron., mas. gen., s. num., 1st per., nom. c. to the v. "valued." |
| valued | A reg. tr. v. (reflexive), act. vo., indic. m., past t., s. num., 1st per., agr. with its nom. "I." |
| myself | A compd. pers. pron., mas. gen., s. num., 1st per., obj. c., gov. by the tr. v. "valued." |
| on | A prep., sh. the rn. bet. "valued" and "being." |
| being | A ger. from the intr. v. "to be," neu. gen., s. num., 3rd per., obj. c., gov. by the prep. "on." |
| strict | An adj. of quality, pos. deg., qual. the n. "monogamist." |
| **monogamist.** | A com. n., mas. gen., s. num., 3rd per., nom. c. after the ger. "being." |
| 3. He | A pers. pron., mas. gen., s. num., 3rd per., nom. c. to the v. "had." |
| had | An irreg. tr. v., act. vo., indic. m., past t., s. num., 3rd per., agr. with its nom. "he." |
| not | An adv. of m. (neg.), mod. the v. "had." |
| sense | An abs. n., neu. gen., s. num., 3rd per., obj. c., gov. by the tr. v. "had." |
| to | A particle, indg. infin. m. |
| to discern | A reg. tr. v., act. vo., infin. m., pres. t., gov. by the n. "sense." |
| impropriety | An abs. n., neu. gen., s. num., 3rd per., obj. c., gov. by the tr. v. "to discern." |
| of | A prep., sh. the rn. bet. "impropriety" and "being." |
| his | A pers. pron., mas. gen., s. num., 3rd per., poss. c., gov. by the ger. "being." |
| being | A ger. from the intr. v. "to be," neu. gen., s. num., 3rd per., obj. c., gov. by the prep. "of." |
| incessant | An adj. of quality, qual. the n. "talker." |
| **talker.** | A com. n., mas. gen., s. num., 3rd per., nom. c. after the ger. "being." |
| 4. He | A pers. pron., mas. gen., s. num., 3rd per., nom. c. to the v. "enjoyed." |
| enjoyed | A reg. tr. v., act. vo., indic. m., past t., s. num., 3rd per., agr. with its nom. "he." |
| privilege | An abs. n., neu. gen., s. num., 3rd per., obj. c., gov. by the tr. v. "enjoyed." |
| of | A prep., sh. the rn. bet. "privilege" and "being." |
| being | A ger. from the intr. v. "to be," neu. gen., s. num., 3rd per., obj. c., gov. by the prep. "of." |
| **chief** | A com. n., mas. gen., s. num., 3rd per., nom. c. after the ger. "being." |
| of | A prep., sh. the rn. bet. "chief" and "party." |

| | |
|---|---|
| his | A pers. pron., mas. gen., s. num., 3rd per., poss. c., gov. by the n. "party." |
| party. | A com. col. n., neu. gen., s. num., 3rd per., obj. c., gov. by the prep. "of." |
| 5. Far | An adv. of deg., mod. the adj. *distant* und. (He far *distant* from.) |
| from | A prep., sh. the rn. bet. *distant* und. and "being." |
| being | A ger. from the intr. v. "to be," neu. gen., s. num., 3rd per., obj. c., gov. by the prep. "from." |
| upright | An adj. of quality, pos. deg., qual. the n. "man." |
| **man** | A com. n., mas. gen., s. num., 3rd per., nom. c. after the ger. "being." |
| he | A pers. pron., mas. gen., s. num., 3rd per., nom. c. to the v. "is possessed." |
| is | An aux. v. to "possessed," indg. pass. vo., pres. t. |
| not | An adv. of m. (neg.), mod. the v. "is possessed." |
| even | An adv. of deg., mod. the v. "is possessed." |
| possessed | A past pl. from the tr. v. "to possess," ref. to "he." |
| is possessed | A reg. tr. v., pass. vo., indic. m., pres. t., s. num., 3rd per., agr. with its nom. "he." |
| of | A prep., sh. the rn. bet. "is possessed" and "honesty." |
| common | An adj. of quality, pos. deg., qual. the n. "honesty." |
| honesty. | An abs. n., neu. gen., s. num., 3rd per., obj. c., gov. by the prep. "of." |
| 6. idle | An adj. of quality, pos. deg., qual. the n. "boy." |
| boy | A com. n., mas. gen., s. num., 3rd per., nom. c. to the v. "was reprimanded." |
| was | An aux. v. to "reprimanded," indg. pass. vo., past t. |
| severely | An adv. of man., mod. the v. "was reprimanded." |
| reprimanded | A past pl. from the tr. v. "to reprimand," ref. to "boy." |
| was reprimanded | A reg. tr. v., pass. vo., indic. m., past t., s. num., 3rd per., agr. with its nom. "boy." |
| for | A prep., sh. the rn. bet. "was reprimanded" and "being." |
| not | An adv. of m. (neg.) mod. the ger. "being." |
| being | A ger. from the intr. v. "to be," neu. gen., s. num., 3rd per., obj. c., gov. by the prep. "for." |
| diligent | An adj. of quality, pos. deg., qual. the n. "scholar." |
| **scholar.** | A com. n., mas. gen., s. num., 3rd per., nom. c. after the ger. "being." |
| 7. How | An adv. of deg., mod. the adv. "loudly." |
| loudly | An adv. of man., mod. the v. "did complain." |
| did | An aux. v. to "complain," indg. past t., emph. form. |
| I | A pers. pron., mas. gen., s. num., 1st per., nom. c. to the v. "did complain." |
| (to) complain | A reg. intr. v., infin. m., pres. t., gov. by the v. "did." |
| did complain | A reg. intr. v., indic. m., past t., emph. form, s. num., 1st per., agr. with its nom. "I." |
| of | A prep., sh. the rn. bet. "did complain" and "being considered." |
| being considered | A compd. ger. from the tr. v. "to consider," neu. gen., s. num., 3rd per., obj. c., gov. by the prep. "of." |
| **traitor** | A com. n., mas. gen., s. num., 3rd per., nom. c. after the ger. "being considered." |
| to | A prep., sh. the rn. bet. "traitor" and "country." |
| country | A com. n., neu. gen., s. num., 3rd per., obj. c., gov. by the prep. "to." |
| for | A prep., sh. the rn. bet. "affection" and "which." |
| which | A rel. pron., neu. gen., s. num., 3rd per., agr. with its ant. "country," obj. c., gov. by the prep. "for." |
| my | A pers. pron., mas. gen., s. num., 1st per., poss. c., gov. by the n. "affection." |
| affection | An abs. n., neu. gen., s. num., 3rd per., nom. c. to the v. "is." |
| is | An irreg. intr. v., indic. m., pres. t., s. num., 3rd per., agr. with its nom. "affection." |
| unbounded. | An adj. of quality, qual. the n. "affection." |
| 8 Instead of | A compd. prep., sh. the rn. bet. "kind and gentle" and "being." (See *Man. of Parsing*, p. 154, for another method.) |
| being | A ger. from the intr. v. "to be," neu. gen., s. num., 3rd per., obj. c., gov. by the prep. "instead of." |

ENGLISH GRAMMAR AND ANALYSIS. 65

| | |
|---|---|
| harsh | An adj. of quality, pos. deg., qual. the n. "father." |
| **father** | A com. n., mas. gen., s. num., 3rd per., nom. c. after the ger. "being." |
| thou | A pers. pron., mas. gen., s. num., 2nd per., nom. c. to the v. "art." |
| art | An irreg. intr. v., indic. m., pres. t., s. num., 2nd per., agr. with its nom. "thou." |
| indeed | An adv. of m. (aff.), mod. the v. "art." |
| kind | An adj. of quality, pos. deg., qual. the pron. "thou." |
| and | A cop. conj., jg. the sents. "thou art indeed kind" and "*thou art indeed* gentle." |
| gentle. | An adj. of quality, pos. deg., qual. the pron. *thou* und. |
| 9. To | A particle, indg. infin. m. |
| To be | An irreg. intr. v., infin. m., pres. t.; used as an abs. n., neu. gen., s. num., 3rd per., nom. c. to the v. "was." |
| good | An adj. of quality, pos. deg., qual. the n. "linguist." |
| **linguist** | A com. n., mas. gen., s. num., 3rd per., nom. c. after the v. "to be." |
| was | An irreg. intr. v., indic. m., past t., s. num., 3rd per., agr. with its nom. "to be." |
| his | A pers. pron., mas. gen., s. num., 3rd per., poss. c., gov. by the n. "aim." |
| sole | An adj. of quality, qual. the n. "aim." |
| aim. | An abs. n., neu. gen., s. num., 3rd per., nom. c. after the v. "was." |
| 10. By | A prep., sh. the rn. bet. "has attained" and "being named." |
| being named | A compd. ger. from the tr. v. "to name," neu. gen., s. num., 3rd per., obj. c., gov. by the prep. "by." |
| **judge** | A com. n., mas. gen., s. num., 3rd per., nom. c. after the ger. "being named." |
| he | A pers. pron., mas. gen., s. num., 3rd per., nom. c. to the v. "has attained." |
| has | An aux. v. to "attained," indg. perf. t. |
| attained | A past pl. from the intr. v. "to attain," ref. to "he." |
| has attained | A reg. intr. v., indic. m., perf. t., s. num., 3rd per., agr. with its nom. "he." |
| to | A prep., sh. the rn. bet. "has attained" and "height." |
| height | An abs. n., neu. gen., s. num., 3rd per., obj. c., gov. by the prep. "to." |
| of | A prep., sh. the rn. bet. "height" and "ambition." |
| his | A pers. pron., mas. gen., s. num., 3rd per., poss. c., gov. by the n. "ambition." |
| ambition. | An abs. n., neu. gen., s. num., 3rd per., obj. c., gov. by the prep. "of." |

### Exercise 111.

| | |
|---|---|
| 1. churches | A com. n., neu. gen., p. num., 3rd per., nom. c. to the v. "crumbled." |
| **lead** | A com. n., neu. gen., s. num., 3rd per., nom. c. absolute. |
| having | A pres. pl. from the tr. v. "to have," ref. to *the tearer* und. and aux. to "been torn," indg. perf. t. |
| been | A past pl. from the intr. v. "to be," ref. to "torn lead," and aux. to "torn," indg. pass. vo. |
| torn | A past pl. from the tr. v. "to tear," ref. to "lead." |
| having been torn | } A perf. pl. from the tr. v. "to tear," ref. to "lead." |
| from | A prep., sh. the rn. bet. "having been torn" and "roofs." |
| roofs | A com. n., neu. gen., p. num., 3rd per., obj. c., gov. by the prep. "from." |
| crumbled | A reg. intr. v., indic. m., past. t., p. num., 3rd per., agr. with its nom. "churches." |
| into | A prep., sh. the rn. bet. "crumbled" and "ruins." |
| ruins. | A com. n., neu. gen., p. num., 3rd per., obj. c., gov. by the prep. "into." |
| 2. My | A pers. pron., com. gen., s. num., 1st per., poss. c., gov. by the n. "thought." |
| whole | An adj. of quantity (bulk or mass), qual. the n. "thought." |

5

| | |
|---|---|
| thought | An abs. n., neu. gen., s. num., 3rd per., nom. c. absolute. |
| being | A pres. pl. from the intr. v. "to be," ref. to "bent thought," and aux. to "bent," indg. pass. vo. |
| now | An adv. of time, mod. the pl. "being bent." |
| bent | A past pl. from the tr. v. "to bend," ref. to "thought." |
| being bent | A pres. pl. from the tr. v. "to bend," pass. vo., ref. to "thought." |
| on | A prep., sh. the rn. bet. "being bent" and "cultivating." |
| cultivating | A ger. from the tr. v., "to cultivate," neu. gen., s. num., 3rd per., obj. c., gov. by the prep. "on." |
| my | A pers. pron., com. gen., s. num., 1st per., poss. c., gov. by the n. "talent." |
| talent | An abs. n., neu. gen., s. num., 3rd per., obj. c., gov. by the tr. ger. "cultivating." |
| I | A pers. pron., com. gen., s. num., 1st per., nom. c. to the v. "applied." |
| applied | A reg. intr. v., indic. m., past t., s. num., 1st per., agr. with its nom. "I." |
| to | A prep., sh. the rn. bet. "applied" and "business." |
| business. | An abs. n., neu. gen., s. num., 3rd per., obj. c., gov. by the prep. "to." |
| 3. My | A pers. pron., com. gen., s. num., 1st per., poss. c., gov. by the n. "study." |
| sole | An adj. of quality, qual. the n. "study." |
| study | An abs. n., neu. gen., s. num., 3rd per., nom. c. absolute. |
| therefore | A cop. conj., introducing the sent. |
| being | A pres. pl. from the intr. v. "to be," ref. to "study." |
| to | A particle, indg. infin. m. |
| to escape | A reg. intr. v., infin. m., pres. t.; used as an abs. n., neu. gen., s. num., 3rd per., nom c. after the pl. "being." |
| with | A prep., sh. the rn. bet. "to escape" and "gods." |
| my | A per. pron., com. gen., s. num., 1st per., poss. c., gov. by the n. "gods." |
| household | A com. n. used as an adj. of quality, qual. the n. "gods." |
| gods | A com. n., mas. gen., p. num., 3rd per., obj. c., gov. by the prep. "with." |
| I | A pers. pron., com. gen., s. num., 1st per., nom. c. to the v. "disappeared." |
| disappeared | A reg. intr. v., indic. m., past t., s. num., 1st per., agr. with its nom. "I." |
| from | A prep., sh. the rn. bet. "disappeared" and "playhouse." |
| playhouse. | A com. n., neu. gen., s. num., 3rd per., obj. c., gov. by the prep. "from." |
| 4. Michaelmas-Eve | An abs. n. used as a prop. n., neu. gen., s. num., 3rd per., nom. c. absolute. |
| happening | A pres. pl. from the intr. v. "to happen," ref. to "Michaelmas-Eve." |
| on | A prep., sh. the rn. bet. "happening" and "day." |
| next | An adj. of quality, superl. deg., qual. the n. "day." |
| day | An abs. n., neu. gen., s. num., 3rd per., obj. c., gov. by the prep. "on." |
| we | A pers. pron., com. gen., p. num., 1st per., nom. c. to the v. "were invited." |
| were | An aux. v. to "invited," indg. pass. vo., past t. |
| invited | A past pl. from the tr. v. "to invite," ref. to "we." |
| were invited | A reg. tr. v., pass. vo., indic. m., past t., p. num., 1st per., agr. with its nom. "we." |
| to | A particle, indg. infin. m. |
| to burn | A reg. tr. v., act. vo., infin. m., pres. t., gov. by the v. "were invited." |
| nuts | A com. n., neu. gen., p. num., 3rd per., obj. c., gov. by the tr. v. "to burn." |
| and | A cop. conj., jg. the sents. "we were invited to burn nuts" and "we were invited to play tricks." |
| to play | A reg. tr. v., act. vo., infin. m., pres. t., gov. by the v. *were invited* und. |
| tricks | An abs. n., neu. gen., p. num., 3rd per., obj. c., gov. by the tr. v. "to play." |
| at | A prep., sh. the rn. bet. "to play" and *house* und. |

| | |
|---|---|
| neighbour | A com. n. used as an adj. of quality, qual. the n. "Flamborough's." |
| Flamborough's. | A prop. n., mas. gen., s. num., 3rd per., poss. c., gov. by the n. *house* und. |
| 5. **business** | An abs. n., neu. gen., s. num., 3rd per., nom. c. absolute. |
| of | A prep., sh. the rn. bet. "business" and "toilet." |
| toilet | A com. n., neu. gen., s. num., 3rd per., obj. c., gov. by the prep. "of." |
| being | A pres. pl. from the intr. v. "to be," ref. to "business." |
| over | An adv. of time, mod. the pl. "being." |
| we | A pers. pron., com. gen., p. num., 1st per., nom. c. to the v. "had." |
| had | An irreg. tr. v., act. vo., indic. m., past t., p. num., 1st per., agr. with its nom. "we." |
| at last | An adverbial phrase of time, mod. the v. "had." (For another method, see *Man. of Parsing*, p. 150). |
| satisfaction | An abs. n., neu. gen., s. num., 3rd per., obj. c., gov. by the tr. v. "had." |
| of | A prep., sh. the rn. bet. "satisfaction" and "seeing." |
| seeing | A ger. from the tr. v. "to see," neu, gen., s. num., 3rd per., obj. c., gov. by the prep. "of." |
| him | A per. pron., mas. gen., s. num., 3rd per., obj. c., gov. by the tr. ger. "seeing." |
| mounted | A past pl. from the tr. v. "to mount," ref. to "him." |
| upon | A prep., sh. the rn. bet. "mounted" and "colt." |
| colt. | A com. n., mas. gen., s. num., 3rd per., obj. c., gov. by the prep. "upon." |
| 6. Her | A per. pron., fem. gen., s. num., 3rd per., poss. c., gov. by the n. "mother." |
| **mother** | A com. n., fem. gen., s. num., 3rd per., nom. c. absolute. |
| dying | A pres. pl. from the intr. v. "to die," ref. to "mother." |
| of | A prep., sh. the rn. bet. "dying" and "gift." |
| gift | A com. n., neu. gen., s. num., 3rd per., obj. c., gov. by the prep. "of." |
| she | A pers. pron., fem. gen., s. num., 3rd per., nom c., to the v. "gave. |
| gave | An irreg. tr. v., act. vo., indic. m., past t., s. num., 3rd per., agr. with its nom. "she." |
| that | A dis. adj., lim. the n. "gift." |
| precious | An adj. of quality, pos. deg., qual. the n. "gift." |
| gift | A com. n., neu. gen., s. num., 3rd per., obj. c., in app. with "gift." |
| what | An interrog. pron., neu. gen., s. num., 3rd per., nom. c. to the v. "remained." |
| else | An indef. nu. adj. of quantity, qual. the pron. "what." |
| remained | A reg. intr. v., indic. m., past t., s. num. 3rd per., agr. with nom. "what." |
| to | A prep., sh. the rn. bet. "remained" and "him." |
| him. | A pers. pron., mas. gen., s. num., 3rd per., obj. c., gov. by the prep. "to." |
| 7. Nothing | A com. n., neu. gen., s. num., 3rd per., nom. c. to the v. "could exceed." |
| could | An aux. v. to "exceed," indg. pot. m., past t. |
| (to) exceed | A reg. tr. v., act. vo., infin. m., pres. t., gov. by the v. "could." |
| could exceed | A reg. tr. v., act. vo., pot. m., past t., s. num., 3rd per., agr. with its nom. "nothing." |
| neatness | An abs. n., neu. gen., s. num., 3rd per., obj. c., gov. by the tr. v. "could exceed." |
| of | A prep., sh. the rn. bet. "neatness" and "enclosures." |
| my | A pers. pron., com. gen., s. num., 1st per., poss. c., gov. by the n. "enclosures." |
| enclosures | A com. n., neu. gen., p. num., 3rd per., obj. c., gov. by the prep. "of." |
| **elms** | A com. n., neu. gen., p. num., 3rd pers., nom. c. absolute. |
| and | A cop. conj., jg. the sents. "Nothing could exceed the neatness of my enclosures, the elms *appearing with inexpressible beauty*" and "*nothing could exceed the neatness of my enclosures, the* hedgerows appearing with inexpressible beauty." |
| **hedgerows** | A com. n., neu. gen., p. num., 3rd pers., nom. c. absolute. |
| appearing | A pres. pl. from the intr. v. "to appear," ref. to "elms" and "hedgerows." |

**68**  KEY TO

| | |
|---|---|
| with | A prep., sh. the rn. bet. "appearing" and "beauty." |
| inexpressible | An adj. of quality, qual. the n. "beauty." |
| beauty. | An abs. n., neu. gen., s. num., 3rd pers., obj. c., gov. by the prep. "with." |
| 8. **day** | An abs. n., neu. gen., s. num., 3rd per., nom. c. absolute. |
| having | A pres. pl. from the tr. v. "to have," ref. to "day," and aux. to "dawned," indg. perf. t. |
| dawned | A past pl. from the intr. v. "to dawn," ref. to "day." |
| having dawned | A perf. pl. from the intr. v. "to dawn," ref. to "day." |
| I | A pers. pron., com. gen., s. num., 1st per., nom. c. to the v. "started." |
| started | A reg. intr. v., indic., m., past t., s. num., 1st per., agr. with its nom. "I." |
| on | A prep. sh. the rn. bet. "started" and "journey." |
| my | A pers. pron., com. gen., s. num., 1st per., poss. c., gov. by the n. "journey." |
| journey. | An abs. n., neu. gen., s. num., 3rd per., obj. c., gov. by the prep. "on." |
| 9. And | A cop. conj., jg. a preceding sent. to "one man... ages." |
| one | A def. card. nu. adj. of quantity, qual. the n. "man." |
| man | A com. n., mas. gen., s. num., 3rd per., nom. c. to the v. "plays." |
| in | A prep., sh. the rn. bet. "plays" and "time." |
| his | A pers. pron., mas. gen., s. num., 3rd per., poss. c., gov. by the n. "time." |
| time | An abs. n., neu. gen., s. num., 3rd per., obj. c., gov. by the prep. "in." |
| plays | A reg. tr. v , act. vo., indic. m., pres. t., s. num., 3rd per., agr. with its nom. "man." |
| many | An indef. nu. adj. of quantity, pos. deg., qual. the n. "parts." |
| parts | An abs. n., neu. gen., p. num., 3rd per., obj. c., gov. by the tr. v. "plays." |
| His | A pers. pron., mas. gen., s. num., 3rd per., poss. c., gov. by the n. "acts." |
| **acts** | An abs. n., neu. gen., p. num., 3rd per., nom. c. absolute. |
| being | A pres. pl. from the intr. v. "to be," ref. to "acts." |
| seven | A def. card. nu. adj. of quantity, qual. the n. "ages." |
| ages. | An abs. n., neu. gen., p. num., 3rd per., nom. c. after "being." |
| 10. So | An adv. of man., mod. the v. "pleads." |
| folly | An abs. n., neu. gen., s. num., 3rd per., nom. c. to the v. "pleads." |
| pleads | A reg. intr. v., indic. m., pres. t., s. num., 3rd per., agr. with its nom. "folly." |
| And | A cop. conj., jg. the sents. "So folly pleads" and " avarice being judge, *folly* with ease succeeds." |
| **avarice** | An abs. n., neu. gen., s. num., 3rd per., nom. c. absolute. |
| being | A pres. pl. from the intr. v. " to be," ref. to "avarice." |
| judge | A com. n., mas. gen., s. num., 3rd per., nom. c. after "being." |
| with | A prop., sh. the rn. bet. "succeeds" and "ease." |
| ease | An abs. n., neu. gen., s. num., 3rd per., obj. c., gov. by the prep. "with." |
| succeeds. | A reg. intr. v., indic. m., pres. t., s. num., 3rd per., agr. with its nom. *folly* und. |

### Exercise 112.

| | |
|---|---|
| 1. O | An interj. |
| **friends** | A com. n., com. gen., p. num., 2nd per., nom. c. of add. |
| I | A pers. pron., com. gen., s. num., 1st per., nom. c. to the v. "hear." |
| hear | An irreg. tr. v., act. vo., indic. m., pres. t., s. num., 1st per., agr. with its nom. " I." |
| tread | An abs. n., neu. gen., s. num., 3rd per., obj. c., gov. by the tr. v. "hear." |
| of | A prep., sh. the rn. bet. "tread " and "feet." |
| nimble | An adj. of quality, pos. deg., qual. the n. "feet." |
| feet | A com. n., neu. gen., p. num., 3rd per., obj. c., gov. by the prep. "of." |
| hasting | A pres. pl. from the intr. v. "to haste," ref. to "feet." |

|  |  |
|---|---|
| this | A dis. adj., lim. the n. "way." |
| way. | A com. n., neu. gen., s. num., 3rd per., obj. c., gov. by the prep. *along* und. |
| 2. These | A dis. adj., lim. the n. *works* und. |
| are | An irreg. intr. v., indic. m., pres. t., p. num., 3rd per., agr. with its nom. *works* und. |
| Thy | A pers. pron., mas. gen., s. num., 2nd per., poss. c., gov. by the n. "works." |
| glorious | An adj. of quality, pos. deg., qual. the n. "works." |
| works | A com. n., neu. gen., p. num., 3rd per., nom. c. after the v. "are." |
| **Parent** | A com. n. tending to prop., mas. gen., s. num., 2nd per., nom. c. of add. |
| of | A prep., sh. the rn. bet. "Parent" and "good." |
| good. | An abs. n., neu. gen., s. num., 3rd per., obj. c., gov. by the prep. "of." |
| 3. Heavenly | An adj. of quality, qual. the n. "stranger." |
| **stranger** | A com. n., com. gen., s. num., 2nd per., nom. c. of add. |
| (to) please | A reg. tr. v., act. vo., infin. m., pres. t., gov. by the v. *may* und. (*May* to taste these bounties please *thee*.) |
| to | A particle, indic. infin. m. |
| to taste | A reg. tr. v., act. v., infin. m. ; used as an abs. n., neu. gen., s. num., 3rd per., nom. c. to the v. "*may* please." |
| these | A dis. adj., lim. the n. "bounties." |
| bounties. | A com. n., neu. gen., p. num., 3rd per., obj. c., gov. by the tr. v. "to taste." |
| 4. Grieve | A reg. intr. v., imper. m., pres. t., s. num., 2nd per., agr. with its nom. *thou* und. |
| not | An adv. of m. (neg.), mod. the v. "grieve." |
| my | A pers. pron., com. gen., s. num., 1st per., poss. c., gov. by the n. "child." |
| **child** | A com. n., com. gen., s. num., 2nd per., nom. c. of add. |
| chase | A reg. tr. v., act. vo., imper. m., pres. t., s. num., 2nd per., agr. with its nom. *thou* und. |
| all | An indef. nu. adj. of quantity, qual. the n. "fears." |
| thy | A pers. pron., com. gen., s. num., 2nd per., poss. c., gov. by the n. "fears." |
| fears | An abs. n., neu. gen., p. num., 3rd per., obj. c., gov. by the tr. v. "chase." |
| away. | An adv. of place, mod. the v. "chase." |
| 5. Wake | A reg. intr. v., imper. m., pres. t., s. num., 2nd per., agr. with its nom. *thou* und. |
| melancholy | An adj. of quality, pos. deg., qual. the n. "mother." |
| **mother** | A com. n., fem. gen., s. num., 2nd per., nom. c. of add. |
| wake | A reg. intr. v., imper. m., pres. t., s. num., 2nd per., agr. with its nom. *thou* und. |
| and | A cop. conj., jg. the sents. "*thou* wake" and "*thou* weep." |
| weep. | An irreg. intr. v., imper. m., pres. t., s. num., 2nd per., agr. with its nom. *thou* und. |
| 6. **England** | A prop. n., fem. gen. by personification, s. num., 2nd per., nom. c. of add. |
| with | A prep., sh. the rn. bet. "thee" and "faults." |
| all | An indef. nu. adj. of quantity, qual. the n. "faults." |
| thy | A pers. pron., fem. gen., s. num., 2nd per., poss. c., gov. by the n. "faults." |
| faults | An abs. n., neu. gen., p. num., 3rd per., obj. c., gov. by the prep. "with." |
| I | A pers. pron., com. gen., s. num., 1st per., nom. c. to the v. "love." |
| love | A reg. tr. v., act. vo., indic. m., pres. t., s. num., 1st per., agr. with its nom. "I." |
| thee | A pers. pron., fem. gen., s. num., 2nd per., obj. c., gov. by the tr. v. "love." |
| still | An adv. of time, mod the v. "love." |
| my | A pers. pron., com. gen., s. num., 1st per., poss. c., gov. by the n. "country." |
| **country.** | A com. n., fem. gen. by personification, s. num., 2nd per., nom. c. of add. |

70   KEY TO

| | | |
|---|---|---|
| 7. | What | An interrog. pron. used as an adj., qual. the n. "wind." |
| | wind | A com. n., neu. gen., s. num., 3rd per., nom. c. to the v. "blew." |
| | blew | An irreg. tr. v., act. vo., indic. m., past t., s. num., 3rd per., agr. with its nom. "wind." |
| | you | A pers. pron., mas. gen., s. num., p. form, 2nd per., obj. c., gov. by the tr. v. "blew." |
| | hither | An adv. of place, mod. the v. "blew." |
| | **Pistol** | A prop. n., mas. gen., s. num., 2nd per., nom. c. of add. |
| 8. | Sweet | An adj. of quality, pos. deg., qual. the n. "Teviot." |
| | **Teviot** | A prop. n., mas. gen. by personification, s. num., 2nd per., nom. c. of add. |
| | on | A prep., sh. the rn. bet. "blaze" and "tide." |
| | thy | A pers. pron., mas. gen., s. num., 2nd per., poss. c., gov. by the n. "tide." |
| | silvery | An adj. of quality, pos. deg., qual. the n. "tide." |
| | tide | A com. n., neu. gen., s. num., 3rd per., obj. c., gov. by the prep. "on." |
| | glaring | A pres. pl. used as an adj. of quality, qual. the n. "bale-fires." |
| | bale-fires | A compd. com. n., neu. gen., p. num., 3rd per., nom. c. to the v. "blaze." |
| | blaze | A reg. intr. v., indic. m., pres. t., p. num., 3rd per., agr. with its nom. "bale-fires." |
| | no | An adv. of m. (neg.), mod. the adv. "more." |
| | more. | An adv. of time, mod. the v. "blaze." |

### Exercise 113.

| | | |
|---|---|---|
| 1. | Poor | An adj. of quality, pos. deg., qual. the n. "creature." |
| | forlorn | An adj. of quality, pos. deg., qual. the n. "creature." |
| | **creature** | A com. n., mas. gen., s. num., 3rd per., nom. c. exclamatory. |
| | where | An interrog. adv. of place, mod. the v. "are." |
| | are | An irreg. intr. v., indic. m., pres. t., p. num., 3rd per., agr. with its nom. "fathers." |
| | now | An adv. of time, mod. the v. "are." |
| | flatterers | A com. n., con. gen., p. num., 3rd per., nom. c. to the v. "are." |
| | that | A rel. pron., com. gen., p. num., 3rd per., agr. with its ant. "flatterers," obj. c., gov. by the tr. v. "could inspire." |
| | he | A pers. pron., mas. gen., s. num., 3rd per., nom. c. to the v. "could inspire." |
| | could | An aux. v. to "inspire," indg. pot. m., past t. |
| | once | An adv. of time, mod. the v. "could inspire." |
| | (to) inspire | A reg. tr. v., act. vo., infin. m., pres. t., gov. by the v. "could." |
| | could inspire | A reg. tr. v., act. vo., pot. m., past t., s. num., 3rd per., agr. with its nom. "he." |
| | and | A cop. conj., jg. the sents. "that he could once inspire," and "that he could once command." |
| | (to) command. | A reg. tr. v., act. vo., infin. m., pres. t., gov. by the v. *could* und. |
| 2. | **Religion** | An abs. n., neu. gen., s. num., 3rd per., nom. c. exclamatory. |
| | what | An interrog. pron. used as an adj., qual. the n. "treasures." |
| | treasures | A com. n., neu. gen., p. num., 3rd per., nom. c. to the v. "reside." |
| | untold | An adj. of quality, qual. the n. "treasures." |
| | reside | A reg. intr. v., indic. m., pres. t., p. num., 3rd per., agr. with its nom. "treasures." |
| | in | A prep., sh. the rn. bet. "reside" and "word." |
| | that | A dis. adj., lim. the n. "word." |
| | heavenly | An adj. of quality, qual. the n. "word." |
| | word. | A com. n., neu. gen., s. num., 3rd per., obj. c., gov. by the prep. "in." |
| 3. | These | A dis. adj., lim. the n. "cowards." |
| | **cowards** | A com. n., mas. gen., p. num., 3rd per., nom. c. exclamatory. |
| | I | A pers. pron., com. gen., s. num., 1st per., nom. c. to the v. "despise." |
| | despise | A reg. tr. v., act. vo., indic. m., pres. t., s. num., 1st per., agr. with its nom. "I." |
| | them. | A pers. pron., mas. gen., p. num., 3rd per., obj. c., gov. by the tr. v. "despise." |
| 4. | **king** | A com. n., mas. gen., s. num., 3rd per., nom. exclamatory. |

| | |
|---|---|
| who | An interrog. pron., mas. gen., s. num., 3rd per., nom. c. to the v. "is." |
| is | An irreg. intr. v., indic. m., pres. t., s. num., 3rd per., agr. with its nom. "who." |
| that. | A dis. adj., lim. the n. *king* und. |
| 5. Your | A pers. pron., com. gen., p. num., 2nd per., poss. c., gov. by the n. "house." |
| **house** | A com. n., neu. gen., s. num., 3rd per., nom. c. exclamatory. |
| It | A pers. pron., neu. gen., s. num., 3rd per., nom. c. to the v. "is left." |
| is | An aux. v. to "left," indg. pass. vo., pres. t. |
| left | A past pl. from the tr. v. "to leave," ref. to "it." |
| is left | An irreg. tr. v., pass. vo., indic. m., pres. t., s. num., 3rd per., agr. with its nom. "it." |
| unto | A prep., sh. the rn. bet. "is left" and "you." |
| you | A pers. pron., com. gen., p. num., 2nd per., obj. c., gov. by the prep. "unto." |
| desolate. | An adj. of quality, pos. deg., qual. the pron. "it." |
| 6. Resplendent | An adj. of quality, pos. deg., qual. the n. "sight." |
| **sight** | An abs. n., neu. gen., s. num., 3rd per., nom. c. exclamatory. |
| Behold | An irreg. tr. v., act. vo., imper. m., pres. t., s. num., 2nd per., agr. with its nom. *thou* und. |
| coxcomb | A com. n. used as an adj. of quality, qual. the n. "Czar." |
| Czar | A prop. n., mas. gen., s. num., 3rd per., obj. c., gov. by the tr. v. "behold." |
| autocrat | A com. n., mas. gen., s. num., 3rd per., obj. c., in app. with "Czar." |
| of | A prep., sh. the rn. bet. "autocrat" and "waltzes." |
| waltzes | An abs. n., neu. gen., p. num., 3rd per., obj. c., gov. by the prep. "of." |
| and | A cop. conj., jg. the sents. "Behold...waltzes" and "*Behold the coxcomb Czar, the autocrat* of war." |
| of | A prep., sh. the rn. bet. *autocrat* und. and "war." |
| war. | An abs. n., neu. gen., s. num., 3rd per., obj. c., gov. by the prep. "of." |

## Exercise 114.

| | |
|---|---|
| 1. There | An expletive adv., mod. the v. "appeared." |
| appeared | A reg. intr. v., indic. m., past t., s. num., 3rd per., agr. with its nom. "light." |
| at | A prep., sh. the rn. bet. "appeared" and "distance." |
| great | An adj. of quality, pos. deg., qual. the n. "distance." |
| distance | An abs. n., neu. gen., s. num., 3rd per., obj. c., gov. by the prep. "at." |
| very | An adv. of deg., mod. the adj. "shining." |
| shining | A pres. pl. used as an adj. of quality, qual. the n. "light." |
| **light** | A com. n., neu. gen., s. num., 3rd per., nom. c. to the v. "appeared." |
| and | A cop. conj., jg. the sents. "There appeared...light" and "*there appeared* in the midst...aspect." |
| in | A prep., sh. the rn. bet. *appeared* und. and "midst." |
| midst | A com. n., neu. gen., s. num., 3rd per., obj. c., gov. by the prep. "in." |
| of | A prep., sh. the rn. bet. "midst" and "it." |
| it | A pers. pron., neu. gen., s. num., 3rd per., obj. c., gov. by the prep. "of." |
| **person** | A com. n., fem. gen., s. num., 3rd per., nom. c. to the v. *appeared* und. |
| of | A prep., sh. the rn. bet. "person" and "aspect." |
| most | An adv. of deg., mod. the adj. "beautiful," indg. superl. deg. |
| most beautiful | An adj. of quality, superl. deg., qual. the n. "aspect." |
| aspect | An abs. n., neu. gen., s. num., 3rd per., obj. c., gov. by the prep. "of." |
| her | A pers. pron., fem. gen., s. num., 3rd per., poss. c., gov. by the n. "name." |
| **name** | A com. n., neu. gen., s. num., 3rd per., nom. c. to the v. "was." |

| | | |
|---|---|---|
| | was | An irreg. intr. v., indic. m., past t., s. num., 3rd per., agr. with its nom. "name." |
| | Truth. | An abs. n. used as a prop. n., fem. gen. by personification, s. num., 3rd per., nom. c. after the v. "was." |
| 2. | Let | An irreg. tr. v., act. vo., imper. m., pres. t., s. num., 2nd per., agr. with its nom. *thou* und. |
| | me | A pers. pron., mas. gen., s. num., 1st per., obj. c., gov. by the tr. v. "let." |
| | (to) pass | A reg. intr. v., infin. m., pres. t., gov. by the v. "let." |
| | cried | A reg. tr. v., act. vo., indic. m., past t., s. num., 3rd per., agr. with its nom. "he." |
| | he | A pers. pron., mas. gen., s. num., 3rd per., nom. c. to the v. "cried." |
| | in | A prep., sh. the rn. bet. "cried" and "voice." |
| | voice | An abs. n., neu. gen., s. num., 3rd per., obj. c., gov. by the prep. "in." |
| | of | A prep., sh. the rn. bet. "voice" and "entreaty." |
| | entreaty. | An abs. n., neu. gen., s. num., 3rd per., obj. c., gov. by the prep. "of." |
| 3. | Beside | A prep., sh. the rn. bet. "stands" and "doors." |
| | portal | An adj. of quality, qual. the n. "doors." |
| | doors | A com. n., neu. gen., p. num., 3rd per., obj. c., gov. by the prep. "beside." |
| | buttress'd | A past pl. from the tr. v. "to buttress," ref. to "doors." |
| | from | A prep., sh. the rn. bet. "buttress'd" and "moonlight." |
| | moonlight | An abs. n., neu. gen., s. num., 3rd per., obj. c., gov. by the prep. "from." |
| | stands | An irreg. intr. v., indic. m., pres. t., s. num., 3rd per., agr. with its nom. "he." |
| | he. | A pers. pron., mas. gen., s. num., 3rd per., nom. c. to the v. "stands." |
| 4. | Such | An adj. of quality, qual. the n. "portrait." |
| | was | An irreg. intr. v., indic. m., past t., s. num., 3rd per., agr. with its nom. "portrait." |
| | **portrait** | A com. n., neu. gen., s. num., 3rd per., nom. c. to the v. "was." |
| | **apostle** | A com. n., mas. gen., s. num., 3rd per., nom. c. to the v. "drew." |
| | drew. | An irreg. tr. v., act. vo., indic. m., past t., s. num., 3rd per., agr. with its nom "apostle." (An apostle drew *which*.) |
| 5. | Of | A prep., sh. the rn. bet. "am" and "train." |
| | their | A pers. pron., com. gen., p. num., 3rd per., poss. c., gov. by the n. "train." |
| | train | A com. n., neu. gen., s. num., 3rd per., obj. c., gov. by the prep. "of." |
| | am | An irreg. intr. v., indic. m., pres. t., s. num., 1st per., agr. with its nom. "I." |
| | **I.** | A pers. pron., com. gen., s. num., 1st per., nom. c. to the v. "am." |
| 6. | So | An adv. of man., mod. the v. "work." |
| | work | A reg. intr. v., indic. m., pres. t., p. num., 3rd per., agr. with its nom. "bees." |
| | honey | A com. n. used as an adj. of quality, qual. the n. "bees." |
| | **bees.** | A com. n., com. gen., p. num., 3rd per., nom. c. to the v. "work." |
| 7. | Down | An adv. of place, mod. the v. "came." |
| | came | An irreg. intr. v., indic. m, past t., p. num., 3rd per., agr. with its nom. "fowl." |
| | by | A prep., sh. the rn. bet. "came" and "hands." |
| | hands | A com. n., neu. gen., p. num., 3rd per., obj. c., gov. by the prep. "by." |
| | of | A prep., sh. the rn. bet. "hands" and *girl* und. |
| | one | A def. card. nu. adj. of quantity, qual. the n. *girl* und. |
| | of | A prep., sh. the rn. bet. *girl* und. and "slave-girls." |
| | Syrian | An adj. of quality, qual. the n. "slave-girls." |
| | slave-girls | A compd. com. n., fem. gen., p. num., 3rd per., obj. c., gov. by the prep. "of." |
| | **fowl** | A com. n., com. gen., p. num., 3rd per., nom. c. to the v. "came." |

| | |
|---|---|
| and | A cop. conj., jg. the sents. "the fowl came down" and "the wine came down." |
| **wine.** | A com. n., neu. gen., s. num., 3rd per., nom. c. to the v. *came* und. |
| 8. Smooth | An adj. of quality, pos. deg., qual. the n. "water." |
| runs | An irreg. intr. v., indic. m., pres. t., s. num., 3rd per., agr. with its nom. "water." |
| **water** | A com. n., ncu. gen., s. num., 3rd per., nom. c. to the v. "runs." |
| where | A cop. conj., jg. the sents. "Smooth runs the water" and "the brook is deep." |
| **brook** | A com. n., neu. gen., s. num., 3rd per., nom. c. to the v. "is." |
| is | An irreg. intr. v., indic. m., pres. t., s. num., 3rd per., agr. with its nom. "brook." |
| deep. | An adj. of quality, pos. deg., qual. the n. "brook." |
| 9. Oh | An interj. |
| could | An aux. v. to "rise," indg. pot. m., past t. |
| their | A pers. pron., com. gen., p. num., 3rd per., poss. c., gov. by the n. "Incas." |
| ancient | An adj. of quality, pos. deg., qual. the n. "Incas." |
| **Incas** | A prop. n., mas. gen., p. num., 3rd per., nom. c. to the v. "could rise." |
| (to) rise | An irreg. intr. v., infin. m., pres. t., gov. by the v. "could." |
| could rise | An irreg. intr. v., pot. m., conditional form, past t., p. num., 3rd per., agr. with its nom. "Incas." (*If* their ancient Incas could rise again.) |
| again | An adv. of time, mod. the v. "could rise." |
| How | An adv. of man., mod. the v. "would take." |
| would | An aux. v. to "take," indg. pot. m., past t. |
| **they** | A pers. pron., mas. gen., p. num., 3rd per., nom. c. to the v. "would take." |
| (to) take | An irreg. tr. v., act. vo., infin. m., pres. t., gov. by the v. "would." |
| would take | An irreg. tr. v., act. vo., pot. m., past t., p. num., 3rd per., agr. with its nom. "they." |
| up | An adv. of place, mod. the v "would take." |
| Israel's | A prop. n., neu. gen., s. num., 3rd per., poss. c., gov. by the n. "strain." |
| taunting | A pres. pl. used as an adj. of quality, qual. the n. "strain." |
| strain | An abs. n., neu. gen., s. num., 3rd per., obj. c., gov. by the tr. v. "would take." |
| Art | An irreg. intr. v., indic. m., pres. t., s. num., 2nd per., agr. with its nom. "thou." |
| **thou** | A pers. pron., fem. gen., s. num., 2nd per., nom. c. to the v. "art." |
| too | An adv. of deg., mod. the v. "art." |
| fallen | A past pl. from the intr. v. "to fall," ref. to "Iberia." |
| Iberia. | A prop. n., fem. gen. by personification, s. num., 2nd per., nom. c. of add. |
| 10. Heavily | An adv. of man., mod. the v. "hangs." |
| hangs | An irreg. intr. v., indic. m., pres. t., s. num., 3rd per., agr. with its nom. "sunflower." |
| broad | An adj. of quality, pos. deg., qual. the n. "sunflower." |
| **sunflower** | A compd. com. n., neu. gen., s. num., 3rd per., nom. c. to the v. "hangs." |
| Over | A prep., sh. the rn. bet. "hangs" and "grave." |
| its | A pers. pron., neu. gen., s. num., 3rd per., poss. c., gov. by the n. "grave." |
| grave | A com. n., neu. gen., s. num., 3rd per., obj. c., gov. by the prep. "over." |
| i'=in | A prep., sh. the rn. bet., "grave" and "earth." |
| earth | A com. n., neu. gen., s. num., 3rd per., obj. c., gov. by the prep. "in." |
| so | An adv. of deg., mod. the adj. "chilly." |
| chilly | An adj. of quality, pos. deg., qual. the n. "earth." |
| Heavily | An adv. of man., mod. the v. "hangs." |
| hangs | An irreg. intr. v., indic. m., pres. t., s. num., 3rd per., agr. with its nom. "holly-hock." |
| **holly-hock** | A compd. com. n., neu. gen., s. num., 3rd per., nom. c. to the v. "hangs." |

74   KEY TO

| Heavily | An adv. of man., mod. the v. "hangs." |
| hangs | An irreg. intr. v., indic. m., pres. t., s. num., 3rd per., agr. with its nom. "lily." |
| tiger | A com. n. used as an adj. of quality, qual. the n. "lily." |
| **lily.** | A com. n., neu. gen., s. num., 3rd per., nom. c. to the v. "hangs." |

## Exercise 115.

1. *Ahab's* house was destroyed. 2. *Raphael's* paintings are renowned. 3. *Shakespeare's* works are an inexhaustible mine. 4. *Napoleon's* victories produced no lasting good. 5. The *farmer's* fields are yellow. 6. The *dealers'* horses are for sale.

## Exercise 116.

| 1. I | A pers. pron., com. gen., s. num., 1st per., nom. c. to the v. "am." |
| am | An irreg. intr. v., indic. m., pres. t., s. num., 1st per., agr. with its nom. "I." |
| out of | A compd. prep., sh. the rn. bet. "am" and "reach." (See also *Man. of Parsing*, p. 154.) |
| **humanity's** | An abs. n., neu. gen., s. num., 3rd per., poss. c., gov. by the n. "reach." |
| reach. | An abs. n., neu. gen., s. num., 3rd per., obj. c., gov. by the compd. prep. "out of." |
| 2. **Men's** | A com. n., mas. gen., p. num., 3rd per., poss. c., gov. by the n. "manners." |
| evil | An adj. of quality, pos. deg., qual. the n. "manners." |
| manners | An abs. n., neu. gen., p. num., 3rd per., nom. c. to the v. "live." |
| live | A reg. intr. v., indic. m., pres. t., p. num., 3rd per., agr. with its nom. "manners." |
| in | A prep., sh. the rn. bet. "live" and "brass." |
| brass | A com. n., neu. gen., s. num., 3rd per., obj. c., gov. by the prep. "in." |
| **their** | A pers. pron., mas. gen., p. num., 3rd per., poss. c., gov. by the n. "virtues." |
| virtues | An abs. n., neu. gen., p. num., 3rd per., obj. c., gov. by the tr. v. "write." |
| we | A pers. pron., com. gen., p. num., 1st per., nom. c. to the v. "write." |
| write | An irreg. tr. v., act. vo., indic. m., pres. t., p. num., 1st per., agr. v i h its nom. "we." |
| in | A prep., sh. the rn. bet. "write" and "water." |
| water. | A com. n., neu. gen., s. num., 3rd per., obj. c., gov. by the prep. "in." |
| 3. **Wolfe's** | A prop. n., mas. gen., s. num., 3rd per., poss. c., gov. by the n. "body." |
| body | A com. n., neu. gen., s. num., 3rd per., nom. c. to the v. "was embalmed." |
| was | An aux. v. to "embalmed," indg. pass. vo., past t. |
| embalmed | A past pl. from the tr. v. "to embalm," ref. to body. |
| was embalmed | A reg. tr. v., pass. vo., indic. m., past t., s. num., 3rd per., agr. with its nom. "body." |
| and | A cop. conj., jg. the sents. "Wolfe's body was embalmed" and "*Wolfe's body was* borne..England." |
| borne | A past pl. from the tr. v. "to bear," ref. to *body* und. |
| to | A prep., sh. the rn. bet. "*was* borne" and "river." |
| river | A com. n., neu. gen., s. num., 3rd per., obj. c., gov. by the prep. "to." |
| for | A prep., sh. the rn. bet. "borne" and "conveyance." |
| conveyance | An abs. n., neu. gen., s. num., 3rd per., obj. c., gov. by the prep. "for." |
| to | A prep., sh. the rn. bet. "conveyance" and "England." |
| England. | A prop. n., neu. gen., s. num., 3rd per., obj. c., gov. by the prep. "to." |
| 4. Basil | A prop. n., mas. gen., s. num., 3rd per., nom. c. to the v. "was." |

# ENGLISH GRAMMAR AND ANALYSIS. 75

| | |
|---|---|
| was | An irreg. intr. v., indic. m., past t., s. num., 3rd per., agr. with its nom. "Basil." |
| **Benedict's** | A prop. n., mas. gen., s. num., 3rd per., poss. c., gov. by the n. "friend." |
| friend. | A com. n., mas. gen., s. num., 3rd per., nom. c. after the v. "was." |
| 5. **Men's** | A com. n., mas. gen., p. num., 3rd per., poss. c., gov. by the n. "happiness." |
| happiness | An abs. n., neu. gen., s. num., 3rd per., nom. c. to the v. *is* und. |
| or | A disj. conj., jg. the sents. "Men's happiness *is for the most part of their own making*" and "*men's* misery is *for the* most part of their own making." |
| misery | An abs. n., neu. gen., s. num., 3rd per., nom. c. to the v. "is." |
| is | An irreg. intr. v., indic. m., pres. t., s. num., 3rd per., agr. with its nom. "misery." |
| most | An adj. of quantity (bulk or mass), qual. the n. "part." |
| part | A com. n., neu. gen., s. num., 3rd per., obj. c., gov. by the prep. *for* und. |
| of | A prep., sh. the rn. bet. "is" and "making." |
| their | A pers. pron., forming with the adj. "own" a compd. pers. pron. |
| own | An intensive adj. of quality, qual. the n. "making." |
| **their own** | A compd. pers. pron., mas. gen., p. num., 3rd per., poss. c., gov. by the n. "making." |
| making. | A verbal or abs. n., neu. gen., s. num., 3rd per., obj. c., gov. by the prep. "of." |
| 6. There | An expletive adv., mod. the v. "was." |
| was | An irreg. intr. v., indic. m., past t., s. num., 3rd per., agr. with its nom. "lack." |
| lack | An abs. n., neu. gen., s. num., 3rd per., nom. c. to the v. "was." |
| of | A prep., sh. the rn. bet. "lack" and "nursing." |
| **woman's** | A com. n., fem. gen., s. num., 3rd per., poss. c., gov. by the n. "nursing." |
| nursing | A verbal or abs. n., neu. gen., s. num., 3rd per., obj. c., gov. by the prep. "of." |
| there | An expletive adv., mod. the v. "was." |
| was | An irreg. intr. v., indic. m., past t., s. num., 3rd per., agr. with its nom. "dearth." |
| dearth | An abs. n., neu. gen., s. num., 3rd per., nom. c. to the v. "was." |
| of | A prep., sh. the rn. bet. "dearth" and "tears." |
| **woman's** | A com. n., fem. gen., s. num., 3rd per., poss. c., gov. by the n. "tears." |
| tears. | A com. n., neu. gen., p. num., 3rd per., obj. c., gov. by the prep. "of." |
| 7. Labour | An abs. n., neu. gen., s. num., 3rd per., nom. c. to the v. "is." |
| for | A prep., sh. the rn. bet. "labour" and "sake." |
| **labour's** | An abs. n., neu. gen., s. num., 3rd per., poss. c., gov. by the n. "sake." |
| sake | An abs. n., neu. gen., s. num., 3rd per., obj. c., gov. by the prep. "for." |
| is | An irreg. intr. v., indic. m., pres. t., s. num., 3rd per., agr. with its nom. "labour." |
| against | A prep., sh. the rn. bet. "is" and "nature." |
| nature. | An abs. n., neu. gen., s. num., 3rd per., obj. c., gov. by the prep. "against." |
| 8. We | A pers. pron., com. gen., p. num., 1st per., nom. c. to the v. "should judge." |
| should | An aux. v. to "judge," indg. pot. m., past t. |
| not | An adv. of m. (neg.), mod. the v. "should judge." |
| (to) judge | A reg. intr. v., infin. m., pres. t., gov. by the v. "should." |
| should judge | A reg. intr. v., pot. m., past t., p. num., 1st per., agr. with its nom. "we." |
| of | A prep., sh. the rn. bet. "should judge" and "things." |
| things | A com. n., neu. gen., p. num., 3rd per., obj. c., gov. by the prep. "of." |
| by | A prep., sh. the rn. bet. "should judge" and "opinions." |
| **men's** | A com. n., mas. gen., p. num., 3rd per., poss. c., gov. by the n. "opinions." |

| | |
|---|---|
| opinions | An abs. n., neu. gen., p. num., 3rd per., obj. c., gov. by the prep. "by." |
| but | A disj. conj., jg. the sents. "We should not judge..opinions" and "*we should judge* of opinions by things." |
| of | A prep., sh. the rn. bet. *should judge* und. and "opinions.' |
| opinions | An abs. n., neu. gen., p. num., 3rd per., obj. c., gov. by the prep. "of." |
| by | A prep., sh. the rn. bet. *should judge* und. and "things." |
| things. | A com. n., neu. gen., p. num., 3rd per., obj. c., gov. by the prep. "by." |
| 9. He | A pers. pron., mas. gen., s. num., 3rd per., nom. c. to the v. "had left." |
| had | An aux. v. to "left," indg. pluperf. t. |
| left | A past pl. from the tr. v. "to leave," ref. to "home." |
| had left | An irreg. tr. v., act. vo., indic. m., pluperf. t., s. num., 3rd per., agr. with its nom. "he." |
| **his** | A pers. pron., mas. gen., s. num., 3rd per., poss. c., gov. by the n. "home." |
| home | A com. n., neu. gen., s. num., 3rd per., obj. c., gov. by the tr. v. "had left." |
| in | A prep., sh. the rn. bet. "had left" and "pride |
| **his** | A pers. pron., mas. gen., s. num., 3rd per., poss. c., gov. by the n. "spirit's." |
| **spirit's** | A com. n., neu. gen., s. num., 3rd per., poss. c., gov. by the n. "pride." |
| pride | An abs. n., neu. gen., s. num., 3rd per., obj. c., gov. by the prep. "in." |
| With | A prep., sh. the rn. bet. "had left" and "sword." |
| **his** | A pers. pron., mas. gen., s. num., 3rd per., poss. c., gov. by the n. "father's." |
| **father's** | A com. n, mas. gen., s. num., 3rd per., poss. c., gov. by the n. "sword." |
| sword | A com. n., neu. gen., s. num., 3rd per., obj. c., gov. by the prep. "with." |
| and | A cop. conj., jg. the sents. "He had left...sword" and "*he had left his home with his father's* blessing." |
| blessing. | An abs. n., neu. gen., s. num., 3rd per., obj. c., gov. by the prep. *with* und. |
| 10. Rome | A prop. n., fem. gen. by personification, s. num., 2nd per., nom. c. of add. |
| thou | A pers. pron., fem. gen., s. num., 2nd per., nom. c. to the v. "art doom'd." |
| art | An aux. v. to "doom'd," indg. pass. vo., pres. t. |
| doom'd | A past pl. from the tr. v. "to doom," ref. to "thou." |
| art doom'd | A reg. tr. v., pass. vo., indic. m., pres. t., s. num., 2nd per., agr. with its nom. "thou." |
| to | A particle, indg. infin. m. |
| to perish | A reg. intr. v., infin. m., pres. t., gov. by the v. "art doom'd." |
| and | A cop. conj., jg. the sents. "thou art doom'd to perish" and "thy days, like mortal man's, are numbered." |
| **thy** | A pers. pron., fem. gen., s. num., 2nd per., poss. c., gov. by the n. "days." |
| days | An abs. n., neu. gen., p. num., 3rd per., nom. c. to the v. "are numbered." |
| like | An adj. of quality, qual. the n. "days." |
| mortal | An adj. of quality, qual. the n. "man's." |
| **man's** | A com. n., mas. gen., s. num., 3rd per., poss. c., gov. by the n. *days* und. |
| are | An aux. v. to "numbered," indg. pass. vo., pres. t. |
| numbered | A past pl. from the tr. v. "to number," ref. to "days." |
| are numbered | A reg. tr. v., pass. vo., indic. m., pres. t., p. num., 3rd per., agr. with its nom. "days." |

## Exercise 117.

| | |
|---|---|
| 1. **Earl** | A com. n tending to prop., mas. gen., s. num., 3rd per., poss. c., gov. by the n. "troops." |
| of | A prep., sh. the rn. bet. "Earl" and "Surrey's." |

| | |
|---|---|
| **Surrey's*** | A prop. n., neu. gen., s. num., 3rd per., obj. c., gov. by the prep. "of." |
| troops | A com. n., neu. gen., p. num., 3rd per., nom. c. to the v. "were." |
| were | An irreg. intr. v., indic. m., past t., p. num., 3rd per., agr. with its nom. "troops." |
| victorious | An adj. of quality, qual. the n. "troops." |
| 2. **Israel** | A prop. n., neu. gen., s. num., 3rd per., poss. c., gov. by the n. *forces* und. |
| and | A cop. conj., jg. the sents. "Israel's *forces fought against Judah*" and "Syria's forces fought against Judah." |
| **Syria's** | A prop. n., neu. gen., s. num., 3rd per., poss. c., gov. by the n. "forces." |
| forces | A com. col. n., neu. gen., p. num., 3rd per., nom. c. to the v. "fought." |
| fought | An irreg. intr. v., indic. m., past t., p. num., 3rd per., agr. with its nom. "forces." |
| against | A prep., sh. the rn. bet. "fought" and "Judah." |
| Judah. | A prop. n., neu. gen., s. num., 3rd per., obj. c., gov. by the prep. "against." |
| 3. Every | A dist. nu. adj. of quantity, qual. the indef. pers. pron. "one." |
| one | An indef. pers. pron., com. gen., s. num., 3rd per., nom. c. to the v. "has heard." |
| has | An aux. v. to "heard," indg. perf. t. |
| heard | A past pl. from the tr. v. "to hear," ref. to *account* und. |
| has heard | An irreg. tr. v., act. vo., indic. m., past t., s. num., 3rd per., agr. with its nom. "one." (Has heard *an account of*.) |
| of | A prep., sh. the rn. bet. "heard" and "Rosinante." |
| Rosinante | A prop. n., mas. gen., s. num., 3rd per., obj. c., gov. by the tr. v. "has heard." |
| **Knight** | A com. n. tending to prop., mas. gen., s. num., 3rd per., poss. c., gov. by the n. "steed." |
| of | A prep., sh. the rn. bet. "Knight" and "La Mancha's." |
| **La Mancha's** | A prop. n., neu. gen., s. num., 3rd per., obj. c., gov. by the prep. "of." |
| steed. | A com n., mas. gen., s. num., 3rd per., obj. c., in app. with "Rosinante." |
| 4. **Duke** | A com. n. tending to prop., mas. gen., s. num., 3rd per., poss. c., gov. by the n. "tactics." |
| of | A prep., sh. the rn. bet. "Duke" and "Wellington's." |
| **Wellington's** | A prop. n., neu. gen., s. num., 3rd per., obj. c., gov. by the prep. "of." |
| tactics | An abs. n., neu. gen., p. num., 3rd per., nom. c. to the v. "were crowned." |
| were | An aux. v. to "crowned," indg. pass. vo., past t. |
| crowned | A past pl. from the tr. v. "to crown," ref. to "tactics." |
| were crowned | A reg. tr. v., pass. vo., indic. m., past t., p. num., 3rd per., agr. with its nom. "tactics." |
| with | A prep., sh. the rn. bet. "were crowned" and "success." |
| success. | An abs. n., neu. gen., s. num., 3rd per., obj. c., gov. by the prep. "with." |
| 5. He | A pers. pron., mas. gen., s. num., 3rd per., nom. c. to the v. "had." |
| had | An irreg. tr. v., act. vo., indic. m., past t., s. num., 3rd per., agr. with its nom. "he." |
| his | A pers. pron., mas. gen., s. num., 3rd per., poss. c., gov. by the n. "father's." |
| **father's** | A com. n., mas. gen., s. num., 3rd per., poss. c., gov. by the n. *assistance* und. |
| and | A cop. conj., jg. the sents. "He had his father's *assistance*" and "*he had* his friend's assistance." |
| his | A pers. pron., mas. gen., s. num., 3rd per., poss. c., gov. by the n. "friend's." |
| **friend's** | A com. n., com. gen., s. num., 3rd per., poss. c., gov. by the n. "assistance." |
| assistance. | An abs. n., neu. gen., s. num., 3rd per., obj. c., gov. by the tr. v. "had." |

* "Earl of Surrey's" and similar expressions may be parsed as compd. prop. nouns.

## 78  KEY TO

| | |
|---|---|
| 6. **Athens** | A prop. n., fem. gen. by personification, s. num., 3rd per., poss. c., gov. by the n. *sons* und. |
| **and** | A cop. conj., jg. the sents. "Athens' *sons*" and "Sparta's sons" into a compd. nom. or subject. |
| **Sparta's** | A prop. n., fem. gen. by personification, s. num., 3rd per., poss. c., gov. by the n. "sons." |
| sons | A com. n., mas. gen., p. num., 3rd per., nom. c. to the v. "fought." |
| fought | An irreg. intr. v., indic. m., past t., p. num., 3rd per., agr. with its nom. "*sons* and sons." |
| side | A com. n., neu. gen., s. num., 3rd per., nom. c. absolute. (Side *being* by side.) |
| by | A prep., sh. the rn. bet. *being* und. and "side." |
| side | A com. n., neu. gen., s. num., 3rd per., obj. c., gov. by the prep. "by." |
| against | A prep., sh. the rn. bet. "fought" and "foe." |
| common | An adj. of quality, qual. the n. "foe." |
| foe. | A com. n., mas. gen., s. num., 3rd per., obj. c., gov. by the prep. "against." |

### Exercise 118.

| | |
|---|---|
| 1. I | A pers. pron., fem. gen., s. num., 1st per., nom. c. to the v. "am." |
| am | An irreg. intr. v., indic. m., pres. t., s. num., 1st per., agr. with its nom. "I." |
| Duke | A com. n. tending to prop., used as an adj. of quality, qual. the n. "Humphrey's." (*Parsing*, p. 13.) |
| **Humphrey's** | A prop. n., mas. gen., s. num., 3rd per., poss. c., gov. by the n. "wife." |
| wife. | A com. n., fem. gen., s. num., 3rd per., nom. c. after the v. "am." |
| 2. Greeks | A prop. n., mas. gen., p. num., 3rd per., nom. c. to the v. "took." |
| took | An irreg. tr. v., act. vo., indic. m., past t., p. num., 3rd per., agr. with its nom. "Greeks." |
| Troy | A prop. n., neu. gen., s. num., 3rd per., obj. c., gov. by the tr. v. "took." |
| after | A prep., sh. the rn. bet. "took" and "siege." |
| ten | A def. card. nu. adj. of quantity, qual. the n. "years'." |
| **years'** | An abs. n., neu. gen., p. num., 3rd per., poss. c., gov. by the n. "siege." |
| siege. | An abs. n., neu. gen., s. num., 3rd per., obj. c., gov. by the prep. "after." |
| 3. In | A prep., sh. the rn. bet. "lie" and "bell." |
| **cowslip's** | A com. n., neu. gen., s. num., 3rd per., poss. c., gov. by the n. "bell." |
| bell | A com. n., neu. gen., s. num., 3rd per., obj. c., gov. by the prep. "in." |
| I | A pers. pron., com. gen., s. num., 1st per., nom. c. to the v. "lie." |
| lie. | An irreg. intr. v., indic. m., pres. t., s. num., 1st per., agr. with its nom. "I." |
| 4. Who | A rel. pron., com. gen., s. num., 3rd per., agr. with its ant. *person* und., nom. c. to the v. "kills." |
| kills | A reg. tr. v., act. vo., indic. m., pres. t., s. num., 3rd per., agr. with its nom. "who." |
| man | A com. n., mas. gen., s. num , 3rd per., obj. c., gov. by the tr. v. "kills." |
| kills | A reg. tr. v., act. vo., indic. m., pres. t., s. num., 3rd per., agr. with its nom. *person* und. |
| reasonable | An adj. of quality, pos. deg., qual. the n. "creature." |
| creature | A com. n., mas. gen., s. num., 3rd per., obj. c., gov. by the tr. v. "kills. |
| **God's** | A prop. n., mas. gen., s. num., 3rd per., poss. c., gov. by the n. "image." |
| image. | A com. n., neu. gen., s. num., 3rd per., obj. c., in app. with "creature." |

ENGLISH GRAMMAR AND ANALYSIS.    79

| | |
|---|---|
| 5. crag | A com. n., neu. gen., s. num., 3rd per., nom. c. to the v. "repeats." |
| repeats | A reg. tr. v., act. vo., indic. m., pres. t., s. num., 3rd per., agr. with its nom. "crag." |
| **raven's** | A com. n., com. gen., s. num., 3rd per., poss. c., gov. by the n. "croak." |
| croak. | An abs. n., neu. gen., s. num., 3rd per., obj. c., gov. by the tr. v. "repeats." |
| 6. **hunter** | A com. n., neu. gen., p. num., 3rd per., obj. c., gov. by the tr. v. "flung." |
| o'er | A prep., sh. the rn. bet. "flung" and "neck." |
| **Malcolm's** | A prop. n., mas. gen., s. num., 3rd per., poss. c., gov. by the n. "neck." |
| neck | A com. n., neu. gen., s. num., 3rd per., obj. c., gov. by the prep. "o'er." |
| he | A pers. pron., mas. gen., s. num., 3rd per., nom. c. to the v. "flung." |
| flung. | An irreg. tr. v., act. vo., indic. m., past t., s. num., 3rd per., agr. with its nom. "he." |
| 7. Old | An adj. of quality, pos. deg., qual. the n. "Kaspar's." |
| **Kaspar's** | A prop. n., mas. gen., s. num., 3rd per., poss. c., gov. by the n. "work." |
| work | An abs. n., neu. gen., s. num., 3rd per., nom. c. to the v. "was done." |
| was | An aux. v. to "done," indg. pass. vo., past t. |
| done | A past pl. from the tr. v. "to do," ref. to "work." |
| was done. | An irreg. tr. v., pass. vo., indic. m., past t., s. num., 3rd per., agr. with its nom. "work." |
| 8. **beehive's** | A compd. com. n., neu. gen., s. num., 3rd per., poss. c., gov. by the n. "hum." |
| hum | An abs. n., neu. gen., s. num., 3rd per., nom. c. to the v. "shall soothe." |
| shall | An aux. v. to "soothe," indg. fut. t., emph. form, expressing certainty. |
| (to) soothe | A reg. tr. v., act. vo., infin. m., pres. t., gov. by the v. "shall." |
| shall soothe | A reg. tr. v., act. vo., infin. m., fut. t., emph. form, s. num., 3rd per., agr. with its nom. "hum." |
| my | A pers. pron., com. gen., s. num., 1st per., poss. c., gov. by the n. "ear." |
| ear. | A com. n., neu. gen., s. num., 3rd per., obj. c., gov. by the tr. v. "shall soothe." |
| 9. O | An interj. |
| open | A reg. tr. v., act. vo., imper. m., pres. t., s. num., 2nd per., agr. with its nom. *thou* und. (*Thou* open *the door*.) |
| for | A prep., sh. the rn. bet. "open" and "sake." |
| our | A pers. pron., com. gen., p. num., 1st per., poss. c., gov. by the n. "lady's." |
| **lady's** | A com. n., fem. gen., s. num., 3rd per., poss. c., gov. by the n. "sake." |
| sake | An abs. n., neu. gen., s. num., 3rd per., obj. c., gov. by the prep. "for." |
| **pilgrim's** | A com. n. mas. gen., s. num., 3rd per., poss. c., gov. by the n. "blessing." |
| blessing | An abs. n., neu. gen., s. num., 3rd per., obj. c., gov. by the tr. v. "win." |
| win. | An irreg. tr. v., act. vo., imper. m., pres. t., s. num., 2nd per., agr. with its nom. *thou* und. |
| 10. In | A prep., sh. the rn. bet. "are allowed" and "change." |
| every | A dist. nu. adj., of quantity, qual. the n. "change." |
| change | An abs. n., neu. gen., s. num., 3rd per., obj. c., gov. by the prep. "in." |
| of | A prep., sh. the rn. bet. "change" and "estate." |
| **Man's** | A com. n. tending to prop., mas. gen., s. num., 3rd per., poss. c., gov. by the n. "estate." |
| estate | An abs. n., neu. gen., s. num., 3rd per., obj. c., gov. by the prep. "of." |
| are | An aux. v. to "allowed," indg. pass. vo., pres. t. |

| | |
|---|---|
| lights | A com. n., neu. gen., p. num., 3rd per., nom. c. to the v. "are allowed" und. |
| nd | A cop. conj., jg. the sents. "...lights are allowed" and "...guides are allowed." |
| guides | A com. n., neu. gen., p. num., 3rd per., nom. c. to the v. "are allowed." |
| allowed | A past pl. from the tr. v. "to allow," ref. to "guides." |
| are allowed. | A reg. tr. v., pass. vo., indic. m., pres. t., p. num., 3rd per., agr. with its nom. "guides." |

### Exercise 119.

| | |
|---|---|
| 1. doctor | A com. n., mas. gen., s. num., 3rd per., nom. c. to the v. "repeated." |
| repeated | A reg. tr. v., act. vo., indic. m., past t., s. num., 3rd per., agr. with its nom. "doctor." |
| his | A pers. pron., mas. gen., s. num., 3rd per., poss. c., gov. by the n. "remarks." |
| **remarks.** | An abs. n., neu. gen., p. num., 3rd per., obj. c., gov. by the tr. v. "repeated." |
| 2. Orestes | A prop. n., mas. gen., s. num., 3rd per., nom. c. to the v. "had spoken." |
| had | An aux. v. to "spoken," indg. pluperf. t. |
| spoken | A past pl. from the tr. v. "to speak," ref. to "truth." |
| had spoken | An irreg. tr. v., act. vo., indic. m., pluperf. t., s. num., 3rd per., agr. with its nom. "Orestes." |
| exact | An adj. of quality, qual. the n. "truth." |
| **truth.** | An abs. n., neu. gen., s. num., 3rd per., obj. c., gov. by the tr. v. "had spoken." |
| 3. Our | A pers. pron., com. gen., p. num., 1st per., poss. c., gov. by the n. "ancestors." |
| ancestors | A com. n., com. gen., p. num., 3rd per., nom. c. to the v. "bought." |
| bought | An irreg. tr. v., act vo., indic. m., past t., p. num., 3rd per., agr. with its nom. "ancestors." |
| **gold** | A com. n., neu. gen., s. num., 3rd per., obj. c., gov. by the tr. v. "bought." |
| with | A prep., sh. the rn. bet. "bought" and "victory." |
| victory. | An abs. n., neu. gen., s. num., 3rd per., obj. c., gov. by the prep. "with." |
| 4. Floating | A pres. pl. used as an adj. of quality, qual. the n. "forests." |
| forests | A com. n., neu. gen., p. num., 3rd per., nom. c. to the v. "paint." |
| paint | A reg. tr. v., act. vo., indic. m., pres. t., p. num., 3rd per., agr. with its nom. "forests." |
| **wave** | A com. n., neu. gen., s. num., 3rd per., obj. c., gov. by the tr. v. "paint." |
| with | A prep., sh. the rn. bet. "paint" and "green." |
| green. | An adj., of quality, used as a com. n., neu. gen., s. num., 3rd per., obj. c., gov. by the prep. "with." |
| 5. Having | A pres. pl. from the tr. v. "to have," ref. to we und., aux. to "engaged," indg. perf. t. (We (nom. absolute) having engaged the limner.) |
| engaged | A past pl. from the tr. v. "to engage," ref. to "limner." |
| having engaged | A perf. pl. from the tr. v. "to engage," ref. to "limner." |
| **limner** | A com. n., mas. gen., s. num., 3rd per., obj. c., gov. by the tr. pl. "having engaged." |
| our | A pers. pron., com. gen., p. num., 1st per., poss. c., gov. by the n. "deliberation." |
| next | An adj. of quality, superl. deg., qual. the n. "deliberation." |
| deliberation | An abs. n., neu. gen., s. num., 3rd per., nom. c. to the v. "was." |
| was | An irreg. intr. v., indic. m., past t., s. num., 3rd per., agr. with its nom. "deliberation." |
| to | A particle, indg. infin. m. |
| to show | A reg. tr. v., act. vo., infin. m., pres. t., used as an abs. n., neu. gen., s. num., 3rd per., nom. c. after the v. "was." |
| **superiority** | An abs. n., neu. gen., s. num., 3rd per., obj. c., gov. by the tr. v. "to show." |
| of | A prep., sh. the rn. bet. "superiority" and "tastes." |

ENGLISH GRAMMAR AND ANALYSIS. 81

| | |
|---|---|
| our | A pers. pron., com. gen., p. num., 1st per., poss. c., gov. by the n. "taste." |
| taste | An abs. n., neu. gen., s. num., 3rd per., obj. c., gov. by the prep. "of." |
| in | A prep., sh. the rn. bet. "to show" and "attitudes." |
| attitudes. | An abs. n., neu. gen., p. num., 3rd per., obj. c., gov. by the prep. "in." |
| 6. Soft | An adj. of quality, pos. deg., qual. the n. "pity." |
| pity | An abs. n., neu. gen., s. num., 3rd per., nom. c. to the v. "heals." |
| heals | A reg. tr. v., act. vo., indic. m., pres. t., s. num., 3rd per., agr. with its nom. "pity." |
| his | A pers. pron., mas. gen., s. num., 3rd. per., poss. c., gov. by the n. "woes." |
| woes. | An abs. n., neu. gen., p. num., 3rd per., obj. c., gov. by the tr. v. "heals." |
| 7. Thought | An abs. n., neu. gen., s. num., 3rd per., nom. c. to the v. "would destroy." |
| would | An aux. v. to "destroy," indg. pot. m., past t. |
| (to) destroy | A reg. tr. v., act. vo., infin. m., pres. t., gov. by the v. "would." |
| would destroy | A reg. tr. v., act. vo., pot. m., past t., s. num., 3rd per., agr. with its nom. "thought." |
| their | A pers. pron., com. gen., p. num., 3rd per., poss. c., gov. by the n. "paradise." |
| paradise. | A com. n., neu. gen., s. num., 3rd per., obj. c., gov. by the tr. v. "would destroy." |
| 8. Cast | An irreg. tr. v., act. vo., imper. m., pres. t., s. num., 2nd per., agr. with its nom. *thou* und. |
| thy | A pers. pron., com. gen., s. num., 2nd per., poss. c., gov. by the n. "bread." |
| bread | A com. n., neu. gen., s. num., 3rd per., obj. c., gov. by the tr. v. "cast." |
| upon | A prep., sh. the rn. bet. "cast" and "waters." |
| waters. | A com. n., neu. gen., p. num., 3rd per., obj. c., gov. by the prep. "upon." |
| 9. midnight | An abs. n., neu. gen., s. num., 3rd per., nom. c. to the v. "brought." |
| brought | An irreg. tr. v., act. vo., indic. m., past t., s. num., 3rd per., agr. with its nom. "midnight." |
| signal | An abs. n., used as an adj. of quality, qual. the n. "sound." |
| sound | An abs. n., neu. gen., s. num., 3rd per., obj. c., gov. by the tr. v. "brought." |
| of | A prep., sh. the rn. bet. "sound" and "strife." |
| strife. | An abs. n., neu. gen., s. num., 3rd per., obj. c., gov. by the prep. "of." |
| 10. She | A pers. pron., fem. gen., s. num., 3rd per., nom. c. to the v. "left." |
| left | An irreg. tr. v., act vo., indic. m., past t., s. num., 3rd per., agr. with its nom. "she." |
| web | A com. n., neu. gen., s. num., 3rd per., obj. c., gov. by the tr. v. "left." |
| she | A pers. pron., fem. gen., s. num., 3rd per., nom. c. to the v. "left." |
| left | An irreg. tr. v., act. vo., indic. m., past t., s. num., 3rd per., agr. with its nom. "she." |
| loom | A com. n., neu. gen., s. num., 3rd per., obj. c., gov. by the tr. v. "left." |
| She | A pers. pron., fem. gen., s. num., 3rd per., nom. c. to the v. "made." |
| made | An irreg. tr. v., act. vo., indic. m., past t., s. num., 3rd per., agr. with its nom. "she." |
| three | A def. card. nu. adj. of quantity, qual. the n. "paces." |
| paces | An abs. n., neu. gen., p. num., 3rd per., obj. c., gov. by the tr. v. "made." |
| through | A prep., sh. the rn. bet. "made" and "room." |
| room | A com. n., neu. gen., s. num., 3rd per., obj. c., gov. by the prep. "through." |
| She | A pers. pron., fem. gen., s. num., 3rd per., nom. c. to the v. "saw." |
| saw | An irreg. tr. v., act. vo., indic. m., past t., s. num., 3rd per., agr. with its nom. "she." |

6

82                KEY TO

| | |
|---|---|
| **water-lily** | A compd. com. n., neu. gen., s. num., 3rd per., obj. c., gov. by the tr. v. "saw." |
| (to) bloom | A reg. intr. v., infin. m., pres. t., gov. by the v. "saw." |
| **she** | A pers. pron., fem. gen., s. num., 3rd per., nom. c. to the v. "saw." |
| **saw** | An irreg. tr. v., act. vo., indic., m., past t., s. num., 3rd per., agr. with its nom. "she." |
| **helmet** | A com. n., neu. gen., s. num., 3rd per., obj. c., gov. by the tr. v. "saw." |
| **and** | A cop. conj., jg. the sents. "She saw the helmet" and "*she saw* the plume." |
| **plume.** | A com. n., neu. gen., s. num., 3rd per., obj. c., gov. by the tr. v. *saw* und. |

## Exercise 120.

| | |
|---|---|
| 1. I | A pers. pron., com. gen., s. num., 1st per., nom. c. to the v. "brought." |
| brought | An irreg. tr. v., act. vo., indic. m., past t., s. num., 1st per., agr. with its nom. "I." |
| **Goldsmith** | A prop. n., mas. gen., s. num., 3rd per., obj. c., gov. by the prep. *to* und. |
| **money.** | A com. n., neu. gen., s. num., 3rd per., obj. c., gov. by the tr. v. "brought.' |
| 2. Then | An adv. of time, mod. the v. "gave." |
| king | A com. n., mas. gen., s. num, 3rd per., nom. c. to the v. "gave." |
| gave | An irreg. tr. v., act. vo., indic. m., past t., s. num., 3rd per., agr. with its nom. "king." |
| **him** | A pers. pron., mas. gen., s. num., 3rd per., obj. c., gov. by the prep. *to* und. |
| **purse** | A com. n., neu. gen., s. num., 3rd per., obj. c., gov. by the tr. v. "gave." |
| of | A prep., sh. the rn. bet. "purse" and "gold." |
| gold | A com. n., neu. gen., s. num., 3rd per., obj. c., gov. by the prep. "of." |
| and | A cop. conj., jg. the sents. "Then the king gave him a purse of gold" and "*then the king* dismissed him." |
| dismissed | A reg. tr. v., act. vo., indic. m., past t., s. num., 3rd per., agr. with its nom. *king* und. |
| him. | A pers. pron., mas. gen., s. num., 3rd per., obj. c., gov. by the tr. v. "dismissed." |
| 3. Friends | A com. n., mas. gen., p. num., 2nd per., nom. c. of add. |
| Romans | A prop. n., mas. gen., p. num., 2nd per., nom. c. of add. |
| countrymen | A com. n., mas. gen., p. num., 2nd per., nom. c. of add. |
| lend | An irreg. tr. v., act. vo., imper. m., pres. t., p. num., 2nd per., agr. with its nom. *you* und. |
| **me** | A pers. pron., mas. gen., s. num., 1st per., obj. c., gov. by the prep. *to* und. (Me=Mark Antony.) |
| your | A pers. pron., mas. gen., p. num., 2nd per., poss. c., gov. by the n. "ears." |
| **ears.** | A com. n., neu. gen., p. num., 3rd per., obj. c., gov. by the tr. v. "lend." |
| 4. Sirrah | A com. n., mas. gen., s. num., 2nd per., nom. c. of add. |
| I | A pers. pron., com. gen., s. num., 1st per., nom. c. to the v. "will teach." |
| 'll=will | An aux. v. to "teach," indg. fut. t., emph. form, expressing "determination." |
| (to) teach | An irreg. tr. v., act. vo., infin. m., pres. t., gov. by the v. "will." |
| will teach | An irreg. tr. v., act. vo., indic. m., fut. t., emph. form, s. num., 1st per., agr. with its nom. "I." |
| **thee** | A pers. pron., mas. gen., s. num., 2nd per., obj. c., gov. by the prep. *to* und. |
| **speech.** | A com. n., neu. gen., s. num., 3rd per., obj. c., gov. by the tr. v. "teach." |
| 5. When | A cop. conj., jg. the sents. "give me mine again" and "*a wise man* gives thee better counsel." |
| wise | An adj. of quality, pos. deg., qual. the n. "man." |
| man | A com. n., mas. gen., s. num., 3rd per., nom. c. to the v. "gives.' |

| | |
|---|---|
| gives | An irreg. tr. v., act. vo., indic. m., pres. t., s. num., 3rd per., agr. with its nom. "man." |
| **thee** | A pers. pron., com. gen., s. num., 2nd per., obj. c., gov. by the prep. *to* und. |
| better | An adj. of quality, comp. deg., qual. the n. "counsel." |
| **counsel** | An abs. n., neu. gen., s. num., 3rd per., obj. c., gov. by the tr. v. "gives." |
| give | An irreg. tr. v., act. vo., imper. m., pres. t., s. num., 2nd per., agr. with its nom. *thou* und. |
| **me** | A pers. pron., com. gen., s. num., 1st per., obj. c., gov. by the prep. *to* und. |
| mine | A pers. pron., com. gen., s. num., 1st per., poss. c., gov. by the n. *counsel* und. |
| again. | An adv. of time, mod. the v. "give." |
| 6. I | A pers. pron., com. gen., s. num., 1st per., nom. c. to the v. "could refuse." |
| could | An aux. v. to "refuse," indg. pot. m., past t. |
| not | An adv. of m. (neg.), mod. the v. "could refuse." |
| (to) refuse | A reg. tr. v., act. vo., infin. m., pres. t., gov. by the v. "could." |
| could refuse | A reg. tr. v., act. vo., pot. m., past t., s. num., 1st per., agr. with its nom. "I." |
| **him** | A pers. pron., mas. gen., s. num., 3rd per., obj. c., gov. by the prep. *to* und. |
| my | A pers. pron., com. gen., s. num., 1st per., poss. c., gov. by the n. "company." |
| **company.** | An abs. n., neu. gen., s. num., 3rd per., obj. c., gov. by the tr. v. "could refuse." |
| 7. My | A pers. pron., com. gen., s. num., 1st per., poss. c., gov. by the n. "father." |
| father | A com. n., mas. gen., s. num., 3rd per., nom. c. to the v. "gave." |
| on | A prep., sh. the rn. bet. "gave" and "birthday." |
| birthday | An abs. n., neu. gen., s. num., 3rd per., obj. c., gov. by the prep. "on." |
| gave | An irreg. tr. v., act. vo., indic. m., past t., s. num., 3rd per., agr. with its nom. "father." |
| **it** | A pers. pron., neu. gen., s. num., 3rd per., obj. c., gov. by the tr. v. "gave." |
| **me.** | A pers. pron., com. gen., s. num., 1st per., obj. c., gov. by the prep. *to* und. |
| 8. My | A pers. pron., mas. gen., s. num., 1st per., poss. c., gov. by the n. "wife." |
| wife | A com. n., fem. gen., s. num., 3rd per., nom. c. to the v. "gave." |
| gave | An irreg. tr. v., act. vo., indic. m., past t., s. num., 3rd per., agr. with its nom. "wife." |
| **him** | A pers. pron., mas. gen., s. num., 3rd per., obj. c., gov. by the prep. *to* und. |
| great | An adj. of quality, pos. deg., qual. the n. "encomiums." |
| **encomiums.** | An abs. n., neu. gen., p. num., 3rd per., obj. c., gov. by the tr. v. "gave." |
| 9. She | A pers. pron., fem. gen., s. num., 3rd per., nom. c. to the v. "left." |
| left | An irreg. tr. v., act. vo., indic. m., past t., s. num., 3rd per., agr. with its nom. "she." |
| **him** | A pers. pron., mas. gen., s. num., 3rd per., obj. c., gov. by the prep. *to* und. |
| her | A pers. pron., fem. gen., s. num., 3rd per., poss. c., gov. by the n. "fortune." |
| **fortune.** | A com. n., neu. gen., s. num., 3rd per., obj. c., gov. by the tr. v. "left." |
| 10. My | A pers. pron., com. gen., s. num., 1st per., poss. c., gov. by the n. "soul." |
| soul | A com. n., neu. gen., s. num., 3rd per., nom. c. to the v. "shall yield." |
| shall | An aux. v. to "yield," indg. fut. t., emph. form, expressing "determination." |
| (to) yield | A reg. tr. v., act. vo., infin. m., pres. t., gov. by the v. "shall." |
| **shall yield** | A reg. tr. v., act. vo., indic. m., fut. t., emph. form, s. num., 3rd per., agr. with its nom. "soul." |

84 KEY TO

| | |
|---|---|
| thee | A pers. pron., com. gen., s. num., 2nd per., obj. c., gov. by the prep. *to* und. |
| willing | An adj. of quality, pos. deg., qual. the n. "thanks." |
| thanks | An abs. n., neu. gen., p. num., 3rd per., obj. c., gov. by the tr. v. "shall yield." |
| and | A cop. conj., jg. the sents. "My soul shall yield thee willing thanks" and "*my soul shall yield thee willing praise.*" |
| praise | An abs. n., neu. gen., s. num., 3rd per., obj. c., gov. by the tr. v. *shall yield* und. |
| For | A prep., sh. the rn. bet. "shall yield" and "blessings." |
| chief | An adj. of quality, qual. the n. "blessings." |
| blessings | An abs. n., neu. gen., p. num., 3rd per., obj. c., gov. by the prep. *for.* |
| of | A prep., sh. the rn. bet. "blessings" and "days." |
| my | A pers. pron., com. gen., s. num., 1st per., poss. c., gov. by the n. "days." |
| fairest | An adj. of quality, superl. deg., qual. the n. "days." |
| day | An abs. n., neu. gen., p. num., 3rd per., obj. c., gov. by the prep. "*of.*" |

## Exercise 121.

| | | |
|---|---|---|
| 1. | We | A pers. pron., com. gen., p. num., 1st per., nom. c. to the v. "were shown." |
| | were | An aux. v. to "shown," indg. pass. vo., past t. |
| | shown | A past pl. from the tr. v. "to show," ref. to "tomb.' |
| | were shown | An irreg. tr. v., pass. vo., indic. m., past t., p. num., 1st per., agr. with its nom. "we." |
| | Edward | A prop. n., mas. gen., s. num., 3rd per., poss. c., gov. by the n. "tomb." |
| | Confessor's | A com. n. tending to prop., mas. gen., s. num., 3rd per., poss. c., in app. with "Edward." |
| | tomb. | A com. n., neu. gen., s. num., 3rd per., obj. c., after the tr. v., pass. vo., "was shown." |
| 2. | He | A pers. pron., mas. gen., s. num., 3rd per., nom. c. to the v. "was owed." |
| | was | An aux. v. to "owed," indg. pass. vo., past t. |
| | owed | A past pl. from the tr. v. "to owe," ref. to "money." |
| | was owed | A reg. tr. v., pass. vo., indic. m., past t., s. num., 3rd per., agr. with its nom. "he." |
| | money | A com. n., neu. gen., s. num., 3rd per., obj. c., after the tr. v., pass. vo., "was owed." |
| | by | A prep., sh. the rn. bet. "was owed" and "Regent." |
| | Regent. | A com. n. tending to prop., mas. gen., s. num., 3rd per., obj. c., gov. by the prep. "by." |
| 3. | We | A pers. pron., com. gen., p. num., 1st per., nom. c. to the v. "were shown." |
| | were | An aux. v. to "shown," indg. pass. vo., past t. |
| | shown | A past pl. from the tr. v. "to show," ref. to "room." |
| | were shown | An irreg. tr. v., pass. vo., indic. m., past t., p. num., 1st per., agr. with its nom. "we." |
| | room. | A com. n., neu. gen., s. num., 3rd per., obj. c., after the tr. v., pass. vo., "were shown." |
| 4. | prisoner | A com. n., com. gen., s. num., 3rd per., nom. c. to the v. "was allowed." |
| | was | An aux. v. to "allowed," indg. pass. vo., past t. |
| | allowed | A past pl. from the tr. v. "to allow," ref. to "advocate." |
| | was allowed | A reg. tr. v., pass. vo., indic. m., past t., s. num., 3rd per., agr. with its nom. "prisoner." |
| | advocate. | A com. n., mas. gen., s. num., 3rd per., obj. c., after the tr. v., pass. vo., "was allowed." |
| 5. | Am | An aux. v. to "denied," indg. pass. vo., pres. t. |
| | I | A pers. pron., com. gen., s. num., 1st per., nom. c. to the v. "am denied." |
| | denied | A past pl. from the tr. v. "to deny," ref. to "favour." |
| | am denied | A reg. tr. v., pass. vo., indic. m., pres. t., s. num., 1st per., agr. with its nom. "I." |

# ENGLISH GRAMMAR AND ANALYSIS. 85

| | |
|---|---|
| this | A dis. adj., lim. the n. "favour." |
| **favour.** | An abs. n., neu. gen., s. num., 3rd per., obj. c., after the tr. v., pass. vo., "am denied." |
| 6. eldest | An adj. of quality, superl. deg., qual. the n. "son." |
| son | A com. n., mas. gen., s. num., 3rd per., nom. c. to the v. "was promised." |
| was | An aux. v. to "promised," indg. pass. vo., past t. |
| promised | A past pl. from the tr. v. "to promise," ref. to "watch." |
| was promised | A reg. tr. v., pass. vo., indic. m., past t., s. num., 3rd per., agr. with its nom. "son." |
| **watch** | A com. n., neu. gen., s. num., 3rd per., obj. c., after the tr. v., pass. vo., "was promised. |
| on | A prep., sh. the rn. bet. "was promised" and "birthday." |
| his | A pers. pron., mas. gen., s. num., 3rd per., poss. c., gov. by the n. "birthday." |
| sixteenth | A def. ord. nu. adj. of quantity, qual. the n. "birthday." |
| birthday. | An abs. n., neu. gen., s. num., 3rd per., obj. c., gov. by the prep. "on." |
| 7. I | A pers. pron., com. gen., s. num., 1st per., nom. c. to the v. "have been told." |
| have | An aux. v. to "been told," indg. perf. t. |
| been | A past pl. from the intr. v. "to be," ref. to "told tale," and aux. to "told," indg. pass. vo. |
| told | A past pl. from the tr. v. "to tell," ref. to "tale." |
| have been told | An irreg. tr. v., pass. vo., indic. m., perf. t., s. num., 1st per., agr. with its nom. "I." |
| this | A dis. adj., lim. the n. "tale." |
| wondrous | An adj. of quality, pos. deg., qual. the n. "tale." |
| **tale.** | A com. n., neu. gen., s. num., 3rd per., obj. c., after the tr. v., pass. vo., "have been told." |
| 8. wily | An adj. of quality, pos. deg., qual. the n. "courtier." |
| courtier | A com. n., mas. gen., s. num., 3rd per., nom. c. to the v. "was offered." |
| was | An aux. v. to "offered," indg. pass. vo., past t. |
| offered | A past pl. from the tr. v. "to offer," ref. to "post." |
| was offered | A reg. tr. v., pass. vo., indic. m., past t., s. num., 3rd per., agr. with its nom. "courtier." |
| **post** | An abs. n., neu. gen., s. num., 3rd per., obj. c., after the tr. v., pass. vo., "was offered." |
| of | A prep., sh. the rn. bet. "post" and "honour." |
| honour. | An abs. n., neu. gen., s. num., 3rd per., obj. c., gov. by the prep. "of." |
| 9. teacher | A com. n., com. gen., s. num., 3rd per., nom. c. to the v. "was asked." |
| was | An aux. v. to "asked," indg. pass. vo., past t. |
| asked | A past pl. from the tr. v. "to ask," ref. to "question." |
| was asked | A reg. tr. v., pass. vo., indic. m., past t., s. num., 3rd per., agr. with its nom. "teacher." |
| **question.** | An abs. n., neu. gen., s. num., 3rd per., obj. c., after the tr. v., pass. vo., "was asked." |
| 10. Nothing | A com. n., neu. gen., s. num., 3rd per., nom. c. to the v. "was denied." |
| was | An aux. v. to "denied," indg. pass. vo., past t. |
| ever | An adv. of time, mod. the v. "was denied." |
| denied | A past pl. from the tr. v. "to deny," ref. to "nothing." |
| was denied | A reg. tr. v., pass. vo., indic. m., past t., s. num., 3rd per., agr. with its nom. "nothing." |
| me | A pers. pron., com. gen., s. num., 1st per., obj. c., gov. by the prep. *to* und. |
| by | A prep., sh. the rn. bet. "was denied" and "master." |
| my | A pers. pron., com. gen., s. num., 1st per., poss. c., gov. by the n. "master." |
| worthy | An adj. of quality, pos. deg., qual. the n. "master." |
| master. | A com. n., mas. gen., s. num., 3rd per., obj. c., gov. by the prep. "by." |

## Exercise 122.

N.B.—For another method of parsing the factitive object, see *Man. of Parsing*, pp. 67, 112.

1. We — A pers. pron., com. gen., p. num., 1st per., nom. c. to the v. "called."
called — A reg. tr. v., act. vo., indic. m., past t., p. num., 1st per., agr. with its nom. "we."
him — A pers. pron., mas. gen., s. num., 3rd per., obj. c., gov. by the tr. v. "called."
poet. — A com. n., mas. gen., s. num., 3rd per., obj. c., in app. with "him." ("Poet" is the factitive object.)

2. She — A pers. pron., fem. gen., s. num., 3rd per., nom. c. to the v. "refused."
refused — A reg. tr. v., act. vo., indic. m., past t., s. num., 3rd per., agr. with its nom. "she."
positively — An adv. of man., mod. the v. "refused."
to — A particle, indg. infin. m.
to name — A reg. tr. v., act. vo., infin. m., pres. t.; used as an abs. n., neu. gen., s. num., 3rd per., obj. c., gov. by the tr. v. "refused."
Mary — A prop. n., fem. gen., s. num., 3rd per., obj. c., gov. by the tr. v. "to name."
Stuart — A prop. n., fem. gen., s. num., 3rd per., obj. c., in app. with "Mary."
Mary Stuart — A compd. prop. n., fem. gen., s. num., 3rd per., obj. c., gov. by the tr. v. "to name."
her — A pers. pron., fem. gen., s. num., 3rd per., poss. c., gov. by the n. "successor."
successor. — A com. n., fem. gen., s. num., 3rd per., poss. c., in app. with "Mary Stuart." ("Successor" is the factitive object.)

3. We — A pers. pron., com. gen., p. num., 1st per., nom. c. to the v. "must declare."
must — An aux. v. to "declare," indg. pot. m., pres. t.
(to) declare — A reg. tr. v., act. vo., infin. m., pres. t., gov. by the v. "must."
must declare — A reg. tr. v., act. vo., pot. m., pres. t., p. num., 1st per., agr. with its nom. "we."
ourselves — A compd. pers. pron., com. gen., p. num., 1st per., obj. c., gov. by the tr. v. "must declare."
his — A pers. pron., mas. gen., s. num., 3rd per., poss. c., gov. by the n. "rivals."
rivals. — A com. n., com. gen., p. num., 3rd per., obj. c., in app. with "ourselves." ("Rivals" is the factitive object.)

4. Who — An interrog. pron., mas. gen., s. num., 3rd per., nom. c. to the v. "calls."
calls — A reg. tr. v., act. vo., indic. m., pres. t., s. num., 3rd per., agr. with its nom. "who."
himself — A compd. pers. pron., mas. gen., s. num., 3rd per., obj. c., gov. by the tr. v. "calls."
friend. — A com. n., mas. gen., s. num., 3rd per., obj. c., in app. with "himself." ("Friend" is the factitive object.)

5. He — A pers. pron., mas. gen., s. num., 3rd per., nom. c. to the v. "considered."
considered — A reg. tr. v., act. vo., indic. m., past t., s. num., 3rd per., agr. with its nom. "he."
transaction — An abs. n., neu. gen., s. num., 3rd per., obj. c., gov. by the tr. v. "considered."
legal — An adj. of quality, qual. the n. "sale."
sale. — An abs. n., neu. gen., s. num., 3rd per., obj. c., in app. with "transaction." ("Sale" is the factitive object.)

6. I — A pers. pron., com. gen., s. num., 1st per., nom. c. to the v. "found."
found — An irreg. tr. v., act. vo., indic. m., past t., s. num., 1st per., agr. with its nom. "I."
you — A pers. pron., fem. gen., s. num., 2nd per., obj. c., gov. by the tr. v. "found."
queen — A com. n., fem. gen., s. num., 3rd per., obj. c., in app. with "you." ("Queen" is the factitive object.)
in — A prep., sh. the rn. bet. "found" and "court."

| | |
|---|---|
| your | A pers. pron., fem. gen., s. num., 2nd per., poss. c., gov. by the n. "court." |
| court. | A com. n., neu. gen., s. num., 3rd per., obj. c., gov. by the prep. "in." |
| 7. I | A pers. pron., com. gen., s. num., 1st per., nom. c. to the v. "will prove." |
| 'll=will | An aux. v. to "prove," indg. fut. t., emph. form, expressing "determination." |
| (to) prove | A reg. tr. v., act. vo., infin. m., pres. t., gov. by the v. "will." |
| will prove | A reg. tr. v., act. vo., indic. m., fut. t., emph. form, s. num., 1st per., agr. with its nom. "I." |
| **thee** | A pers. pron., mas. gen., s. num., 2nd per., obj. c., gov. by the tr. v. "will prove." |
| **traitor.** | A com. n., mas. gen., s. num., 3rd per., obj. c., in app. with "thee." ("Traitor" is the factitive object.) |
| 8. I | A pers. pron., com. gen., s. num., 1st per., nom. c. to the v. "hear." |
| hear | An irreg. tr. v., act. vo., indic. m., pres. t., s. num., 1st per., agr. with its nom. "I." |
| thee | A pers. pron., fem. gen., s. num., 2nd per., obj. c., gov. by the tr. v. "hear." (Thee, *i.e.*, mother.) |
| (to) speak | An irreg. intr. v., infin. m., pres. t., gov. by the v. "hear." |
| of | A prep., sh. the rn. bet. "speak" and "land." |
| better | An adj. of quality, comp. deg., qual. the n. "land." |
| land | A com. n., neu. gen., s. num., 3rd per., obj. c., gov. by the prep. "of." |
| Thou | A pers. pron., fem. gen., s. num., 2nd per., nom. c. to the v. "call'st." |
| call'st | A reg. tr. v., act. vo., indic. m., pres. t., s. num., 2nd per., agr. with its nom. "thou." |
| its | A pers. pron., neu. gen., s. num., 3rd per., poss. c., gov. by the n. "children." |
| **children** | A com. n., com. gen., p. num., 3rd per., obj. c., gov. by the tr. v. "call'st." |
| happy | An adj. of quality, pos. deg., qual. the n. "band." |
| **band.** | A com. col. n., neu. gen., s. num., 3rd per., obj. c., in app. with "children." ("Band" is the factitive object.) |
| 9. Ye | A pers. pron., mas. gen. by personification, p. num., 2nd per., nom. c. of add. |
| winds | A com. n., mas. gen. by personification, p. num., 2nd per., nom. c. in app. with "ye." |
| that | A rel. pron., mas. gen., p. num., 2nd per., agr. with its ant. "winds," nom. c. to the v. "have made." |
| have | An aux. v. to "made," indg. perf. t. |
| made | A past pl. from the tr. v. "to make," ref. to "me." |
| have made | An irreg. tr. v., act. vo., indic. m., perf. t., p. num., 2nd per., agr. with its nom. "that." |
| **me** | A pers. pron., mas. gen., s. num., 1st per., obj. c., gov. by the tr. v. "have made." (Me, *i.e.*, Alexander Selkirk.) |
| your | A pers. pron., mas. gen., p. num., 2nd per., poss. c., gov. by the n. "sport." |
| **sport** | A com. n., neu. gen., s. num., 3rd per., obj. c., in app. with "me." ("Sport" is the factitive object.) |
| Convey | A reg. tr. v., act. vo., imper. m., pres. t., p. num., 2nd per., agr. with its nom. *you* und. |
| to | A prep., sh. the rn. bet. "convey" and "shore." |
| **this** | A dis. adj., lim. the n. "shore." |
| desolate | An adj. of quality, pos. deg., qual. the n. "shore." |
| shore | A com. n., neu. gen., s. num., 3rd per., obj c., gov. by the prep. "to." |
| Some | An indef. nu. adj. of quantity, qual. the n. "report." |
| cordial | An adj. of quality, pos. deg., qual. the n. "report." |
| endearing | An adj. of quality, pos. deg., qual. the n. "report." |
| report | An abs. n., neu. gen., s. num., 3rd per., obj. c., gov. by the tr. v. "convey." |
| Of | A prep., sh. the rn. bet. "report" and "land." |
| land | A com. n., neu gen., s. num., 3rd per., obj. c., gov. by the prep. "of." |
| I | A pers. pron., mas. gen., s. num., 1st per., nom. c. to the v. "shall visit." |

| | |
|---|---|
| shall | An aux. v. to "visit," indg. fut. t. |
| (to) visit | A reg. tr. v., act. vo., infin. m., pros. t., gov. by the v. "shall." (*Which* I shall visit no more.) |
| shall visit | A reg. tr. v., act. vo., indic. m., fut. t., s. num., 1st per., agr. with its nom. "I." |
| no | An adv. of m. (neg.), mod. the adv. "more." |
| more. | An adv. of time, mod. the v. "shall visit." |
| 10. I | A pers. pron., com. gen., s. num., 1st per., nom. c. to the v. "crown." |
| crown | A reg. tr. v., act. vo., indic. m., pres. t., s. num., 1st per., agr. with its nom. "I." |
| thee | A pers. pron., mas. gen., s. num., 2nd per., obj. c., gov. by the tr. v. "crown." |
| king | A com. n., mas. gen., s. num., 3rd per., obj. c., in app. with "thee." ("King" is the factitive object.) |
| of | A prep., sh. the rn. bet. "king" and "delights." |
| intimate | An adj. of quality, pos. deg., qual. the n. "delights." |
| delights | An abs. n., neu. gen., p. num., 3rd per., obj. c., gov. by the prep. "of." |
| Fireside | A com. n. used as an adj. of quality, qual. the n. "enjoyments." |
| enjoyments | An abs. n., neu. gen., p. num., 3rd per., obj. c., gov. by the prep. *of* und. |
| home-born | A compd. adj. of quality, qual. the n. "happiness." |
| happiness | An abs. n., neu. gen., s. num., 3rd per., obj. c., gov. by the prep. *of* und. |
| And | A cop. conj., jg. the sents. "*I crown thee king of* home-born happiness" and "*I crown thee king of* all the comforts." |
| all | An indef. nu. adj. of quantity, qual. the n. "comforts." |
| comforts | An abs. n., neu. gen., p. num., 3rd per., obj. c., gov. by the prep. *of* und. |
| that | A rel. pron., neu. gen., p. num., 3rd per., agr. with its ant. "comforts," obj. c., gov. by the tr. v. *knows* und. |
| lowly | An adj. of quality, pos. deg., qual. the n. "roof." |
| roof | A com. n., neu. gen., s. num., 3rd per., nom. c. to the v. *knows* und. |
| Of | A prep., sh. the rn. bet. "roof" and "retirement." |
| undisturbed | An adj. of quality, qual. the n. "retirement." |
| retirement | An abs. n., neu. gen., s. num., 3rd per., obj. c., gov. by the prep. *of.* |
| and | A cop. conj., jg. the sents. "that the lowly roof of undisturbed retirement *knows*" and "*that* the hours of long, uninterrupted evening know." |
| hours | An abs. n., neu. gen., p. num., 3rd per., nom. c. to the v. "know." |
| of | A prep., sh. the rn. bet. "hours" and "evening." |
| long | An adj. of quality, pos. deg., qual. the n. "evening." |
| uninterrupted | An adj. of quality, qual. the n. "evening." |
| evening | An abs. n., neu. gen., s. num., 3rd per., obj. c., gov. by the prep. "*of.*" |
| know. | An irreg. tr. v., act. vo., indic. m., pres. t., p. num., 3rd per., agr. with its nom. "hours." |

### Exercise 123.

| | |
|---|---|
| 1. He | A pers. pron., mas. gen., s. num., 3rd per., nom. c. to the v. "sang." |
| sang | An irreg. intr. v., indic. m., past t., s. num., 3rd per., agr. with its nom. "he." |
| his | A pers. pron., mas. gen., s. num., 3rd per., poss. c., gov. by the n. "song." |
| song | An abs. n., neu. gen., s. num., 3rd per., obj. c. of cognate signification after the intr. v. "sang." |
| and | A cop. conj., jg. the sents. "He sang his song" and "I replied with mine." |
| I | A pers. pron., com. gen., s. num., 1st per., nom. c. to the v. "replied." |
| replied | A reg. intr. v., indic. m., past t., s. num., 1st per., agr. with its nom. "I." |

| | |
|---|---|
| with | A prep., sh. the rn. bet. "replied" and *song* und. |
| mine. | A pers. pron., com. gen., s num., 1st per., poss. c., gov. by the n. *song* und. |
| 2. scornful | An adj. of quality, pos. deg., qual. the n. "laugh." |
| **laugh** | An abs. n., neu. gen., s. num., 3rd per., obj. c. of cognate signification after the intr. v. "laughed." |
| laughed | A reg. intr. v., indic. m., past t., s. num., 3rd per., agr. with its nom. "he." |
| he. | A pers. pron., mas. gen., s. num., 3rd per., nom. c. to the v. "laughed." |
| 3. We | A pers. pron., com. gen., p. num., 1st per., nom. c. to the v. "lived." |
| lived | A reg. intr. v., indic. m., past t., p. num., 1st per., agr. with its nom. "we." |
| **life** | An abs. n., neu. gen., s. num., 3rd per., obj. c. of cognate signification after the intr. v. "lived." |
| as | An adv. of deg., mod. the adj. "careless." |
| careless | An adj. of quality, pos. deg., qual. the n. "life." |
| as | A cop. conj., jg. the sents. "We lived a life as careless" and "*the life is careless.*" N.B. The construction is: We lived a life as careless as *the life is careless which* birds live. |
| birds. | A com. n., com. gen., p. num., 3rd per., nom c. to the v. *live* und. |
| 4. He | A pers. pron., mas. gen., s. num., 3rd per., nom. c. to the v. "laughed." |
| laughed | A reg. intr. v., indic. m., past t., s. num., 3rd per., agr. with its nom. "he." |
| **laugh** | An abs. n., neu. gen., s. num., 3rd per., obj. c. of cognate signification after the intr. v. "laughed." |
| of | A prep., sh. the rn. bet. "laugh" and "scorn." |
| merry | An adj. of quality, pos. deg., qual. the n. "scorn." |
| scorn. | An abs. n., neu. gen., s. num., 3rd per., obj. c., gov. by the prep. "of." |
| 5. Sing | An irreg. intr. v., imper. m., pres. t., s. num., 2nd per., agr. with its nom. *thou* und. |
| new | An adj. of quality, pos. deg., qual. the n. "song." |
| **song.** | An abs. n., neu. gen., s. num., 3rd per., obj. c. of cognate signification after the intr. v. "sing." |
| 6. Live | A reg. intr. v., imper. m., pres. t., s. num., 2nd per., agr. with its nom. *thou* und. |
| not | An adv. of m. (neg.), mod. the v. "live." |
| **life** | An abs. n., neu. gen., s. num., 3rd per., obj. c. of cognate signification after the intr. v. "live." |
| of | A prep., sh. the rn. bet. "life" and "sloth." |
| sloth. | An abs. n., neu. gen., s. num., 3rd per., obj. c., gov. by the prep. "of." |
| 7. We | A pers. pron., com. gen., p. num., 1st per., nom. c. to the v. "danced." |
| danced | A reg. intr. v., indic. m., past t., p. num., 1st per., agr. with its nom. "we." |
| country | A com. n. used as an adj. of quality, qual. the n. "dance." |
| **dance.** | An abs. n., neu. gen., s. num., 3rd per., obj. c. of cognate signification after the intr. v. "danced." |
| 8. We | A pers. pron., com. gen., p. num., 1st per., nom. c. to the v. "have dreamed." |
| have | An aux. v to "dreamed," indg. perf. t. |
| dreamed | A past pl. from the intr. v. to "dream," ref. to "dream." |
| have dreamed | A reg. intr. v., indic. m., perf. t., p. num., 1st per., agr. with its nom. "we." |
| **dream** | An abs n., neu. gen., s. num., 3rd per., obj. c. of cognate signification after the intr. v. "have dreamed." |
| and | A cop. conj., jg. the sents. "We have dreamed a dream" and "there is no interpreter." |
| there | An expletive adv., mod. the v. "is." |
| is | An irreg intr. v., indic. m., pres. t., s. num., 3rd per., agr. with its nom. "interpreter." |
| no | A def. card. nu. adj of quantity, qual. the n. "interpreter." |
| interpreter. | A com. n., com. gen., s. num., 3rd per., nom. c. to the v. "is" |

90  KEY TO

9. I — A pers. pron., com. gen., s. num., 1st per., nom. c. to the v. "have fought."
have — An aux. v. to "fought," indg. perf. t.
fought — A past pl. from the intr. v. "to fight," ref. to "fight."
have fought — An irreg. intr. v., indic. m., perf. t., s. num., 1st per., agr. with its nom. "I."
good — An adj. of quality, pos. deg., qual. the n. "fight."
**fight.** — An abs. n., neu. gen., s. num., 3rd per., obj. c. of cognate signification after the intr. v. "have fought."
10. She — A pers. pron., fem. gen., s. num., 3rd per., nom. c. to the v. "sleeps."
sleeps — An irreg. intr. v., indic. m., pres. t., s. num., 3rd per., agr. with its nom. "she."
**sleep** — An abs. n., neu. gen., s. num., 3rd per., obj. c. of cognate signification after the intr. v. "sleeps."
of — A prep., sh. the rn. bet. "sleep" and "innocence."
innocence. — An abs. n., neu. gen., s. num., 3rd per., obj. c., gov. by the prep. "of."

## Exercise 124.

1 He — A pers. pron., mas. gen., s. num., 3rd per., nom. c. to the v. "taught."
taught — An irreg. tr. v., act. vo., used intransitively, indic. m., past t., s num., 3rd per., agr. with its nom. "he."
there — An adv. of place, mod. the v. "taught."
forty — A def. card. nu. adj. of quantity, qual. the n. "years."
**years.** — An abs. n., neu. gen., p. num., 3rd per., obj. c., gov. by the prep. *during* und., (or, obj. c. of duration of time after the v. "taught").
2. And — A cop. conj., introducing the sent. "the next day...our party."
next — An adj. of quality, superl. deg., qual. the n. "day."
**day** — An abs. n., neu. gen., s. num., 3rd per., obj. c., gov. by the prep. *during* und., (or, obj. c. of duration of time after the v. "was kept").
both — A cop. conj., introducing the sent. "*he was kept during the* morning."
**morning** — An abs. n., neu. gen., s. num., 3rd per., obj. c., gov. by the prep. *during* und., (or, obj. c. of duration of time after *was kept* und.)
and — A cop. conj., jg. the sents. "*he was kept during the* morning" and "*he was kept during the* afternoon."
**afternoon** — An abs. n., neu. gen., s. num., 3rd per., obj. c., gov. by the prep. *during* und., (or, obj. c. of duration of time after the v. "was kept").
he — A pers. pron., mas. gen., s. num., 3rd per., nom. c. to the v. "was kept."
was — An aux. v. to "kept," indg. pass. vo., past t.
kept — A past pl. from the tr. v. "to keep," ref. to "he."
was kept — An irreg. tr. v., pass. vo., indic. m., past t., s. num., 3rd per., agr. with its nom. "he."
by — A prep., sh. the rn. bet. "was kept" and "party."
our — A pers. pron., com. gen., p. num., 1st per., poss. c., gov. by the n. "party."
party. — A com. col. n., neu. gen., s. num., 3rd per., obj. c., gov. by the prep. "by."
3. Hooper — A prop. n., mas. gen., s. num., 3rd per., nom. c. to the v. "burned."
burned — A reg. tr. v., act. vo., used intransitively, indic. m., past t., s. num., 3rd per., agr. with its nom. "Hooper."
three — A def. card. nu. adj. of quantity, qual. the n. "quarters."
**quarters** — An abs. n., neu. gen., p. num., 3rd per., obj. c., gov. by the prep. *during* und., (or, obj. c. of duration of time after the v. "burned").
of — A prep., sh. the rn. bet. "quarters" and "hour."
hour. — An abs. n., neu. gen., s. num., 3rd per., obj. c., gov. by the prep. "of."
4. man — A com. n., mas. gen., s. num., 3rd per., nom. c. to the v. "requires."

| | |
|---|---|
| usually | An adv. of man., mod. the v. "requires." |
| requires | A reg. tr. v., act. vo., indic. m., pres. t., s. num., 3rd per., agr. with its nom. "man." |
| to | A particle, indg. infin. m. |
| to sleep | An irreg. intr. v., infin. m., pres. t.; used as an abs. n., neu. gen., s. num., 3rd per., obj. c., gov. by the tr. v. "requires." |
| eight | A def. card. nu. adj. of quantity, qual. the n. "hours." |
| **hours** | An abs. n., neu. gen., p. num., 3rd per., obj. c., gov. by the prep. *during* und., (or, obj. c. of duration of time after the v. "to sleep"). |
| out of | A compd. prep., sh. the rn. bet. "hours" and *hours* und. (*Parsing*, p. 154.) |
| twenty-four. | A def. card. nu. adj. of quantity, qual. the n. *hours* und. |
| 5. nugget | A com. n., neu. gen., s. num., 3rd per., nom. c. to the v. "weighed." |
| weighed | A reg. tr. v., act. vo., used intransitively, indic. m., past t., s. num., 3rd per., agr. with its nom. "nugget." |
| sixty | A def. card. nu. adj. of quantity, qual. the n. "ounces." |
| **ounces.** | A com. n., neu. gen., p. num., 3rd per., obj. c., gov. by the prep. *to* und., (or, obj. c. of weight after the v. "weighed"). |
| 6. I | A pers. pron., com. gen., s. num., 1st per., nom. c. to the v. "went." |
| went | An irreg. intr. v., indic. m., past t., s. num., 1st per., agr. with its nom. "I." |
| three | A def. card. nu. adj. of quantity, qual. the n. "times." |
| **times** | An abs. n., neu. gen., p. num., 3rd per., obj. c., gov. by the prep. *at* und., (or, obj. c. of number after the v. "went"). |
| and | A cop. conj., jg. the sents. "I went three times" and "*I* saw him not." |
| saw | An irreg. tr. v., act. vo., indic. m., past t., s. num., 1st per., agr. with its nom. *I* und. |
| him | A pers. pron., mas. gen., s. num., 3rd per., obj. c., gov. by the tr. v. "saw." |
| not. | An adv. of m. (neg.), mod. the v. "saw." |
| 7. mighty | An adj. of quality, pos. deg., qual. the n. "rampart." |
| rampart | A com. n., neu. gen., s. num., 3rd per., nom. c. to the v. "rose." |
| rose | An irreg. intr. v., indic. m., past t., s. num., 3rd per., agr. with its nom. "rampart." |
| six | A def. card. nu. adj. of quantity, qual. the n. "thousand." |
| thousand | A com. n., neu. gen., p. num., 3rd per., obj. c., gov. by the prep. *to* und. |
| feet | A com. n., neu. gen., p. num., 3rd per., obj. c., gov. by the prep. *of* und. |
| Or, six thousand | A def. card. nu. adj. of quantity, qual. the n. "feet." |
| **feet** | A com. n., neu. gen., p. num., 3rd per., obj. c., gov. by the prep. *to* und., (or, obj. c. of space after the v. "rose"). |
| above | A prep., sh. the rn. bet. "rose" and "head." |
| our | A pers. pron., com. gen., p. num., 1st per., poss. c., gov. by the n. "head." |
| head. | A com. n., neu. gen., s. num., 3rd per., obj. c., gov. by the prep. "above." |
| 8. I | A pers. pron., com. gen., s. num., 1st per., nom. c. to the v. "hunted." |
| hunted | A reg. tr. v., act. vo., used intransitively, indic. m., past t., s. num., 1st per., agr. with its nom. "I." |
| some | An indef. nu. adj. of quantity, qual. the n. "years." |
| **years** | An abs. n., neu. gen., p. num., 3rd per., obj. c., gov. by the prep. *during* und., (or, obj. c. of duration of time after the v. "hunted"). |
| with | A prep., sh. the rn. bet. "hunted" and "fox-hounds." |
| Lord | A com. n. tending to prop., mas. gen., s. num., 3rd per., poss. c., gov. by the n. "fox-hounds," (or, used as an adj. of quality, qual. "Darlington's"). |
| Darlington's | A prop. n., mas. gen., s. num., 3rd per., poss. c., in app. with "Lord," (or, gov. by the n. "fox-hounds"). |
| fox-hounds. | A compd. com. n., com. gen., p. num., 3rd per., obj. c., gov. by the prep. "with." |

92                 KEY TO

## Exercise 125.

| | |
|---|---|
| 1. wakeful | An adj. of quality, pos. deg., qual. the n. "trump." |
| trump | A com. n., neu. gen., s. num., 3rd per., nom. c. to the v. "must thunder." |
| **of** | A prep., sh. the rn. bet. "trump" and "doom." |
| **doom** | An abs. n., neu. gen., s. num., 3rd per., obj. c., gov. by the prep. "of." |
| must | An aux. v. to "thunder," indg. pot. m., pres. t. |
| (to) thunder | A reg. intr. v., infin. m., pres. t., gov. by the v. "must." |
| must thunder | A reg. intr. v., pot. m., pres. t., s. num., 3rd per., agr. with its nom. "trump." |
| through | A prep., sh. the rn. bet. "must thunder" and "deep." |
| **deep.** | A com. n., neu. gen., s. num., 3rd per., obj. c., gov. by the prep. "through." |
| 2. I | A pers. pron., com. gen., s. num., 1st per., nom. c. to the v. "spy." |
| spy | A reg. tr. v., act. vo., indic. m., pres. t., s. num., 1st per., agr. with its nom. "I." |
| rock | A com. n., neu. gen., s. num., 3rd per., obj. c., gov. by the tr. v. "spy." |
| beneath | A prep., sh. the rn. bet. "rock" and "sea." |
| smiling | A pres. pl. used as an adj. of quality, qual. the n. "sea." |
| **sea.** | A com. n., neu. gen., s. num., 3rd per., obj. c., gov. by the prep. "beneath." |
| 3. stranger | A com. n., mas. gen., s. num., 3rd per., nom. c. to the v. "is struck." |
| accustomed | A past pl. from the tr. v. "to accustom," ref. to "stranger." |
| to | A prep., sh. the rn. bet. "accustomed" and "crowds." |
| **crowds** | A com. col. n., neu. gen., p. num., 3rd per., obj. c., gov. by the prep. "to." |
| and | A cop. conj., jg. the sents. "A stranger, accustomed to the crowds *of London or Paris*, is struck..." and "*a stranger, accustomed to* the bustle of London or Paris, *is struck*..." |
| **bustle** | An abs. n., neu. gen., s. num., 3rd per., obj. c., gov. by the prep. *to* und. |
| of | A prep., sh. the rn. bet. "bustle" and "London." |
| **London** | A prop. n., neu. gen., s. num. 3rd per., obj. c., gov. by the prep. "of." |
| or | A disj. conj., jg. the sents. "A stranger, accustomed to the crowds and bustle of London, is struck..." and "*a stranger, accustomed to the crowds and bustle of Paris, is struck*..." |
| **Paris** | A prop. n., neu. gen., s. num., 3rd per., obj. c., gov. by the prep. *of* und. |
| is | An aux. v. to "struck," indg. pass. vo., pres. t. |
| struck | A past pl. from the tr. v. "to strike," ref. to "stranger." |
| is struck | An irreg. tr. v., pass. vo., indic. m., pres. t., s. num., 3rd per., agr. with its nom. "stranger." |
| on | A prep., sh. the rn. bet. "is struck" and "arrival." |
| his | A pers. pron., mas. gen, s. num., 3rd per., poss. c., gov. by the n. "arrival." |
| **arrival** | An abs. n., neu. gen., s. num., 3rd per., obj. c., gov. by the prep. "on." |
| at | A prep., sh. the rn. bet. "arrival" and "St. Petersburg." |
| St. | A com. n. tending to prop., used as an adj. of quality, qual. the n. "Peter's" in "Petersburg" (*i.e.*, Peter's burg). |
| **St. Petersburg** | A compd. prop. n., neu. gen., s. num., 3rd per., obj. c., gov. by the prep. "at." |
| by | A prep., sh. the rn. bet. "is struck" and "emptiness." |
| **emptiness** | An abs. n., neu. gen., s. num., 3rd per., obj. c., gov. by the prep. "by." |
| of | A prep., sh. the rn. bet. "emptiness" and "streets." |
| **streets.** | A com. n., neu. gen., p. num., 3rd per., obj. c., gov. by the prep. "of." |
| 4. Our | A pers. pron., com. gen., p. num., 1st per., poss. c., gov. by the n. "hopes." |
| hopes | An abs. n., neu. gen., p. num., 3rd per., nom. c. to the v. "fall." |
| like | An adj. of quality, qual. the n. "hopes." |

ENGLISH GRAMMAR AND ANALYSIS. 93

| | |
|---|---|
| withered | A past pl. from the intr. v. "to wither," used as an adj. of quality, qual. the n. "leaves." |
| **leaves** | A com. n., neu. gen., p. num., 3rd per., obj. c., gov. by the prep. *to* und. |
| fall | An irreg. intr. v., indic. m., pres. t., p. num., 3rd per., agr. with its nom. "hopes." |
| fast. | An adv. of man., mod. the v. "fall." |
| 5. My | A pers. pron., com. gen., s. num., 1st per., poss. c., gov. by the n. "friend." |
| friend | A com. n., com. gen., s. num., 3rd per., nom. c. to the v. "caught." |
| caught | An irreg. tr. v., act. vo., indic. m., past t., s. num., 3rd per., agr. with its nom. "friend." |
| me | A pers. pron., com. gen., s. num., 1st per., obj. c., gov. by the tr. v. "caught." |
| **by** | A prep., sh. the rn. bet. "caught" and "elbow." |
| **elbow** | A com. n., neu. gen., s. num., 3rd per., obj. c., gov. by the prep. "by." |
| and | A cop. conj., jg. the sents. "My friend caught me by the elbow" and "*my friend* led me out of the public walk." |
| led | An irreg. tr. v., act. vo., indic. m., past t., s. num., 3rd per., agr. with its nom. *friend* und. |
| me | A pers. pron., com. gen., s. num., 1st per., obj. c., gov. by the tr. v. "led." |
| out of | A compd. prep., sh. the rn. bet. "led" and "walk." (*Parsing*, p. 154.) |
| public | An adj. of quality, qual. the n. "walk." |
| **walk.** | A com. n., neu. gen., s. num., 3rd per., obj. c., gov. by the compd. prep. "out of." |
| 6. Cataracts | A com. n., neu. gen., p. num., 3rd per., nom. c. to the v. "flooded." |
| of | A prep., sh. the rn. bet. "cataracts" and "water." |
| **water** | A com. n., neu. gen., s. num., 3rd per., obj. c., gov. by the prep. "of." |
| flooded | A reg. tr. v., act. vo., indic. m., past t., p. num., 3rd per., agr. with its nom. "cataracts." |
| houses | A com. n., neu. gen., p. num., 3rd per., obj. c., gov. by the tr. v. "flooded." |
| in | A prep., sh. the rn. bet. "houses" and "city." |
| **city** | A com. n., neu. gen., s. num., 3rd per., obj. c., gov. by the prep. "in." |
| and | A cop. conj., jg. the sents. "Cataracts of water...city" and "*cataracts of water* turned...rivers." |
| turned | A reg. tr. v., act. vo., indic. m., past t., p. num., 3rd per., agr. with its nom. *cataracts* und. |
| streets | A com. n., neu. gen., p. num., 3rd per., obj. c., gov. by the tr. v. "turned." |
| into | A prep., sh. the rn. bet. "streets" and "rivers." |
| **rivers** | A com. n., neu. gen., p. num., 3rd per., obj. c., gov. by the prep. "into." |
| trees | A com. n., neu. gen., p. num., 3rd per., nom. c. to the v. "were torn." |
| were | An aux. v. to "torn," indg. pass. vo., past t. |
| torn | A past pl. from the tr. v. "to tear," ref. to "trees." |
| were torn | An irreg. tr. v., pass. vo., indic. m., past t., p. num., 3rd per., agr. with its nom. "trees." |
| up | An adv. of place, mod. the v. "were torn." |
| by | A prep., sh. the rn. bet. "were torn," and "roots." |
| **roots** | A com. n., neu. gen., p. num., 3rd per., obj. c., gov. by the prep. "by." |
| and | A cop. conj., jg. the sents. "trees were torn...roots," and "*trees were* whirled...air." |
| whirled | A past pl. from the tr. v. "to whirl," ref. to "trees." |
| through | A prep., sh. the rn. bet. "*were* whirled" and "air." |
| **air** | A com. n., neu. gen., s. num., 3rd per., obj. c., gov. by the prep. "through." |
| and | A cop. conj., jg. the sents. "*trees were* whirled...air" and "the forked lightning struck...church." |

## 94  KEY TO

| | |
|---|---|
| more | An adv. of deg., mod. the adj. "awful," indg. comp. deg. |
| more awful | An adj. of quality, comp. deg., qual. the n. "omen." |
| omen | An abs. n., neu. gen., s. num., 3rd per., nom. c. after the v. *was* und. (*Which was* a more awful omen; the ant. to "which" being the sent. "the forked lightning struck, &c." *Parsing*, p. 110.) |
| forked | An adj. of quality, qual. the n. "lightning." |
| lightning | A com. n., neu. gen., s. num., 3rd per., nom. c. to the v. "struck." |
| struck | An irreg. tr. v., act. vo., indic. m., past t., s. num., 3rd per., agr. with its nom. "lightning." |
| down | An adv. of place, mod. the v. "struck." |
| steeple | A com. n., neu. gen., s. num., 3rd per., obj. c., gov. by the tr. v. "struck." |
| of | A prep., sh. the rn. bet. "steeple" and "church." |
| church | A com. n., neu. gen., s. num., 3rd per., obj. c., gov. by the prep. "of." |
| where | A cop. conj., jg. the sents. "the forked lightning struck...church" and "the heretic service had been read...time." |
| heretic | An adj. of quality, qual. the n. "service." |
| service | A com. n., neu. gen., s. num., 3rd per., nom. c. to the v. "had been read." |
| had | An aux. v. to "been read," indg. pluperf. t. |
| been | A past pl. from the intr. v. "to be," ref. to "read service," and aux. to "read," indg. pass. vo. |
| read | A past pl. from the tr. v. "to read," ref. to "service." |
| had been read | An irreg. tr. v., pass. vo., indic. m., pluperf. t., s. num., 3rd per., agr. with its nom. "service." |
| for | A prep., sh. the rn. bet. "had been read" and "time." |
| first | A def. ord. nu. adj. of quantity, qual. the n. "time." |
| time. | An abs. n., neu. gen., s. num., 3rd per., obj. c., gov. by the prep. "for." |

### Exercise 126.

| | |
|---|---|
| 1. mind | A com. n., neu. gen., s. num., 3rd per., nom. c. to the v. "returns." |
| returns | A reg. intr. v., indic. m., pres. t., s. num., 3rd per., agr. with its nom. "mind." |
| to | A prep., sh. the rn. bet. "returns" and "state." |
| its | A pers. pron., neu. gen., s. num., 3rd per., poss. c., gov. by the n. "state." |
| usual | An adj. of quality, pos. deg., qual. the n. "state." |
| state | An abs. n., neu. gen., s. num., 3rd per., obj. c., gov. by the prep. "to." |
| of | A prep., sh. the rn. bet. "state" and "indifference." |
| indifference. | An abs. n., neu. gen., s. num., 3rd per., obj. c., gov. by the prep. "of." |
| 2. This | A dis. adj., lim. the n. *circumstance* und. |
| I | A pers. pron., com. gen., s. num., 1st per., nom. c. to the v. "account." |
| my | A pers. pron., com. gen., s. num., 1st per., poss. c., gov. by the n. "glory." |
| glory | An abs. n., neu. gen., s. num., 3rd per., obj. c., in app. with *circumstance* und., (or, factitive object, gov. by the tr. v. "account"). |
| account | A reg. tr. v., act. vo., indic. m., pres. t., s. num., 1st per., agr. with its nom. "I." |
| my | A pers. pron., com. gen., s. num., 1st per., poss. c., gov. by the n. *exaltation*. |
| exaltation | An abs. n., neu. gen., s. num., 3rd per., obj. c., in app. with *circumstance* und., (or, factitive object, gov. by the tr. v. *account* und ). |
| and | A cop. conj., jg. the sents. "*this circumstance I* my exaltation *account*" and "*this circumstance I* my whole delight *account*." |
| my | A pers. pron., com. gen., s. num., 1st per., poss. c., gov. by the n. "delight." |
| whole | An adj. of quantity (bulk or mass), qual. the n. "delight." |

| | |
|---|---|
| **delight.** | An abs. n., neu. gen., s. num., 3rd per., obj. c., in app. with *circumstance* und., (or, factitive object, gov. by the tr. v. *account* und.). |
| 3. **danger** | An abs. n., neu. gen., s. num., 3rd per., obj. c., gov. by the tr. v. "deny." |
| they | A pers. pron., com. gen., p. num., 3rd per., nom. c. to the v. "discern." |
| discern | A reg. tr. v., act. vo., indic. m., pres. t., p. num., 3rd per., agr. with its nom. "they." (*Which* they discern not.) |
| not | An adv. of m. (neg.), mod. the v. "discern." |
| they | A pers. pron., com. gen., p. num., 3rd per., nom. c. to the v. "deny." |
| deny. | A reg. tr. v., act. vo., indic. m., pres. t., p. num., 3rd per., agr. with its nom. "they." |
| 4. **Words** | A com. n., neu. gen., p. num., 3rd per., obj. c., gov. by the tr. v. "may rehearse." |
| learned | A past pl. from the tr. v. "to learn," ref. to "words." |
| by | A prep., sh. the rn. bet. "learned" and "rote." |
| rote | An abs. n., neu. gen., s. num., 3rd per., obj. c., gov. by the prep. "by." |
| parrot | A com. n., com. gen., s. num., 3rd per., nom. c. to the v. "may rehearse." |
| may | An aux. v. to "rehearse," indg. pot. m., pres. t. |
| (to) rehearse | A reg. tr. v., act. vo., infin. m., pres. t., gov. by the v. "may." |
| may rehearse. | A reg. tr. v., act. vo., pot. m., pres. t., s. num., 3rd per., agr. with its nom. "parrot." |
| 5. **License** | An abs. n., neu. gen., s. num., 3rd per., obj. c., gov. by the tr. v. "mean." |
| they | A pers. pron., com. gen., p. num., 3rd per., nom. c. to the v. "mean." |
| mean | An irreg. tr. v., act. vo., indic. m., pres. t., p. num., 3rd per., agr. with its nom. "they." |
| when | A cop. conj., jg. the sents. "License they mean" and "they cry liberty." |
| they | A pers. pron., com. gen., p. num., 3rd per., nom. c. to the v. "cry." |
| cry | A reg. tr. v., act. vo., indic. m., pres. t., p. num., 3rd per., agr. with its nom. "they." |
| **liberty.** | An abs. n., neu. gen., s. num., 3rd per., obj. c., gov. by the tr. v. "cry." |
| 6. **Whom** | An interrog. pron., com. gen., s. num., 3rd per., obj. c., gov. by the prep. "of." |
| have | An irreg. tr. v., act. vo., indic. m., pres. t., s. num., 1st per., agr. with its nom. "I." |
| I | A pers. pron., com. gen., s. num., 1st per., nom. c. to the v. "have." |
| to | A particle, indg. infin. m. |
| to complain | A reg. intr. v., infln. m., pres. t., gov. by the v. "have." |
| of | A prep., sh. the rn. bet. "to complain" and "whom." |
| but | A disj. conj., jg. the sents. "Whom have I to complain of" and "*I have to complain of* myself." |
| **myself.** | A comp. pers. pron., com. gen., s. num., 1st per., obj. c., gov. by the prep. *of* und. ("But" may also be taken as equivalent to "except," governing "myself" in the obj. c. *Parsing*, p. 165.) |
| 7. Each | A dist. nu. adj. of quantity, qual. the n. "flower." |
| **flower** | A com. n., neu. gen., s. num., 3rd per., obj. c., gov. by the tr. v. "have wet." |
| dews | A com. n., neu. gen., p. num., 3rd per., nom. c. to the v. "have wet." |
| have | An aux. v. to "wet," indg. perf. t. |
| lightly | An adv. of man., mod. the v. "have wet." |
| wet | A past pl. from the tr. v. "to wet," ref. to "flower." |
| have wet. | An irreg. tr. v., act. vo., indic. m., perf. t., p. num., 3rd per., agr. with its nom. "dews." |
| 8. smaller | An adj. of quality, comp. deg., qual. the n. "boon." |
| **boon** | An abs. n., neu. gen., s. num., 3rd per., obj. c., gov. by the tr. v. "can beg." |

| | |
|---|---|
| than | A disj. conj., jg. the sents. "A smaller boon I cannot beg" and "this *boon is small*." |
| this | A dis. adj., lim. the n. *boon* und. |
| I | A pers. pron., com. gen., s. num., 1st per., nom. c. to the v. "can beg." |
| can | An aux. v. to "beg," indg. pot. m., pres. t. |
| not | An adv. of m. (neg.), mod. the v. "can beg." |
| (to) beg | A reg. tr. v., act. vo., infin. m., pres. t., gov. by the v. "can." |
| can beg. | A reg. tr. v., act. vo., pot. m., pres. t., s. num., 1st per., agr. with its nom. "I." |
| 9. **habitation** | A com. n., neu. gen., s. num., 3rd per., obj. c., gov. by the tr. v. "hath." |
| giddy | An adj. of quality, pos. deg., qual. the n. "habitation." |
| and | A cop. conj., jg. the sents. "he hath an habitation giddy" and "*he hath an habitation* unsure." |
| unsure | An adj. of quality, qual. the n. *habitation* und. |
| Hath | An irreg. tr. v., act. vo., indic. m., pres. t., s. num., 3rd per., agr. with its nom. "he." |
| he | A pers. pron., mas. gen., s. num., 3rd per., nom. c. to the v. "hath." |
| that | A rel. pron., mas. gen., s. num., 3rd per., agr. with its ant. "he," nom. c. to the v. "buildeth." |
| buildeth | A reg. tr. v., act. vo., used intransitively, indic. m., pres. t., s. num., 3rd per., agr. with its nom. "that." |
| on | A prep., sh. the rn. bet. "buildeth" and "heart." |
| vulgar | An adj. of quality, pos. deg., qual. the n. "heart." |
| **heart.** | A com. n., neu. gen., s. num., 3rd per., obj. c., gov. by the prep. "on." |
| 10. hounds | A com. n., com. gen., p. num., 3rd per., nom. c. to the v. "ran." |
| ran | An irreg. intr. v., indic. m., past t., p. num., 3rd per., agr. with its nom. "hounds." |
| swiftly | An adv. of man., mod. the v. "ran." |
| through | A prep., sh. the rn. bet. "ran" and "woods." |
| **woods** | A com. n., neu. gen., p. num., 3rd per., obj. c., gov. by the prep. "through." |
| nimble | An adj. of quality, pos. deg., qual. the n. "deer." |
| **deer** | A com. n., com. gen., p. num., 3rd per., obj. c., gov. by the tr. v. "to take." |
| to | A particle, indg. infin. m. |
| to take | An irreg. tr. v., infin. m., pres. t., gov. by the v. "ran." |
| And | A cop. conj., jg. the sents. "The hounds ran...to take" and "with their cries...did make." |
| with | A prep., sh. the rn. bet. *did make* und. and "cries." |
| their | A pers. pron., com. gen., p. num., 3rd per., poss. c., gov. by the n. "cries." |
| **cries** | An abs. n., neu. gen., p. num., 3rd per., obj. c., gov. by the prep. "with." |
| hills | A com. n., neu. gen., p. num., 3rd per., nom. c. to the v. *did make* und. |
| and | A cop. conj., jg. the sents. "with their cries the hills *an echo shrill did make*" and "*with their cries* the dales an echo shrill did make." |
| dales | A com. n., neu. gen., p. num., 3rd per., nom. c. to the v. "did make." |
| echo | An abs. n., neu. gen., s. num., 3rd per., obj. c., gov. by the tr. v. "did make." |
| **shrill** | An adj. of quality, pos. deg., qual. the n. "echo." |
| did | An aux. v. to "make," indg. past t., emph. form. |
| (to) make | An irreg. tr. v., act. vo., infin. m., pres. t , gov. by the v. "did." |
| did make. | An irreg. tr. v., act. vo., indic. m., past t., emph. form, p. num., 3rd per., agr. with its nom. "dales." |

## Exercise 127.

| | |
|---|---|
| 1. Calais | A prop. n., neu. gen., s. num., 3rd per., nom. c. to the v. "was lost." |
| **glory** | An abs n., neu. gen., s. num., 3rd per., nom. c., in app. with "Calais." |

| | |
|---|---|
| of | A prep., sh. the rn. bet. "glory" and "England." |
| England | A prop. n., neu. gen., s. num., 3rd per., obj. c., gov. by the prep. "of." |
| **fear** | An abs. n., neu. gen., s. num., 3rd per., nom. c., in app. with "Calais." |
| of | A prep., sh. the rn. bet. "fear" and "enemies." |
| England's | A prop. n., neu. gen., s. num., 3rd per., poss. c., gov. by the n. "enemies." |
| enemies | A com. n., com. gen., p. num., 3rd per., obj. c., gov. by the prep. "of." |
| was | An aux. v. to "lost," indg. pass. vo., past t. |
| lost | A past pl. from the tr. v. "to lose," ref. to "Calais." |
| was lost. | An irreg. tr. v., pass. vo., indic. m., past t., s. num., 3rd per., agr. with its nom. "Calais." |
| 2. Thus | An adv. of man., mod. the v. "perished." |
| perished | A reg. intr. v., indic. m., past t., s. num., 3rd per., agr. with its nom. "Pythagoras." |
| Pythagoras | A prop. n., mas. gen., s. num., 3rd per., nom. c. to the v. "perished." |
| Samian | A prop. adj. of quality, qual. the n. "philosopher." |
| **philosopher** | A com. n., mas. gen., s. num., 3rd per., nom. c., in app. with "Pythagoras." |
| **founder** | A com. n., mas. gen., s. num., 3rd per., nom. c., in app. with "Pythagoras." |
| of | A prep., sh. the rn. bet. "founder" and "school." |
| Italian | A prop. adj. of quality, qual. the n. "school." |
| school | A com. n., neu. gen., s. num., 3rd per., obj. c., gov. by the prep "of." |
| and | A ccp. conj., jg. the sents. "Thus perished...school" and "thus perished Pythagoras, the great luminary...world." |
| great | An adj. of quality, pos. deg., qual. the n. "luminary." |
| **luminary** | A com. n., mas. gen., s. num., 3rd per., nom. c., in app. with *Pythagoras* und. |
| of | A prep., sh. the rn. bet. "luminary" and "world." |
| heathen | An adj. of quality, qual. the n. "world." |
| world. | A com. n., neu. gen., s. num., 3rd per., obj. c., gov. by the prep. "of." |
| 3. **God** | A prop. n., mas. gen., s. num., 3rd per., nom. c. to the v. "is." |
| **himself** | A compd. pers. pron., mas. gen., s. num., 3rd per., nom. c., in app. with "God." |
| is | An irreg. intr. v., indic. m., pres. t., s. num., 3rd per., agr. with its nom. "God." |
| with | A prep., sh. the rn. bet. "is" and "us." |
| us | A pers. pron., com. gen., p. num., 1st per., obj. c., gov. by the prep. "with." |
| for | A prep., sh. the rn. bet. "is" and "captain." |
| our | A pers. pron., com. gen., p. num., 1st per., poss. c., gov. by the n. "captain." |
| captain. | A com. n., mas. gen., s. num., 3rd per., obj. c., gov. by the prep. "for." |
| 4. **birds** | A com. n., com. gen., p. num., 3rd per., nom. c. to the v. "sing." |
| **they** | A pers. pron., com. gen., p. num., 3rd per., nom. c. in app. with "birds." ("They" is pleonastic.) |
| sing | An irreg. intr. v., indic. m., pres. t., p. num., 3rd per., agr. with its nom. "birds." |
| **deer** | A com. n., com. gen., p. num., 3rd per., nom. c. to the v. "fling." |
| **they** | A pers. pron., com. gen., p. num., 3rd per., nom. c., in app. with "deer." ("They" is pleonastic.) |
| fling. | An irreg. intr. v., indic. m., pres. t., p. num., 3rd per., agr. with its nom. "deer." |
| 5. Lo | An interj. |
| where | A cop. conj., jg. the sents. "you behold" and "the rosy-bosom'd Hours...appear." |
| rosy-bosom'd | A compd. adj. of quality, qual. the n. "Hours." |
| **Hours** | An abs. n. used as a prop. n., fem. gen. by personification, p. num., 3rd per., nom. c. to the v. "appear." |
| Fair | An adj. of quality, pos. deg., qual. the n. "Venus'." |

98　KEY TO

| | |
|---|---|
| Venus' | A prop. n., fem. gen., s. num., 3rd per., poss. c., gov. by the n. "train." |
| **train** | A com. col. n., neu. gen., s. num., 3rd per., nom. c., in app. with "Hours." |
| appear. | A reg. intr. v., indic. m., pres. t., p. num., 3rd per., agr. with its nom. "hours." |
| 6. **Soul** | A com. n., neu. gen., s. num., 2nd per., nom. c. of add. |
| of | A prep., sh. the rn. bet. "soul" and "age." |
| age | An abs. n., neu. gen., s. num., 2nd per., obj. c., gov. by the prep. "of." |
| **applause** | An abs. n., neu. gen., s. num., 2nd per., nom. c., in app. with "soul." |
| **delight** | An abs. n., neu. gen., s. num., 2nd per., nom. c., in app. with "soul." |
| **wonder** | An abs. n., neu. gen., s. num., 2nd per., nom. c., in app. with "soul." |
| of | A prep., sh. the rn. bet. "wonder" and "stage." |
| our | A pers. pron., com. gen., p. num., 1st per., poss. c., gov. by the n. "stage." |
| stage | A com. n., neu. gen., s. num., 3rd per., obj. c., gov. by the prep. "of." |
| My | A pers. pron., com. gen., s. num., 1st per., poss. c., gov. by the n. "Shakespeare." |
| **Shakespeare** | A prop. n., mas. gen., s. num., 2nd per., nom. c. of add. |
| rise. | An irreg. intr. v., imper. m., pres. t., s. num., 2nd per., agr. with its nom. *thou* und. |

## Exercise 128.

| | |
|---|---|
| 1. **Lords** | A com. n. tending to prop., mas. gen., p. num., 3rd per., nom. c. to the v. "reserved." |
| **Justices** | A com. n. tending to prop., mas. gen., p. num., 3rd per., nom. c., in app. with "Lords." |
| **Lords Justices** | A compd. com. n. tending to prop., mas. gen., p. num., 3rd per., nom. c. to the v. "reserved." |
| reserved | A reg. tr. v., act. vo., indic. m., past t., p. num., 3rd per., agr. with its nom. "Lords" (or, agr. with its nom. "Lords Justices"). |
| their | A pers. pron., mas. gen., p. num., 3rd per., poss. c., gov. by the n. "decision." |
| decision. | An abs. n., neu. gen., s. num., 3rd per., obj. c., gov. by the tr. v. "reserved." |
| 2. **Miss** | A com. n. tending to prop., fem. gen., p. num., s. form., 3rd per., nom. c. to the v. "were invited" (or, a com. n. used as an adj. of quality, qual. the n. "Vernons"). |
| **Vernons** | A prop. n. tending to com., fem. gen., p. num., 3rd per., nom. c. in app. with "Miss." |
| **Miss Vernons** | A compd. prop. n., fem. gen., p. num., 3rd per., nom. c. to the v. "were invited." |
| were | An aux. v. to "invited," indg. pass. vo., past t. |
| invited | A past pl. from the tr. v. "to invite," ref. to "Miss," (or, to "Miss Vernons"). |
| were invited. | A reg. tr. v., pass. vo., indic. m., past t., p. num., 3rd per., agr. with its nom. "Miss" (or, "Miss Vernons"). |
| 3. **Lords** | A com. n. tending to prop., mas. gen, p. num., 3rd per., nom. c. to the v. "were appointed." |
| **Wardens** | A com. n. tending to prop., mas. gen., p. num., 3rd per, nom. c., in app. with "Lords." |
| **Lords Wardens** | A compd. com. n. tending to prop., mas. gen., p. num., 3rd per., nom. c. to the v. "were appointed." |
| were | An aux. v. to "appointed," indg. pass. vo., past t. |
| appointed | A past pl. from the tr. v. "to appoint," ref. to "Lords" (or, "Lords Wardens"). |
| were appointed | A reg. tr. v., pass. vo., indic. m., past t., p. num., 3rd per., agr. with its nom. "Lords" (or, "Lords Wardens"). |
| by | A prep., sh. the rn. bet. "were appointed" and "king." |
| king. | A com. n., mas. gen., s. num., 3rd per., obj. c., gov. by the prep. "by." |

| | |
|---|---|
| 4. **Lords** | A com. n. tending to prop., mas. gen., p. num., 3rd per., nom. c. to the v. "prorogued." |
| **Commissioners** | A com. n. tending to prop., mas. gen., p. num., 3rd per., nom. c., in app. with "Lords." |
| **Lords Commissioners** | A compd. com. n. tending to prop., mas. gen., p. num., 3rd per., nom. c. to the v. "prorogued." |
| prorogued | A reg. tr. v., act. vo., indic. m., past t., p. num., 3rd per., agr. with its nom. "Lords" (or, "Lords Commissioners"). |
| parliament. | A com. col. n., neu. gen., s. num., 3rd per., obj. c., gov. by the tr. v. "prorogued." |
| 5. **Miss** | A com. n. tending to prop., fem. gen., p. num., s. form, 3rd per., nom. c. to the v. "were," (or, a com. n. used as an adj. of quality, qual. the n. "Arundels "). |
| **Arundels** | A prop. n. tending to com., fem. gen., p. num., 3rd per., nom. c., in app. with "Miss." |
| **Miss Arundels** | A compd. prop. n., fem. gen., p. num., 3rd per., nom. c. to the v. "were." |
| were | An irreg. intr. v., indic. m., past t., p. num., 3rd per., agr. with its nom. "Miss " (or, "Miss Arundels "). |
| remarkable | An adj. of quality, pos. deg., qual. the n. "Miss " (or, "Miss Arundels "). |
| for | A prep., sh. the rn. bet. "remarkable " and "beauty." |
| their | A pers. pron., fem. gen., p. num., 3rd per., poss. c., gov. by the n. "beauty." |
| beauty. | An abs. n., neu. gen., p. num., 3rd per., obj. c., gov. by the prep. "for." |
| 6. **Messrs.** | A com. n. tending to prop., mas. gen., p. num., 3rd per., nom. c. to the v. "chartered." |
| **Smith** | A prop. n., mas. gen., p. num., s. form, 3rd per., nom. c., in app. with "Messrs." |
| **Messrs. Smith** | A compd. prop. n., mas. gen., p. num., 3rd per., nom. c. to the v. "chartered." |
| chartered | A reg. tr. v., act. vo., indic. m., past t., p. num., 3rd per., agr. with its nom. "Messrs." (or, " Messrs. Smith "). |
| vessel. | A com. n., neu. gen., s. num., 3rd per., obj. c., gov. by the tr. v. "chartered." |

## Exercise 129.

| | |
|---|---|
| 1. **Lord** | A com. n. tending to prop., mas. gen., s. num., 3rd per., poss. c., gov. by the n. "days " (or, a com. n. used as an adj. of quality, qual. the n. "Warwick's "). |
| **Warwick's** | A prop. n., mas. gen., s. num., 3rd per., poss. c., in app. with "Lord." |
| **Lord Warwick's** | A compd. prop. n., mas. gen., s. num., 3rd per., poss. c., gov. by the n. "days." |
| days | An abs. n., neu. gen., p. num., 3rd per., nom. c. to the v. "are." |
| are | An irreg. intr. v., indic. m., past t., p. num., 3rd per., agr. with its nom. "days." |
| o'er. | An adv. of time, mod. the v. "are." |
| 2. **Stephen** | A prop. n., mas. gen., s. num., 3rd per., poss. c., gov. by the n. "carts." |
| **miller's** | A com. n., mas. gen., s. num., 3rd per., poss. c., in app. with "Stephen." |
| carts | A com. n., neu. gen., p. num., 3rd per., nom. c. to the v. "were." |
| were | An irreg. intr. v., indic. m., past t., p. num., 3rd per., agr. with its nom. "carts." |
| in | A prep., sh. the rn. bet. "were " and "front." |
| front | A com. n., neu. gen., s. num., 3rd per., obj. c., gov. by the prep. "in." |
| of | A prep., sh. the rn. bet. "front " and "inn." |
| inn. | A com. n., neu. gen., s. num., 3rd per., obj. c., gov. by the prep. "of." |
| 3. **work** | A com. n., neu. gen., s. num., 3rd per., nom. c. to the v. "is." |
| is | An irreg. intr. v., indic. m., pres. t., s. num., 3rd per., agr. with its nom. "work." |
| **George** | A prop. n., mas. gen., s. num., 3rd per., poss. c., gov. by the n. *work* und. |

| | |
|---|---|
| **Eliot's** | A prop. n., mas. gen., s. num., 3rd per., poss. c., in app. with "George." |
| **George Eliot's** | A compd. prop. n., mas. gen., s. num., 3rd per., poss. c., gov. by the n. *work* und. N.B.—It will be observed that "George Eliot" is a masculine name assumed by a female writer. |
| greatest | An adj. of quality, superl. deg., qual. the n. "novelist." |
| living | A pres. pl. used as an adj. of quality, qual. the n. "novelist." |
| **novelist.** | A com. n., mas. gen., s. num., 3rd per., poss. c., in app. with "George Eliot's." |
| 4. **Henry** | A prop. n., mas. gen., s. num., 3rd per., poss. c., gov. by the n. "policy." (The 's is transferred to the adj. "Eighth.") |
| **Eighth** | A def. ord. nu. adj. of quantity, qual. the n. "Henry." |
| **Henry the Eighth's** | A compd. prop. n., mas. gen., s. num., 3rd per., poss. c., gov. by the n. "policy." |
| policy | An abs. n., neu. gen., s. num., 3rd per., nom. c. to the v. "was." |
| was | An irreg. intr. v., indic. m., past t., s. num., 3rd per., agr. with its nom. "policy." |
| successful. | An adj. of quality, pos. deg., qual. the n. "policy." |
| 5. **My** | A pers. pron., com. gen., s. num., 1st per., poss. c., gov. by the n. "brother." |
| **brother** | A com. n., mas. gen., s. num., 3rd per., poss. c., gov. by the n. "rabbit." (The 's is transferred to the apposition noun "Walter's.") |
| **Walter's** | A prop. n., mas. gen., s. num., 3rd per., poss. c., in app. with "brother." |
| pet | A com. n. used as an adj. of quality, qual. the n. "rabbit." |
| rabbit | A com. n., com. gen., s. num., 3rd per., nom. c. to the v. "is." |
| is | An irreg. intr. v., indic. m., pres. t., s. num., 3rd per., agr. with its nom. "rabbit." |
| dead. | An adj. of quality, qual. the n. "rabbit." |
| 6. **Livy** | A prop. n., mas. gen., s. num., 3rd per., poss. c., gov. by the n. "works." (The 's is transferred to the apposition noun "historian's.") |
| **historian's** | A com. n., mas. gen., s. num., 3rd per., poss. c., in app. with "Livy." |
| works | A com. n., neu. gen., p. num., 3rd per., nom. c. to the v. "are." |
| are | An irreg. intr. v., indic. m., pres. t., p. num., 3rd per., agr. with its nom. "works." |
| of | A prep., sh. the rn. bet. "are" and "interest." |
| great | An adj. of quality, pos. deg., qual. the n. "interest." |
| interest. | An abs. n., neu. gen., s. num., 3rd per., obj. c., gov. by the prep. "of." |

## Exercise 130.

| | |
|---|---|
| 1. Reading | A verbal or abs. n., neu. gen., s. num., 3rd per., nom. c. to the v. "makes." |
| makes | An irreg. tr. v., act. vo., indic. m., pres. t., s. num., 3rd per., agr. with its nom. "reading." |
| **full** | An adj. of quality, qual. the n. "man." |
| man | A com. n., mas. gen., s. num., 3rd per., obj. c., gov. by the tr. v. "makes." |
| speaking | A verbal or abs. n., neu. gen., s. num., 3rd per., nom. c. to the v. *makes* und. |
| **ready** | An adj. of quality, pos. deg., qual. the n. "man." |
| man | A com. n., mas. gen., s. num., 3rd per., obj. c., gov. by the tr. v. *makes* und. |
| writing | A verbal or abs. n., neu. gen., s. num., 3rd per., nom. c. to the v. *makes* und. |
| **correct** | An adj. of quality, pos. deg., qual. the n. "man." |
| man. | A com. n., mas. gen., s. num., 3rd per., obj. c., gov. by the tr. v. *makes* und. |
| 2. Her | A pers. pron., fem. gen., s. num., 3rd per., poss. c., gov. by the n. "arm." |
| **right** | An adj. of quality, qual. the n. "arm." |
| arm | A com. n., neu. gen., s. num., 3rd per., nom. c. to the v. "lay." |
| lay | An irreg. intr. v., indic. m., past t., s. num., 3rd per., agr. with its nom. "arm." |

## ENGLISH GRAMMAR AND ANALYSIS. 101

| | | |
|---|---|---|
| | tolded | A past pl. from the tr. v. "to fold," ref. to "arm." |
| | over | A prep., sh. the rn. bet. "folded" and "bosom." |
| | her | A pers. pron., fem. gen., s. num., 3rd per., poss. c., gov. by the n. "bosom." |
| | bosom. | A com. n., neu. gen., s. num., 3rd per., obj. c., gov. by the prep. "over." |
| 3. | evening | An abs. n., neu. gen., s. num., 3rd per., nom. c. to the v. "was." |
| | was | An irreg. intr. v., indic. m., past t., s. num., 3rd per., agr. with its nom. "evening." |
| | **boisterous.** | An adj. of quality, pos. deg., qual. the n. "evening." |
| 4. | night | An abs. n., neu. gen., s. num., 3rd per., nom. c. to the v. "is." |
| | is | An irreg. intr. v., indic. m., pres. t., s. num., 3rd per., agr. with its nom. "night." |
| | **chill.** | An adj. of quality, pos. deg., qual. the n. "night." |
| 5. | forest | A com. n., neu. gen., s. num., 3rd per., nom. c. to the v. "is." |
| | is | An irreg. intr. v., indic. m., pres. t., s. num., 3rd per., agr. with its nom. "forest." |
| | **bare.** | An adj. of quality, pos. deg., qual. the n. "forest." |
| 6. | dew | A com. n., neu. gen., s. num., 3rd per., nom. c. to the v. "was." |
| | on | A prep., sh. the rn. bet. "dew" and "robe." |
| | his | A pers. pron., mas. gen., s. num., 3rd per., poss. c., gov. by the n. "robe." |
| | robe | A com. n., neu. gen., s. num., 3rd per., obj. c., gov. by the prep. "on." |
| | was | An irreg. intr. v., indic. m., past t., s. num., 3rd per., agr. with its nom. "dew." |
| | **heavy** | An adj. of quality, pos. deg., qual. the n. "dew." |
| | and | A cop. conj., jg. the sents. "The dew...was heavy" and "the dew on his robe was chill." |
| | **chill.** | An adj. of quality, pos. deg., qual. the n. dew und. |
| 7. | He | A pers. pron., mas. gen., s. num., 3rd per., nom. c. to the v. "mounted." |
| | mounted | A reg. tr. v., act. vo., indic. m., past t., s. num., 3rd per., agr. with its nom. "he." |
| | **narrow** | An adj. of quality, pos. deg., qual. the n. "stair." |
| | stair. | A com. n., neu. gen., s. num., 3rd per., obj. c., gov. by the tr. v. "mounted." |
| 8. | **summer** | An abs. n. used as an adj. of quality, qual. the n. "evening." |
| | evening | An abs. n., neu. gen., s. num., 3rd per., nom. c. to the v. "grew." |
| | grew | An irreg. intr. v., indic. m., past t., s. num., 3rd per., agr. with its nom. "evening." |
| | **black** | An adj. of quality, pos. deg., qual. the n. "evening." |
| | as | A cop. conj., jg. the sents. "The summer evening grew black" and "night is black." |
| | night. | An abs. n., neu. gen., s. num., 3rd per., nom. c. to the v. is und. |
| 9. | I | A pers. pron., mas. gen., s. num., 3rd per., nom. c. to the v. "am." |
| | am | An irreg. intr. v., indic. m., pres. t., s. num., 1st per., agr. with its nom. "I." |
| | **booted** | An adj. of quality, qual. the pron. "I." |
| | and | A cop. conj., jg. the sents. "I am booted" and "I am spurred." |
| | **spurred.** | An adj. of quality, qual. the pron. I und. |
| 10. | **miserable** | An adj. of quality, pos. deg., qual. the n. *people* und. |
| | have | An irreg. tr. v., act. vo., indic. m., pres. t., p. num., 3rd per., agr. with its nom. *people* und. |
| | **no** | A def. card. nu. adj. of quantity, qual. "other medicine." |
| | **other** | An indef. nu. adj. of quantity, qual. the n. "medicine." |
| | medicine | A com. n., neu. gen., s. num., 3rd per., obj. c., gov. by the tr. v. "have." |
| | but | A disj. conj., jg. the sents. "The miserable *people* have no other medicine" and "*they have* only hope." |
| | only | An adv. of deg., mod. the v. *have* und. |
| | hope. | An abs. n., neu. gen., s. num., 3rd per., obj. c., gov. by the tr. v. *have* und. |
| 11. | He | A pers. pron., mas. gen., s. num., 3rd per., nom. c. to the v. "had contracted." |
| | had | An aux. v. to "contracted," indg. pluperf. t. |

| | |
|---|---|
| contracted | A past pl. from the tr. v. "to contract," ref. to "passion." |
| had contracted | A reg. tr. v., act. vo., indic. m., pluperf. t., s. num., 3rd per., agr. with its nom. "he." |
| passion | An abs. n., neu. gen., s. num., 3rd per., obj. c., gov. by the tr. v. "had contracted." |
| for | A prep., sh. the rn. bet. "had contracted" and "marvellous." |
| **marvellous** | An adj. of quality, used as an abs. n., neu. gen., s. num., 3rd per., obj. c., gov. by the prep. "for." |
| and | A cop. conj., jg. the sents. "He had contracted...marvellous" and "*he had contracted a passion for the* supernatural." |
| **supernatu-ral.** | } An adj. of quality, used as an abs. n., neu. gen., s. num., 3rd per., obj. c., gov. by the prep. *for* und. |
| 12. We | A pers. pron., com. gen., p. num., 1st per., nom. c. to the v. "received." |
| received | A reg. tr. v., act. vo., indic. m., past t., p. num., 1st per., agr. with its nom. "we." |
| card | A com. n., neu. gen., s. num., 3rd per., obj. c., gov. by the tr. v. "received." |
| from | A prep., sh. the rn. bet. "received" and "ladies." |
| **town** | A com. n. used as an adj. of quality, qual. the n. "ladies." |
| ladies. | A com. n., fem. gen., p. num., 3rd per., obj. c., gov. by the prep. "from." |
| 13. **Mute** | An adj. of quality, qual. the n. "wind." |
| was | An irreg. intr. v., indic. m., past t., s. num., 3rd per., agr. with its nom. "wind." |
| wind | A com. n., neu. gen., s. num., 3rd per., nom. c. to the v. "was." |
| soft | An adv. of man., mod. the v. "fell." |
| fell | An irreg. intr. v., indic. m., past t., s. num., 3rd per., agr. with its nom. "dew." |
| dew. | A com. n., neu. gen., s. num., 3rd per., nom. c. to the v. "fell." |
| 14. I | A pers. pron., mas. gen., s. num., 1st per., nom. c. to the v. "had." |
| had | An irreg. tr. v., act. vo., indic. m., past t., s. num., 1st per., agr. with its nom. "I." |
| message | An abs. n., neu. gen., s. num., 3rd per., obj. c., gov. by the tr. v. "had." |
| to | A particle, indg. infin. m. |
| to send | An irreg. tr. v., act. vo., infin. m., pres. t., gov. by the n. "message." |
| her | A pers. pron., fem. gen., s. num., 3rd per., obj. c., gov. by the prep. *to* und. |
| So | An adv. of deg., mod. the adj. "tender." |
| **tender** | An adj. of quality, pos. deg., qual. the n. "message." |
| and | A cop. conj., jg. the sents. "I had...tender" and "*I had a message to send her so* true." |
| **true** | An adj. of quality, pos. deg., qual. the n. *message* und. |
| and | A cop. conj., jg. the sents. "*I had...*true" and "*I had a message to send her so* sweet." |
| **sweet** | An adj. of quality, pos. deg., qual. the n. *message* und. |
| I | A pers. pron., mas. gen., s. num., 1st per., nom. c. to the v. "longed." |
| longed | A reg. intr. v., indic. m., past t., s. num., 1st per., agr. with its nom. "I." |
| for | A prep., sh. the rn. bet. "longed" and "angel." |
| angel | A com. n., com. gen., s. num., 3rd per., obj. c., gov. by the prep. "for." |
| to | A particle, indg. infin. m. |
| to bear | An irreg. tr. v., act. vo., infin. m., pres. t., gov. by the n. "angel." |
| it | A pers. pron., neu. gen., s. num., 3rd per., obj. c., gov. by the tr. v. "to bear." |
| And | A cop. conj., jg. the sents. "I longed...it" and "*I longed for an angel to lay...feet.*" |
| (to) lay | An irreg. tr. v., act. vo., infin. m., pres. t., gov. by the n. *angel* und. |
| it | A pers. pron., neu. gen., s. num., 3rd per., obj. c., gov. by the tr. v. "*to* lay." |
| down | An adv. of place, mod. the v. "*to* lay." |

| | |
|---|---|
| at | A prep., sh. the rn. bet. "*to lay*" and "feet." |
| her | A pers. pron., fem. gen., s. num., 3rd per., poss. c., gov. by the n. "feet." |
| feet. | A com. n., neu. gen., p. num., 3rd per., obj. c., gov. by the prep. "at." |
| I | A pers. pron., mas. gen., s. num., 1st per., nom. c. to the v. "placed." |
| placed | A reg. tr. v., act. vo., indic. m., past t., s. num., 1st per., agr. with its nom. "I." |
| it | A pers. pron., neu. gen., s. num., 3rd per., obj. c., gov. by the tr. v. "placed." |
| **one** | A def. card. nu. adj. of quantity, qual. "summer's evening." |
| summer's | An abs. n., neu. gen., s. num., 3rd per., poss. c., gov. by the n. "evening." |
| evening | An abs. n., neu. gen., s. num., 3rd per., obj. c., gov. by the prep. *on* und. |
| On | A prep., sh. the rn. bet. "placed" and "breast." |
| **little** | An adj. of quality, pos. deg., qual. the n. "cloud's." |
| **white** | An adj. of quality, pos. deg., qual. the n. "cloud's." |
| cloud's | A com. n., neu. gen., s. num., 3rd per., poss. c., gov. by the n. "breast." |
| breast | A com. n., neu. gen., s. num., 3rd per., obj. c., gov. by the prep. "on." |
| But | A disj. conj., jg. the sents. "I placed it...breast" and "it faded ...splendour." |
| it | A pers. pron., neu. gen., s. num., 3rd per., nom. c. to the v. "faded." |
| faded | A reg. intr. v., indic. m., past t., s. num., 3rd per., agr. with its nom. "it." |
| in | A prep., sh. the rn. bet. "faded" and "splendour." |
| **golden** | An adj. of quality, qual. the n. "splendour." |
| splendour | An abs. n., neu. gen., s. num., 3rd per., obj. c., gov. by the prep. "in." |
| And | A cop. conj., jg. the sents. "it faded...splendour" and "*it* died ...west." |
| died | A reg. intr. v., indic. m., past t., s. num., 3rd per., agr. with its nom. *it* und. |
| in | A prep., sh. the rn. bet. "died" and "west." |
| **crimson** | An adj. of quality, pos. deg., qual. the n. "west." |
| west. | A com. n., neu. gen., s. num., 3rd per., obj. c., gov. by the prep. "in." |
| 15. With | A prep., sh. the rn. bet. "woman" and "fingers." |
| fingers | A com. n., neu. gen., p. num., 3rd per., obj. c., gov. by the prep. "with." |
| **weary** | An adj. of quality, pos. deg., qual. the n. "fingers." |
| and | A cop. conj., jg. the sents. "With fingers weary a woman sat..." and "*with fingers* wan *a woman sat*..." |
| **wan** | An adj. of quality, pos. deg., qual. the n. *fingers* und. |
| With | A prep., sh. the rn. bet. *woman* und. and "eyelids." |
| eyelids | A com. n., neu. gen., p. num., 3rd per., obj. c., gov. by the prep. "with." |
| **heavy** | An adj. of quality, pos. deg., qual. the n. "eyelids." |
| and | A cop. conj., jg. the sents. "With eyelids heavy *a woman sat*..." and "*with eyelids* red *a woman sat*..." |
| **red** | An adj. of quality, pos. deg., qual. the n. *eyelids* und. |
| woman | A com. n., fem. gen., s. num., 3rd per., nom. c. to the v. "sat." |
| sat | An irreg. intr. v., indic. m., past t., s. num., 3rd per., agr. with its nom. "woman." |
| in | A prep., sh. the rn. bet. "sat" and "rags." |
| **unwomanly** | An adj. of quality, pos. deg., qual. the n. "rags." |
| rags | A com. n., neu. gen., p. num., 3rd per., obj. c., gov. by the prep. "in." |
| Plying | A pres. pl. from the tr. v. "to ply," ref. to "woman." |
| her | A pers. pron., fem. gen., s. num., 3rd per., poss. c., gov. by the n. "needle." |
| needle | A com. n., neu. gen., s. num., 3rd per., obj. c., gov. by the tr. pl. "plying." |

| | |
|---|---|
| and | A cop. conj., jg. the sents. "A woman sat..needle" and "*a woman sat..plying her* thread." |
| thread. | A com. n., neu. gen., s. num., 3rd per., obj. c., gov. by the tr. pl. *plying* und. ("Needle and thread" may also be considered as a compd. object. *Parsing*, p. 135, § 22.) |

## Exercise 131.

| | |
|---|---|
| . **grandest** | An adj. of quality, superl. deg., qual. the n. *amphitheatre* und. |
| and | A cop. conj., jg. the sents. "The grandest *amphitheatre of all the ancient amphitheatres is the Coliseum at Rome*" and "*the* most renowned *amphitheatre* of all..Rome." |
| most | An adv. of deg., mod. the adj. "renowned," indg. superl. deg. |
| **most renowned** } | An adj. of quality, superl. deg., qual. the n. *amphitheatre* und. |
| of | A prep., sh. the rn., bet. *amphitheatre* und. and "amphitheatres." |
| all | An indef. nu. adj. of quantity, qual. the n. "amphitheatres." |
| ancient | An adj. of quality, pos. deg., qual. the n. "amphitheatres." |
| amphitheatres | A com. n., neu. gen., p. num., 3rd per., obj. c., gov. by the prep. "of." |
| is | An irreg. intr. v., indic. m., pres. t., s. num., 3rd per., agr. with its nom. *amphitheatre* und. |
| Coliseum | A prop. n., neu. gen., s. num., 3rd per., nom. c. after the v. "is." |
| at | A prep., sh. the rn. bet. "Coliseum" and "Rome." |
| Rome. | A prop. n., neu. gen., s. num., 3rd per., obj. c., gov. by the prep. "of." |
| 2. merle | A com. n., mas. gen., s. num., 3rd per., nom. c. to the v. "may trill." |
| may | An aux. v. to "trill," indg. pot. m., pres. t. |
| (to) trill | A reg. tr. v., act. vo., infin. m., pres. t., gov. by the v. "may." |
| may trill | A reg. tr. v., act. vo., pot. m., pres. t., s. num., 3rd per., agr. with its nom. "merle." |
| his | A pers. pron., mas. gen., s. num., 3rd per., poss. c., gov. by the n. "note." |
| **richest** | An adj. of quality, superl. deg., qual. the n. "note." |
| note | An abs. n., neu. gen., s. num., 3rd per., obj. c., gov. by the tr. v. "may trill." |
| in | A prep., sh. the rn. bet. "may trill" and *manner* und. |
| vain | An adj. of quality, pos. deg., qual. the n. *manner* und. |
| *or*, in vain. | An adverbial phrase of manner, mod. the v. "may trill." |
| 3. Our | A pers. pron., com. gen., p. num., 1st per., poss. c., gov. by the n. "songs." |
| **sweetest** | An adj. of quality, superl. deg., qual. the n. "songs." |
| songs | An abs. n., neu. gen., p. num., 3rd per., nom. c. to the v. "are." |
| are | An irreg. intr. v., indic. m., pres. t., p. num., 3rd per., agr. with its nom. "songs." |
| those | A dis. adj., lim. the n. *songs* und. |
| that | A rel. pron., neu. gen., p. num., 3rd per., agr. with its ant. *songs* und., nom. c. to the v. "tell." |
| tell | An irreg. intr. v., indic. m., pres. t., p. num., 3rd per., agr. with its nom. "that." |
| of | A prep., sh. the rn. bet. "tell" and "thought." |
| **saddest** | An adj. of quality, superl. deg., qual. the n. "thought." |
| thought. | An abs. n., neu. gen., s num., 3rd per., obj. c., gov. by the prep. "of." |
| 4 It | A pers. pron., neu. gen., s. num., 3rd per., nom. c. to the v. "was." |
| was | An irreg. intr. v., indic. m., past t., s. num., 3rd per., agr. with its nom. "it." |
| **nimbler** | An adj. of quality, comp. deg., qual. the pron. "it." |
| much | An adv. of deg., mod. the adj. "nimbler." |
| than | A disj. conj., jg. the sents. "It was nimbler much" and "hinds *are nimble.*" |
| hinds. | A com. n., fem. gen., p. num., 3rd per., nom. c. to the v. *are* und. |
| 5. **darkest** | An adj. of quality, superl. deg., qual. the n. "hour." |
| hour | An abs. n., neu. gen., s. num., 3rd per., nom. c. to the v. "is." |

| | |
|---|---|
| in | A prep., sh. the rn. bet. "hour" and *hours* und. |
| twenty-four | A compd. def. card. nu. adj. of quantity, qual. the n. *hours* und. |
| is | An irreg. intr. v., indic. m., pres. t., s. num., 3rd per., agr. with its nom. "hour." |
| hour | An abs. n., neu. gen., s. num., 3rd per., nom. c. after the v. "is." |
| before | A prep., sh. the rn. bet. "hour" and "day." |
| day. | An abs. n., neu. gen., s. num., 3rd per., obj. c., gov. by the prep. "before." |
| 6. Those | A dis. adj., lim. the n. *persons* und. |
| who | A rel. pron., com. gen., p. num., 3rd per., agr. with its ant. *persons* und., nom. c. to the v. "have observed." |
| have | An aux. v. to "observed," indg. perf. t. |
| never | An adv. of time, mod. the v. "have observed." |
| observed | A past pl. from the tr. v. "to observe," ref. to "coasts." |
| have observed | A reg. tr. v., act. v., indic. m., perf. t., p. num., 3rd per., agr. with its nom. "who." |
| our | A pers. pron., com. gen., p. num., 1st per., poss. c., gov. by the n. "coasts." |
| **boldest** | An adj. of quality, superl. deg., qual. the n. "coasts." |
| coasts | A com. n., neu. gen., p. num., 3rd per., obj. c., gov. by the tr. v. "have observed." |
| have | An irreg. tr. v., act. vo., indic. m., pres. t., p. num., 3rd per., agr. with its nom. *persons* und. |
| no | A def. card. nu. adj. of quantity, qual. the n. "idea." |
| idea | An abs. n., neu. gen., s. num., 3rd per., obj. c., gov. by the tr. v. "have." |
| of | A prep., sh. the rn. bet. "idea" and "sublimity." |
| their | A pers. pron., neu. gen., p. num., 3rd por., poss. c., gov. by the n. "sublimity." |
| tremendous | An adj. of quality, pos. deg., qual. the n. "sublimity." |
| sublimity. | An abs. n., neu. gen., s. num., 3rd per., obj. c., gov. by the prep. "of." |
| 7. circle | A com. n., neu. gen., s. num., 3rd per., nom. c. to the v. "is." |
| is | An irreg. intr. v., indic. m., pres. t., s. num., 3rd per., agr. with its nom. "circle." |
| more | An adv. of deg., mod. the adj. "beautiful," indg. comp. deg. |
| **more beautiful** | An adj. of quality, comp. deg., qual. the n. "circle." |
| than | A disj. conj., jg. the sents. "A circle is more beautiful" and "a square *is beautiful*." |
| square | A com. n., neu. gen., s. num., 3rd per., nom. c. to the v. *is* und. |
| square | A com. n., neu. gen., s. num., 3rd per., nom. c. to the v. "is." |
| is | An irreg. intr. v., indic. m., pres. t., s. num., 3rd per., agr. with its nom. "square." |
| more | An adv. of deg., mod. the adj. "beautiful," indg. comp. deg. |
| **more beautiful** | An adj. of quality, comp. deg., qual. the n. "square." |
| than | A disj. conj., jg. the sents. "a square is more beautiful" and "a parallelogram *is beautiful*." |
| parallelogram. | A com. n., neu. gen., s. num., 3rd per., nom. c. to the v. *is* und. |
| 8. Iceland | A prop. n., neu. gen., s. num., 3rd per., nom. c. to the v. "is." |
| is | An irreg. intr. v., indic. m., pres. t., s. num., 3rd per., agr. with its nom. "Iceland." |
| island | A com. n., neu. gen., s. num., 3rd per., nom. c. after the v. "is." |
| somewhat | An adv. of deg., mod. the adj. "larger." (*Parsing*, p. 177.) |
| **larger** | An adj. of quality, comp. deg., qual. the n. "island." |
| than | A disj. conj., jg. the sents. "Iceland is..larger" and "Ireland *is large*." |
| Ireland. | A prop. n., neu. gen., s. num., 3rd per., nom. c. to the v. *is* und. |
| 9. adventure | An abs. n., neu. gen., s. num., 3rd per., nom. c. to the v. "was." |
| was | An irreg. intr. v., indic. m., past t., s. num., 3rd per., agr. with its nom. "adventure." |
| most | An adv. of deg., mod. the adj. "perilous," indg. superl. deg. |
| **most perilous.** | An adj. of quality, superl. deg., qual. the n. "adventure." |
| 10. **sadder** | An adj. of qual., comp. deg., qual. the n. *man* und. |

| | |
|---|---|
| and | A cop. conj., jg. the sents. "He rose the morrow morn a sadder man" and "*he rose the morrow morn* a wiser man." |
| **wiser** | An adj. of quality, comp. deg., qual. the n. "man." |
| man | A com. n., mas. gen., s. num., 3rd per., nom. c. after the v. "rose." (*Parsing*, p. 65.) |
| He | A pers. pron., mas. gen., s. num., 3rd per., nom. c. to the v. "rose." |
| rose | An irreg. intr. v., indic. m., past t., s. num., 3rd per., agr. with its nom. "he." |
| morrow | An abs. n. used as an adj. of quality, qual. the n. "morn." |
| morn. | An abs. n., neu. gen., s. num., 3rd per., obj. c., gov. by the prep. *on* und., (or, obj. c. of time after the v. "rose"). |

### Exercise 132.

| | |
|---|---|
| 1. My | A pers. pron., com. gen., s. num., 1st per., poss. c., gov. by the n. "effort." |
| **whole** | An adj. of quantity (bulk or mass), qual. the n. "effort." |
| effort | An abs. n., neu. gen., s. num., 3rd per., nom. c. to the v. "was." |
| was | An irreg. intr. v., indic. m., past t., s. num., 3rd per., agr. with its nom. "effort." |
| to | A particle, indg. infin. m. |
| to save | A reg. tr. v., act. vo., infin. m., pres. t. ; used as an abs. n., neu. gen., s. num., 3rd per., nom. c. after the v. "was." |
| life. | An abs. n., neu. gen., s. num., 3rd per., obj. c., gov. by the tr. v. "to save." |
| 2. We | A pers. pron., mas. gen., p. num., 1st per., nom. c. to the v. "landed." |
| landed | A reg. tr. v., act. vo., indic. m., past t., p. num., 1st per., agr. with its nom. "we." |
| **some** | An adj. of quantity (bulk or mass), qual. the n. "hundred." |
| hundred | A com. n., neu. gen., s. num., 3rd per., obj. c., gov. by the tr. v. "landed." |
| men | A com. n., mas. gen., p. num., 3rd per., obj. c., gov. by the prep. *of* und. |
| where | A cop. conj., jg. the sents. "We landed..men" and "we found..water." |
| we | A pers. pron., mas. gen., p. num., 1st per., nom. c. to the v. "found." |
| found | A reg. tr. v., act. vo., indic. m., past t., p. num., 1st per., agr. with its nom. "we." |
| fresh | An adj. of quality, pos. deg., qual. the n. "water." |
| water. | A com. n., neu. gen., s. num., 3rd per., obj. c., gov. by the tr. v. "found." |
| 3. I | A pers. pron., com. gen., s. num., 1st per., nom. c. to the v. "have." |
| have | An irreg. tr. v., act. vo., indic. m., pres. t., s. num., 1st per., agr. with its nom. "I." |
| **no** | An adj. of quantity (bulk or mass), qual. the n. "sympathy." |
| sympathy | An abs. n., neu. gen., s. num., 3rd per., obj. c., gov. by the tr. v. "have." |
| with | A prep., sh. the rn. bet. "sympathy" and "them." |
| them. | A pers. pron., com. gen., p. num., 3rd per., obj. c., gov. by the prep. "with." |
| 4. Who | An interrog. pron., com. gen., s. num., 3rd per., nom. c. to the v. "will show." |
| will | An aux. v. to "show." indg. fut. t. |
| (to) show | An irreg. tr. v., act. vo., infin. m., pres. t., gov. by the v. "will." |
| will show | An irreg. tr. v., act. vo., indic. m., fut. t., s. num., 3rd per., agr. with its nom. "who." |
| us | A pers. pron., com. gen., p. num., 1st per., obj. c., gov. by the prep. *to* und. |
| **any** | An adj. of quantity (bulk or mass), qual. the n. "good." |
| good. | An abs. n., neu. gen., s. num., 3rd per., obj. c., gov. by the tr. v. "will show." |
| 5. Yet | An adv. of time, mod. the v. "show." |
| show | An irreg. tr. v., act. vo., imper. m., pres. t., s. num., 2nd per., agr. with its nom. *thou* und. |

ENGLISH GRAMMAR AND ANALYSIS. 107

| | |
|---|---|
| some | An adj. of quantity (bulk or mass), qual. the n. "pity." |
| pity. | An abs. n., neu. gen., s. num., 3rd per., obj. c., gov. by the tr. v. "show." |
| 6. In | A prep., sh. the rn. bet. "can promise" and "narrative." |
| **whole** | An adj. of quantity (bulk or mass), qual. the n. "narrative." |
| narrative | A com. n., neu. gen., s. num., 3rd per., obj. c., gov. by the prep. "in." |
| I | A pers. pron., com. gen., s. num., 1st per., nom. c. to the v. "can promise." |
| can | An aux. v. to "promise," indg. pot. m., pres. t. |
| scarcely | An adv. of deg., mod. the v. "can promise." |
| (to) promise | A reg. tr. v., act. vo., infin. m., pres. t., gov. by the v. "can." |
| can promise | A reg. tr. v., act. vo., pot. m., pres. t., s. num., 1st per., agr. with its nom. "I." |
| you | A pers. pron., com. gen., p. num., or s. num., p. form, 2nd per., obj. c., gov. by the prep. *to* und. |
| one | A def. card. nu. adj. of quantity, qual. the n. "adventure." |
| adventure. | An abs. n., neu. gen., s. num., 3rd per., obj. c., gov. by the tr. v. "can promise." |
| 7. We | A pers. pron., com. gen., p. num., 1st per., nom. c. to the v. "have." |
| have | An irreg. tr. v., act. vo., indic. m., pres. t., p. num., 1st per., agr. with its nom. "we." |
| space | A com. n., neu. gen., s. num., 3rd per., obj. c., gov. by the tr. v. "have." |
| **enough** | An adj. of quantity (bulk or mass), qual. the n. "space." |
| for | A prep., sh. the rn. bet. "enough" and "purpose." |
| our | A pers. pron., com. gen., p. num., 1st per., poss. c., gov. by the n. "purpose." |
| purpose. | An abs. n., neu. gen., s. num., 3rd per., obj. c., gov. by the prep. "for." |
| 8. He | A pers. pron., mas. gen., s. num., 3rd per., nom. c. to the v. "has." |
| has | An irreg. tr. v., act. vo., indic. m., pres. t., s. num., 3rd per., agr. with its nom. "he." |
| **much** | An adj. of quantity (bulk or mass), qual. the n. "confidence." |
| confidence | An abs. n., neu. gen., s. num., 3rd per., obj. c., gov. by the tr. v. "has." |
| but | A disj. conj., jg. the sents. "He has much confidence" and "he has little *ability*." |
| **little** | An adj. of quantity (bulk or mass), qual. the n. *ability* und. |
| or | A disj. conj., jg. the sents. "he has little *ability*" and "he has no ability." |
| **no** | An adj. of quantity (bulk or mass), qual. the n. "ability." |
| ability. | An abs. n., neu. gen., s. num., 3rd per., obj. c., gov. by the tr. v. *has* und. |
| 9. Here | An adv. of place, mod. the v. "find." |
| we | A pers. pron., com. gen., p. num., 1st per., nom. c. to the v. "find." |
| fi | An irreg. tr. v., act. vo., indic. m., pres. t., p. num., 1st per., agr. with its nom. "we." |
| **little** | An adj. of quantity (bulk or mass), qual. the n. "clay." |
| clay. | A com. n., neu. gen., s. num., 3rd per., obj. c., gov. by the tr. v. "find." |
| 10. We | A pers. pron., com. gen., p. num., 1st per., nom. c. to the v. "have toiled." |
| have | An aux. v. to "toiled," indg. perf. t. |
| toiled | A past pl. from the intr. v. "to toil," ref. to "we." |
| have toiled | A reg. intr. v., indic. m., perf. t., p. num., 1st per., agr. with its nom. "we." |
| **all** | An adj. of quantity (bulk or mass), qual. the n. "night." |
| night. | An abs. n., neu. gen., s. num., 3rd per., obj. c., gov. by the prep. *during* und. |

### Exercise 133.

| | |
|---|---|
| 1. **No** | A def. card. nu. adj. of quantity, qual. the n. "word." |
| word | An abs. n., neu. gen., s. num., 3rd per., obj. c., gov. by the tr. v. "spoke." |

| | |
|---|---|
| spoke | An irreg. tr. v., act. vo., indic. m., past t., s. num., 3rd per., agr. with its nom. "deliverer." |
| deliverer. | A com. n., com. gen., s. num., 3rd per., nom. c. to the v. "spoke." |
| 2. I | A pers. pron., com. gen., s. num., 1st per., nom. c. to the v. "have seen." |
| have | An aux. v. to "seen," indg. perf. t. |
| not | An adv. of m. (neg.), mod. the v. "have seen." |
| seen | A past pl. from the tr. v. "to see," ref. to "him." |
| have seen | An irreg. tr. v., act. vo., indic. m., perf. t., s. num., 1st per., agr. with its nom. "I." |
| him | A pers. pron., mas. gen., s. num., 3rd per., obj. c., gov. by the tr. v. "have seen." |
| for | A prep., sh. the rn. bet. "have seen" and "days." |
| ten | A def. card. nu. adj. of quantity, qual. the n. "days." |
| days. | An abs. n., neu. gen., p. num., 3rd per., obj. c., gov. by the prep. "for." |
| 3. Four | A def. card. nu. adj. of quantity, qual. the n. "armies." |
| armies | A com. col. n., neu. gen., p. num., 3rd per., nom. c. to the v. "were led." |
| to | A prep., sh. the rn. bet. "were led" and "field." |
| field | A com. n., neu. gen., s. num., 3rd per., obj. c., gov. by the prep. "to." |
| were | An aux. v. to "led," indg. pass. vo., past t. |
| led | A past pl. from the tr. v. "to lead," ref. to "armies." |
| were led. | An irreg. tr. v., pass. vo., indic. m., past t., p. num., 3rd per., agr. with its nom. "armies." |
| 4. When | A cop. conj., jg. the scnts. "some twenty oars flashed..pursuit" and "it dashed..stream." |
| it | A pers. pron., neu. gen., s. num., 3rd per., nom. c. to the v. "dashed." |
| dashed | A reg. intr. v., indic. m., past t., s. num., 3rd per., agr. with its nom. "it." |
| madly | An adv. of man., mod. the v. "dashed." |
| across | A prep., sh. the rn. bet. "dashed" and "stream." |
| stream | A com. n., neu., gen., s. num., 3rd per., obj. c., gov. by the prep. "across." |
| some | An indef. nu. adj. of quantity, qual. "twenty oars," (or, adv of man., mod. the adj. "twenty." *Parsing*, p. 119). |
| twenty | A def. card. nu. adj. of quantity, qual. the n. "oars." |
| oars | A com. n., neu. gen., p. num., 3rd per., nom. c. to the v. "flashed." |
| flashed | A reg. intr. v., indic. m., past t., p. num., 3rd per., agr. with its nom. "oars." |
| through | A prep., sh. the rn. bet. "flashed" and "water." |
| water | A com. n., neu. gen., s. num., 3rd per., obj. c., gov. by the prep. "through." |
| in | A prep., sh. the rn. bet. "flashed" and "pursuit." |
| pursuit. | An abs. n., neu. gen., s. num., 3rd per., obj. c., gov. by the prep. "in." |
| 5. Ten | A def. card. nu. adj. of quantity, qual. the n. "thousand." |
| thousand | A com. col. n., neu. gen., p. num., 3rd per., nom. c. to the v. "sweep." |
| fleets | A com. n., neu. gen., p. num., 3rd per., obj. c., gov. by the prep. *of* und. |
| sweep | An irreg. intr. v., indic. m., pres. t., p. num., 3rd per., agr. with its nom. "thousand." |
| over | A prep., sh. the rn. bet. "sweep" and "thee." |
| thee | A pers. pron., neu. gen., s. num., 2nd per., obj. c., gov. by the prep. "over." ("Thee," i.e., son.) |
| in | A prep., sh. the rn. bet. "sweep" and *manner* und. |
| vain | An adj. of quality, pos. deg., qual. the n. *manner* und. |
| in vain. | An adverbial phrase of man., mod. the v. "sweep." |
| 6. At | A prep., sh. the rn. bet. "was discharged" and "expiration." |
| expiration | An abs. n., neu. gen., s. num., 3rd per., obj. c., gov. by the prep. "at." |
| of | A prep., sh. the rn. bet. "expiration" and "days." |
| sixty | A def. card. nu. adj. of quantity, qual. the n. "days." |

ENGLISH GRAMMAR AND ANALYSIS.   109

| | |
|---|---|
| days | An abs. n., neu. gen., p. num., 3rd per., obj. c., gov. by the prep. "of." |
| debt | A com. n., neu. gen., s. num., 3rd per., nom. c. to the v. "was discharged." |
| was | An aux. v. to "discharged," indg. pass. vo., past t. |
| discharged | A past pl. from the tr. v. "to discharge,"ref. to "debt." |
| was discharged | A reg. tr. v., pass. vo., indic. m., past t., s. num., 3rd per., agr. with its nom. "debt." |
| by | A prep., sh. the rn. bet. "was discharged" and "loss." |
| loss | An abs. n., neu. gen., s. num., 3rd per., obj. c., gov. by the prep. "by." |
| of | A prep., sh. the rn. bet. "loss" and "liberty." |
| liberty | An abs. n., neu. gen., s. num., 3rd per., obj. c., gov. by the prep. "of." |
| or | A disj. conj., jg. the sents. "At the expiration..liberty" and "*at the expiration of sixty days the debt was discharged by the loss of* life." |
| life. | An abs. n., neu. gen., s. num., 3rd per., obj. c., gov. by the prep. *of* und. |
| 7. By | A prep., sh. the rn. bet. "hurry" and "hills." |
| **thirty** | A def. card. nu. adj. of quantity, qual. the n. "hills." |
| hills | A com. n., neu. gen., p. num., 3rd per., obj. c., gov. by the prep. "by." |
| I | A pers. pron., mas. gen. by personification, s. num., 1st per., nom. c. to the v. "hurry." ("I," *i.e.*, brook.) |
| hurry | A reg. intr. v., indic. m., pres. t., s. num., 1st per., agr. with its nom. "I." |
| down | An adv. of place, mod. the v. "hurry." |
| or | A disj. conj., jg. the sents. "By thirty hills I hurry down" and "*I slip between the ridges.*" |
| slip | A reg. intr. v., indic. m., pres. t., s. num., 1st per., agr. with its nom. *I* und. |
| between | A prep., sh. the rn. bet. "slip" and "ridges." |
| ridges. | A com. n., neu. gen., p. num., 3rd per., obj. c., gov. by the prep. "between." |
| 8. Greeks | A prop. n., com. gen., p. num., 3rd per., nom. c. to the v. "beheld." |
| beheld | An irreg. tr. v., act. vo., indic. m., past t., p. num., 3rd per., agr. with its nom. "Greeks." |
| with | A prep., sh. the rn. bet. "beheld" and "surprise." |
| surprise | An abs. n., neu. gen., s. num., 3rd per., obj. c., gov. by the prep. "with" |
| **two** | A def. card. nu. adj. of quantity, qual. the n. "sisters." |
| royal | An adj. of quality, qual. the n. "sisters." |
| sisters | A com n., fem. gen., p. num., 3rd per., obj. c., gov. by the tr. v. "beheld." |
| seated | A past pl. from the tr. v. "to seat," ref. to "sisters." |
| on | A prep., sh. the rn. bet. "seated" and "throne." |
| same | A dis. adj., lim. the n. "throne." |
| throne. | A com. n., neu. gen., s. num., 3rd per., obj. c., gov. by the prep. "on." |
| 9. He | A pers. pron., mas. gen., s. num., 3rd per., nom. c. to the v. "left." |
| left | An irreg. tr. v., act. vo., indic. m., past t., s. num., 3rd per., agr. with its nom. "he." |
| **eight** | A def. card. nu. adj. of quantity, qual. the n. "children." |
| children. | A com. n., com. gen., 3rd per., obj. c., gov. by the tr. v. "left." |
| 10. **Seven** | A def. card. nu. adj. of quantity, qual. the n. "days." |
| days | An abs. n., neu. gen., p. num., 3rd per., obj. c., gov. by the prep. *for* or *during* und. |
| **seven** | A def. card. nu. adj. of quantity, qual. the n. "nights." |
| nights | An abs. n., neu. gen., p. num., 3rd per., obj. c., gov. by the prep. *for* or *during* und. |
| I | A pers. pron., mas. gen., s. num., 1st per., nom. c. to the v. "saw." ("I," *i.e.*, the ancient mariner.) |
| saw | An irreg. tr. v., act. vo., indic. m., past t., s. num., 1st per., agr. with its nom. "I." |

| | |
|---|---|
| that | A dis. adj., lim. the n. "curse." |
| curse | An abs. n., neu. gen., s. num., 3rd per., obj. c., gov. by the tr. v. "saw." |
| And | A cop. conj., jg. the sents. "**Seven nights** I saw that curse" and "yet I could not die." |
| yet | An adv. of time, mod. the v. "could die." |
| I | A pers. pron., mas. gen., s. num., 1st per., nom. c. to the v. "could die." |
| could | An aux. v. to "die," indg. pot. m., past t. |
| not | An adv. of m. (neg.), mod. the v. "could die." |
| (to) die | A reg. intr. v., infin. m., pres. t., gov. by the v. "could." |
| could die. | A reg. intr. v., pot. m., past t., s. num., 1st per., agr. with its nom. "I." |

## Exercise 134.

| | |
|---|---|
| 1. **second** | A def. ord. nu. adj. of quantity, qual. the n. "crusade" incl. in "crusades." |
| and | A cop. conj., jg. the sents. "The second crusade *trod...first*" and "the third crusade trod...first." |
| **third** | A def. ord. nu. adj. of quantity, qual. the n. "crusade," incl. in "crusades." |
| crusades | An abs. n., neu. gen., p. num., 3rd per., nom. c. to the v. "trod." |
| trod | An irreg. intr. v., indic. m., past t., p. num., 3rd per., agr. with its nom. "crusades." |
| in | A prep., sh. the rn. bet. "trod" and "footsteps." |
| footsteps | A com. n., neu. gen., p. num., 3rd per., obj. c., gov. by the prep. "in." |
| of | A prep., sh. the rn. bet. "footsteps" and *crusade* und. |
| **first.** | A def. ord. nu. adj. of quantity, qual. the n. *crusade* und. |
| 2. solemn | An adj. of quality, pos. deg., qual. the n. "day," |
| day | An abs. n., neu. gen., s. num., 3rd per., nom. c., to the v. "had been fixed." |
| **twenty-fifth** | A def. ord. nu. adj. of quantity, qual. the n. *day* und. |
| of | A prep., sh. the rn. bet. *day* und. and "December." |
| December | A prop. n., neu. gen., s. num., 3rd per., obj. c., gov. by the prep. "of." |
| had | An aux. v. to "been fixed," indg. pluperf. t. |
| been | A past pl. from the intr. v. "to be," ref. to "fixed day," and aux. to "fixed," indg. pass. vo. |
| fixed | A past pl. from the tr. v. "to fix," ref. to "day." |
| had been fixed | A reg. tr. v., pass. vo., indic. m., pluperf. t., s. num., 3rd per., agr. with its nom. "day." |
| for | A prep., sh. the rn. bet. "had been fixed" and "execution." |
| his | A pers. pron., mas. gen., s. num., 3rd per., poss. c., gov. by the n. "execution." |
| execution. | An abs. n., neu. gen., s. num., 3rd per., obj. c., gov. by the prep. "for." |
| 3. sixty | A def. card. nu. adj. of quantity, qual. the n. "books." |
| books | A com. n., neu. gen., p. num., 3rd per., nom. c. to the v. "were formed" |
| of | A prep., sh. the rn. bet. "books" and "Basilics." |
| Basilics | A prop. n., neu. gen., p. num., 3rd per., obj. c., gov. by the prep. "of." |
| code | A com. n., neu. gen., s. num., 3rd per., nom. c., in app. with "books." |
| and | A cop. conj., jg. the sents. "The sixty books of the Basilics, the code *of civil jurisprudence*, were gradually formed...dynasty" and "*the sixty books of the Basilics*, the pandects of civil jurisprudence, *were gradually formed...dynasty.*" |
| pandects | A com. n., neu. gen., p. num., 3rd per., nom. c., in app. with *books* und. |
| of | A prep., sh. the rn. bet. "pandects" and "jurisprudence." |
| civil | An adj. of quality, qual. the n. "jurisprudence." |
| jurisprudence | An abs. n., neu. gen., s. num., 3rd per., obj. c., gov. by the prep. "of." |
| were | An aux. v. to "formed," indg. pass. vo., past t. |
| gradually | An adv. of man., mod. the v. "were formed." |

ENGLISH GRAMMAR AND ANALYSIS.   111

| | |
|---|---|
| formed | A past pl. from the tr. v. "to form," ref. to "books." |
| were formed | A reg. tr. v., pass. vo., indic. m., past t., p. num., 3rd per., agr. with its nom. "books." |
| in | A prep., sh. the rn. bet. "were formed" and "reigns." |
| three | A def. card. nu. adj. of quantity, qual. "first reigns." |
| **first** | A def. ord. nu. adj. of quantity, qual. the n. "reigns." |
| reigns | An abs. n., neu. gen., p. num., 3rd per., obj. c., gov. by the prep. "in." |
| of | A prep., sh. the rn. bet. "reigns" and "dynasty." |
| that | A dis. adj., lim. the n. "dynasty." |
| prosperous | An adj. of quality, pos. deg., qual. the n. "dynasty." |
| dynasty. | An abs. n., neu. gen., s. num., 3rd per., obj. c., gov. by the prep. "of." |
| 4. Clement | A prop. n., mas. gen., s. num., 3rd per., nom. c. to the v. "was consecrated." |
| **Third** | A def. ord. nu. adj. of quantity, qual. the n. "Clement." |
| was | An aux. v. to "consecrated," indg. pass. vo., past t. |
| consecrated | A past pl. from the tr. v. "to consecrate," ref. to "Clement." |
| was consecrated | A reg. tr. v., pass. vo., indic. m., past t., s. num., 3rd per., agr. with its nom. "Clement." |
| in | A prep., sh. the rn. bet. "was consecrated" and "Lateran." |
| Lateran. | A prop. n., neu. gen., s. num., 3rd per., obj. c., gov. by the prep. "in." |
| 5. In | A prep., sh. the rn. bet. "was intercepted" and "return." |
| his | A pers. pron., mas. gen., s. num., 3rd per., poss. c., gov. by the n. "return." |
| return | An abs. n., neu. gen., s. num., 3rd per., obj. c., gov. by the prep. "in." |
| by | A prep., sh. the rn. bet. "return" and "sea." |
| sea | A com. n., neu. gen., s. num., 3rd per., obj. c., gov. by the prep. "by." |
| from | A prep., sh. the rn. bet. "return" and "crusade." |
| unfortunate | An adj. of quality, pos. deg., qual. the n. "crusade." |
| crusade | An abs. n., neu. gen., s. num., 3rd per., obj. c., gov. by the prep. "from." |
| Louis | A prop. n., mas. gen., s. num., 3rd per., nom. c. to the v. "was intercepted." |
| **Seventh** | A def. ord. nu. adj. of quantity, qual. the n. "Louis." |
| was | An aux. v. to "intercepted," indg. pass. vo., past t. |
| intercepted | A past pl. from the tr. v. "to intercept," ref. to "Louis." |
| was intercepted | A reg. tr. v., pass. vo., indic. m., past t., s. num., 3rd per., agr. with its nom. "Louis." |
| by | A prep., sh. the rn. bet. "was intercepted" and "Greeks." |
| Greeks. | A prop. n., mas. gen., p. num., 3rd per., obj. c., gov. by the prep. "by." |
| 6. Refer | A reg. intr. v., imper. m., pres. t., s. num., 2nd per., agr. with its nom. *thou* und. |
| to | A prep., sh. the rn. bet. "refer" and "page." |
| **eighth** | A def. ord. nu. adj. of quantity, qual. the n. "page." |
| page. | A com. n., neu. gen., s. num., 3rd per., obj. c., gov. by the prep. "to." |
| 7. This | A dis. adj., lim. the n. "event." |
| event | An abs. n., neu. gen., s. num., 3rd per., nom. c. to the v. "may be ascribed." |
| may | An aux. v. to "be ascribed," indg. pot. m., pres. t. |
| be | An aux. v. to "ascribed," indg. pass. vo. |
| ascribed | A past pl. from the tr. v. "to ascribe," ref. to "event." |
| may be ascribed | A reg. tr. v., pass. vo., pot. m., pres. t., s. num., 3rd per., agr. with its nom. "event." |
| to | A prep., sh. the rn. bet. "may be ascribed" and "century." |
| **tenth** | A def. ord. nu. adj. of quantity, qual. the n. "century." |
| century | An abs. n., neu. gen., s. num., 3rd per., obj. c., gov. by the prep. "to." |
| of | A prep., sh. the rn. bet. "century" and "era." |
| Christian | A prop. adj. of quality, qual. the n. "era." |
| era. | An abs. n., neu. gen., s. num., 3rd per., obj. c., gov. by the prep. "of." |
| 8. prudent | An adj. of quality, pos. deg., qual. the n. "Urban." |

| | |
|---|---|
| Urban | A prop. n., mas. gen., s. num., 3rd per., nom. c. to the v. "adjourned." |
| adjourned | A reg. tr. v., act. vo., indic. m., past t., s. num., 3rd per., agr. with its nom. "Urban." |
| decision | An abs. n., neu. gen., s. num., 3rd per., obj. c., gov. by the tr. v. "adjourned." |
| to | A prep., sh. the rn. bet. "adjourned" and "synod." |
| second | A def. ord. nu. adj. of quantity, qual. the n. "synod." |
| synod. | A com. col. n., neu. gen., s. num., 3rd per., obj. c., gov. by the prep. "to." |
| Philip | A prop. n., mas. gen., s. num., 3rd per., nom. c. to the v. "was." |
| First | A def. ord. nu. adj. of quantity, qual. the n. "Philip." |
| was | An irreg. intr. v., indic. m., past t., s. num., 3rd per., agr. with its nom. "Philip." |
| great | An adj. of quality, pos. deg., qual. the n. "grandson." |
| grandson | A com. n., mas. gen., s. num., 3rd per., nom. c. after the v. "was." |
| of | A prep., sh. the rn. bet. "grandson" and "Hugh Capet." |
| Hugh | A prop. n., mas. gen., s. num., 3rd per., obj. c., gov. by the prep. "of." |
| Capet | A prop. n., mas. gen., s. num., 3rd per., obj. c., in app. with "Hugh." |
| Hugh Capet. | A compd. prop. n., mas. gen., s. num., 3rd per., obj. c., gov. by the prep. "of." |
| 10. Jews | A prop. n., com. gen., p. num., 3rd per., nom. c. to the v. "observe." |
| observe | A reg. tr. v., act. vo., indic. m., pres. t., p. num., 3rd per., agr. with its nom. "Jews." |
| seventh | A def. ord. nu. adj. of quantity, qual. the n. "day." |
| day | An abs. n., neu. gen., s. num., 3rd per., obj. c., gov. by the tr. v. "observe." |
| of | A prep., sh. the rn. bet. "day" and "week." |
| week. | An abs. n., neu. gen., s. num., 3rd per., obj. c., gov. by the prep. "of." |

## Exercise 135.

| | |
|---|---|
| 1. Thou | A pers. pron., mas. gen., s. num., 2nd per., nom. c. to the v. "shalt be." |
| shalt | An aux. v. to "be," indg. fut. t., emph. form, expressing "promise." |
| (to) be | An irreg. intr. v., infin. m., pres. t., gov. by the v. "shalt." |
| shalt be | An irreg. intr. v., indic. m., fut. t., emph. form, s. num., 2nd per., agr. with its nom. "thou." |
| father | A com. n., mas. gen., s. num., 2nd per., nom. c. after the v. "shalt be." |
| of | A prep., sh. the rn. bet. "father" and "nations." |
| many | An indef. nu. adj. of quantity, qual. the n. "nations." |
| nations. | A com. col. n., neu. gen., p. num., 3rd per., obj. c., gov. by the prep. "of." |
| 2. Other | An indef. nu. adj. of quantity, qual. the n. "lords." |
| lords | A com. n., mas. gen., p. num., 3rd per., nom. c. to the v. "have had." |
| besides | A prep., sh. the rn. bet. "lords" and "thee." |
| thee | A pers. pron., mas. gen., s. num., 2nd per., obj. c., gov. by the prep. "besides." |
| have | An aux. v. to "had," indg. perf. t. |
| had | A past pl. from the tr. v. "to have," ref. to "dominion." |
| have had | An irreg. tr. v., act. vo., indic. m., past t., p. num., 3rd per., agr. with its nom. "lords." |
| dominion | An abs. n., neu. gen., s. num., 3rd per., obj. c., gov. by the tr. v. "have had." |
| over | A prep., sh. the rn. bet. "have had" and "us." |
| us. | A pers. pron., com. gen., p. num., 1st per., obj. c., gov. by the prep. "over." |
| 3. Thou | A pers. pron., com. gen., s. num., 2nd per., nom. c. to the v. "shalt sow." |

| | |
|---|---|
| shalt | An aux. v. to "sow," indg. fut. t., emph. form, expressing "command." |
| not | An adv. of m. (neg.), mod. the v. "shalt sow." |
| (to) sow | A reg. tr. v., act. vo., infin. m., pres. t., gov. by the v. "shalt." |
| shalt sow | A reg. tr. v., act. vo., indic. m., fut. t., emph. form, s. num., 2nd per., agr. with its nom. "thou." |
| thy | A pers. pron., com. gen., s. num., 2nd per., poss. c., gov. by the n. "fields." |
| fields | A com. n., neu. gen., p. num., 3rd per., obj. c., gov. by the tr. v. "shalt sow." |
| with | A prep., sh. the rn. bet. "shalt sow" and "seeds." |
| **divers** | An indef. nu. adj. of quantity, qual. the n. "seeds." |
| seeds. | A com. n., neu. gen., p. num., 3rd per., obj. c., gov. by the prep. "with." |
| 4. Let | An irreg. tr. v., act. vo., imper. m., pres. t., s. num., 2nd per., agr. with its nom. *thou* und. |
| me | A pers. pron., mas. gen., s. num., 1st per., obj. c., gov. by the tr. v. "let." ("Me," *i.e.*, Esau.) |
| (to) leave | An irreg. tr. v., act. vo., infin. m., pres. t., gov. by the v. "let." |
| **some** | An indef. nu. adj. of quantity, qual. the n. *folk* und. |
| of | A prep., sh. the rn. bet. *folk* und. and "folk." |
| folk | A com. n., mas. gen., p. num., 3rd per., obj. c., gov. by the prep. "of." ("Folk," *i.e.*, Esau's men.) |
| that | A rel. pron., mas. gen., p. num., 3rd per., agr. with its ant. "folk," nom. c. to the v. "are." |
| are | An irreg. intr. v., indic. m., pres. t., p. num., 3rd per., agr. with its nom. "that." |
| with | A prep., sh. the rn. bet. "are" and "me." |
| me. | A pers. pron., mas. gen., s. num., 1st per., obj. c., gov. by the prep. "with." |
| 5. **Several** | An indef. nu. adj. of quantity, qual. the n. *persons* und. |
| of | A prep., sh. the rn. bet. *persons* und. and "them." |
| them | A pers. pron., com. gen., p. num., 3rd per., obj. c., gov. by the prep. "of." |
| neither | A disj. conj., introducing the sent. "Several of them rose... family." |
| rose | An irreg. intr. v., indic. m., past t., p. num., 3rd per., agr. with its nom. *persons* und. |
| from | A prep., sh. the rn. bet. "rose" and "family." |
| **any** | An indef. nu. adj. of quantity, qual. the n. "family." |
| conspicuous | An adj. of quality, pos. deg., qual. the n. "family." |
| family | A com. col. n., neu. gen., s. num., 3rd per., obj. c., gov. by the prep. "from." |
| nor | A disj. conj., cor. to "neither," jg. the sents. "Several...family" and "*several persons of them* left...them." |
| left | An irreg. tr. v., indic. m., past t., p. num., 3rd per., agr. with its nom. *persons* und. |
| **any** | An indef. nu. adj. of quantity, qual. the n. *family* und. |
| behind | A prep., sh. the rn. bet. "left" and "them." |
| them. | A pers. pron., com. gen., p. num., 3rd per., obj. c., gov. by the prep. "behind." |
| 6. This | A dis. adj., lim. the n. "country." |
| country | A com. n., neu. gen., s. num., 3rd per., nom. c. to the v. "is." |
| is | An irreg. intr. v., indic. m., pres. t., s. num., 3rd per., agr. with its nom. "country." |
| large | An adj. of quality, pos. deg., qual. the n. "country." |
| having | A pres. pl. from the tr. v. "to have," ref. to "country." |
| in | A prep., sh. the rn. bet. "having" and "it." |
| it | A pers. pron., neu. gen., s. num., 3rd per., obj. c., gov. by the prep. "in." |
| **many** | An indef. nu. adj. of quantity, qual. the n. "people." |
| people | A com. n., com. gen., p. num., 3rd per., obj. c., gov. by the tr. pl. "having." |
| and | A cop. conj., jg. the sents. "This country is large...people" and "*this country is large, having in it* several kingdoms." |
| **several** | An indef. nu. adj. of quantity, qual. the n. "kingdoms." |
| kingdoms. | A com. n., neu. gen., p. num., 3rd per., obj. c., gov. by the tr. pl. *having* und. |

8

| | |
|---|---|
| 7. Brutus | A prop. n., mas. gen., s. num., 3rd per., nom. c. to the v. "is." |
| is | An irreg. intr. v., indic. m., pres. t., s. num., 3rd per., agr. with its nom. "Brutus." |
| honourable | An adj. of quality, pos. deg., qual. the n. "man." |
| man | A com. n., mas. gen., s. num., 3rd per., nom. c. after the v. "is." |
| so | An adv. of man., mod. the v. "are." |
| are | An irreg. intr. v., indic. m., pres. t., p. num., 3rd per., agr. with its nom. "they." |
| they | A pers. pron., mas. gen., p. num., 3rd per., nom. c. to the v. "are." |
| all | An indef. nu. adj. of quantity, qual. the pron. "they." |
| all | An indef. nu. adj. of quantity, qual. the pron. "they." |
| honourable | An adj. of quality, pos. deg., qual. the n. "men." |
| men. | A com. n., mas. gen., p. num., 3rd per., nom. c. after the v. "are." |
| 8. They | A pers. pron., com. gen., p. num., 3rd per., nom. c. to the v. "embarked." |
| embarked | A reg. intr. v., indic. m., past t., p. num., 3rd per., agr. with its nom. "they." |
| with | A prep., sh. the rn. bet. "embarked" and "goods." |
| all | An indef. nu. adj of quantity, qual. the n. "goods." |
| their | A pers. pron., com. gen., p. num., 3rd per., poss. c., gov. by the n. "goods." |
| goods. | A com. n., neu. gen., p. num., 3rd per., obj. c., gov. by the prep. "with." |
| 9. Atlantic | A prop. adj. of quality, qual. the n. "Ocean." |
| Ocean | A com. n. tending to prop., neu. gen., s. num., 3rd per., nom. c. to the v. "exceeds." |
| Atlantic Ocean | A compd. prop. n., neu. gen., s. num., 3rd per., nom. c. to the v "exceeds." |
| exceeds | A reg. tr. v., act. vo., indic. m., pres. t., s. num., 3rd per., agr. with its nom. "Ocean" (or, "Atlantic Ocean "). |
| all | An indef. nu. adj. of quantity, qual. the n. "oceans." |
| other | An indef. nu. adj. of quantity, qual. the n. "oceans." |
| oceans | A com. n., neu. gen., p. num., 3rd per., obj. c., gov. by the tr. v. "exceeds." |
| in | A prep., sh. the rn. bet. "exceeds" and "number." |
| number | An abs. n., neu. gen., s. num., 3rd per., obj. c., gov. by the prep. "in." |
| of | A prep., sh. the rn. bet. "number" and "seas." |
| its | A pers. pron., neu. gen., s. num., 3rd per., poss. c., gov. by the n. "seas." |
| seas | A com. n., neu. gen., p. num., 3rd per., obj. c., gov. by the prep. "of." |
| and | A cop. conj., jg. the sents. "The Atlantic Ocean exceeds...seas" and "*the Atlantic Ocean exceeds all the other oceans in the number of its gulfs.*" |
| gulfs. | A com n., neu. gen., p. num., 3rd per., obj. c., gov. by the prep. *of* und. |
| 10. Many | A dist. nu. adj. of quantity, qual. the n. "horse." (*Parsing*, p. 118, § 8.) |
| good | An adj. of quality, pos. deg., qual. the n. "horse." |
| horse | A com. n., mas. gen., s. num., 3rd per., nom. c. to the v. "fell." |
| fell | An irreg. intr. v., indic. m., past t., s. num., 3rd per., agr. with its nom. "horse." |
| and | A cop. conj., jg. the sents. "Many a good horse fell" and "*many a good horse* threw .. earth." |
| threw | An irreg. tr. v., act. vo., indic. m., past t., s. num., 3rd per., agr. with its nom. *horse* und. |
| its | A pers. pron., neu. gen., s. num., 3rd per., poss. c., gov. by the n. "rider." (For the gender, see *Parsing*, p. 123, § 1.) |
| rider | A com. n., com. gen., s. num., 3rd per., obj. c., gov. by the tr. v. "threw." |
| to | A prep., sh. the rn. bet. "threw" and "earth." |
| earth. | A com. n., neu. gen., s. num., 3rd per., obj. c., gov. by the prep. "to." |

## Exercise 136.

| | |
|---|---|
| 1. At | A prep., sh. the rn. bet. "fed" and "door." |
| each | A dist. nu. adj. of quantity, qual. the n. "door." |
| door | A com. n., neu. gen., s. num., 3rd per., obj. c., gov. by the prep. "at." |
| neighbour | A com. n., com. gen., s. num., 3rd per., nom. c. to the v. "fed." |
| with | A prep., sh. the rn. bet. "fed" and "neighbour." |
| neighbour | A com. n., com. gen., s. num., 3rd per., obj. c., gov. by the prep. "with." |
| fed. | An irreg. intr. v., indic. m., past t., s. num., 3rd per., agr. with its nom. "neighbour." |
| 2. preaching | A pres. pl. used as an adj. of quality, qual. the n. "friar." |
| friar | A com. n., mas. gen., s. num., 3rd per., nom. c. to the v. "settles." |
| settles | A reg. tr. (reflexive) v., act. vo., indic. m., pres. t., s. num., 3rd per., agr. with its nom. "friar." |
| himself | A compd. pers. pron., mas. gen., s. num., 3rd per., obj. c., gov. by the tr. v. "settles." |
| in | A prep., sh. the rn. bet. "settles" and "village." |
| every | A dist. nu. adj. of quantity, qual. the n. "village." |
| village. | A com. n., neu. gen., s. num., 3rd per., obj. c., gov. by the prep. "in." |
| 3. Each | A dist. nu. adj. of quantity, qual. the n. "horseman." |
| horseman | A com. n., mas. gen., s. num., 3rd per., nom. c. to the v. "drew." |
| drew | An irreg. tr. v., act. vo., indic. m., past t., s. num., 3rd per., agr. with its nom. "horseman." |
| his | A pers. pron., mas. gen., s. num., 3rd per., poss. c., gov. by the n. "battle-blade." |
| battle-blade. | A compd. com. n., neu. gen., s. num., 3rd per., obj. c., gov. by the tr. v. "drew." |
| 4. Every | A dist. nu. adj. of quantity, qual. the n. "house." |
| house | A com. n., neu. gen., s. num., 3rd per., nom. c. to the v. "was." |
| was | An irreg. intr. v., indic. m., past t., s. num., 3rd per., agr. with its nom. "house." |
| inn | A com. n., neu. gen., s. num., 3rd per., nom. c. after the v. "was." |
| where | A cop. conj., jg. the sents. "Every house was an inn." and "all were welcomed." |
| all | An indef. nu. adj. of quantity, qual. the n. *persons* und. |
| were | An aux. v. to "welcomed," indg. pass. vo., past t. |
| welcomed | A past pl. from the tr. v. "to welcome," ref. to *persons* und. |
| were welcomed | A reg. tr. v., pass. vo., indic. m., past t., p. num., 3rd per., agr. with its nom. *persons* und. |
| and | A cop. conj., jg. the sents. "all *persons* were welcomed" and "all *persons* were feasted." |
| feasted. | A past pl. from the tr. v. "to feast," ref. to *persons* und. |
| 5. She | A pers. pron., fem. gen., s. num., 3rd per., nom. c. to the v. "believed." |
| believed | A reg. tr. v., act. vo., indic. m., past t., s. num., 3rd per., agr. with its nom. "she." |
| every | A dist. nu. adj. of quantity, qual. the n. "word." |
| word | An abs. n., neu. gen., s. num., 3rd per., obj. c., gov. by the tr. v. "believed." |
| that | A rel. pron., neu. gen., s. num., 3rd per., agr. with its ant. "word," obj. c., gov. by the v. "said." |
| he | A pers. pron., mas. gen., s. num., 3rd per., nom. c. to the v. "said." |
| said. | An irreg. tr. v., act. vo., indic. m., past t., s. num., 3rd per., agr. with its nom. "he." |
| 6. I | A pers. pron., mas. gen., s. num., 1st per., nom. c. to the v. "will wear." |
| will | An aux. v. to "wear," indg. fut. t., emph. form, expressing "determination." |
| (to) wear | An irreg. tr. v., act. vo., infin. m., pres. t., gov. by the v. "will." |
| will wear | An irreg. tr. v., act. vo., indic. m., fut. t., emph. form, s. num., 1st per., agr. with its nom. "I." |

8—2

116 KEY TO

|  |  |
|---|---|
| **neither** | A dist. nu. adj. of quantity, qual. the n. *sword* und. |
| of | A prep., sh. the rn. bet. *sword* und. and "swords." |
| swords | A com. n., neu. gen., p. num., 3rd per., obj. c., gov. by the prep. "of." |
| 7. Take | An irreg. tr. v., act. vo., imper. m., pres. t., s. num., 2nd per., agr. with its nom. *thou* und. |
| **either** | A dist. nu. adj. of quantity, qual. the n. "road." |
| road. | A com. n., neu. gen., s. num., 3rd per., obj. c., gov. by the tr. v. "take." |
| 8. **Neither** | A dist. nu. adj. of quantity, qual. the n. *man* und. |
| of | A prep., sh. the rn., bet. *man* und. and "men." |
| those | A dis. adj., lim. the n. "men." |
| men | A com. n., mas. gen., p. num., 3rd per., obj. c., gov. by the prep. "of." |
| has | An aux. v. to "done," indg. perf. t. |
| done | A past pl. from the tr. v. "to do," ref. to "duty." |
| has done | An irreg. tr. v., act. vo., indic. m., perf. t., s. num., 3rd per., agr. with its nom. *man* und. |
| his | A pers. pron., mas. gen., s. num., 3rd per., poss. c., gov. by the n. "duty." |
| duty. | An abs. n., neu. gen., s. num., 3rd per., obj. c., gov. by the tr. v. "has done." |
| 9. **Each** | A dist. nu. adj. of quantity, qual. the n. "morning." |
| morning | An abs. n., neu. gen., s. num., 3rd per., nom. c. to the v. "sees." |
| sees | An irreg. tr. v., act. vo., indic. m., pres. t., s. num., 3rd per., agr. with its nom. "morning." |
| some | An indef. nu. adj. of quantity, qual. the n. "task." |
| task | An abs. n., neu. gen., s. num., 3rd per., obj. c., gov. by the tr. v. "sees." |
| begun | A past pl. from the tr. v. "to begin," ref. to "task." |
| **Each** | A dist. nu. adj. of quantity, qual. the n. "evening." |
| evening | An abs. n., neu. gen., s. num., 3rd per., nom. c. to the v. "sees." |
| sees | An irreg. tr. v., act. vo., indic. m., pres. t., s. num., 3rd per., agr. with its nom. "evening." |
| its | A pers. pron., neu. gen., s. num., 3rd per., poss. c., gov. by the n. "close." |
| close. | An abs. n., neu. gen., s. num., 3rd per., obj. c., gov. by the tr. v. "sees." |

### Exercise 137.

|  |  |
|---|---|
| 1. There | An adv. of place, mod. the v. "lies." |
| lies | An irreg. intr. v., indic. m., pres. t., s. num., 3rd per., agr. with its nom. "city." |
| a | A dis. adj., lim. the n. "city." |
| sleeping | A pres. pl. used as an adj. of quality, qual. the n. "city." |
| city. | A com. n., neu. gen., s. num., 3rd per., nom. c. to the v. "lies." |
| 2. A | A dis. adj., lim. the n. "sound." |
| sound | An abs. n., neu. gen., s. num., 3rd per., nom. c. to the v. "came." |
| came | An irreg. intr. v., indic. m., past t., s. num., 3rd per., agr. with its nom. "sound." |
| from | A prep., sh. the rn. bet. "came" and "land." |
| land. | A com. n., neu. gen., s. num., 3rd per., obj. c., gov. by the prep. "from." |
| 3. I | A pers. pron., com. gen., s. num., 1st per., nom. c. to the v. "see." |
| see | An irreg. tr. v., act. vo., indic. m., pres. t., s. num., 1st per., agr. with its nom. "I." |
| a | A dis. adj., lim. the n. "star." |
| star. | A com. n., neu. gen., s. num., 3rd per., obj. c., gov. by the tr. v. "see." |
| 4. Lo | An interj. |
| o'er | A prep., sh. the rn. bet. "rose" and "city." |
| city | A com. n., neu. gen., s. num., 3rd per., obj. c., gov. by the prep. "o'er." |
| a | A dis. adj., lim. the n. "tempest." |
| tempest | An abs. n., neu. gen., s. num., 3rd per., nom. c. to the v. "rose." |

ENGLISH GRAMMAR AND ANALYSIS. 117

| | |
|---|---|
| rose. | An irreg. intr. v., indic. m., past t., s. num., 3rd per., agr. with its nom. "tempest." |
| 5. You | A pers. pron., com. gen., s. num., p. form, 2nd per., nom. c. to the v. "are." |
| are | An irreg. intr. v., indic. m., pres. t., s. num., p. form., 2nd per., agr. with its nom. "you." |
| a | A dis. adj., lim. the n. "counsellor." |
| counsellor. | A com. n., com. gen., s. num., 3rd per., nom. c. after the v. "are." |
| 6. I | A pers. pron., com. gen., s. num., 1st per., nom. c. to the v. "see." |
| see | An irreg. tr. v., act. vo., indic. m., pres. t., s. num., 1st per., agr. with its nom. "I." |
| a | A dis. adj., lim. the n. "fountain." |
| fountain | A com. n., neu. gen., s. num., 3rd per., obj. c., gov. by the tr. v. "see." |
| large | An adj. of quality, pos. deg., qual. the n. "fountain." |
| and | A cop. conj., jg. the sents. "I see a fountain large" and "I see a fountain fair." |
| fair | An adj. of quality, pos. deg., qual. the n. fountain und. |
| A | A dis. adj., lim. the n. "willow." |
| willow | A com. n., neu. gen., s. num., 3rd per., obj. c., gov. by the tr. v. see und. |
| and | A cop. conj., jg. the sents. "I see a willow" and "I see a ruined hut." |
| a | A dis. adj., lim. the n. "hut." |
| ruined | An adj. of quality, qual. the n. "hut." |
| hut. | A com. n., neu. gen., s. num., 3rd per., obj. c., gov. by the tr. v. see und. |

### Exercise 138.

| | |
|---|---|
| 1. Man | A com. n., mas. gen., s. num., 3rd per., nom. c. to the v. "hath." |
| hath | An irreg. tr. v., act. vo., indic. m., pres. t., s. num., 3rd per., agr. with its nom. "man." |
| a | A dis. adj., lim. the n. "pilgrimage." |
| weary | An adj. of quality, pos. deg., qual. the n. "pilgrimage." |
| pilgrimage. | An abs. n., neu. gen., s. num., 3rd per., obj. c., gov. by the tr. v. "hath." |
| 2. Virtue | An abs. n., neu. gen., s. num., 3rd per., nom. c. to the v. "is." |
| is | An irreg. intr. v., indic. m., pres. t., s. num., 3rd per., agr. with its nom. "virtue." |
| its | A pers. pron., forming with the adj. "own" a compd. pers. pron. |
| own | An intensive adj. of quality, qual. the n. "reward." |
| its own | A compd. pers. pron., neu. gen., s. num., 3rd per., poss. c., gov. by the n. "reward." |
| reward. | An abs. n., neu. gen., s. num., 3rd per., obj. c., gov. by the tr. v. "hath." |
| 3. There | An expletive adv., mod. the v. "is." |
| is | An irreg. intr. v., indic. m., pres. t., s. num., 3rd per., agr. with its nom. "virtue." |
| not | An adv. of m. (neg.), mod. the v. "is." |
| a | A dis. adj., lim. the n. "virtue." |
| virtue | An abs. n., neu. gen., s. num., 3rd per., nom. c. to the v. "is." |
| which | A rel. pron., neu. gen., s. num., 3rd per., agr. with its ant. "virtue," nom. c. to the v. "does ennoble." |
| does | An aux. v. to "ennoble," indg. pres. t., and completing the negative form of the v. |
| not | An adv. of m. (neg.), mod. the v. "does ennoble." |
| (to) ennoble | A reg. tr. v., act. vo., infin. m., pres. t., gov. by the v. "does." |
| does ennoble | A reg. tr. v., act. vo., indic. m., pres. t., s. num., 3rd per., agr. with its nom. "which." |
| a | A dis. adj., lim. the n. "man." |
| man. | A com. n., mas. gen., s. num., 3rd per., obj. c., gov. by the tr. v. "does ennoble." |
| 4. man | A com. n., mas. gen., s. num., 3rd per., nom. c. to the v. "is." |

118　　　　　　　　　　　KEY TO

|  |  |
|---|---|
| is | An irreg. intr. v., indic. m., pres. t., s. num., 3rd per., agr. with its nom. "man." |
| a | A dis. adj., lim. the n. "Nestor." |
| Nestor. | A prop. n., tending to com., mas. gen., s. num., 3rd per., nom. c. after the v. "is." |
| 5. A | A dis. adj., lim. the n. "murder." |
| murder | An abs. n., neu. gen., s. num., 3rd per., nom. c. to the v. "has been done." |
| has | An aux. v. to "been done," indg. perf. t. |
| been | A past pl. from the intr. v. "to be," ref. to "done murder," and aux. to "done," indg. pass. vo. |
| done | A past pl. from the tr. v. "to do," ref. to "murder.' |
| has been done. | An irreg. tr. v., pass. vo., indic. m., perf. t., s. num., 3rd per., agr. with its nom. "murder." |
| 6. Murder | An abs. n., neu. gen., s. num., 3rd per., nom. c. to the v. "may pass." |
| may | An aux. v. to "pass," indg. pot. m., pres. t. |
| (to) pass | A reg. intr. v., infin. m., pres. t., gov. by the v. "may." |
| may pass | A reg. intr. v., pot. m., pres. t., s. num., 3rd per., agr. with its nom. "murder." |
| unpunish'd | A negative form of the past pl. from the tr. v. "to punish," ref. to "murder." |
| for | A prep., sh. the rn. bet. "unpunish'd" and "time." |
| time | An abs. n., neu. gen., s. num., 3rd per., obj. c., gov. by the prep. "for." |
| But | A disj. conj., jg. the sents. "Murder may pass .. time" and "tardy justice ... crime." |
| tardy | An adj. of quality, pos. deg., qual. the n. "justice." |
| justice | An abs. n., neu. gen., s. num., 3rd per., nom. c. to the v. "will o'ertake." |
| will | An aux. v. to "o'ertake," indg. fut. t. |
| (to) o'ertake | An irreg. tr. v., act. vo., infin. m., pres. t., gov. by the v. "will." |
| will o'ertake | An irreg. tr. v., act. vo., indic. m., fut. t., s. num., 3rd per., agr. with its nom. "justice." |
| crime. | An abs. n., neu. gen., s. num., 3rd per., obj. c., gov. by the tr. v. "will o'ertake." |

## Exercise 139.

|  |  |
|---|---|
| 1. The | A dis. adj., lim. the n. "house-martin." |
| house-martin | A compd. com. n., mas. gen., s num., 3rd per., nom. c. to the v. "makes." |
| makes | An irreg. tr. v., act. vo., indic. m., pres. t., s. num., 3rd per., agr. with its nom. "house-martin." |
| his | A pers. pron., mas. gen., s. num., 3rd per., poss. c., gov. by the n. "nest." |
| nest | A com. n., neu. gen., s. num., 3rd per., obj. c., gov. by the tr. v. "makes." |
| against | A prep., sh. the rn. bet. "makes" and "sides." |
| the | A dis. adj., lim. the n. "sides." |
| sides | A com. n., neu. gen., p. num., 3rd per., obj. c., gov. by the prep. "against." |
| of | A prep., sh. the rn. bet. "sides" and "houses." |
| houses. | A com. n., neu. gen., p. num., 3rd per., obj. c., gov. by the prep. "of." |
| 2. Round | An adv. of place, mod. the v. *were cast* und. |
| and | A cop. conj., jg. the sents. "Round *the sounds were cast*" and "round the sounds were cast." |
| round | An adv. of place, mod. the v. "were cast." |
| the | A dis. adj., lim. the n. "sounds." |
| sounds | An abs. n., neu. gen., p. num., 3rd per., nom. c. to the v. "were cast." |
| were | An aux. v. to "cast," indg. pass. vo., past t. |
| cast | A past pl. from the tr. v. "to cast," ref. to "sounds." |
| were cast. | An irreg. tr. v., pass. vo., indic. m., past t., p. num., 3rd per., agr. with its nom. "sounds." |
| 3. The | A dis. adj., lim. the n. *people* und. |

# ENGLISH GRAMMAR AND ANALYSIS. 119

| | |
|---|---|
| unfortunate | An adj. of quality, pos. deg., qual. the n. *people* und. |
| are | An irreg. intr. v., indic. m., pres. t., p. num., 3rd per., agr. with its nom. *people* und. |
| loud | An adj. of quality, pos. deg., qual. the n. *people* und. |
| and | A cop. conj., jg. the sents. "The unfortunate *people* are loud in their complaints" and "*the unfortunate people are* loquacious .. complaints." |
| loquacious | An adj. of quality, pos. deg., qual. the n. *people* und. |
| in | A prep., sh. the rn. bet. "loquacious" and "complaints." |
| their | A pers. pron., com. gen., p. num., 3rd per., poss. c., gov. by the n. "complaints." |
| complaints. | An abs. n., neu. gen., p. num., 3rd per., obj. c., gov. by the prep. "in." |
| 4. The | An adv. of deg., mod. the adv. "less." |
| less | An adv. of deg., mod. the adj. "kind." |
| kind | An adj. of quality, pos. deg., qual. the n. "Fortune." |
| I | A pers. pron., com. gen., s. num., 1st per., nom. c. to the v. "found." |
| found | An irreg. tr. v., act. vo., indic. m., past t., s. num., 1st per., agr. with its nom. "I." |
| Fortune | An abs. n. used as a prop. n., fem. gen., s. num., 3rd per., obj. c., gov. by the tr. v. "found." |
| at | A prep., sh. the rn. bet. "found" and "time." |
| one | A def. card. nu. adj. of quantity, qual. the n. "time." |
| time | An abs. n., neu. gen., s. num., 3rd per., obj. c., gov. by the prep. "at." |
| the | An adv. of deg., mod. the adj. "more." |
| more | An adj. of quantity (bulk or mass), comp. deg., qual. the n. *advantage* und. |
| I | A pers. pron., com. gen., s. num., 1st per., nom. c. to the v. "expected." |
| expected | A reg. tr. v., act. vo., indic. m., past t., s. num., 1st per., agr. with its nom. "I." |
| from | A prep., sh. the rn. bet. "expected" and "her." |
| her | A pers. pron., fem. gen., s. num., 3rd per., obj. c., gov. by the prep. "from." |
| at | A prep., sh. the rn. bet. "expected" and *time* und. |
| another. | An indef. nu. adj. of quantity, qual. the n. *time* und. |
| 5. Weave | An irreg. tr. v., act. vo., imper. m., pres. t., p. num., 2nd per., agr. with its nom. *you* und. |
| the | A dis. adj., lim. the n. "warp." |
| warp | A com. n., neu. gen., s. num., 3rd per., obj. c., gov. by the tr. v. "weave" |
| and | A cop. conj., jg. the sents. "weave the warp" and "weave the woof." |
| weave | An irreg. tr. v., act. vo., imper. m., pres. t., p. num., 2nd per., agr. with its nom. *you* und. |
| the | A dis. adj., lim. the n. "woof." |
| woof | A com. n., neu. gen., s. num., 3rd per., obj. c., gov. by the tr. v. "weave." |
| The | A dis. adj., lim. the n. "winding-sheet." |
| winding-sheet | A compd. com. n., neu. gen., s. num., 3rd per., obj. c., in app. with "warp and woof" taken as a compd. |
| of | A prep., sh. the rn. bet. "winding-sheet" and "race." |
| Edward's | A prop. n., mas. gen., s. num., 3rd per., poss. c., gov. by the n. "race." |
| race. | A com. n., neu. gen., s. num., 3rd per., obj. c., gov. by the prep. "of." |
| 6. By | A prep., sh. the rn. bet. "stays" and "bank." |
| the | A dis. adj., lim. the n. "bank." |
| rushy-fringed | A compd. adj. of quality, qual. the n. "bank." |
| bank | A com. n., neu. gen., s. num., 3rd per., obj. c., gov. by the prep. "by." |
| Where | A cop. conj., jg. the sents. "My sliding chariot stays by the rushy-fringed bank" and "the willow grows." |
| grows | An irreg. intr. v., indic. m., pres. t., s. num., 3rd per., agr. with its nom. "willow." |

| | |
|---|---|
| the | A dis. adj., lim. the n. "willow." |
| willow | A com. n., neu. gen., s. num., 3rd per., nom. c. to the v. "grows." |
| and | A cop. conj., jg. the sents. "the willow grows" and "the osier dank grows." |
| the | A dis. adj., lim. the n. "osier." |
| osier | A com. n., neu. gen., s. num., 3rd per., nom. c. to the v. grows und. |
| dank | An adj. of quality, pos. deg., qual. the n. "osier." |
| My | A pers. pron., com. gen., s. num., 1st per., poss. c., gov. by the n. "chariot." |
| sliding | A pres. pl. used as an adj. of quality, qual. the n. "chariot." |
| chariot | A com. n., neu. gen., s. num., 3rd per., nom. c. to the v. "stays." |
| stays. | A reg. intr. v., indic. m., pres. t., s. num., 3rd per., agr. with its nom. "chariot." |

## Exercise 140.

| | |
|---|---|
| 1. Liege | A prop. n., neu. gen., s. num., 3rd per., nom. c. to the v. "is." |
| is | An irreg. intr. v., indic. m., pres. t., s. num., 3rd per., agr. with its nom. "Liege." |
| the | A dis. adj., lim. the n. "Birmingham." |
| Birmingham | A prop. n. tending to com., neu. gen., s. num., 3rd per., nom. c. after the v. "is." |
| of | A prep., sh. the rn. bet. "Birmingham" and "Belgium." |
| Belgium. | A prop. n., neu. gen., s. num., 3rd per., obj. c., gov. by the prep. "of." |
| 2. The | A dis. adj., lim. the n. ship und. |
| Royal | An adj. of quality, qual. the n. "George." |
| George | A prop. n., forming with the adj. "Royal" a compd. prop. n. |
| Royal George | A compd. prop. n., neu. gen., s. num., 3rd per., nom. c., in app. with ship und. |
| sank. | An irreg. intr. v., indic. m., past t., s. num., 3rd per., agr. with its nom. ship und. |
| 3. Homer | A prop. n., mas. gen., s. num., 3rd per., nom. c. to the v. "was." |
| was | An irreg. intr. v., indic. m., past t., s. num., 3rd per., agr. with its nom. "Homer." |
| greatest | An adj. of quality, superl. deg., qual. the n. "poet." |
| epic | An adj. of quality, qual. the n. "poet." |
| poet. | A com. n., mas. gen., s. num., 3rd per., nom. c. after the v. "was." |
| 4. He | A pers. pron., mas. gen., s. num., 3rd per., nom. c. to the v. "is." |
| is | An irreg. intr. v., indic. m., pres. t., s. num., 3rd per., agr. with its nom. "he." |
| the | A dis. adj., lim. the n. "Homer." |
| Homer | A prop. n. tending to com., mas. gen., s. num., 3rd per., nom. c. after the v. "is." |
| of | A prep., sh. the rn. bet. "Homer" and "country." |
| his | A pers. pron., mas. gen., s. num., 3rd per., poss. c., gov. by the n. "country." |
| country | A com. n., neu. gen., s. num., 3rd per., obj. c., gov. by the prep. "of." |
| 5. We | A pers. pron., com. gen., p. num., 1st per., nom. c. to the v. "read." |
| read | An irreg. tr. v., act. vo., indic. m., pres. or past t., p. num., 1st per., agr. with its nom. "we." |
| lives | A com. n., neu. gen., p. num., 3rd per., obj. c., gov. by the tr. v. "read." |
| of | A prep., sh. the rn. bet. "lives" and "Cæsars." |
| the | A dis. adj., lim. the n. "Cæsars." |
| Cæsars. | A prop. n. tending to com., mas. gen., p. num., 3rd per., obj. c., gov. by the prep. "of." |
| 6. The | A dis. adj., lim. the n. river und. |
| Volga | A prop. n., neu. gen., s. num., 3rd per., nom. c., in app. with river und. |

| | |
|---|---|
| flows | A reg. intr. v., indic. m., pres. t., s. num., 3rd per., agr. wih its nom. *river* und. |
| into | A prep., sh. the rn. bet. "flows" and "Caspian Sea." |
| **the** | A dis. adj., lim. the n. "sea." |
| Caspian | A prop. n. used as an adj. of quality, qual. the n. "Sea." |
| Sea | A com. n. tending to prop., forming with "Caspian" a compd prop. n. |
| Caspian Sea. | A compd. prop. n., neu. gen., s. num., 3rd per., obj. c., gov. by the prep. "into." |

## Exercise 141.

| | |
|---|---|
| 1. In | A prep., sh. the rn. bet. "kept" and *field* und. |
| **this** | A dis. adj., lim. the n. *field* und. |
| glorious | An adj. of quality, pos. deg., qual. the n. *field* und. |
| and | A cop. conj., jg. the sents. "In this glorious *field we kept together in our chivalry*" and "*in this* well-foughten field we kept.. chivalry." |
| well-foughten | A compd. adj. of quality, qual. the n. "field." |
| field | A com. n., neu. gen., s. num., 3rd per., obj. c., gov. by the prep. *in* und. |
| we | A pers. pron., mas. gen., p. num., 1st per., nom. c. to the v. "kept." |
| kept | An irreg. intr. v., indic. m., past t., p. num., 1st per., agr. with its nom. "we." |
| together | An adv. of man., mod. the v. "kept." |
| in | A prep., sh. the rn. bet. "kept" and "chivalry." |
| our | A pers. pron., mas. gen., p. num., 1st per., poss. c., gov. by the n. "chivalry." |
| chivalry | An abs. n., neu. gen., s. num., 3rd per., obj. c., gov. by the prep. "in." |
| 2 **The** | A dis. adj., lim. the n. *manner* und. |
| pretty | An adj. of quality, pos. deg., qual. the n. *manner* und. |
| and | A cop. conj., jg. the sents. "The pretty *manner of it forced those waters from me*" and "*the* sweet manner of it forced.. me." |
| sweet | An adj. of quality, pos. deg., qual. the n. "manner." |
| manner | An abs. n., neu. gen., s. num., 3rd per., nom. c. to the v. "forc'd." |
| of | A prep., sh. the rn. bet. "manner" and "it." |
| it | A pers. pron., neu. gen., s. num., 3rd per., obj. c., gov. by the prep. "of." |
| forc'd | A reg. tr. v., act. vo., indic. m., past t., s. num., 3rd per., agr. with its nom. "manner." |
| those | A dis. adj., lim. the n. "waters." |
| waters | A com. n., neu. gen., p. num., 3rd per., obj. c., gov. by the tr. v. "forc'd." |
| from | A prep., sh. the rn. bet. "forc'd" and "me." |
| me. | A pers. pron., com. gen., s. num., 1st per., obj. c., gov. by the prep. "from." |
| 3. **An** | A dis. adj., lim. the n. *father* und. |
| ancient | An adj. of quality, pos. deg., qual. the n. *father* und. |
| and | A cop. conj., jg. the sents. "An ancient *father now appeared*" and "*a venerable* father now appeared." |
| venerable | An adj. of quality, pos. deg., qual. the n. "father." |
| father | A com. n., mas. gen., s. num., 3rd per., nom. c. to the v. "appeared." |
| now | An adv. of time, mod. the v. "appeared." |
| appeared. | A reg. intr. v., indic. m., past t., s. num., 3rd per., agr. with its nom. "father." |
| 4. Trevor | A prop. n., mas. gen., s. num., 3rd per., nom. c. to the v. "was." |
| was | An irreg. intr. v., indic. m., past t., s. num., 3rd per., agr. with its nom. "Trevor." |
| **the** | A dis. adj., lim. the n. "secretary." |
| secretary | A com. n., mas. gen., s. num., 3rd per., nom. c. after the v. "was." |
| and | A cop. conj., jg. the sents. "Trevor was the secretary *of the company*" and "*Trevor was the* treasurer..company." |

| | |
|---|---|
| treasurer | A com n., mas. gen., s. num., 3rd per., nom. c. after the v. *was* und. |
| of | A prep., sh. the rn. bet. "treasurer" and "company." |
| company. | A com. col. n., neu. gen., s. num., 3rd per., obj. c., gov. by the prep. "of." |
| 5. He | A pers. pron., mas. gen., s. num., 3rd per., nom. c. to the v. "was." |
| was | An irreg. intr. v., indic. m., past t., s. num., 3rd per., agr. with its nom. "he." |
| a | A dis. adj., lim. the n. "scholar." |
| better | An adj. of quality, comp. deg., qual. the n. "scholar." |
| scholar | A com. n., mas. gen., s. num., 3rd per., nom. c. after the v. "was." |
| than | A disj. conj., jg. the sents. "He was a better scholar" and "*he was a good* statesman." |
| statesman. | A com. n., mas. gen., s. num., 3rd per., nom. c. after the v. *was* und. |
| 6. Nor | A disj. conj., jg. a sent. und. and the sent. "He doth dedicate.. the weary *night*." |
| doth | An aux. v. to "dedicate," indg. pres. t., and completing the negative form of the v. |
| he | A pers. pron., mas. gen., s. num., 3rd per., nom. c. to the v. "doth dedicate." |
| (to) dedicate | A reg. tr. v., act. vo., infin. m., pres. t., gov. by the v. "doth." |
| doth dedicate | A reg. tr. v., act. vo., indic. m., pres. t., s. num., 3rd per., agr. with its nom. "he." |
| one | A def. card. nu. adj. of quantity, qual. the n. "jot." |
| jot | A com. n., neu. gen., s. num., 3rd per., obj. c., gov. by the tr. v. "doth dedicate" |
| of | A prep., sh. the rn. bet. "jot" and "colour." |
| colour | An abs. n., neu. gen., s. num., 3rd per., obj. c., gov. by the prep. "of." |
| Unto | A prep., sh. the rn. bet. "doth dedicate" and *night* und. |
| the | A dis. adj., lim. the n. *night* und. |
| weary | An adj. of quality, pos. deg., qual. the n. *night* und. |
| and | A cop. conj., jg. the sents. "he doth dedicate... weary *night*" and "*he doth dedicate one jot of colour unto the* all-watched night." |
| all-watched | A compd. adj. of quality, qual. the n. "night." |
| night. | An abs. n., neu. gen., s. num., 3rd per., obj. c., gov. by the prep. *unto* und. |

## Exercise 142.

| | |
|---|---|
| 1 I | A pers. pron., com. gen., s. num., 1st per., nom. c. to the v. "planted." |
| planted | A reg. tr. v., act. vo., indic. m., past t., s. num., 1st per., agr. with its nom. "I." |
| this | A dis. adj., lim. the n. "rose." |
| rose | A com. n., neu. gen., s. num., 3rd per., obj. c., gov. by the tr. v. "planted." |
| and | A cop. conj., jg. the sents. "I planted this rose" and "*I planted this lily.*" |
| this | A dis. adj., lim. the n. "lily." |
| lily. | A com. n., neu. gen., s. num., 3rd per., obj. c., gov. by the tr. v. *planted* und. |
| 2. A | A dis. adj., lim. the n. "elephant." |
| tame | An adj. of quality, pos. deg., qual. the n. *elephant* und. |
| and | A cop. conj., jg. the sents. "A tame *elephant was placed in the same enclosure*" and "a wild elephant was placed in the same enclosure." |
| a | A dis. adj., lim. the n. "elephant." |
| wild | An adj. of quality, pos. deg., qual. the n. "elephant." |
| elephant | A com. n., com. gen., s. num., 3rd per., nom. c. to the v. "was placed" incl. in "were placed." |
| were | An aux. v. to "placed," ind. pass. vo., past t. |
| placed | A past pl. from the tr. v. "to place," ref. to "elephant." |

| | |
|---|---|
| were placed | A reg. tr. v., pass. vo., indic. m., past t., p. num., 3rd per., agr. with its noms. *elephant* und. and "elephant." |
| in | A prep., sh. the rn. bet. "were placed" and "enclosure." |
| same | A dis. adj., lim. the n. "enclosure." |
| enclosure. | A com. n., neu. gen., s. num., 3rd per., obj. c., gov. by the prep. "in." |
| 3. The | A dis. adj., lim. the n. *people* und. |
| noble | An adj. of quality, pos. deg., qual. the n. *people* und. |
| and | A cop. conj., cor. to "both," jg. the sents. "the noble *people are alike to him*" and "the lowly-born *people* are alike to him." |
| the | A dis. adj., lim. the n. *people* und. |
| lowly | An adv. of man., mod. the adj. "born." |
| born | A past pl. used as an adj. of quality, qual. the n. *people* und. |
| lowly-born | A compd. adj. of quality, pos. deg., qual. the n. *people* und. |
| are | An irreg. intr. v., indic. m., pres. t., p. num., 3rd per., agr. with its noms. *people* and *people* und. |
| both | A cop. conj., introducing the sent. "the noble &c." |
| alike | An adj. of quality, pos. deg., qual. the n. *people* und. and *people* und. |
| to | A prep., sh. the rn. bet. "alike" and "him." |
| him. | A pers. pron., mas. gen., s. num., 3rd per., obj. c., gov. by the prep. "to." |
| 4. trumpets | A com. n., neu. gen., p. num., 3rd per., nom. c. to the v. "sound." |
| sound | A reg. tr. v., act. vo., indic. m., pres. t., p. num., 3rd per., agr. with its nom. "trumpets." |
| the | A dis. adj., lim. the n. "charge." |
| charge | An abs. n., neu. gen., s. num., 3rd per., obj. c., gov. by the tr. v. "sound." |
| and | A cop. conj., jg. the sents. "The trumpets sound the charge" and "*the trumpets sound* the retreat." |
| the | A dis. adj., lim. the n. "retreat." |
| retreat. | An abs. n., neu. gen., s. num., 3rd per., obj. c., gov. by the tr. v. *sound* und. |
| 5. A | A dis. adj., lim. the n. "horse." |
| horse | A com. n., com. gen., s. num., 3rd per., nom. c. to the v. "was jogging" incl. in "were jogging." |
| and | A cop. conj., jg. the sents. "A horse was jogging *along together with an ass*" and "an ass was jogging along together *with a horse.*" |
| an | A dis. adj., lim. the n. "ass." |
| ass | A com. n., com. gen., s. num., 3rd per., nom. c. to the v. "was jogging" incl. in "were jogging." |
| were | An aux. v. to "jogging," indg. past t., prog. form. |
| jogging | A pres. pl. from the intr. v. "to jog," ref. to "horse" and "ass." |
| were jogging | A reg. intr. v., indic. m., past t., prog. form, p. num., 3rd per., agr. with its noms. "horse" and "ass." |
| along | An adv. of place, mod. the v. "were jogging." |
| together. | An adv. of man., mod. the v. "were jogging." |
| 6. The | A dis. adj., lim. the n. "pope." |
| pope | A com. n., mas. gen., s. num., 3rd per., nom. c. to the v. "was" incl. in the v. "were." |
| and | A cop. conj., jg. the sents. "The pope was *at variance with the emperor*" and "the emperor was at variance *with the pope.*" |
| the | A dis. adj., lim. the n. "emperor." |
| emperor | A com. n., mas. gen., s. num., 3rd per., nom. c. to the v. "was" incl. in the v. "were." |
| were | An irreg. intr. v., indic. m., past t., p. num., 3rd per., agr. with its noms. "pope" and "emperor." |
| at | A prep., sh. the rn. bet. "were" and "variance." |
| variance. | An abs. n., neu. gen., s. num., 3rd per., obj. c., gov. by the prep. "at." |

## Exercise 143.

| | |
|---|---|
| 1. **That** | A dis. adj., lim. the n. *difficulty* und. |
| is | An irreg. intr. v., indic. m., pres. t., s. num., 3rd per., agr. with its nom. *difficulty* und. |
| difficulty | An abs. n., neu. gen., s. num., 3rd per., nom. c. after the v. "is." |
| next | An adj. of quality, superl. deg., qual. the n. "difficulty." |
| to | A prep., sh. the rn. bet. "next" and *thing* und. |
| impossible. | An adj. of quality, qual. the n. *thing* und. ("Next to" may be treated as equivalent to "nearly," an adv. mod. "impossible;" in that case the adj. "impossible" qualifies "difficulty.") |
| 2. How | An adv. of deg., mod. the adj. "fit." |
| fit | An adj. of quality, pos. deg., qual. the n. "retreat." |
| is | An irreg. intr. v., indic. m., pres. t., s. num., 3rd per., agr. with its nom. "retreat." |
| **this** | A dis. adj., lim. the n. "retreat." |
| retreat | A com. n., neu. gen., s. num., 3rd per., nom. c. to the v. "is." |
| for | A prep., sh. the rn. bet. "fit" and "study." |
| uninterrupted | The negative form of the past pl. of the tr. v. "to interrupt," used as an adj. of quality, qual. the n. "study." |
| study. | An abs. n., neu. gen., s. num., 3rd per., obj. c., gov. by the prep. "for." |
| 3. Nothing | A com. n., neu. gen., s. num., 3rd per., nom. c. to the v. "can give." |
| can | An aux. v. to "give," indg. pot. m., pres. t. |
| (to) give | An irreg. tr. v., act. vo., infin. m., pres. t., gov. by the v. "can." |
| can give | An irreg. tr. v., act. vo., pot. m., pres. t., s. num., 3rd per., agr. with its nom. "nothing." |
| **that** | A dis. adj., lim. the n. *thing* und. |
| to | A prep., sh. the rn. bet. "can give" and *thing* und. |
| another | An indef. nu. adj. of quantity, qual. the n. *thing* und. |
| which | A rel. pron., neu. gen., s. num., 3rd per., agr. with its ant. *thing* und. (that *thing*), obj. c., gov. by the tr. v. "hath." |
| it | A pers. pron., neu. gen., s. num., 3rd per., nom. c. to the v. "hath." |
| hath | An irreg. tr. v., act. vo., indic. m., pres. t., s. num., 3rd per., agr. with its nom. "it." |
| not | An adv. of m. (neg.), mod. the v. "hath." |
| itself. | A compd. pers. pron., neu. gen., s. num., 3rd per., nom. c., in app. with "it." |
| 4. **This** | A dis. adj., lim. the n. "world." |
| world | A com. n., neu. gen., s. num., 3rd per., nom. c. to the v. "is." |
| is | An irreg. intr. v., indic. m., pres. t., s. num., 3rd per., agr. with its nom. "world." |
| region | A com. n., neu. gen., s. num., 3rd per., nom. c. after the v. "is." |
| of | A prep., sh. the rn. bet. "region" and "danger." |
| danger | An abs. n., neu. gen., s. num., 3rd per., obj. c., gov. by the prep. "of." |
| in | A prep., sh. the rn. bet. "is possessed" and "which." |
| which | A rel. pron., neu. gen., s. num., 3rd per., agr. with its ant. "region," obj. c., gov. by the prep. "in." |
| perfect | An adj. of quality, qual. the n. "safety." |
| safety | An abs. n., neu. gen., s. num., 3rd per., nom. c. to the v. "is possessed." |
| is | An aux. v. to "possessed," indg. pass. vo., pres. t. |
| possessed | A past pl. from the tr. v. "to possess," ref. to "safety." |
| is possessed | A reg. tr. v., pass. vo., indic. m., pres. t., s. num., 3rd per., agr. with its nom. "safety." |
| by | A prep., sh. the rn. bet. "is possessed" and "man." |
| no | A def. card. nu. adj. of quantity, qual. the n. "man." |
| man. | A com. n., mas. gen., s. num., 3rd per., obj. c., gov. by the prep. "by." |
| 5. **That** | A dis. adj., lim. the n. *notion* und. |
| is | An irreg. intr. v., indic. m., pres. t., s. num., 3rd per., agr. with its nom. *notion* und. |
| another | An indef. nu. adj. of quantity, qual. the n. *notion* und. |
| of | A prep., sh. the rn. bet. *notion* und. and "notions." |

| | |
|---|---|
| your | A pers. pron., com. gen., s. num., p. form, 2nd per., poss. c., gov. by the n. "notions." |
| odd | An adj. of quality, pos. deg., qual. the n. "notions." |
| notions. | An abs. n., neu. gen., p. num., 3rd per., obj. c., gov. by the prep. "of." |
| 6. I | A pers. pron., com. gen., s. num., 1st per., nom. c. to the v. "had be" (would be). |
| had (=would) | An aux. v. to "be," indg. pot. m., past t. |
| rather | An adv. of deg., mod. the v. "had be" (would be). |
| (to) be | An irreg. intr. v., infin. m., pres. t., gov. by the v. "had" (would). |
| had be=would be | An irreg. intr. v., pot. m., past t., s. num., 1st per., agr. with its nom. "I." |
| kitten | A com. n., com. gen., s. num., 3rd per., nom. c. after the v. "had be" (would be). |
| and | A cop. conj., jg. the sents. "I had rather be a kitten" and "I had rather cry mew." |
| (to) cry | A reg. tr. v., act. vo., infin. m., pres. t., gov. by the v. had (would) und. |
| mew | An abs. n., neu. gen., s. num., 3rd per., obj. c., gov. by the tr. v. "had cry" (would cry). |
| Than | A disj. conj., jg. the sents. "I had rather cry mew" and "I would be one...ballad-mongers." |
| one | A def. card. nu. adj. of quantity, qual. the n. ballad-monger und. |
| of | A prep., sh. the rn. bet. ballad-monger und. and "ballad-mongers." |
| these | A dis. adj., lim. the n. "ballad-mongers." |
| same | A dis. adj., lim. the n. "ballad-mongers." |
| metre | A com. n. used as an adj. of quality, qual. the n. "ballad-mongers." |
| ballad-mongers. | A compd. com. n., mas. gen., p. num., 3rd per., nom. c. after the v. would be und. |

### Exercise 144.

| | |
|---|---|
| 1. Through | A prep., sh. the rn. bet. "is passing" and "valley." |
| yonder | A dis. adj., lim. the n. "valley." |
| valley | A com. n., neu. gen., s. num., 3rd per., obj. c., gov. by the prep. "through." |
| shower | A com. n., neu. gen., s. num., 3rd per., nom. c. to the v. "is passing." |
| is | An aux. v. to "passing," indg. pres. t., prog. form. |
| passing | A pres. pl. from the intr. v. "to pass," ref. to "shower." |
| is passing. | A reg. intr. v., indic. m., pres. t., prog. form, s. num., 3rd per., agr. with its nom. "shower." |
| 2. At | A prep., sh. the rn. bet. "to swell" and "time." |
| same | A dis. adj., lim. the n. "time." |
| time | An abs. n., neu. gen., s. num., 3rd per., obj. c., gov. by the prep. "at." |
| waters | A com. n., neu. gen., p. num., 3rd per., nom. c. to the v. "began." |
| in | A prep., sh. the rn. bet. "waters" and "river." |
| river | A com. n., neu. gen., s. num., 3rd per., obj. c., gov. by the prep. "in." |
| began | An irreg. tr. v., act. vo., indic. m., past t., p. num., 3rd per., agr. with its nom. "waters." |
| to swell | A reg. intr. v., infin. m., pres. t.; used as an abs. n., neu. gen., s. num., 3rd per., obj. c., gov. by the tr. v. "began." |
| again. | An adv. of time, mod. the v. "to swell." |
| 3. His | A pers. pron., mas. gen., s. num., 3rd per., poss. c., gov. by the n. "servant." |
| servant | A com. n., mas. gen., s. num., 3rd per., nom. c. to the v. "was healed." |
| was | An aux. v. to "healed," indg. pass. vo., past t. |
| healed | A past pl. from the tr. v. "to heal," ref. to "servant." |
| was healed | A reg. tr. v., pass. vo., indic. m., past t., s. num., 3rd per., agr. with its nom. "servant." |
| in | A prep., sh. the rn. bet. "was healed" and "hour." |

| | |
|---|---|
| self-same | A dis. adj., lim. the n. "hour." |
| hour. | An abs. n., neu. gen., s. num., 3rd per., obj. c., gov. by the prep. "in." |
| 4. same | A dis. adj., lim. the n. "mother." |
| fond | An adj. of quality, pos. deg., qual. the n. "mother." |
| mother | A com. n., fem. gen., s. num., 3rd per., nom. c. to the v. "bent." |
| bent | An irreg. intr. v., indic. m., past t., s. num., 3rd per., agr. with its nom. "mother." |
| at | A prep., sh. the rn. bet. "bent" and "night." |
| night. | An abs. n., neu. gen., s. num., 3rd per., obj. c., gov. by the prep. "at." |
| O'er | A prep., sh. the rn. bet. "bent" and "brow." |
| each | A dist. nu. adj. of quantity, qual. the n. "brow." |
| fair | An adj. of quality, pos. deg., qual. the n. "brow." |
| sleeping | A pres. pl. from the intr. v. "to sleep," used as an adj. of quality, qual. the n. "brow." |
| brow. | A com. n., neu. gen., s. num., 3rd per., obj. c., gov. by the prep. "o'er." |
| 5. But | A disj. conj., introducing the sent. "look thou." |
| look | A reg. intr. v., imper. m., pres. t., s. num., 2nd per., agr. with its nom. *thou* und. |
| morn | An abs. n., neu. gen., s. num., 3rd per., nom. c. to the v. "walks." |
| in | A prep., sh. the rn. bet. "clad" and "mantle." |
| russet | An adj. of quality, qual. the n. "mantle." |
| mantle | A com. n., neu. gen., s. num., 3rd per., obj. c., gov. by the prep. "in." |
| clad | A past pl. from the tr. v. "to clothe," ref. to "morn." |
| Walks | A reg. intr. v., indic. m., pres. t., s. num., 3rd per., agr. with its nom. "morn." |
| o'er | A prep., sh. the rn. bet. "walks" and "dew." |
| dew | A com. n., neu. gen., s. num., 3rd per., obj. c., gov. by the prep. "o'er." |
| of | A prep., sh. the rn. bet. "dew" and "hill." |
| yon | A dis. adj., lim. the n. "hill." |
| high | An adj. of quality, pos. deg., qual. the n. "hill." |
| eastern | An adj. of quality, qual. the n. "hill." |
| hill. | A com. n., neu. gen., s. num., 3rd per., obj. c., gov. by the prep. "of." |
| 6. Pray | A reg. intr. v., imper. m., pres. t., s. num., 2nd per., agr. with its nom. *thou* und. |
| Alice | A prop. n., fem. gen., s. num., 2nd per., nom. c. of add. |
| pray | A reg. intr. v., imper. m., pres. t., s. num., 2nd per., agr. with its nom. *thou* und. |
| my | A pers. pron., mas. gen., s. num., 1st per., poss. c., gov. by the n. "wife." |
| darling | A com. n. used as an adj. of quality, qual. the n. "wife." |
| wife | A com. n., fem. gen., s. num., 2nd per., nom. c. of add. |
| That | A cop. conj., jg. the sents. "*Thou* pray" and "we may die... day." |
| we | A pers. pron., com. gen., p. num., 1st per., nom. c. to the v. "may die." |
| may | An aux. v. to "die," indg. pot. m., pres. t. |
| (to) die | A reg. intr. v., infin. m., pres. t., gov. by the v. "may." |
| may die | A reg. intr. v., pot. m., pres. t., p. num., 1st per., agr. with its nom. "we." |
| self-same | A dis. adj., lim. the n. "day." |
| day. | An abs. n., neu. gen., s. num., 3rd per., obj. c., gov. by the prep. *in* und. |

## Exercise 145.

| | |
|---|---|
| 1. The | A dis. adj., lim. the n. "birds." |
| smaller | An adj. of quality, comp. deg., qual. the n. "birds." |
| birds | A com. n., com. gen., p. num., 3rd per., nom. c. to the v. "were." |
| were | An irreg. intr. v., indic. m., past t., p. num., 3rd per., agr. with its nom. "birds." |
| not | An adj. of m. (neg.), mod. the v. "were." |

| | |
|---|---|
| **afraid** | An adj. of quality, pos. deg., qual. the n. "birds." |
| of | A prep., sh. the rn. bet. "afraid" and "me." |
| me. | A pers. pron., com. gen., s. num., 1st per., obj. c., gov. by the prep. "of." |
| 2. **The** | A dis. adj., lim. the n. "man." |
| **poor** | An adj. of quality, pos. deg., qual. the n. "man." |
| man | A com. n., mas. gen., s. num., 3rd per., nom. c. to the v. "is." |
| is | An irreg. intr. v., indic. m., pres. t., s. num., 3rd per., agr. with its nom. "man." |
| **hungry** | An adj. of quality, pos. deg., qual. the n. "man." |
| and | A cop. conj., jg. the sents. "The poor man is hungry" and "*the poor man is* athirst." |
| **athirst.** | An adj. of quality, pos. deg., qual. the n. *man* und. |
| 3. **Beautiful** | An adj. of quality, pos. deg., qual. the pron. "it." |
| it | A pers. pron., neu. gen., s. num., 3rd per., nom. c. to the v. "is." |
| is | An irreg. intr. v., indic. m., pres. t., s. num., 3rd per., agr. with its nom. "it." |
| to | A particle, indg. infin. m. |
| to understand | An irreg. intr. v., infin m., pres. t.; used as an abs. n., neu. gen., s. num., 3rd per., nom. c., in app. with "it." |
| and | A cop. conj., jg. the sents. "Beautiful it is to understand" and "*beautiful it is to* know." |
| (to) know | An irreg. tr. v., act. vo., infin. m., pres. t.; used as an abs. n., neu. gen., s. num., 3rd per., nom. c., in app. with *it* und. |
| that | A cop. conj., jg. the sents. "*beautiful it is to* know" and "a thought did...die." |
| a | A dis. adj., lim. the n. "thought." |
| thought | An abs. n., neu. gen., s. num., 3rd per., nom. c. to the v. "did die." |
| did | An aux. v. to "die," indg. past t., and completing the negative form of the v. |
| never | An adv. of time, mod. the v. "did die." |
| yet | An adv. of time, mod. the v. "did die." |
| (to) die | A reg. intr. v., infin. m., pres. t., gov. by the v. "did." |
| did die. | A reg. intr. v., indic. m., past t., s. num., 3rd per., agr. with its nom. "thought." |
| 4. **Last** | An adj. of quality, superl. deg., qual. the n. "noon." |
| noon | An abs. n., neu. gen., s. num., 3rd per., nom. c. to the v. "beheld." |
| beheld | An irreg. tr. v., act. vo., indic. m., past t., s. num., 3rd per., agr. with its nom. "noon." |
| them | A pers. pron., mas. gen., p. num., 3rd per., obj. c., gov. by the tr. v. "beheld." |
| **full** | An adj. of quality, qual. the pron. "them." |
| of | A prep., sh. tho rn. bet. "full" and "life." |
| **lusty** | An adj. of quality, pos. deg., qual. the n. "life." |
| life. | An abs. n., neu. gen., s. num., 3rd per., obj. c., gov. by the prep. "of." |
| 5. **The** | A dis. adj., lim. the n. "wizards." |
| **star-led** | A compd. adj. of quality, qual. the n. "wizards." |
| wizards | A com. n., mas. gen., p. num., 3rd per., nom. c. to the v. "haste." |
| haste | A reg. intr. v., indic. m., pres. t., p. num., 3rd per., agr. with its nom. "wizards." |
| with | A prep., sh. the rn. bet. "haste" and "odours." |
| odours | A com. n., neu. gen., p. num., 3rd per., obj. c., gov. by the prep. "with." |
| **sweet.** | An adj. of quality, pos. deg., qual. the n. "odours." |
| 6. O | An interj. |
| **what** | A compd. rel. pron. used as an adj., qual. the n. "mind." |
| a | A dis. adj., lim. the n. "mind." |
| **noble** | An adj. of quality, pos. deg., qual. the n. "mind." |
| mind | A com. n., neu. gen., s. num., 3rd per., nom. c. to the v. "is o'erthrown." |
| is | An aux. v. to "o'erthrown," indg. pass. vo., pres. t. |
| here | An adv. of place, mod. the v. "is o'erthrown." |
| o'erthrown | A past pl. from the tr. v. "to o'erthrow," ref. to "mind." |
| is o'erthrown. | An irreg. tr. v., pass. vo., indic. m., pres. t., s. num., 3rd per., agr. with its nom. "mind." |

| | | |
|---|---|---|
| 7. It | | A pers. pron., neu. gen., s. num., 3rd per., nom. c. to the v. "is." |
| | is | An irreg. intr. v., indic. m., pres. t., s. num., 3rd per., agr. with its nom. "it." |
| | a | A dis. adj., lim. the n. "evening." |
| | **beauteous** | An adj. of quality, pos. deg., qual. the n. "evening." |
| | evening | An abs. n., neu. gen., s. num., 3rd per., nom. c. after the v. "is." |
| | **calm** | An adj. of quality, pos. deg., qual. the n. "evening." |
| | and | A cop. conj., jg. the sents. "It is..calm" and "*it is a beauteous evening* free." |
| | **free**. | An adj. of quality, pos. deg., qual. the n. *evening* und. |
| 8. But | | A disj. conj., introducing the sent. "pangs..wound their *sympathetic Queen.*" |
| | pangs | An abs. n., neu. gen., p. num., 3rd per., nom. c. to the v. "wound." |
| | more | An adv. of deg., mod. the adj. "cruel" and indg. comp. deg. |
| | **more cruel** | An adj. of quality, comp. deg., qual. the n. "pangs." |
| | more | An adv. of deg., mod. the adv. "intensely," indg. comp. deg. |
| | intensely | An adv. of deg., mod. the adj. "keen." |
| | more intensely | An adv. of deg., comp. deg., mod. the adj. "keen." |
| | **keen** | An adj. of quality, pos. deg., qual. the n. "pangs." |
| | Wound | A reg. tr. v., act. vo., indic. m., pres. t., p. num., 3rd per., agr. with its nom. "pangs." |
| | and | A cop. conj., jg. the sents. "pangs..wound their sympathetic Queen" and "*pangs more cruel more intensely keen,* distr. c.. Queen." |
| | distract | A reg. tr. v., act. vo., indic. m., pres. t., p. num., 3rd per., agr. with its nom. *pangs* und. |
| | their | A pers. pron., com. gen., p. num., 3rd per., poss. c., gov. by the n. "Queen." |
| | **sympathetic** | An adj. of quality, pos. deg., qual. the n. "Queen." |
| | Queen. | A com. n., tending to prop., fem. gen., s. num., 3rd per., obj. c., gov. by the tr. v. "distract." |
| 9. Who | | An interrog. pron., com. gen., s. num., 3rd per., nom. c. to the v. "would wish." |
| | o'er | A prep., sh. the rn. bet. "to reign" and "herd." |
| | the | A dis. adj., lim the n. "herd." |
| | herd | A com. col. n., neu. gen., s. num., 3rd per., obj. c., gov. by the prep. "o'er." |
| | would | An aux. v. to "wish," indg. pot. m., past t. |
| | (to) wish | A reg. intr. v., infin. m., pres. t., gov. by the v. "would." |
| | would wish | A reg. intr. v., pot. m., past t., s. num, 3rd per., agr. with its nom. "who." |
| | to | A particle, indg. infin. m. |
| | to reign | A reg. intr. v., infin. m., pres. t., gov. by the v. "would wish." |
| | **Fantastic** | An adj. of quality, pos. deg., qual. the n. "herd." |
| | **fickle** | An adj. of quality, pos. deg., qual. the n. "herd." |
| | **fierce** | An adj. of quality, pos. deg., qual. the n. "herd." |
| | and | A cop. conj., jg. the sents. "Who o'er the fierce herd would wish to reign" and "*who o'er the* vain *herd would wish to reign.*" |
| | **vain**. | An adj. of quality, pos. deg. qual. the n. *herd* und. |
| 10. **Broad** | | An adj. of quality, pos. deg., qual. the n. "shadows." |
| | shadows | A com. n., neu. gen., p. num., 3rd per., nom. c. to the v. "fell." |
| | o'er | A prep., sh. the rn. bet. "fell" and "passage." |
| | their | A pers. pron., com. gen., p. num., 3rd per., poss. c., gov. by the n. "passage." |
| | passage | A com. n., neu. gen., s. num., 3rd per., obj. c., gov. by the prep. "o'er." |
| | fell | An irreg. intr. v., indic. m., past t., p. num., 3rd per., agr. with its nom. "shadows." |
| | **Deeper** | An adj. of quality, comp. deg., qual. the n. *dell* und. |
| | and | A cop. conj., jg. the sents. "Deeper *grew the dell*" and "narrower grew the dell." |
| | **narrower** | An adj. of quality, comp. deg., qual. the n. "dell." |
| | grew | An irreg. intr. v., indic. m., past t., s. num., 3rd per., agr. with its nom. "dell." |
| | the | A dis. adj., lim. the n. "dell." |
| | dell. | A com. n., neu. gen., s. num., 3rd per., nom. c. to the v. "grew." |

ENGLISH GRAMMAR AND ANALYSIS. 129

## Exercise 146.

| | |
|---|---|
| 1. Sweet | An adj. of quality, pos. deg., qual. the n. "heaps." |
| to | A prep., sh. the rn. bet. "sweet" and "miser." |
| miser | A com. n., mas. gen., s. num., 3rd per., obj. c., gov. by the prep. "to." |
| are | An irreg. intr. v., indic. m., pres. t., p. num., 3rd per., agr. with its nom. "heaps." |
| **his** | A pers. pron., mas. gen., s. num., 3rd per., poss. c., gov. by the n. "heaps." |
| glittering | A pres. pl. from the intr. v. "to glitter," used as an adj. of quality, pos. deg., qual. the n. "heaps." |
| heaps. | A com. n., neu. gen., p. num., 3rd per., nom. c. to the v. "are." |
| 2. Deep | An adj. of quality, pos. deg., qual. the n. "sleep." |
| is | An irreg. intr. v., indic. m., pres. t., s. num., 3rd per., agr. with its nom. "sleep." |
| sleep | An abs. n., neu. gen., s. num., 3rd per., nom. c. to the v. "is." |
| of | A prep., sh. the rn. bet. "sleep" and *persons* und. |
| dead | An adj. of quality, qual. the n. *persons* und. |
| low | An adj. of quality, pos. deg., qual. the n. "pillow." |
| **their** | A pers. pron., com. gen., p. num., 3rd per., poss. c., gov. by the n. "pillow." |
| pillow | A com. n., neu. gen., s. num., 3rd per., nom. c. to the v. *is* und. |
| of | A prep., sh. the rn. bet. "pillow" and "dust." |
| dust. | A com. n., neu. gen., s. num., 3rd per., obj. c., gov. by the prep. "of." |
| 3. Can | An aux. v. to "change," indg. pot. m., pres. t. |
| Ethiopian | A prop. n., mas. gen., s. num., 3rd per., nom. c. to the v. "can change." |
| (to) change | A reg. tr. v., act. vo., infin. m., pres. t., gov. by the v. "can." |
| can change | A reg. tr. v., act. vo., pot. m., pres. t., s. num., 3rd per., agr. with its nom. "Ethiopian." |
| **his** | A pers. pron., mas. gen., s. num., 3rd per., poss. c., gov. by the n. "skin." |
| skin | A com. n., neu. gen., s. num., 3rd per., obj. c., gov. by the tr. v. "can change." |
| or | A disj. conj., jg. the sents. "Can the Ethiopian change his skin" and "can the leopard *change* his spots." |
| leopard | A com. n., mas. gen., s. num., 3rd per., nom. c. to the v. *can change* und. |
| **his** | A pers. pron., mas. gen., s. num., 3rd per., poss. c., gov. by the n. "spots." |
| spots. | A com. n., neu. gen., p. num., 3rd per., obj. c., gov. by the tr. v. *can change* und. |
| 4. Behold | An irreg. tr. v., act. vo., imper. m., pres. t., s. num., 2nd per., agr. with its nom. *thou* und. |
| how | A cop. conj., jg. the sents. "*Thou* behold" and "*it is* good *for brethren to dwell together in unity.*" |
| good | An adj. of quality, pos. deg., qual. the pron. *it* und. |
| and | A cop. conj., jg. the sents. "*thou* behold" and *thou behold* und. |
| how | A cop. conj., jg. the sents. *thou behold* und. and "it is pleasant.. unity." |
| pleasant | An adj. of quality, pos. deg., qual. the pron. "it." |
| it | A pers. pron., neu. gen., s. num., 3rd per., nom. c. to the v. "is." |
| is | An irreg. intr. v., indic. m., pres. t., s. num., 3rd per., agr. with its nom. "it." |
| for | A prep., sh. the rn. bet. "pleasant" and "brethren." |
| brethren | A com. n., mas. gen., p. num., 3rd per., obj. c., gov. by the prep. "for." |
| to | A particle, indg. infin. m. |
| to dwell | An irreg. intr. v., infin. m., pres. t., gov. by the n. "brethren" (or, used as a n. in app. with "it"). |
| together | An adv. of man., mod. the v. "to dwell." |
| in | A prep., sh. the rn. bet. "to dwell" and "unity." |
| unity. | An abs. n., neu. gen., s. num., 3rd per., obj. c., gov. by the prep. "in." |

| | |
|---|---|
| 5. assembly | A com. col. n., com. gen., p. num., 3rd per., nom. c. to the v. "resumed." |
| then | An adv. of time, mod. the v. "resumed." |
| resumed | A reg. tr. v., act. vo., indic. m., past t., p. num., 3rd per., agr. with its nom. "assembly." |
| **their** | A pers. pron., com. gen., p. num., 3rd per., poss. c., gov. by the n. "places." |
| places. | A com. n., neu. gen., p. num., 3rd per., obj. c., gov. by the tr. v. "resumed." |
| 6. Lapland | A prop. n., neu. gen., s. num., 3rd per., nom. c. to the v. "has" incl. in "have." |
| and | A cop. conj., jg. the sents. "Lapland has its *historians*" and "Iceland has its historians." |
| Iceland | A prop. n., neu. gen., s. num., 3rd per., nom. c. to the v. "has" incl. in "have." |
| have | An irreg. tr. v., act. vo., indic. m., pres. t., p. num., 3rd per., agr. with its noms. "Lapland" and "Iceland." |
| **their** | A pers. pron., neu. gen., p. num., 3rd per., poss. c., gov. by the n. "historians." |
| historians | A com. n., com. gen., p. num., 3rd per., obj. c., gov. by the tr. v. "have." |
| **their** | A pers. pron., neu. gen., p. num., 3rd per., poss. c., gov. by the n. "critics." |
| critics | A com. n., com. gen., p. num., 3rd per., obj. c., gov. by the tr. v. *have* und. |
| and | A cop. conj., jg. the sents. "*Lapland and Iceland have* their critics" and "*Lapland and Iceland have* their poets." |
| **their** | A pers. pron., neu. gen., p. num., 3rd per., poss. c., gov. by the n. "poets." |
| poets. | A com. n., com. gen., p. num., 3rd per., obj. c., gov. by the tr. v. *have* und. |
| 7. improvidence | An abs. n., neu. gen., s. num., 3rd per., nom. c. to the v. "reduces." |
| of | A prep., sh. the rn. bet. "improvidence" and "Esquimaux." |
| Esquimaux | A prop. n., com. gen., p. num., 3rd per., obj. c., gov. by the prep. "of." |
| often | An adv. of time, mod. the v. "reduces." |
| reduces | A reg. tr. v., act. vo., indic. m., pres. t., s. num., 3rd per., agr. with its nom. "improvidence." |
| **them** | A pers. pron., com. gen., p. num., 3rd per., obj. c., gov. by the tr. v. "reduces." |
| t | A prep., sh. the rn. bet. "reduces" and "straits." |
| terrible | An adj. of quality, pos. deg., qual. the n. "straits." |
| straits. | A com. n., neu. gen., p. num., 3rd per., obj. c., gov. by the prep. "to." |
| 8. Friend | A com. n., com. gen., s. num., 2nd per., nom. c. of add. |
| of | A prep., sh. the rn. bet. "friend" and "soul." |
| **my** | A pers. pron., com. gen., s. num., 1st per., poss. c., gov. by the n. "soul." |
| soul | A com. n., neu. gen., s. num., 3rd per., obj. c., gov. by the prep. "of." |
| this | A dis. adj., lim. the n. "goblet." |
| goblet | A com. n., neu. gen., s. num., 3rd per., obj. c., gov. by the tr. v. "sip." |
| sip | A reg. tr. v., act. vo., imper. m., pres. t., s. num., 2nd per., agr. with its nom. *thou* und. |
| **It** | A pers. pron., neu. gen., s. num., 3rd per., nom. c. to the v. "will chase." |
| will | An aux. v. to "chase," indg. fut. t. |
| (to) chase | A reg. tr. v., act. vo., infin. m., pres. t., gov. by the v. "will." |
| will chase | A reg. tr. v., act. vo., indic. m., fut. t., s. num., 3rd per., agr. with its nom. "it." |
| that | A dis. adj., lim. the n. "tear." |
| pensive | An adj. of quality, pos. deg., qual. the n. "tear." |
| tear. | A com. n., neu. gen., s. num., 3rd per., obj. c., gov. by the tr. v. "will chase." |
| 9. Nought | A com. n., neu. gen., s. num., 3rd per., nom. c. to the v. "shall make." |

| | |
|---|---|
| shall | An aux. v. to "make," indg. fut. t., emph. form, expressing "certainty." |
| (to) make | An irreg. tr. v., act. vo., infin. m., pres. t., gov. by the v. "shall." |
| shall make | An irreg. tr. v., act. vo., indic. m., fut. t., emph. form, s. num., 3rd per., agr. with its nom. "nought." |
| us | A pers. pron., com. gen., p. num., 1st per., obj. c., gov. by the tr. v. "shall make." |
| (to) rue | A reg. intr. v., infin. m., pres. t., gov. by the v. "shall make." |
| If | A cop. conj., jg. the sents. "Nought shall rue" and "England to itself.. true," and indg. subj. m. |
| England | A prop. n., neu. gen., s. num., 3rd per., nom. c. to the v. "do rest." |
| to | A prep , sh. the rn. bet. "true" and "itself." |
| itself | A compd. pers. pron., neu. gen., s. num., 3rd per., obj. c., gov. by the prep. "to." |
| do | An aux. v. to "rest," indg. pres. t., emph. form. |
| (to) rest | A reg. intr. v., infin. m., pres. t., gov. by the v. "do." |
| do rest | A reg. intr. v., subj. m., pres. t., emph. form, s. num., 3rd per. agr. with its nom. "England." |
| but = only | An adv. of deg., mod. the v. "do rest." |
| true. | An adj. of quality, pos. deg., qual. the n. "England." |
| 10. western | An adj. of quality, qual. the n. "waves." |
| waves | A com. n., neu. gen., p. num., 3rd per., nom. c. to the v. "roll'd." |
| of | A prep., sh. the rn. bet. "waves" and "day." |
| ebbing | A pres. pl. from the intr. v. "to ebb," used as an adj. of quality, qual. the n. "day." |
| day | An abs. n., neu. gen., s. num., 3rd per., obj. c., gov. by the prep. "of." |
| Roll'd | A reg. intr. v., indic. m., past t., p. num., 3rd per., agr. with its nom. "waves." |
| o'er | A prep., sh. the rn. bet. "roll'd" and "glen." |
| glen | A com. n., neu. gen., s. num., 3rd per., obj. c., gov. by the prep. "o'er." |
| their | A pers. pron., neu. gen., p. num., 3rd per., poss. c., gov. by the n. "way." |
| level | An adj. of quality, qual. the n. "way." |
| way. | A com. n., neu. gen., s. num., 3rd per., obj. c., gov. by the prep. on und. |

## Exercise 147.

| | |
|---|---|
| 1. Saul | A prop. n., mas. gen., s. num., 3rd per., nom. c. to the v. "was" incl. in "were." |
| and | A cop. conj., jg. the sents. "Saul was *lovely*" and "Jonathan was lovely." |
| Jonathan | A prop. n., mas. gen., s. num., 3rd per., nom. c. to the v. "was" incl. in "were." |
| were | An irreg. intr. v., indic. m., past t., p. num., 3rd per., agr. with its noms. "Saul" and "Jonathan." |
| lovely | An adj. of quality, pos. deg., qual. the nouns "Saul" and "Jonathan." |
| and | A cop. conj., jg. the sents. "Saul and Jonathan were lovely in *their lives*" and "*Saul and Jonathan were* pleasant in their lives." |
| pleasant | An adj. of quality, pos. deg., qual. the nouns *Saul* and *Jonathan* und. |
| in | A prep., sh. the rn. bet. "pleasant" and "lives." |
| their | A pers. pron., mas. gen., p. num., 3rd per., poss. c., gov. by the n. "lives." |
| lives | An abs. n., neu. gen., p. num., 3rd per., obj. c., gov. by the prep. "in." |
| and | A cop. conj., jg. the sents. "Saul and Jonathan...lives" and "in their death..divided." |
| in | A prep., sh. the rn. bet. "were divided" and "death." |
| their | A pers. pron., mas. gen., p. num., 3rd per., poss. c., gov. by the n. "death." |

| | |
|---|---|
| death | An abs. n., neu. gen., s. num., 3rd per., obj. c., gov. by the prep. "in." |
| **they** | A pers. pron., mas. gen., p. num., 3rd per., nom. c. to the v. "were divided." |
| were | An aux. v. to "divided," indg. pass. vo., past t. |
| not | An adv. of m. (neg.), mod. the v. "were divided." |
| divided | A past pl. from the tr. v. "to divide," ref. to "they." |
| were divided | A reg. tr. v., pass. vo., indic. m., past t., p. num., 3rd per., agr. with its nom. "they." |
| **they** | A pers. pron., mas. gen., p. num., 3rd per., nom. c. to the v. "were." |
| were | An irreg. intr. v., indic. m., past t., p. num., 3rd per., agr. with its nom. "they." |
| swifter | An adj. of quality, comp. deg., qual. the pron. "they." |
| than | A disj. conj., jg. the sents. "they were swifter" and "eagles are swift." |
| eagles | A com. n., com. gen., p. num., 3rd per., nom. c. to the v. are und. |
| **they** | A pers. pron., mas. gen., p. num., 3rd per., nom. c. to the v. "were." |
| were | An irreg. intr. v., indic. m., past t., p. num., 3rd per., agr. with its nom. "they." |
| stronger | An adj. of quality, comp. deg., qual. the pron. "they." |
| than | A disj. conj., jg. the sents. "they were stronger" and "lions are strong." |
| lions. | A com. n., com. gen., p. num., 3rd per., nom. c. to the v. are und. |
| 2. two | A def. card. nu. adj. of quantity, qual. the n. "sons." |
| sons | A com. n., mas. gen., p. num., 3rd per., nom. c. to the v. "maintained." |
| of | A prep., sh. the rn. bet. "sons" and "Alexius." |
| Alexius | A prop. n., mas. gen., s. num., 3rd per., obj. c., gov. by the prep. "of." |
| John | A prop. n., mas. gen., s. num., 3rd per., nom. c., being, together with "Isaac," in app. with "sons" (or, nom. c. to *maintained* und.). |
| and | A cop. conj., jg. the implied sents. "John *maintained the fraternal concord*" and "Isaac *maintained the fraternal concord*." |
| Isaac | A prop. n., mas. gen., s. num., 3rd per., nom. c., being, together with "John," in app. with "sons" (or, nom. c. to *maintained* und.). |
| maintained | A reg. tr. v., act. vo., indic. m., past t., p. num., 3rd per., agr. with its nom. "sons." |
| fraternal | An adj. of quality, qual. the n. "concord." |
| concord | An abs. n., neu. gen., s. num., 3rd per., obj. c., gov. by the tr. v. "maintained." |
| hereditary | An adj. of quality, qual. the n. "virtue." |
| virtue | An abs. n., neu. gen., s. num., 3rd per., obj. c., in app. with "concord." |
| of | A prep., sh. the rn. bet. "virtue" and "race." |
| **their** | A pers. pron., mas. gen., p. num., 3rd per., poss. c., gov. by the n. "race." |
| race. | A com. col. n., neu. gen., s. num., 3rd per., obj. c., gov. by the prep. "of." |
| 3. Simeon | A prop. n., mas. gen., s. num., 3rd per., nom. c. to the v. "is" incl. in "are." |
| and | A cop. conj., jg. the sents. "Simeon is a brother of Levi" and "Levi is a brother of Simeon." (See also *Parsing*, p. 85.) |
| Levi | A prop. n., mas. gen., s. num., 3rd per., nom. c. to the v. "is" incl. in "are." |
| are | An irreg. intr. v., indic. m., pres. t., p. num., 3rd per., agr. with its noms. "Simeon" and "Levi." |
| brethren | A com. n., mas. gen., p. num., 3rd per., nom. c. after the v. "are." |
| instruments | A com. n., neu. gen., p. num., 3rd per., nom. c. to the v. "are." |
| of | A prep., sh. the rn. bet. "instruments" and "cruelty." |
| cruelty | An abs. n., neu. gen., s. num., 3rd per., obj. c., gov. by the prep. "of." |

| | |
|---|---|
| are | An irreg. intr. v., indic. m., pres. t., p. num., 3rd per., agr. with its nom. "instruments." |
| in | A prep., sh. the rn. bet. "are" and "habitations." |
| **their** | A pers. pron., mas. gen., p. num., 3rd per., poss. c., gov. by the n. "habitations." |
| habitations. | A com. n., neu. gen., p. num., 3rd per., obj. c., gov. by the prep. "in." |
| 4. sword | A com. n., neu. gen., s. num., 3rd per., nom. c. to the v. "has done" incl. in "have done." |
| and | A cop. conj., jg. the sents. "The sword has done its work" and "the dagger has done its work." |
| dagger | A com. n., neu. gen., s. num., 3rd per., nom. c. to the v. "has done" incl. in "have done." |
| have | An aux. v. to "done," indg. perf. t. |
| done | A past pl. from the tr. v. "to do," ref. to "work." |
| have done | An irreg. tr. v., act. vo., indic. m., perf. t., p. num., 3rd per., agr. with its noms. "sword" and "dagger." |
| **their** | A pers. pron., neu. gen., p. num., 3rd per., poss. c., gov. by the n. "work." |
| work. | An abs. n., neu. gen., s. num., 3rd per., obj. c., gov. by the tr. v. "have done." |
| 5. Famine | An abs. n., neu. gen., s. num., 3rd per., nom. c. to the v. "stalked" incl. in "stalked." |
| and | A cop. conj., jg. the sents. "Famine stalked through the land" and "pestilence stalked through the land." |
| pestilence | An abs. n., neu. gen., s. num., 3rd per., nom. c. to the v. "stalked" incl. in "stalked." |
| stalked | A reg. intr. v., indic. m., past t., p. num., 3rd per., agr. with its noms. "famine" and "pestilence." |
| through | A prep., sh. the rn. bet. "stalked" and "land." |
| land | A com. n., neu. gen., s. num., 3rd per., obj. c., gov. by the prep. "through." |
| thousands | A com. n., neu. gen., p. num., 3rd per., nom. c. to the v. "were destroyed." |
| were | An aux. v. to "destroyed," indg. pass. vo., past t. |
| destroyed | A past pl. from the tr. v. "to destroy," ref. to "thousands." |
| were destroyed | A reg. tr. v., pass. vo., indic. m., past t., p. num., 3rd per., agr. with its nom. "thousands." |
| by | A prep., sh. the rn. bet. "were destroyed" and "them." |
| **them.** | A pers. pron., neu. gen., p. num., 3rd per., obj. c., gov. by the prep. "by." |
| 6. Foxglove | A com. n., neu. gen., s. num., 3rd. per., nom. c. to the v. "grouped" incl. in "grouped." |
| and | A cop. conj., jg. the sents. "Foxglove, *side by side with night-shade, emblem of punishment and pride*, grouped its *dark hues with every stain*" and "night-shade, side by side *with foxglove*, emblem of...stain." |
| night-shade | A compd. com. n., neu. gen., s. num., 3rd per., nom. c. to the v. "grouped" incl. in "grouped." |
| side | A com. n., neu. gen., s. num., 3rd per., nom. c. absolute. (*Being* is und. See *Parsing*, p. 107.) |
| by | A prep., sh. the rn. bet. *being* und. and "side." |
| side | A com. n., neu. gen., s. num., 3rd pers., obj. c., gov. by the prep. "by." |
| Emblems | A com. n., neu. gen., p. num., 3rd per., nom. c., in app. with "foxglove" and "night-shade." |
| of | A prep., sh. the rn. bet. "emblems" and "punishment." |
| punishment | An abs. n., neu. gen., s. num., 3rd per., obj. c., gov. by the prep. "of." |
| and | A cop. conj., jg. the sents. "Foxglove and night-shade, side by side, emblems of punishment, grouped *their dark hues with every stain*" and "*foxglove and night-shade, side by side, emblems of* pride, grouped...stain." |
| pride | An abs. n., neu. gen., s. num., 3rd per., obj. c., gov. by the prep. *of* und. |
| Grouped | A reg. tr. v., act. vo., indic. m., past t., p. num., 3rd per., agr. with its noms. "foxglove" and "night-shade." |

| | |
|---|---|
| their | A pers. pron., neu. gen., p. num., 3rd per., poss. c., gov. by the n. "hues." |
| dark | An adj. of quality, pos. deg., qual. the n. "hues." |
| hues | An abs. n., neu. gen., p. num., 3rd per., obj. c., gov. by the tr. v. "grouped." |
| with | A prep., sh. the rn. bet. "grouped" and "stain." |
| every | A dist. nu. adj. of quantity, qual. the n. "stain." |
| stain | A com. n., neu. gen., s. num., 3rd per., obj. c., gov. by the prep. "with." |
| weather-beaten | A compd. adj. of quality, pos. deg., qual. the n. "crags." |
| crags | A com. n., neu. gen., p. num., 3rd per., nom. c. to the v. "retain." |
| retain. | A reg. tr. v., act. vo., indic. m., pres. t., p. num., 3rd per., agr. with its nom. "crags." |

## Exercise 148.

| | |
|---|---|
| 1. Either | A disj. conj., introducing the sent. "the captain *will lose his life in this fearful struggle*." |
| captain | A com. n., mas. gen., s. num., 3rd per., nom. c. to the v. *will lose* und. |
| or | A disj. conj., cor. to "either," jg. the sents. "the captain *will lose ...struggle*" and "the sailor...struggle." |
| sailor | A com. n., mas. gen., s. num., 3rd per., nom. c. to the v. "will lose." |
| will | An aux. v. to "lose," indg. fut. t. |
| (to) lose | An irreg. tr. v., act. vo., infin. m., pres. t., gov. by the v. "will." |
| will lose | A reg. tr. v., act. vo., indic. m., fut. t., s. num., 3rd per., agr. with its nom. "sailor." |
| his | A pers. pron., mas. gen., s. num., 3rd per., poss. c., gov. by the n. "life." |
| life | An abs. n., neu. gen., s. num., 3rd per., obj. c., gov. by the tr. v. "will lose." |
| in | A prep., sh. the rn. bet. "will lose" and "struggle." |
| this | A dis. adj., lim. the n. "struggle." |
| fearful | An adj. of quality, pos. deg., qual. the n. "struggle." |
| struggle. | An abs. n., neu. gen., s. num., 3rd per., obj. c., gov. by the prep. "in." |
| 2. Literature | An abs. n., neu. gen., s. num., 3rd per., nom. c. to the v. *has had* und. |
| or | A disj. conj., jg. the sents. "Literature *has had its influence on this poet's mind*" and "art has had...mind." |
| art | An abs. n., neu. gen., s. num., 3rd per., nom. c. to the v. "has had." |
| has | An aux. v. to "had," indg. perf. t. |
| had | A past pl. from the tr. v. "to have," ref. to "influence." |
| has had | An irreg. tr. v., act. vo., indic. m., perf. t., s. num., 3rd per., agr. with its nom. "art." |
| its | A pers. pron., neu. gen., s. num., 3rd per., poss. c., gov. by the n. "influence." |
| influence | An abs. n., neu. gen., s. num., 3rd per., obj. c., gov. by the tr. v. "has had." |
| on | A prep., sh. the rn. bet. "has had" and "mind." |
| this | A dis. adj., lim. the n. "poet's." |
| poet's | A com. n., mas. gen., s. num., 3rd per., poss. c., gov. by the n. "mind." |
| mind. | A com. n., neu. gen., s. num., 3rd per., obj. c., gov. by the prep. "on." |
| 3. hero | A com. n., mas. gen., s. num., 3rd per., nom. c. to the v. *may have incited* und. |
| or | A disj. conj., jg. the sents. "A hero *may, by his example, have incited the heathen to noble deeds*" and "a demi-god...deeds." |
| demi-god | A com. n., mas. gen., s. num., 3rd per., nom. c. to the v. "may have incited." |
| may | An aux. v. to "have incited," indg. pot m. |
| by | A prep., sh. the rn. bet. "may have incited" and "example." |
| his | A pers. pron., mas. gen., s. num., 3rd per., poss. c., gov. by the n. "example." |

| | |
|---|---|
| example | An abs. n., neu. gen., s. num., 3rd per., obj. c., gov. by the prep. "by." |
| have | An aux. v. to "incited," indg. perf. t. |
| incited | A past pl. from the tr. v. "to incite," ref. to "heathen." |
| may have in- cited | A reg. tr. v., act. vo., pot. m., perf. t., s. num., 3rd per., agr. with its nom. "demi-god." |
| heathen | A com. n., com. gen., p. num., 3rd per., obj. c., gov. by the tr. v. "may have incited." |
| to | A prep., sh. the rn. bet. "may have incited" and "deeds." |
| noble | An adj. of quality, pos. deg., qual. the n. "deeds." |
| deeds. | An abs. n., neu. gen., p. num., 3rd per., obj. c., gov. by the prep. "to." |
| 4. Neither | A disj. conj., introducing the sent. "the king *governed his subjects well.*" |
| king | A com. n., mas. gen., s. num., 3rd per., nom. c. to the v. *governed* und. |
| nor | A disj. conj., cor. to "neither," jg. the sents. "the king *governed ...well*" and "the emperor ..well." |
| emperor | A com. n., mas. gen., s. num., 3rd per., nom. c. to the v. "governed." |
| governed | A reg. tr. v., act. vo., indic. m., past t., s. num., 3rd per., agr. with its nom. "emperor." |
| **his** | A pers. pron., mas. gen., s. num., 3rd per., poss. c., gov. by the n. "subjects." |
| subjects | A com. n., com. gen., p. num., 3rd per., obj. c., gov. by the tr. v. "governed." |
| well. | An adv. of man., mod. the v. "governed." |
| 5. Either | A disj. conj., introducing the sent. "Lucy *has lost her purse.*" |
| Lucy | A prop. n., fem. gen., s. num., 3rd per., nom. c. to the v. *has lost* und. |
| or | A disj. conj., cor. to "either," jg. the sents. "Lucy *has lost her purse*" and "Caroline...purse." |
| Caroline | A prop. n., fem. gen., s. num., 3rd per., nom. c. to the v. "has lost." |
| has | An aux. v. to "lost," indg. perf. t. |
| lost | A past pl. from the tr. v. "to lose," ref. to "purse." |
| has lost | An irreg. tr. v., act. vo., indic. m., perf. t., s. num., 3rd per., agr. with its nom. "Caroline." |
| **her** | A pers. pron., fem. gen., s. num., 3rd per., poss. c., gov. by the n. "purse." |
| purse. | A com. n., neu. gen., s. num., 3rd per., obj. c., gov. by the tr. v. "has lost." |
| 6. senator | A com. n., mas. gen., s. num., 3rd per., nom. c. to the v. *must overstep* und. |
| or | A disj. conj., jg. the sents. "A senator *must not overstep his duty*" and "a counsellor...duty." |
| counsellor | A com. n., mas. gen., s. num., 3rd per., nom. c. to the v. "must overstep." |
| must | An aux. v. to "overstep," indg. pot. m., pres. t. |
| not | An adv. of m. (neg.), mod. the v. "must overstep." |
| (to) overstep | A reg. tr. v., act. vo., infin. m., pres. t., gov. by the v. "must." |
| must overstep | A reg. tr. v., act. vo., pot. m., pres. t., s. num., 3rd per., agr. with its nom. "counsellor." |
| **his** | A pers. pron., mas. gen., s. num., 3rd per., poss. c., gov. by the n. "duty." |
| duty. | An abs. n., neu. gen., s. num., 3rd per., obj. c., gov. by the tr. v. "must overstep." |

## Exercise 149.

| | |
|---|---|
| 1. You | A pers. pron., com. gen., p. num., or s. num., p. form, 2nd per., nom. c. to the v. "have met" incl. in "have met." |
| and | A cop. conj., jg. the sents. "You have met *me at last*" and "I have met *you* at last." |
| I | A pers. pron., com. gen., s. num., 1st per., nom. c. to the v. "have met" incl. in "have met." |
| have | An aux. v. to "met," indg. perf. t. |
| met | A past pl. from the tr. v. "to meet," ref. to "you." |

136  KEY TO

| | |
|---|---|
| have met | An irreg. tr. v., act. vo., indic. m. perf. t., p. num., 1st per., agr. with its noms. "you" and "I" ("you and I"=we). |
| at last | A comp. adv. of time, mod. the v. "have met." (See also *Parsing* p. 150.) |
| **we** | A pers. pron., com. gen., p. num., 1st per., nom. c. to the v. "must settle." |
| must | An aux. v. to "settle," indg. pot. m., pres. t. |
| now | An adv. of time, mod. the v. "must settle." |
| **our** | A pers. pron., com. gen., p. num., 1st per., poss. c., gov. by the n. "quarrel." |
| quarrel | An abs. n., neu. gen., s. num., 3rd per., obj. c., gov. by the tr. v. "must settle." |
| (to) settle | A reg. tr. v., act. vo., infin. m., pres. t., gov. by the v. "must." |
| must settle. | A reg. tr. v., act. vo., pot. m., pres. t., p. num., 1st per., agr. with its nom. "we." |
| 2. He | A pers. pron., mas. gen., s. num., 3rd per., nom. c. to the v. "has done" incl. in "have done." |
| and | A cop. conj., jg. the sents. "He has done his *best endeavour*" and "I have done my best *endeavour*." |
| I | A pers. pron., com. gen., s. num., 1st per., nom. c. to the v. "have done," incl. in "have done." |
| have | An aux. v. to "done," indg. perf. t. |
| done | A past p. from the tr v. "to do," ref. to *endeavour* und. |
| have done | An irreg. tr. v., act. vo., indic. m., perf. t., p. num., 1st. per., agr. with its noms. "he" and "I" ("he and I"=we). |
| **our** | A pers. pron., com. gen., p. num., 1st per., poss. c., gov. by the n. *endeavour* und. |
| best. | An adj. of quality, superl. deg., qual. the n. *endeavour* und. |
| 3. My | A pers. pron., com. gen., s. num., 1st per., poss. c., gov. by the n. "servant." |
| servant | A com. n., com. gen., s. num., 3rd per., nom. c. to the v. "fought," incl. in "fought." |
| and | A cop. conj., jg. the sents. "My servant fought his (or her) *way through the crowd*" and "I fought my way...crowd." |
| I | A pers. pron., com. gen., s. num., 1st per., nom. c. to the v. "fought," incl. in "fought." |
| fought | An irreg. tr. v., act. vo., indic. m., past t., p. num., 1st per., agr. with its noms. "servant" and "I" ("servant and I"=we). |
| **our** | A pers. pron., com. gen., p. num., 1st per., poss. c., gov. by the n. "way." |
| way | A com. n., neu. gen., s. num., 3rd per., obj. c., gov. by the tr. v. "fought." |
| through | A prep., sh. the rn. bet. "fought" and "crowd." |
| crowd. | A com. col. n., neu. gen., s. num., 3rd per., obj. c., gov. by the prep. "through." |
| 4. My | A pers. pron., com. gen., s. num., 1st per., poss. c., gov. by the n. "son." |
| son | A com. n., mas gen., s. num., 3rd per., nom. c. to the v. "does bequeath" incl. in "do bequeath." |
| and | A cop. conj., jg. the sents. "My son doth bequeath *to you* his faithful services" and "I do bequeath to you my faithful services." |
| I | A pers. pron., com. gen., s. num., 1st per., nom. c. to the v. "do bequeath" incl. in "do bequeath." |
| do | An aux. v. to "bequeath," indg. pres t., emph. form. |
| (to) bequeath | A reg. tr. v., act. vo., infin. m., pres. t., gov. by the v. "do." |
| do bequeath | A reg. tr. v., act. vo., indic. m., pres. t., emph. form, p. num., 1st per., agr. with its noms. "son" and "I" ("son and I" = we). |
| to | A prep., sh. the rn. bet. "do bequeath" and "you." |
| you | A pers. pron., com. gen., p. num., or s. num., p. form, 2nd per., obj. c., gov. by the prep. "to." |
| **our** | A pers. pron., com. gen., p. num., 1st per., poss. c., gov. by the n. "services." |
| faithful | An adj. of quality, pos. deg., qual. the n. "services." |
| services. | An abs. n., neu. gen., p. num., 3rd per., obj. c., gov. by the tr. v. "do bequeath." |
| 5. You | A pers. pron., com. gen., s. num., p. form, 2nd per., nom. c. to the v. "has followed" incl. in "have followed." |

| | |
|---|---|
| and | A cop. conj., jg. the sents. "You have *thus far* followed *the bent of* your *own inclinations*" and "your brother has thus far followed the bent of his own inclinations." |
| your | A pers. pron., com. gen., s. num., p. form, 2nd per., poss. c., gov. by the n. "brother." |
| brother | A com. n., mas. gen., s. num., 3rd per., nom. c. to the v. "has followed" incl. in "have followed." |
| have | An aux. v. to "followed," indg. perf. t. |
| thus | An adv. of deg., mod. the adv. "far." |
| far | An adv. of place, mod. the v. "have followed." |
| followed | A past pl. from the tr. v. "to follow." ref. to the n. "bent." |
| have followed | A reg. tr. v., act. vo., indic. m., past t., p. num., 2nd per., agr. with its noms. "you" and "brother" ("you and brother" = you). |
| bent | An abs. n., neu. gen., s. num., 3rd per., obj. c., gov. by the tr. v. "have followed." |
| of | A prep., sh. the rn. bet. "bent" and "inclinations." |
| **your** | A pers. pron., forming with the adj. "own" a compd. pers. pron. |
| own | An intensive adj. of quality, qual. the n. "inclinations." |
| **your own** | A compd. pers. pron., com. gen., p. num., 2nd per., poss. c., gov. by the n. "inclinations." |
| inclinations. | An abs. n., neu. gen., p. num., 3rd per., obj. c., gov. by the prep. "of." |
| 6. You | A pers. pron., com. gen., s. num., p. form, 2nd per., nom. c. to the v. "seem" incl. in "seem." |
| and | A cop. conj., jg. the sents. "You seem *to live by* your *wits*" and "Frederick seems to live by his wits." |
| Frederick | A prop. n., mas. gen., s. num., 3rd per., nom. c. to the v. "seems" incl. in "seem." |
| seem | A reg. intr. v., indic. m., pres. t., p. num., 2nd per., agr. with its noms. "you" and "Frederick" ("you and Frederick" = you). |
| to | A particle, indg. infin. m. |
| to live | A reg. intr. v., infin. m., pres. t., gov. by the v. "seem." |
| by | A prep., sh. the rn. bet. "to live" and "wits." |
| **your** | A pers. pron., com. gen., p. num., 2nd per., poss. c., gov. by the n. "wits." |
| wits. | An abs. n., neu. gen., p. num., 3rd per., obj. c., gov. by the prep. "by." |

## Exercise 150.

| | |
|---|---|
| 1. **You** | A pers. pron., com. gen., s. num., p. form., 2nd per., nom. c. to the v. "must say" incl. in "must say." |
| and | A cop. conj., jg. the sents. "You must say *farewell*" and "I must say farewell." |
| **I** | A pers. pron., com. gen., s. num., 1st per., nom. c. to the v. "must say" incl. in "must say." |
| must | An aux. v. to "say," indg. pot m., pres. t. |
| (to) say | An irreg. tr. v., act. vo., infin. m., pres. t., gov. by the v. "must." |
| must say | An irreg. tr. v., act. vo., pot. m., pres. t., p. num., 1st per., agr. with its noms. "you" and "I" ("you and I" = we). |
| farewell. | An abs. n., neu. gen., s. num., 3rd per., obj. c., gov. by the tr. v. "must say." |
| 2. **You** | A pers. pron., com. gen., s. num., p. form, 2nd per., nom. c. to the v. "must take" incl. in "must take." |
| and | A cop. conj., jg. the sents. "You must take your chance" and "he must take his chance." |
| **he** | A pers. pron., mas. gen., s. num., 3rd per., nom. c. to the v. "must take" incl. in "must take." |
| must | An aux. v. to "take," indg. pot. m., pres. t. |
| (to) take | An irreg. tr. v., act. vo., infin. m., pres. t., gov. by the v. "must." |
| must take | An irreg. tr. v., act. vo., pot. m., pres. t., p. num., 2nd per., agr. with its noms. "you" and "he" ("you and he" = you). |
| your | A pers. pron., com. gen., p. num., 2nd per., poss. c., gov. by the n. "chance." |

138                        KEY TO

| | |
|---|---|
| chance. | An abs. n., neu. gen., s. num., 3rd per., obj. c., gov. by the tr. v. "must take." |
| 3. **She** | A pers. pron., fem. gen., s. num., 3rd per., nom. c. to the v. "gathered" incl. in "gathered." |
| and | A cop. conj., jg. the sents. "She gathered *flowers in the wood*" and "I gathered...wood." |
| **I** | A pers. pron., com. gen., s. num., 1st per., nom. c. to the v. "gathered" incl. in "gathered." |
| gathered | A reg. tr. v., act. vo., indic. m., past t., p. num., 1st per., agr. with its noms. "She" and "I" ("she and I"== we). |
| flowers | A com. n., neu. gen., p. num., 3rd per., obj. c., gov. by the tr. v. "gathered." |
| in | A prep., sh. the rn. bet. "gathered" and "wood." |
| wood. | A com. n., neu. gen., s. num., 3rd per., obj. c., gov. by the prep. "in." |
| 4. Even | An adv. of man., mod. the phrase "for that." |
| for | A prep., sh. the rn. bet. "thank" and *favour* und. |
| that | A dis. adj., lim. the n. *favour* und. |
| **he** | A pers. pron., mas. gen., s. num., 3rd per., nom. c. to the v. *thanks* incl. in "thank." |
| and | A cop. conj., jg. the sents. "Even for that he thanks *you*" and "*even for that* I thank you." |
| **I** | A pers. pron., com. gen., s. num., 1st per., nom. c. to the v. "thank" incl. in "thank." |
| thank | A reg. tr. v., act. vo., indic. m., pres. t., p. num., 1st per., agr. with its noms. "he" and "I" ("he and I"==we). |
| you. | A pers. pron., com. gen., p. num., (or s. num., p. form,) 2nd per., obj. c., gov. by the tr. v. "thank." |
| 5. Let | An irreg. tr. v., act. vo., imper. m., pres. t., s. num., 2nd per., agr. with its nom. *thou* und. |
| **thee** | A pers. pron., com. gen., s. num., 2nd per., obj. c., gov. by the tr. v. "let." |
| and | A cop. conj., jg. the sents. "Let thee *this feat attempt*" and "*let me...attempt*." |
| **me** | A pers. pron., com. gen., s. num., 1st per., obj. c., gov. by the tr. v. *let* und. |
| this | A dis. adj., lim. the n. "feat." |
| feat | An abs. n., neu. gen., s. num., 3rd per., obj. c., gov. by the tr. v. "*to* attempt." |
| (to) attempt. | A reg. tr. v., act. vo., infin. m., pres. t., gov. by the v. "let." |
| 6. Such | An adj. of quality, qual. the n. "kindness." |
| was | An irreg. intr. v., indic. m., past t., s. num., 3rd per., agr. with its nom. "kindness." |
| kindness | An abs. n., neu. gen., s. num., 3rd per., nom. c. to the v. "was." |
| they | A pers. pron., com. gen., p. num., 3rd per., nom. c. to the v. "showed." |
| showed | A reg. tr. v., act. vo., indic. m., past t., p. num., 3rd per., agr. with its nom. "they." (*Which* they showed.) |
| to | A prep., sh. the rn. bet. "showed" and "her." |
| **her** | A pers. pron., fem. gen., s. num., 3rd per., obj. c., gov. by the prep. "to." |
| and | A cop. conj., jg. the sents. "*which* they showed to her" and "*which they showed to* me." |
| **me.** | A pers. pron., com. gen., s. num., 1st per., obj. c., gov. by the prep. *to* und. |

## Exercise 151.

| | |
|---|---|
| 1. Be | An aux. v. to "assured," indg. pass. vo., pres. t. |
| assured | A past pl. from the tr. v. "to assure," ref. to *you* und. |
| be assured | A reg. tr. v., pass. vo., imper. m., pres. t., p. num., 2nd per., agr. with its nom. *you* und. |
| **you** | A pers. pron., com. gen., p. num., 2nd per., nom. c. to the v. "will be set" incl. in "will be set." |
| and | A cop. conj., jg. the sents. "you will be set *free*" and "they... free." |
| **they** | A pers. pron., com. gen., p. num., 3rd per., nom. c. to the v. "will be set" incl. in "will be set." |

ENGLISH GRAMMAR AND ANALYSIS. 139

| | |
|---|---|
| will | An aux. v. to "be set," indg. fut. t. |
| be | An aux. v. to "set," indg. pass. vo. |
| set | A past pl. from the tr. v. "to set," ref. to "you" and "they." |
| will be set | An irreg. tr. v., pass. vo., indic. m., past t., p. num., 2nd per., agr. with its noms. "you" and "they" ("you and they"= you). |
| free. | An adj. of quality, pos. deg., qual. the prons. "you" and "they." |
| 2. wise | An adj. of quality, pos. deg., qual. the n. *virgins* und. |
| answered | A reg. intr. v., indic. m., past t., p. num., 3rd per., agr. with its nom. *virgins* und. |
| saying | A pres. pl. from the tr. v. "to say," ref. to *virgins* und. |
| Not | An adv. of m. (neg.), mod. the v. *can do* und. (*We can* not *do* so.) |
| so | An adv. of man., mod. the v. *can do* und. |
| lest | A disj. conj., jg. the sents. "*We can* not *do* so" and "there be …you," and indg. subj. m. |
| there | An expletive adv., mod. the v. "be." |
| be | An irreg. intr. v., subj. m., pres. t., s. num., 3rd per., agr. with its nom. *oil* und. |
| not | An adv. of m. (neg.), mod. the v. "be." |
| enough | An adj. of quantity (bulk or mass), qual. the n. *oil* und. |
| for | A prep., sh. the rn. bet. *oil* und. and "us." |
| **us** | A pers. pron., fem. gen., p. num., 1st per., obj. c., gov. by the prep. "for." |
| and | A cop. conj., jg. the sents. "there be not enough for us" and "there be not enough *for* you." |
| **you.** | A pers. pron., fem. gen., p. num., 2nd per., obj. c., gov. by the prep. *for* und. |
| 3. **We** | A pers. pron., com. gen., p. num., 1st per., nom. c. to the v. "have acted" incl. in "have acted." |
| and | A cop. conj., jg. the sents. "We have acted" and "they have acted." |
| **they** | A pers. pron., com. gen., p. num., 3rd per., nom. c. to the v. "have acted" incl. in "have acted." |
| have | An aux. v. to "acted," indg. perf. t. |
| acted | A past pl. from the intr. v. "to act," ref. to "they." |
| have acted | A reg. intr. v., indic. m., perf. t., p. num., 1st per., agr. with its noms. "we" and "they" ("we and they"=we). |
| as | A cop. conj., jg. the sents. "we…acted" and "you desired." |
| you | A pers. pron., com. gen., p. num. (or s. num., p. form), 2nd per., nom. c. to the v. "desired." |
| desired. | A reg. intr. v., indic. m., past t., p. num. (or s. num., p. form), 2nd per., agr. with its nom. "you." |
| 4. **We** | A pers. pron., com. gen., p, num., 1st per., nom. c. to the v. "must denounce" incl. in "must denounce." |
| **you** | A pers. pron., com. gen., p. num., 2nd per., nom. c. to the v. "must denounce" incl. in "must denounce." |
| and | A cop. conj., jg. the sents. "you must denounce *this villany*" and "they must denounce this villany." |
| **they** | A pers. pron., com. gen., p. num., 3rd per., nom. c. to the v. "must denounce" incl. in "must denounce." |
| must | An aux. v. to "denounce," indg. pot. m., pres. t. |
| (to) denounce | A reg. tr. v., act vo., infin. m., pres. t., gov. by the v. "must." |
| must denounce | A reg. tr. v., act. vo., pot. m., pres. t., p. num., 1st per., agr. with its noms. "we," "you," and "they" ("we, you, and they"=we). |
| this | A dis. adj., lim. the n. "villany." |
| villany. | An abs. n., neu. gen., s. num., 3rd per., obj. c., gov. by the tr. v. "must denounce." |
| 5. **You** | A pers. pron., com. gen., p. num., 2nd per., nom. c. to the v. "seem" incl. in "seem." |
| and | A cop. conj., jg. the sents. "You seem *to mock us*" and "they seem to mock us." |
| **they** | A pers. pron., com. gen., p. num., 3rd per., nom. c. to the v. "seem" incl. in "seem." |
| seem | A reg. intr. v., indic. m., pres. t., p. num., 2nd per., agr. with its noms. "you" and "they" ("you and they"=you.) |
| to | A particle, indg. infin. m. |
| to mock | A reg. tr. v., act. vo., infin. m., pres. t., gov. by the v. "seem." |

| | |
|---|---|
| us. | A pers. pron., com. gen., p. num., 1st per., obj. c., gov. by the tr. v. "to mock." |
| 6. He | A pers. pron., mas. gen., s. num., 3rd per., nom. c. to the v. "has showered." |
| has | An aux. v. to "showered," indg. perf. t. |
| showered | A past pl. from the tr. v. "to shower," ref. to "benefits." |
| has showered | A reg. tr. v., act. vo., indic. m., perf. t., s. num., 3rd per., agr. with its nom. "he." |
| benefits | An abs. n., neu. gen., p. num., 3rd per., obj. c., gov. by the tr. v. "has showered." |
| on | A prep., sh. the rn. bet. "has showered" and "you." |
| you | A pers. pron., com. gen., p. num., 2nd per., obj. c., gov. by the prep. "on." |
| and | A cop. conj., jg. the sents. "He has showered...you" and "he has showered benefits on them." |
| them. | A pers. pron., com. gen., p. num., 3rd per., obj. c., gov. by the prep. on und. |

## Exercise 152.

| | |
|---|---|
| 1. It | A pers. pron., neu. gen., s. num., 3rd per., nom. c. to the v. "had pleased." |
| had | An aux. v. to "pleased," indg. pluperf. t. |
| pleased | A past pl. from the tr. v. "to please," ref. to "Heaven." |
| had pleased | A reg. tr. v., act. vo., indic. m., pluperf. t., s. num., 3rd per., agr. with its nom. "it." |
| Heaven | A prop. n., mas. gen. by personification, s. num., 3rd per., obj. c., gov. by the tr. v. "had pleased." |
| he | A pers. pron., mas. gen., s. num., 3rd per., nom. c. to the v. "said." |
| said | An irreg. tr. v., act. vo., indic. m., pres. t., s. num., 3rd per., agr. with its nom. "he." |
| to | A particle, indg. infin. m. |
| to bless | A reg. tr. v., act. vo., infin. m., pres. t.; used as an abs. n., neu. gen., s. num., 3rd per., nom. c., in app. with "it." |
| him | A pers. pron., mas. gen., s. num., 3rd per., obj. c., gov. by the tr. v. "to bless." |
| with | A prep., sh. the rn. bet. "to bless" and "sons." |
| three | A def. card. nu. adj. of quantity, qual. the n. "sons." |
| sons. | A com. n., mas. gen., p. num., 3rd per., obj. c., gov. by the prep. "with." |
| 2. O | An interj. |
| it | A pers. pron., neu. gen., s. num., 3rd per., nom. c. to the v. "is." |
| is | An irreg. intr. v., indic. m., pres. t., s. num., 3rd per., agr. with its nom. "it." |
| excellent | An adj. of quality, qual. the pron. "it." |
| to | A particle, indg. infin. m. |
| to have | An irreg. tr. v., act. vo., infin. m., pres. t.; used as an abs. n., neu. gen., s. num., 3rd per., nom. c., in app. with "it." |
| giant's | A com. n., mas. gen., s. num., 3rd per., poss. c., gov. by the n. "strength." |
| strength | An abs. n., neu. gen., s. num., 3rd per., obj. c., gov. by the tr. v. "to have." |
| but | A disj. conj., jg. the sents. "It is...strength" and "it is...giant." |
| it | A pers. pron., neu. gen., s. num., 3rd per., nom. c. to the v. "is." |
| is | An irreg. intr. v., indic. m., pres. t., s. num., 3rd per., agr. with its nom. "it." |
| tyrannous | An adj. of quality, pos. deg., qual. the pron. "it." |
| to | A particle, indg. infin. m. |
| to use | A reg. tr. v., act. vo., infin. m., pres. t.; used as an abs. n., neu. gen., s. num., 3rd per., nom. c., in app. with "it." |
| it | A pers. pron., neu. gen., s. num., 3rd per., obj. c., gov. by the tr. v. "to use." |
| like | An adv. of man., mod. the v. "to use." |
| giant. | A com. n., mas. gen., s. num., 3rd per., obj. c., gov. by the prep. to und. |

## ENGLISH GRAMMAR AND ANALYSIS. 141

3. It — A pers. pron., neu. gen., s. num., 3rd per., nom. c. to the v. "can be."
can — An aux. v. to "be," indg. pot. m., pres. t.
(to) be — An irreg. intr. v., infin. m., pres. t., gov. by the v. "can."
can be — An irreg. intr. v., pot. m., pres. t., s. num., 3rd per., agr. with its nom. "it."
no — An adv. of m. (neg.), mod. the adj. "more."
more — An adj. of quantity (bulk or mass), comp. deg., qual. the n. "sin."
sin — An abs. n., neu. gen., s. num., 3rd per., nom. c. after the v. "can be."
to — A particle, indg. infin. m.
to ask — A reg. tr. v., act. vo., infin. m., pres. t.; used as an abs. n., neu. gen., s. num., 3rd per., nom. c., in app. with "it."
what — A compd. rel. pron., including both the rel. and the ant., neu. gen., s. num., 3rd per. "What" is equiv. to "the thing which," "thing" being obj. c., gov. by the tr. v. "to ask," and "which," obj. c., gov. by the tr. v. "grants."
God — A prop. n., mas. gen., s. num., 3rd per., nom. c. to the v. "grants."
grants — A reg. tr. v., act. vo., indic. m., pres. t., s. num., 3rd per., agr. with its nom. "God."

4. It — A pers. pron., neu. gen., s. num., 3rd per., nom. c. to the v. "was."
was — An irreg. intr. v., indic. m., past t., s. num., 3rd per., agr. with its nom. "it."
her — A pers. pron., fem. gen., s. num., 3rd per., poss. c., gov. by the n. "fingers."
fingers — A com. n., neu. gen., p. num., 3rd per., nom. c. after the v. "was."
which — A rel. pron., neu. gen., p. num., 3rd per., agr. with its ant. "fingers," nom. c. to the v. "gave."
gave — An irreg. tr. v., act. vo., indic. m., past t., p. num., 3rd per., agr. with its nom. "which."
pickles — A com. n., neu. gen., p. num., 3rd per., obj. c., gov. by the prep. *to* und.
their — A pers. pron., neu. gen., p. num., 3rd per., poss. c., gov. by the n. *colour* und.
peculiar — An adj. of quality, pos. deg., qual. the n. *colour* und.
green. — An adj. of quality, pos. deg., qual. the n. *colour* und.

5. I — A pers. pron., com. gen., s. num., 1st per., nom. c. to the v. "am."
am — An irreg. intr. v., indic. m., pres. t., s. num., 1st per., agr. with its nom. "I."
not — An adv. of m. (neg.), mod. the v. "am."
what — A compd. rel. pron., including both the rel. and the ant., neu. gen., s. num., 3rd per. "What" is equiv. to "the thing which," "thing" being nom. c. after the v. "am," and "which" obj. c., gov. by the prep. "for."
you — A pers. pron., com. gen., p. num. (or s. num., p. form), 2nd per., nom. c. to the v. "take."
take — An irreg. tr. v., act. vo., indic. m., pres. t., p. num. (or s. num., p. form), 2nd per., agr. with its nom. "you."
me — A pers. pron., com. gen., s. num., 1st per., obj. c., gov. by the tr. v. "take."
for. — A prep., sh. the rn. bet. "take" and "which" incl. in "what."

6. Who — An interrog. pron., com. gen., s. num., 3rd per., nom. c. after the v. "are."
are — An irreg. intr. v., indic. m., pres. t., s. num., p. form, 2nd per., agr. with its nom. "you."
you — A pers. pron., com. gen., s. num., p. form, 2nd per., nom. c. to the v. "are."
You — A pers. pron., com. gen., s. num., p. form, 2nd per., nom. c. to the v. "know."
know — An irreg. tr. v., act. vo., indic. m., pres. t., s. num., p. form, 2nd per., agr. with its nom. "you."
me. — A pers. pron., com. gen., s. num., 1st per., obj. c., gov. by the tr. v. "know."

| | |
|---|---|
| 7. **Your** | A pers. pron., com. gen., s. num., p. form, 2nd per., poss. c., gov. by the n. "son." |
| son | A com. n., mas. gen., s. num., 3rd per., nom. c. to the v. "has used." |
| has | An aux. v. to "used," indg. perf. t. |
| not | An adv. of m. (neg.), mod. the v. "has used." |
| used | A past pl. from the tr. v. "to use," ref. to "me." |
| has used | A reg. tr. v., act. vo., indic. m., perf. t., s. num., 3rd per., agr. with its nom. "son." |
| **me** | A pers. pron., com. gen., s. num., 1st per., obj. c., gov. by the tr. v. "has used." |
| well. | An adv. of man., mod. the v. "has used." |
| 8. **They** | A pers. pron., com. gen., p. num., 3rd per., nom. c. to the v. "shall reap." |
| that | A rel. pron., com. gen., p. num., 3rd per., agr. with its ant. "they," nom. c. to the v. "sow." |
| sow | A reg. (or, sometimes, irreg.) intr. v., indic. m., pres. t., p. num., 3rd per., agr. with its nom. "that." |
| in | A prep., sh. the rn. bet. "sow" and "tears." |
| tears | A com. n., neu. gen., p. num., 3rd per., obj. c., gov. by the prep. "in." |
| shall | An aux. v. to "reap," indg. fut. t., emph. form, expressing "certainty" or "promise." |
| (to) reap | A reg. intr. v., infin. m., pres. t., gov. by the v. "shall." |
| shall reap | A reg. intr. v., indic. m., fut. t., emph. form, p. num., 3rd per., agr. with its nom. "they." |
| in | A prep., sh. the rn. bet. "shall reap" and "joy." |
| joy. | An abs. n., neu. gen., s. num., 3rd per., obj. c., gov. by the prep. "in." |
| 9. colony | A com. n., neu. gen., s. num., 3rd per., nom. c. to the v. "is." |
| is | An irreg. intr. v., indic. m., pres. t., s. num., 3rd per., agr. with its nom. "colony." |
| under | A prep., sh. the rn. bet. "is" and "obligations." |
| personal | An adj. of quality, qual. the n. "obligations." |
| obligations | An abs. n., neu. gen., p. num., 3rd per., obj. c., gov. by the prep. "under." |
| to | A prep., sh. the rn. bet. "obligations" and "you." |
| **you.** | A pers. pron., com. gen., p. num. (or s. num., p. form), 2nd per., obj. c., gov. by the prep. "to." |
| 10. **We** | A pers. pron., com. gen., p. num., 1st per., nom. c. to the v. "look." |
| look | An irreg. intr. v., indic. m., pres. t., p. num., 1st per., agr. with its nom. "we." |
| before | An adv. of place, mod. the v. "look." |
| and | A cop. conj., jg. the sents. "We look before" and "*we look* after." |
| after | An adv. of place, mod. the v. *look* und. |
| And | A cop. conj., jg. the sents. "*we look* after" and "we pine for the thing." |
| pine | A reg. intr. v., indic. m., pres. t., p. num., 1st per., agr. with its nom. *we* und. |
| for | A prep., sh. the rn. bet. "pine" and "thing" incl. in "what." |
| what | A compd. rel. pron., including both the rel. and the ant., neu. gen., s. num., 3rd per. "What" is equiv. to "the thing which," "thing" being obj. c., gov. by the prep. "for," and "which" nom. c. to the v. "is." |
| is | An irreg. intr. v., indic. m., pres. t., s. num., 3rd per., agr. with its nom. "which" incl. in "what." |
| not. | An adv. of m. (neg.), mod. the v. "is." |

### Exercise 153.

| | |
|---|---|
| 1. sun | A com. n., mas. gen. by personification, s. num., 3rd per., nom. c. to the v. "withheld." |
| **himself** | A compd. pers. pron., mas. gen., s. num., 3rd per., nom. c., in app. with "sun." |
| withheld | An irreg. tr. v., act. vo., indic. m., past t., s. num., 3rd per., agr. with its nom. "sun." |

| | |
|---|---|
| **his** | A pers. pron., mas. gen., s. num., 3rd per., poss. c., gov. by the n. "speed." |
| wonted | An adj. of quality, qual. the n. "speed." |
| speed. | An abs. n., neu. gen., s. num., 3rd per., obj. c., gov. by the tr. v. "withheld." |
| 2. priests | A com. n., mas. gen., p. num., 3rd per., nom. c. to the v. "had." |
| had | An irreg. tr. v., act. vo., indic. m., past t., p. num., 3rd per., agr. with its nom. "priests." |
| portion | A com. n., neu. gen., s. num., 3rd per., obj. c., gov. by the tr. v. "had." |
| assigned | A past pl. from the tr. v. "to assign," ref. to "portion." |
| **them.** | A pers. pron., mas. gen., p. num., 3rd per., obj. c., gov. by the prep. *to* und. |
| 3. Men | A com. n., mas. gen., p. num., 3rd per., nom. c. to the v. "befool." |
| befool | A reg. tr. v., act. vo., indic. m., pres. t., p. num., 3rd per., agr. with its nom. "men." |
| **themselves.** | A compd. pers. pron., mas. gen., p. num., 3rd per., obj. c., gov. by the tr. v. "befool." |
| 4. boy's | A com. n., mas. gen., s. num., 3rd per., poss. c., gov. by the n. "eye." |
| eye | A com. n., neu. gen., s. num., 3rd per., nom. c. to the v. "is fixed." |
| is | An aux. v. to "fixed," indg. pass. vo., pres. t. |
| fixed | A past pl. from the tr. v. "to fix," ref. to "eye." |
| is fixed | A reg. tr. v., pass. vo., indic. m., pres. t., s. num., 3rd per., agr. with its nom. "eye." |
| towards | A prep., sh. the rn. bet. "is fixed" and "Heaven." |
| Heaven | A com. n. tending to prop., neu. gen., s. num., 3rd per., obj. c., gov. by the prep. "towards." |
| and | A cop. conj., jg. the sents. "The boy's eye...Heaven" and "his young heart *is fixed* on Him." |
| **his** | A pers. pron., mas. gen., s. num., 3rd per., poss. c., gov. by the n. "heart." |
| young | An adj. of quality, pos. deg., qual. the n. "heart." |
| heart | A com. n., neu. gen., s. num., 3rd per., nom. c. to the v. *is fixed* und. |
| on | A prep., sh. the rn. bet. *is fixed* und. and "Him." |
| Him | A pers. pron., mas. gen., s. num., 3rd per., obj. c., gov. by the prep. "on." |
| who | A rel. pron., mas. gen., s. num., 3rd per., agr. with its ant. "Him," nom. c. to the v. "reigns." |
| reigns | A reg. intr. v., indic. m., pres. t., s. num., 3rd per., agr. with its nom. "who." |
| there. | An adv. of place, mod. the v. "reigns." |
| 5. Bruce | A prop. n., mas. gen., s. num., 3rd per., nom. c. to the v. "was." |
| was | An irreg. intr. v., indic. m., past t., s. num., 3rd per., agr. with its nom. "Bruce." |
| in | A prep., sh. the rn. bet. "was" and "front." |
| front | A com. n., neu. gen., s. num., 3rd per., obj. c., gov. by the prep. "in." |
| of | A prep., sh. the rn. bet. "front" and "line." |
| **his** | A pers. pron., forming with the adj. "own" a compd. pers. pron. |
| own | An intensive adj. of quality, qual. the n. "line." |
| **his own** | A compd. pers. pron., mas. gen., s. num., 3rd per., poss. c., gov. by the n. "line." |
| line | A com. n., neu. gen., s. num., 3rd per., obj. c., gov. by the prep. "of." |
| arranging | A pres. pl. from the tr. v. "to arrange," ref. to "Bruce." |
| **his** | A pers. pron., mas. gen., s. num., 3rd per., poss. c., gov. by the n. "men." |
| men. | A com. n., mas. gen., p. num., 3rd per., obj. c., gov. by the tr. pl. "arranging." |
| 6. man | A com. n., mas. gen., s. num., 3rd per., nom. c. to the v. "becomes." |
| who | A rel. pron., mas. gen., s. num., 3rd per., agr. with its ant. "man," nom. c. to the v. "dedicates." |

| | |
|---|---|
| dedicates | A reg. tr. v., act. vo., indic. m., pres. t., s. num., 3rd per., agr. with its nom. "who." |
| his | A pers. pron., mas. gen., s. num., 3rd per., poss. c., gov. by the n. "life." |
| life | An abs. n., neu. gen., s. num., 3rd per., obj. c., gov. by the tr. v. "dedicates." |
| to | A prep., sh. the rn. bet. "dedicates" and "knowledge." |
| knowledge | An abs. n., neu. gen., s. num., 3rd per., obj. c., gov. by the prep. "to." |
| becomes | An irreg. intr. v., indic. m., pres. t., s. num., 3rd per., agr. with its nom. "man." |
| habituated | A past pl. from the tr. v. "to habituate," ref. to "man." |
| to | A prep., sh. the rn. bet. "habituated" and "pleasure." |
| pleasure | An abs. n., neu. gen., s. num., 3rd per., obj. c., gov. by the prep. "to." |
| which | A rel. pron., neu. gen., s. num., 3rd per., agr. with its ant. "pleasure," nom. c. to the v. "carries." |
| carries | A reg. tr. v., act. vo., indic. m., pres. t., s. num., 3rd per., agr. with its nom. "which." |
| with | A prep., sh. the rn. bet. "carries" and "it." |
| it | A pers. pron., neu. gen., s. num., 3rd per., obj. c., gov. by the prep. "with." |
| no | A def. card. nu. adj. of quantity, qual. the n. "reproach." |
| reproach. | An abs. n., neu. gen., s. num., 3rd per., obj. c., gov. by the tr. v. "carries." |
| 7. Many | An indef. nu. adj. of quantity, qual. the n. "tribes." |
| tribes | A com. col. n., neu. gen., p. num., 3rd per., nom. c. to the v. "are." |
| of | A prep., sh. the rn. bet. "tribes" and "Indians." |
| Indians | A prop. n., com. gen., p. num., 3rd per., obj. c., gov. by the prep. "of." |
| are | An irreg. intr. v., indic. m., pres. t., p. num., 3rd per., agr. with its nom. "tribes." |
| indebted | An adj. of quality, pos. deg., qual. the n. "tribes." |
| to | A prep., sh. the rn. bet. "indebted" and "bison." |
| bison | A com. n., com. gen., s. num., 3rd per., obj. c., gov. by the prep. "to." |
| for | A prep., sh. the rn. bet. "indebted" and "means." |
| their | A pers. pron., neu. gen., p. num., 3rd per., poss. c., gov. by the n. "means." |
| means | An abs. n., neu. gen., p. num., 3rd per., obj. c., gov. by the prep. "for." |
| of | A prep., sh. the rn. bet. "means" and "living." |
| living. | A verbal or abs. n., neu. gen., s. num., 3rd per., obj. c., gov. by the prep. "of." |
| 8. path | A com. n., neu. gen., s. num., 3rd per., nom. c. to the v. "is." |
| is | An irreg. intr. v., indic. m., pres. t., s. num., 3rd per., agr. with its nom. "path." |
| narrow | An adj. of quality, pos. deg., qual. the n. "path." |
| and | A cop. conj., jg. the sents. "The path is narrow" and "it narrows still." |
| it | A pers. pron., neu. gen., s. num., 3rd per., nom. c. to the v. "narrows." |
| narrows | A reg. intr. v., indic. m., pres. t., s. num., 3rd per., agr. with its nom. "it." |
| still. | An adv. of time, mod. the v. "narrows." |
| 9. great | An adj. of quality, pos. deg., qual. the n. "skill." |
| skill | An abs. n., neu. gen., s. num., 3rd per., nom. c. to the v. "is." |
| of | A prep., sh. the rn. bet. "skill" and "teacher." |
| teacher | A com. n., mas. gen., s. num., 3rd per., obj. c., gov. by the prep. "of." |
| is | An irreg. intr. v., indic. m., pres. t., s. num., 3rd per., agr. with its nom. "skill." |
| to | A particle, indg. infin. m. |
| to get | An irreg. tr. v., act. vo., infin. m., pres. t.; used as an abs. n., neu. gen., s. num., 3rd per., nom. c. after the v. "is." |
| and | A cop. conj., jg. the sents. "The great skill of a teacher is to get |

|  |  |
|---|---|
|  | *the attention of his scholar*" and "*the great skill of a teacher is to keep the attention of his scholar.*" |
| (to) keep | An irreg. tr. v., act. vo., infin. m., pres. t.; used as an abs. n., neu. gen., s. num., 3rd per., nom. c. after the v. *is* und. |
| attention | An abs. n., neu. gen., s. num., 3rd per., obj. c., gov. by the tr. v. "*to* keep." |
| of | A prep., sh. the rn. bet. "attention" and "scholar." |
| **his** | A pers. pron., mas. gen., s. num., 3rd per., poss. c., gov. by the n. "scholar." |
| scholar. | A com. n., com. gen., s. num., 3rd per., obj. c., gov. by the prep. "of." |
| 10. **It** | A pers. pron., neu. gen., s. num., 3rd per., nom. c. to the v. "was." |
| was | An irreg. intr. v., indic. m., past t., s. num., 3rd per., agr. with its nom. "it." |
| time | An abs. n., neu. gen., s. num., 3rd per., nom. c. after the v. "was." |
| of | A prep., sh. the rn. bet. "time" and "roses." |
| roses | A com. n., neu. gen., p. num., 3rd per., obj. c., gov. by the prep. "of." |
| We | A pers. pron., com. gen., p. num., 1st per., nom. c. to the v. "pluck'd." |
| pluck'd | A reg. tr. v., act. vo., indic. m., past t., p. num., 1st per., agr. with its nom. "we." |
| **them** | A pers. pron., neu. gen., p. num., 3rd per., obj. c., gov. by the tr. v. "pluck'd." |
| as | A cop. conj., jg. the sents. "We pluck'd them" and "we pass'd." |
| we | A pers. pron., com. gen., p. num., 1st per., nom. c. to the v. "pass'd." |
| pass'd. | A reg. intr. v., indic. m., past t., p. num., 1st per., agr. with its nom. "we." |

### Exercise 154.

|  |  |
|---|---|
| 1. husbandman | A com. n., mas. gen., s. num., 3rd per., nom. c. to the v. "pays." |
| pays | An irreg. tr. v., act. vo., indic. m., pres. t., s. num., 3rd per., agr. with its nom. "husbandman." |
| respect | An abs. n., neu. gen., s. num., 3rd per., obj. c., gov. by the tr. v. "pays." |
| to | A prep., sh. the rn. bet. "pays" and "redbreast." |
| redbreast | A com. n., com. gen., s. num., 3rd per., obj. c., gov. by the prep. "to." |
| **which** | A rel. pron., com. gen., s. num., 3rd per., agr. with its ant. "redbreast," nom. c. to the v. "predicts." |
| predicts | A reg. tr. v., act. vo., indic. m., pres. t., s. num., 3rd per., agr. with its nom. "which." |
| fine | An adj. of quality, pos. deg., qual. the n. "weather." |
| weather. | An abs. n., neu. gen., s. num., 3rd per., obj. c., gov. by the tr. v. "predicts." |
| 2. Then | An adv. of time, mod. the v. "must speak." |
| must | An aux. v. to "speak," indg. pot. m., pres. t. |
| you | A pers. pron., mas. gen., p. num., 2nd per., nom. c. to the v. "must speak." ("You," *i.e.*, the officers sent to recall Othello.) |
| (to) speak | An irreg. intr. v., infin. m., pres. t., gov. by the v. "must." |
| must speak | An irreg. intr. v., pot. m., pres. t., p. num., 2nd per., agr. with its nom. "you." |
| of | A prep., sh. the rn. bet. "must speak" and "one." |
| one | An indef. pers. pron., mas. gen., s. num., 3rd per., obj. c., gov. by the prep. "of." ("One," *i.e.*, Othello.) |
| **that** | A rel. pron., mas. gen., s. num., 3rd per., agr. with its ant. "one," nom. c. to the v. "lov'd." |
| lov'd | A reg. intr. v., indic. m., past t., s. num., 3rd per., agr. with its nom. "that." |
| not | An adv. of m. (neg.), mod. the adv. "wisely." |
| wisely | An adv. of man., mod. the v. "lov'd." |

| | |
|---|---|
| but | A cnj. conj., jg. the sents. "that lov'd not wisely" and "*that lov'd too well.*" |
| too | An adv. of deg., mod. the adv. "well." |
| well. | An adv. of man., mod. the v. *lov'd* und. |
| 3. He | A pers. pron., mas. gen., s. num., 3rd per., nom. c. to the v. "requested." |
| then | An adv. of time, mod. the v. "requested." |
| requested | A reg. tr. v., act. vo., indic. m., past t., s. num., 3rd per., agr. with its nom. "he." |
| her | A pers. pron., fem. gen., s. num., 3rd per., obj. c., gov. by the tr. v. "requested." |
| to | A particle, indg. infin. m. |
| to stand | An irreg. intr. v., infin. m., pres. t., gov. by the v. "requested." |
| on | A prep., sh. the rn. bet. "to stand" and "straw." |
| straw | A com. n., neu. gen., s. num., 3rd per., obj. c., gov. by the prep. on. |
| **which** | A rel. pron., neu. gen., s. num., 3rd per., agr. with its ant. the sent. "He then requested..straw," obj. c., gov. by the tr. v. "did." |
| she | A pers. pron., fem. gen., s. num., 3rd per., nom. c. to the v. "did." |
| did. | An irreg. tr. v., act. vo., indic. m., past t., s. num., 3rd per., agr. with its nom. "she." |
| 4. My | A pers. pron., com. gen., s. num., 1st per., poss. c., gov. by the n. "mistress." |
| mistress | A com. n., fem. gen., s. num., 3rd per., nom. c. to the v. "chides." |
| gently | An adv. of man., mod. the v. "chides." |
| chides | An irreg. tr. v., act. vo., indic. m., pres. t., s. num., 3rd per., agr. with its nom. "mistress." |
| fault | An abs. n., neu. gen., s. num., 3rd per., obj. c., gov. by the tr. v. "chides." |
| I | A pers. pron., com. gen., s. num., 1st per., nom. c. to the v. "made." |
| made. | An irreg. tr. v., act. vo., indic. m., past t., s. num., 1st per., agr. with its nom. "I." (*Which* I made.) |
| 5. None | A def. card. nu. adj. of quantity, qual. the n. *persons* und. |
| love | A reg. tr. v., act. vo., indic. m., pres. t., p. num., 3rd. per., agr. with its nom. *persons* und. |
| their | A pers. pron., com. gen., p. num., 3rd per., poss. c., gov. by the n. "country." |
| country | A com. n., neu. gen., s. num., 3rd per., obj. c., gov. by the tr. v. "love." |
| but=except | A prep., sh. the rn. bet. *persons* und. and *persons* und. (No persons but *the persons.*) |
| **who** | A rel. pron., com. gen., p. num., 3rd per., agr. with its ant. *persons* und., nom. c. to the v. "love." |
| love | A reg. tr. v., act. vo., indic. m., pres. t., p. num., 3rd per., agr. with its nom. "who." |
| their | A pers. pron., com. gen., p. num., 3rd per., poss. c., gov. by the n. "home." |
| home. | A com. n., neu. gen., s. num., 3rd per., obj. c., gov. by the tr. v. "love." |
| 6. Thrice | An adv. of num., mod. the v. "is arm'd." |
| is | An aux. v. to "arm'd," indg. pass. vo., pres. t. |
| he | A pers. pron., mas. gen., s. num., 3rd per., nom. c. to the v. "is arm'd." |
| arm'd | A past pl. from the tr. v. "to arm," ref. to "he." |
| is arm'd | A reg. tr. v., pass. vo., indic. m., pres. t., s. num., 3rd per., agr. with its nom. "he." |
| **that** | A rel. pron., mas. gen., s. num., 3rd per., agr. with its ant. "he," nom. c. to the v. "hath." |
| hath | An irreg. tr. v., act. vo., indic. m., pres. t., s. num., 3rd per., agr. with its nom. "that." |
| his | A pers. pron., mas. gen., s. num., 3rd per., poss. c., gov. by the n. "quarrel." |
| quarrel | An abs. n., neu. gen., s. num., 3rd per., obj. c., gov. by the tr. v. "hath." |

| | |
|---|---|
| just. | An adj. of quality, pos. deg., qual. the n. "quarrel." |
| 7. Cork | A com. n., neu. gen., s. num., 3rd per., nom. c. to the v. "is." |
| is | An irreg. intr. v., indic. m., pres. t., s. num., 3rd per., agr. with its nom. "cork." |
| outer | An adj. of quality, comp. deg., qual. the n. "bark." |
| bark | A com. n., neu. gen., s. num., 3rd per., nom. c. after the v. "is." |
| of | A prep., sh. the rn. bet. "bark" and "oak." |
| large | An adj. of quality, pos. deg., qual. the n. "oak." |
| oak | A com. n., neu. gen., s. num., 3rd per., obj. c., gov. by the prep. "of." |
| **which** | A rel. pron., neu. gen., s. num., 3rd per., agr. with its ant. "oak," nom. c. to the v. "grows." |
| grows | An irreg. intr. v., indic. m., pres. t., s. num., 3rd per., agr. with its nom. "which." |
| in | A prep., sh. the rn. bet. "grows" and "countries." |
| countries | A com. n., neu. gen., p. num., 3rd per., obj. c., gov. by the prep. "in." |
| around | A prep., sh. the rn. bet. "countries" and "Mediterranean." |
| Mediterranean. | A prop. n., neu. gen., s. num., 3rd per., obj. c., gov. by the prep. "around." |
| 8. Let | An irreg. tr. v., act. vo., imper. m., pres. t., s. or p. num., 2nd per., agr. with its nom. *thou* or *you* und. |
| not | An adv. of m. (neg.), mod. the v. "let." |
| men | A com. n., mas. gen., p. num., 3rd per., obj. c., gov. by the tr. v. "let." |
| (to) think | An irreg. intr. v., infin. m., pres. t., gov. by the v. "let." |
| there | An expletive adv., mod. the v. "is." |
| is | An irreg. intr. v., indic. m., pres. t., s. num., 3rd per., agr. with its nom. "truth." |
| no | An adj. of quantity (bulk or mass), qual. the n. "truth." |
| truth | An abs. n., neu. gen., s. num., 3rd per., nom. c. to the v. "is." |
| but | A disj. conj., jg. the sents. "there is no truth" and "*it be* in the sciences" (or, jg. the sents. "there is no truth" and "*there is truth* in the sciences.") |
| in | A prep., sh. the rn. bet. *be* und. and "sciences" (or, bet. *is* und. and "sciences.") |
| sciences | An abs. n., neu. gen., p. num., 3rd per., obj. c., gov. by the prep. "in." |
| **that** | A rel. pron., neu. gen., p. num., 3rd per., agr. with its ant. "sciences," obj. c., gov. by the tr. v. "study." |
| they | A pers. pron., mas. gen., p. num., 3rd per., nom. c. to the v. "study." |
| study | A reg. tr. v., act. vo., indic. m., pres. t., p. num., 3rd per., agr. with its nom. "they." |
| or | A disj. conj., jg. the sents. "but (=except) *it be* in the sciences" and "*but* (=except) *it be in* the books" (or, jg. the sents. "*there is truth* in the sciences" and "*there is truth in* the books.") |
| books | A com. n., neu. gen., p. num., 3rd per., obj. c., gov. by the prep. *in* und. |
| **that** | A rel. pron., neu. gen., p. num., 3rd per., agr. with its ant. "books," obj. c., gov. by the tr. v. "read." |
| they | A pers. pron., mas. gen., p. num., 3rd per., nom. c. to the v. "read." |
| read. | An irreg. tr. v., act. vo., indic. m., pres. t., p. num., 3rd per., agr. with its nom. "they." |
| 9. Who | A rel. pron., com. gen., s. num., 3rd per., agr. with its ant. *person* und., nom. c. to the v. "will pant." |
| will | An aux. v. to *pant* und., indg. fut. t. |
| may | An aux. v. to "pant," indg. pot. m., pres. t. |
| (to) pant | A reg. intr. v., infin. m., pres. t., gov. by the v. "may." |
| may pant | A reg. intr. v., pot. m., pres. t., s. num., 3rd per., agr. with its nom. *person* und. |
| for | A prep., sh. the rn. bet. "may pant" and "glory." |
| glory. | An abs. n., neu. gen., s. num., 3rd per., obj. c., gov. by the prep. "for." |
| 10. It | A pers. pron., neu. gen., s. num., 3rd per., nom. c. to the v. "was reserved." |
| was | An aux. v. to "reserved," indg. pass. vo., past t. |

| | |
|---|---|
| reserved | A past pl. from the tr. v. "to reserve," ref. to "it." |
| was reserved | A reg. tr. v., pass. vo., indic. m., past t., s. num., 3rd per., agr. with its nom. "it." |
| for | A prep., sh. the rn. bet. "was reserved" and "Portugal." |
| Portugal | A prop. n., neu. gen., s. num., 3rd per., obj. c., gov. by the prep. "for." |
| to | A particle, indg. infin. m. |
| to tear | An irreg. tr. v., act. vo., infin. m., pres. t.; used as an abs. n., neu. gen., s. num., 3rd per., nom. c., in app. with "it." |
| aside | An adv. of place, mod. the v. "to tear." |
| veil | A com. n., neu. gen., s. num., 3rd per., obj. c., gov. by the tr. v. "to tear." |
| **which** | A rel. pron., neu. gen., s. num., 3rd per., agr. with its ant. "veil," nom. c. to the v. "hung." |
| hung | An irreg. intr. v., indic. m., past t., s. num., 3rd per., agr. with its nom. "which." |
| over | A prep., sh. the rn. bet. "hung" and "part." |
| greater | An adj. of quality, comp. deg., qual. the n. "part." |
| part | A com. n., neu. gen., s. num., 3rd per., obj. c., gov. by the prep. "over." |
| of | A prep., sh. the rn. bet. "part" and "Africa." |
| Africa. | A prop. n., neu. gen., s. num., 3rd per., obj. c., gov. by the prep. "of." |
| 11. Every | A dist. nu. adj. of quantity, qual. the n. "joint." |
| joint | A com. n., neu. gen., s. num., 3rd per., nom. c. to the v. "can be shown." |
| in | A prep., sh. the rn. bet. "joint" and "frame." |
| animal | A com. n. used as an adj. of quality, qual. the n. "frame." |
| frame | A com. n., neu. gen., s. num., 3rd per., obj. c., gov. by the prep. "in." |
| can | An aux. v. to "be shown," indg. pot. m., pres. t. |
| be | An aux. v. to "shown," indg. pass. vo. |
| shown | A past pl. from the tr. v. "to show," ref. to "joint." |
| can be shown | An irreg. tr. v., pass. vo., pot. m., pres. t., s. num., 3rd per., agr. with its nom. "joint." |
| to | A particle, indg. infin. m. |
| be | An aux. v. to "suited," indg. pass. vo. |
| exactly | An adv. of man., mod. the v. "to be suited." |
| suited | A past pl. from the tr. v. "to suit," ref. to "joint." |
| to be suited | A reg. tr. v., pass. vo., infin. m., pres. t., gov. by the v. "can be shown." |
| to | A prep., sh. the rn. bet. "to be suited" and "function." |
| function | An abs. n., neu. gen., s. num., 3rd per., obj. c., gov. by the prep. "to." |
| **which** | A rel. pron., neu. gen., s. num., 3rd per., agr. with its ant. "function," obj. c., gov. by the tr. v. "to perform." |
| it | A pers. pron., neu. gen., s. num., 3rd per., nom. c. to the v. "has." |
| has | An irreg. tr. v., act. vo., indic. m., pres. t., s. num., 3rd per., agr. with its nom. "it." |
| to | A particle, indg. infin. m. |
| to perform | A reg. tr. v., act. vo., infin. m., pres. t., gov. by the v. "has." |
| 12. In | A prep., sh. the rn. bet. "spent" and "manner." |
| this | A dis. adj., lim. the n. "manner." |
| manner | An abs. n., neu. gen., s. num., 3rd per., obj. c., gov. by the prep. "in." |
| we | A pers. pron., com. gen., p. num., 1st per., nom. c. to the v. "spent." |
| spent | An irreg. tr. v., act. vo., indic. m., past t., p. num., 1st per., agr. with its nom. "we." |
| forenoon | An abs. n., neu. gen., s. num., 3rd per., obj. c., gov. by the tr. v. "spent." |
| till | A cop. conj., jg. the sents. "In this manner..forenoon" and "the bell...dinner." |
| bell | A com. n., neu. gen., s. num., 3rd per., nom. c. to the v. "summoned." |
| summoned | A reg. tr. v., act. vo., indic. m., past t., s. num., 3rd per., agr. with its nom. "bell." |

| | |
|---|---|
| us | A pers. pron., com. gen., p. num., 1st per., obj. c., gov. by the tr. v. "summoned." |
| to | A prep., sh. the rn. bet. "summoned" and "dinner." |
| dinner | A com. n., neu. gen., s. num., 3rd per., obj. c., gov. by the prep. "to." |
| where | A cop. conj., jg. the sents. "the bell...dinner" and "we found ...company." |
| we | A pers. pron., com. gen., p. num., 1st per., nom. c. to the v. "found." |
| found | An irreg. tr. v., act. vo., indic. m., past t., p. num., 1st per., agr. with its nom. "we." |
| manager | A com. n., mas. gen., s. num., 3rd per., obj. c., gov. by the tr. v. "found." |
| of | A prep., sh. the rn. bet. "manager" and "company." |
| strolling | A pres. pl. from the intr. v. "to stroll," used as an adj. of quality, qual. the n. "company." |
| company | A com. col. n., neu. gen., s. num., 3rd per., obj. c., gov. by the prep. "of." |
| **that** | A rel. pron., neu. gen., s. num., 3rd per., agr. with its ant. "company," obj. c., gov. by the tr. v. "mentioned." |
| I | A pers. pron., com. gen., s. num., 1st per., nom. c. to the v. "mentioned." |
| mentioned | A reg. tr. v., act. vo., indic. m., past t., s. num., 1st per., agr. with its nom. "I." |
| before | An adv. of time, mod. the v. "mentioned." |
| **who** | A rel. pron., mas. gen., s. num., 3rd per., agr. with its ant. "manager," nom. c. to the v. "was come." |
| was | An aux. v. to "come," indg. pluperf. t. (Was=had.) |
| come | A past pl. from the intr. v. "to come," ref. to "who." |
| was come | An irreg. intr. v., indic. m., pluperf. t., s. num., 3rd per., agr. with its nom. "who." (Was come = had come.) |
| to | A particle, indg. infin. m. |
| to dispose | A reg. intr. v., infin. m., pres. t., gov. by the v. "was come." |
| of | A prep., sh. the rn. bet. "to dispose" and "tickets." |
| tickets | A com. n., neu. gen., p. num., 3rd per., obj. c., gov. by the prep. "of." |
| for | A prep., sh. the rn. bet. "tickets" and "Penitent." |
| Fair | An adj. of quality, pos. deg., qual. the n. "Penitent." |
| Penitent | A prop. n., forming with the adj. "Fair" a compd. prop. n. |
| Fair Penitent | A compd. prop. n., neu. gen., s num., 3rd per., obj. c., gov. by the prep. "for." ("Fair Penitent" is here neu. gen., because it is the name of a play.) |
| **which** | A rel. pron., neu. gen., s. num., 3rd per., agr. with its ant. "Fair Penitent," nom. c. to the v. "was." |
| was | An irreg. intr. v., indic. m., past t., s. num., 3rd per., agr. with its nom. "which." |
| to | A particle, indg. infin. m. |
| be | An aux. v. to "acted," indg. pass. vo. |
| acted | A past pl. from the tr. v. "to act," ref. to "which." |
| to be acted | A reg. tr. v., pass. vo., infin. m., pres. t., gov. by the v. "was." |
| that | A dis. adj., lim. the n. "evening." |
| evening | An abs. n., neu. gen., s. num., 3rd per., obj. c., gov. by the prep. *during* und. |
| part | A com. n., neu. gen., s. num., 3rd per., nom. c. absolute. (The part *being to be acted*.) |
| of | A prep., sh. the rn. bet. "part" and "Horatio." |
| Horatio | A prop. n., mas. gen., s. num., 3rd per., obj. c., gov. by the prep. "of." |
| by | A prep., sh. the rn. bet. *to be acted* und. and "gentleman." |
| young | An adj. of quality, pos. deg., qual. the n. "gentleman." |
| gentleman | A com. n., mas. gen., s. num., 3rd per., obj. c., gov. by the prep "by." |
| **who** | A rel. pron., mas. gen., s. num., 3rd per., agr. with its ant. "gentleman," nom. c. to the v. "had appeared." |
| had | An aux. v. to "appeared," indg. pluperf. t. |
| never | An adv. of time, mod. the v. "had appeared." |
| appeared | A past pl. from the intr. v. "to appear," ref. to "who." |

|   |   |
|---|---|
| had appeared | A reg. intr. v., indic. m., pluperf. t., s. num., 3rd per., agr. with its nom. "who." |
| on | A prep., sh. the rn. bet. "had appeared" and "stage." |
| any | An indef. nu. adj. of quantity, qual. the n. "stage." |
| stage. | A com. n., neu. gen., s. num., 3rd per., obj. c., gov. by the prep. "on." |
| 13. I | A pers. pron., com. gen., s. num., 1st per., nom. c. to the v. "have revealed." |
| have | An aux. v. to "revealed," indg. perf. t. |
| revealed | A past pl. from the tr. v. "to reveal," ref. to "discord.' |
| have revealed | A reg. tr. v., act. vo., indic. m., perf. t., s. num., 1st per., agr. with its nom. "I." |
| discord | An abs. n., neu. gen., s. num., 3rd per., obj. c., gov. by the tr. v. "have revealed." |
| **which** | A rel. pron., neu. gen., s. num., 3rd per., agr. with its ant. "discord," nom. c. to the v. "befel." |
| befel. | An irreg. intr. v., indic. m., past t., s. num., 3rd per., agr. with its nom. "which." |
| 14. It | A pers. pron., neu. gen., s. num., 3rd per., nom. c. to the v. "was." |
| was | An irreg. intr. v., indic. m., past t., s. num., 3rd per., agr. with its nom. "it." |
| English | A prop. n., mas. gen., p. num., 3rd per., nom. c. after the v. "was." |
| Kaspar | A prop. n., mas. gen., s. num., 3rd per., nom. c. to the v. "cried." |
| cried | A reg. tr. v., act. vo., indic. m., past t., s. num., 3rd per., agr. with its nom. "Kaspar." |
| **That** | A rel. pron., mas. gen., p. num., 3rd per., agr. with its ant. "English," nom. c. to the v. "put." |
| put | An irreg. tr. v., act. vo., indic. m., past t., p. num., 3rd per., agr. with its nom. "that." |
| French | A prop. n., mas. gen., p. num., 3rd per., obj. c., gov. by the tr. v. "put." |
| to | A prep., sh. the rn. bet. "put" and "rout." |
| rout. | An abs. n., neu. gen., s. num., 3rd per., obj. c., gov. by the prep. "to." |
| 15. We | A pers. pron., com. gen., p. num., 1st per., nom. c. to the v. "beg." |
| ignorant | An adj. of quality, pos. deg., qual. the pron. "we." |
| of | A prep., sh. the rn. bet. "ignorant" and "ourselves." |
| ourselves | A compd. pers. pron., com. gen., p. num., 1st per., obj. c., gov. by the prep. "of." |
| Beg | A reg. tr. v., act. vo., indic. m., pres. t., p. num., 1st per., agr. with its nom. "we." |
| often | An adv. of time, mod. the v. "beg." |
| our | A pers. pron., forming with the adj. "own" a compd. pers. pron. |
| own | An intensive adj. of quality, qual. the n. "harms." |
| our own | A compd. pers. pron., com. gen., p. num., 1st per., poss. c., gov. by the n. "harms." |
| harms | An abs. n., neu. gen., p. num., 3rd per., obj. c., gov. by the tr. v. "beg." |
| **which** | A rel. pron., neu. gen., p. num., 3rd per., agr. with its ant. "harms," obj. c., gov. by the tr. v. "deny." |
| wise | An adj. of quality, pos. deg., qual. the n. "powers." |
| powers | A com. n., com. gen., p. num., 3rd per., nom. c. to the v. "deny." |
| Deny | A reg. tr. v., act. vo., indic. m., pres. t., p. num., 3rd per., agr. with its nom. "powers." |
| us | A pers. pron., com. gen., p. num., 1st per., obj. c., gov. by the prep. *to* und. |
| for | A prep., sh. the rn. bet. "deny" and "good." |
| our | A pers. pron., com. gen., p. num., 1st per., poss. c., gov. by the n. "good." |
| good. | An abs. n., neu. gen., s. num., 3rd per., obj. c., gov. by the prep. "for." |

## Exercise 155.

| | |
|---|---|
| 1. Thou | A pers. pron., mas. gen., s. num., 2nd per., nom. c. to the v. "art." |
| art | An irreg. intr. v., indic. m., pres. t., s. num., 2nd per., agr. with its nom. "thou." |
| man | A com. n., mas. gen., s. num., 3rd per., nom. c. after the v. "art." |
| **that** | A rel. pron., mas. gen., s. num., 3rd per., agr. with its ant. "man," nom. c. to the v. "should guide." |
| should | An aux. v. to "guide," indg. pot. m., past t. |
| (to) guide | A reg. tr. v., act. vo., infin. m., pres. t., gov. by the v. "should." |
| should guide | A reg. tr. v., act. vo., pot. m., pres. t., s. num., 3rd per., agr. with its nom. "that." |
| ship. | A com. n., neu. gen., s. num., 3rd per., obj. c., gov. by the tr. v. "should guide." |
| 2. You | A pers. pron., com. gen., s. num., p. form, 2nd per., nom. c. to the v. "are." |
| are | An irreg. intr. v., indic. m., pres. t., s. num., p. form, 2nd per., agr. with its nom. "you." |
| person | A com. n., com. gen., s. num., 3rd per., nom. c. after the v. "are." |
| **who** | A rel. pron., com. gen., s. num., 3rd per., agr. with its ant. "person," nom. c. to the v. "was implicated." |
| was | An aux. v. to "implicated," indg. pass. vo., past t. |
| implicated | A past pl. from the tr. v. "to implicate," ref. to "who." |
| was implicated | A reg. tr. v., pass. vo., indic. m., past t., s. num., 3rd per., agr. with its nom. "who." |
| in | A prep., sh. the rn. bet. "was implicated" and "conspiracy." |
| conspiracy. | An abs. n., neu. gen., s. num., 3rd per., obj. c., gov. by the prep. "in." |
| 3. I | A pers. pron., com. gen., s. num., 1st per., nom. c. to the v. "am." |
| am | An irreg. intr. v., indic. m., pres. t., s. num., 1st per., agr. with its nom. "I." |
| unfortunate | An adj. of quality, pos. deg., qual. the n. "victim." |
| victim | A com. n., com. gen., s. num., 3rd per., nom. c. after the v. "am." |
| **who** | A rel. pron., com. gen., s. num., 3rd per., agr. with its ant. "victim," nom. c. to the v. "has felt." |
| has | An aux. v. to "felt," indg. perf. t. |
| felt | A past pl. from the tr. v. "to feel," ref. to "injustice." |
| has felt | An irreg. tr. v., act. vo., indic. m., perf. t., s. num., 3rd per., agr. with its nom. "who." |
| tyrant's | A com. n., com. gen., s. num., 3rd per., poss. c., gov. by the n. "injustice." |
| injustice. | An abs. n., neu. gen., s. num., 3rd per., obj. c., gov. by the tr. v. "has felt." |
| 4. deliverer | A com. n., com. gen., s. num., 3rd per., nom. c. to the v. "was." |
| on | A prep., sh. the rn. bet. "was" and "occasion." |
| that | A dis. adj., lim. the n. "occasion." |
| occasion | An abs. n., neu. gen., s. num., 3rd per., obj. c., gov. by the prep. "on." |
| was | An irreg. intr. v., indic. m., past t., s. num., 3rd per., agr. with its nom. "deliverer." |
| I | A pers. pron., com. gen., s. num., 1st per., nom. c. after the v. "was." |
| **who** | A rel. pron., com. gen., s. num., 1st per., agr. with its ant. "I," nom. c. to the v. "am." |
| am | An irreg. intr. v., indic. m., pres. t., s. num., 1st per., agr. with its nom. "who." |
| still | An adv. of time, mod. the v. "am." |
| ready | An adj. of quality, pos. deg., qual. the pron. "who." |
| to | A particle, indg. infin. m. |
| to be | An irreg. intr. v., infin. m., pres. t., gov. by the adj. "ready." |
| your | A pers. pron., com. gen., p. num., 2nd per., poss. c., gov. by the n. "leader." |
| leader. | A com. n., com. gen., s. num., 3rd per., nom. c. after the v. "to be." |

| | |
|---|---|
| 5. Thou | A pers. pron., mas. gen., s. num., 2nd per., nom. c. to the v. "art." |
| art | An irreg. intr. v., indic. m., pres. t., s. num., 2nd per., agr. with its nom. "thou." |
| he | A pers. pron., mas. gen., s. num., 3rd per., nom. c. after the v. "art." |
| **who** | A rel. pron., mas. gen., s. num., 3rd per., agr. with its ant. "he,' nom. c. to the v. "points." |
| points | A reg. tr. v., act. vo., indic. m., pres. t., s. num., 3rd per., agr. with its nom. "who." |
| out | An adv. of place, mod. the v. "points." |
| to | A prep., sh. the rn. bet. "points" and "us." |
| us | A pers. pron., com. gen., p. num., 1st per., obj. c., gov. by the prep. "to." |
| path | A com. n., neu. gen., s. num., 3rd per., obj. c., gov. by the tr. v. "points." |
| of | A prep., sh. the rn. bet. "path" and "duty." |
| duty. | An abs. n., neu. gen., s. num., 3rd per., obj. c., gov. by the prep. "of." |
| 6. I | A pers. pron., fem. gen., s. num., 1st per., nom. c. to the v. "am." |
| am | An irreg. intr. v., indic. m., pres. t., s. num., 1st per., agr. with its nom. "I." |
| she | A pers. pron., fem. gen., s. num., 3rd per., nom. c. after the v. "am." |
| **who** | A rel. pron., fem. gen., s. num., 3rd per., agr. with its ant. "she," nom. c. to the v. "devotes." |
| devotes | A reg. tr. v., act. vo., indic. m., pres. t., s. num., 3rd per., agr. with its nom. "who." |
| herself | A compd. pers. pron., fem. gen., s. num., 3rd per., obj. c., gov. by the tr. v. "devotes." |
| willingly | An adv. of man., mod. the v. "devotes." |
| to | A prep., sh. the rn. bet. "devotes" and "cause." |
| this | A dis. adj., lim. the n. "cause." |
| sacred | An adj. of quality, pos. deg., qual. the n. "cause." |
| cause. | An abs. n., neu. gen., s. num., 3rd per., obj. c., gov. by the prep. "to." |

## Exercise 156.

1. Our aim must be such [a thing] as [the thing is which] our motive is.

| | |
|---|---|
| Such | An adj. of quality, qual. the n. *thing* und. |
| as | A cop. conj., cor. to "such," jg. the sents. "Our aim...*thing*" and "*the thing is*." |
| our | A pers. pron., com. gen., p. num., 1st per., poss. c., gov. by the n. "motive." |
| motive | An abs. n., neu. gen., s. num., 3rd per., nom. c., to the v. "is." |
| is | An irreg. intr. v., indic. m., pres. t., s. num., 3rd per., agr. with its nom. "motive." |
| our | A pers. pron., com. gen., p. num., 1st per., poss. c., gov. by the n. "aim." |
| aim | An abs. n., neu. gen., s. num., 3rd per., nom. c. to the v. "must be." |
| must | An aux. v. to "be," indg. pot. m., pres. t. |
| (to) be | An irreg. intr. v., infin. m., pres. t., gov. by the v. "must." |
| must be. | An irreg. intr. v., pot. m., pres. t., s. num., 3rd per., agr. with its nom. "aim." |

2. He was ready enough to look at such curiosities on the way as [the curiosities were which] could be seen for nothing.

| | |
|---|---|
| Such | An indef. nu. adj. of quantity, qual. the n. "curiosities." |
| curiosities | A com. n., neu. gen., p. num., 3rd per., obj. c., gov. by the prep. "at." |
| on | A prep., sh. the rn. bet. "curiosities" and "way." |
| way | A com. n., neu. gen., s. num., 3rd per., obj. c., gov. by the prep. "on." |
| as | A cop. conj., cor. to "such," jg. the sents. "He was ready..way" and "*the curiosities were*." |

| | |
|---|---|
| could | An aux. v. to "be seen," indg. pot. m., past t. |
| be | An aux. v. to "seen," indg. pass. vo. |
| seen | A past pl. from the tr. v. "to see," ref. to *which* und. |
| could be seen | An irreg. tr. v., pass. vo., pot. m., past t., p. num., 3rd per., agr. with its nom. *which* und. |
| for | A prep., sh. the rn. bet. "could be seen" and "nothing." |
| nothing | A com. n., neu. gen., s. num., 3rd per., obj. c., gov. by the prep. "for." |
| he | A pers. pron., mas. gen., s. num., 3rd per., nom. c. to the v. "was." |
| was | An irreg. intr. v., indic. m., past t., s. num., 3rd per., agr. with its nom. "he." |
| ready | An adj. of quality, pos. deg., qual. the pron. "he." |
| enough | An adv. of mea., mod. the adj. "ready." |
| to | A particle, indg. infin. m. |
| to look | A reg. ntr. v., infin. m., pres. t., gov. by the adj. "ready." |
| at. | A prep., sh. the rn. bet. "to look" and "curiosities." |

3. This [liquor] is not such a liquor as [the liquor is which] Homer speaketh of, which ran from Venus' hand, when it was pierced by Diomedes.

| | |
|---|---|
| This | A dis. adj., lim. the n. *liquor* und. |
| is | An irreg. intr. v., indic. m., pres. t., s. num., 3rd per., agr. with its nom. *liquor* und. |
| not | An adv. of m. (neg.), mod. the v. "is." |
| such | An adj. of quality, qual. the n. "liquor." |
| liquor | A com. n., neu. gen., s. num., 3rd per., nom. c. after the v. "is." |
| as | A cop. conj., cor. to "such," jg. the sents. "This..liquor" and "*the liquor is*." |
| Homer | A prop. n., mas. gen., s. num., 3rd per., nom. c. to the v. "speaketh." |
| speaketh | An irreg. intr. v., indic. m., pres. t., s. num., 3rd per., agr. with its nom. "Homer." |
| of | A prep., sh. the rn. bet. "speaketh" and *which* und. |
| which | A rel. pron., neu. gen., s num., 3rd per., agr. with its ant. *liquor* und., nom. c. to the v. "ran." |
| ran | An irreg. intr. v., indic. m., past t., s. num., 3rd per., agr. with its nom. "which." |
| from | A prep., sh. the rn. bet. "ran" and "hand." |
| Venus' | A prop. n., fem. gen., s. num., 3rd per., poss. c., gov. by the n. "hand." |
| hand | A com. n., neu. gen., s. num., 3rd per., obj. c., gov. by the prep. "from." |
| when | A cop. conj., jg. the sents. "which ran..hand" and "it was..Diomedes." |
| it | A pers. pron., neu. gen., s. num., 3rd per., nom. c. to the v. "was pierced." |
| was | An aux. v. to "pierced," indg. pass. vo., past t. |
| pierced | A past pl. from the tr. v. "to pierce," ref. to "it." |
| was pierced | A reg. tr. v., pass. vo., indic. m., past t., s. num., 3rd per., agr. with its nom. "it." |
| by | A prep., sh. the rn. bet. "was pierced" and "Diomedes." |
| Diomedes. | A prop. n., mas. gen., s. num., 3rd per., obj. c., gov. by the prep. "by." |

4. Such [persons] as [the persons were who] were so disposed might give themselves to histories, [such persons might give themselves to] modern languages, [such persons might give themselves to] books of policy, and [such persons might give themselves to] civil discourses.

| | |
|---|---|
| Such | An indef. nu. adj. of quantity, qual. the n. *persons* und. |
| as | A cop. conj., cor. to "such," jg. the sents. "Such *persons* might give themselves to histories" and "*the persons were*." |
| were | An aux. v. to "disposed," indg. pass. vo., past t. |
| so | An adv. of man., mod. the v. "were disposed." |
| disposed | A past pl. from the tr. v. "to dispose," ref. to *who* und. |
| were disposed | A reg. tr. v., pass. vo., indic. m., past t., p. num., 3rd per., agr. with its nom. *who* und. |
| might | An aux. v. to "give," indg. pot. m., past t. |
| (to) give | An irreg. tr. v., act. vo., infin. m., pres. t., gov. by the v. "might." |

| | |
|---|---|
| might give | An irreg. tr. v., act. vo., pot. m., past t., p. num., 3rd per., agr. with its nom. *persons* und. |
| themselves | A compd. pers. pron., com. gen., p. num., 3rd per., obj. c., gov. by the tr. v. "might give." |
| to | A prep., sh. the rn. bet. "might give" and "histories." |
| histories | A com. n., neu. gen., p. num., 3rd per., obj. c., gov. by the prep. "to." |
| modern | An adj. of quality, pos. deg., qual. the n. "languages." |
| languages | A com. n., neu. gen., p. num., 3rd per., obj. c., gov. by the prep. *to* und. |
| books | A com. n., neu. gen., p. num., 3rd per., obj. c., gov. by the prep. *to* und. |
| of | A prep., sh. the rn. bet. "books" and "policy." |
| policy | An abs. n., neu. gen., s. num., 3rd per., obj. c., gov. by the prep. "of." |
| and | A cop. conj., jg. the sents. "*such persons might*.. policy" and "*such persons might..to* civil discourses." |
| civil | An adj. of quality, qual. the n. "discourses." |
| discourses. | A com. n., neu. gen., p. num., 3rd pers., obj. c., gov. by the prep. *to* und. |

5. He followed the same line of action as [the line of action was which] his predecessor [followed].

| | |
|---|---|
| He | A pers. pron., mas. gen., s. num., 3rd per., nom. c. to the v. "followed." |
| followed | A reg. tr. v., act. vo., indic. m., past t., s. num., 3rd per., agr. with its nom. "he." |
| same | A dis. adj., lim. the n. "line." |
| line | An abs. n., neu. gen., s. num., 3rd per., obj. c., gov. by the tr. v. "followed." |
| of | A prep., sh. the rn. bet. "line" and "action." |
| action | An abs. n., neu. gen., s. num., 3rd per., obj. c., gov. by the prep. "of." |
| as | A cop. conj., cor. to "same," jg. the sents. "He followed...action" and "*the line of action was.*" |
| his | A pers. pron., mas. gen., s. num., 3rd per., poss. c., gov. by the n. "predecessor." |
| predecessor. | A com. n., mas. gen., s. num., 3rd per., nom. c., to the v. *followed* und. |

6. In at this gate none pass the vigilance here placed but (=except) such [persons] as [the persons are who] come well known from heaven.

| | |
|---|---|
| In | An adv. of place, mod. the v. "pass." |
| at | A prep., sh. the rn. bet. "pass" and "gate." |
| this | A dis. adj., lim. the n. "gate." |
| gate | A com. n., neu. gen., s. num., 3rd per., obj. c., gov. by the prep. "at." |
| none | A def. card. nu. adj. of quantity, qual. the n. *persons* und. |
| pass | A reg. tr. v., act. vo., indic. m., pres. t., p. num., 3rd per., agr. with its nom. *persons* und. |
| vigilance | An abs. n., neu. gen., s. num., 3rd per., obj. c., gov. by the tr. v. "pass." |
| here | An adv. of place, mod. the pl. "plac'd." |
| plac'd | A past pl. from the tr. v. "to place," ref. to "vigilance." |
| but | A prep., sh. the rn. bet. *persons* und. and *persons* und. (No *persons* except such *persons*.) |
| such | An indef. nu. adj. of quantity, qual. the n. *persons* und. |
| as | A cop. conj., cor. to "such," jg. the sents. "In at this gate...such *persons*" and "*the persons are.*" |
| come | An irreg. intr. v., indic. m., pres. t., p. num., 3rd per., agr. with its nom. *who* und. |
| Well | An adv. of man., mod the past pl. "known." |
| known | A past pl. from the tr. v. "to know," ref. to *who* und. |
| from | A prep., sh. the rn. bet. "come" and "heaven." |
| heaven. | A com. n., neu. gen., s. num., 3rd per., obj. c., gov. by the prep. "from." |

## Exercise 157.

**1. He** — A pers. pron., mas. gen., s. num., 3rd per., nom. c. to the v. "was buried."

was — An aux. v. to "buried," indg. pass. vo., past t.

buried — A past pl. from the tr. v. "to bury," ref. to "he."

was buried — A reg. tr. v., pass. vo., indic. m., past t., s. num., 3rd per., agr. with its nom. "he."

beside — A prep., sh. the rn. bet. "was buried" and "father."

his — A pers. pron., mas. gen., s. num., 3rd per., poss. c., gov. by the n. "father."

father — A com. n., mas. gen., s. num., 3rd per., obj. c., gov. by the prep. "beside."

**who** — A rel. pron., mas. gen., s. num., 3rd per., agr. with its ant. "father," nom. c. to the v. "had died."

had — An aux. v. to "died," indg. pluperf. t.

died — A past pl. from the intr. v. "to die," ref. to "who."

had died — A reg. intr. v., indic. m., pluperf. t., s. num., 3rd per., agr. with its nom. "who."

but — An adv. of deg., mod. the adj. "few."

few — An indef. nu. adj. of quantity, qual. the n. "months."

months — An abs. n., neu. gen., p. num., 3rd per., obj. c., gov. by the prep. *at* or *in* und.

before — An adv. of time, mod. the v. "had died" (or, a prep., gov. *time* und.).

**2. My** — A pers. pron., com. gen., s. num., 1st per., poss. c., gov. by the n. "account."

account — An abs. n., neu. gen., s. num., 3rd per., nom. c. to the v. "is."

is — An irreg. intr. v., indic. m., pres. t., s. num., 3rd per., agr. with its nom. "account."

rather — An adv. of deg., mod. the v. "is."

of — A prep., sh. the rn. bet. "is" and "thing" incl. in "what" (or, bet. "is" and the sent. "what I saw").

**what** — A compd. rel. pron., including both the rel. and the ant., neu. gen., s. num., 3rd per. "What" is equiv. to "the thing which," "thing" being obj. c., gov. by the prep. "of," and "which," obj. c., gov. by the tr. v. "saw."

I — A pers. pron., com. gen., s. num., 1st per., nom. c. to the v. "saw."

saw — An irreg. tr. v., act. vo., indic. m., past t., s. num., 1st per., agr. with its nom. "I."

than — A disj. conj., cor. to "rather," jg. the sents. "My account is rather of the thing" and "*it is of* the thing." ("My account is rather of the thing which I saw than *it is of* the thing which I did.")

**what** — A compd. rel. pron., including both the rel. and the ant., neu. gen., s. num., 3rd per. "What" is equiv. to "the thing which," "thing" being obj. c., gov. by the prep. *of* und., and "which" being obj. c., gov. by the tr. v. "did."

I — A pers. pron., com. gen., s. num., 1st per., nom. c. to the v. "did."

did. — An irreg. tr. v., act. vo., indic. m., past t., s. num., 1st per., agr. with its nom. "I."

**3. Of** — A prep., sh. the rn. bet. "most ardent" and "affections."

all — An indef. nu. adj. of quantity, qual. the n. "affections."

affections — An abs. n., neu. gen., p. num., 3rd per., obj. c., gov. by the prep. "of."

**which** — A rel. pron., neu. gen., p. num., 3rd per., agr. with its ant. "affections," nom. c. to the v. "attend."

attend — A reg. tr. v., act. vo., indic. m., pres. t., p. num., 3rd per., agr. with its nom. "which."

human — An adj. of quality, qual. the n. "life."

life — An abs. n., neu. gen., s. num., 3rd per., obj. c., gov. by the tr. v. "attend."

love — An abs. n., neu. gen., s. num., 3rd per., nom. c. to the v. "is."

of — A prep., sh. the rn. bet. "love" and "glory."

glory — An abs. n., neu. gen., s. num., 3rd per., obj. c., gov. by the prep. "of."

| | |
|---|---|
| is | An irreg. intr. v., indic. m., pres. t., s. num., 3rd per., agr. with its nom. "love." |
| most | An adv. of deg., mod. the adj. "ardent," indg. superl. deg. |
| most ardent. | An adj. of quality, superl. deg., qual. the n. *affection* und. |
| 4. He | A pers. pron., mas. gen., s. num., 3rd per., nom. c. to the v. "has assented." |
| that | A rel. pron., mas. gen., s. num., 3rd per., agr. with its ant. "he," nom. c. to the v. "has." |
| has | An irreg. tr. v., act. vo., indic. m., pres. t., s. num., 3rd per., agr. with its nom. "that." |
| mind | An abs. n., neu. gen., s. num., 3rd per., obj. c., gov. by the tr. v. "has." |
| to | A particle, indg. infin. m. |
| to believe | A reg. intr. v., indic. m., pres. t., gov. by the n. "mind." |
| has | An aux. v. to "assented," indg. perf. t. |
| half | An adv. of mea., mod. the v. "has assented." |
| assented | A past pl. from the intr. v. "to assent," ref. to "he." |
| has assented | A reg. intr. v., indic. m., perf. t., s. num., 3rd per., agr. with its nom. "he." |
| already | An adv. of time, mod. the v. "has assented." |
| and | A cop. conj., jg. the sents. "He...already" and "he..himself." |
| he | A pers. pron., mas. gen., s. num., 3rd per., nom. c. to the v. "is." |
| that | A rel. pron., mas. gen., s. num., 3rd per., agr. with its ant. "he," nom. c. to the v. "imposes." |
| by | A prep., sh. the rn. bet. "imposes" and "arguing." |
| often | An adv. of time, mod. the ger. "arguing." |
| arguing | A ger. from the intr. v. "to argue," neu. gen., s. num., 3rd per., obj. c., gov. by the prep. "by." |
| against | A prep., sh. the rn. bet. "arguing" and "sense." |
| his | A pers. pron., forming with the adj. "own" a compd. pers. pron. |
| own | An intensive adj. of quality, qual. the n. "sense." |
| his own | A compd. pers. pron., mas. gen., s. num., 3rd per., poss. c., gov. by the n. "sense." |
| sense | An abs. n., neu. gen., s. num., 3rd per., obj. c., gov. by the prep. "against." |
| imposes | A reg. tr. v., act. vo., indic. m., pres. t., s. num., 3rd per., agr. with its nom. "that." |
| falsehoods | An abs. n., neu. gen., p. num., 3rd per., obj. c., gov. by the tr. v. "imposes." |
| on | A prep., sh. the rn. bet. "imposes" and "others." |
| others | An indef. nu. adj. used as a com. n., com. gen., p. num., 3rd per., obj. c., gov. by the prep. "on." |
| is | An irreg. intr v., indic. m., pres. t., s. num., 3rd per., agr. with its nom. "he." |
| not | An adv. of m. (neg.), mod. the adv. "far." |
| far | An adv. of place, mod. the v. "is." |
| from | A prep., sh. the rn. bet. "is" and "believing." |
| believing | A ger. from. the intr. v. "to believe," neu. gen., s. num., 3rd per., obj. c., gov. by the prep. "from." |
| himself. | A compd. pers. pron., mas. gen., s. num., 3rd per., nom. c., in app. with "he." |
| 5. population | A com. col. n., neu. gen., s. num., 3rd per., nom. c. to the v. "is." |
| of | A prep., sh. the rn. bet. "population" and "St. Petersburg." |
| St. | An adj. of quality, qualifying the n. "Peter's" incl. in "Petersburg." |
| Petersburg | A prop. n., forming with "St." a compd. prop. n. |
| St. Petersburg | A compd. prop. n., neu. gen., s. num., 3rd per., obj. c., gov. by the prep. "of." |
| is | An irreg. intr. v., indic. m., pres. t., s. num., 3rd per., agr. with its nom. "population." |
| most | An adv. of deg., mod. the adj. "varied," indg. superl. deg. |
| most varied | An adj. of quality, superl. deg., qual. the n. *population* und. |
| and | A cop. conj., jg. the sents. "The population .. varied *population*" and "*the population of St. Petersburg is the most motley population.*" |
| most motley | An adj. of quality, superl. deg., qual. the n. *population* und. |

| | |
|---|---|
| that | A rel. pron., neu. gen., s. num., 3rd per., agr. with its ant. *population* und., obj. c., gov. by the tr. v. "can imagine." |
| mind | A com. n., neu. gen., s. num., 3rd per., nom c. to the v. "can imagine." |
| can | An aux. v. to "imagine," indg. pot. m., pres. t. |
| (to) imagine | A reg. tr. v., act. vo., infin. m., pres. t., gov. by the v. "can." |
| can imagine. | A reg. tr. v., act. vo., pot. m., pres. t., s. num., 3rd per., agr. with its nom. "mind." |
| 6. Southward | An adv. of place, mod. the v. "rose." |
| mountain | A com. n., neu. gen., s. num., 3rd per., nom. c. to the v. "rose." |
| rose | An irreg. intr. v., indic. m., past t., s. num., 3rd per., agr. with its nom. "mountain." |
| with | A prep., sh. the rn. bet. "rose" and "swell." |
| easy | An adj. of quality, pos. deg., qual. the n. "swell." |
| swell | An abs. n., neu. gen., s. num., 3rd per., obj. c., gov. by the prep. "with." |
| Whose | A rel. pron., neu. gen., s. num., 3rd per., agr. with its ant. "mountain," poss. c., gov. by the n. "groves." |
| long | An adj. of quality, pos. deg., qual. the n. "groves." |
| long | An adj. of quality, pos. deg., qual. the n. "groves." |
| groves | A com. n., neu. gen., p. num., 3rd per., nom. c. to the v. "made." |
| eternal | An adj. of quality, qual. the n. "murmurs." |
| murmurs | An abs. n., neu. gen., p. num., 3rd per., obj. c., gov. by the tr. v. "made." |
| made. | An irreg. tr. v., act. vo., indic. m., past t., p. num., 3rd per., agr. with its nom. "groves." |
| 7. For | A cop. conj., introducing the sent. "our..stirrers." |
| our | A pers. pron., com. gen., p. num., 1st per., poss. c., gov. by the n. "neighbour." |
| bad | An adj. of quality, pos. deg., qual. the n. "neighbour." |
| neighbour | A com. n., com. gen., s. num., 3rd per., nom. c. to the v. "makes." |
| makes | An irreg. tr. v., act. vo., indic. m., pres. t., s. num., 3rd per., agr. with its nom. "neighbour." |
| us | A pers. pron., com. gen., p. num., 1st per., obj. c., gov. by the tr. v. "makes." |
| early | An adj. of quality, pos. deg., qual. the n. "stirrers." |
| stirrers | A com. n., com. gen., p. num., 3rd per., obj. c., in app. with "us." ("Stirrers" is the factitive object.) |
| Which | A rel. pron., neu. gen., s. num., 3rd per., agr. with its ant. the sent. "our..stirrers," nom. c. to the v. "is." |
| is | An irreg. intr. v., indic. m., pres. t., s. num., 3rd per., agr. with its nom. "which." |
| both | A cop. conj., introducing the sent. "which is healthful." |
| healthful | An adj. of quality, pos. deg., qual. the pron. "which." |
| and | A cop. conj., cor. to "both," jg. the sents. "Which is healthful and "*which is* good husbandry." |
| good | An adj. of quality, pos. deg., qual. the n. "husbandry." |
| husbandry. | An abs. n., neu. gen., s. num., 3rd per., nom. c. after the v. *is* und. |
| 8. And | A cop. conj., introducing the sent. "In his..brand." |
| in | A prep., sh. the rn. bet. "shakes" and "hand." |
| his | A pers. pron., mas. gen., s. num., 3rd per., poss. c., gov. by the n. "hand." |
| hand | A com. n., neu. gen., s. num., 3rd per., obj. c., gov. by the prep. "in." |
| he | A pers. pron., mas. gen., s. num., 3rd per., nom. c. to the v. "shakes." |
| shakes | An irreg. tr. v., act. vo., indic. m., pres. t., s. num., 3rd per., agr. with its nom. "he." |
| brand | A com. n., neu. gen., s. num., 3rd per., obj. c., gov. by the tr. v. "shakes." |
| Which | A rel. pron., neu. gen., s. num., 3rd per., agr. with its ant. "brand," obj. c., gov. by the tr. v. "can wield." |
| none | A def. card. nu. adj. of quantity, qual. the n. *person* und. |
| but | A disj. conj., jg. the sents. "Which none *can wield*" and "*which* he can wield." |

| | |
|---|---|
| he | A pers. pron., mas. gen., s. num., 3rd per., nom. c. to the v. "can wield." |
| can (to) wield | An aux. v. to "wield," indg. pot. m., pres. t. |
| | A reg. tr. v., act. vo., infin. m., pres. t., gov. by the v. "can." |
| can wield. | A reg. tr. v., act. vo., pot. m., pres. t., s. num., 3rd per., agr. with its nom. "he." |
| 9. To | A particle, indg. infin. m. |
| To climb | A reg. tr. v., act. vo., infin. m., pres. t. ; used as an abs. n., neu. gen., s. num., 3rd per., nom. c. to the v. "requires." |
| steep | An adj. of quality, pos. deg., qual. the n. "hills." |
| hills | A com. n., neu. gen., p. num., 3rd per., obj. c., gov. by the tr. v. "to climb." |
| Requires | A reg. tr. v., act. vo., indic. m., pres. t., s. num., 3rd per., agr. with its nom. "to climb." |
| slow | An adj. of quality, pos. deg., qual. the n. "pace." |
| pace | An abs. n., neu. gen., s. num., 3rd per., obj. c., gov. by the tr. v. "requires." |
| at | A prep., sh. the rn. bet. "requires" and *time* und. |
| first | An adj. of quality, superl. deg., qual. the n. *time* und. |
| at first | An adverbial phrase of time, mod. the v. "requires." (See *Parsing*, p. 150.) |
| anger | An abs. n., neu. gen., s. num., 3rd per., nom. c. to the v. "is." |
| is | An irreg. intr. v., indic. m., pres. t., s. num., 3rd per., agr. with its nom. "anger." |
| like | An adj. of quality, pos. deg., qual. the n. "anger." |
| full | An adj. of quality, pos. deg., qual. the n. "horse." |
| hot | An adj. of quality, pos. deg., qual. the n. "horse." |
| horse | A com. n., mas. gen., s. num., 3rd per., obj. c., gov. by the prep. *to* und. |
| **who** | A rel. pron., mas. gen., s. num., 3rd per., agr. with its ant. "horse," nom. c. absolute. |
| being | A pres. pl. from the intr. v. "to be," ref. to "allowed who," and aux. to "allowed," indg. pass. vo. |
| allowed | A past pl. from the tr. v. "to allow," ref. to "who." |
| being allowed | A pres. pl. from the tr. v. "to allow," pass. vo., ref. to "who." |
| his | A pers. pron., mas. gen., s. num., 3rd per., poss. c., gov. by the n. "way." |
| way | A com. n., neu. gen., s. num., 3rd per., obj. c., gov. by the tr. v. *to have* und. (or, after the pl. "being allowed," *Gr.* § 308.) |
| Self-mettle | A compd. abs. n., neu. gen., s. num., 3rd per., nom. c. to the v. "tires." |
| tires | A reg. tr. v., act. vo., indic. m., pres. t., s. num., 3rd per., agr. with its nom. "self-mettle." |
| him. | A pers. pron., mas. gen., s. num., 3rd per., obj. c., gov. by the tr. v. "tires." |
| 10. Love | An abs. n., neu. gen., s. num., 3rd per., obj. c., gov. by the tr. v. "had found." |
| had | An aux. v. to "found," indg. pluperf. t. |
| he | A pers. pron., mas. gen., s. num., 3rd per., nom. c. to the v. "had found." |
| found | A past pl. from the tr. v. "to find," ref. to "love." |
| had found | An irreg. tr. v., act. vo., indic. m., pluperf. t., s. num., 3rd per., agr. with its nom. "he." |
| in | A prep., sh. the rn. bet. "had found" and "huts." |
| huts | A com. n., neu. gen., p. num., 3rd per., obj. c., gov. by the prep. "in." |
| where | A cop. conj., jg. the sents. "Love...huts" and "poor men lie." |
| poor | An adj. of quality, pos. deg., qual. the n. "men." |
| men | A com. n., mas. gen., p. num., 3rd per., nom. c. to the v. "lie." |
| lie | An irreg. intr. v., indic. m., pres. t., p. num., 3rd per., agr. with its nom. "men." |
| His | A pers. pron., mas. gen., s. num., 3rd per., poss. c., gov. by the n. "teachers." |
| daily | An adj. of quality, qual. the n. "eachers." |
| teachers | A com. n., neu. gen., p. num., 3rd per., nom. c. to the v. "had been." |
| had | An aux. v. to "been," indg. pluperf. t. |
| been | A past pl. from the intr. v. "to be," ref. to "teachers." |

| | |
|---|---|
| had been | An irreg. intr. v., indic. m., pluperf. t., p. num., 3rd per., agr. with its nom. "teachers." |
| woods | A com. n., neu. gen., p. num., 3rd per., nom. c. after the v. "had been." |
| and | A cop. conj., jg. the sents. "His daily..woods" and "*his daily teachers had been* rills." |
| rills | A com. n., neu. gen., p. num., 3rd per., nom. c. after the v. *had been* und. |
| silence | An abs. n., neu. gen., s. num., 3rd per., nom. c. after the v. *had been* und. |
| **that** | A rel. pron., neu. gen., s. num., 3rd per., agr. with its ant. "silence," nom. c. to the v. "is." |
| is | An irreg. intr. v., indic. m., pres. t., s. num., 3rd per., agr. with its nom. "that." |
| in | A prep., sh. the rn. bet. "is" and "sky." |
| starry | An adj. of quality, pos. deg., qual. the n. "sky." |
| sky | A com. n., neu. gen., s. num., 3rd per., obj. c., gov. by the prep. "in." |
| sleep | An abs. n., neu. gen., s. num., 3rd per., nom. c. after the v. *had been* und. |
| **that** | A rel. pron., neu. gen., s. num., 3rd per., agr. with its ant. "sleep," nom. c. to the v. "is." |
| is | An irreg. intr. v., indic. m., pres. t., s. num., 3rd per., agr. with its nom. "that." |
| among | A prep., sh. the rn. bet. "is" and "hills." |
| lonely | An adj. of quality, pos. deg., qual. the n. "hills." |
| hills. | A com. n., neu. gen., p. num., 3rd per., obj. c., gov. by the prep. "among." |

## Exercise 158.

| | |
|---|---|
| 1. **What** | An interrog. pron., neu. gen., s. num., 3rd per., obj. c., gov. by the tr. v. "do want." |
| do | An aux. v. to "want," indg. pres. t., and completing the interrog. form of the v. |
| you | A pers. pron., com. gen., p. num., or s. num., p. form, 2nd per., nom. c. to the v. "do want." |
| (to) want | A reg. tr. v., act. vo., infin. m., pres. t., gov. by the v. "do." |
| do want. | A reg. tr. v., act. vo., indic. m., pres. t., p. num., or s. num., p. form, 2nd per., agr. with its nom. "you." |
| 2. **Who** | An interrog. pron., com. gen., s. num., 3rd per., nom. c. to the v. "knows." |
| knows | An irreg. tr. v., act. vo., indic. m., pres. t., s. num., 3rd per., agr. with its nom. "who." |
| **what** | An interrog. pron., neu. gen., s. num., 3rd per., nom. c. to the v. "may happen." |
| may | An aux. v. to "happen," indg. pot. m., pres. t. |
| (to) happen | A reg. intr. v., infin. m., pres. t., gov. by the v. "may." |
| may happen. | A reg. intr. v., pot. m., pres. t., s. num., 3rd per., agr. with its nom. "what." |
| 3. Ah | An interj. |
| **who** | An interrog. pron., com. gen., s. num., 3rd per., nom. c. to the v. "can tell." |
| melodies | An abs. n., neu. gen., p. num., 3rd per., obj. c., gov. by the tr. v. "can tell." |
| of | A prep., sh. the rn. bet. "melodies" and "morn." |
| morn | An abs. n., neu. gen., s. num., 3rd per., obj. c., gov. by the prep. "of." |
| can | An aux. v. to "tell," indg. pot. m., pres. t. |
| (to) tell | An irreg. tr. v., act. vo., infin. m., pres. t., gov. by the v. "can." |
| can tell. | An irreg. tr. v., act. vo., pot. m., pres. t., s. num., 3rd per., agr. with its nom. "who." |
| 4. **Who** | An interrog. pron., com. gen., s. num., 3rd per., nom. c. to the v. "hath lost." |
| hath | An aux. v. to "lost," indg. perf. t. |
| not | An adv. of m. (neg.), mod. the v. "hath lost." |
| lost | A past pl. from the tr. v. "to lose," ref. to "friend." |
| hath lost | An irreg. tr. v., act. vo., indic. m., perf. t., s. num., 3rd per., agr. with its nom. "who." |

| | |
|---|---|
| friend. | A com. n., com. gen., s. num., 3rd per., obj. c., gov. by the tr. v "hath lost." |
| 5. **Who** | An interrog. pron., com. gen., s. num., 3rd per., nom. c. to the v. "shall decide." |
| shall | An aux. v. to "decide," indg. fut. t., emph. form, expressing "determination." |
| (to) decide | A reg. intr. v., infin. m., pres. t., gov. by the v. "shall." |
| shall decide | A reg. intr. v., indic. m., fut. t., emph. form, s. num., 3rd per., agr. with its nom. "who." |
| when | A cop. conj., jg. the sents. "Who shall decide" and "doctors disagree." |
| doctors | A com. n., mas. gen., p. num., 3rd per., nom. c. to the v. "disagree." |
| disagree. | A reg. intr. v., indic. m., pres. t., p. num., 3rd per., agr. with its nom. "doctors." |
| 6. **Who** | An interrog. pron., mas. gen., s. num., 3rd per., nom. c. to the v. "is." |
| is | An irreg. intr. v., indic. m., pres. t., s. num., 3rd per., agr. with its nom. "who." |
| here | An adv. of place, mod. the v. "is." |
| so | An adv. of deg., mod. the adj. "base." |
| base | An adj. of quality, pos. deg., qual. the pron. "who." |
| that | A rel. pron., mas. gen., s. num., 3rd per., agr. with its ant. "who," nom. c. to the v. "would be." |
| would | An aux. v. to "be," indg. pot. m., past t. |
| (to) be | An irreg. intr. v., infin. m., pres. t., gov. by the v. "would." |
| would be | An irreg. intr. v., pot. m., past t., s. num., 3rd per., agr. with its nom. "that." |
| bondman | A com. n., mas. gen., s. num., 3rd per., nom. c. after the v. "would be." |
| If | A cop. conj., jg. the sents. "*You* speak" and "*there be* any *man so base*," and indg. subj. m. |
| any | An indef. nu. adj. of quantity, qual. the n. *man* und. |
| speak | An irreg. intr. v., imper. m., pres. t., p. num., 2nd per., agr. with its nom. *you* und. |
| for | A cop. conj., jg. the sents. "*you* speak" and "him have I offended." |
| him | A pers. pron., mas. gen., s. num., 3rd per., obj. c., gov. by the tr. v. "have offended." |
| have | An aux. v. to "offended," indg. perf. t. |
| I | A pers. pron., mas. gen., s. num., 1st per., nom. c. to the v. "have offended." ("I," i.e., Mark Antony.) |
| offended | A past pl. from the tr. v. "to offend," ref. to "him." |
| have offended | A reg. tr. v., act. vo., indic. m., perf. t., s. num., 1st per., agr. with its nom. "I." |
| **Who** | An interrog. pron., mas. gen., s. num., 3rd per., nom. c. to the v. "is." |
| is | An irreg. intr. v., indic. m., pres. t., s. num., 3rd per., agr. with its nom. "who." |
| here | An adv. of place, mod. the v. "is." |
| so | An adv. of deg., mod. the adj. "rude." |
| rude | An adj. of quality, pos. deg., qual. the pron. "who." |
| that | A rel. pron., mas. gen., s. num., 3rd per., agr. with its ant. "who," nom. c. to the v. "would be." |
| would | An aux. v. to "be," indg. pot. m., past t. |
| not | An adv. of m. (neg.), mod. the v. "would be." |
| (to) be | An irreg. intr. v., infin. m., pres. t., gov. by the v. "would." |
| would be | An irreg. intr. v., pot. m., past t., s. num., 3rd per., agr. with its nom. *he* und. |
| Roman | A prop. n., mas. gen., s. num., 3rd per., nom. c. after the v. "would be." |
| If | A cop. conj., jg. the sents."*you* speak" and "*there be* any *man so rude*," and indg. subj. m. |
| any | An indef. nu. adj. of quantity, qual. the n. *man* und. |
| speak | An irreg. intr. v., imper. m., pres. t., p. num., 2nd per., agr. with its nom. *you* und. |
| for | A cop. conj., jg. the sents. "*you* speak" and "him have I offended." |

| | |
|---|---|
| him | A pers. pron., mas. gen., s. num., 3rd per., obj. c., gov. by the tr. v. "have offended." |
| have | An aux. v. to "offended," indg. perf. t. |
| I | A pers. pron., mas. gen., s. num., 1st per., nom. c. to the v. "have offended." |
| offended | A past pl. from the tr. v. "to offend," ref. to "him." |
| have offended. | A reg. tr. v., act. vo., indic. m., perf. t., s. num., 1st per., agr. with its nom. "I." |
| 7. **What** | An interrog. pron. used as an adj., qual. the n. "bird." |
| bird | A com. n., com. gen., s. num., 3rd per., nom. c. after the v. "is." |
| is | An irreg. intr. v., indic. m., pres. t., s. num., 3rd per., agr. with its nom. *bird* und. |
| this. | A dis. adj., lim. the n. *bird* und. |
| 8. **Whoever** | A compd. interrog. pron., com. gen., s. num., 3rd per., nom. c. to the v. "gazed." |
| gazed | A reg. intr. v., indic. m., past t., s. num., 3rd per., agr. with its nom. "whoever." |
| upon | A prep., sh. the rn. bet. "gazed" and "sea." |
| broad | An adj. of quality, pos. deg., qual. the n. "sea." |
| sea | A com. n., neu. gen., s. num., 3rd per., obj. c., gov. by the prep. "upon." |
| without | A prep., sh. the rn. bet. "gazed" and "emotion." |
| emotion. | An abs. n., neu. gen., s. num., 3rd per., obj. c., gov. by the prep. "without." |
| 9. **What** | An interrog. pron., neu. gen., s. num., 3rd per., nom. c. after the v. "were." |
| were | An irreg. intr. v., indic. m., past t., p. num., 3rd per., agr. with its nom. "orders." |
| my | A pers. pron., com. gen., s. num., 1st per., poss. c., gov. by the n. "orders." |
| orders. | An abs. n., neu. gen., p. num., 3rd per., nom. c. to the v. "were." |
| 10. After | A prep., sh. the rn. bet. "is come" and "whom." |
| **whom** | An interrog. pron., com. gen., s. num., 3rd per., obj. c., gov. by the prep. "after." |
| is | An aux. v. to "come," indg. perf. t. |
| king | A com. n., mas. gen., s. num., 3rd per., nom. c. to the v. "is come." |
| of | A prep., sh. the rn. bet. "king" and "Israel." |
| Israel | A prop. n., neu. gen., s. num., 3rd per., obj. c., gov. by the prep. "of." |
| come | A past pl. from the intr. v. "to come," ref. to "king." |
| is come | An irreg. intr. v., indic. m., perf. t., s. num., 3rd per., agr. with its nom. "king." (Is come=has come.) |
| out. | An adv. of place, mod. the v. "is come." |

## Exercise 159.

| | |
|---|---|
| 1. **What** | An interrog. pron. used as an adj., qual. the n. "warmth." |
| warmth | An abs. n., neu. gen., s. num., 3rd per., nom. c. to the v. "is." |
| is | An irreg. intr. v., indic. m., pres. t., s. num., 3rd per., agr. with its nom. "warmth." |
| there | An expletive adv., mod. the v. "is." |
| in | A prep., sh. the rn. bet. "is" and "affection." |
| your | A pers. pron., com. gen., p. num., or s. num., p. form, 2nd per., poss. c., gov. by the n. "affection." |
| affection | An abs. n., neu. gen., s. num., 3rd per., obj. c., gov. by the prep. "in." |
| towards | A prep., sh. the rn. bet. "affection" and *suitors* und. |
| any | An indef. nu. adj. of quantity, qual. the n. *suitors* und. |
| of | A prep., sh. the rn. bet. *suitors* und. and "suitors." |
| these | A dis. adj., lim. the n. "suitors." |
| princely | An adj. of quality, pos. deg., qual. the n. "suitors." |
| suitors. | A com. n., mas. gen., p. num., 3rd per., obj. c., gov. by the prep. "of." |
| 2 **Who** | An interrog. pron., com. gen., s. num., 3rd per., nom. c. to the v. "goes." |
| goes | An irreg. intr. v., indic. m., pres. t., s. num., 3rd per., agr. with its nom. "who." |
| there. | An adv. of place, mod. the v. "**goes.**" |

KEY TO

3. **What** — An interrog. pron., neu. gen., s. num., 3rd per., nom. c. to the v. "is."
is — An irreg. intr. v., indic. m., pres. t., s. num., 3rd per., agr. with its nom. "what."
most — An adv. of deg., mod. the adj. "like," indg. superl. deg.
most like — An adj. of quality, superl. deg., qual. the pron. "what."
thee. — A pers. pron., com. gen., s. num., 2nd per., obj. c., gov. by the prep. to und.

4. Watchman — A com. n., mas. gen., s. num., 2nd per., nom. c. of add.
**what** — An interrog. pron. used as an adj., qual. the n. *news* und.
of — A prep., sh. the rn. bet. *news* und. and "night."
night. — An abs. n., neu. gen., s. num., 3rd per., obj. c., gov. by the prep. "of."

5. **Which** — An interrog. pron., used as an adj., qual. the n. "way."
way — A com. n., neu. gen., s. num., 3rd per., obj. c., gov. by the prep. *by* und.
went — An irreg. intr. v., indic. m., past t., s. num., 3rd per., agr. with its nom. "he."
he. — A pers. pron., mas. gen., s. num., 3rd per., nom. c. to the v. "went."

6. **Who** — An interrog. pron., com. gen., s. num., 3rd per., nom. c. to the v. "is."
is — An irreg. intr. v., indic. m., pres. t., s. num., 3rd per., agr. with its nom. "who."
on — A prep., sh. the rn. bet. "is" and "side."
our — A pers. pron., com. gen., p. num., 1st per., poss. c., gov. by the n. "side."
side. — A com. n., neu. gen., s. num., 3rd per., obj. c., gov. by the prep. "on."

7. **What** — An interrog. pron. used as an adj., qual. the n. "request."
ill — An adj. of quality, pos. deg., qual. the n. "request."
request — An abs. n., neu. gen., s. num., 3rd per., obj. c., gov. by the tr. v. "did make."
did — An aux. v. to "make," indg. past t., and completing the interrog. form of the v.
Brutus — A prop. n., mas. gen., s. num., 3rd per., nom. c. to the v. "did make."
(to) make — An irreg. tr. v., act. vo., infin. m., pres. t., gov. by the v. "did."
did make — An irreg. tr. v., act. vo., indic. m., past t., s. num., 3rd per., agr. with its nom. "Brutus."
to — A prep., sh. the rn. bet. "did make" and "thee."
thee. — A pers. pron., com. gen., s. num., 2nd per., obj. c., gov. by the prep. "to."

8. **What** — An interrog. pron., neu. gen., s. num., 3rd per., nom. c. to the v. "is."
is — An irreg. intr. v., indic. m., pres. t., s. num., 3rd per., agr. with its nom. "what."
your — A pers. pron., mas. gen., s. num., 2nd per., poss. c., gov. by the n. "pleasure."
pleasure — An abs. n., neu. gen., s. num., 3rd per., nom. c. after the v. "is."
sir. — A com. n., mas. gen., s. num., 2nd per., nom. c. of add.

9. **What** — An interrog. pron. used as an adj., qual. the n. "hope."
hope — An abs. n., neu. gen., s. num., 3rd per., nom. c. to the v. *is* und.
or — A disj. conj., jg. the sents. "What hope *is thine*" and "*what* fear *is thine.*"
fear — An abs. n., neu. gen., s. num., 3rd per., nom. c. to the v. *is* und.
or — A disj. conj., jg. the sents. "*what fear is thine*" and "*what joy* is thine."
joy — An abs. n., neu. gen., s. num., 3rd per., nom. c. to the v. "is."
is — An irreg. intr. v., indic. m., pres. t., s. num., 3rd per., agr. with its nom. "joy."
thine — A pers. pron., fem. gen., s. num., 2nd per., poss. c., gov. by the n. "joy."

| | |
|---|---|
| Who | An interrog. pron., com. gen., s. num., 3rd per., nom. c. to the v. "talketh." |
| talketh | A reg. intr. v., indic. m., pres. t., s. num., 3rd per., agr. with its nom. "who." |
| with | A prep., sh. the rn. bet. "talketh" and "thee." |
| thee | A pers. pron., fem. gen., s. num., 2nd per., obj. c., gov. by the prep. "with." |
| Adeline. | A prop. n., fem. gen., s. num., 2nd per., nom. c. of add. |
| 10. And | A cop. conj., introducing the sent. "still I would sing." |
| still | An adv. of time, mod. the v. "would sing." |
| as | A cop. conj., jg. the sents. "I would sing" and "I comb'd." |
| I | A pers. pron., fem. gen., s. num., 1st per., nom. c. to the v. "comb'd." |
| comb'd | A reg. tr. v., indic. m., past t., s. num., 1st per., agr. with its nom. "I." |
| I | A pers. pron., fem. gen., s. num., 1st per., nom. c. to the v. "would sing." |
| would | An aux. v. to "sing," indg. pot. m., past t. |
| (to) sing | An irreg. intr. v., infin. m., pres. t., gov. by the v. "would." |
| would sing | An irreg. intr. v., pot. m., past t., s. num., 1st per., agr. with its nom. "I." |
| and | A cop. conj., jg. the sents. "I would sing" and "*I would* say." |
| (to) say | An irreg. tr. v., act. vo., infin. m., pres. t., gov. by the v. *would* und. |
| Who | An interrog. pron., mas. gen., s. num., 3rd per., nom. c. to the v. "is." |
| is | An irreg. intr. v., indic. m., pres. t., s. num., 3rd per., agr. with its nom. "who." |
| it | A pers. pron., neu. gen., s. num., 3rd per., nom. c. after the v. "is." |
| loves | A reg. tr. v., act. vo., indic. m., pres. t., s. num., 3rd per., agr. with its nom. *that* und. |
| me | A pers. pron., fem. gen., s. num., 1st per., obj. c., gov. by the tr. v. "loves." |
| Who | An interrog. pron., mas. gen., s. num., 3rd per., nom. c. to the v. "loves." |
| loves | A reg. tr. v., act. vo., indic. m., pres. t., s. num., 3rd per., agr. with its nom. "who." |
| not | An adv. of m. (neg.), mod. the v. "loves." |
| me. | A pers. pron., fem. gen., s. num., 1st per., obj. c., gov. by the tr. v. "loves." |

## Exercise 160.

| | |
|---|---|
| 1. reindeer | A com. n., com. gen., s. num., 3rd per., nom. c. to the v. "is." |
| is | An irreg. intr. v., indic. m., pres. t., s. num., 3rd per., agr. with its nom. "reindeer." |
| tractable | An adj. of quality, pos. deg., qual. the n. "reindeer." |
| and | A cop. conj., jg. the sents. "The reindeer is tractable" and "*the reindeer is* easily tamed." |
| easily | An adv. of man., mod. the v. "*is* tamed." |
| tamed. | A past pl. from the tr. v. "to tame," ref. to the n. *reindeer* und. |
| 2. marmot | A com. n., com. gen., s. num., 3rd per., nom. c. to the v. "absconds." |
| absconds | A reg. intr. v., indic. m., pres. t., s. num., 3rd per., agr. with its nom. "marmot." |
| in | A prep., sh. the rn. bet. "absconds" and "winter." |
| winter. | An abs. n., neu. gen., s. num., 3rd per., obj. c., gov. by the prep. "in." |
| 3. Ripe | An adj. of quality, pos. deg., qual. the n. "apples." |
| apples | A com. n., neu. gen., p. num., 3rd per., nom. c. to the v. "drop." |
| drop | A reg. intr. v., indic. m., pres. t., p. num., 3rd per., agr. with its nom. "apples." |
| about | A prep., sh. the rn. bet. "drop" and "head." |
| my | A pers. pron., com. gen., s. num., 1st per., poss. c., gov. by the n. "head." |
| head. | A com. n., neu. gen., s. num., 3rd per., obj. c., gov. by the prep. "about." |

# KEY TO

4. allies — A com. n., com. gen., p. num., 3rd per., nom. c. to the v. "were."
of — A prep., sh. the rn. bet. "allies" and "Rome."
Rome — A prop. n., neu. gen., s. num., 3rd per., obj. c., gov. by the prep. "of."
**were** — An irreg. intr. v., indic. m., past t., p. num., 3rd per., agr. with its nom. "allies."
slaves. — A com. n., com. gen., p. num., 3rd per., nom. c. after the v. "were."

5. native — An adj. of quality, qual. the n. "inhabitants."
inhabitants — A com. n., com. gen., p. num., 3rd per., nom. c. to the v. "are."
of — A prep., sh. the rn. bet. "inhabitants" and "Greenland."
Greenland — A prop. n., neu. gen., s. num., 3rd per., obj. c., gov. by the prep. "of."
**are** — An irreg. intr. v., indic. m., pres. t., p. num., 3rd per., agr. with its nom. "inhabitants."
true — An adj. of quality, qual. the n. "Esquimaux."
Esquimaux. — A prop. n., com. gen., p. num., 3rd per., nom. c. after the v. "are."

6. Warwick — A prop. n., mas. gen., s. num., 3rd per., nom. c. to the v. "is."
**is** — An irreg. intr. v., indic. m., pres. t., s. num., 3rd per., agr. with its nom. "Warwick."
hoarse — An adj. of quality, pos. deg., qual. the n. "Warwick."
with — A prep., sh. the rn. bet. "hoarse" and "calling."
calling — A ger. from the tr. v. "to call," neu. gen., s. num., 3rd per., obj. c., gov. by the prep. "with."
thee — A pers. pron., mas. gen., s. num., 2nd per., obj. c., gov. by the tr. ger. "calling."
to — A prep., sh. the rn. bet. "calling" and "arms."
arms. — A com. n., neu. gen., p. num., 3rd per., obj. c., gov. by the prep. "to."

7. smallest — An adj. of quality, superl. deg., qual. the n. "worm."
worm — A com. n., com. gen., s. num., 3rd per., nom. c. to the v. "will turn."
will — An aux. v. to "turn," indg. fut. t.
(to) turn — A reg. intr. v., infin. m., pres. t., gov. by the v. "will."
**will turn** — A reg. intr. v., indic. m., fut. t., s. num., 3rd per., agr. with its nom. "worm."
being — A pres. pl. from the intr. v. "to be," ref. to "trodden worm," aux. to "trodden," indg. pass. vo.
trodden — A past pl. from the tr. v. "to tread," ref. to "worm."
being trodden — A pres. pl. from the tr. v. "to tread," pass vo., ref. to "worm."
on. — An adv. of place, mod. the pl. "being trodden." ("On" may also be taken along with the pl. "being trodden" as the pres. pass. pl. of the prep. v. "to tread–on." See *Gr.* § 369; *Parsing*, p. 148.)

8. Things — A com. n., neu. gen., p. num., 3rd per., nom. c. to the v. "had."
ill-got — A compd. adj. of quality, pos. deg., qual. the n. "things."
**had** — An irreg. tr. v., act. vo., indic. m., past. t., p. num., 3rd per., agr. with its nom. "things."
ever — An adv. of time, mod. the v. "had."
bad — An adj. of quality, pos. deg., qual. the n. "success."
success. — An abs. n., neu. gen., s. num., 3rd per., obj. c., gov. by the tr. v. "had."

9. Ill — An adv. of man., mod. the v. "blows."
**blows** — An irreg. intr. v., indic. m., pres. t., s. num., 3rd per., agr. with its nom. "wind."
wind — A com. n., neu. gen., s. num., 3rd per., nom. c. to the v. "blows."
that — A rel. pron., neu. gen., s. num., 3rd per., agr. with its ant. "wind," nom. c. to the v. "profits."
**profits** — A reg. tr. v., act. vo., indic. m., pres. t., s. num., 3rd per., agr. with its nom. "that."
nobody. — A com. n., com. gen., s. num., 3rd per., obj. c., gov. by the tr. v. "profits."

10. panting — A pres. pl. from the intr. v. "to pant," used as an adj. of quality, qual. the n. "herds."
herds — A com. col. n., neu. gen., p. num., 3rd per., nom. c. to the v. "repose."

| | |
|---|---|
| repose. | A reg. intr. v., indic., m., pres. t., p. num., 3rd per., agr. with its nom. "herds." |
| 11. One | A def. card. nu. adj. of quantity, qual. the n. "touch." |
| touch | An abs. n., neu. gen., s. num., 3rd per., nom. c. to the v. "makes." |
| of | A prep., sh. the rn. bet. "touch" and "nature." |
| nature | An abs. n., neu. gen., s. num., 3rd per., obj. c., gov. by the prep. "of." |
| makes | An irreg. tr. v., act. vo., indic. m., pres. t., s. num., 3rd per., agr. with its nom. "touch." |
| whole | An adj., of quantity (bulk or mass), qual. the n. "world." |
| world | A com. n., neu. gen., s. num., 3rd per., obj. c., gov. by the tr. v. "makes." |
| kin. | A com. n., neu. gen., p. num., 3rd per., obj. c., in app. with "world." |
| 12. Wisdom | An abs. n., neu. gen., s. num., 3rd per., nom. c. to the v. "cries." |
| cries | A reg. intr. v., indic. m., pres. t., s. num., 3rd per., agr. with its nom. "wisdom." |
| out | An adv. of man., mod. the v. "cries." |
| in | A prep., sh. the rn. bet. "cries" and "streets." |
| streets | A com. n., neu. gen., p. num., 3rd per., obj. c., gov. by the prep. "in." |
| and | A cop. conj., jg. the sents. "Wisdom..streets" and "no man regards." |
| no | A def. card. nu. adj. of quantity, qual. the n. "man." |
| man | A com. n., mas. gen., s. num., 3rd per., nom. c. to the v. "regards." |
| regards. | A reg. intr. v., indic. m., pres. t., s. num., 3rd per., agr. with its nom. "man." |
| 13. I | A pers. pron., com. gen., s. num., 1st per., nom. c. to the v. "can call." |
| can | An aux. v. to "call," indg. pot. m., pres. t. |
| (to) call | A reg. tr. v., act. vo., infin. m., pres. t., gov. by the v. "can." |
| can call | A reg. tr. v., act. vo., pot. m., pres. t., s. num., 1st per., agr. with its nom. "I." |
| spirits | A com. n., com. gen., p. num., 3rd per., obj. c., gov. by the tr. v. "can call." |
| from | A prep., sh. the rn. bet. "can call" and "deep." |
| vasty | An adj. of quality, qual. the n. "deep." |
| deep. | A com. n., neu. gen., s. num., 3rd per., obj. c., gov. by the prep. "from." |
| 14. Two | A def. card. nu. adj. of quantity, qual. the n. "stars." |
| stars | A com. n., neu. gen., p. num., 3rd per., nom. c. to the v. "keep." |
| keep | An irreg. tr. v., act. vo., indic. m., pres. t., p. num., 3rd per., agr. with its nom. "stars." |
| not | An adv. of m. (neg.), mod. the v. "keep." |
| their | A pers. pron., neu. gen., p. num., 3rd per., poss. c., gov. by the n. "motion." |
| motion | An abs. n., neu. gen., s. num., 3rd per., obj. c., gov. by the tr. v. "keep." |
| in | A prep., sh. the rn. bet. "keep" and "sphere." |
| one | A def. card. nu. adj. of quantity, qual. the n. "sphere." |
| sphere. | A com. n., neu. gen., s. num., 3rd per., obj. c., gov. by the prep. "in." |
| 15. better | An adj. of quality, comp. deg., qual. the n. "part." |
| part | A com. n., neu. gen., s. num., 3rd per., nom. c. to the v. "is." |
| of | A prep., sh. the rn. bet. "part" and "valour." |
| valour | An abs. n., neu. gen., s. num., 3rd per., obj. c., gov. by the prep. "of." |
| is | An irreg. intr. v., indic. m., pres. t., s. num., 3rd per., agr. with its nom. "part." |
| discretion. | An abs. n., neu. gen., s. num., 3rd per., nom. c. after the v. "is." |
| 16. We | A pers. pron., com. gen., p. num., 1st per., nom. c. to the v. "must be." |
| must | An aux. v. to "be," indg. pot. m., pres. t. |
| (to) be | An irreg. intr. v., infin. m., pres. t., gov. by the v. "must." |

| | |
|---|---|
| must be | An irreg. intr. v., pot. m., pres. t., p. num., 1st per., agr. with its nom. "we." |
| brief | An adj. of quality, pos. deg., qual. the pron. "we." |
| when | A cop. conj., jg. the sents. "We...brief" and "traitors..field." |
| traitors | A com. n., mas. gen., p. num., 3rd per., nom. c. to the v. "brave." |
| **brave** | A reg. tr. v., act. vo., indic. m., pres. t., p. num., 3rd per., agr. with its nom. "traitors." |
| field. | A com. n., neu. gen., s. num., 3rd per., obj. c., gov. by the tr. v. "brave." |
| 17. **Fling** | An irreg. tr. v., act. vo., imper. m., pres. t., s. num., 2nd per., agr. with its nom. *thou* und. |
| away | An adv. of place, mod. the v. "fling." |
| ambition. | An abs. n., neu. gen., s. num., 3rd per., obj. c., gov. by the tr. v. "fling." |
| 18. But | A disj. conj., introducing the sent. "to throw...water, is an imprudence." |
| to | A particle, indg. infin. m. |
| to throw | An irreg. tr. v., act. vo., infin. m., pres. t. ; used as an abs. n., neu. gen., s. num., 3rd per., nom. c. to the v. "is." |
| one's | An indef. pers. pron., com. gen., s. num., 3rd per., poss. c., gov. by the n. "self." |
| self | A com. n., neu. gen., s. num., 3rd per., obj. c., gov. by the tr. v. "to throw." |
| one's self | A compd. pers. pron., com. gen., s. num., 3rd per., obj. c., gov. by the tr. v. "to throw." |
| into | A prep, sh. the rn. bet. "to throw" and "water." |
| cold | An adj. of quality, pos. deg., qual. the n. "water." |
| spring | A com. n. used as an adj. of quality, qual. the n. "water." |
| water | A com. n., neu. gen., s. num., 3rd per., obj. c., gov. by the prep. "into." |
| when | A cop. conj., jg. the sents. "to throw..imprudence" and "the body..sun." |
| body | A com. n., neu. gen., s. num., 3rd per., nom. c. to the v. "has been heated." |
| has | An aux. v. to "been heated," indg. perf. t. |
| been | A past pl. from the intr. v. "to be," ref. to "heated body" and aux. to "heated," indg. pass. vo. |
| heated | A past pl. from the tr. v. "to heat," ref. to "body." |
| **has been** heated | A reg. tr. v., pass. vo., indic. m., perf. t., s. num., 3rd per., agr. with its nom. "body." |
| by | A prep., sh. the rn. bet. "has been heated" and "exercise." |
| exercise | An abs. n., neu. gen., s. num., 3rd per., obj. c., gov. by the prep. "by." |
| of | A prep., sh. the rn. bet. "exercise" and "sun." |
| sun | A com. n., neu. gen., s. num., 3rd per., obj. c., gov. by the prep. "of." |
| **is** | An irreg. intr. v., indic. m., pres. t., s. num., 3rd per., agr. with its nom. "to throw." |
| imprudence | An abs. n., neu. gen., s. num., 3rd per., nom. c. after the v. "is." |
| which | A rel. pron., neu. gen., s. num., 3rd per., agr. with its ant. "imprudence," nom. c. to the v. "may prove." |
| may | An aux. v. to "prove," indg. pot. m., pres. t. |
| (to) prove | A reg. intr. v., infin. m., pres. t., gov. by the v. "may." |
| **may prove** | A reg. intr. v., pot. m., pres. t., s. num., 3rd per., agr. with its nom. "which." |
| fatal. | An adj. of quality, pos. deg., qual. the pron. "which." |
| 19. Lives | An abs. n. used as a prop. n., neu. gen., s. num., p. form, 3rd per., nom. c. to the v. "is." |
| of | A prep., sh. the rn. bet. "Lives" and "Chancellors." |
| Chancellors | A com. n. tending to prop. n., mas. gen., p. num., 3rd per., obj. c., gov. by the prep. "of." |
| Lives of the Chancellors | A compd. prop. n., neu. gen., s. num., p. form, 3rd per., nom. c. to the v "is." |
| **is** | An irreg. intr. v., indic. m., pres. t., s. num., 3rd per., agr. with its nom. "Lives of the Chancellors." |
| voluminous | An adj. of quality, pos. deg., qual. the n. "work." |

ENGLISH GRAMMAR AND ANALYSIS. 167

| | | |
|---|---|---|
| | work. | A com. n., neu. gen., s. num., 3rd per., nom. c. after the v. "is." |
| 20. | **Methought** | An irreg. impersonal v., indic. m., past t., s. num., 3rd per., the true nom. being the sent. "I saw...lay." (See also *Parsing*, pp. 138, 139.) |
| | I | A pers. pron., com. gen., s. num., 1st per., nom. c. to the v. "saw." |
| | **saw** | An irreg. tr. v., act. vo., indic. m., past t., s. num., 1st per., agr. with its nom. "I." |
| | grave | A com. n., neu. gen., s. num., 3rd per., obj. c., gov. by the tr. v. "saw." |
| | where | A cop. conj., jg. the sents. "I...grave" and "Laura lay." |
| | Laura | A prop. n., fem. gen., s. num., 3rd per., nom. c. to the v. "lay." |
| | **lay.** | An irreg. intr. v., indic. m., past t., s. num., 3rd per., agr. with its nom. "Laura." |

## Exercise 161.

| | | |
|---|---|---|
| 1. | Innocence | An abs. n., neu. gen., s. num., 3rd per., nom. c. to the v. "makes" incl. in "make." |
| | and | A cop. conj., jg. the sents. "Innocence *along with independence* makes *a brave spirit*" and "independence *along with innocence* makes a brave spirit." |
| | independence | An abs. n., neu. gen., s. num., 3rd per., nom. c. to the v. "makes" incl. in "make." |
| | **make** | An irreg. tr. v., act. vo., indic. m., pres. t., p. num., 3rd per., agr. with its noms. "innocence" and "independence." |
| | brave | An adj. of quality, pos. deg., qual. the n. "spirit." |
| | spirit. | A com. n., neu. gen., s. num., 3rd per., obj. c., gov. by the tr. v. "make." |
| 2. | Both | A cop. conj., introducing the sent. "He is still within my power." |
| | he | A pers. pron., mas. gen., s. num., 3rd per., nom. c. to the v. "is" incl. in "are." |
| | and | A cop. conj., cor. to "both," jg. the sents. "He is still *within my power*" and "she is still within my power." |
| | she | A pers. pron., fem. gen., s. num., 3rd per., nom. c. to the v. "is" incl. in "are." |
| | **are** | An irreg. intr. v., indic. m., pres. t., p. num., 3rd per., agr. with its noms. "he" and "she." |
| | still | An adv. of time, mod. the v. "are." |
| | within | A prep., sh. the rn. bet. "are" and "power." |
| | my | A pers. pron., com. gen., s. num., 1st per., poss. c., gov. by the n. "power." |
| | power. | An abs. n., neu. gen., s. num., 3rd per., obj. c., gov. by the prep. "within." |
| 3. | At | A prep., sh. the rn. bet. "are" and "point." |
| | one | A def. card. nu. adj. of quantity, qual. the n. "point." |
| | point | A com. n., neu. gen., s. num., 3rd per., obj. c., gov. by the prep. "at." |
| | Danube | A prop. n., neu. gen., s. num., 3rd per., nom. c. to the v. "is" incl. in "are." |
| | and | A cop. conj., jg. the sents. "At one point the Danube is *only twelve miles apart from the Rhine*" and "*at one point* the Rhine is *only twelve miles* apart *from the Danube*." |
| | Rhine | A prop. n., neu. gen., s. num., 3rd per., nom. c. to the v. "is" incl. in "are." |
| | **are** | An irreg. intr. v., indic. m., pres. t., p. num., 3rd per., agr. with its noms. "Danube" and "Rhine." |
| | only | An adv. of deg., mod. the adj. "twelve." |
| | twelve | A def. card. nu. adj. of quantity, qual. the n. "miles." |
| | miles | A com. n., neu. gen., p. num., 3rd per., obj. c., gov. by the prep. *at* und. |
| | apart. | An adv. of place, mod. the v. "are." |
| 4. | piece | A com. n., neu. gen., s. num., 3rd per., nom. c. to the v. "was" incl. in "were." |
| | of | A prep., sh. the rn. bet. "piece" and "bread." |

| | |
|---|---|
| bread | A com. n., neu. gen., s. num., 3rd per., obj. c., gov. by the prep. "of." |
| and | A cop. conj., jg. the sents. "a piece of bread *along with a draught of water* was *often his sole repast*" and "a draught of water *along with a piece of bread* was often his sole *repast*." |
| draught | A com. n., neu. gen., s. num., 3rd per., nom. c. to the v. "was" incl. in "were." |
| of | A prep., sh. the rn. bet. "draught" and "water." |
| water | A com. n., neu. gen., s. num., 3rd per., obj. c., gov. by the prep. "of." |
| **were** | An irreg. intr. v., indic. m., past t., p. num., 3rd per., agr. with its noms. "piece" and "draught." |
| often | An adv. of time, mod. the v. "were." |
| his | A pers. pron., mas. gen., s. num., 3rd per., poss. c., gov. by the n. *repast* und. |
| sole | An adj. of quality, qual. the n. *repast* und. |
| and | A cop. conj., jg. the sents. "A piece..sole *repast*" and "*a piece.. evening repast.*" |
| evening | An abs. n., used as an adj. of quality, qual. the n. "repast." |
| repast. | A com. n., neu. gen., s. num., 3rd per., nom. c. after the v. *were* und. |
| 5. Wolfe | A prop. n., mas. gen., s. num., 3rd per., nom. c. to the v. "landed" incl. in "landed." |
| Monckton | A prop. n., mas. gen., s. num., 3rd per., nom. c. to the v. "landed" incl. in "landed." |
| and | A cop. conj., jg. the sents. "Monckton landed *with the first division*" and "Murray landed with the first division." |
| Murray | A prop. n., mas. gen., s. num., 3rd per., nom. c. to the v. "landed" incl. in "landed." |
| **landed** | A reg. intr. v., indic. m., past t., p. num., 3rd per., agr. with its noms. "Wolfe," "Monckton," and "Murray." |
| with | A prep., sh. the rn. bet. "landed" and "division." |
| first | A def. ord. nu. adj. of quantity, qual. the n. "division." |
| division. | A com. col. n., neu. gen., s. num., 3rd per., obj. c., gov. by the prep. "with." |
| 6. I | A pers. pron., com. gen., s. num., 1st per., nom. c. to the v. "heard." |
| heard | An irreg. tr. v., act. vo., indic. m., past t., s. num., 1st per., agr. with its nom. "I." |
| wrack | An abs. n., neu. gen., s. num., 3rd per., obj. c., gov. by the tr. v. "heard." |
| as | A cop. conj., jg. the sents. "I..wrack" and "*I should hear it.*" |
| if | A cop. conj., jg. the sents. "*I should hear it*" and "earth..mingle *with the sky*," and indg. conditional form. |
| as if | A compd. cop. conj., jg. the sents. "I..wrack" and "earth..mingle." |
| earth | A com. n., neu. gen., s. num., 3rd per., nom. c. to the v. "would mingle." incl. in "would mingle." |
| and | A cop. conj., jg. the sents. "earth would mingle *with the sky*" and "sky would mingle *with the earth.*" |
| sky | A com. n., neu. gen., s. num., 3rd per., nom. c. to the v. "would mingle" incl. in "would mingle." |
| would | An aux. v. to "mingle," indg. pot. m., past t. |
| (to) mingle | A reg. intr. v., infin. m., pres. t., gov. by the v. "would." |
| would mingle | A reg. intr. v., pot. m., past t., p. num., 3rd per., agr. with its noms. "earth" and "sky." |
| 7. Sheba | A prop. n., neu. gen., s. num., 3rd per., nom. c. to the v. "borders" incl. in "border." |
| and | A cop. conj., jg. the sents. "Sheba borders *on the Persian Gulf*" and "Raamah borders on the Persian Gulf." |
| Raamah | A prop. n., neu. gen., s. num., 3rd per., nom. c. to the v. "borders" incl. in "border." |
| **border** | A reg. intr. v., indic. m., pres. t., p. num., 3rd per., agr. with its noms. "Sheba" and "Raamah." |
| Persian | A prop. adj. of quality, qual. the n. "gulf." |
| gulf. | A com. n., neu. gen., s. num., 3rd per., obj. c., gov. by the prep. *on* und. |

| | |
|---|---|
| 8. Copper | A com. n., neu. gen., s. num., 3rd per., nom. c. to the v. "is" incl. in "are." |
| and | A cop. conj., jg. the sents. "Copper is a soft metal" and "tin is a soft metal." |
| tin | A com. n., neu. gen., s. num., 3rd per., nom. c. to the v. "is" incl. in "are." |
| **are** | An irreg. intr. v., indic. m., pres. t., p. num., 3rd per., agr. with its noms. "copper" and "tin." |
| soft | An adj. of quality, pos. deg., qual. the n. "metals." |
| metals. | A com. n., neu. gen., p. num., 3rd per., nom. c. after the v. "are." |
| 9. Rocks | A com. n., neu. gen., p. num., 3rd per., nom. c. to the v. *rise* und. |
| torrents | A com. n., neu. gen., p. num., 3rd per., nom. c. to the v. *rise* und. |
| gulfs | A com. n., neu. gen., p. num., 3rd per., nom. c. to the v. *rise* und. |
| and | A cop. conj., jg. the sents. "gulfs rise" and "shapes of giant size *rise*." |
| shapes | A com. n., neu. gen., p. num., 3rd per., nom. c. to the v. *rise* und. |
| of | A prep., sh. the rn. bet. "shapes" and "size." |
| giant | A com. n. used as an adj. of quality, qual. the n. "size." |
| size | An abs. n., neu. gen., s. num., 3rd per., obj. c., gov. by the prep. "of." |
| And | A cop. conj., jg. the sents. "shapes of giant size *rise*" and "glittering cliffs on cliffs *rise*." |
| glittering | A pres. pl. from the intr. v. "to glitter," used as an adj. of quality, pos. deg., qual. the n. "cliffs." |
| cliffs | A com. n., neu. gen., p. num., 3rd per., nom. c. to the v. *rise* und. |
| on | A prep., sh. the rn. bet. "cliffs" and "cliffs." |
| cliffs | A com. n., neu. gen., p. num., 3rd per., obj. c., gov. by the prep. "on." |
| and | A cop. conj., jg. the sents. "glittering cliffs on cliffs *rise*" and "fiery ramparts *rise*." |
| fiery | An adj. of quality, pos. deg., qual. the n. "ramparts." |
| ramparts | A com. n., neu. gen., p. num., 3rd per., nom. c. to the v. "rise." |
| **rise.** | An irreg. intr. v., indic. m., pres. t., p. num., 3rd per., agr. with its nom. "ramparts." |
| 10. Here | An adv. of place, mod. the v. "sit." |
| I | A pers. pron., com. gen., s. num., 1st per., nom. c. to the v. "sit" incl. in "sit." |
| and | A cop. conj., jg. the sents. "Here I sit" and "*here* sorrow sits." |
| sorrow | An abs. n., neu. gen., s. num., 3rd per., nom. c. to the v. "sits" incl. in "sit." |
| **sit** | An irreg. intr. v., indic. m., pres. t., p. num., 1st per., agr. with its noms. "I" and "sorrow" ("I and sorrow"=we). |
| Here | An adv. of place, mod. the v. "is." |
| is | An irreg. intr. v., indic. m., pres. t., s. num., 3rd per., agr. with its nom. "throne." |
| thy | A pers. pron., com. gen., s. num., 2nd per., poss. c., gov. by the n. "throne." |
| throne | A com. n., neu. gen., s. num., 3rd per., nom. c. to the v. "is." |
| bid | An irreg. tr. v., act. vo., imper. m., pres. t., s. num., 2nd per., agr with its nom. *thou* und. |
| kings | A com. n., mas. gen., p. num., 3rd per., obj. c., gov. by the tr. v. "bid." |
| (to) come | An irreg. intr. v., infin. m., pres. t., gov. by the v. "bid." |
| (to) bow | A reg. intr. v., infin. m., pres. t., gov. by the v. "to come." |
| to | A prep., sh. the rn. bet. "to bow" and "it." |
| it. | A pers. pron., neu. gen., s. num., 3rd per., obj. c., gov. by the prep. "to." |

## Exercise 162.

| | |
|---|---|
| 1. Pride | An abs. n., neu. gen., s. num., 3rd per., nom. c. to the v. *will carry* und. |
| or | A disj. conj., jg. the sents. "Pride *will carry a man to great lengths*" and "passion will....lengths." |

| | |
|---|---|
| passion | An abs. n., neu. gen., s. num., 3rd per., nom. c. to the v. "**will carry**." |
| will | An aux. v. to "carry," indg. fut. t. |
| (to) carry | A reg. tr. v., act. vo., infin. m., pres. t., gov. by the v. "will." |
| **will carry** | A reg. tr. v., act. vo., indic. m., fut. t., s. num., 3rd per., agr. with its nom. "passion." |
| man | A com. n., mas. gen., s. num., 3rd per., obj. c., gov. by the tr. v. "will carry." |
| to | A prep., sh. the rn. bet. "will carry" and "lengths." |
| great | An adj. of quality, pos. deg., qual. the n. "lengths." |
| lengths. | An abs. n., neu. gen., p. num., 3rd per., obj. c., gov. by the prep. "to." |
| 2. No | A def. card. nu. adj. of quantity, qual. the n. "nook." |
| nook | A com. n., neu. gen., s. num., 3rd per., nom. c. to the v. was left und. |
| or | A disj. conj., jg. the sents. "no nook *was left unexplored*" and "*no corner..unexplored.*" |
| corner | A com. n., neu. gen., s. num., 3rd per., nom. c. to the v. "was left." |
| was | An aux. v. to "left," indg. pass. vo., past t. |
| left | A past pl. from the tr. v. "to leave," ref. to "corner." |
| **was left** | An irreg. tr. v., pass. vo., indic. m., past t., s. num., 3rd per., agr. with its nom. "corner." |
| unexplored. | A negative form of the past pl. from the tr. v. "to explore," ref. to "corner." |
| 3. There | An expletive adv., mod. the v. "was." |
| **was** | An irreg. intr. v., indic., m., past t., s. num., 3rd per., agr. with its nom. "sound." |
| neither | A disj. conj., introducing the sent. "There was sound." |
| sound | An abs. n., neu. gen., s. num., 3rd per., nom. c. to the v. "was." |
| nor | A disj. conj., cor. to "neither," jg. the sents. "There was sound" and "*there was* sight." |
| sight | An abs. n., neu. gen., s. num., 3rd per., nom. c. to the v. was und. |
| To | A particle, indg. infin. m. |
| To serve | A reg. tr. v., act. vo., infin. m., pres. t., gov. by the n. "sight." |
| them | A pers. pron., com. gen., p. num., 3rd per., obj. c., gov. by the tr. v. "to serve." |
| for | A prep., sh. the rn. bet. "to serve" and "guide." |
| guide. | A com. n., neu. gen., s. num., 3rd per., obj. c., gov. by the prep. "for." |
| 4. No | A def. card. nu. adj. of quantity, qual. the n. "noise." |
| other | An indef. nu. adj. of quantity, qual. the n. "noise." |
| noise | An abs. n., neu. gen., s. num., 3rd per., nom. c. to the v. *might be heard* und. |
| or | A disj. conj., jg. the sents. "No other noise *might there be heard*" and "*no people's troubled cries might there be heard.*" |
| people's | A com. n., com. gen., p. num., 3rd per., poss. c., gov. by the n. "cries." |
| troublous | An adj. of quality, pos. deg., qual. the n. "cries." |
| cries | An abs. n., neu. gen., p. num., 3rd per., nom. c. to the v. "might be heard." |
| As | A cop. conj., jg. the sents. "*no people's troublous cries might there be heard*" and "*the cries are.*" |
| still | An adv. of time, mod. the v. "are." |
| are | An irreg. intr. v., indic. m., pres. t., p. num., 3rd per., agr. with its nom. *which* und. |
| wont | A past pl. from the obsolete v. "wunian" (to dwell, to abide, to do habitually), ref. to *which* und. (*Parsing*, p. 182.) |
| to | A particle, indg. infin. m. |
| to annoy | A reg. tr. v., act. vo., infin. m., pres. t., gov. by the pl. "wont." |
| walled | An adj. of quality, qual. the n. "town." |
| town | A com. n., neu. gen., s. num., 3rd per., obj. c., gov. by the tr. v. "to annoy." |
| Might | An aux. v. to "be heard," indg. pot. m., past t. |
| there | An adv. of place, mod. the v. "might be heard." |
| be | An aux. v. to "heard," indg. pass. vo. |
| heard. | A past pl. from the tr. v. "to hear," ref. to "cries." |

| | |
|---|---|
| might be } heard } | An irreg. tr. v., pass. vo., pot. m., past t., p. num., 3rd per., agr. with its nom. "cries." |
| but | A disj. conj., jg. the sents. "*no* people's...heard" and "careless... enemies." |
| careless | An adj. of quality. pos. deg., qual. the n. "quiet." |
| quiet | An abs. n., neu. gen., s. num., 3rd per., nom. c. to the v. "lies." |
| lies | An irreg. intr. v., indic. m., pres. t., s. num., 3rd per., agr. with its nom. "quiet." |
| Wrapt | A past pl. from the tr. v. "to wrap," ref. to "quiet." |
| in | A prep., sh. the rn. bet. "wrapt" and "silence." |
| eternal | An adj. of quality, qual. the n. "silence." |
| silence | An abs. n., neu. gen., s. num., 3rd per., obj. c., gov. by the prep. "in." |
| far | An adv. of place, mod. the v. "lies." |
| from | A prep., sh. the rn. bet. "lies" and "enemies." |
| enemies. | A com. n., com. gen., p. num., 3rd per., obj. c., gov. by the prep. "from." |
| 5. Whether | A disj. conj., jg. the sents. "Each..cause" and "love *thy royal thoughts did move*," and indg. subj. m. |
| love | An abs. n., neu. gen., s. num., 3rd per., nom. c., to the v. *did move* und. |
| Or | A disj. conj., cor. to "whether," jg. the sents. "love *did move thy royal thoughts*" and "victory did move thy royal thoughts." |
| victory | An abs. n., neu. gen., s. num., 3rd per., nom. c. to the v. "did move." |
| thy | A pers. pron., mas. gen., s. num., 2nd per., poss. c., gov. by the n. "thoughts." |
| royal | An adj. of quality, qual. the n. "thoughts." |
| thoughts | An abs. n., neu. gen., p. num., 3rd per., obj. c., gov. by the tr. v. "did move." |
| did | An aux. v. to "move," indg. past t., emph. form. |
| (to) move | A reg. tr. v., act. vo., infin. m., pres. t., gov. by the v. "did." |
| **did move** | A reg. tr. v., act. vo., subj. m., past t., emph. form, s. num., 3rd per., agr. with its nom. "victory." |
| Each | A dist. nu. adj. of quantity, qual. the n. *cause* und. |
| was | An irreg. intr. v., indic. m., past t., s. num., 3rd per., agr. with its nom. *cause* und. |
| noble | An adj. of quality, pos. deg., qual. the n. "cause." |
| cause. | An abs. n., neu. gen., s. num., 3rd per., nom. c. after the v. "was." |
| 6. breezy | An adj. of quality, qual. the n. "call." |
| call | An abs. n., neu. gen., s. num., 3rd per., nom. c. to the v. *shall rouse* und. |
| of | A prep., sh. the rn. bet. "call" and "morn." |
| incense- breathing } | A compd. adj. of quality, qual. the n. "morn." |
| morn | An abs. n., neu. gen., s. num., 3rd per., obj. c., gov. by the prep. "of." |
| swallow | A com. n., com. gen., s. num., 3rd per., nom. c. to the v. *shall rouse* und. |
| twittering | A pres. pl. from the intr. v. "to twitter," ref. to "swallow." |
| from | A prep., sh. the rn. bet. "twittering" and "shed." |
| straw-built | A compd. adj. of quality, qual. the n. "shed." |
| shed | A com. n., neu. gen., s. num., 3rd per., obj. c., gov. by the prep. "from." |
| cock's | A com. n., mas. gen., s. num., 3rd per., poss. c., gov. by the n. "clarion." |
| shrill | An adj. of quality, pos. deg., qual. the n. "clarion." |
| clarion | A com. n., neu. gen., s. num., 3rd per., nom. c. to the v. *shall rouse* und. |
| or | A disj. conj., jg. the sents. "The cock's shrill clarion *no more shall rouse them from their lowly bed*" and "the echoing horn... bed." |
| echoing | A pres. pl. from the intr. v. "to echo," used as an adj. of quality, qual. the n. "horn." |
| horn | A com. n., neu. gen., s. num., 3rd per., nom. c. to the v. "shall rouse." |
| No | An adv. of m. (neg.), mod. the adv. "more." |

172 KEY TO

| | |
|---|---|
| more | An adv. of time, mod. the v. "shall rouse." |
| shall | An aux. v. to "rouse," indg. fut. t., emph. form, expressing "certainty." |
| (to) rouse | A reg. tr. v., act. vo., infin. m., pres. t., gov. by the v. "shall." |
| **shall rouse** | A reg. tr. v., act. vo., indic. m., fut. t., emph. form, s. num., 3rd per., agr. with its nom. "horn." |
| them | A pers. pron., mas. gen., p. num., 3rd per., obj. c., gov. by the tr. v. "shall rouse." ("Them," i.e. the forefathers of the hamlet.) |
| from | A prep., sh. the rn. bet. "shall rouse" and "bed." |
| their | A pers. pron., mas. gen., p. num., 3rd per., poss. c., gov. by the n. "bed." |
| lowly | An adj. of quality, pos. deg., qual. the n. "bed." |
| bed. | A com. n., neu. gen., s. num., 3rd per., obj. c., gov. by the prep. "from." |

## Exercise 163.

| | |
|---|---|
| 1. council | A com. col. n., mas. gen., p. num., 3rd per., nom. c. to the v. "rubbed." |
| being | A pres. pl. from the intr. v. "to be," ref. to "awakened council," aux. to "awakened," and indg. pass. vo. |
| awakened | A past pl. from the tr. v. "to awaken," ref. to "council." |
| being awakened | A pres. pl. from the tr. v. "to awaken," pass. vo., ref. to "council." |
| by | A prep., sh. the rn. bet. "being awakened" and "serjeant-at-arms." |
| serjeant-at-arms | A compd. com. n., mas. gen., s. num., 3rd per., obj. c., gov. by the prep. "by." |
| **rubbed** | A reg. tr. v., act. vo., indic. m., past. t., p. num., 3rd per., agr. with its n. "council." |
| their | A pers. pron., mas. gen., p. num., 3rd per., poss. c., gov. by the n. "eyes." |
| eyes. | A com. n., neu. gen., p. num., 3rd per., obj. c., gov. by the tr. v. "rubbed." |
| 2. jury | A com. col. n., mas. gen., p. num., 3rd per., nom. c. to the v. "were discharged." |
| were | An aux. v. to "discharged," indg. pass. vo., past t. |
| discharged | A past pl. from the intr. v. "to discharge," ref. to "jury." |
| **were discharged** | A reg. tr. v., pass. vo., indic. m., past t., p. num., 3rd per., agr. with its nom. "jury." |
| 3. multitude | A com. col. n., com. gen., p. num., 3rd per., nom. c. to the v. "were divided." |
| were | An aux. v. to "divided," indg. pass. vo., past t. |
| divided | A past pl. from the tr. v. "to divide," ref. to "multitude." |
| **were divided** | A reg. tr. v., pass. vo., indic. m., past t., p. num., 3rd per., agr. with its nom. "multitude." |
| in | A prep., sh. the rn. bet. "were divided" and "opinion." |
| opinion. | An abs. n., neu. gen., s. num., 3rd per., obj. c., gov. by the prep. "in." |
| 4. parliament | A com. col. n., neu. gen., s. num., 3rd per., nom. c. to the v. "has elected." |
| has | An aux. v. to "elected," indg. perf. t. |
| elected | A past pl. from the tr. v. "to elect," ref. to "Speaker." |
| **has elected** | A reg. tr. v., act. vo., indic. m., perf. t., s. num., 3rd per., agr. with its nom. "parliament." |
| its | A pers. pron., neu. gen., s. num., 3rd per., poss. c., gov. by the n. "Speaker." |
| Speaker. | A com. n. tending to prop., mas. gen., s. num., 3rd per., obj. c., gov. by the tr. v. "has elected." |
| 5. meeting | A com. col. n., neu. gen., s. num., 3rd per., nom. c. to the v. "has chosen." |
| has | An aux. v. to "chosen," indg. perf. t. |
| chosen | A past pl. from the tr. v. "to choose," ref. to "president." |
| **has chosen** | An irreg. tr. v., act. vo., indic. m., perf. t., s. num., 3rd per., agr. with its nom. "meeting." |
| president. | A com. n., mas. gen., s. num., 3rd per., obj. c., gov. by the tr. v. "has chosen." |

| | |
|---|---|
| 6. House | A com. col. n. tending to prop., mas. gen., p. num., 3rd per., nom. c. to the v. " were agreed." |
| of | A prep., sh. the rn. bet. " House " and " Commons." |
| Commons | A com. n. tending to prop., mas. gen., p. num., 3rd per., obj. c., gov. by the prep. " of." |
| were | An aux. v. to " agreed," used for " had," indg. pluperf. t. |
| well | An adv. of man., mod. the v. " were agreed." |
| agreed | A past pl. from the intr. v. " to agree," ref. to " House." |
| **were agreed** | A reg. intr. v., indic. m., pluperf. t., p. num., 3rd per., agr. with its nom. " House." (Were agreed = had agreed. *Parsing*, p. 135.) |
| in | A prep., sh. the rn. bet. " were agreed " and " passing." |
| passing | A ger. from the tr. v. " to pass," neu. gen., s. num., 3rd per., obj. c., gov. by the prep. " in." |
| bill. | A com. n., neu. gen., s. num., 3rd per., obj. c., gov. by the tr. ger. " passing." |

## Exercise 164.

| | |
|---|---|
| 1. my | A pers. pron., com. gen., s. num., 1st per., poss. c., gov. by the n. " father." |
| father | A com. n., mas. gen., s. num., 3rd per., nom. c. to the v. " has lived," incl. in " have lived." |
| and | A cop. conj., jg. the sents. " My father has lived *here fifteen years*" and " I have lived here fifteen years.' |
| I | A pers. pron., com. gen., s. num., 1st per., nom. c. to the v. " have lived " incl. in " have lived." |
| have | An aux. v. to " lived," indg. perf. t. |
| lived | A past pl. from the intr. v. " to live," ref. to " father " and " I." |
| **have lived** | A reg. intr. v., indic. m., perf. t., p. num., 1st per., agr. with its noms. " father " and " I " (father and I=we). |
| here | An adv. of place, mod. the v. " have lived." |
| fifteen | A def. card. nu. adj. of quantity, qual. the n. " years." |
| years. | An abs. n., neu. gen., p. num., 3rd per., obj. c., gov. by the prep. *during* und. |
| 2. We | A pers. pron., com. gen., p. num., 1st per., nom. c. to the v. " landed " incl. in " landed." |
| and | A cop. conj., jg. the sents. " We landed *yesterday*" and " they landed yesterday." |
| they | A pers. pron., com. gen., p. num., 3rd per., nom. c. to the v. " landed " incl. in " landed." |
| **landed** | A reg. intr. v., indic. m., past t., p. num., 1st per., agr. with its noms. " we " and " they " (we and they = we). |
| yesterday. | An adv. of time, mod. the v. " landed." |
| 3. bishop | A com. n., mas. gen., s. num., 3rd per., nom. c. to the v. " undertook " incl. in " undertook." |
| and | A cop. conj., jg. the sents. " The bishop undertook *the work* " and " I undertook the work." |
| I | A pers. pron., com. gen., s. num., 1st per., nom. c. to the v. " undertook " incl. in " undertook." |
| **undertook** | An irreg. tr. v., act. vo., indic. m., past t., p. num., 1st per., agr. with its noms. " bishop " and " I " (bishop and I = we). |
| work. | A com. n., neu. gen., s. num., 3rd per., obj. c., gov. by the tr. v. " undertook." |
| 4. You | A pers. pron., fem. gen., s. num., p. form, 2nd per., nom. c. to the v. " might pass " incl. in " might pass." |
| and | A cop. conj., jg. the sents. " You might pass for her sister " and " she might pass for your sister." |
| she | A pers. pron., fem. gen., s. num., 3rd per., nom. c. to the v. " might pass " incl. in " might pass." |
| might | An aux v. to " pass," indg. pot. m., past t. |
| (to) pass | A reg. intr. v., infin. m., pres. t., gov. by the v. " might." |
| **might pass** | A reg. intr. v., pot. m., past t., p. num., 2nd per., agr. with its noms. " you " and " she " (you and she = you). |
| for | A prep., sh. the rn. bet. " might pass " and " sisters." |
| sisters. | A com. n., fem. gen., p. num., 3rd per., obj. c., gov. by the prep. " for." |

| | |
|---|---|
| 5. You | A pers. pron., com. gen., s. num., p. form, 2nd per., nom. c. to the v. "must protect" incl. in "must protect." |
| and | A cop. conj., jg. the sents. "You must protect *these orphans*" and "I must protect these orphans." |
| I | A pers. pron., com. gen., s. num., 1st per., nom. c. to the v. "must protect" incl. in "must protect." |
| must | An aux. v. to "protect." indg. pot. m., pres. t. |
| (to) protect | A reg. tr. v., act. vo., infin. m., pres. t., gov. by the v. "must." |
| **must protect** | A reg. tr. v., act. vo., pot. m., pres. t., p. num., 1st per., agr. with its noms. "You" and "I" (you and I = we). |
| these | A dis. adj., lim. the n. "orphans." |
| orphans. | A com. n., com. gen., p. num., 3rd per., obj. c., gov. by the tr. v. "must protect." |
| 6. You | A pers. pron., com. gen., p. num., or s. num., p. form, 2nd per., nom. c. to the v. "are" incl. in "are." |
| and | A cop. conj., jg. the sents. "You are *now in a position to pay the debt*" and "they are..debt." |
| they | A pers. pron., com. gen., p. num., 3rd per., nom. c. to the v. "are" incl. in "are." |
| **are** | An irreg. intr. v., indic. m., pres. t., p. num., 2nd per., agr. with its noms. "you" and "they" (you and they = you). |
| now | An adv. of time, mod. the v. "are." |
| in | A prep. sh. the rn. bet. "are" and "position." |
| position | An abs. n., neu. gen., s. num., 3rd per., obj. c., gov. by the prep. "in." |
| to | A particle, indg. infin. m. |
| to pay | An irreg. tr. v., act. vo., infin. m., pres. t., gov. by the n. "position." |
| debt. | A com. n., neu. gen., s. num., 3rd per., obj. c., gov. by the tr. v. "to pay." |

## Exercise 165.

| | |
|---|---|
| 1. Neither | A disj. conj., introducing the sent. "you *have witnessed the new play*." |
| you | A pers. pron., com. gen., p. num., or s. num., p. form, 2nd per., nom. c. to the v. *have witnessed* und. |
| nor | A disj. conj., cor. to "neither," jg. the sents. "you *have witnessed the new play*," and "he has..play." |
| he | A pers. pron., mas. gen., s. num., 3rd per., nom. c. to the v. "has witnessed." |
| has | An aux. v. to "witnessed," indg. perf. t. |
| witnessed | A past pl. from the tr. v. "to witness," ref. to "play." |
| **has witnessed** | A reg. tr. v., act. vo., indic. m., perf. t., s. num., 3rd per., agr. with its nom. "he." |
| new | An adj. of quality, pos. deg., qual. the n. "play." |
| play. | A com. n., neu. gen., s. num., 3rd per., obj. c., gov. by the tr. v. "has witnessed." |
| 2. Either | A disj. conj., introducing the sent. "she *is deceived*." |
| she | A pers. pron., fem. gen., s. num., 3rd per., nom. c. to the v. *is deceived* und. |
| or | A disj. conj., cor. to "either," jg. the sents. "she *is deceived*" and "I am deceived." |
| I | A pers. pron., com. gen., s. num., 1st per., nom. c. to the v. "am deceived." |
| am | An aux. v. to "deceive," indg. pass. vo., pres. t. |
| deceived | A past pl. from the tr. v. "to deceive," ref. to "I." |
| **am deceived.** | A reg. tr. v., pass. vo., indic. m., pres. t., s. num., 1st per., agr. with its nom. "I." |
| 3. Either | A disj. conj., introducing the sent. "you *have been at the masquerade*." |
| you | A pers. pron., com. gen., p. num., or s. num., p. form, 2nd per., nom. c. to the v. *have been* und. |
| or | A disj. conj., cor. to "either," jg. the sents. "you *have been at the masquerade*" and "Lovell..masquerade." |
| Lovell | A prop. n., mas. gen., s. num., 3rd per., nom. c. to the v. "has been." |
| has | An aux. v. to "been," indg. perf. t. |
| be | A past pl. from the intr. v. "to be," ref. to "Lovell." |

ENGLISH GRAMMAR AND ANALYSIS.   175

| | |
|---|---|
| **has been** | An irreg. intr. v. indic. m., perf. t., s. num., 3rd per., agr. with its nom. "Lovell." |
| at | A prep., sh. the rn. bet. "has been," and "masquerade." |
| masquerade. | A com. n., neu. gen., s. num., 3rd per., obj. c., gov. by the prep. "at." |
| 4. Neither | A disj. conj., introducing the sent. "you *can realise the appalling truth.*" |
| you | A pers. pron., com. gen., p. num., or s. num., p. form, 2nd per., nom. c. to the v. *can realise* und. |
| nor | A disj. conj., cor. to "neither," jg. the sents. "you *can realise the appalling truth*" and "I can..truth." |
| I | A pers. pron., com. gen., s. num., 1st per., nom. c. to the v. "can realise." |
| can | An aux. v. to "realise," indg. pot. m., pres. t. |
| (to) realise | A reg. tr. v., act. vo., infin. m., pres. t., gov. by the v. "can." |
| **can realise** | A reg. tr. v., act. vo., pot. m., pres. t., s. num., 1st per., agr. with its nom. "I." |
| appalling | A pres. pl. from the tr. v. "to appal," used as an adj. of quality, qual. the n. "truth." |
| truth. | An abs. n., neu. gen., s. num., 3rd per., obj. c., gov. by the tr. v. "can realise." |
| 5. Neither | A disj. conj., introducing the sent. "you *were in the right.*" |
| you | A pers. pron., com. gen., p. num., or s. num., p. form, 2nd per., nom. c. to the v. *were* und. |
| nor | A disj. conj., cor. to "neither," jg. the sents. "you *were in the right*" and the priest..right." |
| priest | A com. n., mas. gen., s. num., 3rd per., nom. c. to the v. "was." |
| **was** | An irreg. intr. v., indic. m., past t., s. num., 3rd per., agr. with its nom. "priest." |
| in | A prep., sh. the rn. bet. "was" and "right." |
| right. | An abs. n., neu. gen., s. num., 3rd per., obj. c., gov. by the prep. "in." |
| 6. Either | A disj. conj., introducing the sent. "he *is sadly changed.*" |
| he | A pers. pron., mas. gen., s. num., 3rd per., nom. c. to the v. *is changed* und. |
| or | A disj. conj., cor. to "either," jg. the sents. "he *is sadly changed*" and "I..changed." |
| I | A pers. pron., com. gen., s. num., 1st per., nom. c. to the v. "am changed." |
| am | An aux. v. to "changed," indg. pass. vo., pres. t. |
| sadly | An adv. of man., mod. the v. "am changed." |
| changed | A past pl. from the tr. v. "to change," ref. to "I." |
| **am changed.** | A reg. tr. v., pass. vo., indic. m., pres. t., s. num., 1st per., agr. with its nom. "I." |

## Exercise 166.

| | |
|---|---|
| 1. If | A cop. conj., jg. the sents. "You touch all" and "you touch one," and indg. subj. m. |
| you | A pers. pron., com. gen., p. num., or s. num., p. form, 2nd per., nom. c. to the v. "touch." |
| **touch** | A reg. tr. v., act. vo., subj. m., pres. t., p. num., or s. num., p. form, 2nd per., agr. with its nom. "you." |
| one | A def. card. nu. adj. of quantity, qual. the n. *person* or *thing* und. |
| you | A pers. pron., com. gen., p. num., or s. num., p. form, 2nd per., nom. c. to the v. "touch." |
| touch | A reg. tr. v., act. vo., indic. m., pres. t., p. num., or s. num., p. form, 2nd per., agr. with its nom. "you." |
| all. | An indef. nu. adj. of quantity, qual. the n. *persons* or *things* und. |
| 2. Life | An abs. n., neu. gen., s. num., 3rd per., nom. c. to the v. "is." |
| is | An irreg. intr. v., indic. m., pres. t., s. num., 3rd per., agr. with its nom. "life." |
| no | A def. card. nu. adj. of quantity, qual. the n. "trifle." |
| trifle | A com. n., neu. gen., s. num., 3rd per., nom. c. after the v. "is." |
| howsoever | A disj. conj., jg. the sents. "Life is no trifle" and "short it seem," and indg. subj. m. |

| | |
|---|---|
| short | An adj. of quality, pos. deg., qual. the pron. "it." |
| it | A pers. pron., neu. gen., s. num., 3rd per., nom. c. to the v. "seem." |
| **seem.** | A reg. intr. v., subj. m., pres. t., s. num., 3rd per., agr. with its nom. "it." |
| 3. What | An interrog. pron., neu. gen., s. num., 3rd per., obj. c., gov. by the tr. v. *does matter* und. (What *does it matter.*) |
| though | A disj. conj., jg. the sents. "What *does it matter*" and "no real voice *amid their radiant orbs be found*," and indg. subj. m. |
| no | A def. card. nu. adj. of quantity, qual. the n. "voice." |
| real | An adj. of quality, qual. the n. "voice." |
| voice | An abs. n., neu. gen., s. num., 3rd per., nom. c. to the v. *be found* und. |
| nor | A disj. conj., jg. the sents. "no real voice *amid their radiant orbs be found*" and "*no* sound amid their radiant orbs be found." |
| sound | An abs. n., neu. gen., s. num., 3rd per., nom. c. to the v. "be found." |
| amid | A prep., sh. the rn. bet. "be found" and "orbs." |
| their | A pers. pron., neu. gen., p. num., 3rd per., poss. c., gov. by the n. "orbs." |
| radiant | An adj. of quality, pos. deg., qual. the n. "orbs." |
| orbs | A com. n., neu. gen., p. num., 3rd per., obj. c., gov. by the prep. "amid." |
| be | An aux. v. to "found," indg. pass. vo., pres. t. |
| found | A past pl. from the tr. v. "to find," ref. to "sound." |
| **be found.** | An irreg. tr. v., pass. vo., subj. m., pres. t., s. num., 3rd per., agr. with its nom. "sound." |
| 4. Though | A disj. conj., jg. the sents. "be not amazed" and "they to one be ten," and indg. subj. m. |
| they | A pers. pron., com. gen., p. num., 3rd per., nom. c. to the v. "be." |
| to | A prep., sh. the rn. bet. "be" and *person* und. |
| one | A def. card. nu. adj. of quantity, qual. the n. *person* und. |
| be | An irreg. intr. v., subj. m., pres. t., p. num., 3rd per., agr. with its nom. "they." |
| ten | A def. card. nu. adj. of quantity, qual. the n. *persons* und. |
| be | An aux. v. to "amazed," indg. pass. vo., pres. t. |
| not | An adv. of m. (neg.), mod. the v. "be amazed." |
| amazed | A past pl. from the tr. v. "to amaze," ref. to *you* und. |
| **be amazed.** | A reg. tr. v., pass. vo., imper. m., pres. t., p. num., 2nd per., agr. with its nom. *you* und. |
| 5 He | A pers. pron., mas. gen., s. num., 3rd per., nom. c. to the v. "will come." |
| will | An aux. v. to "come," indg. fut. t. |
| not | An adv. of m. (neg.), mod. the v. "will come." |
| (to) come | An irreg. intr. v., infin. m., pres. t., gov. by the v. "will." |
| will come | An irreg. intr. v., indic. m., fut. t., s. num., 3rd per., agr. with its nom. "he." |
| till | A cop. conj., jg. the sents. "He..come" and "she be gone," and indg. subj. m. |
| she | A pers. pron., fem. gen., s. num., 3rd per., nom. c. to the v. "be gone." |
| be | An aux. v. to "gone," used for "have," indg. perf. t. |
| gone | A past pl. from the intr. v. "to go," ref. to "she." |
| **be gone.** | An irreg. intr. v., subj. m., perf. t., s. num., 3rd per., agr. with its nom. "she." |
| 6. If | A cop. conj., jg. the sents. "it should be otherwise" and "I were a king," and indg. subj. m. |
| I | A pers. pron., mas. gen., s. num., 1st per., nom. c. to the v. "were." |
| **were** | An irreg. intr. v., subj. m, past t., s. num., 1st per., agr. with its nom. "I." |
| king | A com. n., mas. gen., s. num., 3rd per., nom. c. after the v. "were." |
| it | A pers. pron., neu. gen., s. num., 3rd per., nom. c. to the v. "should be." |
| should | An aux. v. to "be," indg. pot. m., past t. |

## ENGLISH GRAMMAR AND ANALYSIS. 177

| | |
|---|---|
| (to) be | An irreg. intr. v., infin. m., pres. t., gov. by the v. "should." |
| should be | An irreg. intr. v., pot. m., past t., s. num., 3rd per., agr. with its nom. "it." |
| otherwise. | An adv. of man., mod. the v. "should be." |
| 7. Though | A disj. conj., jg. the sents. "we do..strength" and "all the winds..earth," and indg. subj. m. |
| all | An indef. nu. adj. of quantity, qual. the n. "winds." |
| winds | A com. n., neu. gen., p. num., 3rd per., nom. c. to the v. "were let." |
| of | A prep., sh. the rn. bet. "winds" and "doctrine." |
| doctrine | An abs. n., neu. gen., s. num., 3rd per., obj. c., gov. by the prep. "of." |
| were | An aux. v. to "let," indg. pass. vo., past t. |
| let | A past pl. from the tr. v. "to let," ref. to "winds." |
| **were let** | An irreg. tr. v., pass. vo., indic. m., past t., p. num., 3rd per., agr. with its nom. "winds." |
| loose | An adj. of quality, pos. deg., qual. the n. "winds." |
| to | A particle, indg. infin. m. |
| to play | A reg. intr. v., infin. m., pres. t., gov. by the adj. "loose." |
| upon | A prep., sh. the rn. bet. "to play" and "earth." |
| earth | A com. n., neu. gen., s. num., 3rd per., obj. c., gov. by the prep. "upon." |
| so | A cop. conj., jg. the sents. "we do..strength" and "Truth be in the field," and indg. subj. m. |
| Truth | An abs. n. used as a prop. n., fem. gen. by personification, s. num. 3rd per., nom. c. to the v. "be." |
| **be** | An irreg. intr. v., subj. m., pres. t., s. num., 3rd per., agr. with its nom. "Truth." |
| in | A prep., sh. the rn. bet. "be" and "field." |
| field | A com. n., neu. gen., s. num., 3rd per., obj. c., gov. by the prep. "in." |
| we | A pers. pron., com. gen., p. num., 1st per., nom. c. to the v. "do." |
| do | An irreg. intr. v., indic. m., pres. t., p. num., 1st per., agr. with its nom. "we." |
| injuriously | An adv. of man., mod. the v. "do." |
| by | A prep., sh. the rn. bet. "do" and "licensing." |
| licensing | A ger. from the tr. v. "to license," neu. gen., s. num., 3rd per., obj. c., gov. by the prep. "by." |
| and | A cop. conj., jg. the sents. "we do injuriously by licensing, *to mis-doubt her strength*" and "*we do injuriously by* prohibiting, to mis-doubt her strength." |
| prohibiting | A ger. from the tr. v. "to prohibit," neu. gen., s. num., 3rd per., obj. c., gov. by the prep. *by* und. |
| to | A particle, indg. infin. m. |
| to mis-doubt | A reg. tr. v., act. vo., infin. m., pres. t., gov. by the v. "do." |
| her | A pers. pron., fem. gen., s. num., 3rd per., poss. c., gov. by the n. "strength." |
| strength. | An abs. n., neu. gen., s. num., 3rd per., obj. c., gov. by the tr. v. "to mis-doubt." |
| 8. In | A prep., sh. the rn. bet. "lurk" and "shape." |
| whatsoever | A compd. rel. pron. used as an adj., qual. the n. "shape," and indg. subj. m. |
| shape | An abs. n., neu. gen., s. num., 3rd per., obj. c., gov. by the prep. "in." |
| he | A pers. pron., mas. gen., s. num., 3rd per., nom. c. to the v. "lurk." |
| **lurk** | A reg. intr. v., subj. m., pres. t., s. num., 3rd per., agr. with its nom. "he." |
| I | A pers. pron., com. gen., s. num., 1st per., nom. c. to the v. "will know." |
| 'll=will | An aux. v. to "know," indg. fut. t., emph. form, expressing "determination." |
| (to) know | An irreg. tr. v., act. vo., infin. m., pres. t., gov. by the v. "will." |
| will know. | An irreg. tr. v., act. vo., indic. m., fut. t., emph. form, s. num., 1st per., agr. with its nom. "I." |
| 9. Saw | An irreg. tr. v., act. vo., subj. m., past t., s. num., 1st per., agr. with its nom. "I." (*If I saw.*) |

| | |
|---|---|
| I | A pers. pron., com. gen., s. num., 1st per., nom. c. to the v. "saw." |
| that | A dis. adj., lim. the n. "insect." |
| insect | A com. n., com. gen., s. num., 3rd per., obj. c., gov. by the tr. v. "saw." |
| on | A prep., sh. the rn. bet. "saw" and "brim." |
| this | A dis. adj., lim. the n. "goblet's." |
| goblet's | A com. n., neu. gen., s. num., 3rd per., poss. c., gov. by the n. "brim." |
| brim | A com. n., neu. gen., s. num., 3rd per., obj. c., gov. by the prep. "on." |
| I | A pers. pron., com. gen., s. num., 1st per., nom. c. to the v. "would remove." |
| would | An aux. v. to "remove," indg. pot. m., past t. |
| (to) remove | A reg. tr. v., act. vo., infin. m., pres. t., gov. by the v. "would." |
| would remove | A reg. tr. v., act. vo., pot. m., past t., s. num., 1st per., agr. with its nom. "I." |
| it | A pers. pron., neu. gen., s. num., 3rd per., obj. c., gov. by the tr. v. "would remove." |
| with | A prep., sh. the rn. bet. "would remove" and "pity." |
| anxious | An adj. of quality, pos. deg., qual. the n. "pity." |
| pity. | An abs. n., neu. gen., s. num., 3rd per., obj. c., gov. by the prep. "with." |
| 10. This | A dis. adj., lim. the n. "sword." |
| sword | A com. n., neu. gen., s. num., 3rd per., nom. c. to the v. "hath ended." |
| hath | An aux. v. to "ended," indg. perf. t. |
| ended | A past pl. from the tr. v. "to end," ref. to "him." |
| hath ended | A reg. tr. v., act. vo., indic. m., perf. t., s. num., 3rd per., agr. with its nom. "sword." |
| him | A pers. pron., mas. gen., s. num., 3rd per., obj. c., gov. by the tr. v. "hath ended." |
| so | An adv. of man., mod. the v. "shall end." |
| shall | An aux. v. to end und., indg. fut. t., emph. form, expressing "certainty." |
| it | A pers. pron., neu. gen., s. num., 3rd per., nom. c. to the v. "shall end." |
| thee | A pers. pron., com. gen., s. num., 2nd per., obj. c., gov. by the tr. v. "shall end." |
| Unless | A disj. conj., jg. the sents. "so shall it end thee" and "thou yield thee," and indg. subj. m. |
| thou | A pers. pron., com. gen., s. num., 2nd per., nom. c. to the v. "yield." |
| **yield** | A reg. tr. v., act. vo., subj. m., pres. t., s. num., 2nd per., agr. with its nom. "thou." |
| thee | A pers. pron., com. gen., s. num., 2nd per., obj. c., gov. by the tr. v. "yield." |
| as | A cop. conj., jg. the sents. "thou yield thee" and "my prisoner yields." |
| my | A pers. pron., com. gen., s. num., 1st per., poss. c., gov. by the n. "prisoner." |
| prisoner. | A com. n., com. gen., s. num., 3rd per., nom. c. to the v. *yields* und. |

N.B.—"As" may be treated as redundant or as an appositive conjunction, in either of which cases, "prisoner" will be obj. c., in app. with "thee."

## Exercise 167.

| | |
|---|---|
| 1. Now | An adv. of time, mod. the v. "sing." |
| let | An irreg. tr. v., act. vo., imper. m., pres. t., s. num., 2nd per., agr. with its nom. *thou* und. |
| us | A pers. pron., com. gen., p. num., 1st per., obj. c., gov. by the tr. v. "let." |
| (to) sing | An irreg. tr. v., act. vo., infin. m., pres. t., gov. by the v. "let." |
| Long | An adv. of time, mod. the v. "live." |
| **live** | A reg. intr. v., imper. m., pres. t., s. num., 3rd per., agr. with its nom. "king." (*Parsing*, p. 129.) |

ENGLISH GRAMMAR AND ANALYSIS. 179.

| | |
|---|---|
| king. | A com. n., mas. gen., s. num., 3rd per., nom. c. to the v. "live." |
| 2. people | A com. n., com. gen., p. num., 3rd per., nom. c. to the v. "shouted." |
| shouted | A reg. tr. v., act. vo., indic. m., past t., p. num., 3rd per., agr. with its nom. "people." |
| God | A prop. n., mas. gen., s. num., 3rd per., nom. c. to the v. "save." |
| **save** | A reg. tr. v., act. vo., imper. m., pres. t., s. num., 3rd per., agr. with its nom. "God." |
| king. | A com. n., mas. gen., s. num., 3rd per., obj. c., gov. by the tr. v. "save." |
| 3. hostile | An adj. of quality, pos. deg., qual. the n. "army." |
| army | A com. col. n., neu. gen., s. num., 3rd per., nom. c. to the v. "is." |
| is | An irreg. intr. v., indic. m., pres. t., s. num., 3rd per., agr. with its nom. "army." |
| immense | An adj. of quality, pos. deg., qual. the n. "army." |
| consisting | A pres. pl. from the intr. v. "to consist," ref. to "army." |
| of | A prep., sh. the rn. bet. "consisting" and "hundred" (or, bet. "consisting" and "men "). |
| **say** | An irreg. tr. v., act. vo., imper. m., pres. t., used absolutely. (*Parsing*, p. 129.) |
| one | A def. card. nu. adj. of quantity, qual. the n. "hundred." |
| hundred | A com. n., neu. gen., s. num., 3rd per., obj. c., gov. by the prep. "of." |
| thousand | A com. n., neu. gen., p. num., s. form, 3rd per., obj. c., gov. by the prep. *of* und. |
| one hundred thousand | } A def. card. nu. adj. of quantity, qual. the n. "men." |
| men. | A com. n., mas. gen., p. num., 3rd per., obj. c., gov. by the prep. *of* und. (or, gov. by the prep. "of"). (Consisting of one hundred *of* thousand*s of* men ; or, consisting of one-hundred-thousand men.) |
| 4. distance | An abs. n., neu. gen., s. num., 3rd per., nom. c. to the v. "is." |
| is | An irreg. intr. v., indic. m., pres. t., s. num., 3rd per., agr. with its nom. "distance." |
| great | An adj. of quality, pos. deg., qual. the n. "distance." |
| **say** | An irreg. tr. v., act. vo., imper. m., pres. t., used absolutely. |
| fifteen | A def. card. nu. adj. of quantity, qual. the n. "thousand." |
| thousand | A com. n., neu. gen., p. num., s. form, 3rd per., obj. c., gov. by the tr. v. "say." |
| fifteen thousand | A def. card. nu. adj. of quantity, qual. the n. "paces." |
| paces. | A com. n., neu. gen., p. num., 3rd per., obj. c., gov. by the prep. *of* und. (or, gov. by the tr. v. "say.") (Say fifteen thousand*s of* paces ; or, say fifteen thousand paces.) |
| 5. Many | An indef. nu. adj. of quantity, qual. the n. "nobles." |
| nobles | A com. n., mas. gen., p. num., 3rd per., nom. c. to the v. "were." |
| **say** | An irreg. tr. v., act. vo., imper. m., pres. t., used absolutely. |
| fifty | A def. card. nu. adj. of quantity, qual. the n. *nobles* und. |
| were | An irreg. intr. v., indic. m., past t., p. num., 3rd per., agr. with its nom. "nobles." |
| in | A prep., sh. the rn. bet. "were" and "assembly." |
| assembly. | A com. col. n., neu. gen., s. num., 3rd per., obj. c., gov. by the prep. "in." |
| 6. And | A cop. conj., introducing the sent. "be..me." |
| be | An irreg. intr. v., imper. m., pres. t., s. num., 3rd per., agr. with its nom. "epitaph." |
| Spartan's | A prop. n., mas. gen., s. num., 3rd per., poss. c., gov. by the n. "epitaph." |
| epitaph | A com. n., neu. gen., s. num., 3rd per., nom. c. to the v. "be." |
| on | A prep., sh. the rn. bet. "be" and "me." |
| me | A pers. pron., mas. gen., s. num., 1st per., obj. c., gov. by the prep. "on." |
| Sparta | A prop. n., neu. gen., s. num., 3rd per., nom. c. to the v. "hath." |
| hath | An irreg. tr. v , act. vo., indic. m., pres. t., s. num., 3rd per., agr. with its nom. "Sparta." |

12—2

| | |
|---|---|
| many | A dist. nu. adj. of quantity, qual. the n. "son." (*Gr.* § 66, iv *Obs.*; *Parsing*, p. 118.) |
| worthier | An adj. of quality, comp. deg., qual. the n. "son." |
| son | A com. n., mas. gen., s. num., 3rd per., obj. c., gov. by the tr. v. "hath." |
| than | A disj. conj., jg. the sents. "Sparta..son" and "he *was a worthy son.*" |
| he. | A pers. pron., mas. gen., s. num., 3rd per., nom. c. to the v. *was* und. |

## Exercise 168.

| | |
|---|---|
| 1. Bailie | A com. n. tending to prop., mas. gen., s. num., 3rd per., nom. c. to the v. "found." |
| found | An irreg. tr. v., act. vo., indic. m., past t., s. num., 3rd per., agr. with its nom. "Bailie." |
| way | A com. n., neu. gen., s. num., 3rd per., obj. c., gov. by the tr. v. "found." |
| to | A particle, indg. infin. m. |
| **to make** | An irreg. tr. v., act. vo., infin. m., pres. t., gov. by the n. "way." |
| them | A pers. pron., com. gen., p. num., 3rd per., obj. c., gov. by the tr. v. "to make." |
| (to) speak | An irreg. tr. v., act. vo., infin. m., pres. t., gov. by the v. "to make." |
| English. | A prop. n., neu. gen., s. num., 3rd per., obj. c., gov. by the tr. v. "*to* speak." |
| 2. bishops | A com. n., mas. gen., p. num., 3rd per., nom. c. to the v. "agreed." |
| agreed | A reg. intr. v., indic. m., past t., p. num., 3rd per., agr. with its nom. "bishops." |
| to | A particle, indg. infin. m. |
| **to proceed.** | A reg. intr. v., infin. m., pres. t., gov. by the v. "agreed." |
| 3. Newton | A prop. n., mas. gen., s. num., 3rd per., nom. c. to the v. "has learned." |
| has | An aux. v. to "learned," indg. perf. t. |
| learned | A past pl. from the tr. v. "to learn," ref. to "to see." |
| has learned | A reg. tr. v., act. vo., indic. m., perf. t., s. num., 3rd per., agr. with its nom. "Newton." |
| to | A particle, indg. infin. m. |
| **to see** | An irreg. tr. v., act. vo., infin. m., pres. t.; used as an abs. n., neu. gen., s. num., 3rd per., obj. c., gov. by the tr. v. "has learned." |
| what | A compd. rel. pron., including both the rel. and the ant., neu. gen., s. num., 3rd per. "What" is equiv. to "the thing which," "thing" being obj. c., gov. by the tr. v. "to see," and "which," obj. c., gov. by the tr. v. "saw." |
| Kepler | A prop. n., mas. gen., s. num., 3rd per., nom. c. to the v. "saw." |
| saw. | An irreg. tr. v., act. vo., indic. m., past t., s. num., 3rd per., agr. with its nom. "Kepler." |
| 4. He | A pers. pron., mas. gen., s. num., 3rd per., nom. c. to the v. "was." |
| was | An irreg. intr. v., indic. m., past t., s. num., 3rd per., agr. with its nom. "he." |
| ready | An adj. of quality, pos. deg., qual. the pron. "he." |
| to | A particle, indg. infin. m. |
| **to die** | A reg. intr. v., infin. m., pres. t., gov. by the adj. "ready." |
| in | A prep., sh. the rn. bet. "to die" and "defence." |
| her | A pers. pron., fem. gen., s. num., 3rd per., poss. c., gov. by the n. "defence." |
| defence. | An abs. n., neu. gen., s. num., 3rd per., obj. c., gov. by the prep. "in." |
| 5. bishop | A com. n., mas. gen., s. num., 3rd per., nom. c. to the v. "consented." |
| consented | A reg. intr. v., indic. m., past t., s. num., 3rd per., agr. with its nom. "bishop." |
| to | A particle, indg. infin. m. |
| **to reply.** | A reg. intr. v., infin. m., pres. t., gov. by the v. "consented." |

# ENGLISH GRAMMAR AND ANALYSIS.

| | |
|---|---|
| 6. They | A pers. pron., com. gen., p. num., 3rd per., nom. c. to the v. "agreed." |
| agreed | A reg. intr. v., indic. m., past t., p. num., 3rd per., agr. with its nom. "they." |
| to | A particle, indg. infin. m. |
| **to give** | An irreg. tr. v., act. vo., infin. m., pres. t., gov. by the v. "agreed." |
| four | A def. card. nu. adj. of quantity, qual. the n. "shillings." |
| shillings | A com. n., neu. gen., p. num., 3rd per., obj. c., gov. by the tr. v. "to give." |
| in | A prep., sh. the rn. bet. "to give" and "pound." ("In" here means "for.") |
| pound | A com. n., neu. gen., s. num., 3rd per., obj. c., gov. by the prep. "in." |
| for | A prep., sh. the rn. bet. "to give" and "year." |
| one | A def. card. nu. adj. of quantity, qual. the n. "year." |
| year. | An abs. n., neu. gen., s. num., 3rd per., obj. c., gov. by the prep. "for." |
| 7. voice | An abs. n., neu. gen., s. num., 3rd per., nom. c. to the v. "is." |
| of | A prep., sh. the rn. bet. "voice" and "man." |
| that | A dis. adj., lim. the n. "man." |
| one | A def. card. nu. adj. of quantity, qual. the n. "man." |
| man | A com. n., mas. gen., s. num., 3rd per., obj. c., gov. by the prep. "of." |
| is | An irreg. intr. v., indic. m., pres. t., s. num., 3rd per., agr. with its nom. "voice." |
| able | An adj. of quality, pos. deg., qual. the n. "voice." |
| to | A particle, indg. infin. m. |
| **to put** | An irreg. tr. v., act. vo., infin. m., pres. t., gov. by the adj. "able." |
| more | An adj. of quantity (bulk or mass), comp. deg., qual. the n. "life." |
| life | An abs. n., neu. gen., s. num., 3rd per., obj. c., gov. by the tr. v. "to put." |
| in | A prep., sh. the rn. bet. "to put" and "us." |
| us. | A pers. pron., com. gen., p. num., 1st per., obj. c., gov. by the prep. "in." |
| 8. I | A pers. pron., com. gen., s. num., 1st per., nom. c. to the v. "drew." |
| drew | An irreg. tr. v., act. vo., indic. m., past t., s. num., 1st per., agr. with its nom. "I." |
| my | A pers. pron., com. gen., s. num., 1st per., poss. c., gov. by the n. "knife." |
| knife | A com. n., neu. gen., s. num., 3rd per., obj. c., gov. by the tr. v. "drew." |
| and | A cop. conj., jg. the sents. "I..knife" and "I began..flint." |
| began | An irreg. tr. v., act. vo., indic. m., past t., s. num., 1st per., agr. with its nom. I und. |
| to | A particle, indg. infin. m. |
| **to pick** | A reg. tr. v., act. vo. infin. m., pres. t.; used as an abs. n., neu. gen., s. num., 3rd per., obj. c., gov. by the tr. v. "began." |
| flint. | A com. n., neu. gen., s. num., 3rd per., obj. c., gov. by the tr. v. "to pick." |
| 9. It | A pers. pron., neu. gen., s. num., 3rd per., nom. c. to the v. "is." |
| is | An irreg. intr. v., indic. m., pres. t., s. num., 3rd per., agr. with its nom. "it." |
| no | A def. card. nu. adj. of quantity, qual. the n. "time." |
| time | An abs. n., neu. gen., s. num., 3rd per., nom. c. after the v. "is." |
| to | A particle, indg. infin. m. |
| **to joke.** | A reg. intr. v., infin. m., pres. t., gov. by the n. "time." |
| 10. Sir | A com. n. tending to prop., mas. gen., s. num., 3rd per., nom. c. to the v. "was advised." |
| Henry | A prop. n., mas. gen., s. num., 3rd per., nom. c., in app. with "Sir." N.B.—"Sir" may be parsed as an adj., qual. the n. "Henry" and "Henry" nom. c. to the v. "was advised"; or, "Sir Henry" may be parsed as a compd. prop. n., nom. c. to the v. "was advised." (*Parsing*, pp. 11, 12.) |
| was | An aux. v. to "advised," indg. pass vo., past t. |

| | |
|---|---|
| advised | A past pl. from the tr. v. "to advise," ref. to "Sir" (or "Sir Henry"). |
| was advised | A reg. tr. v., pass. vo., indic. m., past t., s. num., 3rd per., agr. with its nom. "Sir" (or "Sir Henry"). |
| to | A particle, indg. infin. m. |
| to defer | A reg. tr. v., act. vo., infin. m., pres. t., gov. by the v. "was advised." |
| his | A pers. pron., mas. gen., s. num., 3rd per., poss. c., gov. by the n. "attack." |
| attack. | An abs. n., neu. gen., s. num., 3rd per., obj. c., gov. by the tr. v. "to defer." |
| 11. He | A pers. pron., mas. gen., s. num., 3rd per., nom. c. to the v. "liked." |
| rather | An adv. of deg., mod. the v. "liked." |
| liked | A reg. tr. v., act. vo., indic. m., past t., s. num., 3rd per., agr. with its nom. "he." |
| to | A particle, indg. infin. m. |
| to talk. | A reg. intr. v., infin. m., pres. t.; used as an abs. n., neu. gen., s. num., 3rd per., obj. c., gov. by the v. "liked." |
| 12. When | A cop. conj., jg. the sents. "he stopped..tribute" and "the mourner..story." |
| mourner | A com. n., mas. gen., s. num., 3rd per., nom. c. to the v. "had got." |
| had | An aux. v. to "got," indg. pluperf. t. |
| got | A past pl. from the intr. v. "to get," ref. to "mourner." |
| had got | An irreg. intr. v., indic. m., pluperf. t., s. num., 3rd per., agr. with its nom. "mourner." |
| thus | An adv. of deg., mod. the adv. "far." |
| far | An adv. of place, mod. the v. "had got." |
| in | A prep., sh. the rn. bet. "had got" and "story." |
| his | A pers. pron., mas. gen., s. num., 3rd per., poss. c., gov. by the n. "story." |
| story | A com. n., neu. gen., s. num., 3rd per., obj. c., gov. by the prep. "in." |
| he | A pers. pron., mas. gen., s. num., 3rd per., nom. c. to the v. "stopped." |
| stopped | A reg. intr. v., indic. m., past t., s. num., 3rd per., agr. with its nom. "he." |
| to | A particle, indg. infin. m. |
| to pay | An irreg. tr. v., act. vo., infin. m., pres. t., gov. by the v. "stopped." |
| Nature | An abs. n. used as a prop. n., fem. gen. by personification, s. num., 3rd per., obj. c., gov. by the prep. *to* und. |
| her | A pers. pron., fem. gen., s. num., 3rd per., poss. c., gov. by the n. "tribute." |
| tribute | A com. n., neu. gen., s. num., 3rd per., obj. c., gov. by the tr. v. "to pay." |
| and | A cop. conj., jg. the sents. "he..tribute" and "*he* wept bitterly." |
| wept | An irreg. intr. v., indic. m., past t., s. num., 3rd per., agr. with its nom. *he* und. |
| bitterly. | An adv. of man., mod. the v. "wept." |
| 13. She | A pers. pron., fem. gen., s. num., 3rd per., nom. c. to the v. "dropped." |
| dropped | A reg. tr. v., act. vo., indic. m., past t., s. num., 3rd per., agr. with its nom. "she." |
| her | A pers. pron., fem. gen., s. num., 3rd per., poss. c., gov. by the n. "glove." |
| glove | A com. n., neu. gen., s. num., 3rd per., obj. c., gov. by the tr. v. "dropped." |
| to | A particle, indg. infin. m. |
| to prove | A reg. tr. v., act. vo., infin. m., pres. t., gov. by the v. "dropped." |
| his | A pers. pron., mas. gen., s. num., 3rd per., poss. c., gov. by the n. "love." |
| love | An abs. n., neu. gen., s. num., 3rd per., obj. c., gov. by the tr. v. "to prove." |
| then | An adv. of time, mod. the v. "looked." |
| looked | A reg. intr. v., indic. m., past t., s. num., 3rd per., agr. with its nom. *she* und. |

| | |
|---|---|
| at | A prep., sh. the rn. bet. "looked" and "him." |
| him | A pers. pron., mas. gen., s. num., 3rd per., obj. c., gov. by the prep. "at." |
| and | A cop. conj., jg. the sents. "*she* then looked at him" and "*she* smiled." |
| smiled. | A reg. intr. v., indic. m., past t., s. num., 3rd per., agr. with its nom. *she* und. |
| 14. Thy | A pers. pron., fem. gen. by personification, s. num., 2nd per., poss. c., gov. by the n. "triumphs." |
| triumphs | An abs. n., neu. gen., p. num., 3rd per., obj. c., gov. by the tr. v. "shall see." |
| Rome | A prop. n., fem. gen. by personification, s. num., 2nd per., nom. c. of add. |
| I | A pers. pron., com. gen., s. num., 1st per., nom. c. to the v. "shall see." |
| shall | An aux. v. to "see," indg. fut. t. |
| not | An adv. of m. (neg.), mod. the v. "shall see." |
| **(to) see** | An irreg. tr. v., act. vo., infin. m., pres. t., gov. by the v. "shall." |
| shall see | An irreg. tr. v., act. vo., indic. m., fut. t., s. num., 1st per., agr. with its nom. "I." |
| For | A cop. conj., jg. the sents. "Thy triumphs..see" and "I..die." |
| I | A pers. pron., com. gen., s. num., 1st per., nom. c. to the v. "return." |
| return | A reg. intr. v., indic. m., pres. t., s. num., 1st per., agr. with its nom. "I." |
| to | A particle, indg. infin. m. |
| **to die.** | A reg. intr. v., infin. m., pres. t., gov. by the v. "return." |
| 15. Where | An interrog. adv. of place, mod. the v. "is." |
| 's=is | An irreg. intr. v., indic. m., pres. t., s. num., 3rd per., agr. with its nom, "coward." |
| coward | A com. n., mas. gen., s. num., 3rd per., nom. c. to the v. "is." |
| that | A rel. pron., mas. gen., s. num., 3rd per., agr. with its ant. "coward," nom. c. to the v. "would dare." |
| would | An aux. v. to "dare," indg. pot. m., past t. |
| not | An adv. of m. (neg.), mod. the v. "would dare." |
| **(to) dare** | An irreg. intr. v., infin. m., pres. t., gov. by the v. "would." |
| would dare | An irreg. intr. v., pot. m., past t., s. num., 3rd per., agr. with its nom. "that." |
| To | A particle, indg. infin. m. |
| **To fight** | An irreg. intr. v., infin. m., pres. t., gov. by the v. "would dare." |
| for | A prep., sh. the rn. bet. "to fight" and "land." |
| such | An adj. of quality, qual. the n. "land." |
| land. | A com. n., neu. gen., s. num., 3rd per., obj. c., gov. by the prep. "for." |

## Exercise 169.

| | |
|---|---|
| 1. To | A particle, indg. infin. m. |
| **To do** | An irreg. tr. v., act. vo., infin. m., pres. t., used absolutely. |
| her | A pers. pron., fem. gen., s. num., 3rd per., obj. c., gov. by the prep. *to* und. |
| justice | An abs. n., neu. gen., s. num., 3rd per., obj. c., gov. by the tr. v. "to do." |
| she | A pers. pron., fem. gen., s. num., 3rd per., nom. c. to the v. "was." |
| was | An irreg. intr. v., indic. m., past t., s. num., 3rd per., agr. with its nom. "she." |
| good-natured | A compd. adj. of quality, pos. deg., qual. the n. "woman." |
| notable | An adj. of quality, pos. deg., qual. the n. "woman." |
| woman. | A com. n., fem. gen., s. num., 3rd per., nom. c. after the v. "was." |
| 2. To | A particle, indg. infin. m. |
| **To say** | An irreg. tr. v., act. vo., infin. m., pres. t., used absolutely. |
| truth | An abs. n., neu. gen., s. num., 3rd per., obj. c., gov. by the tr. v. "to say." |

| | |
|---|---|
| I | A pers. pron., com. gen., s. num., 1st per., nom. c. to the v. "was." |
| was | An irreg. intr. v., indic. m., past t., s. num., 1st per., agr. with its nom. "I." |
| tired | An adj. of quality, pos. deg., qual. the pron. "I." |
| of | A prep., sh. the rn. bet. "tired" and "being." |
| being | A ger. from the intr. v. "to be," neu. gen., s. num., 3rd per., obj. c., gov. by the prep. "of." |
| always | An adv. of time, mod. the ger. "being." |
| wise. | An adj. of quality, pos. deg., qual. the n. *person* und. |
| 3. To | A particle, indg. infin. m. |
| **To confess** | A reg. tr. v., act. vo., infin. m., pres. t., used absolutely. |
| truth | An abs. n., neu. gen., s. num., 3rd per., obj. c., gov. by the tr. v. "to confess." |
| this | A dis. adj., lim. the n. "man's." |
| man's | A com. n., mas. gen., s. num., 3rd per., poss. c., gov. by the n. "mind." |
| mind | A com. n., neu. gen., s. num., 3rd per., nom. c. to the v. "seems." |
| seems | A reg. intr. v., indic. m., pres. t., s. num., 3rd per., agr. with its nom. "mind." |
| fitted | A past pl. from the tr. v. "to fit," ref. to "mind." |
| to | A prep., sh. the rn. bet. "fitted" and "station." |
| his | A pers. pron., mas. gen., s. num., 3rd per., poss. c., gov. by the n. "station." |
| station. | An abs. n., neu. gen., s. num., 3rd per., obj. c., gov. by the prep. "to." |
| 4. To | A particle, indg. infin. m. |
| **To say** | An irreg. tr. v., act. vo., infin. m., pres. t., used absolutely. |
| truth | An abs. n., neu. gen., s. num., 3rd per., obj. c., gov. by the tr. v. "to say." |
| I | A pers. pron., com. gen., s. num., 1st per., nom. c. to the v. "do know." |
| do | An aux. v. to "know," indg. pres. t., and completing the negative form of the v. |
| not | An adv. of m. (neg.), mod. the v. "do know." |
| (to) know | An irreg. tr. v., act. vo., infin. m., pres. t., gov. by the v. "do." |
| do know | An irreg. tr. v., act. vo., indic. m., pres. t., s. num., 1st per., agr. with its nom. "I." |
| that | A cop. conj., jg. the sents. "To say..know" and "they..all." |
| they | A pers. pron., com. gen., p. num., 3rd per., nom. c. to the v. "imitate." |
| imitate | A reg. tr. v., act. vo., indic. m., pres. t., p. num., 3rd per., agr. with its nom. "they." |
| anything | A com. n., neu. gen., s. num., 3rd per., obj. c., gov. by the tr. v. "imitate." |
| at | A prep., sh. the rn. bet. "imitate" and *time* und. |
| all | An indef. nu. adj. of quantity, qual. the n. *time* und. |
| at all. | A compd. adv. of time, mod. the v. "imitate." (*Parsing*, p. 150.) |
| 5. It | A pers. pron., neu. gen., s. num., 3rd per., nom. c. to the v. "is." |
| is | An irreg. intr. v., indic. m., pres. t., s. num., 3rd per., agr. with its nom. "it." |
| admirable | An adj. of quality, pos. deg., qual. the n. "sword." |
| sword | A com. n., neu. gen., s. num., 3rd per., nom. c. after the v. "is." |
| to | A particle, indg. infin. m. |
| **to be** | An irreg. intr. v., infin. m., pres. t., used absolutely. |
| sure. | An adj. of quality, pos. deg., qual. the n. *person* und. |
| 6. To | A particle, indg. infin. m. |
| **To be** | An irreg. intr. v., infin. m., pres. t., used absolutely. |
| short | An adj. of quality, pos. deg., qual. the n. *person* und. (i.e., a person short in speech). |
| for | A prep., sh. the rn. bet. "was divorced" and "appearance." |
| not | An adv. of m. (neg.), used as an adj., qual. the n. "appearance." ("Appearance" is equiv. to the ger. or verbal n. "appearing." See *Parsing*, p. 142.) |

| | |
|---|---|
| appearance | An abs. n., neu. gen., s. num., 3rd per., obj. c., gov. by the prep. "for." |
| and | A cop. conj., jg. the sents. "*by the main assent..divorced* for not appearance" and "by the main assent..divorced *for* the king's late scruple." |
| king's | A com. n., mas. gen., s. num., 3rd per., poss. c., gov. by the n. "scruple." |
| late | An adj. of quality, pos. deg., qual. the n. "scruple." |
| scruple | An abs. n., neu. gen., s. num., 3rd per., obj. c., gov. by the prep. *for* und. |
| by | A prep., sh. the rn. bet. "was divorced" and "assent." |
| main | An adj. of quality, qual. the n. "assent." |
| assent | An abs. n., neu. gen., s. num., 3rd per., obj. c., gov. by the prep. "by." |
| Of | A prep., sh. the rn. bet. "assent" and "men." |
| all | An indef. nu. adj. of quantity, qual. the n. "men." |
| these | A dis. adj., lim. the n. "men." |
| learned | An adj. of quality, pos. deg., qual. the n. "men." |
| men | A com. n., mas. gen., p. num., 3rd per., obj. c., gov. by the prep. "of." |
| she | A pers. pron., fem. gen., s. num., 3rd per., nom. c. to the v. "was divorced." |
| was | An aux. v. to "divorced," indg. pass. vo., past t. |
| divorced | A past pl. from the tr. v. "to divorce," ref. to "she." |
| was divorced. | A reg. tr. v., pass. vo., indic. m., past t., s. num., 3rd per., agr. with its nom. "she." |

## Exercise 170.

| | |
|---|---|
| 1. My | A pers. pron., mas. gen., s. num., 1st per., poss. c., gov. by the n. "Phœbe." |
| gentle | An adj. of quality, pos. deg., qual. the n. "Phœbe." |
| Phœbe | A prop. n., fem. gen., s. num., 3rd per., nom. c. to the v. "did bid." |
| did | An aux. v. to "bid," indg. past t., emph. form. |
| (to) bid | An irreg. tr. v., act. vo., infin. m., pres. t., gov. by the v. "did." |
| did bid | An irreg. tr. v., act. vo., indic. m., past t., emph. form, s. num., 3rd per., agr. with its nom. "Phœbe." |
| me | A pers. pron., mas. gen., s. num., 1st per., obj. c., gov. by the tr. v. "did bid." |
| (to) give | An irreg. tr. v., act. vo., infin. m., pres. t., gov. by the v. "did bid." |
| you | A pers. pron., com. gen., s. num., p. form, 2nd per., obj. c., gov. by the prep. *to* und. |
| this. | A dis. adj., lim. the n. *present* und. |
| 2. English | A prop. adj. of quality, qual. the n. "vessels." |
| vessels | A com. n., neu. gen., p. num., 3rd per., nom. c. to the v. "saw." |
| saw | An irreg. tr. v., act. vo., indic. m., past t., p. num., 3rd per., agr. with its nom. "vessels." |
| their | A pers. pron., neu. gen., p. num., 3rd per., poss. c., gov. by the n. "prey." |
| prey | A com. n., neu. gen., s. num., 3rd per., obj. c., gov. by the tr. v. "saw." |
| (to) pass | A reg. intr. v., infin. m., pres. t., gov. by the v. "saw." |
| by. | An adv. of place, mod. the v. "to pass." |
| 3. At | A prep., sh. the rn. bet. "heard" and *time* und. |
| first | A def. ord. nu. adj. of quantity, qual. the n. *time* und. |
| At first | An adverbial phrase of time, mod. the v. "heard." (*Parsing*, p. 150.) |
| I | A pers. pron., com. gen., s. num., 1st per., nom. c. to the v. "heard." |
| heard | An irreg. tr. v., act. vo., indic. m., past t., s. num., 1st per., agr. with its nom. "I." |
| every | A dist. nu. adj. of quantity, qual. the n. "man." |
| man | A com. n., mas. gen., s. num., 3rd per., obj. c., gov. by the tr. v. "heard." |

| | |
|---|---|
| (to) say | An irreg. tr. v., act. vo., infin. m., pres. t., gov. by the v. "heard." |
| Let | An irreg. tr. v., act. vo., imper. m., pres. t., s. num., 2nd per. agr. with its nom. *thou* und. |
| us | A pers. pron., com. gen., p. num., 1st per., obj. c., gov. by the tr. v. "let." |
| (to) hang | A reg. tr. v., act. vo., infin. m., pres. t., gov. by the v. "let." |
| priest. | A com. n., mas. gen., s. num., 3rd per., obj. c., gov. by the tr. v. "*to* hang." |
| 4. I | A pers. pron., com. gen., s. num., 1st per., nom. c. to the v. "dare." |
| dare | An irreg. intr. v., indic. m., pres. t., s. num., 1st per., agr. with its nom. "I." |
| (to) assure | A reg. tr. v., act. vo., infin. m., pres. t., gov. by the v. "dare." |
| you | A pers. pron., mas. gen., s. num., 2nd per., obj. c., gov. by the tr. v. "to assure." |
| sir | A com. n., mas. gen., s. num., 2nd per., nom. c. of add. |
| 't=it | A pers. pron., neu. gen., s. num., 3rd per., nom. c. to the v. "is." |
| is | An irreg. intr. v., indic. m., pres. t., s. num., 3rd per., agr. with its nom. "it." |
| almost | An adv. of deg., mod. the v. "is." |
| two. | A def. card. nu. adj. of quantity, qual. the n. *hours* und. (or, a com. n., neu. gen., s. num., 3rd per., nom. c. after the v. "is "). |
| 5. You | A pers. pron., com. gen., p. num., or s. num., p. form, 2nd per., nom. c. to the v. "can hear." |
| can | An aux. v. to "hear," indg. pot. m., pres. t. |
| (to) hear | An irreg. tr. v., act. vo., infin. m., pres. t., gov. by the v. "can." |
| can hear | An irreg. tr. v., act. vo., pot. m., pres. t., p. num., or s. num., p. form, 2nd per., agr. with its nom. "you." |
| him | A pers. pron., mas. gen., s. num., 3rd per., obj. c., gov. by the tr. v. "can hear." |
| (to) swing | An irreg. tr. v., act. vo., infin. m., pres. t., gov. by the v. "can hear." |
| his | A pers. pron., mas. gen., s. num., 3rd per., poss. c., gov. by the n. "sledge." |
| heavy | An adj. of quality, pos. deg., qual. the n. "sledge." |
| sledge. | A com. n., neu. gen., s. num., 3rd per., obj. c., gov. by the tr. v. "to swing." |
| 6. Let | An irreg. tr. v., act. vo., imper. m., pres. t., s. num., 2nd per. agr. with its nom. *thou* und. |
| (to) go | An irreg. intr. v., infin. m., pres. t., gov. by the v. "let." |
| thy | A pers. pron., com. gen., s. num., 2nd per., poss. c., gov. by the n. "hold." |
| hold | An abs. n., neu. gen., s. num., 3rd per., obj. c., gov. by the tr. v. "let." |
| when | A cop. conj., jg. the sents. "Let..hold" and "a great..hill." |
| great | An adj. of quality, pos. deg., qual. the n. "wheel." |
| wheel | A com. n., neu. gen., s. num., 3rd per., nom. c. to the v. "runs." |
| runs | An irreg. intr. v., indic. m., pres. t., s. num., 3rd per., agr. with its nom. "wheel." |
| down | A prep, sh. the rn. bet. "runs" and "hill." |
| hill. | A com. n., neu. gen., s. num., 3rd per., obj. c., gov. by the prep. "down." |
| 7. I | A pers. pron., com. gen., s. num., 1st per., nom. c. to the v. "knew." |
| never | An adv. of time, mod. the v. "knew." |
| know | An irreg. tr. v., act. vo., indic. m., past t., s. num., 1st per., agr. with its nom. "I." |
| one | A def. card. nu. adj. of quantity, qual. the n. *person* und. |
| of | A prep., sh. the rn. bet. *person* und. and "them." |
| them | A pers. pron., com. gen., p. num., 3rd per., obj. c., gov. by the prep. "of." |

| | |
|---|---|
| (to) find | An irreg. tr. v., act. vo., infin. m., pres. t., gov. by the v. "knew." |
| fault | An abs. n., neu. gen., s. num., 3rd per., obj. c., gov. by the tr. v. "to find." |
| with | A prep., sh. the rn. bet. "to find" and "it." |
| it. | A pers. pron., neu. gen., s. num., 3rd per., obj. c., gov. by the prep. "with." |
| 8. good-natured | A compd. adj. of quality, pos. deg., qual. the n. "girl." |
| girl | A com. n., fem. gen., s. num., 3rd per., nom. c. to the v. "let." |
| let | An irreg. tr. v., act. vo., indic. m., past t., s. num., 3rd per., agr. with its nom. "girl." |
| (to) fall | An irreg. intr. v., infin. m., pres. t., gov. by the v. "let." |
| tear | A com. n., neu. gen., s. num., 3rd per., obj. c., gov. by the tr. v. "let." |
| at | A prep., sh. the rn. bet. "to fall" and "account. |
| this | A dis. adj., lim. the n. "account." |
| account. | An abs. n., neu. gen., s. num., 3rd per., obj. c., gov. by the prep. "at." |
| 9. I | A pers. pron., com. gen., s. num., 1st per., nom. c. to the v. "bid." |
| bid | An irreg. tr. v., act. vo., indic. m., pres. t., s. num., 1st per., agr. with its nom. "I." |
| you | A pers. pron., com. gen., p. num., or s. num., p. form, 2nd per., obj. c., gov. by the tr. v. "bid." |
| (to) spurn | A reg. tr. v., act. vo., infin. m., pres. t., gov. by the v. "bid." |
| gilded | A past pl. from the tr. v. "to gild," used as an adj. of quality, qual. the n. "bait." |
| bait | A com. n., neu. gen., s. num., 3rd per., obj. c., gov. by the tr. v. "to spurn." |
| they | A pers. pron., com. gen., p. num., 3rd per., nom. c. to the v. "bear." |
| bear. | An irreg. tr. v., act. vo., indic. m., pres. t., p. num., 3rd per., agr. with its nom. "they." (They bear *which*.) |
| 10. bleak | An adj. of quality, pos. deg., qual. the n. "wind." |
| wind | A com. n., neu. gen., s. num., 3rd per., nom. c. to the v. "made." |
| of | A prep., sh. the rn. bet. "wind" and "March." |
| March | A prop. n., neu. gen., s. num., 3rd per., obj. c., gov. by the prep. "of." |
| Made | An irreg. tr. v., act. vo., indic. m., past t., s. num., 3rd per., agr. with its nom. "wind." |
| her | A pers. pron., fem. gen., s. num., 3rd per., obj. c., gov. by the tr. v. "made." |
| (to) tremble | A reg. intr. v., infin. m., pres. t., gov. by the v. "made." |
| and | A cop. conj., jg. the sents. "The bleak..trembled" and "*the bleak wind of March made her* shiver." |
| (to) shiver | A reg. intr. v., infin. m., pres. t., gov. by the v. *made* und. |
| But | A disj. conj., jg. the sents. "*the bleak wind..*shiver" and "not the dark arch *made her shiver*." |
| not | An adv. of m. (neg.), mod. the v. *made* und. |
| dark | An adj. of quality, pos. deg., qual. the n. "arch." |
| arch | A com. n., neu. gen., s. num., 3rd per., nom. c. to the v. *made* und. |
| Or | A disj. conj., jg. the sents. "not the dark arch *made her shiver*" and "*not* the black-flowing river *made her shiver*." |
| black-flowing | A compd. adj. of quality, qual. the n. "river." |
| river. | A com. n., neu. gen., s. num., 3rd per., nom. c. to the v. *made* und. |

## Exercise 171.

| | |
|---|---|
| 1. To | A particle, indg. infin. m. |
| To measure | A reg. tr. v., act. vo., infin. m., pres. t.; used as an abs. n., neu. gen., s. num., 3rd per., obj. c., gov. by the tr. v. "learn." |
| life | An abs. n., neu. gen., s. num., 3rd per., obj. c., gov. by the tr. v. "to measure." |
| learn | An irreg. tr. v., act. vo., imper. m., pres. t., s. num., 2nd per., agr. with its nom. "thou." |
| thou | A pers. pron., com. gen., s. num., 2nd per., nom. c. to the v. "learn." |

| | |
|---|---|
| betimes. | An adv. of time, mod. the v. "learn." |
| 2. trees | A com. n., neu. gen., p. num., 3rd per., nom. c. to the v. "began." |
| began | An irreg. tr. v., act. vo., indic. m., past t., p. num., 3rd per., agr. with its nom. "trees." |
| to | A particle, indg. infin. m. |
| (to) whisper | A reg. intr. v., infin. m., pres. t.; used as an abs. n., neu. gen., s. num., 3rd per., obj. c., gov. by the tr. v. "began." |
| and | A cop. conj., jg. the sents. "The trees..whisper" and "the wind..roll." |
| wind | A com. n., neu. gen., s. num., 3rd per., nom. c. to the v. "began." |
| began | An irreg. tr. v., act. vo., indic. m., past t., s. num., 3rd per., agr. with its nom. "wind." |
| to | A particle, indg. infin. m. |
| to roll. | A reg. intr. v., infin. m., pres. t.; used as an abs. n., neu. gen., s. num., 3rd per., obj. c., gov. by the tr. v. "began." |
| 3. To | A particle, indg. infin. m. |
| To have | An irreg. tr. v., act. vo., infin. m., pres. t.; used as an abs. n., neu. gen., s. num., 3rd per., nom. c. to the v. *is* und. |
| open | An adj. of quality, pos. deg., qual. the n. "ear." |
| ear | A com. n., neu. gen., s. num., 3rd per., obj. c., gov. by the tr. v. "to have." |
| quick | An adj. of quality, pos. deg., qual. the n. "eye." |
| eye | A com. n., neu. gen., s. num., 3rd per., obj. c., gov. by the tr. v. *to have* und. |
| and | A cop. conj., jg. the sents. "*to have* a quick eye *is necessary for a cut-purse*" and "*to have* a nimble hand..cut-purse." |
| nimble | An adj. of quality, pos. deg., qual. the n. "hand." |
| hand | A com. n., neu. gen., s. num., 3rd per., obj. c., gov. by the tr. v. *to have* und. |
| is | An irreg. intr. v., indic. m., pres. t., s. num., 3rd per., agr. with its nom. *to have* und. |
| necessary | An adj. of quality, pos. deg., qual. *to have* und. |
| for | A prep., sh. the rn. bet. "necessary" and "cut-purse." |
| cut-purse. | A compd. com. n., mas. gen., s. num., 3rd per., obj. c., gov. by the prep. "for." |
| 4. It | A pers. pron., neu. gen., s. num., 3rd per., nom. c. to the v. "is." |
| is | An irreg. intr. v., indic. m., pres. t., s. num., 3rd per., agr. with its nom. "it." |
| noble | An adj. of quality, pos. deg., qual. the pron. "it." |
| to | A particle, indg. infin. m. |
| to seek | An irreg. tr. v., act. vo., infin. m., pres. t.; used as an abs. n., neu. gen., s. num., 3rd per., nom. c., in app. with "it." |
| truth | An abs. n., neu. gen., s. num., 3rd per., obj. c., gov. by the tr. v. "to seek." |
| and | A cop. conj., jg. the sents. "it is..truth" and "it is..it." |
| it | A pers. pron., neu. gen., s. num., 3rd per., nom. c. to the v. "is." |
| is | An irreg. intr. v., indic. m., pres. t., s. num., 3rd per., agr. with its nom. "it." |
| beautiful | An adj. of quality, pos. deg., qual. the pron. "it." |
| to | A particle, indg. infin. m. |
| to find | An irreg. tr. v., act. vo., infin. m., pres. t.; used as an abs. n., neu. gen., s. num., 3rd per., nom. c., in app. with "it." |
| it. | A pers. pron., neu. gen., s. num., 3rd per., obj. c., gov. by the tr. v. "to find." |
| 5. T=It | A pers. pron., neu. gen., s. num., 3rd per., nom. c. to the v. "is." |
| is | An irreg. intr. v., indic. m., pres. t., s. num., 3rd per., agr. with its nom. "it." |
| cruelty | An abs. n., neu. gen., s. num., 3rd per., nom. c. after the v. "is." |
| to | A particle, indg. infin. m. |
| to load | A reg. tr. v., act. vo., infin. m., pres. t.; used as an abs. n., neu. gen., s. num., 3rd per., nom. c., in app. with "it." |
| falling | A pres. pl. from the intr. v. "to fall," used as an adj. of quality, qual. the n. "man." |
| man. | A com. n., mas. gen., s. num., 3rd per., obj. c., gov. by the tr. v. "to load." |
| 6. How | An adv. of deg., mod. the adj. "hard." |
| hard | An adj. of quality, pos. deg., qual. the pron. "it." |

| | |
|---|---|
| it | A pers. pron., neu. gen., s. num., 3rd per., nom. c. to the v. "is." |
| is | An irreg. intr. v., indic. m., pres. t., s. num., 3rd per., agr. with its nom. "it." |
| to | A particle, indg. infin. m. |
| **to hide** | An irreg. tr. v., act. vo., infin. m., pres. t.; used as an abs. n., neu. gen., s. num., 3rd per., nom. c., in app. with "it." |
| sparks | A com. n., neu. gen., p. num., 3rd per., obj. c., gov. by the tr. v. "to hide." |
| of | A prep., sh. the rn. bet. "sparks" and "nature." |
| nature. | An abs. n., neu. gen., s. num., 3rd per., obj. c., gov. by the prep. "of." |
| 7. It | A pers. pron., neu. gen., s. num., 3rd per., nom. c. to the v. "is." |
| is | An irreg. intr. v., indic. m., pres. t., s. num., 3rd per., agr. with its nom. "it." |
| not | An adv. of m. (neg.), mod. the v. "is." |
| safe | An adj. of quality, pos. deg., qual. the pron. "it." |
| to | A particle, indg. infin. m. |
| **to play** | A reg. intr. v., infin. m., pres. t.; used as an abs. n., neu. gen., s. num., 3rd per., nom. c., in app. with "it." |
| with | A prep., sh. the rn. bet. "to play" and "error." |
| error | An abs. n., neu. gen., s. num., 3rd per., obj. c., gov. by the prep. "with." |
| and | A cop. conj., jg. the sents. "It is..error" and "*it is not safe to dress it up to ourselves in the shape of truth.*" |
| (to) **dress** | A reg. tr. v., act. vo., infin. m., pres. t.; used as an abs. n., neu. gen., s. num., 3rd per., nom. c., in app. with it und. |
| it | A pers. pron., neu. gen., s. num., 3rd per., obj. c., gov. by the tr. v. "*to* dress." |
| up | An adv. of man., mod. the v. "*to* dress." |
| to | A prep., sh. the rn. bet. "*to* dress" and "ourselves." |
| ourselves | A compd. pers. pron., com. gen., p. num., 1st per., obj. c., gov. by the prep. "to." |
| or | A disj. conj., jg. the sents. "*it is not safe to* dress it up to ourselves *in the shape of truth*" and "*it is not safe to dress it up to* others ..truth." |
| others | A com. n., com. gen., p. num., 3rd per., obj. c., gov. by the prep. *to* und. |
| in | A prep., sh. the rn. bet. *to dress* und. and "shape." |
| shape | An abs. n., neu. gen., s. num., 3rd per., obj. c., gov. by the prep. "in." |
| of | A prep., sh. the rn. bet. "shape" and "truth." |
| truth. | An abs. n., neu. gen., s. num., 3rd per., obj. c., gov. by the prep. "of." |
| 8. I | A pers. pron., com. gen., s. num., 1st per., nom. c. to the v. "thought." |
| thought | An irreg. tr. v., act. vo., indic. m., past t., s. num., 1st per., agr. with its nom. "I." |
| to | A particle, indg. infin. m. |
| **to stand** | An irreg. intr. v., infin. m., pres. t.; used as an abs. n., neu. gen., s. num., 3rd per., obj. c., gov. by the tr. v. "thought" (*i.e.*, expected). |
| where | A cop. conj., jg. the sents. "I..stand" and "banners waved." |
| banners | A com. n., neu. gen., p. num., 3rd per., nom. c. to the v. "waved." |
| waved. | A reg. intr. v., indic. m., past t., p. num., 3rd per., agr. with its nom. "banners." |
| 9. To | A particle, indg. infin. m. |
| **To copy** | A reg. tr. v., act. vo., infin. m., pres. t.; used as an abs. n., neu. gen., s. num., 3rd per., nom. c. to the v. "forfeits." |
| beauties | An abs. n., neu. gen., p. num., 3rd per., obj. c., gov. by the tr. v. "to copy." |
| forfeits | A reg. tr. v., act. vo., indic. m., pres. t., s. num., 3rd per., agr. with its nom. "to copy." |
| all | An adj. of quantity (bulk or mass), qual. the n. "pretence." |
| pretence | An abs. n., neu. gen., s. num., 3rd per., obj. c., gov. by the tr. v. "forfeits." |
| to | A prep., sh. the rn. bet. "pretence" and "fame." |

| | |
|---|---|
| fame | An abs. n., neu. gen., s. num., 3rd per., obj. c., gov. by the prep. "to." |
| To | A particle, indg. infin. m. |
| **To copy** | A reg. tr. v., act. vo., infin. m., pres. t.; used as an abs. n., neu. gen., s. num., 3rd per., nom. c. to the v. "is." |
| faults | An abs. n., neu. gen., p. num., 3rd per., obj. c., gov. by the tr. v. "to copy." |
| is | An irreg. intr. v., indic. m., pres. t., s. num., 3rd per., agr. with its nom. "to copy." |
| want | An abs. n., neu. gen., s. num., 3rd per., nom. c. after the v. "is." |
| of | A prep., sh. the rn. bet. "want" and "sense." |
| sense. | An abs. n., neu. gen., s. num., 3rd per., obj. c., gov. by the prep. "of." |
| 10. To | A particle, indg. infin. m. |
| **To gild** | A reg. tr. v., act. vo., infin. m., pres. t.; used as an abs. n., neu. gen., s. num., 3rd per., nom. c. to the v. *is* und. |
| refined | A past pl. from the tr. v. "to refine," used as an adj. of quality, pos. deg., qual. the n. "gold." |
| gold | A com. n., neu. gen., s. num., 3rd per., obj. c., gov. by the tr. v. "to gild." |
| to | A particle, indg. infin. m. |
| **to paint** | A reg. tr. v., act. vo., infin. m., pres. t.; used as an abs. n., neu. gen., s. num., 3rd per., nom. c. to the v. *is* und. |
| lily | A com. n., neu. gen., s. num., 3rd per., obj. c., gov. by the tr. v. "to paint." |
| To | A particle, indg. infin. m. |
| **To throw** | An irreg. tr. v., act. vo., infin. m., pres. t.; used as an abs. n., neu. gen., s. num., 3rd per., nom. c. to the v. *is* und. |
| perfume | A com. n., neu. gen., s. num., 3rd per., obj. c., gov. by the tr. v. "to throw." |
| on | A prep., sh. the rn. bet. "to throw" and "violet." |
| violet | A com. n., neu. gen., s. num., 3rd per., obj. c., gov. by the prep. "on." |
| To | A particle, indg. infin. m. |
| **To smooth** | A reg. tr. v., act. vo., infin. m., pres. t.; used as an abs. n., neu. gen., s. num., 3rd per., nom. c. to the v. *is* und. |
| ice | A com. n., neu. gen., s. num., 3rd per., obj. c., gov. by the tr. v. "to smooth." |
| or | A disj. conj., jg. the sents. "To smooth the ice *is wasteful and ridiculous excess*" and "*to* add another hue unto the rainbow *is wasteful and ridiculous excess.*" |
| **(to) add** | A reg. tr. v., act. vo., infin. m., pres. t.; used as an abs. n., neu. gen., s. num., 3rd per., nom. c. to the v. *is* und. |
| another | An indef. nu. adj. of quantity, qual. the n. "hue." |
| hue | A com. n., neu. gen., s. num., 3rd per., obj. c., gov. by the tr. v. "to add." |
| Unto | A prep., sh. the rn. bet. "*to* add" and "rainbow." |
| rainbow | A com. n., neu. gen., s. num., 3rd per., obj. c., gov. by the prep. "unto." |
| or | A disj. conj., jg. the sents. "*To* add another hue unto the rainbow *is wasteful and ridiculous excess*" and "with a taper..excess." |
| with | A prep., sh. the rn. bet. "to garnish" and "light." |
| taper | A com. n. used as an adj. of quality, qual. the n. "light." |
| light | A com. n., neu. gen., 3rd per., obj. c., gov. by the prep. "with." |
| To | A particle, indg. infin. m. |
| **To seek** | An irreg. tr. v., act. vo., infin. m., pres. t.; used as an abs. n., neu. gen., s. num., 3rd per., nom. c. to the v. "is." |
| beauteous | An adj. of quality, pos. deg., qual. the n. "eye." |
| eye | A com. n., neu. gen., s. num., 3rd per., obj. c., gov. by the tr. v. "to garnish." |
| of | A prep., sh. the rn. bet. "eye" and "heaven." |
| heaven | A com. n., neu. gen., s. num., 3rd per., obj. c., gov. by the prep. "of." |
| to | A particle, indg. infin. m. |
| **to garnish** | A reg. tr. v., act. vo., infin. m., pres. t.; used as an abs. n., neu. gen., s. num., 3rd per., obj. c., gov. by the tr. v. "to seek." |

| | |
|---|---|
| Is | An irreg. intr. v., indic. m., pres. t., s. num., 3rd per., agr. with its nom. "to seek." |
| wasteful | An adj. of quality, pos. deg., qual. the n. *excess* und. |
| and | A cop. conj., jg. the sents. "To seek...wasteful *excess*" and "*to seek the beauteous eye of heaven to garnish is* ridiculous excess." |
| ridiculous | An adj. of quality, pos. deg., qual. the n. "excess." |
| excess. | An abs. n., neu. gen., s. num., 3rd per., nom. c. after the v. *is* und. |

## Exercise 172.

| | |
|---|---|
| 1. **Fanned** | A past pl. from the tr. v. "to fan," ref. to "blaze." |
| by | A prep., sh. the rn. bet. "fanned" and "breeze." |
| fresh | An adj. of quality, pos. deg., qual. the n. "breeze." |
| breeze | A com. n., neu. gen., s. num., 3rd per., obj. c., gov. by the prep. "by." |
| blaze | A com. n., neu. gen., s. num., 3rd per., nom. c. to the v. "rose." |
| rose | An irreg. intr. v., indic. m., past t., s. num., 3rd per., agr. with its nom. "blaze." |
| into | A prep., sh. the rn. bet. "rose" and "sky." |
| sky. | A com. n., neu. gen., s. num., 3rd per., obj. c., gov. by the prep. "into." |
| 2. So | A cop. conj., introducing the sent. "purposing..linger'd still." |
| **purposing** | A pres. pl. from the tr. v. to "purpose," ref. to "she." |
| each | A dist. nu. adj. of quantity, qual. the n. "moment." |
| moment | An abs. n., neu. gen., s. num., 3rd per., obj. c., gov. by the prep. *at* und. |
| to | A particle, indg. infin. m. |
| to retire | A reg. intr. v., infin. m., pres. t.; used as an abs. n., neu. gen., s. num., 3rd per., obj. c., gov. by the tr. pl. "purposing." |
| she | A pers. pron., fem. gen., s. num., 3rd per., nom. c. to the v. "linger'd." |
| linger'd | A reg. intr. v., indic. m., past t., s. num., 3rd per., agr. with its nom. "she." |
| still. | An adv. of time, mod. the v. "linger'd." |
| 3. Being | A pres. pl. from the intr. v. "to be," ref. to "apprised neighbourhood," and aux. to "apprised," indg. pass. vo. |
| apprised | A past pl. from the tr. v. "to apprise," ref. to "neighbourhood." |
| **being apprised** | A pres. pl. from the tr. v. "to apprise," pass. vo., ref. to "neighbourhood." |
| of | A prep., sh. the rn. bet. "being apprised" and "approach." |
| our | A pers. pron., com. gen., p. num., 1st per., poss. c., gov. by the n. "approach." |
| approach | An abs. n., neu. gen., s. num., 3rd per., obj. c., gov. by the prep. "of." |
| whole | An adj. of quantity (bulk or mass), qual. the n. "neighbourhood." |
| neighbourhood | A com. col. n., com. gen., p. num., 3rd per., nom. c. to the v. "came." |
| came | An irreg. intr. v., indic. m., past t., p. num., 3rd per., agr. with its nom. "neighbourhood." |
| out | An adv. of place, mod. the v. "came." |
| to | A particle, indg. infin. m. |
| to meet | An irreg. tr. v., act. vo., infin. m., pres. t., gov. by the v. "came." |
| their | A pers. pron., com. gen., p. num., 3rd per., poss. c., gov. by the n. "minister." |
| minister | A com. n., mas. gen., s. num., 3rd per., obj. c., gov. by the tr. v. "to meet." |
| **dressed** | A past pl. from the tr. v. "to dress," ref. to "neighbourhood." |
| in | A prep., sh. the rn. bet. "dressed" and "clothes." |
| their | A pers. pron., com. gen., p. num., 3rd per., poss. c., gov. by the n. "clothes." |
| fine | An adj. of quality, pos. deg., qual. the n. "clothes." |

## 192 KEY TO

| | |
|---|---|
| clothes | A com. n., neu. gen., p. num., 3rd per., obj. c., gov. by the prep. "in." |
| and | A cop. conj., jg. the sents. "Being apprised..clothes" and "*being apprised of our approach. the whole neighbourhood came out to meet their minister*, preceded by a pipe." |
| **preceded** | A past pl. from the tr. v. "to precede," ref. to *neighbourhood* und. |
| by | A prep., sh. the rn. bet. "preceded" and "pipe." |
| pipe | A com. n., neu. gen., s. num., 3rd per., obj. c., gov. by the prep. "by." |
| and | A cop. conj., jg. the sents. "*being apprised*..pipe" and "*being apprised...preceded by a* tabor." |
| tabor. | A com. n., neu. gen., s. num., 3rd per., obj. c., gov. by the prep. *by* und. |
| 4. Birds | A com. n., com. gen., p. num., 3rd per., nom. c. to the v. "sit." |
| of | A prep., sh. the rn. bet. "birds" and "calm." |
| calm | An abs. n., neu. gen., s. num., 3rd per., obj. c., gov. by the prep. "of." |
| sit | An irreg. intr. v., indic. m., pres. t., p. num., 3rd per., agr. with its nom. "birds." |
| **brooding** | A pres. pl. from the intr. v. "to brood," ref. to "birds." |
| on | A prep., sh. the rn bet. "sit" and "wave." |
| **charmed** | A past pl. from the tr. v. "to charm," used as an adj. of quality, qual. the n. "wave." |
| wave. | A com. n., neu. gen., s. num., 3rd per., obj. c., gov. by the prep. "on." |
| 5. Hope | An abs. n., neu. gen., s. num., 3rd per., nom. c. to the v. "maketh." |
| **deferred** | A past pl. from the tr. v. "to defer," ref. to "hope." |
| maketh | An irreg. tr. v., act. vo., indic. m., pres. t., s. num., 3rd per., agr. with its nom. "hope." |
| heart | A com. n., neu. gen., s. num., 3rd per., obj. c., gov. by the tr. v. "maketh." |
| sick. | An adj. of quality, pos. deg., qual. the n. "heart." |
| 6. **living** | A pres. pl. from the intr. v. "to live," used as an adj. of quality, qual. the n. "dog." |
| dog | A com. n., com. gen., s. num., 3rd per., nom. c. to the v. "is." |
| is | An irreg. intr. v., indic. m., pres. t., s. num., 3rd per., agr. with its nom. "dog." |
| better | An adj. of quality, comp. deg., qual. the n. "dog." |
| than | A disj. conj., jg. the sents. "A living dog is better" and "a dead lion *is good*." |
| dead | An adj. of quality, qual. the n. "lion." |
| lion. | A com. n., com. gen., s. num., 3rd per., nom. c. to the v. *is* und. |
| 7. Thou | A pers. pron., com. gen., s. num., 2nd per., nom. c. to the v. "art." |
| art | An irreg. intr. v., indic. m., pres. t., s. num., 2nd per., agr. with its nom. "thou." |
| **unseen** | A negative form of the past pl. from the tr. v. "to see," ref. to "thou." |
| but | A disj. conj., jg. the sents. "Thou art unseen" and "I..delight." |
| yet | An adv. of time, mod. the v. "hear." |
| I | A pers. pron., com. gen., s. num., 1st per., nom. c. to the v. "hear." |
| hear | An irreg. tr. v., act. vo., indic. m., pres. t., s. num., 1st per., agr. with its nom. "I." |
| thy | A pers. pron., com. gen., s. num., 2nd per., poss. c., gov. by the n. "delight." |
| shrill | An adj. of quality, pos. deg., qual. the n. "delight." |
| delight. | An abs. n., neu. gen., s. num., 3rd per., obj. c., gov. by the tr. v. "hear." |
| 8. We | A pers. pron., com. gen., p. num., 1st per., nom. c. to the v. "wander." |

ENGLISH GRAMMAR AND ANALYSIS. 193

| | |
|---|---|
| wander | A reg. intr. v., indic. m., pres. t., p. num., 1st per., agr. with its nom. "we." |
| o'er | A prep., sh. the rn. bet. "wander" and "soil." |
| sunburnt | A compd. adj. of quality, pos. deg., qual. the n. "soil." |
| thirsty | An adj. of quality, pos. deg., qual. the n. "soil." |
| soil | A com. n., neu. gen., s. num., 3rd per., obj. c., gov. by the prep. "o'er." |
| **Murmuring** | A pres. pl. from the intr. v. "to murmur," ref. to "we." |
| and | A cop. conj., jg. the sents. "We wander..murmuring" and "*we wander o'er a sunburnt thirsty soil*, weary of our daily toil." |
| weary | An adj. of quality, pos. deg., qual. the pron. *we* und. |
| of | A prep., sh. the rn. bet. "weary" and "toil." |
| our | A pers. pron., com. gen., p. num., 1st per., poss. c., gov. by the n. "toil." |
| daily | An adj. of quality, qual. the n. "toil." |
| toil. | An abs. n., neu. gen., s. num., 3rd per., obj. c., gov. by the prep. "of." |
| 9. **Waiting** | A pres. pl. from the intr. v. "to wait," ref. to "clouds." |
| till | A cop. conj., jg. the sents. "The freighted..lie waiting" and "the west-wind blows." |
| west-wind | A compd. com. n., neu. gen., s. num., 3rd per., nom. c. to the v. "blows." |
| blows | An irreg. intr. v., indic. m., pres. t., s. num., 3rd per., agr. with its nom. "west-wind." |
| **freighted** | A past pl. from the tr. v. "to freight," used as an adj. of quality, qual. the n. "clouds." |
| clouds | A com. n., neu. gen., p. num., 3rd per., nom. c. to the v. "lie." |
| at | A prep., sh. the rn. bet. "lie" and "anchor." |
| anchor | A com. n., neu. gen., s. num., 3rd per., obj. c., gov. by the prep. "at." |
| lie. | An irreg. intr. v., indic. m., pres. t., p. num., 3rd per., agr. with its nom. "clouds." |
| 10. Then | An adv. of time, mod. the v. "came." |
| came | An irreg. intr. v., indic. m., past t., s. num., 3rd per., agr. with its nom. "May." |
| fair | An adj. of quality, pos. deg., qual. the n. "May." |
| May | A prop. n., fem. gen. by personification, s. num., 3rd per., nom. c. to the v. "came." |
| fairest | An adj. of quality, superl. deg., qual. the n. "maid." |
| maid | A com. n., fem. gen., s. num., 3rd per., nom. c., in app. with "May." |
| on | A prep., sh. the rn. bet. "maid" and "ground." |
| ground | A com. n., neu. gen., s. num., 3rd per., obj. c., gov. by the prep. "on." |
| **Deck'd** | A past pl. from the tr. v. "to deck," ref. to "May." |
| all | An adv. of deg., mod. the pl. "deck'd." |
| with | A prep., sh. the rn. bet. "deck'd" and "dainties." |
| dainties | A com. n., neu. gen., p. num., 3rd per., obj. c., gov. by the prep. "with." |
| of | A prep., sh. the rn. bet. "dainties" and "pride." |
| her | A pers. pron., fem. gen., s. num., 3rd per., poss. c., gov. by the n. "season's." |
| season's | An abs. n., neu. gen., s. num., 3rd per., poss. c., gov. by the n. "pride." |
| pride | An abs. n., neu. gen., s. num., 3rd per., obj. c., gov. by the prep. "of." |
| And | A cop. conj., jg. the sents. "Then came..pride" and "*then came fair May, the fairest maid on ground, throwing..around.*" |
| **throwing** | A pres. pl. from the tr. v. "to throw," ref. to *May* und. |
| flowers | A com. n., neu. gen., p. num., 3rd per., obj. c., gov. by the tr. pl. "throwing." |
| out of | A compd. prep., sh. the rn. bet. "throwing" and "lap." (*Pars- ing*, p. 154.) |
| her | A pers. pron., fem. gen., s. num., 3rd per., poss. c., gov. by the n. "lap." |
| lap | A com. n., neu. gen., s. num., 3rd per., obj. c., gov. by the prep. "out of." |
| around. | An adv. of place, mod. the pl. "throwing." |

13

## Exercise 173.

| | |
|---|---|
| 1. Generally | An adv. of man., mod. the pl. "speaking." |
| **speaking** | A pres. pl. from the intr. v. "to speak," used absolutely. |
| this | A dis. adj., lim. the n. "physician." |
| physician | A com. n., mas. gen., s. num., 3rd per., nom. c. to the v. "rises." |
| rises | An irreg. intr. v., indic. m., pres. t., s. num., 3rd per., agr. with its nom. "physician." |
| at | A prep., sh. the rn. bet. "rises" and *hours* und. |
| five | A def. card. nu. adj. of quantity, qual. the n, *hours* und. |
| in | A prep., sh. the rn. bet. "rises" and "morning." |
| morning. | An abs. n., neu. gen., s. num., 3rd per., obj. c., gov. by the prep. "in." |
| 2. **Considering** | A pres. pl. from the tr. v. "to consider" used absolutely. |
| by | A prep., sh. the rn. bet. "considering" and "means." |
| what | An interrog. pron. used as an adj., qual. the n. "means." |
| means | An abs. n., neu. gen., p. num., 3rd per., obj. c., gov. by the prep. "by." |
| he | A pers. pron., mas. gen., s. num., 3rd per., nom. c. to the v. "gained." |
| gained | A reg. tr. v., act. vo., indic. m., past t., s. num., 3rd per., agr. with its nom. "he." |
| his | A pers. pron., mas. gen., s. num., 3rd per., poss. c., gov. by the n. "ends." |
| ends | An abs. n., neu. gen., p. num., 3rd per., obj. c., gov. by the tr. v. "gained." |
| he | A pers. pron., mas. gen., s. num., 3rd per., nom. c. to the v. "must be condemned." |
| must | An aux. v. to "be condemned," indg. pot. m., pres. t. |
| be | An aux. v. to "condemned," indg. pass. vo. |
| condemned | A past pl. from the tr. v. "to condemn," ref. to "he." |
| must be condemned. | A reg. tr. v., pass. vo., pot. m., pres. t., s. num., 3rd per., agr. with its nom. "he." |
| 3. **Seeing** | A pres. pl. from the tr. v. "to see," used absolutely. |
| straits | An abs. n., neu. gen., p. num., 3rd per., obj. c., gov. by the tr. pl. "seeing." |
| to | A prep., sh. the rn. bet. "was pushed" and "which." |
| which | A rel. pron., neu. gen., p. num., 3rd per., agr. with its ant. "straits," obj. c., gov. by the prep. "to." |
| he | A pers. pron., mas. gen., s. num., 3rd per., nom. c. to the v. "was pushed." |
| was | An aux. v. to "pushed," indg. pass. vo., past t. |
| pushed | A past pl. from the tr. v. "to push," ref. to "he." |
| was pushed | A reg. tr. v., pass. vo., indic. m., past t., s. num., 3rd per., agr. with its nom. "he." |
| it | A pers. pron., neu. gen., s. num., 3rd per., nom. c. to the v. "was." |
| was | An irreg. intr. v., indic. m., past t., s. num., 3rd per., agr. with its nom. "it." |
| natural | An adj. of quality, qual. the pron. "it." |
| for | A prep., sh. the rn. bet. "natural" and "him." |
| him | A pers. pron., mas. gen., s. num., 3rd per., obj. c., gov. by the prep. "for." |
| to | A particle, indg. infin. m. |
| to invoke | A reg. tr. v., act. vo., infin. m., pres. t.; used as an abs. n., neu. gen., s. num., 3rd per., nom. c., in app. with "it." |
| your | A pers. pron., com. gen., p. num., or s. num., p. form, 2nd per., poss. c., gov. by the n. "aid." |
| aid. | An abs. n., neu. gen., s. num., 3rd per., obj. c., gov. by the tr. v. "to invoke." |
| 4. **Judging** | A pres. pl. from the intr. v. "to judge," used absolutely. |
| at | A prep., sh. the rn. bet. "judging" and *manner* und. |
| random | An adj. of quality, pos. deg., qual. the n. *manner* und. |
| at random | An adverbial phrase of man., mod. the pl. "judging." |
| there | An expletive adv., mod. the v. "are." |
| are | An irreg. intr. v., indic. m., pres. t., p. num., 3rd per., agr. with its nom. *kine* und. |

| | |
|---|---|
| threescore | A def. card. nu. adj. of quantity, qual. the n. *kine* und. |
| and | A cop. conj., jg. the sents. "Judging...threescore *kine in the meadow*" and "*judging at random there are* ten kine in the meadow." |
| ten | A def. card. nu. adj. of quantity, qual. the n. "kine." |
| kine | A com. n., fem. gen., p. num., 3rd per., nom. c. to the v. *are* und. |
| in | A prep., sh. tho rn. bet. *are* und. and "meadow." |
| meadow. | A com. n., neu. gen., s. num., 3rd per., obj. c., gov. by the prep. "in." |
| 5. Generally | An adv. of man., mod. the pl. "speaking." |
| **speaking** | A pres. pl. from the intr. v. "to speak," used absolutely. |
| Godfrey | A prop. n., mas. gen., s. num., 3rd per., nom. c. to the v. "excels." |
| excels | A reg. tr. v., act. vo., indic. m., pres. t., s. num., 3rd per., agr. with its nom. "Godfrey." |
| his | A pers. pron., mas. gen., s. num., 3rd per., poss. c., gov. by the n. "rivals." |
| rivals. | A com. n., mas. gen., p. num., 3rd per., obj. c., gov. by the tr. v. "excels." |
| 6. **Speaking** | A pres. pl. from the intr. v. "to speak," used absolutely. |
| in | A prep., sh. the rn. bet. "speaking" and "numbers." |
| round | An adj. of quality, qual. the n. "numbers." |
| numbers | A com. n., neu. gen., p. num., 3rd per., obj. c., gov. by the prep. "in." |
| this | A dis. adj., lim. the n. *event* und. |
| happened | A reg. intr. v., indic. m., past t., s. num., 3rd per., agr. with its nom. *event* und. |
| three | A def. card. nu. adj. of quantity, qual. the n. "centuries." |
| centuries | An abs. n., neu. gen., p. num., 3rd per., obj. c., gov. by the prep. *at* or *in* und. |
| ago. | An adv. of time, mod. the v. "happened." |

## Exercise 174.

| | |
|---|---|
| 1. **Lamenting** | A pres. pl. from the tr. v. "to lament," ref. to "I." |
| barren | An adj. of quality, pos. deg., qual. the n. "superfluity." |
| superfluity | An abs. n., neu. gen., s. num., 3rd per., obj. c., gov. by the tr. pl. "lamenting." |
| of | A prep., sh. the rn. bet. "superfluity" and "materials." |
| materials | A com. n., neu. gen., p. num., 3rd per., obj. c., gov. by the prep. "of." |
| I | A pers. pron., com. gen., s. num., 1st per., nom. c. to the v. "have studied." |
| have | An aux. v. to "studied," indg. perf. t. |
| studied | A past pl. from the tr. v. "to study," ref. to "to compress." |
| have studied | A reg. tr. v., act. vo., indic. m., perf. t., s. num., 1st per., agr. with its nom. "I." |
| to | A particle, indg. infin. m. |
| to compress | A reg. tr. v., act. vo., infin. m., pres. t.; used as an abs. n., neu. gen., s. num., 3rd per., obj. c., gov. by the tr. v. "have studied." |
| narrative | A com. n., neu. gen., s. num., 3rd per., obj. c., gov. by the tr. v. "to compress." |
| of | A prep., sh. the rn. bet. "narrative" and "transactions." |
| these | A dis. adj., lim. the n. "transactions." |
| uninteresting | An adj. of quality, pos. deg., qual. the n. "transactions." |
| transactions. | An abs. n., neu. gen., p. num., 3rd per., obj. c., gov. by the prep. "of." |
| 2. **Elated** | A past pl. from the tr. v. "to elate," ref. to "he." |
| by | A prep., sh. the rn. bet. "elated" and "success." |
| his | A pers. pron., mas. gen., s. num., 3rd per., poss. c., gov. by the n. "success." |
| recent | An adj. of quality, pos. deg., qual. the n. "success." |
| success | An abs. n., neu. gen., s. num., 3rd per., obj. c., gov. by the prep. "by." |
| he | A pers. pron., mas. gen., s. num., 3rd per., nom. c. to the v. "despatched." |

| | |
|---|---|
| despatched | A reg. tr. v., act. vo., indic. m., past t., s. num., 3rd per., agr. with its nom. "he." |
| herald | A com. n., mas. gen., s. num., 3rd per., obj. c., gov. by the tr. v. "despatched." |
| with | A prep., sh. the rn. bet. "despatched" and "defiance." |
| bold | An adj. of quality, pos. deg., qual. the n. "defiance." |
| defiance | An abs. n., neu. gen., s. num., 3rd per., obj. c., gov. by the prep. "with." |
| to | A prep., sh. the rn. bet. "despatched" and "camp." |
| camp | A com. n., neu. gen., s. num., 3rd per., obj. c., gov. by the prep. "to." |
| of | A prep., sh. the rn. bet. "camp" and "Romans." |
| Romans | A prop. n., mas. gen., p. num., 3rd per., obj. c., gov. by the prep. "of." |
| **requesting** | A pres. pl. from the tr. v. "to request," ref. to "herald." |
| them | A pers. pron., mas. gen., p. num., 3rd per., obj. c., gov. by the tr. pl. "requesting." |
| to | A particle, indg. infin. m. |
| to fix | A reg. tr. v., act. vo., infin. m., pres. t., gov. by the pl. "requesting." |
| day | An abs. n., neu. gen., s. num., 3rd per., obj. c., gov. by the tr. v. "to fix." |
| of | A prep., sh. the rn. bet. "day" and "battle." |
| battle. | An abs. n., neu. gen., s. num., 3rd per., obj. c., gov. by the prep. "of." |
| 3. Manifestoes | A com. n., neu. gen., p. num., 3rd per., nom. c. to the v. "were circulated." |
| were | An aux. v. to "circulated," indg. pass. vo., past t. |
| diligently | An adv. of man., mod. the v. "were circulated." |
| circulated | A past pl. from the tr. v. "to circulate," ref. to "manifestoes." |
| were circulated | A reg. tr. v., pass. vo., indic. m., past t., p. num., 3rd per., agr. with its nom. "manifestoes." |
| **exhorting** | A pres. pl. from. the tr. v. "to exhort," ref. to "manifestoes." |
| Persians | A prop. n., mas. gen., p. num., 3rd per., obj. c., gov. by the tr. pl. "exhorting." |
| to | A particle, indg. infin. m. |
| to assert | A reg. tr. v., act. vo., infin. m., pres. t., gov. by the pl. "exhorting." |
| their | A pers. pron., mas. gen., p. num., 3rd per., poss. c., gov. by the n. "freedom." |
| freedom | An abs. n., neu. gen., s. num., 3rd per., obj. c., gov. by the tr. v. "to assert." |
| against | A prep., sh. the rn. bet. "to assert" and *tyrant* und. |
| odious | An adj. of quality, pos. deg., qual. the n. *tyrant* und. |
| and | A cop. conj., jg. the sents. "Manifestoes...odious *tyrant*" and "*manifestoes were diligently circulated, exhorting the Persians to assert their freedom against a contemptible tyrant.*" |
| contemptible | An adj. of quality, pos. deg., qual. the n. "tyrant." |
| tyrant. | A com. n., mas. gen., s. num., 3rd per., obj. c., gov. by the prep. *against* und. |
| 4. I | A pers. pron., com. gen., s. num., 1st per., nom. c. to the v. "shook." |
| shook | An irreg. intr. v., act. vo., indic. m., past t., s. num., 1st per., agr. with its nom. "I." |
| each | A dist. nu. adj. of quantity, qual. the n. *person* und. |
| tenderly | An adv. of man., mod. the v. "shook." |
| by | A prep., sh. the rn. bet. "shook" and "hand." |
| hand | A com. n., neu. gen., s. num., 3rd per., obj. c., gov. by the prep. "by." |
| and | A cop. conj., jg. the sents. "I...hand" and "*I, leaving...interruption.*" |
| **leaving** | A pres. pl. from the tr. v. "to leave," ref. to *I* und. |
| them | A pers. pron., com. gen., p. num., 3rd per., obj. c., gov. by the prep. *to* und. |
| my | A pers. pron., com. gen., s. num., 1st per., poss. c., gov. by the n. "blessing." |
| blessing | An abs. n., neu. gen., s. num., 3rd per., obj. c., gov. by the tr. pl. "leaving." |

| | |
|---|---|
| proceeded | A reg. intr. v., indic. m., past t., s. num., 1st per., agr. with its nom. *I* und. |
| forward | An adv. of place, mod. the v. "proceeded." |
| without | A prep., sh. the rn. bet. "proceeded" and "meeting." |
| meeting | A ger. from the tr. v. "to meet," neu. gen., s. num., 3rd per., obj. c., gov. by the prep. "without." |
| any | An indef. nu. adj. of quantity, qual. the n. "interruption." |
| further | An adj. of quality, comp. deg., qual. the n. "interruption." |
| interruption. | An abs. n., neu. gen., s. num., 3rd per., obj. c., gov. by the tr. ger. "meeting." |
| 5. Having | A pres. pl. from the tr. v. "to have," ref. to "I," aux. to "instructed," indg. perf. t. |
| thus | An adv. of man., mod. the pl. "having instructed." |
| instructed | A past pl. from the tr. v. "to instruct," ref. to "him." |
| **having instructed** | A perf. pl. from the tr. v. "to instruct," ref. to "him." |
| him | A pers. pron., mas. gen., s. num., 3rd per., obj. c., gov. by the tr. pl. "having instructed." |
| and | A cop. conj., jg. the sents. "Having thus instructed him, *I walked down to the common prison*" and "*having settled the rest, I.. prison.*" |
| settled | A past pl. from the tr. v. "to settle," ref. to "rest." |
| rest | A com. n., neu. gen., s. num., 3rd per., obj. c., gov. by the tr. pl. "*having* settled." |
| I | A pers. pron., com. gen., s. num., 1st per., nom. c. to the v. "walked." |
| walked | A reg. intr. v., indic. m., past t., s. num., 1st per., agr. with its nom. "I." |
| down | An adv. of place, mod. the v. "walked." |
| to | A prep., sh. the rn. bet. "walked" and "prison." |
| common | An adj. of quality, qual. the n. "prison." |
| prison. | A com. n., neu. gen., s. num., 3rd per., obj. c., gov. by the prep. "to." |
| 6. From | A prep., sh. the rn. bet. "see" and "study." |
| my | A pers. pron., com. gen., s. num., 1st per., poss. c., gov. by the n. "study." |
| study | A com. n., neu. gen., s. num., 3rd per., obj. c., gov. by the prep. "from." |
| I | A pers. pron., com. gen., s. num., 1st per., nom. c. to the v. "see." |
| see | An irreg. tr. v., act. vo., indic. m., pres. t., s. num., 1st per., agr. with its nom. "I." |
| lamplight | A compd. com. n., neu. gen., s. num., 3rd per., obj. c., gov. by the tr. v. "see." |
| **descending** | A pres. pl. from the tr. v. "to descend," ref. to "lamplight." |
| broad | An adj. of quality, pos. deg., qual. the n. "hall-stair." |
| hall-stair. | A compd. com. n., neu. gen., s. num., 3rd per., obj. c., gov, by the tr. pl. "descending." |
| 7. **Waving** | A pres. pl. from the tr. v. "to wave," ref. to "she." |
| wide | An adv. of man., mod. the pl. "waving." |
| her | A pers. pron., fem. gen., s. num., 3rd per., poss. c., gov. by the n. "wand." |
| myrtle | A com. n. used as an adj. of quality, qual. the n. "wand." |
| wand | A com. n., neu. gen., s. num., 3rd per., obj. c., gov. by the tr. pl. "waving." |
| She | A pers. pron., fem. gen., s. num., 3rd per., nom. c. to the v. "strikes." |
| strikes | An irreg. tr. v., act. vo., indic. m., pres. t., s. num., 3rd per., agr. with its nom. "she." |
| universal | An adj. of quality, qual. the n. "peace." |
| peace | An abs. n., neu. gen., s. num., 3rd per., obj. c., gov. by the tr. v. "strikes." |
| through | A prep., sh. the rn. bet. "strikes" and "sea." |
| sea | A com. n., neu. gen., s. num., 3rd per., obj. c., gov. by the prep. "through." |
| and | A cop. conj., jg. the sents. "Waving..sea" and "*waving wide her myrtle wand, she strikes a universal peace through* land." |

## KEY TO

|  |  |
|---|---|
| land. | A com. n., neu. gen., s. num., 3rd per., obj. c., gov. by the prep. *through* und. |
| 8. **Whispering** | A pres. pl. from the tr. v. "to whisper," ref. to "zephyrs." |
| pleasure | An abs. n., neu. gen., s. num., 3rd per., obj. c., gov. by the tr. pl. "whispering." |
| as | A cop. conj., jg. the sents. "Cool zephyrs..fling, whispering pleasure" and "they fly." |
| they | A pers. pron., neu. gen., p. num., 3rd per., nom. c. to the v. "fly." |
| fly | An irreg. intr. v., indic. m., pres. t., p. num., 3rd per., agr. with its nom. "they." |
| Cool | An adj. of quality, pos. deg., qual. the n. "zephyrs." |
| zephyrs | A com. n., neu. gen., p. num., 3rd per., nom. c. to the v. "fling." |
| through | A prep., sh. the rn. bet. "fling" and "sky." |
| clear | An adj. of quality, pos. deg., qual. the n. "sky." |
| blue | An adj. of quality, pos. deg., qual. the n. "sky." |
| sky | A com. n., neu. gen., s. num., 3rd per., obj. c., gov. by the prep. "through." |
| Their | A pers. pron., neu. gen., p. num., 3rd per., poss. c., gov. by the n. "fragrance." |
| gathered | A past pl. from the tr. v. "to gather," used as an adj. of quality, qual. the n. "fragrance." |
| fragrance | An abs. n., neu. gen., s. num., 3rd per., obj. c., gov. by the tr. v. "fling." |
| fling. | An irreg. tr. v., act. vo., indic. m., pres. t., p. num., 3rd per., agr. with its nom. "zephyrs." |
| 9. We | A pers. pron., mas. gen., p. num., 1st per., nom. c. to the v. "buried." |
| buried | A reg. tr. v., act. vo., indic. m., past t., p. num., 1st per., agr. with its nom. "we." |
| him | A pers. pron., mas. gen., s. num., 3rd per., obj. c., gov. by the tr. v. "buried." |
| darkly | An adv. of man., mod. the v. "buried." |
| at | A prep., sh. the rn. bet. "buried" and "dead." |
| dead | An abs. n., neu. gen., s. num., 3rd per., obj. c., gov. by the prep. "at." |
| of | A prep., sh. the rn. bet. "dead" and "night." |
| night | An abs. n., neu. gen., s. num., 3rd per., obj. c., gov. by the prep. "of." |
| sods | A com. n., neu. gen., p. num., 3rd per., obj. c., gov. by the tr. pl. "turning." |
| with | A prep., sh. the rn. bet. "turning" and "bayonets." |
| our | A pers. pron., mas. gen., p. num., 1st per., poss. c., gov. by the n. "bayonets." |
| bayonets | A com. n., neu. gen., p. num., 3rd per., obj. c., gov. by the prep. "with." |
| turning. | A pres. pl. from the tr. v. "to turn," ref. to "we." |
| 10. It | A pers. pron., neu. gen., s. num., 3rd per., nom. c. to the v. "was." |
| was | An irreg. intr. v., indic. m., past t., s. num., 3rd per., agr. with its nom. "it." |
| vain | An adj. of quality, pos. deg., qual. the pron. "it." |
| loud | An adj. of quality, pos. deg., qual. the n. "waves." |
| waves | A com. n., neu. gen., p. num., 3rd per., nom. c. to the v. "lashed." |
| lashed | A reg. tr. v., act. vo., indic. m., past. t., p. num., 3rd per., agr. with its nom. "waves." |
| shore | A com. n., neu. gen., s. num., 3rd per., obj. c., gov. by the tr. v. "lashed." |
| Return | An abs. n., neu. gen., s. num., 3rd per., obj. c., gov. by the tr. pl. *preventing* und. |
| or | A disj. conj., jg. the sents. "the loud..return *preventing*" and "*the loud waves lashed the shore*, aid preventing." |
| aid | An abs. n., neu. gen., s. num., 3rd per., obj. c., gov. by the tr. pl. "preventing." |
| **preventing.** | A pres. pl. from the tr. v. "to prevent," ref. to "waves." |

## Exercise 175.

| | |
|---|---|
| **1. Once** | An adv. of time, mod. the ger. "carrying." |
| I | A pers. pron., com. gen., s. num., 1st per., nom. c. to the v. "remember." |
| remember | A reg. tr. v., act. vo., indic. m., pres. t., s. num., 1st per., agr. with its nom. "I." |
| **carrying** | A ger. from the tr. v. "to carry," neu. gen., s. num., 3rd per., obj. c., gov. by the tr. v. "remember." |
| my | A pers. pron., forming with the adj. "own" a compd. pers. pron. |
| own | An intensive adj. of quality, qual. the n. "bread." |
| my own | A compd. pers. pron., com. gen., s. num , 1st per., poss. c., gov. by the n. "bread." |
| bread | A com. n., neu. gen., s. num., 3rd per., obj. c., gov. by the tr. ger. "carrying." |
| under | A prep., sh. the rn. bet. "carrying" and "arm." |
| my | A pers. pron., com. gen., s. num., 1st per., poss. c., gov. by the n. "arm." |
| arm. | A com. n., neu. gen., s. num., 3rd per., obj. c., gov. by the prep. "under." |
| **2. My** | A pers. pron., com. gen., s. num., 1st per., poss. c., gov. by the n. "sensations." |
| sensations | An abs. n., neu. gen., p. num., 3rd per., nom. c. to the v. "were." |
| were | An irreg. intr. v., indic. m., past t., p. num., 3rd per., agr. with its nom. "sensations." |
| ever | An adv. of time, mod. the v. "were." |
| too | An adv. of deg., mod. the adj. "violent." |
| violent | An adj. of quality, pos. deg., qual. the n. "sensations." |
| to | A particle, indg. infin. m. |
| to permit | A reg. tr. v., act. vo., infin. m., pres. t., gov. by the adj. "violent." |
| my | A pers. pron., com. gen., s. num., 1st per., poss. c., gov. by the ger. "attempting." |
| **attempting** | A ger. from the tr. v. "to attempt," neu. gen., s. num., 3rd per., obj. c., gov. by the tr. v. "to permit." |
| her | A pers. pron., fem. gen., s. num., 3rd per., poss. c., gov. by the n. "rescue." |
| rescue. | An abs. n., neu. gen., s. num., 3rd per., obj. c., gov. by the tr. ger. "attempting." |
| **3. By** | A prep., sh. the rn. bet. "got" and "taking." |
| **taking** | A ger. from the tr. v. "to take," neu. gen., s. num., 3rd per., obj. c., gov. by the prep. "by." |
| current | A com. n., neu. gen., s. num., 3rd per., obj. c., gov. by the tr. ger. "taking." |
| little | An adj. of quantity (bulk or mass), pos. deg., qual. the n. *distance* und. |
| farther | An adj. of quality, comp. deg., qual. the n. *distance* und. |
| up | An adv. of place, mod. the adj. "farther." |
| rest | A com. col. n., neu. gen., s. num., 3rd per., nom. c. to the v. "got." |
| of | A prep., sh. the rn. bet. "rest" and "family." |
| family | A com. col. n., neu. gen., s. num., 3rd per., obj. c., gov. by the prep. "of." |
| got | An irreg. intr. v., indic. m., past t., s. num., 3rd per., agr. with its nom. "rest." |
| safely | An adv. of man., mod. the v. "got." |
| over. | A prep., sh. the rn. bet. "got" and *it* und. |
| **4. Talking** | A verbal or abs. n., neu. gen., s. num., 3rd per., nom. c. to the v. "is." |
| is | An irreg. intr. v., indic. m., pres. t., s. num., 3rd per., agr. with its nom. "talking." |
| not | An adv. of m. (neg.), mod. the adv. "always." |
| always | An adv. of time, mod. the v. "is." |
| to | A particle, indg. infin. m. |
| to converse. | A reg. intr. v., infin. m., pres. t. ; used as an abs. n., neu. gen., s. num., 3rd per., nom. c. after the v. "is." |

| | |
|---|---|
| 5. I | A pers. pron., com. gen., s. num., 1st per., nom. c. to the v. "did consider." |
| did | An aux. v. to "consider," indg. past t., and completing the negative form of the v. |
| not | An adv. of m. (neg.), mod. the v. "did consider." |
| (to) consider | A reg. tr. v., act. vo., infin. m., pres. t., gov. by the v. "did." |
| did consider | A reg. tr. v., act. vo., indic. m., past t., s. num., 1st per., agr. with its nom. "I." |
| impropriety | An abs. n., neu. gen., s. num., 3rd per., obj. c., gov. by the tr. v. "did consider." |
| of | A prep., sh. the rn. bet. "impropriety" and "being." |
| my | A pers. pron., com. gen., s. num., 1st per., poss. c., gov. by the ger. "being." |
| **being** | A ger. from the intr. v. "to be," neu. gen., s. num., 3rd per., obj. c., gov. by the prep. "of." |
| in | A prep., sh. the rn. bet. "being" and "company." |
| such | An adj. of quality, qual. the n. "company." |
| company | A com. col. n., neu. gen., s. num., 3rd per., obj. c., gov. by the prep. "in." |
| till | A cop. conj., jg. the sents. "I..company" and "I...me." |
| I | A pers. pron., com. gen., s. num., 1st per., nom. c. to the v. "saw." |
| saw | An irreg. tr. v., act. vo., indic. m., past t., s. num., 1st. per., agr. with its nom. "I." |
| mob | A com. col. n., neu. gen., s. num., 3rd per., obj. c., gov. by the tr. v. "saw." |
| (to) gather | A reg. intr. v., infin. m., pres. t., gov. by the v. "saw." |
| about | A prep., sh. the rn. bet. "to gather" and "me." |
| me. | A pers. pron., com. gen., s. num., 1st per., obj. c., gov. by the prep. "about." |
| 6 I | A pers. pron., com. gen., s. num., 1st per., nom. c. to the v. "comforted." |
| comforted | A reg. tr. v., act. vo., indic. m., past t., s. num., 1st per., agr. with its nom. "I." |
| myself | A compd. pers. pron., com. gen., s. num., 1st per., obj. c., gov. by the tr. v. "comforted." |
| with | A prep., sh. the rn. bet. "comforted" and "reflecting." |
| **reflecting** | A ger. from the tr. v. "to reflect," neu. gen., s. num., 3rd per., obj. c., gov. by the prep. "with." |
| that | A cop. conj., jg. the sents. "I...reflecting" and "London..mart." |
| London | A prop. n., neu. gen., s. num., 3rd per., nom. c. to the v. "was." |
| was | An irreg. intr. v., indic. m., past t., s. num., 3rd per., agr. with its nom. "London." |
| mart | A com. n., neu. gen., s. num., 3rd per., nom. c. after the v. "was." |
| where | A cop. conj., jg. the sents. "London...mart" and "abilities...distinction." |
| abilities | An abs. n., neu. gen., p. num., 3rd per., nom. c. to the v. "were." |
| of | A prep., sh. the rn. bet. "abilities" and "kind." |
| every | A dist. nu. adj. of quantity, qual. the n. "kind." |
| kind | An abs. n., neu. gen., s. num., 3rd per., obj. c., gov. by the prep. "of." |
| were | An irreg. intr. v., indic. m., past t., p. num., 3rd per., agr. with its nom. "abilities." |
| sure | An adj. of quality, pos. deg., qual. the n. "abilities." |
| of | A prep., sh. the rn. bet. "sure" and "meeting." |
| **meeting** | A ger. from the tr. v. "to meet," neu. gen., s. num., 3rd per., obj. c., gov. by the prep. "of." |
| distinction | An abs. n., neu. gen., s. num., 3rd per., obj. c., gov. by the tr. ger. "meeting." |
| and | A cop. conj., jg. the sents. "abilities...distinction," and "*abilities of every kind were sure of meeting* reward." |
| reward. | An abs. n., neu. gen., s. num., 3rd per., obj. c., gov. by the tr. ger. *meeting* und. |
| 7. Captain | A com. n. tending to prop., mas. gen., s. num., 3rd per., nom. c. to the v. "congratulated" (or, a com. n. used as an adj. of quality, qual. the n. "Hardy"). |

| | |
|---|---|
| Hardy | A prop. n., mas. gen., s. num., 3rd per., nom. c., in app. with "Captain." |
| Captain Hardy | A compd. prop. n., mas. gen., s. num., 3rd per., nom. c. to the v. "congratulated." |
| congratulated | A reg. tr. v., act. vo. indic. m., past t., s. num., 3rd per., agr. with its nom. "Captain" (or, "Captain Hardy"). |
| him | A pers. pron., mas. gen., s. num., 3rd per., obj. c., gov. by the tr. v. "congratulated." |
| on | A prep., sh. the rn. bet. "congratulated" and "having gained." |
| **having gained** } | A compd. ger. from the tr. v. "to gain," neu. gen., s. num., 3rd per., obj. c., gov. by the prep. "on." |
| complete | An adj. of quality, qual. the n. "victory." |
| victory. | An abs. n., neu. gen., s. num., 3rd per., obj. c., gov. by the tr. ger. "having gained." |
| 8. Upon | A prep., sh. the rn. bet. "seemed" and "entering." |
| Mr. | A com. n. tending to prop., mas. gen., s. num., 3rd per., poss. c., gov. by the n. "entering" (or, a com. n. used as an adj. of quality, qual. the n. "Thornhill's"). |
| Thornhill's | A prop. n., mas. gen., s. num., 3rd per., poss. c., in app. with "Mr." |
| Mr. Thornhill's | A compd. prop. n., mas. gen., s. num., 3rd per., poss. c., gov. by the n. "entering." |
| **entering** | A verbal or abs. n., neu. gen., s. num., 3rd per., obj. c., gov. by the prep. "upon." |
| he | A pers. pron., mas. gen., s. num., 3rd per., nom. c. to the v. "seemed." |
| seemed | A reg. intr. v., indic. m., past t., s. num., 3rd per., agr. with its nom. "he." |
| at | A prep., sh. the rn. bet. "to start" and "seeing." |
| **seeing** | A ger. from the tr. v. "to see," neu. gen., s. num., 3rd per., obj. c., gov. by the prep. "at." |
| my | A pers. pron., mas. gen., s. num., 1st per., poss. c., gov. by the n. "son" (my, *i.e.* Vicar of Wakefield's). |
| son | A com. n., mas. gen., s. num., 1st per., obj. c., gov. by the tr. ger. "seeing." |
| and | A cop. conj., jg. the sents. "Upon...son, *to start back*" and "*upon Mr. Thornhill's entering, he seemed, at seeing* me, to start back." |
| me | A pers. pron., mas. gen., s. num., 1st per., obj. c., gov. by the tr. ger. *seeing* und. |
| to | A particle, indg. infin. m. |
| to start | A reg. intr. v., infin. m., pres. t., gov. by the v. "seemed." |
| back. | An adv. of place, mod. the v. "to start." |
| 9. Upon | A prep., sh. the rn. bet. "called" and "bleeding." |
| **bleeding** | A verbal or abs. n., neu. gen., s. num., 3rd per., obj. c., gov by the prep. "upon." |
| of | A prep., sh. the rn. bet. "bleeding" and "wounds." |
| his | A pers. pron., mas. gen., s. num., 3rd per., poss. c., gov. by the n. "wounds." |
| wounds | A com. n., neu. gen., p. num., 3rd per., obj. c., gov. by the prep. "of." |
| he | A pers. pron., mas. gen., s. num., 3rd per., nom. c. to the v "called." |
| called | A reg. tr. v., act. vo., indic. m., past t., s. num., 3rd per., agr., with its nom. "he." |
| unto | A prep., sh. the rn. bet. "called" and "him." |
| him | A pers. pron., mas. gen., s. num., 3rd per., obj. c., gov. by the prep. "unto." |
| one | A def. card. nu. adj. of quantity, qual. the n *flatterer* und. |
| of | A prep., sh. the rn. bet. *flatterer* und. and "flatterers." |
| his | A pers. pron., mas. gen., s. num., 3rd per., poss. c., gov. by the n. "flatterers." |
| flatterers. | A com. n., com. gen., p. num., 3rd per., obj. c., gov. by the prep. "of." |
| 10. We | A pers. pron., com. gen., p. num., 1st per., nom. c. to the v. "rode." |
| rode | An irreg. intr. v., indic. m., past t., p. num., 1st per., agr. with its nom. "we." |
| over | A prep., sh. the rn. bet. "rode" and "Downs." |

| | |
|---|---|
| Castlewood | A prop. adj. of quality, qual. the n. "Downs." |
| Downs | A com. n. tending to prop., neu. gen., p. num., 3rd per., obj. c., gov. by the prep. "over." |
| Castlewood } Downs } | A compd. prop. n., neu. gen., p. num., 3rd per., obj. c., gov. by the prep. "over." |
| before | A prep., sh. the rn. bet. "rode" and "breaking." |
| **breaking** | A verbal or abs. n., neu. gen., s. num., 3rd per., obj. c., gov. by the prep. "before." |
| of | A prep., sh. the rn. bet. "breaking" and "dawn." |
| dawn. | An abs. n., neu. gen., s. num., 3rd per., obj. c., gov. by the prep. "of." |

## Exercise 176.

| | |
|---|---|
| 1. Cassius | A prop. n., mas. gen., s. num., 3rd per., nom. c. to the v. "hath." |
| **hath** | An irreg. tr. v., act. vo., indic. m., pres. t., s. num., 3rd per., agr. with its nom. "Cassius." |
| lean | An adj. of quality, pos. deg., qual. the n. *look* und. |
| and | A cop. conj., jg. the sents. "Cassius hath a lean *look*" and "*Cassius hath a* hungry look." |
| hungry | An adj. of quality, pos. deg., qual. the n. "look." |
| look. | An abs. n., neu. gen., s. num., 3rd per., obj. c., gov. by the tr. v. *hath* und. |
| 2. Maidens | A com. n., fem. gen., p. num., 3rd per., nom. c. to the v. "wear." |
| still | An adv. of time, mod. the v. "wear." |
| **wear** | An irreg. tr. v., act. vo., indic. m., pres. t., p. num., 3rd per., agr. with its nom. "maidens." |
| their | A pers. pron., fem. gen., p. num., 3rd per., poss. c., gov. by the n. "caps." |
| Norman | A prop. adj. of quality, qual. the n. "caps." |
| caps. | A com. n., neu. gen., p. num., 3rd per., obj. c., gov. by the tr. v. "wear." |
| 3. One | A def. card. nu. adj. of quantity, qual. the n. "step." |
| devious | An adj. of quality, pos. deg., qual. the n. "step." |
| step | An abs. n., neu. gen., s. num., 3rd per., nom. c. to the v. "may lead." |
| at | A prep., sh. the rn. bet. *made* und. and *start* und. |
| first | A def. ord. nu. adj. of quantity, qual. the n. *start* und. |
| at first | An adverbial phrase of time, mod. the pl. *made* und. |
| may | An aux. v. to "lead," indg. pot. m., pres. t. |
| (to) lead | An irreg. intr. v., infin. m., pres. t., gov. by the v. "may." |
| **may lead** | An irreg. intr. v., pot. m., pres. t., s. num., 3rd per., agr. with its nom. "step." |
| into | A prep., sh. the rn. bet. "may lead" and "course." |
| **course** | An abs. n., neu. gen., s. num., 3rd per., obj. c., gov. by the prep. "into." |
| of | A prep., sh. the rn. bet. "course" and "vice." |
| habitual | An adj. of quality, qual. the n. "vice." |
| vice. | An abs. n., neu. gen., s. num., 3rd per., obj. c., gov. by the prep. "of." |
| 4. Icebergs | A com. n., neu. gen., p. num., 3rd per., nom. c. to the v. "are." |
| **are** | An irreg. intr. v., indic. m., pres. t., p. num., 3rd per., agr. with its nom. "icebergs." |
| of | A prep., sh. the rn. bet. "are" and "sizes." |
| various | An adj. of quality, qual. the n. "sizes." |
| sizes. | An abs. n., neu. gen., p. num., 3rd per., obj. c., gov. by the prep. "of." |
| 5. Sir | A com. n. tending to prop., mas. gen., s. num., 3rd per., nom. c. to the v. "was struck" (or, a com. n. tending to prop., used as an adj. of quality, qual. the n. "John"). |
| John | A prop. n., mas. gen., s. num., 3rd per., nom. c., in app. with "Sir" (or, a prop. n., forming with "Sir" a compd. prop. n. which is used as an adj. of quality, qual. the n. "Moore"). |
| Moore | A prop. n., mas. gen., s. num., 3rd per., nom. c., in app. with "John." |
| Sir John Moore | A compd. prop. n., mas. gen., s. num., 3rd per., nom. c. to the v. "was struck." |

ENGLISH GRAMMAR AND ANALYSIS. 203

| | |
|---|---|
| while | A cop. conj., jg. the sents. "Sir John Moore was struck...shot" and "*he was* earnestly...fight." |
| earnestly | An adv. of man., mod. the v. "*was* watching." |
| **watching** | A pres. pl. from the tr. v. "to watch," ref. to *he* und. |
| result | An abs. n., neu. gen., s. num., 3rd per., obj. c., gov. by the tr. v. "*was* watching." |
| of | A prep., sh. the rn. bet. "result" and "fight." |
| fight | An abs. n., neu. gen., s. num., 3rd per., obj. c., gov. by the prep. "of." |
| was | An aux. v. to "struck," indg. pass. vo., past t. |
| struck | A past pl. from the tr. v. "to strike," ref. to "Sir" (or "Sir John Moore"). |
| **was struck** | An irreg. tr. v., pass. vo., indic. m., past t., s. num., 3rd per., agr. with its nom. "Sir" (or "Sir John Moore"). |
| on | A prep., sh. the rn. bet. "was struck" and "breast." |
| left | An adj. of quality, qual. the n. "breast." |
| breast | A com. n., neu. gen., s. num., 3rd per., obj. c., gov. by the prep. "on." |
| by | A prep., sh. the rn. bet. "was struck" and "shot." |
| cannon | A com. n. used as an adj. of quality, qual. the n. "shot." |
| shot. | A com. n., neu. gen., s. num., 3rd per., obj. c., gov. by the prep. "by." |
| 6. It | A pers. pron., neu. gen., s. num., 3rd per., nom. c. to the v. "is." |
| **is** | An irreg. intr. v., indic. m., pres. t., s. num., 3rd per., agr. with its nom. "it." |
| one | A def. card. nu. adj. of quantity, qual. the n. "thing." |
| thing | A com. n., neu. gen., s. num., 3rd per., nom. c. after the v. "is." |
| to | A particle, indg. infin. m. |
| be | An aux. v. to "tempted," indg. pass. vo. |
| tempted | A past pl. from the tr. v. "to tempt," ref. to *person* und. |
| **to be tempted** | A reg. tr. v., pass. vo., infin. m., pres. t. ; used as an abs. n., neu. gen., s. num., 3rd per., nom. c., in app. with "it." |
| Escalus | A prop. n., mas. gen., s. num., 2nd per., nom. c. of add. |
| another | An indef. nu. adj. of quantity, qual. the n. "thing." |
| thing | A com. n., neu. gen., s. num., 3rd per., nom. c. after the v. *is* und. |
| to | A particle, indg. infin. m. |
| **to fall.** | An irreg. intr. v., infin. m., pres. t. ; used as an abs. n., neu. gen., s. num., 3rd per., nom. c., in app. with *it* und. (*It*, viz., to fall, *is* another thing.) |

## Exercise 177.

| | |
|---|---|
| 1. **Where** | An interrog. adv. of place, mod. the v. "shall meet." |
| shall | An aux. v. to "meet," indg. fut. t. |
| we | A pers. pron., com. gen., p. num., 1st per., nom. c. to the v. "shall meet." |
| **sometimes** | An adv. of time, mod. the v. "shall meet." |
| (to) meet | An irreg. intr. v., infin. m., pres. t., gov. by the v. "shall." |
| shall meet. | An irreg. intr. v., indic. m., fut. t., p. num., 1st per., agr. with its nom. "we." |
| 2. He | A pers. pron., mas. gen., s. num., 3rd per., nom. c. to the v. "speaks." |
| speaks | An irreg. intr. v., indic. m., pres. t., s. num., 3rd per., agr. with its nom. "he." |
| **like** | An adv. of man., mod. the v. "speaks." |
| man. | A com. n., mas. gen., s. num., 3rd per., obj. c., gov. by the prep. *to* und. |
| 3. I | A pers. pron., com. gen., s. num., 1st per., nom. c. to the v. "had forgotten." |
| had | An aux. v. to "forgotten," indg. pluperf. t. |
| **almost** | An adv. of deg., mod. the v. "had forgotten." |
| forgotten | A past pl. from the tr. v. "to forget," ref. to "him." |
| had forgotten | An irreg. tr. v., act. vo., indic. m., pluperf. t., s. num., 1st per., agr. with its nom. "I." |
| him. | A pers. pron., mas. gen., s. num., 3rd per., obj. c., gov. by the tr. v. "had forgotten." |

| | |
|---|---|
| 4. Command | A reg. tr. v., act. vo., imper. m., pres. t., s. or p. num., 2nd per. agr. with its nom. *thou* or *you* und. |
| me | A pers. pron., com. gen., s. num., 1st per., obj. c., gov. by the tr. v. "command." |
| **absolutely** | An adv. of man., mod. the v. "command." |
| **not** | An adv. of m. (neg.), mod. the v. "to go." |
| to | A particle, indg. infin. m. |
| to go. | An irreg. intr. v., infin. m., pres. t., gov. by the v. "command." |
| 5. Instances | An abs. n., neu. gen., p. num., 3rd per., nom. c. to the v. "are." |
| of | A prep., sh. the rn. bet. "instances" and "longevity." |
| longevity | An abs. n., neu. gen., s. num., 3rd per., obj. c., gov. by the prep. "of." |
| are (=exist) | An irreg. intr. v., indic. m., pres. t., p. num., 3rd per., agr. with its nom. "instances." |
| **chiefly** | An adv. of deg., mod. the v. "are." |
| among | A prep., sh. the rn. bet. "are" and *persons* und. |
| abstemious. | An adj. of quality, pos. deg., qual. the n. *persons* und. |
| 6. Act | A reg. tr. v., act. vo., imper. m., pres. t., s. num., p. form, 2nd per., agr. with its nom. *you* und. |
| **well** | An adv. of man., mod. the v. "act." |
| your | A pers. pron., com. gen., s. num., p. form, 2nd per., poss. c., gov. by the n. "part." |
| part | An abs. n., neu. gen., s. num., 3rd per., obj. c., gov. by the tr. v. "act." |
| **there** | An adv. of place, mod. the v. "lies." |
| all | An adj. of quantity (bulk or mass), qual. the n. "honour." |
| honour | An abs. n., neu. gen., s. num., 3rd per., nom. c. to the v. "lies." |
| lies. | An irreg. intr. v., indic. m., pres. t., s. num., 3rd per., agr. with its nom. "honour." |
| 7. storm | A com. n., neu. gen., s. num., 3rd per., nom. c. to the v. "bursts." |
| bursts | An irreg. intr. v., indic. m., pres. t., s. num., 3rd per., agr. with its nom. "storm." |
| **overhead.** | An adv. of place, mod. the v. "bursts." |
| 8. Penn | A prop. n., mas. gen., s. num., 3rd per., nom. c. to the v. "dealt." |
| dealt | An irreg. intr. v., indic. m., past t., s. num., 3rd per., agr. with its nom. "Penn." |
| **justly** | An adv. of man., mod. the v. "dealt." |
| and | A cop. conj., jg. the sents. "Penn dealt justly *with the Indians*" and "*Penn dealt* kindly with the Indians." |
| **kindly** | An adv. of man., mod. the v. *dealt* und. |
| with | A prep., sh. the rn. bet. *dealt* und. and "Indians." |
| Indians. | A prop. n., com. gen., p. num., 3rd per., obj. c., gov. by the prep. "with." |
| 9. I | A pers. pron., com. gen., s. num., 1st per., nom. c. to the v. "missed." |
| missed | A reg. tr. v., act. vo., indic. m., past t., s. num., 1st per., agr. with its nom. "I." |
| him | A pers. pron., mas. gen., s. num., 3rd per., obj. c., gov. by the tr. v. "missed." |
| all | An adj. of quantity (bulk or mass), qual. the n. "day." |
| day | An abs. n., neu. gen., s. num., 3rd per., obj. c., gov. by the prep. *during* und. |
| long | An adj. of quality, pos. deg., qual. the n. "day." |
| and | A cop. conj., jg. the sents. "I..long" and "*I* knew..then." |
| knew | An irreg. tr. v., act. vo., indic. m., past t., s. num., 1st per., agr. with its nom. *I* und. |
| **not** | An adv. of m. (neg.), mod. the v. "knew." |
| till | A prep., sh. the rn. bet. "knew" and *time* und. (or bet. "knew" and "then.") |
| **then** | An adv. of time, mod. the pl. *existing*\* und. (or, an adv. used as an abs. n., neu. gen., s. num., 3rd per., obj. c., gov. by the prep. "till.") |
| **till then** | An adverbial phrase of time, mod. the v. "knew." |

\* Till *time* then *existing*. *Parsing*, p. 152.

| | |
|---|---|
| how | A cop. conj., jg. the sents. "*I* knew..then" and "much..him." |
| much | An adv. of deg., mod. the v. "had loved." |
| I | A pers. pron., com. gen., s. num., 1st per., nom. c. to the v. "had loved." |
| had | An aux. v. to "loved," indg. pluperf. t. |
| loved | A past pl. from the tr. v. "to love," ref. to "him." |
| had loved | A reg. tr. v., act. vo., indic. m., pluperf. t., s. num., 1st per., agr. with its nom. "I." |
| him. | A pers. pron., mas. gen., s. num., 3rd per., obj. c., gov. by the tr. v. "had loved." |
| 10. **Smoothly** | An adv. of man., mod. the v. "glides." |
| but | A disj. conj., jg. the sents. "Smoothly he glides over" and "quickly *he glides over*." |
| **quickly** | An adv. of man., mod. the v. *glides* und. |
| as | A cop. conj., jg. the sents. "quickly *he glides over*" and "an arrow's flight *glides over*." |
| arrow's | A com. n., neu. gen., s. num., 3rd per., poss. c., gov. by the n. "flight." |
| flight | An abs. n., neu. gen., s. num., 3rd per., nom. c. to the v. *glides* und. |
| he | A pers. pron., mas. gen., s. num., 3rd per., nom. c. to the v. "glides." |
| glides | A reg. intr. v., indic. m., pres. t., s. num., 3rd per., agr. with its nom. "he." |
| **over** | An adv. of place, mod. the v. "glides." |
| and | A cop. conj., jg. the sents. "smoothly..over" and "*he is*..more." |
| is | An aux. v. to "seen," indg. pass. vo., pres. t. |
| seen | A past pl. from the tr. v. "to see," ref. to *he* und. |
| is seen | An irreg. tr. v., pass. vo., indic. m., pres. t., s. num., 3rd per., agr. with its nom. *he* und. |
| **no** | An adv. of m. (neg.), mod. the adv. "more." |
| **more.** | An adv. of time, mod. the v. "is seen." |
| 11. **Now** | An adv. of time, mod. the v. "close." |
| my | A pers. pron., com. gen., s. num., 1st per., poss. c., gov. by the n. "lips." |
| weary | An adj. of quality, pos. deg., qual. the n. "lips." |
| **lips** | A com. n., neu. gen., p. num., 3rd per., obj. c., gov. by the tr. v. "close." |
| I | A pers. pron., com. gen., s. num., 1st per., nom. c. to the v. "close." |
| close. | A reg. tr. v., act. vo., indic. m., pres. t., s. num., 1st per., agr. with its nom "I." |
| 12. He | A pers. pron., mas. gen., s. num., 3rd per., nom. c. to the v. "had loved." |
| had | An aux. v. to "loved," indg. pluperf. t. |
| **always** | An adv. of time, mod. the v. "had loved." |
| loved | A past pl. from the tr. v. "to love," ref. to "books." |
| had loved | A reg. tr. v., act. vo., indic. m., pluperf. t., s. num., 3rd per., agr. with its nom. "he." |
| books | A com. n., neu. gen., p. num., 3rd per., obj. c., gov. by the tr. v. "had loved." |
| and | A cop. conj., jg. the sents. "He..books" and "they..him." |
| they | A pers. pron., neu. gen., p. num., 3rd per., nom. c. to the v. "were." |
| were | An irreg. intr. v., indic. m., past t., p. num., 3rd per., agr. with its nom. "they." |
| **now** | An adv. of time, mod. the v. "were." |
| necessary | An adj. of quality, pos. deg., qual. the pron. "they." |
| to | A prep., sh. the rn. bet. "necessary" and "him." |
| him. | A pers. pron., mas. gen., s. num., 3rd per., obj. c., gov. by the prep. "to." |
| 13. **Where** | An interrog. adv. of place, mod. the v. "is." |
| is | An irreg. intr. v., indic. m., pres. t., s. num., 3rd per., agr. with its nom. "mother." |
| mother | A com. n., fem. gen., s. num., 3rd per., nom. c. to the v. "is." |
| that | A rel. pron., fem. gen., s. num., 3rd per., agr. with its ant. "mother," nom. c. to the v. "looked." |

| | |
|---|---|
| looked | A reg. intr. v., indic. m., past t., s. num., 3rd per., agr. with its nom. "that." |
| on | A prep., sh. the rn. bet. "looked" and "childhood." |
| my | A pers. pron., com. gen., s. num., 1st per., poss. c., gov. by the n. "childhood." |
| childhood. | An abs. n., neu. gen., s. num., 3rd per., obj. c., gov. by the prep. "on." |
| 14. **Whence** | An interrog. adv. of place, mod. the v. "come." |
| come | An irreg. intr. v., indic. m., pres. t., p. num., or s. num., p. form, 2nd per., agr. with its nom. "you." |
| you. | A pers. pron., com. gen., p. num., or s. num., p. form, 2nd per., nom. c. to the v. "come." |
| 15. thing | A com. n., neu. gen., s. num., 3rd per., nom. c. to the v. "is." |
| of | A prep., sh. the rn. bet. "thing" and "beauty." |
| beauty | An abs. n., neu. gen., s. num., 3rd per., obj. c., gov. by the prep. "of." |
| is | An irreg. intr. v., indic. m., pres. t., s. num., 3rd per., agr. with its nom. "thing." |
| joy | An abs. n., neu. gen., s. num., 3rd per., nom. c. after the v. "is." |
| for | A prep., sh. the rn. bet. "is" and *time* und. (For *time* ever continuing.) |
| **ever** | An adv. of time, mod. the pl. *continuing* und. |
| **for ever.** | An adverbial phrase of time, mod. the v. "is." |
| 16. They | A pers. pron., com. gen., p. num., 3rd per., nom. c. to the v. "strolled." |
| strolled | A reg. intr. v., indic. m., past t., p. num., 3rd per., agr. with its nom. "they." |
| up | A prep., sh. the rn. bet. "strolled" and *walks* und. |
| and | A cop. conj., jg. the sents. "They strolled up *the terrace walks, talking incessantly*" and "*they strolled* down..incessantly." |
| down | A prep., sh. the rn. bet. *strolled* und. and "walks." |
| terrace | A com. n. used as an adj. of quality, qual. the n. "walks." |
| walks | A com. n., neu. gen., p. num., 3rd per., obj. c., gov. by the prep. "down." |
| talking | A pres. pl. from the tr. v. "to talk," ref. to "they." |
| **incessantly.** | An adv. of man., mod. the pl. "talking." |
| 17. She | A pers. pron., fem. gen., s. num., 3rd per., nom. c. to the v. "did know." |
| did | An aux. v. to "know," indg. past t., and completing the negative form of the v. |
| **not** | An adv. of m. (neg.), mod. the v. "did know." |
| (to) know | An irreg. tr. v., act. vo., infin. m., pres. t., gov. by the v. "did." |
| did know | An irreg. tr. v., act. vo., indic. m., past t., s. num., 3rd per., agr. with its nom. "she." |
| him. | A pers. pron., mas. gen., s. num., 3rd per., obj. c., gov. by the tr. v. "did know." |
| 18. **Yea** | An adv. of m. (aff.) |
| slimy | An adj. of quality, pos. deg., qual. the n. "things." |
| things | A com. n., com. gen., p. num., 3rd per., nom. c. to the v. "did crawl." |
| did | An aux. v. to "crawl," indg. past t., emph. form. |
| (to) crawl | A reg. intr. v., infin. m., pres. t., gov. by the v. "did." |
| did crawl | A reg. intr. v., indic. m., past t., p. num., 3rd per., agr. with its nom. "things." |
| with | A prep., sh. the rn. bet. "did crawl" and "legs." |
| legs | A com. n., neu. gen., p. num., 3rd per., obj. c., gov. by the prep. "with." |
| Upon | A prep., sh. the rn. bet. "did crawl" and "sea." |
| slimy | An adj. of quality, pos. deg., qual. the n. "sea." |
| sea. | A com. n., neu. gen., s. num., 3rd per., obj. c., gov. by the prep. "upon." |
| 19. Touch | A reg. tr. v., act. vo., imper. m., pres. t., s. or p. num., 2nd per., agr. with its nom *thou* or *you* und. |
| her | A pers. pron., fem. gen., s. num., 3rd per., obj. c., gov. by the tr. v. "touch." |
| **not** | An adv. of m. (neg.), mod. the v. "touch." |
| **scornfully** | An adv. of man., mod. the v. "touch." |

| | | |
|---|---|---|
| | Think | An irreg. intr. v., imper. m., pres. t., s. or p. num., 2nd per., agr. with its nom. *thou* or *you* und. |
| | of | A prep., sh. the rn. bet. "think" and "her." |
| | her | A pers. pron., fem. gen., s. num., 3rd per., obj. c., gov. by the prep. "of." |
| | **mournfully** | An adv. of man., mod. the v. "think." |
| | **Gently** | An adv. of man., mod. the v. "think." |
| | and | A cop. conj., jg. the sents. "*think of her* gently" and "*think of her* humanly." |
| | **humanly.** | An adv. of man., mod. the v. *think* und. |
| 20. | **Swiftly** | An adv. of man., mod. the v. "flew." |
| | **swiftly** | An adv. of man., mod. the v. "flew." |
| | flew | An irreg. intr. v., indic. m., past t., s. num., 3rd per., agr. with its nom. "ship." |
| | ship | A com. n., fem. gen. by personification, s. num., 3rd per., nom. c. to the v. "flew." |
| | Yet | A disj. conj., jg. the sents. "Swiftly..ship" and "she..too." |
| | she | A pers. pron., fem. gen., s. num., 3rd per., nom. c. to the v. "sailed." |
| | sailed | A reg. intr. v., indic. m., past t., s. num., 3rd per., agr. with its nom. "she." |
| | **softly** | An adv. of man., mod. the v. "sailed." |
| | **too** | An adv. of deg., mod. the v. "sailed. |
| | **Sweetly** | An adv. of man., mod. the v. "blew." |
| | **sweetly** | An adv. of man., mod. the v. "blew." |
| | blew | An irreg. intr. v., indic. m., past t., s. num., 3rd per., agr. with its nom. "breeze." |
| | breeze | A com. n., neu. gen., s. num., 3rd per., nom. c. to the v. "blew." |
| | On | A prep., sh. the rn. bet. "blew" and "me." |
| | me | A pers. pron., mas. gen., s. num., 1st per., obj. c., gov. by the prep. "on." (Me, *i.e.*, the ancient mariner.) |
| | alone | An adj. of qual., qual. the pron. "me." |
| | it | A pers. pron., neu. gen., s. num., 3rd. per., nom. c. to the v. "blew." |
| | blew. | An irreg. intr. v., indic. m., past t., s. num., 3rd per., agr. with its nom. "it." |

## Exercise 178.

| | | |
|---|---|---|
| 1. | **Then** | An adv. of time, mod. the v. "ceased." |
| | ceased | A reg. intr. v., indic. m., past t., s. num., 3rd per., agr. with its nom. "storm." |
| | storm. | A com. n., neu. gen., s. num., 3rd per., nom. c. to the v. "ceased." |
| 2. | His | A pers. pron., mas. gen., s. num., 3rd per., poss. c., gov. by the n. "hands." |
| | hands | A com. n., neu. gen., p. num., 3rd per., nom. c. to the v. "were." |
| | were | An irreg. intr. v., indic. m., past t., p. num., 3rd per., agr. with its nom. "hands." |
| | **enormously** | An adv. of deg., mod. the adj. "large." |
| | large. | An adj. of quality, pos. deg., qual. the n. "hands." |
| 3. | I | A pers. pron., com. gen., s. num., 1st per., nom. c. to the v. "linger." |
| | linger | A reg. intr. v., indic. m., pres. t., s. num., 1st. per., agr. with its nom. "I." |
| | **yet** | An adv. of time, mod. the v. "linger." |
| | with | A prep., sh. the rn. bet. "linger" and "nature." |
| | nature. | An abs. n., neu. gen., s. num., 3rd per., obj. c., gov. by the prep. "with." |
| 4. | Put | An irreg. tr. v., act. vo., imper. m., pres. t., p. num., 2nd per., agr. with its nom. "*you*" und. |
| | **not** | An adv. of m. (neg.), mod. the v. "put." |
| | your | A pers. pron., com. gen., p. num., 2nd per., poss. c., gov. by the n. "trust." |
| | trust | An abs. n., neu. gen., s. num., 3rd per., obj. c., gov. by the tr. v. "put." |
| | in | A prep., sh. the rn. bet. "put" and "princes." |

| | | |
|---|---|---|
| | princes. | A com. n., mas. gen., p. num., 3rd per., obj. c., gov. by the prep. "in." |
| 5. | **How** | An interrog. adv. of man., mod. the v. "came." |
| | came | An irreg. intr. v., indic. m., past t., s. num., 3rd per., agr. with its nom. "it." |
| | it | A pers. pron., neu. gen., s. num., 3rd per., nom. c. to the v. "came." |
| | **there.** | An adv. of place, mod. the v. "came." |
| 6. | To | A prep., sh. the rn. bet. "true" and "self." |
| | thine | A pers. pron., forming with the adj. "own" a compd. pers. pron. |
| | own | An intensive adj. of quality, qual. the n. "self." |
| | thine own | A compd. pers. pron., mas. gen., s. num., 2nd per., poss. c., gov. by the n. "self." |
| | self | A com. n., neu. gen., s. num., 3rd per., obj. c., gov. by the prep. "to." |
| | be | An irreg. intr. v., imper. m., pres. t., s. num., 2nd per., agr. with its nom. *thou* und. |
| | true | An adj. of quality, pos. deg., qual. the pron. *thou* und. |
| | and | A cop. conj., jg. the sents. "To..true" and "it must follow." |
| | it | A pers. pron., neu. gen., s. num., 3rd per., nom. c. to the v. "must follow." |
| | must | An aux. v. to "follow," indg. pot. m., pres. t. |
| | (to) follow | A reg. intr. v., infin. m., pres. t., gov. by the v. "must." |
| | must follow | A reg. intr. v., pot. m., pres. t., s. num., 3rd per., agr. with its nom. "it." |
| | as | A cop. conj., jg. the sents. "it must follow" and "the night *follows* the day." |
| | night | An abs. n., neu. gen., s. num., 3rd per., nom. c. to the v. *follows* und. |
| | day | An abs. n., neu. gen., s. num., 3rd per., obj. c., gov. by the tr. v. *follows* und. |
| | thou | A pers. pron., mas. gen., s. num., 2nd per., nom. c. to the v. "canst be." |
| | canst | An aux. v. to "be," indg. pot. m., pres. t. |
| | **not** | An adv. of m. (neg.), mod. the v. "canst be." |
| | then | An adv. of time, mod. the v. "canst be." |
| | (to) be | An irreg. intr. v., infin. m., pres. t., gov. by the v. "canst." |
| | canst be | An irreg. intr. v., pot. m., pres. t., s. num., 2nd per., agr. with its nom. "thou." |
| | false | An adj. of quality, qual. the pron. "thou." |
| | to | A prep., sh. the rn. bet. "false" and "man." |
| | any | An indef. nu. adj. of quantity, qual. the n. "man." |
| | man. | A com. n., mas. gen., s. num., 3rd per., obj. c., gov. by the prep. "to." |
| 7. | I | A pers. pron., com. gen., s. num., 1st per., nom. c. to the v. "cry." |
| | cry | A reg. intr. v., indic. m., pres. t., s. num., 1st per., agr. with its nom. "I." |
| | out | An adv. of man., mod. the v. "cry." |
| | too | An adv. of deg., mod. the adv. "late." |
| | late | An adv. of time, mod. the v. "cry." |
| | to | A particle, indg. infin. m. |
| | to save. | A reg. intr. v., infin. m., pres. t., gov. by the n. *order* und. (Too late *in order* to save.) N.B.—"To save" may be called infin. of purpose, gov. by the v. "cry." |
| 8. | Duncan | A prop. n., mas. gen., s. num., 3rd per., nom c. to the v. "comes." |
| | comes | An irreg. intr. v., indic. m., pres. t., s. num., 3rd per., agr. with its nom. "Duncan." |
| | here | An adv. of place, mod. the v. "comes." |
| | to-night. | An adv. of time, mod the v. "comes." |
| 9. | They | A pers. pron., com. gen., p. num., 3rd per., nom. c. to the v. "were overtaken." |
| | were | An aux. v. to "overtaken," indg. pass. vo., past t. |
| | **soon** | An adv. of time, mod. the v. "were overtaken." |
| | overtaken | A past pl. from the tr. v. "to overtake," ref. to "they." |
| | were overtaken. | An irreg. tr. v., pass. vo., indic. m., past t., p. num., 3rd per., agr. with its nom. "they." |
| 10. | **Merrily** | An adv. of man., mod. the v. "goes." |
| | merrily | An adv. of man., mod. the v. "goes." |

| | |
|---|---|
| goes | An irreg. intr. v., indic. m., pres. t., s. num., 3rd per., agr. with its nom. "bark." |
| bark | A com. n., neu. gen., s. num., 3rd per., nom. c. to the v. "goes." |
| On | A prep., sh. the rn. bet. "goes" and "breeze." |
| breeze | A com. n., neu. gen., s. num., 3rd per., obj. c., gov. by the prep. "on." |
| from | A prep., sh. the rn. bet. "breeze" and "northward." |
| northward | A com. n., neu. gen., s. num., 3rd per., obj. c., gov. by the prep. "from." |
| free. | An adj. of quality, pos. deg., qual. the n. "breeze." |

## Exercise 179.

N.B.—The preposition-verbs are here parsed as such ; but it should be borne in mind that the verb and preposition may be parsed separately in the ordinary way. See *Parsing*, p. 148.

| | |
|---|---|
| 1. He | A pers. pron., mas. gen., s. num., 3rd per., nom. c. to the prep. v. "spoke-of." |
| **spoke-of** | An irreg. tr. prep.-v., act. vo., indic. m., past t., s. num., 3rd per., agr. with its nom. "he." |
| Queen | A com. n. tending to prop., fem. gen., s. num., 3rd per., obj. c., gov. by the tr. prep.-v. "spoke-of." |
| of | A prep., sh. the rn. bet. "Queen" and "Scots." |
| Scots. | A prop. n., com. gen., p. num., 3rd per., obj. c., gov. by the prep. "of." |
| 2. He | A pers. pron., mas. gen., s. num., 3rd per., nom. c. to the prep.-v. "spake-to." |
| **spake-to** | An irreg. tr. prep.-v., act. vo., indic. m., past t., s. num., 3rd per., agr. with its nom. "he." |
| deaf | An adj. of quality, qual. the n. "audience." |
| audience. | A com. col. n., neu. gen., s. num., 3rd per., obj. c., gov. by the tr. prep.-v. "spake-to." |
| 3. He | A pers. pron., mas. gen., s. num., 3rd per., nom. c. to the prep.-v. "spoke-of." |
| **spoke-of** | An irreg. tr. prep.-v., act. vo., indic. m., past t., s. num., 3rd per., agr. with its nom. "he." |
| many | An indef. nu. adj. of quantity, pos. deg., qual. the n. "places." |
| strange | An adj. of quality, pos. deg., qual. the n. "places." |
| places. | A com. n., neu. gen., p. num., 3rd per., obj. c., gov. by the tr. prep.-v. "spoke-of." |
| 4. We | A pers. pron., com. gen., p. num., 1st per., nom. c. to the prep.-v. "despair-of." |
| **despair-of** | A reg. tr. prep.-v., act. vo., indic. m., pres. t., p. num., 1st per., agr. with its nom. "we." |
| even | An adv. of deg., mod. the prep.-v. "despair-of." |
| life. | An abs. n., neu. gen., s. num., 3rd per., obj. c., gov. by the tr. prep.-v. "despair-of." |
| 5. voyagers | A com. n., com. gen., p. num., 3rd per., nom. c. to the prep.-v. "met-with." |
| **met-with** | An irreg. tr. prep.-v., act. vo., indic. m., past t., p. num., 3rd per., agr. with its nom. "voyagers." |
| many | An indef. nu. adj. of quantity, pos. deg., qual. the n. "disasters." |
| disasters | An abs. n., neu. gen., p. num., 3rd per., obj. c., gov. by the tr. prep.-v. "met-with." |
| on | A prep., sh. the rn. bet. "met-with" and "way." |
| way. | A com. n., neu. gen., s. num., 3rd per., obj. c., gov. by the prep. "on." |
| 6. rustics | A com. n., com. gen., p. num., 3rd per., nom. c. to the prep.-v. "wondered-at." |
| **wondered-at** | A reg. tr. prep.-v., act. vo., indic. m., past t., p. num., 3rd per., agr. with its nom. "rustics." |
| his | A pers. pron., mas. gen., s. num., 3rd per., poss. c., gov. by the n. "agility." |
| agility. | An abs. n., neu. gen., s. num., 3rd per., obj. c., gov. by the tr. prep.-v. "wondered-at." |

| | |
|---|---|
| 7. We | A pers. pron., mas. gen., p. num., 1st per., nom. c. to the prep.-v. "thought-of." |
| bitterly | An adv. of man., mod. the prep.-v. "thought-of." |
| **thought-of** | An irreg. tr. prep.-v., act. vo., indic. m., past t., p. num., 1st per., agr. with its nom. "we." |
| morrow. | An abs. n., neu. gen., s. num., 3rd per., obj. c., gov. by the tr. prep.-v. "thought-of.' |
| 8. prince | A com. n., mas. gen., s. num., 3rd per., nom. c. to the v. "affected." |
| affected | A reg. tr. v., act. vo., indic. m., past t., s. num., 3rd per., agr. with its nom. "prince." |
| to | A particle, indg. infin. m. |
| **to com-plain-of** } | A reg. tr. prep.-v., act. vo., infin. m., pres. t. ; used as an abs. n., neu. gen., s. num., 3rd per., obj. c., gov. by the tr. v. "affected." |
| insincerity | An abs. n., neu. gen., s. num., 3rd per., obj. c., gov. by the tr. prep.-v. "to complain-of." |
| of | A prep., sh. the rn. bet. "insincerity" and "Greeks." |
| Greeks. | A prop. n., com. gen., p. num., 3rd per., obj. c., gov. by the prep. "of." |
| 9. king | A com. n., mas. gen., s. num., 3rd per., nom. c. to the prep.-v. "sided-with." |
| **sided-with** | A reg. tr. prep.-v., act. vo., indic. m., past t., s. num., 3rd per., agr. with its nom. "king." |
| bolder | An adj. of quality, comp. deg., qual. the n. "party." |
| party. | A com. col. n., neu. gen., s. num., 3rd per., obj. c., gov. by the tr. prep.-v. "sided-with." |
| 10. governor | A com. n., mas. gen., s. num., 3rd per., nom. c. to the prep.-v. "connived-at." |
| **connived-at** | A reg. tr. prep.-v., act. vo., indic. m., past t., s. num., 3rd per., agr. with its nom. "governor." |
| his | A pers. pron., mas. gen., s. num., 3rd per., poss. c., gov. by the n. "escape." |
| escape. | An abs. n., neu. gen., s. num., 3rd per., obj. c., gov. by the tr. prep.-v. "connived-at." |

## Exercise 180.

Regard *for, to* ; worthy *of* ; resolve *on, upon* ; confer *on, upon, with* ; avert *from* ; averse *to, from* ; deficient *in* ; correspond *with, to* ; triumph *over* ; accuse *of* ; devolve *on, upon* ; dissent *from* ; differ *with, from* ; glad *of* ; bestow *upon* ; warn *of* ; expert *at, in* ; profit *by* ; sympathy *with* ; smile *at, upon*.

## Exercise 181.

| | |
|---|---|
| 1. He | A pers. pron., mas. gen., s. num., 3rd per., nom. c. to the v. "was." |
| was | An irreg. intr. v., indic. m., past t., s. num., 3rd per., agr. with its nom. "he." |
| ignorant | An adj. of quality, pos. deg., qual. the pron. "he." |
| **of** | A prep., sh. the rn. bet. "ignorant" and "letters." |
| letters. | A com. n., neu. gen., p. num., 3rd per., obj. c., gov. by the prep. "of." |
| 2. hero | A com. n., mas. gen., s. num., 3rd per., nom. c. to the v. "could depend." |
| could | An aux. v. to "depend," indg. pot. m., past t. |
| not | An adv. of m. (neg.), mod. the v. "could depend." |
| (to) depend | A reg. intr. v., infin. m., pres. t., gov. by the v. "could." |
| could depend | A reg. intr. v., pot. m., past t., s. num., 3rd per., agr. with its nom. "hero." |
| **on** | A prep., sh. the rn. bet. "could depend" and "faith." |
| faith | An abs. n., neu. gen., s. num., 3rd per., obj. c., gov. by the prep. "on." |

| | |
|---|---|
| of | A prep., sh. the rn. bet. "faith" and "tyrant." |
| tyrant. | A com. n., mas. gen., s. num., 3rd per., obj. c., gov. by the prep. "of." |
| 3. He | A pers. pron., mas. gen., s. num., 3rd per., nom. c. to the v. "was beheaded." |
| was | An aux. v. to "beheaded," indg. pass. vo., past t. |
| beheaded | A past pl. from the tr. v. "to behead," ref. to "he." |
| was beheaded | A reg. tr. v., pass. vo., indic. m., past t., s. num., 3rd per., agr. with its nom. "he." |
| at | A prep., sh. the rn. bet. "was beheaded" and "Nice." |
| Nice. | A prop. n., neu. gen., s. num., 3rd per., obj. c., gov. by the prep. "at." |
| 4. He | A pers. pron., mas. gen., s. num., 3rd per., nom. c. to the v. "was deprived." |
| was | An aux. v. to "deprived," indg. pass. vo., past t. |
| deprived | A past pl. from the tr. v. "to deprive," ref. to "he." |
| was deprived | A reg. tr. v., pass. vo., indic. m., past t., s. num., 3rd per., agr. with its nom. "he." |
| of | A prep., sh. the rn. bet. "was deprived" and "friend." |
| his | A pers. pron., mas. gen., s. num., 3rd per., poss. c., gov. by the n. "friend." |
| only | A def. card. nu. adj. of quantity, qual. the n. "friend." |
| friend. | A com. n., com. gen., s. num., 3rd per., obj. c., gov. by the prep. "of." |
| 5. fugitives | A com. n., com. gen., p. num., 3rd per., nom. c. to the v. "were entertained." |
| of | A prep., sh. the rn. bet. "fugitives" and "Palestine." |
| Palestine | A prop. n., neu. gen., s. num., 3rd per., obj. c., gov. by the prep. "of." |
| were | An aux. v. to "entertained," indg. pass. vo., past t. |
| entertained | A past pl. from the tr. v. "to entertain," ref. to "fugitives." |
| were entertained | A reg. tr. v., pass. vo., indic. m., past t., p. num., 3rd per., agr. with its nom. "fugitives." |
| at | A prep., sh. the rn. bet. "were entertained" and "Alexandria." |
| Alexandria. | A prop. n., neu. gen., s. num., 3rd per., obj. c., gov. by the prep "at." |
| 6. I | A pers. pron., com. gen., s. num., 1st per., nom. c. to the v. "am." |
| am | An irreg. intr. v., indic. m., pres. t., s. num. 1st per., agr. with its nom. "I." |
| not | An adv. of m. (neg.), mod. the v. "am." |
| worthy | An adj. of quality, pos. deg., qual. the pron. "I." |
| of | A prep., sh. the rn. bet. "worthy" and *mercy* und. |
| least | An adj. of quality, superl. deg., qual. the n. *mercy* und. |
| of | A prep., sh. the rn. bet. *mercy* und. and "mercies." |
| all | An indef. nu. adj. of quantity, qual. the n. "mercies." |
| these | A dis. adj., lim. the n. "mercies." |
| mercies. | An abs. n., neu. gen., p. num., 3rd per., obj. c., gov. by the prep. "of." |
| 7. insidious | An adj. of quality, pos. deg., qual. the n. "smile." |
| smile | An abs. n., neu. gen., s. num., 3rd per., ncm. c. to the v. "would warn." |
| upon | A prep., sh. the rn. bet. "smile" and "cheek." |
| cheek | A com. n., neu. gen., s. num., 3rd per., obj. c., gov. by the prep. "upon." |
| would | An aux. v. to "warn," indg. pot. m., past t. |
| (to) warn | A reg. tr. v., act. vo., infin. m., pres. t., gov. by the v. "would." |
| would warn | A reg. tr. v., act. vo., pot. m., past t., s. num., 3rd per., agr. with its nom. "smile." |
| him | A pers. pron., mas. gen., s. num., 3rd per., obj. c., gov. by the tr. v. "would warn." |
| of | A prep., sh. the rn. bet. "would warn" and "canker." |
| canker | A com. n., neu. gen., s. num., 3rd per., obj. c., gov. by the prep. "of." |
| in | A prep., sh. the rn. bet. "canker" and "heart." |
| heart. | A com. n., neu. gen., s. num., 3rd per., obj. c., gov. by the prep. "in." |

| | |
|---|---|
| 8. title | A com. n., neu. gen., s. num., 3rd per., nom. c. to the v. "was bestowed." |
| of | A prep., sh. the rn. bet. "title" and "Lord Protector." |
| Lord | A com. n. tending to prop., mas. gen., s. num., 3rd per., obj. c., gov. by the prep. "of." |
| Protector | A com. n. tending to prop., mas. gen., s. num., 3rd per., obj. c., in app. with "Lord." |
| Lord Protector | A compd. com. n. tending to prop., mas. gen., s. num., 3rd per., obj. c., gov. by the prep. "of." |
| was | An aux. v. to "bestowed," indg. pass. vo., past t. |
| bestowed | A past pl. from the tr. v. "to bestow," ref. to "title." |
| was bestowed | A reg. tr. v., pass. vo., indic. m., past t., s. num., 3rd per., agr. with its nom. "title." |
| on | A prep., sh. the rn. bet. "was bestowed" and "Cromwell." |
| Cromwell. | A prop. n., mas. gen., s. num., 3rd per., obj. c., gov. by the prep. "on." |
| 9. Do | An aux. v. to "acquiesce," indg. pres. t., and completing the negative form of the v. |
| not | An adv. of m. (neg.), mod. the v. "do acquiesce." |
| (to) acquiesce | A reg. intr. v., infin. m., pres. t., gov. by the v. "do." |
| Do acquiesce | A reg. intr. v., imper. m., pres. t., s. or p. num., 2nd per., agr. with its nom. *thou* or *you* und. |
| in | A prep., sh. the rn. bet. "do acquiesce" and "opinion." |
| every | A dist. nu. adj. of quantity, qual. the n. "opinion." |
| opinion. | An abs. n., neu. gen., s. num., 3rd per., obj. c., gov. by the prep. "in." |
| 10. If | A cop. conj., jg. the sents. "their troops..deserted" and "they..him," and indg. subj. m. |
| they | A pers. pron., com. gen., p. num., 3rd per., nom. c. to the v. "had waited." |
| had | An aux. v. to "waited," indg. pluperf. t. |
| waited | A past pl. from the intr. v. "to wait," ref. to "they." |
| had waited | A reg. intr. v., subj. m., pluperf. t., p. num., 3rd per., agr. with its nom. "they." |
| for | A prep., sh. the rn. bet. "had waited" and "him." |
| him | A pers. pron., mas. gen., s. num., 3rd per., obj. c., gov. by the prep. "for." |
| their | A pers. pron., com. gen., p. num., 3rd per., poss. c., gov. by the n. "troops." |
| troops | A com. col. n., neu. gen., p. num., 3rd per., nom. c. to the v. "would have deserted." |
| would | An aux. v. to "have deserted," indg. pot. m. |
| have | An aux. v. to "deserted," and together with "would," indg. pluperf. t. |
| deserted | A past pl. from the tr. v. "to desert," ref. to "troops." |
| would have deserted. | A reg. intr. v., pot. m., pluperf. t., p. num., 3rd per., agr. with its nom. "troops." |
| 11. I | A pers. pron., com. gen., s. num., 1st per., nom. c. to the v. "have found." |
| have | An aux. v. to "found," indg. perf. t. |
| found | A past pl. from the tr. v. "to find," ref. to "history." |
| have found | An irreg. tr. v., act. vo., indic. m., perf. t., s. num., 1st per., agr. with its nom. "I." |
| history | An abs. n., neu. gen., s. num., 3rd per., obj. c., gov. by the tr. v. "have found." |
| that | A rel. pron., neu. gen., s. num., 3rd per., agr. with its ant. "history," nom. c. to the v. "has." |
| has | An irreg. tr. v., act. vo., indic. m., pres. t., s. num., 3rd per., agr. with its nom. "that." |
| great | An adj. of quality, pos. deg., qual. the n. "resemblance." |
| resemblance | An abs. n., neu. gen., s. num., 3rd per., obj. c., gov. by the tr. v. "has." |
| to | A prep., sh. the rn. bet. "resemblance" and *history* und. |
| hers. | A pers. pron., fem. gen., s. num., 3rd per., poss. c., gov. by the n. *history* und. |
| 12. She | A pers. pron., fem. gen., s. num., 3rd per., nom. c. to the v. "came." |

| | |
|---|---|
| came | An irreg. intr. v., indic. m., past t., s. num., 3rd per., agr. with its nom. "she." |
| to | A prep., sh. the rn. bet. "came" and "Paris." |
| Paris. | A prop. n., neu. gen., s. num., 3rd per., obj. c., gov. by the prep. "to." |
| 13. When | A cop. conj., jg. the sents. "he..hat" and "our..ended." |
| our | A pers. pron., com. gen., p. num., 1st per., poss. c., gov. by the n. "visit." |
| visit | An abs. n., neu. gen., s. num., 3rd per., nom. c. to the v. "was ended." |
| was | An aux. v. to "ended," indg. pass. vo., past t. |
| ended | A past pl. from the tr. v. "to end," ref. to "visit." |
| was ended | A reg. tr. v., pass. vo., indic. m., past t., s. num., 3rd per., agr. with its nom. "visit." |
| he | A pers. pron., mas. gen., s. num., 3rd per., nom. c. to the v. "called." |
| called | A reg. intr. v., indic. m., past t., s. num., 3rd per., agr. with its nom. "he." |
| for | A prep., sh. the rn. bet. "called" and "hat." |
| his | A pers. pron., mas. gen., s. num., 3rd per., poss. c., gov. by the n. "hat." |
| hat. | A com. n., neu. gen., s. num., 3rd per., obj. c., gov. by the prep. "for." |
| 14. Many | An indef. nu. adj. of quantity, qual. the n. *persons* und. |
| are | An irreg. intr. v., indic. m., pres. t., p. num., 3rd per., agr. with its nom. *persons* und. |
| desirous | An adj. of quality, pos. deg., qual. the n. *persons* und. |
| of | A prep., sh. the rn. bet. "desirous" and "testifying." |
| testifying | A ger. from the tr. v. "to testify," neu. gen., s. num., 3rd per., obj. c., gov. by the prep. "of." |
| their | A pers. pron., com. gen., p. num., 3rd per., poss. c., gov. by the n. "respect." |
| respect | An abs. n., neu. gen., s. num., 3rd per., obj. c., gov. by the tr. ger. "testifying." |
| by | A prep., sh. the rn. bet. "testifying" and "attending." |
| attending. | A ger. from the intr. v. "to attend," neu. gen., s. num., 3rd per., obj. c., gov. by the prep. "by." |
| 15. great | An adj. of quality, pos. deg., qual. the n. "beauty." |
| beauty | An abs. n., neu. gen., s. num., 3rd per., nom. c. to the v. "depends." |
| of | A prep., sh. the rn. bet. "beauty" and *things* und. |
| both | A def. card. nu. adj. of quantity, qual. the n. *things* und. |
| depends | A reg. intr. v., indic. m., pres. t., s. num., 3rd per., agr. with its nom. "beauty." |
| on | A prep., sh. the rn. bet. "depends" and "contrast." |
| contrast | An abs. n., neu. gen., s. num., 3rd per., obj. c., gov. by the prep. "on." |
| between | A prep., sh. the rn. bet. "contrast" and "splendour and obscurity." |
| splendour | An abs. n., neu. gen., s. num., 3rd per., obj. c., in conjunction with "obscurity" (with which it forms a compd. object), gov. by the prep. "between." |
| and | A cop. conj., jg. "splendour" and "obscurity" into a compd. object. |
| obscurity. | An abs. n., neu. gen., s. num., 3rd per., obj. c., in conjunction with "splendour," gov. by the prep. "between." |

## Exercise 182.

| | |
|---|---|
| 1. **On** | A prep., sh. the rn. bet. "haste" and "wings." |
| fickle | An adj. of quality, pos. deg., qual. the n. "wings." |
| wings | A com. n., neu. gen., p. num., 3rd per., obj. c., gov. by the prep. "on." |
| minutes | An abs. n., neu. gen., p. num., 3rd per., nom. c. to the v. "haste." |
| haste. | A reg. intr. v., indic. m., pres. t., p. num., 3rd per., agr. with its nom. "minutes." |

## KEY TO

| | |
|---|---|
| 2. father | A com. n., mas. gen., s. num., 3rd per., nom. c. to the v. "bends." |
| bends | An irreg. intr. v., indic. m., pres. t., s. num., 3rd per., agr. with its nom. "father." |
| o'er | A prep., sh. the rn. bet. "bends" and "him." |
| him | A pers. pron., mas. gen., s. num., 3rd per., obj. c., gov. by the prep. "o'er." |
| with | A prep., sh. the rn. bet. "bends" and "looks." |
| looks | An abs. n., neu. gen., p. num., 3rd per., obj. c., gov. by the prep. "with." |
| of | A prep., sh. the rn. bet. "looks" and "delight." |
| delight. | An abs. n., neu. gen., s. num., 3rd per., obj. c., gov. by the prep. "of." |
| 3. I | A pers. pron., com. gen. by personification, s. num., 1st per., nom. c. to the v. "steal." |
| steal | An irreg. intr. v., indic. m., pres. t., s. num., 1st per., agr. with its nom. "I." |
| by | A prep., sh. the rn. bet. "steal" and "lawns." |
| lawns | A com. n., neu. gen., p. num., 3rd per., obj. c., gov. by the prep. "by." |
| and | A cop. conj., jg. the sents. "I..lawns" and "I steal by grassy plots." |
| grassy | An adj. of quality, qual. the n. "plots." |
| plots. | A com. n., neu. gen., p. num., 3rd per., obj. c., gov. by the prep. by und. |
| 4. gorse | A com. n., neu. gen., s. num., 3rd per., nom. c. to the v. "is." |
| is | An irreg. intr. v., indic. m., pres. t., s. num., 3rd per., agr. with its nom. "gorse." |
| yellow | An adj. of quality, pos. deg., qual. the n. "gorse." |
| on | A prep., sh. the rn. bet. "gorse" and "heath." |
| heath. | A com. n., neu. gen., s. num., 3rd per., obj. c., gov. by the prep. "on." |
| 5. tradesman | A com. n., mas. gen., s. num., 3rd per., nom. c. to the v. "has failed." |
| that | A rel. pron., mas. gen., s. num., 3rd per., agr. with its ant. "tradesman," obj. c., gov. by the prep. "with." |
| you | A pers. pron., com. gen., p. num., or s. num., p. form., 2nd per., nom. c. to the v. "were acquainted." |
| were | An aux. v. to "acquainted," indg. pass. vo., past t. |
| acquainted | A past pl. from the tr. v. "to acquaint," ref. to "you." |
| were acquainted | A reg. tr. v., pass. vo., indic. m., past t., p. num., or s. num. p. form., 2nd per., agr. with its nom. "you." |
| with | A prep., sh. the rn. bet. "were acquainted" and "that." |
| has | An aux. v. to "failed," indg. perf. t. |
| failed | A past pl. from the intr. v. "to fail," ref. to "tradesman." |
| has failed. | A reg. intr. v., indic. m., perf. t., s. num., 3rd per., agr. with its nom. "tradesman." |
| 6. I | A pers. pron., com. gen., s. num., 1st per., nom. c. to the v. "have." |
| have | An irreg. tr. v., act. vo., indic. m., pres. t., s. num., 1st per., agr. with its nom. "I." |
| you | A pers. pron., com. gen., p. num., or s. num., p. form, 2nd per., obj. c., gov. by the tr. v. "have." |
| fast | An adj. of quality, pos. deg., qual. the pron. "you." |
| in | A prep., sh. the rn. bet. "have" and "fortress." |
| my | A pers. pron., com. gen., s. num., 1st per., poss. c., gov. by the n. "fortress." |
| fortress. | A com. n., neu. gen., s. num., 3rd per., obj. c., gov. by the prep. "in." |
| 7. Echo | An abs. n. used as a prop. n., fem. gen. by personification, s. num., 3rd per., nom. c. to the v. "walks." |
| walks | A reg. intr. v., indic. m., pres. t., s. num., 3rd per., agr. with its nom. "Echo." |
| steep | An adj. of quality, pos. deg., qual. the n. "hills." |
| hills | A com. n., neu. gen., p. num., 3rd per., obj. c., gov. by the prep. "among." |
| among. | A prep., sh. the rn. bet. "walks" and "hills." |

ENGLISH GRAMMAR AND ANALYSIS.   215

| | |
|---|---|
| 8. **With** | A prep., sh. the rn. bet. "comes" and "glory." |
| what | An interrog. pron. used as an adj. of quality, qual. the n. "glory." |
| glory | An abs. n., neu. gen., s. num., 3rd per., obj. c., gov. by the prep. "with." |
| comes | An irreg. intr. v., indic. m., pres. t., s. num., 3rd per., agr. with its nom. *year* und. |
| and | A cop. conj., jg. the sents. "With..comes *the year*" and "*with what a glory* goes the year." |
| goes | An irreg. intr. v., indic. m., pres. t., s. num., 3rd per., agr. with its nom. "year." |
| year. | An abs. n., neu. gen., s. num., 3rd per., nom. c. to the v. "goes." |
| 9. Thou | A pers. pron., com. gen., s. num., 2nd per., nom. c. to the v. "wast." |
| wast | An irreg. intr. v., indic. m., past t., s. num., 2nd per., agr. with its nom. "thou." |
| bauble | A com. n., neu. gen., s. num., 3rd per., nom. c. after the v. "wast." |
| once | An adv. of time, mod. the v. "wast." |
| cup | A com. n., neu. gen., s. num., 3rd per., nom. c. after the v. *wast* und. |
| and | A cop. conj., jg. the sents. "*thou wast* a cup" and "*thou wast a ball.*" |
| ball | A com. n., neu. gen., s. num., 3rd per., nom. c. after the v. *wast* und. |
| Which | A rel. pron., neu. gen., s. num., 3rd per., agr. with its ant. "bauble," obj. c., gov. by the prep. "with." |
| babes | A com. n., com. gen., p. num., 3rd per., nom. c. to the v. "might play." |
| might | An aux. v. to "play," indg. pot. m., past t. |
| (to) play | A reg. intr. v., infin. m., pres. t., gov. by the v. "might." |
| might play | A reg. intr. v., pot. m., past t., p. num., 3rd per., agr. with its nom. "babes." |
| **with.** | A prep., sh. the rn. bet. "might play" and "which." |
| 10. **Around** | A prep., sh. the rn. bet. "bound" and "sovereign." |
| their | A pers. pron., com. gen. by personification, p. num., 3rd per., poss. c., gov. by the n. "sovereign." |
| sovereign | A com. n., com. gen., s. num., 3rd per., obj. c., gov. by the prep. "around." |
| on | A prep., sh. the rn. bet. "bound" and "ground." |
| verdant | An adj. of quality, pos. deg., qual. the n. "ground." |
| ground | A com. n., neu. gen., s. num., 3rd per., obj. c., gov. by the prep. "on." |
| Sweet | An adj. of quality, pos. deg., qual. the n. "forms." |
| airy | An adj. of quality, qual. the n. "forms." |
| forms | A com. n., com. gen. by personification, p. num., 3rd per., nom. c. to the v. "bound." |
| **in** | A prep., sh. the rn. bet. "bound" and "measures." |
| mystic | An adj. of quality, pos. deg., qual. the n. "measures." |
| measures | An abs. n., neu. gen., p. num., 3rd per., obj. c., gov. by the prep. "in." |
| bound. | A reg. intr. v., indic. m., pres. t., p. num., 3rd per., agr. with its nom. "forms." |

## Exercise 183.

| | |
|---|---|
| 1. wolves | A com. n., com. gen., p. num., 3rd per., nom. c. to the v. "howled." |
| howled | A reg. intr. v., indic. m., past t., p. num., 3rd per., agr. with its nom. "wolves." |
| **and** | A cop. conj., jg. the sents. "The wolves howled" and "*the wolves* whined." |
| whined. | A reg. intr. v., indic. m., past t., p. num., 3rd per., agr. with its nom. *wolves* und. |
| 2. Ill | An adj. of quality, pos. deg., qual. the n. "news." |
| news | A com. n., neu. gen., s. num., p. form, 3rd per., nom. c. to the v. "is" |

| | |
|---|---|
| is | An irreg. intr. v., indic. m., pres. t., s. num., 3rd per., agr. with its nom. "news." |
| winged | An adj. of quality, qual. the n. "news." |
| with | A prep., sh. the rn. bet. "winged" and "fate." |
| fate | An abs. n., neu. gen., s. num., 3rd per., obj. c., gov. by the prep. "with." |
| and | A cop. conj., jg. the sents. "Ill...fate" and "*ill news* flies apace." |
| flies | An irreg. intr. v., indic. m., pres. t., s. num., 3rd per., agr. with its nom. *news* und. |
| apace. | An adv. of man., mod. the v. "flies." |
| 3. Thou | A pers. pron., com. gen., s. num., 2nd per., nom. c. to the v. "wert." |
| wert | An irreg. intr. v., indic. m., past t., s. num., 2nd per., agr. with its nom. "thou." |
| my | A pers. pron., com. gen., s. num., 1st per., poss. c., gov. by the n. "guide." |
| guide | A com. n., com. gen., s. num., 3rd per., nom. c. after the v. "wert." |
| philosopher | A com. n., com. gen., s. num., 3rd per., nom. c. after the v. *wert* und. |
| and | A cop. conj., jg. the sents. "thou wert my philosopher" and "*thou wert my* friend." |
| friend. | A com. n., com. gen., s. num., 3rd per., nom. c. after the v. "wert." |
| 4. He | A pers. pron., mas. gen., s. num., 3rd per., nom. c. to the v. "was." |
| was | An irreg. intr. v., indic. m., past t., s. num., 3rd per., agr. with its nom. "he." |
| scholar | A com. n., mas. gen., s. num., 3rd per., nom. c. after the v. "was." |
| and | A cop. conj., jg. the sents. "He...scholar" and "he was a good one." |
| good | An adj. of quality, pos. deg., qual. the pron. "one." |
| one. | An indef. pers. pron., mas. gen., s. num., 3rd per., nom. c. after the v. *was* und. |
| 5. Many | An indef. nu. adj. of quantity, pos. deg., qual. the n. *persons* und. |
| were | An irreg. intr. v., indic. m., past t., p. num., 3rd per., agr. with its nom. *persons* und. |
| in | A prep., sh. the rn. bet. "were" and "tears." |
| tears | A com. n., neu. gen., p. num., 3rd per., obj. c., gov. by the prep. "in." |
| and | A cop. conj., jg. the sents. "Many...tears" and "many...him." |
| many | An indef. nu. adj. of quantity, pos. deg., qual. the n. *persons* und. |
| knelt | An irreg. intr. v., indic. m., past t., p. num., 3rd per., agr. with its nom. *persons* und. |
| before | A prep., sh. the rn. bet. "knelt" and "him." |
| him | A pers. pron., mas. gen., s. num., 3rd per., obj. c., gov. by the prep. "before." |
| and | A cop. conj., jg. the sents. "many...him" and "*many* blessed him." |
| blessed | A reg. tr. v., act. vo., indic. m., past t., p. num., 3rd per., agr. with its nom. *persons* und. |
| him | A pers. pron., mas. gen., s. num., 3rd per., obj. c., gov. by the tr. v. "blessed." |
| as | A cop. conj., jg. the sents. "*many* blessed him" and "he passed." |
| he | A pers. pron., mas. gen., s. num., 3rd per., nom. c. to the v. "passed." |
| passed. | A reg. intr. v., indic. m., past t., s. num., 3rd per., agr. with its nom. "he." |
| 6. Shame | An abs. n., neu. gen., s. num., 3rd per., nom. c. to the v. "hurts." |
| greatly | An adv. of deg., mod. the v. "hurts." |
| hurts | An irreg. tr. v., act. vo., indic. m., pres. t, s. num., 3rd per., agr. with its nom. "shame." |

## ENGLISH GRAMMAR AND ANALYSIS. 217

| | |
|---|---|
| or | A disj. conj., jg. the sents. "shame greatly hurts *mankind*" and "*shame* greatly helps mankind." |
| greatly | An adv. of deg., mod. the v. "helps." |
| helps | A reg. tr. v., act. vo., indic. m., pres. t., s. num., 3rd per., agr. with its nom. *shame* und. |
| mankind. | A com. col. n., com. gen., p. num., 3rd per., obj. c., gov. by the tr. v. "helps." |
| 7. He | A pers. pron., mas. gen., s. num., 3rd per., nom. c. to the v "plied." |
| plied | A reg. tr. v., act. vo., indic. m., past t., s. num., 3rd per., agr. with its nom. "he." |
| his | A pers. pron., mas. gen., s. num., 3rd per., poss. c., gov. by the n. "work." |
| work | An abs. n., neu. gen., s. num., 3rd per., obj. c., gov. by the tr. v. "plied." |
| and | A cop. conj., jg. the sents. "He...work" and "Lucy...hand." |
| Lucy | A prop. n., fem. gen., s. num., 3rd per., nom. c. to the v. "took." |
| took | An irreg. tr. v., act. vo., indic. m., past t., s. num., 3rd per., agr. with its nom. "Lucy." |
| lantern | A com. n., neu. gen., s. num., 3rd per., obj. c., gov. by the tr. v. "took." |
| in | A prep., sh. the rn. bet. "took" and "hand." |
| her | A pers. pron., fem. gen., s. num., 3rd per., poss. c., gov. by the n. "hand." |
| hand. | A com. n., neu. gen., s. num., 3rd per., obj. c., gov. by the prep. "in." |
| 8. In | A prep., sh. the rn. bet. "doth bleed" and *manner* und. |
| vain | An adj. of quality, pos. deg., qual. the n. *manner* und. |
| In vain | An adverbial phrase of man., mod. the v. "doth bleed." |
| doth | An aux. v. to "bleed," indg. pres. t., emph. form. |
| valour | An abs. n., neu. gen., s. num., 3rd per., nom. c. to the v. "doth bleed." |
| (to) bleed | An irreg. intr. v., infin. m., pres. t., gov. by the v. "doth." |
| doth bleed | An irreg. intr. v., indic. m., pres. t., emph. form, s. num., 3rd per., agr. with its nom. "valour." |
| While | A cop. conj., jg. the sents. "In vain...bleed" and "avarice...land." |
| avarice | An abs. n., neu. gen., s. num., 3rd per., nom. c. to the v. "shares," incl. in "share." |
| and | A cop. conj., jg. the sents. "avarice shares *the land with rapine*" and "rapine shares the land *with avarice*." |
| rapine | An abs. n., neu. gen., s. num., 3rd per., nom. c. to the v. "shares" incl. in "share." |
| share | A reg. tr. v., act. vo., indic. m., pres. t., p. num., 3rd per., agr. with its noms. "avarice" and "rapine." |
| land. | A com. n., neu. gen., s. num., 3rd per., obj. c., gov. by the tr. v. "share." |
| 9. He | A pers. pron., mas. gen., s. num., 3rd per., nom. c. to the v. "looks." |
| looks | A reg. intr. v., indic. m., pres. t., s. num., 3rd per., agr. with its nom. "he." |
| to | A prep., sh. the rn. bet. "looks" and "her." |
| her | A pers. pron., fem. gen., s. num., 3rd per., obj. c., gov. by the prep. "to." |
| and | A cop. conj., jg. the sents. "He...her" and "*he* rushes on." |
| rushes | A reg. intr. v., indic. m., pres. t., s. num., 3rd per., agr. with its nom. *he* und. |
| on | An adv. of place, mod. the v. "rushes." |
| Where | A cop. conj., jg. the sents. "*he* rushes on" and "life is lost." |
| life | An abs. n., neu. gen., s. num., 3rd per., nom. c. to the v. "is lost." |
| is | An aux. v. to "lost," indg. pass. vo., pres. t. |
| lost | A past pl. from the tr. v. "to lose," ref. to "life." |
| is lost | An irreg. tr. v., pass. vo., indic. m., pres. t., s. num., 3rd per., agr. with its nom. "life." |
| or | A disj. conj., jg. the sents. "life is lost" and "freedom is won." |

218　KEY TO

| | |
|---|---|
| freedom | An abs. n., neu. gen., s. num., 3rd per., nom. c. to the v. "*is won*." |
| won. | A past pl. from the tr. v. "to win," ref. to "freedom." |
| 10. Here | An adv. of place, mod. the v. *dwell* und. |
| in | A prep., sh. the rn. bet. *dwell* und. and "grot." |
| cool | An adj. of quality, pos. deg., qual. the n. "grot." |
| grot | A com. n., neu. gen., s. num., 3rd per., obj. c., gov. by the prep. "in." |
| **and** | A cop. conj., jg. the sents. "we rural fays *dwell* here in cool grot' and " *we rural fays dwell here in* mossy cell." |
| mossy | An adj. of quality, qual. the n. "cell." |
| cell | A com. n., neu. gen., s. num., 3rd per., obj. c., gov. by the prep. *in* und. |
| We | A pers. pron., com. gen., p. num., 1st per., nom. c. to the v. *dwell* und. |
| rural | An adj. of quality, qual. the n. "fays." |
| fays | A com. n., com. gen., p. num., 1st per., nom. c., in app. with "we." |
| **and** | A cop. conj., jg. the sents. "We rural fays dwell…" and "*we* fairies dwell…" |
| fairies | A com. n., com. gen., p. num., 1st per., nom. c., in app. with *we* und. |
| dwell. | An irreg. intr. v., indic. m., pres. t., p. num., 1st per., agr. with its nom. *we* und. |

### Exercise 184.

| | |
|---|---|
| 1. No | A def. card. nu. adj. of quantity, qual. the n. "person." |
| person | A com. n., com. gen., s. num., 3rd per., nom. c. to the v. "had." |
| ever | An adv. of time, mod. the v. "had." |
| had | An irreg. tr. v., act. vo., indic. m., past t., s. num., 3rd per., agr. with its nom. "person." |
| better | An adj. of quality, comp. deg. qual., the n. "knack." |
| knack | An abs. n., neu. gen., s. num., 3rd per., obj. c., gov. by the tr. v. "had." |
| of | A prep., sh. the rn. bet. "knack" and "hoping." |
| hoping | A ger. from the intr. v. "to hope," neu. gen., s. num., 3rd per., obj. c., gov. by the prep. "of." |
| **than** | A disj. conj., jg. the sents. "No..hoping" and "I *had a good knack of hoping.*" |
| I. | A pers. pron., com. gen., s. num., 1st per., nom. c. to the v. *had* und. |
| 2. My | A pers. pron., com. gen., s. num., 1st per., poss. c., gov. by the n. "skill." |
| skill | An abs. n., neu. gen., s. num., 3rd per., nom. c. to the v. "availed." |
| in | A prep., sh. the rn. bet. "skill" and "music." |
| music | An abs. n., neu. gen., s. num., 3rd per., obj. c., gov. by the prep. "in." |
| availed | A reg. tr. v., act. vo., indic. m., past t., s. num., 3rd per., agr. with its nom. "skill." |
| me | A pers. pron., com. gen., s. num., 1st per., obj. c., gov. by the tr. v. "availed." |
| nothing | A com. n., neu. gen., s. num., 3rd per., obj. c., gov. by the prep. *in* und. (or, a com. n. used as an adv., mod. the v. "availed"). |
| in | A prep., sh. the rn. bet. "availed" and "country." |
| country | A com. n., neu. gen., s. num., 3rd per., obj. c., gov. by the prep. "in." |
| where | A cop. conj., jg. the sents. "My skill..country" and "every.. musician." |
| every | A dist. nu. adj. of quantity, qual. the n. "peasant." |
| peasant | A com. n., com. gen., s. num., 3rd per., nom. c. to the v. "was." |
| was | An irreg. intr. v., indic. m., past t., s. num., 3rd per., agr. with its nom. "peasant." |
| better | An adj. of quality, comp. deg., qual. the n. "musician." |
| musician | A com. n., com. gen., s. num., 3rd per., nom. c. after the v. "was." |

| | |
|---|---|
| than | A disj. conj., jg. the sents. "every..musician" and "I *was a good musician.*" |
| I. | A pers. pron., com. gen., s. num., 1st per., nom. c. to the v. *was* und. |
| 3. They | A pers. pron., com. gen., p. num., 3rd per., nom. c. to the v. "wrote." |
| wrote | An irreg. intr. v., indic. m., past t., p. num., 3rd per., agr. with its nom. "they." |
| faster | An adv. of man., comp. deg., mod. the v. "wrote." |
| than | A disj. conj., jg. the sents. "They wrote faster" and "I *wrote fast.*" |
| I. | A pers. pron., com. gen., s. num., 1st per., nom. c. to the v. *wrote* und. |
| 4. frigate-bird | A compd. com. n., mas. gen., s. num., 3rd per., nom. c. to the v. "is." |
| is | An irreg. intr. v., indic. m., pres. t., s. num., 3rd per., agr. with its nom. "frigate-bird." |
| little | An adv. of mea., mod. the adv. "more." |
| more | An adj. of quantity (bulk or mass), comp. deg., qual. the n. *substance* und. |
| than | A disj. conj., jg. the sents. "The frigate-bird..more *substance*" and "wings *are much substance.*" |
| wings | A com. n., neu. gen., p. num., 3rd per., nom. c. to the v. *are* und. |
| he | A pers. pron., mas. gen., s. num., 3rd per., nom. c. to the v. "has." |
| has | An irreg. tr. v., act. vo., indic. m., pres. t., s. num., 3rd per., agr. with its nom. "he." |
| scarcely | An adv. of deg., mod. the adj. "any." |
| any | An adj. of quantity (bulk or mass), qual. the n. "body." |
| body | A com. n., neu. gen., s. num., 3rd per., obj. c., gov. by the tr. v. "has." |
| 5. I | A pers. pron., com. gen., s. num., 1st per., nom. c. to the v. "love." |
| love | A reg. tr. v., act. vo., indic. m., pres. t., s. num., 1st per., agr. with its nom. "I." |
| you | A pers. pron., com. gen., p. num., or s. num., p. form, 2nd per., obj. c., gov. by the tr. v. "love." |
| better | An adv. of man., comp. deg., mod. the v. "love." |
| than | A disj. conj., jg. the sents. "I..better" and "he *loves you.*" |
| he. | A pers. pron., mas. gen., s. num., 3rd per., nom. c. to the v. *loves* und. |
| 6. I | A pers. pron., com. gen., s. num., 1st per., nom. c. to the v. "love." |
| love | A reg. tr. v., act. vo., indic. m., pres. t., s. num., 1st per., agr. with its nom. "I." |
| you | A pers. pron., com. gen., p. num., or s. num., p. form, 2nd per., obj. c., gov. by the tr. v. "love." |
| better | An adv. of man., comp. deg., mod. the v. "love." |
| than | A disj. conj., jg. the sents. "I..better" and "*I love him.*" |
| him. | A pers. pron., mas. gen., s. num., 3rd per., obj. c., gov. by the tr. v. *love* und. |

## Exercise 185.

| | |
|---|---|
| 1. Hesiod | A prop. n., mas. gen., s. num., 3rd per., nom. c. to the v. "was." |
| was | An irreg. intr. v., indic. m., past t., s. num., 3rd per., agr. with its nom. "Hesiod." |
| **either** | A disj. conj., introducing the sent. "Hesiod..Homer." |
| contemporary | An adj. of quality, qual. the n. "Hesiod." |
| with | A prep., sh. the rn. bet. "contemporary" and "Homer." |
| Homer | A prop. n., mas. gen., s. num., 3rd per., obj. c., gov. by the prep. "with." |
| or | A disj. conj., cor. to "either," jg. the sents. "Hesiod..Homer" and "Hesiod lived..him." |
| lived | A reg. intr. v., indic. m., past t., s. num., 3rd per., agr. with its nom. *Hesiod* und. |
| immediately | An adv. of time, mod. the v. "lived." |

## 220            KEY TO

| | |
|---|---|
| after | A prop., sh. the rn. bet. "lived" and "him." |
| him. | A pers. pron., mas. gen., s. num., 3rd per., obj. c., gov. by the prep. "after." |
| **2. He** | A pers. pron., mas. gen., s. num., 3rd per., nom. c. to the v. "understands." |
| understands | An irreg. tr. v., act. vo., indic. m., pres. t., s. num., 3rd per., agr. with its nom. "he." |
| how | A cop. conj., jg. the sents. "He understands" and "*he ought* to manage public *concerns*." |
| to | A particle, indg. infin. m. |
| to manage | A reg. tr. v., act. vo., infin. m., pres. t., gov. by the v. *ought* und. |
| **both** | A cop. conj., introducing the sent. "how *he ought* to manage public *concerns*." |
| public | An adj. of quality, qual. the n. *concerns* und. |
| **and** | A cop. conj., cor. to "both," jg. the sents. "how *he ought* to manage public *concerns*" and "*how he ought to manage* private concerns." |
| private | An adj. of quality, qual. the n. "concerns." |
| concerns. | An abs. n., neu. gen., p. num., 3rd per., obj. c., gov. by the tr. v. *to manage* und. |
| **3. It** | A pers. pron., neu. gen., s. num., 3rd per., nom. c. to the v. "is." |
| is | An irreg. intr. v., indic. m., pres. t., s. num., 3rd per., agr. with its nom. "it." |
| **neither** | A disj. conj., introducing the sent. "it is here." |
| here | An adv. of place, mod. the v. "is." |
| **nor** | A disj. conj., cor. to "neither," jg. the sents. "'Tis here" and "*'tis* there." |
| there. | An adv. of place, mod. the v. *is* und. |
| **4. Though** | A disj. conj., introducing the sent. "her father.. Naples," and indg. subj. m. |
| her | A pers. pron., fem. gen., s. num., 3rd per., poss. c., gov. by the n. "father." |
| father | A com. n., mas. gen., s. num., 3rd per., nom. c. to the v. "be." |
| be | An irreg. intr. v., subj. m., pres. t., s. num., 3rd per., agr. with its nom. "father." |
| king | A com. n., mas. gen., s. num., 3rd per., nom. c. after the v. "be." |
| of | A prep., sh. the rn. bet. "king" and "Naples." |
| Naples | A prop. n., neu. gen., s. num., 3rd per., obj. c., gov. by the prep. "of." |
| Duke | A com. n. tending to prop., mas. gen., s. num., 3rd per., nom. c. after the v. *be* und. |
| of | A prep., sh. the rn. bet. "Duke" and "Anjou." |
| Anjou | A prop. n., neu. gen., s. num., 3rd per., obj. c., gov. by the prep. "of." |
| and | A cop. conj., jg. the sents. "*though her father be* Duke of Anjou" and "*though her father be Duke of* Maine." |
| Maine | A prop. n., neu. gen., s. num., 3rd per., obj. c., gov. by the prep. *of* und. |
| **yet** | A disj. conj., cor. to *though* und., jg. the sents. "*though her father be Duke of* Maine" and "he is poor." |
| is | An irreg. intr. v., indic. m., pres. t., s. num., 3rd per., agr. with its nom. "he." |
| he | A pers. pron., mas. gen., s. num., 3rd per., nom. c. to the v. "is." |
| poor. | An adj. of quality, pos. deg., qual. the pron. "he." |
| **5. I** | A pers. pron., com. gen., s. num., 1st per., nom. c. to the v. "could read." |
| could | An aux. v. to "read," indg. pot. m., past t. |
| **neither** | A disj. conj., introducing the sent. "I could read *with satisfaction*." |
| (to) read | An irreg. intr. v., infin. m., pres. t., gov. by the v. "could." |
| could read | An irreg. intr. v., pot. m., past t., s. num., 1st per., agr. with its nom. "I." |
| **nor** | A disj. conj., cor. to "neither," jg. the sents. "I could read *with satisfaction*" and "*I could* write with satisfaction." |
| (to) write | An irreg. intr. v., infin. m., pres. t., gov. by the v. *could* und. |
| with | A prep., sh. the rn. bet. "*could* write" and "satisfaction." |

ENGLISH GRAMMAR AND ANALYSIS. 221

| | | |
|---|---|---|
| | satisfaction. | An abs. n., neu. gen., s. num., 3rd per., obj. c., gov. by the prep. "with." |
| 6. | **Whether** | A disj. conj., introducing the sent. "is the lion *the stronger.*" |
| | is | An irreg. intr. v., indic. m., pres. t., s. num., 3rd per., agr. with its nom. "lion." |
| | lion | A com. n., mas. gen., s. num., 3rd per., nom. c. to the v. "is." |
| | **or** | A disj. conj., cor. to "whether," jg. the sents. "is the lion *the stronger*" and "*is* the ox the stronger." |
| | ox | A com. n., mas. gen., s. num., 3rd per., nom. c. to the v. *is* und. |
| | stronger. | An adj. of quality, comp. deg., qual. the n. *animal* und. |
| 7. | **As** | A cop. conj., introducing the sent. "the lion..Africa." |
| | lion | A com. n., mas. gen., s. num., 3rd per., nom. c. to the v. "reigns." |
| | reigns | A reg. intr. v., indic. m., pres. t., s. num., 3rd per., agr. with its nom. "lion." |
| | in | A prep., sh. the rn. bet. "reigns" and "Africa." |
| | Africa | A prop. n., neu. gen., s. num., 3rd per., obj. c., gov. by the prep. "in." |
| | **so** | A cop. conj., cor. to "as," jg. the sents. "the lion..Africa" and "the tiger..jungles." |
| | tiger | A com. n., mas. gen., s. num., 3rd per., nom. c. to the v. "is." |
| | is | An irreg. intr. v., indic. m., pres. t., s. num., 3rd per., agr. with its nom. "tiger." |
| | lord | A com. n., mas. gen., s. num., 3rd per., nom. c. after the v. "is. |
| | and | A cop. conj., jg. the sents. "the tiger is lord *of the Indian jungles*" and "*the tiger is* master..jungles." |
| | master | A com. n., mas. gen., s. num., 3rd per., nom. c. after the v. *is* und. |
| | of | A prep., sh. the rn. bet. "master" and "jungles." |
| | Indian | A prop. adj. of quality, qual. the n. "jungles." |
| | jungles. | A com. n., neu. gen., p. num., 3rd per., obj. c., gov. by the prep. "of." |
| 8. | **Though** | A disj. conj., introducing the sent. "it..move." |
| | it | A pers. pron., neu. gen., s. num., 3rd per., nom. c. to the v. "does seem." |
| | does | An aux. v. to "seem," indg. pres. t., and completing the negative form of the v. |
| | not | An adv. of m. (neg.), mod. the v. "does seem." |
| | (to) seem | A reg. intr. v., infin. m., pres. t., gov. by the v. "does." |
| | does seem | A reg. intr. v., indic. m., pres. t., s. num., 3rd per., agr. with its nom. "it." |
| | to | A particle, indg. infin. m. |
| | to move | A reg. intr. v., infin. m., pres. t., gov. by the v. "does seem." |
| | **yet** | A disj. conj., cor. to "though," jg. the sents. "it..move" and "it..valley." |
| | it | A pers. pron., neu. gen., s. num., 3rd per., nom. c. to the v. "forces." |
| | slowly | An adv. of man., mod. the v. "forces." |
| | forces | A reg. tr. v., act. vo., indic. m., pres. t., s. num., 3rd per., agr. with its nom. "it." |
| | its | A pers. pron., neu. gen., s. num., 3rd per., poss. c., gov. by the n. "way." |
| | way | A com. n., neu. gen., s. num., 3rd per., obj. c., gov. by the tr. v. "forces." |
| | down | A prep., sh. the rn. bet. "forces" and "valley." |
| | valley | A com. n., neu. gen., s. num., 3rd per., obj. c., gov. by the prep. "down." |
| | till | A cop. conj., jg. the sents. "it..valley" and "it..sea." |
| | it | A pers. pron., neu. gen., s. num., 3rd per., nom. c. to the v. "reaches." |
| | reaches | A reg. tr. v., act. vo., indic. m., pres. t., s. num., 3rd per., agr. with its nom. "it." |
| | sea. | A com. n., neu. gen., s. num., 3rd per., obj. c., gov. by the tr. v. "reaches." |
| 9. | crow | A com. n., com. gen., s. num., 3rd per., nom. c. to the v. "doth sing." |
| | doth | An aux. v. to "sing," indg. pres. t., emph. form. |
| | (to) sing | An irreg. intr. v., infin. m., pres. t., gov. by the v. "doth." |

| | |
|---|---|
| doth sing | An irreg. intr. v., indic. m., pres. t., smph. form, s. num., 3rd per., agr. with its nom. "crow." |
| as | An adv. of deg., mod. the adv. "sweetly." |
| sweetly | An adv. of man., mod. the v. "doth sing." |
| as | A cop. conj., cor. to "as," jg. the sents. "The crow..sweetly" and "the lark *doth sing sweetly.*" |
| lark | A com. n., com. gen., s. num., 3rd per., nom. c. to the v. *sings* und. |
| When | A cop. conj., jg. the sents. "The crow..lark *doth sing*" and "neither is attended." |
| neither | A dist. nu. adj. of quantity, qual. the n. *bird* und. |
| is | An aux. v. to "attended," indg. pass. vo., pres. t. |
| attended | A past pl. from the tr. v. "to attend," ref. to *bird* und. |
| is attended. | A reg. tr. v., pass. vo., indic. m., pres. t., s. num., 3rd per., agr. with its nom. *bird* und. |
| 10. Romans | A prop. n., mas. gen., p. num., 3rd per., nom. c. to the v. "spared." |
| in | A prep., sh. the rn. bet. "spared" and "quarrel." |
| Rome's | A prop. n., neu. gen., s. num., 3rd per., poss. c., gov. by the n. "quarrel." |
| quarrel | An abs. n., neu. gen., s. num., 3rd per., obj. c., gov. by the prep. "in." |
| Spared | A reg. tr. v., act. vo., indic. m., past t., p. num., 3rd per., agr. with its nom. "Romans." |
| **neither** | A disj. conj., introducing the sent. "the Romans, in Rome's quarrel, spared land." |
| land | A com. n., neu. gen., s. num., 3rd per., obj. c., gov. by the tr. v. "spared." |
| **nor** | A disj. conj., cor. to "neither," jg. the sents. "the Romans..land" and "*the Romans, in Rome's quarrel, spared* gold." |
| gold | A com. n., neu. gen., s. num., 3rd per., obj. c., gov. by the tr. v. *spared* und. |
| **Nor** | A disj. conj., cor. to "neither," jg. the sents. "*the Romans, in Rome's quarrel, spared* gold" and "*the Romans, in Rome's quarrel, spared* son." |
| son | A com. n., mas. gen., s. num., 3rd per., obj. c, gov. by the tr. v. *spared* und. |
| **nor** | A disj. conj., cor. to "neither," jg. the sents. "*the Romans, in Rome's quarrel, spared* son" and "*the Romans, in Rome's quarrel, spared* wife." |
| wife | A com. n., fem. gen., s. num., 3rd per., obj. c., gov. by the tr. v. *spared* und. |
| **nor** | A disj. conj., cor. to "neither," jg. the sents. "*the Romans, in Rome's quarrel, spared* wife" and "*the Romans, in Rome's quarrel, spared* limb." |
| limb | A com. n., neu. gen., s. num., 3rd per., obj. c., gov. by the tr. v. *spared* und. |
| **nor** | A disj. conj., cor. to "neither," jg. the sents. "*the Romans, in Rome's quarrel, spared* limb" and "*the Romans, in Rome's quarrel, spared* life." |
| life | An abs. n., neu. gen., s. num., 3rd per., obj. c., gov. by the tr. v. *spared* und. |
| In | A prep., sh. the rn. bet. "spared" and "days." |
| brave | An adj. of quality, pos. deg., qual. the n. "days." |
| days | An abs. n., neu. gen., p. num., 3rd per., obj. c., gov. by the prep. "in." |
| of | A prep., sh. the rn. bet. "days" and *time* und. |
| old. | An adj. of quality, pos. deg., qual. the n. *time* und. |

## Exercise 186.

| | |
|---|---|
| 1. warders | A com. n., mas. gen., p. num., 3rd per., nom. c. to the v. "waved." |
| waved | A reg. tr. v., act. vo., indic. m., past t., p. num., 3rd per., agr. with its nom. "warders." |
| their | A pers. pron., mas. gen., p. num., 3rd per., poss. c., gov. by the n. "caps." |

| | |
|---|---|
| caps | A com. n., neu. gen., p. num., 3rd per., obj. c., gov. by the tr. v. "waved." |
| **and** | A cop. conj., jg. the sents. "The warders..caps" and "*the warders* cheered." |
| cheered | A reg. intr. v., indic. m., past t., p. num., 3rd per., agr. with its nom. *warders* und. |
| **but** | A disj. conj., jg. the sents. "*the warders* cheered" and "the crowd..impassively." |
| crowd | A com. col. n., neu. gen., s. num., 3rd per., nom. c. to the v. "looked." |
| looked | A reg. intr. v., indic. m., past t., s. num., 3rd per., agr. with its nom. "crowd." |
| on | An adv. of place, mod. the v. "looked." |
| impassively. | An adv. of man., mod. the v. "looked." |
| 2. Our | A pers. pron., com. gen., p. num., 1st per., poss. c., gov. by the n. "soldiers." |
| soldiers | A com. n., mas. gen., p. num., 3rd per., nom. c. to the v. "performed." |
| performed | A reg. tr. v., act. vo., indic. m., past t., p. num., 3rd per., agr. with its nom. "soldiers." |
| such | An adj. of quality, qual. the n. "feats." |
| feats | An abs. n., neu. gen., p. num., 3rd per., obj. c., gov. by the tr. v. "performed." |
| **as** | A cop. conj., cor. to "such," jg. the sents. "Our soldiers..feats" and "*the feats are*." (Such feats as *the feats are which* they are not able to express.) |
| they | A pers. pron., mas. gen., p. num., 3rd per., nom. c. to the v. "are." |
| are | An irreg. intr. v., indic. m., pres. t., p. num., 3rd per., agr. with its nom. "they." |
| not | An adv. of m. (neg.), mod. the v. "are." |
| able | An adj. of quality, pos. deg., qual. the pron. "they." |
| to | A particle, indg. infin. m. |
| to express. | A reg. tr. v., act. vo., infin. m., pres. t., gov. by the adj. "able." |
| 3. bay | A com. n., neu. gen., s. num., 3rd per., nom. c. to the v. "is." |
| is | An irreg. intr. v., indic. m., pres. t., s. num., 3rd per., agr. with its nom. "bay." |
| wide | An adj. of quality, pos. deg., qual. the n. "bay." |
| **but** | A disj. conj., jg. the sents. "The bay is wide" and "*the bay is* dangerous from shoals." |
| dangerous | An adj. of quality, pos. deg., qual. the n. *bay* und. |
| from | A prep., sh. the rn. bet. "dangerous" and "shoals." |
| shoals. | A com. n., neu. gen., p. num., 3rd per., obj. c., gov. by the prep. "from." |
| 4. He | A pers. pron., mas. gen., s. num., 3rd per., nom. c. to the v. "took." |
| took | An irreg. tr. v., act. vo., indic. m., past t., s. num., 3rd per., agr. with its nom. "he." |
| her | A pers. pron., fem. gen., s. num., 3rd per., poss. c., gov. by the n. "hand." |
| soft | An adj. of quality, pos. deg., qual. the n. "hand." |
| hand | A com. n., neu. gen., s. num., 3rd per., obj. c., gov. by the tr. v. "took." |
| **ere** | A cop. conj., jg. the sents. "He..hand" and "her mother could bar." |
| her | A pers. pron., fem. gen., s. num., 3rd per., poss. c., gov. by the n. "mother." |
| mother | A com. n., fem. gen., s. num., 3rd per., nom. c. to the v. "could bar." |
| could | An aux. v. to "bar," indg. pot. m., past t. |
| (to) bar | A reg. intr. v., infin. m., pres. t., gov. by the v. "could." |
| could bar. | A reg. intr. v., pot. m., past t., s. num., 3rd per., agr. with its nom. "mother." |
| 5. Wrath | An abs. n., neu. gen., s. num., 3rd per., nom. c. to the v. "is." |
| is | An irreg. intr. v., indic. m., pres. t., s. num., 3rd per., agr. with its nom. "wrath." |
| cruel | An adj. of quality, pos. deg., qual. the n. "wrath." |

| | |
|---|---|
| and | A cop. conj., jg. the sents. "Wrath is cruel" and "anger is outrageous." |
| anger | An abs. n., neu. gen., s. num., 3rd per., nom. c. to the v. "is." |
| is | An irreg. intr. v., indic. m., pres. t., s. num., 3rd per., agr. with its nom. "anger." |
| outrageous | An adj. of quality, pos. deg., qual. the n. "anger." |
| **but** | A disj. conj., jg. the sents. "anger is outrageous" and "who..envy." |
| who | An interrog. pron., com. gen., s. num., 3rd per., nom. c. to the v. "is." |
| is | An irreg. intr. v., indic. m., pres. t., s. num., 3rd per., agr. with its nom. "who." |
| able | An adj. of quality, pos. deg., qual. the pron. "who." |
| to | A particle, indg. infin. m. |
| to stand | An irreg. intr. v., infin. m., pres. t., gov. by the adj. "able." |
| before | A prep., sh. the rn. bet. "to stand" and "envy." |
| envy. | An abs. n., neu. gen., s. num., 3rd per., obj. c., gov. by the prep. "before." |
| 6. Be | An irreg. intr. v., imper. m., pres. t., s. num., p. form, 2nd per., agr. with its nom. *you* und. |
| swift | An adj. of quality, pos. deg., qual. the pron. *you* und. |
| to | A particle, indg. infin. m. |
| to hear | An irreg. intr. v., infin. m., pres. t., gov. by the adj. "swift." |
| **but** | A disj. conj., jg. the sents. "Be..hear" and "be cautious..tongue." |
| cautious | An adj. of quality, pos. deg., qual. the pron. *you* und. |
| of | A prep., sh. the rn. bet. "cautious" and "tongue." |
| your | A pers. pron., com. gen., s. num., p. form, 2nd per., poss. c., gov. by the n. "tongue." |
| tongue | A com. n., neu. gen., s. num., 3rd per., obj. c., gov. by the prep. "of." |
| **lest** | A disj. conj., jg. the sents. "be cautious..tongue" and "you..ignorance," and indg. subj. m. |
| you | A pers. pron., com. gen., s. num., p. form, 2nd per., nom. c. to the v. "betray." |
| betray | A reg. tr. v., act. vo., subj. m., pres. t., s. num., p. form, 2nd per., agr. with its nom. "you." |
| your | A pers. pron., com. gen., s. num., p. form, 2nd per., poss. c., gov. by the n. "ignorance." |
| ignorance. | An abs. n., neu. gen., s. num., 3rd per., obj. c., gov. by the tr. v. "betray." |
| 7. To-morrow | An adv. of time, mod. the v. "do." |
| let | An irreg. tr. v., act. vo., imper. m., pres. t., s. num., 2nd per., agr. with its nom. *thou* und. |
| us | A pers. pron., com. gen., p. num., 1st per., obj. c., gov. by the tr. v. "let." |
| (to) do | An irreg. intr. v., infin. m., pres. t., gov. by the v. "let." |
| **or** | A disj. conj., jg. the sents. "To-morrow..do" and "*to-morrow let us die.*" |
| (to) die. | A reg. intr. v., infin. m., pres. t., gov. by the v. *let* und. |
| 8. They | A pers. pron., com. gen., p. num., 3rd per., nom. c. to the v. "serve." |
| also | A cop. conj., introducing the sent. "They serve." |
| serve | A reg. intr. v., indic. m., pres. t., p. num., 3rd per., agr. with its nom. "the *y*." |
| who | A rel. pron., com. gen., p. num., 3rd per., agr. with its ant. "they," nom. c. to the v. "stand." |
| only | An adv. of deg., mod. the v. "stand." |
| stand | An irreg. intr. v., indic. m., pres. t., p. num., 3rd per., agr. with its nom. "who." |
| **and** | A cop. conj., jg. the sents. "who only stand" and "*who only wait.*" |
| wait. | A reg. intr. v., indic. m., pres. t., p. num., 3rd per., agr. with its nom. *who* und. |
| 9. cold | An adj. of quality, pos. deg., qual. the n. "sweat." |
| sweat | A com. n., neu. gen., s. num., 3rd per., nom. c. to the v. "melted." |

ENGLISH GRAMMAR AND ANALYSIS. 225

| | |
|---|---|
| melted | A reg. intr. v., indic. m., past t., s. num., 3rd per., agr. with its nom. "sweat." |
| from | A prep., sh. the rn. bet. "melted" and "limbs." |
| their | A pers. pron., mas. gen., p. num., 3rd per., poss. c., gov. by the n. "limbs." (Their, *i.e.* sailors'.) |
| limbs | A com. n., neu. gen., p. num., 3rd per., obj. c., gov. by the prep. "from." |
| **Nor** | A disj. conj., jg. the sents. "The cold...limbs" and "*they did rot.*" |
| (to) rot | A reg. intr. v., infin. m., pres. t., gov. by the v. *did* und. |
| **nor** | A disj. conj., jg. the sents. "*they did* rot" and "they did reck." |
| (to) reck | A reg. intr. v., infin. m., pres. t., gov. by the v. "did." |
| did | An aux. v. to "reck," indg. past t., and completing the negative form of the v. |
| did reck | A reg. intr. v., indic. m., past t., p. num., 3rd per., agr. with its nom. "they." |
| they. | A pers. pron., mas. gen., p. num., 3rd per., nom. c. to the v. "did reck." |
| 10. Lives | An abs. n., neu. gen., p. num., 3rd per., nom. c. to the v. "remind." |
| of | A prep., sh. the rn. bet. "lives" and "men." |
| great | An adj. of quality, pos. deg., qual. the n. "men." |
| men | A com. n., mas. gen., p. num., 3rd per., obj. c., gov. by the prep. "of." |
| all | An indef. nu. adj. of quantity, qual. the n. "lives." |
| remind | A reg. tr. v., act. vo., indic. m., pres. t., p. num., 3rd per., agr. with its nom. "lives." |
| us | A pers. pron., com. gen., p. num., 1st per., obj. c., gov. by the tr. v. "remind." |
| We | A pers. pron., com. gen., p. num., 1st per., nom. c. to the v. "can make." |
| can | An aux. v. to "make," indg. pot. m., pres. t. |
| (to) make | An irreg. tr. v., act. vo., infin. m., pres. t., gov. by the v. "can." |
| can make | An irreg. tr. v., act. vo., pot. m., pres. t., p. num., 1st per., agr. with its nom. "we." |
| our | A pers. pron., com. gen., p. num., 1st per., poss. c., gov. by the n. "lives." |
| lives | An abs. n., neu. gen., p. num., 3rd per., obj. c., gov. by the tr. v. "can make." |
| sublime. | An adj. of quality, qual. the n. "lives." |

## Exercise 187.

| | |
|---|---|
| 1. **Alas** | An interj. |
| how | An adv. of deg., mod. the adj. "little." |
| little | An adj. of quantity (bulk or mass), qual. the n. *knowledge* und. |
| can | An aux. v. to "be known," indg. pot. m., pres. t. |
| be | An aux. v. to "known," indg. pass. vo. |
| known | A past pl. from the tr. v. "to know," ref. to *knowledge* und. |
| can be known. | An irreg. tr. v., pass. vo., pot. m., pres. t., s. num., 3rd per., agr. with its nom. *knowledge* und. |
| 2. **Oh** | An interj. |
| that | A cop. conj., jg. the sents. "*I wish*" and "those lips had language," and indg. subj. m. |
| those | A dis. adj., lim. the n. "lips." |
| lips | A com. n., neu. gen., p. num., 3rd per., nom. c. to the v. "had." |
| had | An irreg. tr. v., subj. m., past t., p. num., 3rd per., agr. with its nom. "lips." |
| language. | An abs. n., neu. gen., s. num., 3rd per., obj. c., gov. by the tr. v. "had." |
| 3. **Oh** | An interj. |
| take | An irreg. tr. v., act. vo., imper. m., pres. t., s. num., 2nd per., agr. with its nom. *thou* und. |
| wanderer | A com. n., com. gen., s. num., 3rd per., obj. c., gov. by the tr. v. "take." |
| home. | A com. n., neu. gen., s. num., 3rd per., obj. c., gov. by the prep. *to* und. |

4. **Alas** — An interj.
how — An adv. of deg., mod. the adv. "soon."
soon — An adv. of time, mod. the v. "will end."
thy — A pers. pron., com. gen., s. num., 2nd per., poss. c., gov. by the n. "course."
little — An adj. of quality, pos. deg., qual. the n. "course."
course — An abs. n., neu. gen., s. num., 3rd per., nom. c. to the v. "will end."
will — An aux. v. to "end," indg. fut. t.
(to) end — A reg. intr. v., infin. m., pres. t., gov. by the v. "will."
will end. — A reg. intr. v., indic. m., fut. t., s. num., 3rd per., agr. with its nom. "course."

5. My — A pers. pron., com. gen., s. num., 1st per., poss. c., gov. by the n. "cheek."
cheek — A com. n., neu. gen., s. num., 3rd per., nom. c. to the v. "is."
is — An irreg. intr. v., indic. m., pres. t., s. num., 3rd per., agr. with its nom. "cheek."
cold — An adj. of quality, pos. deg., qual. the n. "cheek."
and — A cop. conj., jg. the sents. "My...cold" and "*my cheek is white.*"
white — An adj. of quality, pos. deg., qual. the n. *cheek* und.
**alas.** — An interj.

6. **O** — An interj.
brother — A com. n., mas. gen., s. num., 2nd per., nom. c. of add.
say — An irreg. tr. v., act. vo., imper. m., pres. t., s. num., 2nd per., agr. with its nom. *thou* und.
not — An adv. of m. (neg.), mod. the v. "say."
so. — An adv. of man., mod. the v. "say."

7. **Ah** — An interj.
me — A pers. pron., com. gen., s. num., 1st per., obj. c., gov. by the prep. *to* und. (or gov. by the prep. *for* und., or gov. by the tr. v. *pity* und. *Parsing*, pp. 86, 127.)
how — An adv. of deg., mod. the adv. "wearily."
wearily — An adv. of man., mod. the v. "pass."
pass — A reg. intr. v., indic. m., pres. t., p. num., 3rd per., agr. with its nom. "hours."
hours. — An abs. n., neu. gen., p. num., 3rd per., nom. c. to the v. "pass."

8. **O** — An interj.
lift — A reg. tr. v., act. vo., imper. m., pres. t., s. num., 2nd per., agr. with its nom. *thou* und.
me — A pers. pron., com. gen., s. num., 1st per., obj. c., gov. by the tr. v. "lift."
from — A prep., sh. the rn. bet. "lift" and "grass."
grass. — A com. n., neu. gen., s. num., 3rd per., obj. c., gov. by the prep. "from."

9. **Lo** — An interj.
lilies — A com. n., neu. gen., p. num., 3rd per., nom. c. exclamatory (or, obj. c., gov. by the tr. v. *behold* und.).
of — A prep., sh. the rn. bet. "lilies" and "field."
field — A com. n., neu. gen., s. num., 3rd per., obj. c., gov. by the prep. "of."
How — An adv. of man., mod. the v. "yield."
their — A pers. pron., neu. gen., p. num., 3rd per., poss. c., gov. by the n. "leaves."
leaves — A com. n., neu. gen., p. num., 3rd per., nom. c. to the v. "yield."
instruction — An abs. n., neu. gen., s. num., 3rd per., obj. c., gov. by the tr. v. "yield."
yield. — A reg. tr. v., act. vo., indic. m., pres. t., p. num., 3rd per., agr. with its nom. "leaves."

10. **Ah** — An interj.
**well-a-day** — An interj.
what — An interrog. pron. used as an adj. of quality, qual. the n. "looks."
evil — An adj. of quality, pos. deg., qual. the n. "looks."
looks — An abs. n., neu. gen., p. num., 3rd per., obj. c., gov. by the tr. v. "had."

| | |
|---|---|
| Had | An irreg. tr. v., act. vo., indic. m., past t., s. num., 1st per., agr. with its nom. "I." |
| I | A pers. pron., com. gen., s. num., 1st per., nom. c. to the v. "had." |
| from | A prep., sh. the rn. bet. "had" and *persons* und. |
| old | An adj. of quality, pos. deg., qual. the n.*persons* und. |
| and | A cop. conj., jg. the sents. "what...old *persons*" and "*What evil looks had I from young persons.*" |
| young. | An adj. of quality, pos. deg., qual. the n. *persons* und. |

## Exercise 188.

1. Gray hairs = old age; *metonymy (effect for cause)*. 2. Twenty sail = twenty ships; *synecdoche*. 3. (1) Thou art the gale of spring = thou art gentle like the gale of spring; *metaphor:* (2) thou art the mountain storm = thou art terrible and destructive like the mountain storm; *metaphor*. 4. Milton = the works of Milton; *metonymy (cause for effect)*. 5. (1) The whole passage forms a *climax:* (2) In action how like an angel; *simile:* (3) In apprehension, how like a god; *simile*. 6. (1) They were swifter than eagles = they were very swift; *hyperbole:* (2) they were stronger than lions = they were very strong; *hyperbole*. 7. (1) He waged more wars than others had read; *antithesis:* (2) [he] conquered more provinces than others had governed; *antithesis:* (3) [he] had been trained, &c., not by the precepts of others, but by his own commands; *antithesis:* (4) [he had been trained] not by miscarriages in the field, but by victories; *antithesis:* (5) [he had been trained] not by campaigns, but triumphs; *antithesis*. 8. The whole passage forms a *climax*. 9. This passage forms an *antithesis*. 10. Thirty head = thirty bodies; *synecdoche*. 11. Cicero = the works of Cicero; *metonymy (cause for effect)*. 12. Fair Penelopes = women as fair as Penelope; *metaphor*. 13. The kettle = the water in the kettle; *metonymy (container for thing contained)*. 14. Hannibal = Hannibal's men; *metonymy (effect for cause)*. 15. Frothing bowl = frothing liquor in the bowl; *metonymy (container for thing contained)*. 16. Beauty like lapse of summer day's light; *simile*. 17. I saw the Pleiads glitter like a swarm of fire-flies; *simile*. 18. (1) Oh, night; *apostrophe:* (2) [Oh] storm; *apostrophe:* (3) [Oh] darkness; *apostrophe*. 19. (1) Love took up, &c.; *prosopopœia* or *personification:* (2) Time; *prosopopœia* or *personification:* (3) Life; *prosopopœia* or *personification:* (4) Self; *prosopopœia* or *personification:* (5) golden sands = sands like gold; *metaphor*. 20. There is a tide = there is a crisis like a tide; *metaphor*. The metaphor is continued: taken at the flood; voyage of their life is bound in shallows; on such a full sea are we now afloat; we must take the current; or [we must] lose our ventures.

## Exercise 189.

| | |
|---|---|
| 1. But | A disj. conj., introducing the sent. "I should ill...Peers." |
| I | A pers. pron., mas. gen., s. num., 1st per., nom. c. to the v "should become." ("I," *i.e.*, Satan.) |
| should | An aux. v. to "become," indg. pot. m., past t. |
| ill | An adv. of m., mod. the v. "should become." |
| (to) become | An irreg. tr. v., act. vo., infin. m., pres. t., gov. by the v. "should." |
| should become | An irreg. tr. v., act. vo., pot. m., past t., s. num., 1st per., agr. with its nom. "I." |
| this | A dis. adj., lim. the n. "throne." |
| throne | A com. n., neu. gen., s. num., 3rd per., obj. c., gov. by the tr. v. "should become." |

| | |
|---|---|
| O | An interj. |
| Peers | A com. n. tending to prop., mas. gen., p. num., 2nd per., nom. c. of add. |
| And | A cop. conj., jg. the sents. "I should ill...Peers" and "*I should ill become* this imperial...power." |
| this | A dis. adj., lim. the n. "sov'reignty." |
| imperial | An adj. of quality, qual. the n. "sov'reignty." |
| sov'reignty | An abs. n., neu. gen., s. num., 3rd per., obj. c., gov. by the tr. v. *should become* und. |
| adorn'd | A past pl. from the tr. v. "to adorn," ref. to "sov'reignty." |
| With | A prep., sh. the rn. bet. "adorn'd" and "splendour." |
| splendour | An abs. n., neu. gen., s. num., 3rd per., obj. c., gov. by the prep. "with." |
| armed | A past pl. from the tr. v. "to arm," ref. to "sov'reignty." |
| with | A prep., sh. the rn. bet. "armed" and "power." |
| power | An abs. n., neu. gen., s. num., 3rd per., obj. c., gov. by the prep. "with." |
| if | A cop. conj., jg. the sents. "*I should ill become* this imperial ..power" and "aught propos'd *in the shape of difficulty could deter me from attempting*." |
| aught | A com. n., neu. gen., s. num., 3rd per., nom. c. to the v. *could deter* und. |
| propos'd | A past pl. from the tr. v. "to propose," ref. to "aught." |
| And | A cop. conj., jg. the sents. "aught propos'd *in the shape of difficulty could deter me from attempting*" and "aught judg'd of public moment, in the shape of difficulty *could deter me from attempting*." |
| judg'd | A past pl. from the tr. v. "to judge," ref. to *aught* und. |
| of | A prep., sh. the rn. bet. "judg'd" and "moment." |
| public | An adj. of quality, qual. the n. "moment." |
| moment | An abs. n., neu. gen., s. num., 3rd per., obj. c., gov. by the prep. "of." |
| in | A prep., sh. the rn. bet. *aught* und. and "shape." |
| shape | An abs. n., neu. gen., s. num., 3rd per., obj. c., gov. by the prep. "in." |
| Of | A prep., sh. the rn. bet. "shape" and "difficulty." |
| difficulty | An abs. n., neu. gen., s. num., 3rd per., obj. c., gov. by the prep. "of." |
| or | A disj. conj., jg. the sents. "aught judg'd of public moment, in the shape of difficulty *could deter me from attempting*" and "aught judg'd *of public moment in the shape of* danger..attempting." |
| danger | An abs. n., neu. gen., s. num., 3rd per., obj. c., gov. by the prep. *of* und. |
| could | An aux. v. to "deter," indg. pot. m., past t. |
| (to) deter | A reg. tr. v., act. vo., infin. m., pres. t., gov. by the v. "could." |
| could deter | A reg. tr. v., act. vo., pot. m., past t., s. num., 3rd per., agr. with its nom. *aught* und. |
| Me | A pers. pron., mas. gen., s. num., 1st per., obj. c., gov. by the tr. v. "could deter." |
| from | A prep., sh. the rn. bet. "could deter" and "attempting." |
| attempting. | A ger. from the intr. v. "to attempt," neu. gen., s. num., 3rd per., obj. c., gov. by the prep. "from." |
| Wherefore | An interrog. adv. of cause, mod. the v. "do assume." |
| do | An aux. v. to "assume," indg. pres. t., and completing the interrog. form of the v. |
| I | A pers. pron., mas. gen., s. num., 1st per., nom. c. to the v. "do assume." |
| (to) assume | A reg. tr. v., act. vo., infin. m., pres. t., gov. by the v. "do." |
| do assume | A reg. tr. v., act. vo., indic. m., pres. t., s. num., 1st per., agr. with its nom. "I." |
| These | A dis. adj., lim. the n. "royalties." |
| royalties | An abs. n., neu. gen., p. num., 3rd per., obj. c., gov. by the tr. v. "do assume." |
| and | A cop. conj., jg. the sents. "Wherefore do I..royalties" and "*wherefore do I not..reign*." |
| no | An adv. of m. (neg.), mod. the v. "do refuse." |

| | |
|---|---|
| (to) refuse | A reg. tr. v., act. vo., infin. m., pres. t., gov. by the v. *do* und. |
| to | A particle, indg. infin. m. |
| to reign | A reg. intr. v., infin. m., pres. t., gov. by the v. "*do* refuse." |
| Refusing | A pres. pl. from the tr. v. "to refuse," ref. to "I." |
| to | A particle, indg. infin. m. |
| to accept | A reg. tr. v., act. vo., infin. m., pres. t., gov. by the tr. pl. "refusing." |
| so | An adv. of deg., mod. the adj. "great." |
| great | An adj. of quality, pos. deg., qual. the n. "share." |
| share | An abs. n., neu. gen., s. num., 3rd per., obj. c., gov. by the tr. v. "to accept." |
| of | A prep., sh. the rn. bet. "share" and "hazard." |
| hazard | An abs. n., neu. gen., s. num., 3rd per., obj. c., gov. by the prep. "of." |
| as | A cop. conj., jg. the sents. "*wherefore do I* not refuse to reign.. hazard" and "*the share* of honour *is great*." |
| of | A prep., sh. the rn. bet. *share* und. and "honour." |
| honour | An abs. n., neu. gen., s. num., 3rd per., obj. c., gov. by the prep. "of." |
| due | An adj. of quality, qual. the pron. *which* und. (*which are* due alike). |
| alike | An adv. of man., mod. the adj. "due." |
| To | A prep., sh. the rn. bet. "due" and "him." |
| him | A pers. pron., mas. gen., s. num., 3rd per., obj. c., gov. by the prep. "to." |
| who | A rel. pron., mas. gen., s. num., 3rd per., agr. with its ant. "him," nom. c. to the v. "reigns." |
| reigns | A reg. intr. v., indic. m., pres. t., s. num., 3rd per., agr. with its nom. "who." |
| and | A cop. conj., jg. the sents. "*which are* due alike to him" and "so much *share* to him *is* due of hazard more." |
| so | An adv. of deg., mod. the adv. "much." |
| much | An adv. of deg., mod. the adj. "more." |
| to | A prep., sh. the rn. bet. "due" and "him." |
| him | A pers. pron., mas. gen., s. num., 3rd per., obj. c., gov. by the prep. "to." |
| due | An adj. of quality, pos. deg., qual. the n. *share* und. |
| Of | A prep., sh. the rn. bet. *share* und. and "hazard." |
| hazard | An abs. n., neu. gen., s. num., 3rd per., obj. c., gov. by the prep. "of." |
| more | An adj. of quantity (bulk or mass), comp. deg., qual. the n. *share* und. |
| as | A cop. conj., jg. the sents. "so much more *share* of hazard *is* due to him" and "he...sits." |
| he | A pers. pron., mas. gen., s. num., 3rd per., nom. c. to the v. "sits." |
| above | A prep., sh. the rn. bet. "sits" and "rest." |
| rest | A com. col. n., mas. gen. p. num., 3rd per., obj. c., gov. by the prep. "above." |
| High | An adj. of quality, used as an adv. of man., mod. the pl. "honour'd." |
| honour'd | A past pl. from the tr. v. "to honour," ref. to "he." |
| sits. | An irreg. intr. v., indic. m., pres. t., s. num., 3rd per., agr. with its nom. "he." |
| 2. When | A cop. conj., jg. the sents. "give thy soul...like *act*" and "first thine eyes unveil." |
| first | An adv. of time, mod. the v. "unveil." |
| thine | A pers. pron., com. gen., s. num., 2nd per., poss. c., gov. by the n. "eyes." |
| eyes | A com. n., neu. gen., p. num., 3rd per., nom. c. to the v. "unveil." |
| unveil | A reg. intr. v., indic. m., pres. t., p. num., 3rd per., agr. with its nom. "eyes." |
| give | An irreg. tr. v., act. vo., imper. m., pres. t., s. num., 2nd per., agr. with its nom. *thou* und. |
| thy | A pers. pron., com. gen., s. num., 2nd per., poss. c., gov. by the n. "soul." |

| | |
|---|---|
| soul | A com. n., neu. gen., s. num., 3rd per., obj. c., gov. by the prep. *to* und. |
| leave | An abs. n., neu. gen., s. num., 3rd per., obj. c., gov. by the tr. v. "give." |
| To | A particle, indg. infin. m. |
| To do | An irreg. tr. v., act. vo., infin. m., pres. t., gov. by the n. "leave." |
| like | An adj. of quality, pos. deg., qual. the n. *act* und. |
| our | A pers. pron., com. gen., p. num., 1st per., poss. c., gov. by the n. "bodies." |
| bodies | A com. n., neu. gen., p. num., 3rd per., nom. c. to the v. "forerun." |
| but | An adv. of deg., mod. the v. "forerun." |
| forerun | An irreg. tr. v., act. vo., indic. m., pres. t., p. num., 3rd per., agr. with its nom. "bodies." |
| spirit's | A com. n., neu. gen., s. num., 3rd per., poss. c., gov. by the n. "duty." |
| duty | An abs. n., neu. gen., s. num., 3rd per., obj. c., gov. by the tr. v. "forerun." |
| true | An adj. of quality, pos. deg., qual. the n. "hearts." |
| hearts | A com. n., neu. gen., p. num., 3rd per., nom. c. to the v. "spread." |
| spread | An irreg. intr. v., indic. m., pres. t., p. num., 3rd per., agr. with its nom. "hearts." |
| and | A cop. conj., jg. the sents. "true hearts spread" and "*true hearts* heave unto their God." |
| heave | An irreg. intr. v., indic. m., pres. t., p. num., 3rd per., agr. with its nom. *hearts* und. |
| Unto | A prep., sh. the rn. bet. "heave" and "God." |
| their | A pers. pron., neu. gen., p. num., 3rd per., poss. c., gov. by the n. "God." |
| God | A prop. n., mas. gen., s. num., 3rd per., obj. c., gov. by the prep. "unto." |
| as | A cop. conj., jg. the sents. "*true hearts* heave unto their God" and "flowers do *heave* to the sun." |
| flowers | A com. n., neu. gen., p. num., 3rd per., nom. c. to the v. "do heave." |
| do | An aux. v. to *heave* und., indg. pres. t., emph. form. |
| to | A prep., sh. the rn. bet. "do" and "sun." |
| sun. | A com. n., neu. gen., s. num., 3rd per., obj. c., gov. by the prep. "to." |
| 3. There | An expletive adv., mod. the v. "is." |
| is | An irreg. intr. v., indic. m., pres. t., s. num., 3rd per., agr. with its nom. *person* und. |
| none | A def. card. nu. adj. of quantity, qual. the n. *person* und. (no person). |
| of | A prep., sh. the rn. bet. *person* und. and "you." |
| you | A pers. pron., com. gen., p. num., 2nd per., obj. c., gov. by the prep. "of." |
| so | An adv. of deg., mod. the adj. "mean." |
| mean | An adj. of quality, pos. deg., qual. the n. *person* und. |
| and | A cop. conj., jg. the sents. "there is..mean" and "*there is none of you so* base." |
| base | An adj. of quality, pos. deg., qual. the n. *person* und. |
| That | A rel. pron., com. gen., s. num., 3rd per., agr. with its ant. *person* und., nom. c. to the v. "hath." |
| hath | An irreg. tr. v., act. vo., indic. m., pres. t., s. num., 3rd per., agr. with its nom. "that." |
| not | An adv. of m. (neg.), mod. the v. "hath." |
| noble | An adj. of quality, pos. deg., qual. the n. "lustre." |
| lustre | An abs. n., neu. gen., s. num., 3rd per., obj. c., gov. by the tr. v. "hath." |
| in | A prep., sh. the rn. bet. "hath" and "eyes." |
| your | A pers. pron., com. gen., p. num., 2nd per., poss. c., gov. by the n. "eyes." |
| eyes | A com. n., neu. gen., p. num., 3rd per., obj. c., gov. by the prep. "in." |

| | |
|---|---|
| I | A pers. pron., com. gen., s. num., 1st per., nom. c. to the v. "see." |
| see | An irreg. tr. v., act. vo., indic. m., pres. t., s. num., 1st per., agr. with its nom. "I." |
| you | A pers. pron., com. gen., p. num., 2nd per., obj. c., gov. by the tr. v. "see." |
| (to) stand | An irreg. intr. v., infin. m., pres. t., gov. by the v. "see." |
| like | An adj. of quality, pos. deg., qual. the pron. "you." |
| greyhounds | A com. n., com. gen., p. num., 3rd per., obj. c., gov. by the prep. *to* und. |
| in | A prep., sh. the rn. bet. "greyhounds" and "slips." |
| slips | A com. n., neu. gen., p. num., 3rd per., obj. c., gov. by the prep. "in." |
| Straining | A pres. pl. from the intr. v. "to strain," ref. to "greyhounds." |
| upon | A prep., sh. the rn. bet. "straining" and "start." |
| start. | An abs. n., neu. gen., s. num., 3rd per., obj. c., gov. by the prep. "upon." |
| 4. But | A disj. conj., introducing the sent. "some..notice of it." |
| some | An indef. nu. adj. of quantity, qual. the n. *friends* und. |
| of | A prep., sh. the rn. bet. *friends* und. and "friends." |
| Cicero's | A prop. n., mas. gen., s. num., 3rd per., poss. c., gov. by the n. "friends." |
| friends | A com. n., com. gen., p. num., 3rd per., obj. c., gov. by the prep. "of." |
| found | An irreg. tr. v., act. vo., indic. m., past t., p. num., 3rd per., agr. with its nom. *friends* und. |
| means | An abs. n., neu. gen., s. or p. num., 3rd per., obj. c., gov. by the tr. v. "found." |
| to | A particle, indg. infin. m. |
| to give | An irreg. tr. v., act. vo., infin. m., pres. t., gov. by the n. "means." |
| him | A pers. pron., mas. gen., s. num., 3rd per., obj. c., gov. by the prep. *to* und. |
| early | An adj. of quality, pos. deg., qual. the n. "notice." |
| notice | An abs. n., neu. gen., s. num., 3rd per., obj. c., gov. by the tr. v. "to give." |
| of | A prep., sh. the rn. bet. "notice" and "it." |
| it | A pers. pron., neu. gen., s. num., 3rd per., obj. c., gov. by the prep. "of." |
| upon | A prep., sh. the rn. bet. "set" and "which." |
| which | A rel. pron., neu. gen., s. num., 3rd per., agr. with its ant. the preceding sent., obj. c., gov. by the prep. "upon." |
| he | A pers. pron., mas. gen., s. num., 3rd per., nom. c. to the v. "set." |
| set | An irreg. intr. v., indic. m., past t., s. num., 3rd per., agr. with its nom. "he." |
| forward | An adv. of place, mod. the v. "set." |
| presently | An adv. of time, mod. the v. "set." |
| with | A prep., sh. the rn. bet. "set" and "brother." |
| his | A pers. pron., mas. gen., s. num., 3rd per., poss. c., gov. by the n. "brother." |
| brother | A com. n., mas. gen., s. num., 3rd per., obj. c., gov. by the prep. "with." |
| and | A cop. conj., jg. the sents. "upon which...brother" and "*upon which he set forward presently with his* nephew." |
| nephew | A com. n., mas. gen., s. num., 3rd per., obj. c., gov. by the prep. *with* und. |
| towards | A prep., sh. the rn. bet. "set" and "Astura." |
| Astura | A prop. n., neu. gen., s. num., 3rd per., obj. c., gov. by the prep. "towards." |
| nearest | An adj. of quality, superl. deg., qual. the n. "villa." |
| villa | A com. n., neu. gen., s. num., 3rd per., obj. c., in app. with "Astura." |
| which | A rel. pron., neu. gen., s. num., 3rd per., agr. with its ant. "villa," obj. c., gov. by the tr. v. "had." |
| he | A pers. pron., mas. gen., s. num., 3rd per., nom. c. to the v. "had." |

| | |
|---|---|
| had | An irreg. tr. v., act. vo., indic. m., past t., s. num., 3rd per., agr. with its nom. "he." |
| upon | A prep., sh. the rn. bet. "had" and "sea." |
| sea | A com. n., neu. gen., s. num., 3rd per., obj. c., gov. by the prep. "upon." |
| with | A prep., sh. the rn. bet. "set" and "intent." |
| intent | An abs. n., neu. gen., s. num., 3rd per., obj. c., gov. by the prep. "with." |
| to | A particle, indg. infin. m. |
| to transport | A reg. tr. v., act. vo., infin. m., pres. t., gov. by the n. "intent." |
| themselves | A compd. pers. pron., mas. gen., p. num., 3rd per., obj. c., gov. by the tr. v. "to transport." |
| directly | An adv. of time, mod. the v. "to transport." |
| out of | A compd. prep., sh. the rn. bet. "to transport" and "reach." (See also *Parsing*, p. 154.) |
| reach | An abs. n., neu. gen., s. num., 3rd per., obj. c., gov. by the prep. "out of." |
| of | A prep., sh. the rn. bet. "reach" and "enemies." |
| their | A pers. pron., mas. gen., p. num., 3rd per., poss. c., gov. by the n. "enemies." |
| enemies. | A com. n., com. gen., p. num., 3rd per., obj. c., gov. by the prep. "of." |
| But | A disj. conj., jg. the sents. "some...enemies" and "Quintus...abroad." |
| Quintus | A prop. n., mas. gen., s. num., 3rd per., nom. c. to the v. "resolved." |
| being | A pres. pl. from the intr. v. "to be," ref. to "unprepared Quintus." |
| wholly | An adv. of deg., mod. the pl. "unprepared." |
| unprepared | A negative form of the past pl. from the tr. v. "to prepare," ref. to "Quintus." |
| for | A prep., sh. the rn. bet. "unprepared" and "voyage." |
| so | An adv. of deg., mod. the adj. "long." |
| long | An adj. of quality, pos. deg., qual. the n. "voyage." |
| voyage | An abs. n., neu. gen., s. num., 3rd per., obj. c., gov. by the prep. "for." |
| resolved | A reg. tr. v., act. vo., indic. m., past t., s. num., 3rd per., agr. with its nom. "Quintus." |
| to | A particle, indg. infin. m. |
| to turn | A reg. intr. v., infin. m., pres. t., gov. by the v. "resolved." |
| back | An adv. of place, mod. the v. "to turn." |
| with | A prep., sh. the rn. bet. "to turn" and "son." |
| his | A pers. pron., mas. gen., s. num., 3rd per., poss. c., gov. by the n. "son." |
| son | A com. n., mas. gen., s. num., 3rd per., obj. c., gov. by the prep. "with." |
| to | A prep., sh. the rn. bet. "to turn" and "Rome." |
| Rome | A prop. n., neu. gen., s. num., 3rd per., obj. c., gov. by the prep. "to." |
| in | A prep., sh. the rn. bet. "resolved" and "confidence." |
| confidence | An abs. n., neu. gen., s. num., 3rd per., obj. c., gov. by the prep. "in." |
| of | A prep., sh. the rn. bet. "confidence" and "lying." |
| lying | A ger. from the intr. v. "to lie," neu. gen., s. num., 3rd per., obj. c., gov. by the prep. "of." |
| concealed | A past pl. from the tr. v. "to conceal," ref. to "Quintus." |
| there | An adv. of place, mod. the ger. "lying." |
| till | A cop. conj., jg. the sents. "Quintus...there" and "they...abroad." |
| they | A pers. pron., mas. gen., p. num., 3rd per., nom. c. to the v. "could provide." |
| could | An aux. v. to "provide," indg. pot. m., past t. |
| (to) provide | A reg. tr. v., act. vo., infin. m., pres. t., gov. by the v. "could." |
| could provide | A reg. tr. v., act. vo., pot. m., past t., p. num., 3rd per., agr. with its nom. "they." |
| money | A com. n., neu. gen., s. num., 3rd per., obj. c., gov. by the tr. v "could provide." |

ENGLISH GRAMMAR AND ANALYSIS. 233

| | |
|---|---|
| and | A cop. conj., jg. the sents. "they could provide money *for their support abroad*" and "*they could provide* necessaries for their support abroad." |
| necessaries | A com. n., neu. gen., p. num., 3rd per., obj. c., gov. by the tr. v. *could provide* und. |
| for | A prep., sh. the rn. bet. *could provide* und. and "support." |
| their | A pers. pron., mas. gen., p. num., 3rd per., poss. c., gov. by the n. "support." |
| support | An abs. n., neu. gen., s. num., 3rd per., obj. c., gov. by the prep. "for." |
| abroad. | An adv. of place, mod. the v. *should be* und. (*Whilst they should be* abroad.) |
| 5. But | A disj. conj., introducing the sent. "thou revisit'st not these eyes." |
| thou | A pers. pron., neu. gen., s. num., 2nd per., nom. c. to the v. "revisit'st." (Thou, *i.e.*, light.) |
| Revisit'st | A reg. tr. v., act. vo., indic. m., pres. t., s. num., 2nd per., agr. with its nom. "thou." |
| not | An adv. of m. (neg.), mod. the v. "revisit'st." |
| these | A dis. adj., lim. the n. "eyes." |
| eyes | A com. n., neu. gen., p. num., 3rd per., obj. c., gov. by the tr. v. "revisit'st." |
| that | A rel. pron., neu. gen., p. num., 3rd per., agr. with its ant. "eyes," nom. c. to the v. "roll." |
| roll | A reg. intr. v., indic. m., pres. t., p. num., 3rd per., agr. with its nom. "that." |
| in | A prep., sh. the rn. bet. "roll" and *manner* und. |
| vain | An adj. of quality, pos. deg., qual. the n. *manner* und. |
| in vain | An adverbial phrase of man., mod. the v. "roll." (*Parsing*, p. 150.) |
| To | A particle, indg. infin. m. |
| To find | An irreg. tr. v., act. vo., infin. m., pres. t., gov. by the v. "roll." |
| thy | A pers. pron., neu. gen., s. num., 2nd per., poss. c., gov. by the n. "ray." |
| piercing | A pres. pl. from the tr. v. "to pierce," used as an adj. of quality, qual. the n. "ray." |
| ray | A com. n., neu. gen., s. num., 3rd per., obj. c., gov. by the tr. v. "to find." |
| and | A cop. conj., jg. the sents. "that roll...ray" and "*that* find no dawn." |
| find | An irreg. tr. v., act. vo., indic. m., pres. t., p. num., 3rd per., agr. with its nom. *that* und. |
| no | A def. card. nu. adj. of quantity, qual. the n. "dawn." |
| dawn | A com. n., neu. gen., s. num., 3rd per., obj. c., gov. by the tr. v. "find." |
| So | An adv. of deg., mod. the adj. "thick." |
| thick | An adj. of quality, pos. deg., qual. the n. "drop." |
| drop | A com. n., neu. gen., s. num., 3rd per., nom. c. to the v. "hath quench'd." |
| serene | An adj. of quality, pos. deg., qual. the n. "drop." |
| hath | An aux. v. to "quench'd," indg. perf. t. |
| quench'd | A past pl. from the tr. v. "to quench," ref. to "orbs." |
| hath quench'd | A reg. tr. v., act. vo., indic. m., perf. t., s. num., 3rd per., agr. with its nom. "drop." |
| their | A pers. pron., neu. gen., p. num., 3rd per., poss. c., gov. by the n. "orbs." |
| orbs | A com. n., neu. gen., p. num., 3rd per., obj. c., gov. by the tr. v. "hath quench'd." |
| Or | A disj. conj., jg. the sents. "So thick...orbs" and "dim suffusion *hath* veil'd *their orbs.*" |
| dim | An adj. of quality, pos. deg., qual. the n. "suffusion." |
| suffusion | An abs. n., neu. gen., s. num., 3rd per., nom. c. to the v. "*hath* veil'd." |
| veil'd | A past pl. from the tr. v. "to veil," ref. to *orbs* und. |
| Yet | A disj. conj., jg. the preceding paragraph to the following sent. |
| not | An adv. of m. (neg.), mod. the v. "cease." |
| the | An adv. of deg., mod. the adv. "more." |
| more | An adv. of time, mod. the v. "cease." |

| | |
|---|---|
| Cease | A reg. tr. v., act. vo., indic. m., pres. t., s. num., 1st per., agr. with its nom. "I." |
| I | A pers. pron., mas. gen., s. num., 1st per., nom. c. to the v. "cease." |
| to | A particle, indg. infin. m. |
| to wander | A reg. intr. v., infin. m., pres. t.; used as an abs. n., neu. gen., s. num., 3rd per., obj. c., gov. by the tr. v. "cease." |
| where | A cop. conj., jg. the sents. "not the more...wander" and "the Muses...spring." |
| Muses | A prop. n., fem. gen., p. num., 3rd per., nom. c. to the v. "haunt." |
| haunt | A reg. tr. v., act. vo., indic. m., pres. t., p. num., 3rd per., agr. with its nom. "Muses." |
| Clear | An adj. of quality, pos. deg., qual. the n. "spring." |
| spring | A com. n., neu. gen., s. num., 3rd per., obj. c., gov. by the tr. v. "haunt." |
| or | A disj. conj., jg. the sents. "where the Muses...spring" and "*where the Muses haunt* shady grove." |
| shady | An adj. of quality, pos. deg., qual. the n. "grove." |
| grove | A com. n., neu. gen., s. num., 3rd per., obj. c., gov. by the tr. v. *haunt* und. |
| or | A disj. conj., jg. the sents. "*where the Muses haunt* shady grove" and "*where the Muses haunt* sunny hill." |
| sunny | An adj. of quality, pos. deg., qual. the n. "hill." |
| hill | A com. n., neu. gen., s. num., 3rd per., obj. c., gov. by the tr. v. *haunt* und. |
| Smit | A past pl. from the tr. v. "to smite," ref. to "I." (Smit= smitten.) |
| with | A prep., sh. the rn. bet. "smit" and "love." |
| love | An abs. n., neu. gen., s. num., 3rd per., obj. c., gov. by the prep. "with." |
| of | A prep., sh. the rn. bet. 'love" and "song." |
| sacred | An adj. of quality, pos. deg., qual. the n. "song." |
| song | An abs. n., neu. gen., s. num., 3rd per., obj. c., gov. by the prep. "of." |
| but | A disj. conj., jg. the sents. "not the more..song" and "chief.. visit." |
| chief=chiefly | An adv. of man., mod. the v. *visit* und. |
| Thee | A pers. pron., fem. gen. by personification, s. num., 2nd per., obj. c., gov. by the tr. v. *visit* und. |
| Sion | A prop. n., fem. gen. by personification, s. num., 2nd per., nom. c. of add. |
| and | A cop. conj., jg. the sents. "chief thee, Sion, *nightly I visit*" and "*chief* the flowery brooks beneath *thee* nightly I visit." |
| flowery | An adj. of quality, pos. deg., qual. the n. "brooks." |
| brooks | A com. n., neu. gen., p. num., 3rd per., obj. c., gov. by the tr. v. "visit." |
| beneath | A prep., sh. the rn. bet. "brooks" and *thee* und. |
| That | A rel. pron., neu. gen., p. num., 3rd per., agr. with its ant. "brooks," nom. c. to the v. "wash'd." |
| wash'd | A reg. tr. v., act. vo., indic. m., past t., p. num., 3rd per., agr. with its nom. "that." |
| thy | A pers. pron., fem. gen. by personification, s. num., 2nd per., poss. c., gov. by the n. "feet." |
| hallow'd | An adj. of quality, pos. deg., qual. the n. "feet." |
| feet | A com. n., neu. gen., p. num., 3rd per., obj. c., gov. by the tr. v. "wash'd." |
| and | A cop. conj., jg. the sents. "That..feet" and "*that* warbling flow." |
| warbling | A pres. pl. from the intr. v. "to warble," ref. to *that* und. ("Warbling" may be parsed as an adv. See *Parsing*, p. 145, § 7.) |
| flow | A reg. intr. v., indic. m., pres. t., p. num., 3rd per., agr. with its nom. *that* und. |
| Nightly | An adv. of time, mod. the v. "visit." |
| I | A pers. pron., mas. gen., s. num., 1st per., nom. c. to the v. "visit." |
| visit. | A reg. tr. v., act. vo. indic. m., pres. t., s. num., 1st per., agr. with its nom. "I." |

# ENGLISH GRAMMAR AND ANALYSIS. 235

| | |
|---|---|
| 6. Once | An adv. of num., mod. the v. *advance* und. |
| more | An adv. of time, mod. the v. *advance* und. |
| unto | A prep., sh. the rn. bet. *advance* und. and "breach." |
| breach | A com. n., neu. gen., s. num., 3rd per., obj. c., gov. by the prep. "unto." |
| dear | An adj. of quality, pos. deg., qual. the n. "friends." |
| friends | A com. n., mas. gen., p. num., 2nd per., nom. c. of add. |
| once | An adv. of num., mod. the v. *advance* und. |
| more | An adv. of time, mod. the v. *advance* und. |
| Or | A disj. conj., jg. the sents. "*advance* once more unto the breach" and "close..dead." |
| close | A reg. tr. v., act. vo., imper. m., pres. t., p. num., 2nd per., agr. with its nom. *you* und. |
| wa | A com. n., neu. gen., s. num., 3rd per., obj. c., gov. by the tr. v. "close." |
| up | An adv. of man., mod. the v. "close." |
| with | A prep., sh. the rn. bet. "close" and *soldiers* und. |
| our | A pers. pron., mas. gen., p. num., 1st per., poss. c., gov. by the n. *soldiers* und. |
| English | A prop. adj. of quality, qual. the n. *soldiers* und. |
| dead | An adj. of quality, qual. the n. *soldiers* und. |
| In | A prep., sh. the rn. bet. "is" and "peace." |
| peace | An abs. n., neu. gen., s. num., 3rd per., obj. c., gov. by the prep "in." |
| there | An expletive adv., mod. the v. "is." |
| 's = is | An irreg. intr. v., indic. m., pres. t., s. num., 3rd per., agr. with its nom. "nothing." |
| nothing | A com. n., neu. gen., s. num., 3rd per., nom. c. to the v. "is." |
| so | An adv. of deg., mod. the v. "becomes." |
| becomes | An irreg. tr. v., act. vo., indic. m., pres. t., s. num., 3rd per., agr. with its nom. *which* und. |
| man | A com. n., mas. gen., s. num., 3rd per., obj. c., gov. by the tr. v. "becomes." |
| As | A cop. conj., jg. the sents. "*which* so becomes a man" and "modest stillness *becomes him.*" |
| modest | An adj. of quality, pos. deg., qual. the n. "stillness." |
| stillness | An abs. n., neu. gen., s. num., 3rd per., nom. c. to the v. *becomes* und. |
| and | A cop. conj., jg. the sents. "modest stillness *becomes him*" and "humility *becomes him.*" |
| humility | An abs. n., neu. gen., s. num., 3rd per., nom. c. to the v. *becomes* und. |
| But | A disj. conj., jg. the sents. "In peace...nothing" and "Then imitate..tiger." |
| when | A cop. conj., cor. to the adv. "then," jg. the sents. "Then imitate..tiger" and "the blast..ears." |
| blast | An abs. n., neu. gen., s. num., 3rd per., nom. c. to the v. "blows." |
| of | A prep., sh. the rn. bet. "blast" and "war." |
| war | An abs. n., neu. gen., s. num., 3rd per., obj. c., gov. by the prep. "of." |
| blows | An irreg. intr. v., indic. m., pres. t., s. num., 3rd per., agr. with its nom. "blast." |
| in | A prep., sh. the rn. bet. "blows" and "ears." |
| our | A pers. pron., mas. gen., p. num., 1st per., poss. c., gov. by the n. "ears." |
| ears | A com. n., neu. gen., p. num., 3rd per., obj. c., gov. by the prep. "in." |
| Then | An adv. of time, mod. the v. "imitate." |
| imitate | A reg. tr. v., act. vo., imper. m., pres. t., p. num., 2nd per., agr. with its nom. *you* und. |
| action | An abs. n., neu. gen., s. num., 3rd per., obj. c., gov. by the tr. v. "imitate." |
| of | A prep., sh. the rn. bet. "action" and "tiger." |
| tiger | A com. n., com. gen., s. num., 3rd per., obj. c., gov. by the prep. "of." |
| Stiffen | A reg. tr. v., act. vo., imper. m., pres. t., p. num., 2nd per., agr. with its nom. *you* und. |

# 236 KEY TO

| | |
|---|---|
| sinews | A com. n., neu. gen., p. num., 3rd per., obj. c., gov. by the tr. v. "stiffen." |
| summon | A reg. tr. v., act. vo., imper. m., pres. t., p num., 2nd per., agr. with its nom. *you* und. |
| up | An adv. of man., mod. the v. "summon." |
| blood | A com. n., neu. gen., s. num., 3rd per., obj. c., gov. by the tr. v. "summon." |
| Disguise | A reg. tr. v., act. vo., imper. m., pres. t., p. num., 2nd per., agr. with its nom. *you* und. |
| fair | An adj. of quality, pos. deg., qual. the n. "nature." |
| nature | An abs. n., neu. gen., s. num., 3rd per., obj. c., gov. by the tr. v. "disguise." |
| with | A prep., sh. the rn. bet. "disguise" and "rage." |
| hard-favour'd | A compd. adj. of quality, pos. deg., qual. the n. "rage." |
| rage | An abs. n., neu. gen., s. num., 3rd per., obj. c., gov. by the prep. "with." |
| Then | An adv. of time, mod. the v. "lend." |
| lend | An irreg. tr. v., act. vo., imper. m., pres. t., p. num., 2nd per., agr. with its nom. *you* und. |
| eye | A com. n., neu. gen., s. num., 3rd per., obj. c., gov. by the prep. *to* und. |
| terrible | An adj. of quality, pos. deg., qual. the n. "aspect." |
| aspect | An abs. n., neu. gen., s. num., 3rd per., obj. c., gov. by the tr. v. "lend." |
| Let | An irreg. tr. v., act. vo., imper. m., pres. t., p. num., 2nd per., agr. with its nom. *you* und. |
| it | A pers. pron., neu. gen., s. num., 3rd per., obj. c., gov. by the tr. v. "let." |
| (to) pry | A reg. intr. v., infin. m., pres. t., gov. by the v. "let." |
| through | A prep., sh. the rn. bet. "to pry" and "portage." |
| portage | A com. n., neu. gen., s. num., 3rd per., obj. c., gov. by the prep. "through." |
| of | A prep., sh. the rn. bet. "portage" and "head." |
| head | A com. n., neu. gen., s. num., 3rd per., obj. c., gov. by the prep. "of." |
| Like | An adj. of quality, pos. deg., qual. the pron. "it." |
| brass | A com. n. used as an adj. of quality, qual. the n. "cannon." |
| cannon | A com. n., neu. gen., s. num., 3rd per., obj. c., gov. by the prep. *to* und. |
| let | An irreg. tr. v., act. vo., imper. m., pres. t., p. num., 2nd per., agr. with its nom. *you* und. |
| brow | A com. n., neu. gen., s. num., 3rd per., obj. c., gov. by the tr. v. "let." |
| (to) o'erwhelm | A reg. tr. v., act. vo., infin. m., pres. t., gov. by the v. "let." |
| it | A pers. pron., neu. gen., s. num., 3rd per., obj. c., gov. by the tr. v. "to o'erwhelm." |
| As | An adv. of deg., mod. the adv. "fearfully." |
| fearfully | An adv. of man., mod. the v. "to o'erwhelm." |
| as | A cop. conj., cor. to the adv. "as," jg. the sents. "let the brow ...fearfully" and "doth a galled rock o'erhang *his confounded base...Ocean.*" |
| doth | An aux. v. to "o'erhang," indg. pres. t. |
| galled | A past pl. from the tr. v. "to gall," used as an adj. of quality, qual. the n. "rock." |
| rock | A com. n., neu. gen., s. num., 3rd per., nom. c. to the v. "doth o'erhang." |
| (to) O'erhang | An irreg. tr. v., act. vo., infin. m., pres. t., gov. by the v. "doth." |
| doth o'erhang | An irreg. tr. v., act. vo., indic. m., pres. t., s. num., 3rd per., agr. with its nom. "rock." |
| and | A cop. conj., jg. the sents. "a galled rock doth o'erhang *his confounded base*" and "*a galled rock doth* jutty his confounded base." |
| (to) jutty | A reg. tr. v., act. vo., infin. m., pres. t., gov. by the v. *doth* und. |
| his | A pers. pron., neu. gen., s. num., 3rd per., poss. c., gov. by the n. "base." (See *Parsing*, p. 123, § 1, Ex. 2.) |

ENGLISH GRAMMAR AND ANALYSIS. 237

| | |
|---|---|
| confounded | A past pl. from the tr. v. "to confound," used as an adj. of quality, qual. the n. "base." |
| base | A com. n., neu. gen., s. num., 3rd per., obj. c., gov. by the tr. v. "doth jutty." |
| Swill'd | A past pl. from the tr. v. "to swill," ref. to "base." |
| with | A prep., sh. the rn. bet. "swill'd" and *Ocean* und. |
| wild | An adj. of quality, pos. deg., qual. the n. *Ocean* und. |
| and | A cop. conj., jg. the sents. "a galled rock doth o'erhang...wild Ocean" and "a galled rock doth o'erhang...swill'd with the wasteful Ocean." |
| wasteful | An adj. of quality, pos. deg., qual. the n. "Ocean." |
| Ocean. | A com. n. tending to prop., neu. gen., s. num., 3rd per., obj. c., gov. by the prep. *with* und. |
| Now | An adv. of time, mod. the v. "set." |
| set | An irreg. tr. v., act. vo., imper. m., pres. t., p. num., 2nd per., agr. with its nom. *you* und. |
| teeth | A com. n., neu. gen., p. num., 3rd per., obj. c., gov. by the tr. v. "set." |
| and | A cop. conj., jg. the sents. "Now...teeth" and "stretch...wide." |
| stretch | A reg. tr. v., act. vo., imper. m., pres. t., p. num., 2nd per., agr. with its nom. *you* und. |
| nostril | A com. n., neu. gen., s. num., 3rd per., obj. c., gov. by the tr. v. "stretch." |
| wide | An adj. of quality, pos. deg., qual. the n. "nostril." |
| Hold | An irreg. tr. v., act. vo., imper. m., pres. t., p. num., 2nd per., agr. with its nom. *you* und. |
| hard | An adv. of man., mod. the v. "hold." |
| breath | A com. n., neu. gen., s. num., 3rd per., obj. c., gov. by the tr. v. "hold." |
| and | A cop. conj., jg. the sents. "Hold...breath" and "bend...height." |
| bend | An irreg. tr. v., act. vo., imper. m., pres. t., p. num., 2nd per., agr. with its nom. *you* und. |
| up | An adv. of place, mod. the v. "bend." |
| every | A dist. nu. adj. of quantity, qual. the n. "spirit." |
| spirit | A com. n., neu. gen., s. num., 3rd per., obj. c., gov. by the tr. v. "bend." |
| to | A prep., sh. the rn. bet. "bend" and "height." |
| his | A pers. pron., neu. gen., s. num., 3rd per., poss. c., gov. by the n. "height." |
| full | An adj. of quality, qual. the n. "height." |
| height | An abs. n., neu. gen., s. num., 3rd per., obj. c., gov. by the prep. "to." |
| on | An adv. of place, mod. the v. *go* und. |
| on | An adv. of place, mod. the v. *go* und. |
| you | A pers. pron., mas. gen., p. num., 2nd per., nom. c. of add. |
| noblest | An adj. of quality, superl. deg., qual. the n. "English." |
| English | A prop. n., mas. gen., p. num., 2nd per., nom. c., in app. with "you." |
| Whose | A rel. pron., mas. gen., p. num., 2nd per., agr. with its ant. "English," poss. c., gov. by the n. "blood." |
| blood | A com. n., neu. gen., s. num., 3rd per., nom. c. to the v. "is fet." |
| is | An aux. v. to "fet," indg. pass. vo., pres. t. |
| fet = fetched | A past pl. from the tr. v. "to fet" (= to fetch), ref. to "blood." |
| is fet | An irreg. tr. v., pass. vo., indic. m., pres. t., s. num., 3rd per., agr. with its nom. "blood." ("Fet" is from O.E. "Fetian," to bring to. Its modern form, "fetch" is regular.) |
| from | A prep., sh. the rn. bet. "is fet" and "fathers." |
| fathers | A com. n., mas. gen., p. num., 3rd per., obj. c., gov. by the prep. "from." |
| of | A prep., sh. the rn. bet. "fathers" and "war-proof." |
| war-proof. | A compd. abs. n., neu. gen., s. num., 3rd per., obj. c., gov. by the prep. "of." |
| 7. Imagination | An abs. n., neu. gen., s. num., 3rd per., nom. c. to the v. "is." |
| in | A prep., sh. the rn. bet. "imagination" and "poet." |

| | |
|---|---|
| poet | A com. n., mas. gen., s. num., 3rd per., obj. c., gov. by the prep. "in." |
| is | An irreg. intr. v., indic. m., pres. t., s. num., 3rd per., agr. with its nom. "imagination." |
| faculty | An abs. n., neu. gen., s. num., 3rd per., nom. c. after the v. "is." |
| so | An adv. of deg., mod. the adj. "wild." |
| wild | An adj. of quality, pos. deg., qual. the n. "faculty." |
| and | A cop. conj., jg. the sents. "Imagination...wild" and "*imagination in a poet is a faculty so* lawless." |
| lawless | An adj. of quality, pos. deg., qual. the n. *faculty* und. |
| that | A cop. conj., jg. the sents. "Imagination...lawless" and "it needs...upon it." |
| it | A pers. pron., neu. gen., s. num., 3rd per., nom. c. to the v. "needs." |
| needs | A reg. tr. v., act. vo., indic. m., pres. t., s. num., 3rd per., agr. with its nom. "it." |
| to | A particle, indg. infin. m. |
| to have | An irreg. tr. v., act. vo., infin. m., pres. t.; used as an abs. n., neu. gen., s. num., 3rd per., obj. c., gov. by the tr. v. "needs." |
| some | An indef. nu. adj. of quantity, qual. the n. "check." |
| check | An abs. n., neu. gen., s. num., 3rd per., obj. c., gov. by the tr. v. "to have." |
| put | A past pl. from the tr. v. "to put," ref. to "check." |
| upon | A prep., sh. the rn. bet. "put" and "it." |
| it | A pers. pron., neu. gen., s. num., 3rd per., obj. c., gov. by the prep. "upon." |
| lest | A disj. conj., jg. the sents. "it needs...upon it" and "it...judgment," and indg. subj. m. |
| it | A pers. pron., neu. gen., s. num., 3rd per., nom. c. to the v. "outrun." |
| outrun | An irreg. tr. v., act. vo., subj. m., pres. t., s. num., 3rd per., agr. with its nom. "it." |
| judgment. | An abs. n., neu. gen., s. num., 3rd per., obj. c., gov. by the tr. v. "outrun." |
| great | An adj. of quality, pos. deg., qual. the n. "easiness." |
| easiness | An abs. n., neu. gen., s. num., 3rd per., nom. c. to the v. "renders." |
| of | A prep., sh. the rn. bet. "easiness" and "verse." |
| blank | An adj. of quality, qual. the n. "verse." |
| verse | A com. n., neu. gen., s. num., 3rd per., obj. c., gov. by the prep. "of." |
| renders | A reg. tr. v., act. vo., indic. m., pres. t., s. num., 3rd per., agr. with its nom. "easiness." |
| poet | A com. n., mas. gen., s. num., 3rd per., obj. c., gov. by the tr. v. "renders." |
| too | An adv. of deg., mod. the adj. "luxuriant." |
| luxuriant | An adj. of quality, pos. deg., qual. the n. "poet." |
| he | A pers. pron., mas. gen., s. num., 3rd per., nom. c. to the v. "is tempted." |
| is | An aux. v. to "tempted," indg. pass. vo., pres. t. |
| tempted | A past pl. from the tr. v. "to tempt," ref. to "he." |
| is tempted | A reg. tr. v., pass. vo., indic. m., pres. t., s. num., 3rd per., agr. with its nom. "he." |
| to | A particle, indg. infin. m. |
| to say | An irreg. tr. v., act. vo., infin. m., pres. t., gov. by the v. "is tempted." |
| many | An indef. nu. adj. of quantity, pos. deg., qual. the n. "things." |
| things | A com. n., neu. gen., p. num., 3rd per., obj. c., gov. by the tr. v. "to say." |
| which | A rel. pron., neu. gen., p. num., 3rd per., agr. with its ant. "things," nom. c. to the v. "might be omitted." |
| might | An aux. v. to "be omitted," indg. pot. m., past t. |
| better | An adv. of man., comp. deg., mod. the v. "might be omitted." |
| be | An aux. v. to "omitted," indg. pass. vo. |
| omitted | A past pl. from the tr. v. "to omit," ref. to "which." |

| | |
|---|---|
| might be omitted | A reg. tr. v., pass. v., pot. m., past t., p. num., 3rd per., agr. with its nom. "which." |
| or | A disj. conj., jg. the sents. "which..omitted" and "which might at least be shut up in fewer words." |
| at least | A compd. adv. of deg., mod. the v. "might be shut." (See also Parsing, p. 150.) |
| shut | A past pl. from the tr. v. "to shut," ref. to *which* und. |
| up | An adv. of place, mod. the v. "might be shut." |
| in | A prep., sh. the rn. bet. "might be shut" and "words." |
| fewer | An indef. nu. adj. of quantity, comp. deg., qual. the n. "words." |
| words. | A com. n., neu. gen., p. num., 3rd per., obj. c., gov. by the prep. "in." |
| But | A disj. conj., jg. the sents. "he is tempted..omitted" and "the fancy then..to come in." |
| when | A cop. conj., cor. to the adv. "then," jg. the sents. "the fancy then..to come in" and "the difficulty..is interposed." |
| difficulty | An abs. n., neu. gen., s. num., 3rd per., nom. c. to the v. "is interposed." |
| of | A prep., sh. the rn. bet. "difficulty" and "rhyming." |
| artful | An adj. of quality, pos. deg., qual. the n. "rhyming." |
| rhyming | An abs. n., neu. gen., s. num., 3rd per., obj. c., gov. by the pre "of." |
| is | An aux. v. to "interposed," indg. pass. vo., pres. t. |
| interposed | A past pl. from the tr. v. "to interpose," ref. to "difficulty." |
| is interposed | A reg. tr. v., pass. vo., indic. m., pres. t., s. num., 3rd per., agr. with its. nom. "difficulty." |
| where | A cop. conj., jg. the sents. "the difficulty..is interposed" and "the poet..couplet." |
| poet | A com. n., mas. gen., s. num., 3rd per., nom. c. to the v. "confines." |
| confines | A reg. tr. v., act. vo., indic. m., pres. t., s. num., 3rd per., agr. with its nom. "poet." |
| his | A pers. pron., mas. gen., s. num., 3rd per., poss. c., gov. by the n. "sense." |
| sense | An abs. n., neu. gen., s. num., 3rd per., obj. c., gov. by the tr. v. "confines." |
| to | A prep., sh. the rn. bet. "confines" and "couplet." |
| his | A pers. pron., mas. gen., s. uum., 3rd per., poss. c., gov. by the n. "couplet." |
| couplet | A com. n., neu. gen., s. num., 3rd per., obj. c., gov. by the prep. "to." |
| and | A cop. conj., jg. the sents. "where the poet..couplet" and "*where the poet* must contrive..words." |
| must | An aux. v. to "contrive," indg. pot. m., pres. t. |
| (to) contrive | A reg. tr. v., act. vo., infin. m., pres. t., gov. by the v. "must." |
| must contrive | A reg. tr. v., act. vo., pot. m., pres. t., s. num., 3rd per., agr. with its nom. *poet* und. |
| that | A dis. adj., lim. the n. "sense." |
| sense | An abs. n., neu. gen., s. num., 3rd per., obj. c., gov. by the tr. v. "must contrive." |
| into | A prep., sh. the rn. bet. "must contrive" and "words." |
| such | An adj. of quality, qual. the n. "words." |
| words | A com. n., neu. gen., p. num., 3rd per., obj. c., gov. by the prep. "into." |
| that | A cop. conj., jg. the sents. "*the poet* must contrive..words" and "the rhyme..them." |
| rhyme | A com. n., neu. gen., s. num., 3rd per., nom. c. to the v. "shall follow." |
| shall | An aux. v. to "follow," indg. fut. t., emph. form, expressing "certainty." |
| naturally | An adv. of man. mod. the v. "shall follow." |
| (to) follow | A reg. tr. v., act. vo., infin. m., pres. t., gov. by the v. "shall." |
| shall follow | A reg. tr. v., act. vo., indic. m., fut. t., emph. form, s. num., 3rd per., agr. with its nom. "rhyme." |
| them | A pers. pron., neu. gen., p. num., 3rd per., obj. c., gov. by the tr. v. "shall follow." |

240  KEY TO

| | |
|---|---|
| nor | A disj. conj., jg. the sents. "the rhyme..them" and that *sense shall follow* the rhyme." |
| that | A dis. adj., lim. the n. *sense* und. |
| rhyme | A com. n., neu. gen., s. num., 3rd per., obj. c., gov. by the tr. v. *shall follow* und. |
| fancy | An abs. n., neu. gen., s. num., 3rd per., nom. c. to the v. "gives." |
| then | An adv. of time, mod. the v. "gives." |
| gives | An irreg. tr. v., act. vo., indic. m., pres. t., s. num., 3rd per., agr. with its nom. "fancy." |
| leisure | An abs. n., neu. gen., s. num., 3rd per., obj. c., gov. by the tr. v. "gives." |
| to | A prep., sh. the rn. bet. "gives" and "judgment." |
| judgment | An abs. n., neu. gen., s. num., 3rd per., obj. c., gov. by the prep. "to." |
| to | A particle, indg. infin. m. |
| to come | An irreg. intr. v., infin. m., pres. t., gov. by the n. "leisure." |
| in | An adv. of place, mod. the v. "to come." |
| which | A rel. pron., neu. gen., s. num., 3rd per., agr. with its ant. "judgment," nom. c. to the v. "is." |
| seeing | A pres. pl. from the tr. v. "to see," ref. to "which." |
| so | An adv. of deg., mod. the adj. "heavy." |
| heavy | An adj. of quality, pos. deg., qual. the n. "tax." |
| tax | A com. n., neu. gen., s. num., 3rd per., obj. c., gov. by the tr. pl. "seeing." |
| imposed | A past pl. from the tr. v. "to impose," ref. to "tax." |
| is | An irreg. intr. v., indic. m., pres. t., s. num., 3rd per., agr. with its nom. "which." |
| ready | An adj. of quality, pos. deg., qual. the pron. "which." |
| to | A particle, indg. infin. m. |
| to cut | An irreg. tr. v., act. vo., infin. m., pres. t., gov. by the adj. "ready." |
| off | An adv. of place, mod. the v. "to cut." |
| all | An indef. nu. adj. of quantity, qual. the n. "expenses." |
| unnecessary | An adj. of quality, pos. deg., qual. the n. "expenses." |
| expenses. | A com. n., neu. gen., p. num., 3rd per., obj. c., gov. by the tr. v. "to cut." |
| 8. There | An adv. of place, mod. the v. *will enjoy* und. |
| love | An abs. n., neu. gen., s. num., 3rd per., obj. c., gov. by the tr. v. *will enjoy* und. |
| and | A cop. conj., jg. the sents. "There *we'll enjoy* love *in* peace" and "*there* we'll enjoy freedom in peace." |
| freedom | An abs. n., neu. gen., s. num., 3rd per., obj. c., gov. by the tr. v. "will enjoy." |
| we | A pers. pron., com. gen., p. num., 1st per., nom. c. to the v. "will enjoy." |
| 'll=will | An aux. v. to "enjoy," indg. fut. t., emph. form, expressing "certainty." |
| in | A prep., sh. the rn. bet. "will enjoy" and "peace." |
| peace | An abs. n., neu. gen., s. num., 3rd per., obj. c., gov. by the prep. "in." |
| (to) enjoy | A reg. tr. v., act. vo., infin. m., pres. t., gov. by the v. "will." |
| will enjoy | A reg. tr. v., act. vo., indic. m., fut. t., emph. form, p. num., 1st per., agr. with its nom. "we." |
| No | A def. card. nu. adj. of quantity, qual. the n. "Spaniards." |
| Spaniards | A prop. n., com. gen., p. num., 3rd per., nom. c. to the v. "will destroy." |
| will | An aux. v. to "destroy," indg. fut. t. |
| that | A dis. adj., lim. the n. "colony." |
| colony | A com. n., neu. gen., s. num., 3rd per., obj. c., gov. by the tr. v. "will destroy." |
| (to) destroy | A reg. tr. v., act. vo., infin. m., pres. t., gov. by the v. "will." |
| will destroy | A reg. tr. v., act. vo., indic. m., fut. t., p. num., 3rd per., agr. with its nom. "Spaniards." |
| We | A pers. pron., com. gen., p. num., 1st per., nom. c. to the v. "will grant." |
| to | A prep., sh. the rn. bet. "will grant" and "ourselves." |

| | |
|---|---|
| ourselves | A compd. pers. pron., com. gen., p. num., 1st per., obj. c., gov. by the prep. "to." |
| will | An aux. v. to "grant," indg. fut. t., emph. form, expressing "determination." |
| all | An indef. nu. adj. of quantity, qual. the n. "wishes." |
| our | A pers. pron., com. gen., p. num., 1st per., poss. c., gov. by the n. "wishes." |
| wishes | An abs. n., neu. gen., p. num., 3rd per., obj. c., gov. by the tr. v. "will grant." |
| (to) grant | A reg. tr. v., act. vo., infin. m., pres. t., gov. by the v. "will." |
| will grant | A reg. tr. v., act. vo., indic. m., fut. t., emph. form, p. num., 1st per., agr. with its nom. "we." |
| And | A cop. conj., jg. the sents. "We...grant" and "we nothing...want." |
| nothing | A com. n., neu. gen., s. num., 3rd per., obj. c., gov. by the tr. pl. "coveting." |
| coveting | A pres. pl. from the tr. v. "to covet," ref. to we und. |
| can | An aux. v. to "want," indg. pot. m., pres. t. |
| nothing | A com. n., neu. gen., s. num., 3rd per., obj. c., gov. by the tr. v. "can want." |
| (to) want | A reg. tr. v., act. vo., infin. m., pres. t., gov. by the v. "can." |
| can want. | A reg. tr. v., act. vo., pot. m., pres. t., p. num., 1st per., agr. with its nom. we und. |
| 9. Heaven | A com. n. tending to prop., mas. gen. by personification, s. num., 3rd per., nom. c. to the v. "hides." |
| from | A prep., sh. the rn. bet. "hides" and "creatures." |
| all | An indef. nu. adj. of quantity, qual. the n. "creatures." |
| creatures | A com. n., com. gen., p. num., 3rd per., obj. c., gov. by the prep. "from." |
| hides | An irreg. tr. v., act. vo., indic. m., pres. t., s. num., 3rd per., agr. with its nom. "Heaven." |
| book | A com. n., neu. gen., s. num., 3rd per., obj. c., gov. by the tr. v. "hides." |
| of | A prep., sh. the rn. bet. "book" and "fate." |
| fate | An abs. n., neu. gen., s. num., 3rd per., obj. c., gov. by the prep. "of." |
| All | An adj. of quantity (bulk or mass), qual. the n. "book." |
| but=except | A prep., sh. the rn. bet. "all" and "page." |
| page | A com. n., neu. gen., s. num., 3rd per., obj. c., gov. by the prep. "but." |
| prescribed | A past pl. from the tr. v. "to prescribe," ref. to "page." |
| their | A pers. pron., com. gen., p. num., 3rd per., poss. c., gov. by the n. "state." |
| present | An adj. of quality, qual. the n. "state." |
| state | An abs. n., neu. gen., s. num., 3rd per., obj. c., in app. with "page." |
| From | A prep., sh. the rn. bet. *hides* und. and "brutes." |
| brutes | A com. n., com. gen., p. num., 3rd per., obj. c., gov. by the prep. "from." |
| what | A compd. rel. pron., including both the rel. and the ant., neu. gen., s. num., 3rd per. "What" is equiv. to "the thing which," "thing" being obj. c., gov. by the tr. v. *hides* und., and "which" obj. c., gov. by the tr. v. *know* und. |
| men | A com. n., mas. gen., p. num., 3rd per., nom. c. to the v. *know* und. |
| from | A prep., sh. the rn. bet. *hides* und. and "men." |
| men | A com. n., mas. gen., p. num., 3rd per., obj. c., gov. by the prep. "from." |
| what | A compd. rel. pron., including both the rel. and the ant., neu. gen., s. num., 3rd per. "What" is equiv. to "the thing which," "thing" being obj. c., gov. by the tr. v. *hides* und., and "which" obj. c., gov. by the tr. v. "know." |
| spirits | A com. n., com. gen., p. num., 3rd per., nom. c. to the v. "know." |
| know | An irreg. tr. v., act. vo., indic. m., pres. t., p. num., 3rd per., agr. with its nom. "spirits." |
| Or | A disj. conj., jg. the sents. "Heaven...state" and "who...below." |

| | |
|---|---|
| who | An interrog. pron., com. gen., s. num., 3rd per., nom. c. to the v "could suffer." |
| could | An aux. v. to "suffer," indg. pot. m., past t. |
| (to) suffer | A reg. tr. v., act. vo., infin. m., pres. t., gov. by the v. "could." |
| could suffer | A reg. tr. v., act. vo., pot. m., past t., s. num., 3rd per., agr. with its nom. "who." |
| being | A ger. from the intr. v. "to be," neu. gen., s. num., 3rd per., obj. c., gov. by the tr. v. "could suffer." |
| here | An adv. of place, mod. the ger. "being." |
| below. | An adv. of place, mod. the ger. "being." |
| lamb | A com. n., mas. gen., s. num., 3rd per., nom. c. to the v. "would skip." |
| thy | A pers. pron., com. gen., s. num., 2nd per., poss. c., gov. by the n. "riot." |
| riot | An abs. n., neu. gen., s. num., 3rd per., nom. c. to the v. "dooms." |
| dooms | A reg. tr. v., act. vo., indic. m., pres. t., s. num., 3rd per., agr. with its nom. "riot." (*Which* thy riot dooms to bleed to-day.) |
| to bleed | A particle, indg. infin. m. |
| to bleed | An irreg. intr. v., infin. m., pres. t., gov. by the v. "dooms." |
| to-day | An adv. of time, mod. the v. "to bleed." |
| Had | An irreg. tr. v., subj. m., past t., s. num., 3rd per., agr. with its nom. "he." (*If* he had thy reason.) |
| he | A pers. pron., mas. gen., s. num., 3rd per., nom. c. to the v. "had." |
| thy | A pers. pron., com. gen., s. num., 2nd per., poss. c., gov. by the n. "reason." |
| reason | An abs. n., neu. gen., s. num., 3rd per., obj. c., gov. by the tr. v. "had." |
| would | An aux. v. to "skip," indg. pot. m., past t. |
| he | A pers. pron., mas. gen., s. num., 3rd per., nom. c., in app. with "lamb." ("He" is redundant. See *Gr.* ₴314, *Obs.* 6.) |
| (to) skip | A reg. intr. v., infin. m., pres. t., gov. by the v. "would." |
| would skip | A reg. intr. v., pot. m., past t., s. num., 3rd per., agr. with its nom. "lamb." |
| and | A cop. conj., jg. the sents. "would the lamb skip" and "*would the lamb* play." |
| (to) play. | A reg. intr. v., infin. m., pres. t., gov. by the v. *would* und. |
| Have | An irreg. tr. v., act. vo., indic. m., pres. t., s. num., 1st per., agr. with its nom. "I." |
| I | A pers. pron., mas. gen., s. num., 1st per., nom. c. to the v. "have." ("I," i.e. King Edward the Fourth.) |
| tongue | A com. n., neu. gen., s. num., 3rd per., obj. c., gov. by the tr. v. "have." |
| to | A particle, indg. infin. m. |
| to doom | A reg. tr. v., act. vo., infin. m., pres. t., gov. by the n. "tongue." |
| my | A pers. pron., mas. gen., s. num., 1st per., poss. c., gov. by the n. "brother's." |
| brother's | A com. n., mas. gen., s. num., 3rd per., poss. c., gov. by the n. "death." |
| death | An abs. n., neu. gen., s. num., 3rd per., obj. c., gov. by the tr. v. "to doom." |
| And | A cop. conj., jg. the sents. "Have I...death" and "shall..slave." |
| shall | An aux. v. to "give," indg. fut. t., emph. form, expressing "certainty." |
| that | A dis. adj., lim. the n. "tongue." |
| tongue | A com. n., neu. gen., s. num., 3rd per., nom. c. to the v. "shall give." |
| (to) give | An irreg. tr. v., act. vo., infin. m., pres. t., gov. by the v. "shall." |
| shall give | An irreg. tr. v., act. vo., indic. m., fut. t., emph. form, s. num., 3rd per., agr. with its nom. "tongue." |
| pardon | An abs. n., neu. gen., s. num., 3rd per., obj. c., gov. by the tr. v. "shall give." |
| to | A prep., sh. the rn. bet. "shall give" and "slave." |

| | |
|---|---|
| lave | A com. n., mas. gen., s. num., 3rd per., obj. c., gov. by the prep. "to." |
| My | A pers. pron., mas. gen., s. num., 1st per., poss. c., gov. by the n. "brother." |
| brother | A com. n., mas. gen., s. num., 3rd per., nom. c. to the v. "killed." |
| killed | A reg. tr. v., act. vo., indic. m., past t., s. num., 3rd per., agr. with its nom. "brother." |
| no | A def. card. nu. adj. of quantity, qual. the n. "man." |
| man | A com. n., mas. gen., s. num., 3rd per., obj. c., gov. by the tr. v. "killed." |
| his | A pers. pron., mas. gen., s. num., 3rd per., poss. c., gov. by the n. "fault." |
| fault | An abs. n., neu. gen., s. num., 3rd per., nom. c. to the v. "was." |
| was | An irreg. intr. v., indic. m., past t., s. num., 3rd per., agr. with its nom. "fault." |
| thought | An abs. n., neu. gen., s. num., 3rd per., nom. c. after the v. "was." |
| And | A cop. conj., jg. the sents. "his fault was thought" and "yet.. death." |
| yet | An adv. of time, mod. the v. "was." |
| his | A pers. pron., mas. gen., s. num., 3rd per., poss. c., gov. by the n. "punishment." |
| punishment | An abs. n., neu. gen., s. num., 3rd per., nom. c. to the v. "was." |
| was | An irreg. intr. v., indic. m., past t., s. num., 3rd per., agr. with its nom. "punishment." |
| bitter | An adj. of quality, pos. deg., qual. the n. "death." |
| death | An abs. n., neu. gen., s. num., 3rd per., nom. c. after the v. "was." |
| Who | An interrog. pron., com. gen., s. num., 3rd per., nom. c. to the v. "sued." |
| sued | A reg. intr. v., indic. m., past t., s. num., 3rd per., agr. with its nom. "who." |
| to | A prep., sh. the rn. bet. "sued" and "me." |
| me | A pers. pron., mas. gen., s. num., 1st per., obj. c., gov. by the prep. "to." |
| for | A prep., sh. the rn. bet. "sued" and "him." |
| him | A pers. pron., mas. gen., s. num., 3rd per., obj. c., gov. by the prep. "for." |
| who | An interrog. pron., com. gen., s. num., 3rd per., nom. c. to the v. "kneel'd." |
| in | A prep., sh. the rn. bet. "kneel'd" and "wrath." (In=during.) |
| my | A pers. pron., mas. gen., s. num., 1st per., poss. c., gov. by the n. "wrath." |
| wrath | An abs. n., neu. gen., s. num., 3rd per., obj. c., gov. by the prep. "in." |
| Kneel'd | A reg. intr. v., indic. m., past t., s. num., 3rd per., agr. with its nom. "who." |
| at | A prep., sh. the rn. bet. "kneel'd" and "feet." |
| my | A pers. pron., mas. gen., s. num., 1st per., poss. c., gov. by the n. "feet." |
| feet | A com. n., neu. gen., p. num., 3rd per., obj. c., gov. by the prep. "at." |
| and | A cop. conj., jg. the sents. "who..feet" and "*who* bade me be advised." |
| bade | An irreg. tr. v., act. vo., indic. m., past t., s. num., 3rd per., agr. with its nom. *who* und. |
| me | A pers. pron., mas. gen., s. num., 1st per., obj. c., gov. by the tr. v. "bade." |
| be | An aux. v. to "advised," indg. pass. vo., pres. t. |
| advised | A past pl. from the tr. v. "to advise," ref. to "me." |
| (to) be advised | A reg. tr. v., pass. vo., infin. m., pres. t., gov. by the v. "bade." |
| Who | An interrog. pron., com. gen., s. num., 3rd per., nom. c. to the v. "spoke." |
| spoke | An irreg. intr. v., indic. m., past t., s. num., 3rd per., agr. with its nom. "who." |

| | |
|---|---|
| of | A prep., sh. the rn. bet. "spoke" and "brotherhood." |
| brotherhood | An abs. n., neu. gen., s. num., 3rd per., obj. c., gov. by the prep. "of." |
| who | An interrog. pron., com. gen., s. num., 3rd per., nom. c. to the v. "spoke." |
| spoke | An irreg. intr. v., indic. m., past t., s. num., 3rd per., agr. with its nom. "who." |
| of | A prep., sh. the rn. bet. "spoke" and "love." |
| love | An abs. n., neu. gen., s. num., 3rd per., obj. c., gov. by the prep. "of." |
| Who | An interrog. pron., com. gen., s. num., 3rd per., nom. c. to the v. "told." |
| told | An irreg. tr. v., act. vo., indic. m., past t., s. num., 3rd per., agr. with its nom. "who." |
| me | A pers. pron., mas. gen., s. num., 1st per., obj. c., gov. by the prep. *to* und. |
| how | A cop. conj., jg. the sents. "Who told me" and "the poor soul.. Warwick." |
| poor | An adj. of quality, pos. deg., qual. the n. "soul." |
| soul | A com. n., mas. gen., s. num., 3rd per., nom. c. to the v. "did forsake." ("Soul" here is equivalent to "man.") |
| did | An aux. v. to "forsake," indg. past t., emph. form. |
| (to) forsake | An irreg. tr. v., act. vo., infin. m., pres. t., gov. by the v. "did." |
| did forsake | An irreg. tr. v., act. vo., indic. m., past t., emph. form, s. num., 3rd per., agr. with its nom. "soul." |
| mighty | An adj. of quality, pos. deg., qual. the n. "Warwick." |
| Warwick | A prop. n., mas. gen., s. num., 3rd per., obj. c., gov. by the tr. v. "did forsake." |
| and | A cop. conj., jg. the sents. "how the poor soul.. Warwick" and "how the poor soul did fight for me." |
| did | An aux. v. to "fight," indg. past t., emph. form. |
| (to) fight | An irreg. intr. v., infin. m., pres. t., gov. by the v. "did." |
| did fight | An irreg. intr. v., indic. m., past t., emph. form, s. num., 3rd per., agr. with its nom. *soul* und. |
| for | A prep., sh. the rn. bet. "did fight" and "me." |
| me. | A pers. pron., mas. gen., s. num., 1st per., obj. c., gov. by the prep. "for." |

## Exercise 190.

1. The heather *blooms*. 2. The fish *swims*. 3. The wood *burns*. 4. The bell *rings*. 5. The ship *sails*. 6. The sea *foams*. 7. The spring *advances*. 8. The boy *learns*. 9. The star *twinkles*. 10. The angel *guards*. 11. The snow *falls*. 12. The river *flows*. 13. The forest *shakes*. 14. The night *darkens*. 15. The branches *spread*. 16. The lion *roars*. 17. The Thames *is crossed*. 18. The sand *is scattered*. 19. The reaper *rests*. 20. The lamp *glimmers*. 21. The door *creaks*. 22. The fields *are parched*. 23. The blossom *fades*. 24. The drum *beats*. 25. The man *works*. 26. The eye *sees*. 27. The wind *sighs*. 28. The king *rules*. 29. The glass *is broken*. 30. The leaves *decay*. 31. The sun *shines*. 32. The lance *is shivered*.

## Exercise 191.

1. *The gate* swings. 2. *The chain* hangs. 3. *A voice* was heard. 4. *The reed* shakes. 5. *The cup* breaks. 6. *Rain* falls. 7. *The moon* rose. 8. *The stars* shone. 9. *The labourer* awakes. 10. *Summer* came. 11. *The hero* stood. 12. *The flower* decays. 13. *The tables* were laid. 14. *The miser* grasps. 15. *The breeze* blows. 16. *The lilies* bloom. 17. *The earth* moves. 18. *The guide* shouts. 19. *The child* blushes. 20. *The strangers* speak. 21. *Plants* grow. 22. *The cock* crows. 23. *The*

*Indians* gaze. 24. *The boy* lives. 25. *The brig* sailed. 26. *The windows* open. 27. *The warrior* smites. 28. *The prisoners* tremble. 29. *The bells* ring. 30. *The enemy* struck.

## Exercise 192.

| | Subject. | Predicate. | | Subject. | Predicate. |
|---|---|---|---|---|---|
| 1. | She | paused. | 11. | The doe | awoke. |
| 2. | The hall | was cleared. | 12. | The blackbird | warbled. |
| 3. | He | woke. | 13. | The fold | was guarded. |
| 4. | The bark | glides. | 14. | The shout | was hushed. |
| 5. | The dog | barked. | 15. | Wolves | howl. |
| 6. | The maid | replied. | 16. | The lark | carols. |
| 7. | The war-pipes | ceased. | 17. | The rose | blooms. |
| 8. | The boatman | rows. | 18. | The father | called. |
| 9. | The lightning | flashes. | 19. | The bull | was slain. |
| 10. | Time | flies. | 20. | The bows | are bent. |

## Exercise 193.

1. *Lands*, n. 2. *Skipper*, n. 3. *This*, adj. (sight und.). 4. *Storm*, n. 5. *Ship*, n. 6. *They*, pron. 7. *She*, pron. 8. *You*, pron. 9. *I*, pron. 10. *To delay longer*, infin. phrase. 11. *Mighty*, adj. (men und.). 12. "*Dust thou art, to dust returnest*," quotation. 13. *Boat*, n. 14. *Dew*, n. 15. *Each*, adj. (man und.). 16. *I*, pron. 17. *What*, pron. 18. *Roaming among the hills*, participial or gerundial phrase. 19. *Many*, adj. (persons und.). 20. *Sleeping*, pl. (persons und.). 21. *To dream of the past*, infin. phrase. 22. *They*, pron. 23. *To yield to remedies*, infin. phrase. 24. *Sleep*, n. 25. *I*, pron.

## Exercise 194.

1. *A*, adj.; *most celestial*, adj.; *of dainty music*, prepositional phrase; **sound.** 2. *The*, adj.; *of heaven*, prepositional phrase; **gentleness.** 3. *The*, adj.; *rising*, adj.; **moon.** 4. *Those*, adj.; *aged*, adj.; *olive*, adj.; **trees.** 5. *The wealthiest farmer of Grand-Pré*, n. in app. enlarged by adjectives (*the wealthiest*) and prepositional phrase (*of Grand-Pré*); **Benedict Bellefontaine.** 6. *The*, adj.; *being moved with compassion towards me*, participial phrase; **Genius.** 7. *The*, adj.; *of England*, prepositional phrase; **rose.** 8. *Some men's*, n. in poss. c. enlarged by adj. (*some*); **tempers.** 9. *A*, adj.; *breaking out in the cellar*, participial phrase; **fire.** 10. *Feeling it chilly*, participial phrase; **I.** 11. *Musing upon many things*, participial phrase; **I.** 12. *To see the evening star appear*, infin. phrase used as a n. in app.; **it.** 13. *The*, adj.; *sable*, adj.; *of the silent night*, prepositional phrase; **mantle.** 14. *Rich*, adj.; *fruitless*, adj.; *from wanton glory waged*, participial phrase; **war.** 15. *This*, adj.; *ruthless*, adj.; *in her jungle raging*, participial phrase; **tiger.**

## Exercise 195.

1. *Seemed a garden green*, a cop. v., followed by a n. in the nom. c. (the n. being enlarged by adjs. *a* and *green*). 2. *Are plentiful*, the v. "to be," followed by an adj. 3. *Stood open*, a cop. v., followed by an adj. 4. *Is short*, the v. "to be," followed by an adj. 5. *Is scorning to revenge an injury*, the v. "to be," followed by a participial or gerundial

phrase. 6. *Are open*, the v. "to be," followed by an adj. 7. *Am no pilot*, the v. "to be," followed by a n. in the nom. c. (the n. being enlarged by adj. *no*). 8. *Are of that sort*, the v. "to be," followed by a phrase: (In full, "we are *persons* of that sort ourselves"). 9. *Is of a religious nature*, the v. "to be," followed by a phrase: (In full, Work is *a thing* of a religious nature"). 10. *Had been to land in the Highlands*, the v. "to be," followed by an infin. phrase. 11. *Were gathering*, a finite v. 12. *Are good men and true*, the v. "to be," followed by a n. in the nom. c. (the n. being enlarged by *good and true*). 13. *Look'd sad and strange*, a cop. v., followed by adjs. 14. *Was in a deplorable condition*, the v. "to be," followed by a phrase: (In full, "The whole army was *an army* in a deplorable condition). 15. *Is of the same opinion*, the v. "to be," followed by a phrase: (In full, "A man convinced against his will is *a man* of the same opinion still").

## Exercise 196.

| | Subject. | Predicate. |
|---|---|---|
| 1. | The mob | recoiled. |
| 2. | Fierce cries | arose. |
| 3. | The French | appeared to be resting. |
| 4. | She | was [a princess] of the blood royal of England. |
| 5. | The sky | grew black. |
| 6. | Death | is bitter. |
| 7. | Life | is sweet. |
| 8. | The dykes | were frozen. |
| 9. | The marriage | was to pass quietly. |
| 10. | The weather | was wild |
| 11. | It | is a day of rain. |
| 12. | Glory built on selfish principles | is shame and guilt. |
| 13. | Work | is [a thing] of a brave nature. |
| 14. | The moon | is down. |
| 15. | To-day | is ours. |

## Exercise 197.

1. *Me*, pron. 2. *Field*, n. 3. "*God bless us*," quotation. 4. *To have my cause deferred*, infin. phrase. 5. "*To arms*," quotation. 6. *Thee*, pron. 7. *Pyramids*, n. 8. *Benefactor*, n. 9. *Stones*, n. 10. *Them*, pron. 11. *Prudent*, adj. (persons und.). 12. *To hear my counsel*, infin. phrase. 13. *Giving alms*, participial or gerundial phrase. 14. *Brave*, adj. (persons und.). 15. *To labour and to wait*, verbs in the infin. m.

## Exercise 198.

1. *His*, pron. in poss. c.; *watery*, adj.; **nest**. 2. *Most*, adj.; *of blessing*, prepositional phrase; **need**. 3. *A*, adj.; *gold*, adj.; **bow**. 4. *A*, adj.; *fairer*, adj.; **mortal**. 5. *A*, adj.; *to measure out the wind*, infin. phrase; **way**. 6. *The mind's*, n. in poss. c., enlarged by adj. (*the*); *cage*, adj.; **door**. 7. *No*, adj.; *help*. 8. *His*, pron. in poss. c.; **shop**. 9. *What*, pron. used as adj.; *modest*, adj.; **thoughts**. 10. *A*, adj.; *to mow*, v. in the infin. m.; **field**. 11. *The*, adj.; *quick*, adj.;

**kite.** 12. *The*, adj.; *of their lances*, prepositional phrase; **points.** 13. *My*, pron. in poss. c.; *flowing*, pl. used as adj.; **hair.** 14. *The*, adj.; *communicating with the Prince's room*, participial phrase; **door.** 15. *The*, adj.; *coming in to help his wearied hounds*, participial phrase; **hunter.**

### Exercise 199.

1. *The owl*, dir. [*to*] *scream*, indir. 2. *Us*, dir.; *mad* [*persons*], indir. 3. [*To*] *me*, indir.; *counsel*, dir. 4. [*To*] *him*, indir.; *eyes*, dir. 5. *Me*, dir.; [*to*] *accompany them in their search*, indir. 6. *You*, dir.; *to go away with it*, indir. 7. *An old man of fourscore*, dir.; *a child*, indir. 8. *Her*, dir.; [*to*] *dash with rapid wing*, indir. 9. *My ear*, dir.; [*to*] *catch your music*, indir. 10. *The apostle John*, dir.; [*to be*] *living in exile*, indir. 11. *The wind*, dir.; *to the shorn lamb*, indir. 12. *The echoes*, dir.; [*to*] *throng through the mountains*, indir. 13. *Three men*, dir.; [*to be*] *raising him up*, indir. 14. [*To*] *his landlord*, indir.; *no rent*, dir. 15. (*To*) *him*, indir.; *a hearty welcome*, dir. 16. *Me*, dir.; [*to*] *bear the blame for ever*, indir. 17. *The cares of empire*, dir.; *to his wiser colleague*, indir. 18. *Us*, dir.; *dull* [*persons*], indir. 19. *The trailing garments of the night*, dir.; [*to*] *sweep through her marble halls*, indir. 20. *The lights of the village*, dir.; [*to*] *gleam through the rain and the mist*, indir.

### Exercise 200.

1. *To thee*, object after prep.-v. 2. *Of your misfortunes*, object after prep.-v. 3. *To temporise*, infin. 4. *To sleep*, infin. 5. *With the tenets of Irenæus*, object after prep.-v. 6. *Of the trust*, genitive. 7. *For himself*, dative. 8. *To be obedient to the elders*, infin. 9. *Of the past*, object after prep.-v. 10. *Of the fleet's coming to Portsmouth*, object after prep.-v. 11. *Of robbery*, genitive. 12. *With his match*, object after prep.-v. 13. *Of my own native land*, object after prep.-v. 14. *Of fearful winds*, object after prep.-v. 15. *To him*, dative.

### Exercise 201.

1. *Across her mind*, prepositional phrase. 2. *How long*, adverbial phrase; *between two opinions*, prepositional phrase. 3. *Why*, adv.; *yet*, adv. 4. *Not*, adv. 5. *In a moment*, prepositional phrase; *with the wind cutting keenly at him sideways*, prepositional phrase; *down*, adv.; *to his boat*, prepositional phrase. 6. *Still*, adv.; *to thy side*, prepositional phrase. 7. *Still*, adv.; *in the depths of the valleys*, prepositional phrase. 8. *In twilight shade of tangled thickets*, prepositional phrase. 9. *For my sin*, prepositional phrase. 10. *The day having dawned*, nom. absolute; *down*, adv.; *to the beach*, prepositional phrase. 11. *Again*, adv. 12. *Now*, adv.; *beneath the skies*, prepositional phrase. 13. *Next morning, being Friday the third day of August, in the year* 1492, n. in the obj. c., with enlargements: *a little* [*time*] *before sunrise*, n. in the obj. c., with enlargements; *in presence of a vast crowd of spectators*, prepositional phrase. 14. *To-day*, adv.; *from the rock*, prepositional phrase. 15. *From the cool cistern of the midnight air*, prepositional phrase.

248 KEY TO

### Exercise 202.

1. How soon. 2. In such a night. 3. Some time. 4. On a starry night. 5. In a few moments. 6. This night. 7. At an early hour next morning. 8. For three nights. 9. At the instant. 10. In his early years; occasionally. 11. One morning in the month of May. 12. In the hours of prayer. 13. For a moment. 14. At midnight hour. 15. Ten years ago; ten years ago.

### Exercise 203.

1. At home; by thy quiet fire. 2. On his garments. 3. In the second chamber. 4. Across the sea. 5. In Asia. 6. At my feet. 7. From France. 8. Into the drawing-room. 9. To the curate's house in Kensington. 10. O'er Egypt's dark sea. 11. To Chalcedon. 12. From his sanctuary. 13. Round about him. 14. Under a spreading chestnut-tree.

### Exercise 204.

1. Like minutes. 2. In a wrong light. 3. With pleasure of her own. 4. With rapid gesticulations. 5. In silence. 6. Like the wolf on the folds. 7. Fast. 8. Very much. 9. Pleasantly. 10. Well. 11. With nimble glide. 12. By Mr. Pollard. 13. By a cannon shot. 14. With their colours displayed.

### Exercise 205.

1. To see you haste away so soon. 2. With delight. 3. To live alone. 4. With the cooling wind. 5. With impatience. 6. For a lowly flight. 7. For offending thee. 8. To bring you news. 9. For myself alone. 10. To sell their goods. 11. From fear (extension of cause to indir. obj., *to act*). 12. For delight. 13. To contradict. 14. Notwithstanding all their efforts. 15. With application.

### Exercise 206.

| | Subject. | Predicate. | Object. | Extension. |
|---|---|---|---|---|
| 1. | The moonlight | sleeps | | how sweet[ly] upon this bank |
| 2. | The word of Cæsar | might have stood | | but yesterday against the world |
| 3. | I | love | to stand by the foaming surge of ocean | |
| 4. | He | reads | of a shipwreck on the coast of Bohemia (*Indir. Obj.*) | perhaps |
| 5. | I | waited | for the train (*Indir. Obj.*) | at Coventry |

| | Subject. | Predicate. | Object. | Extension. |
|---|---|---|---|---|
| 6. | He | sat | | pondering over the strange chances of the day |
| 7. | I | breathe | this prayer (viz., Peace ! Peace !) | Orestes-like |
| 8. | To put the power of sovereign rule into the good man's hand | is giving peace and happiness to millions | | |
| 9. | We | were conducted | | immediately into the little chapel on the right hand |
| 10. | I, having often received an invitation from my friend Sir Roger de Coverley to pass away a month with him in the country | accompanied | him | last week thither |
| 11. | The lamed soldier, begging alms | hops | | here on timber-leg painfully along |
| 12. | He | went | | on speaking with great animation of gesture |
| 13. | I | tamed | the ger-falcon | far in the northern land by the wild Baltic strand with my childish hand |
| 14. | The cliffs | did reverberate | the sound of parted fragments tumbling from on high | oft |
| 15. | Dido | stood | | in such a night with a willow in her hand upon the wild sea-banks |

N.B.—In sent. 4, "reads-of" may be put as the pred., in which case "a shipwreck ... Bohemia" is dir. obj. In sent. 5, "waited-for" may be put as the pred., in which case "the train" is dir. obj.

## Exercise 207.

1. [That] they have awaked. 2. Whose power condemns me. 3. I have loved this lady long. 4. Whether supper would be ready soon.

5. "I have no need of thee." 6. That all this is mainly owing. 7. That about noon the rain would slacken. 8. Whether the mental powers of women be equal to those of men. 9. How they could deliver themselves. 10. (1) What they will; (2) what she list. 11. The design is to avoid the dreadful imputation of pedantry. 12. "It is good." 13. How our princely father 'scaped. 14. This aspect of mine hath feared the valiant. 15. (1) What you can make her do; (2) What [you can make her] to speak.

### Exercise 208.

1. Which I remember. 2. Whereof the chief stands in their metropolis. 3. Which was the best in the town. 4. Which is left. 5. Wherein Solyman's councils were revealed. 6. That beside her grows. 7. That ever burst into that silent sea. 8. [Which] I never entered. 9. Who was the darling of the tenants. 10. Which the Roman empire received. 11. When lilies blow. 12. Whose sound was like the sea. 13. Wherein the spirit held his wont to walk. 14. At which I knock in vain. 15. (1) Which thou behold'st; (2) but (=which not) in his motion like an angel sings, still quiring to the young-eyed cherubim.

### Exercise 209.

1. When Greeks joined Greeks. 2. When the mourner had got thus far in his story. 3. As they lowered the body into the earth. 4. While his life-blood ebbed away. 5. As they looked on him with astonishment. 6. When beggars die. 7. As he went. 8. Till I have pleased my discontented peers. 9. When I hear sweet music. 10. When the ice broke up. 11. Since I heard thee last. 12. After the storm of cavalry had passed. 13. As we went up the body of the church. 14. When first she gleamed upon my sight. 15. When the breeze of a joyful dawn blew free in the silken sail of infancy.

### Exercise 210.

1. Where ignorance is bliss. 2. Where'er we dwell. 3. Where your treasure is. 4. Where he lay. 5. Where the breakers roll'd. 6. Where the bee sucks. 7. Wheresoever the carcase is. 8. Where thou wilt. 9. Where thou art commanded. 10. Where the violets grow. 11. Where you will. 12. Where it best fits to be. 13. Wheresoe'er thou art in this world's globe. 14. Where all paves the way for death. 15. Where bleed the many to enrich the few.

### Exercise 211.

1. As the dew [is shed]. 2. As Moses did [use] his rod. 3. As curs mouth a bone. 4. (1) That, instead of paralysing his tongue, it even rendered him eloquent; (2) as [it did] on ordinary occasions. 5. Than sacrifice [is good]. 6. That I pulled out my purse. 7. The more I honour thee. 8. As water [is unstable]. 9. As [it] could be sad. 10. As children [deal] with their play. 11. As the rose [blossoms]. 12. As the forest is [thy lyre]. 13. As if they had heard of the loss of a dear friend—as [*they would turn pale*] if they had heard of the loss of

a dear friend. The sent. in italics is the adverbial sent. of man. 14. Than where castles mounted stand = *than* [*he shall be safe*] where castles mounted stand. The sent. in italics is the adverbial sent. of man. 15. Than are dreamt of in your philosophy = *than* [*the things are which*] are dreamt of in your philosophy. The sent. in italics is the adverbial sent. of man.

## Exercise 212.

1. If good fortune came. 2. If I forget thee. 3. That ye be not judged. 4. Though I could not broach it. 5. Though I thought it doubtful. 6. Although there is little or no rain in Egypt. 7. Lest he should be thought a coward. 8. For of it we make bread. 9. If an armed foe were near. 10. Because [it is] a very incorrect expression. 11. That I may live at ease. 12. (1) Though this proposal did not at all suit my inclination ; (2) Lest I should disoblige the only friend. 13. If parts allure thee. 14. If thou wouldst view fair Melrose aright. 15. [If] thy sunny realm and flowery gardens were mine.

## Exercise 213.

| | | Sentence. | Kind of Sentence. | Connective. | Subject. | Predicate. | Object. | Extension. |
|---|---|---|---|---|---|---|---|---|
| 1. | a. | The moving light had proved | Prin. sent. | | The moving light | had proved | | |
| | b. | which he beheld | Adj. sent. to *light* in a. | Rel. pron. | he | beheld | which | |
| | c. | that it was the residence of man. | Noun sent., object to a. | that | it | was the residence of man | | |
| 2. | a. | Then the road passes straight on through a waste moor | Prin. sent. | Then (introducing sent.) | the road | passes | | straight on through a waste moor |
| | b. | till at length the towers of a distant city appear before the traveller. | Adv. sent. (time) to a. | till | the towers of a distant city | appear | | before the traveller at length |
| 3. | a. | Our conductor pointed to that monument | Prin. sent. | | Our conductor | pointed | | to that monument |
| | b. | where there is the figure of one of our English kings without a head. | Adj. sent. to *monument* in a. | where (= on which) | the figure of one of our English kings without a head | is there | | |
| 4. | a. | As the evening darkened | Adv. sent. (time) to a. | As | the evening | darkened | | |
| | b. | Columbus took his station on the top of the castle or cabin in the high poop of his vessel. | Prin. sent. | | Columbus | took | his station | on the top of the castle or cabin in the high poop of his vessel |

| | | Sentence. | Kind of Sentence. | Connective. | Subject. | Predicate. | Object. | Extension. |
|---|---|---|---|---|---|---|---|---|
| 5. | a. | The bison is so sure-footed | Prin. sent. | | The bison | is so sure-footed | | |
| | b. | that he can pass over ground | Adv. sent. (manner) to a. | that | he | can pass | | over ground |
| | c. | where no horse could follow. | Adj. sent. to *ground* in b. | where (= on which) | no horse | could follow | | |
| 6. | a. | Plants must wait | Prin. sent. | | Plants | must wait | | |
| | b. | till their food comes to them. | Adv. sent. (time) to a. | till | their food | comes | | to them |
| 7. | a. | Whoever lost his footing in that fierce tumult | Noun sent., subject to b. | Compd. rel. | *Noun sent.* | lost | his footing | in that fierce tumult |
| | b. | ...never rose again. | Prin. sent. | | | rose | | never again |
| 8. | a. | Every milder method is to be tried | Prin. sent. | | Every milder method | is to be tried | | |
| | b. | before a nation makes an appeal to arms. | Adv. sent. (time) to a. | before | a nation | makes | an appeal to arms | |
| 9. | a. | She struck | Prin. sent. | | She | struck | | |
| | b. | where the white and fleecy waves look'd soft | Adv. sent. (place) to a. | where | the white and fleecy waves | look'd soft | | |
| | c. | as carded wool [is soft]. | Adv. sent. (manner) to b. | as | carded wool | [is soft] | | |

254　KEY TO

| | | Sentence. | Kind of Sentence. | Connection. | Subject. | Predicate. | Object. | Extension. |
|---|---|---|---|---|---|---|---|---|
| 10. | a. | While thus I sing | Adv. sent. (time) to b. | While | I | sing | | thus |
| | b. | I am a king | Prin. sent. | | I | am a king | | |
| | c. | Although [I am] a poor blind boy. | Adv. sent. (cause) to b. | Although | [I] | [am] a poor blind boy | | |
| 11. | a. | Yet some there be | Prin. sent. | Yet | some [persons] | be there | | |
| | b. | that by due steps aspire To lay their just hands on that golden key | Adj. sent. to (persons) in a. | Rel. pron. | that | aspire | to lay their just hands on that golden key | by due steps |
| | c. | That opes the palace of eternity. | Adj. sent. to key in b. | Rel. pron. | that | opes | the palace of eternity | |
| 12. | a. | When thou wouldst gather solace | Adv. sent. (time) to c. | When | thou | wouldst gather | solace | |
| | b. | When our child's first accents flow | Adv. sent. (time) to c, co-ord. to a. | When | our child's first accents | flow | | |
| | c. | Wilt thou teach her to say "Father" | Prin. sent. | | thou | wilt teach | her (Indir. Obj.) to say "Father" (Dir. Obj.) | |
| | d. | Though his care she must forego? | Adv. sent. (cause) to c. | Though | she | must forego | his care | |
| 13. | a. | Such were the sounds | Prin. sent. | | the sounds | were such | | |

| Sentence. | Kind of Sentence. | Connection. | Subject. | Predicate. | Object. | Extension. |
|---|---|---|---|---|---|---|
| b. that o'er the crested pride Of the first Edward scattered wild dismay | Adj. sent. to *scands* in *a*. | Rel. pron. | that | scattered | wild dismay | o'er the crested pride of the first Edward |
| c. As down the steep of Snowdon's shaggy side He wound with toilsome march his long array. | Adv. sent. (time) to *b*. | As | He | wound | his long array | down the steep of Snowdon's shaggy side with toilsome march |
| 14. a. That on yon bloomy spray Warblest at eve | Adj. sent. to nom. of add., *nightingale*. | Rel. pron. | that | warblest | | on yon bloomy spray at eve |
| b. when all the woods are still | Adv. sent. (time) to *a*. | when | all the woods | are still | | |
| c. Thou with fresh hope the lover's heart dost fill | Prin. sent. | | Thou | dost fill | the lover's heart | with fresh hope |
| d. While the jolly hours lead on propitious May. | Adv. sent. (time) to *c*. | While | the jolly hours | lead | propitious May | on |
| 15. a. I heard a thousand blended notes | Prin. sent. | | I | heard | a thousand blended notes | |
| b. While in a grove I sate reclin'd, In that sweet mood | Adv. sent. (time) to *a*. | While | I | sate | | in a grove reclined in that sweet mood |
| c. when pleasant thoughts Bring sad thoughts to the mind. | Adj. sent. to *mood* in *b*. | when (=in which) | pleasant thoughts | bring | sad thoughts (Dir. Obj.) to the mind (Indir. Obj.) | |

## Exercise 214.

1. (a) The fair breeze blew, (b) the white foam flew, (c) the furrow followed free. 2. (a) They drew off *and* (b) [they] encamped. 3. (a) [You] receive me, *and* (b) [you] shield my vexed spirit. 4. (a) Her little bird was stirring nimbly in its cage; *and* (b) the strong heart of its child-mistress was mute [for ever] *and* (c) [the strong heart of its child-mistress was] motionless for ever. 5. (a) They heard *and* (b) [they] were abashed. 6. (a) Another ranger dismounted *and* (b) [this ranger] came to his assistance. 7. (a) He is old; *moreover*, (b) he was confided to my care. 8. (a) He is not only bold *but* (b) *likewise* he is unscrupulous. 9. (a) He cannot deny it *nor* (=and not) (b) will he attempt to do so. 10. (a) They were exposed to an oblique fire from the batteries on the hills on both sides, *as well as* (b) [they were exposed] to a direct fire of musketry. 11. (a) They have been at a feast of languages, *and* (b) [they] have stolen the scraps. 12. (a) His directions were obeyed *and* (b) they pulled ashore directly. 13. (a) Your praise the birds shall chant in every grove, *And*, (b) winds shall waft it to the powers above. 14. (a) The whistling ploughman stalks afield; (b) Down the rough slope the ponderous waggon rings; (c) Through rustling corn the hare astonished springs; (d) Slow tolls the village clock the drowsy hour; (e) The partridge bursts away on whirring wings; (f) Deep mourns the turtle in sequester'd bower; *And* (g) shrill lark carols clear from her aërial tower.

## Exercise 215.

1. (a) I did not feel afraid, *or* (b) [I did not feel] *sorry*, *or* (c) [I did not feel] glad. 2. (a) What is Hecuba to him, *or* (b) [what is] he to Hecuba. 3. (a) *Neither* [thou be] a borrower, *nor* (b) [thou] be a lender. 4. (a) He received an appointment, *or* (b) [he received] the offer of a commission. 5. (a) *Either* we cannot absolutely approve willingness to die, *or* (b) [we cannot absolutely approve] forwardness to die. 6. (a) *Neither* we had a relation [in the world] *nor* (b) we had a friend in the world. 7. (a) He was singing [all the day] *or* (b) [he was] flirting all the day. 8. (a) *Either* it is sixteen [years ago] *or* (b) [it is] seventeen years ago. 9. (a) [Thou] drink deep, *or* (b) [thou] taste not the Pierian spring. 10. (a) [You] walk quickly, *else* (b) you will not overtake him. 11. (a) [You] awake, *or* (b) [you] be for ever fallen. (c) [You] arise [or (d) you be for ever fallen]. 12. (a) [You] let us do *or* (b) [you let us] die. 13. (a) *Either* he is drowned *or* (b) some passing ship has saved him. 14. (a) Was I deceived *or* (b) did a sable cloud Turn forth her silver lining on the night. 15. (a) *Either* he fears his fate too much *or* (b) his deserts are small. The adj. sents. are co-ord. (disjunc.), viz., (c) who dares not put it to the touch to gain [it all] *or* (d) [who dares not put it to the touch to] lose it all.

## Exercise 216.

F. 1. (a) Our wants are many and grievous, *but* (b) [they are] quite of another kind. 2. (a) I called him, *but* (b) he gave me no answer. 3. (a) In no wise [thou] speak against the truth, *but* (b) [thou] be abashed of the error of thy ignorance. 4. (a) [Thou] take each man's censure, *but* (b) [thou] reserve thy judgment. 5. (a) I will speak daggers to her, *but* (*b*) [I will] use none. 6. (*a*) His comrade bent to lift him, *but* (*b*) the spark of life had fled. 7. (*a*) Hatred stirreth up strifes, *but* (*b*) love covereth all sins. 8. (*a*) Some natural tears they dropped, *but* (*b*) [they] wiped them soon. 9. (*a*) Men may go, *But* (*b*) I go on for ever. 10. (*a*) My hasting days fly on with full career, *But* (*b*) my late spring [showeth] no bud. 11. (*a*) Not a sound rose from the city at that early morning hour, *But* (*b*) I heard a heart of iron beating in the ancient tower. 12. (*a*) Fitz-James looked round—*yet* (*b*) [he] scarce believed the witness. 13. (*a*) Her little hand lay lightly, confidingly in mine, *But* (*b*) we'll meet no more at Bingen—loved Bingen on the Rhine. 14. (*a*) [To them] his griefs were given, *But* (*b*) all his serious thoughts had rest in heaven. 15. (*a*) My thoughts still cling to the mouldering Past, *But* (*b*) the hopes of youth fall thick in the blast.

## Exercise 217.

1. (*a*) The smoke by no means escaped from its legitimate aperture, *for* (*b*) you might observe little clouds of it bursting out of the doors and windows. 2. (*a*) He blushes; *therefore* (*b*) he is guilty. 3. (*a*) Your rhetoric is too moving, *for* (*b*) it makes your auditory weep. 4. (*a*) Gewtrey seemed wounded, *for* (*b*) he staggered forward. 5. (*a*) [You] take courage *for* (*b*) this grief availeth nothing. 6. (*a*) She is a woman, *and therefore* (*b*) [she is] to be wooed. (*c*) She is a woman, *and therefore* (*d*) [she is] to be won. 7. (*a*) The squire is old, *for* (*b*) his hair is silver-grey. 8. (*a*) It will be fine weather to-day, *for* (*b*) the sky is red and lowering. 9. (*a*) The land is good, *for* (*b*) the crop is heavy. 10. (*a*) The crop is heavy, *therefore* (*b*) the land is good. 11. (*a*) [Thou] boast not thyself of to-morrow, *for* (*b*) thou knowest not. 12. (*a*) The angles are equal, *consequently* (*b*) the sides are equal. 13. (*a*) His friends must have deserted him; *for* (*b*) he was alone in the world. 14. (*a*) He must have done his duty, *for* (*b*) he is a good man. 15. (*a*) [You] take the instant way, *For* (*b*) honour travels in a strait so narrow.

## Exercise 218.

| | | Sentence. | Kind of Sentence. | Connective. | Subject. | Predicate. | Object. | Extension. |
|---|---|---|---|---|---|---|---|---|
| 1.(1) | a. | The man is one | Prin. sent. | | The man | is one | | |
| | b. | whom I call worthy of the name | Adj. sent. to *man* in a. | Rel. pron. | I | call | whom (Dir. Obj.) worthy of the name (Indir. Obj.) | |
| | c. | whose thoughts [are for others rather] | Adj. sent. to *one* in a. | Rel. pron. | whose thoughts | [are for others] | | [rather] |
| | d. | and [whose] exertions are for others rather | Adj. sent. to *one* in a, co-ord. to c. | and [Rel. pron.] | [whose] exertions | are for others | | rather |
| | e. | than [they are] for himself | Adv. sent. (manner) to c and d. | than | [they] | [are] for himself | | |
| | f. | whose high purpose is adopted on just principles | Adj. sent. to *one* in a, co-ord. to c, d. | Rel. pron. | whose high purpose | is adopted | | on just principles |
| | g. | and [whose high purpose] is never abandoned | Adj. sent. to *one* in a, co-ord. to c, d, f. | and [Rel. pron.] | [whose high purpose] | is abandoned | | never |
| | h. | while heaven and earth afford means of accomplishing it. | Adv. sent. (time) to g. | while | heaven and earth | afford | means of accomplishing it | |
| (2) | a. | He is one | Prin. sent. | | He | is one | | |
| | b. | who will neither seek an indirect advantage by a specious road | Adj. sent. to *one* in a. | Rel. pron. neither (introductory) | who | will seek | an indirect advantage | by a specious road |

## ENGLISH GRAMMAR AND ANALYSIS. 259

| | Sentence. | Kind of Sentence. | Connective. | Subject. | Predicate. | Object. | Extension. |
|---|---|---|---|---|---|---|---|
| c. | nor [who will] take an evil path to secure a really good purpose. | Adj. sent. to *one* in *a*, co-ord to *b*. | nor [Rel. pron.] | [who] | [will] take | an evil path | to secure a really good purpose |
| 2.(1) a. | Some blue peaks in the distance rose | Prin. sent. | | Some blue peaks | rose | | in the distance |
| b. | And white against the cold-white sky Shone out their crowning snows. | Prin. sent., co-ord. (cop.) to *a*. | And | their crowning snows | shone white | | out against the cold-white sky |
| (2) a. | One willow over the river wept | Prin. sent. | | one willow | wept | | over the river |
| b. | And [one willow] shook the wave | Prin. sent., co-ord. (cop.) to *a*. | and | [one willow] | shook | the wave | |
| c. | as the wind did sigh | Adv. sent. (time) to *b*. | as | the wind | did sigh | | |
| d. | Above, in the wind, was the swallow, Chasing itself at its own wild will | Prin. sent., co-ord. (cop.) to *a*, *b*. | | the swallow, chasing itself at its own wild will | was above in the wind | | |
| e. | And far through the marish green and still, The water-courses slept, Shot over with purple, and green, and yellow. | Prin. sent., co-ord. (cop.) to *a, b, d*. | And | The water-courses, shot over with purple, and green, and yellow | slept | | far through the marish green and still |
| 3.(1) a. | The oracles are dumb | Prin. sent | | The oracles | are dumb | | |
| b. | No voice runs through the arched roof in words deceiving | Prin. sent., co-ord. (cop.) to *a*. | | No voice | runs | | through the arched roof in words deceiving |

| | Sentence. | Kind of Sentence. | Connection. | Subject. | Predicate. | Object. | Extension. |
|---|---|---|---|---|---|---|---|
| c. | or [no] hideous hum [runs through the arched roof in words deceiving] | Prin. sent., co-ord. (disj.) | or | [no] hideous hum | runs | | [through the arched roof] [in words deceiving] |
| (2) a. | Apollo from his shrine Can no more divine, With hollow shriek the steep of Delphos leaving. | Prin. sent. | | Apollo, leaving the steep of Delphos with hollow shriek | can divine | | from his shrine no more |
| (3) a. | No nightly trance Inspires the pale-eyed priest from the prophetic cell | Prin. sent. | | No nightly trance | inspires | the pale-eyed priest | from the prophetic cell |
| b. | or [no] breathed spell [inspires the pale-eyed priest from the prophetic cell]. | Prin. sent., co-ord. (disj.) to a. | or | [no] breathed spell | [inspires] | [the pale-eyed priest] | [from the prophetic cell] |
| 4.(1) a. | But yesterday, the word of Cæsar might Have stood against the world | Prin. sent. | | the word of Cæsar | might have stood | | but (= only) yesterday against the world |
| b. | now lies he there | Prin. sent., co-ord. (advers.) | | he | lies | | there now |
| c. | and none [is] so poor to do him reverence. | Prin. sent., co-ord. (cop.) to b. | and | none | [is] so poor to do him reverence | | |
| (2) a. | If I were disposed to stir Your hearts and minds to mutiny and rage | Adv. sent. (cause) to b. | if | I | were disposed | to stir your hearts and minds to mutiny and rage (Indir. Obj.) | |

| | Sentence. | Kind of Sentence. | Connective. | Subject. | Predicate. | Object. | Extension. |
|---|---|---|---|---|---|---|---|
| 1. b. | Oh, masters! I should do Brutus wrong | Prin. sent. | | I | should do | wrong (Dir. Obj.) [to] Brutus (Indir. Obj.) | |
| c. | and [I should do] Cassius wrong | Prin. sent., co-ord. (cop.) to b. | and | [I] | [should do] | wrong (Dir. Obj.) [to] Cassius (Indir. Obj.) | |
| d. | Who are honourable men | Adj. sent. to Brutus in b, and Cassius in c. | Rel. pron. | who | are honourable men | | |
| e*. | [as] you all know. | Adv. sent. (manner) to d. | [as] | you all | know | | |
| 2. a. | Our young gentleman, by his insinuating behaviour, acquired the full confidence of the doctor | Prin. sent. | | Our young gentleman | acquired | the full confidence of the doctor | by his insinuating behaviour |
| b. | who invited him to an entertainment | Prin. sent., co-ord. (cop.) to a. | Rel. pron. | who (= and the doctor) | invited | him | to an entertainment |
| c. | which he intended to prepare in the manner of the ancients. | Adj. sent. to entertainment in b. | Rel. pron. | he | intended | to prepare which in the manner of the ancients | |
| 3. a. | Sickness is a sort of early old age | Prin. sent. | | Sickness | is a sort of early old age | | |

| | Sentence. | Kind of Sentence. | Connective. | Subject. | Predicate. | Object. | Extension. |
|---|---|---|---|---|---|---|---|
| b. | it teaches us a diffidence in our earthly state [better] | Prin. sent., co-ord. (cop.) to a. | | it | teaches | [to] us (*Indir. Obj.*) a diffidence in our earthly state (*Dir. Obj.*) | [better] |
| c. | and [it] inspires us with the thoughts of a future better | Prin. sent., co-ord. (cop.) to a, b. | and | [it] | inspires | us | with the thoughts of a future better |
| d. | than a thousand volumes of philosophers and divines [teach] | Adv. sent. (manner) to b. | than | a thousand volumes of philosophers and divines | [teach] | | |
| e. | [than a thousand volumes of philosophers and divines inspire] | Adv. sent. (manner) to c. | [than] | [a thousand volumes of philosophers and divines] | [inspire] | | |
| a. | As I looked more attentively | Adv. sent. (time) to b. | As | I | looked | | more attentively |
| b. | I saw several of the passengers dropping through the bridge into the great tide | Prin. sent. | | I | saw | several of the passengers (*Dir. Obj.*) [to be] dropping through the bridge into the great tide (*Indir. Obj.*) | |
| c. | that flowed underneath it | Adj. sent. to *tide* in b. | Rel. pron. | that | flowed | | underneath it |

| Sentence. | Kind of Sentence. | Connective. | Subject. | Predicate. | Object. | Extension. |
|---|---|---|---|---|---|---|
| d. and, upon further examination, [I] perceived | Prin. sent., co-ord. (cop.) to b. | and | [I] | perceived | | upon further examination |
| e. (that) there were innumerable trap-doors | Noun sent., object to d. | [that] | innumerable trap-doors | were there | | |
| f. that lay concealed in the bridge | Adj. sent. to trap-doors in e. | Rel. pron. | that | lay | | in the bridge concealed |
| g. which the passengers no sooner trod upon | Adj. sent. to trap-doors in e. | Rel. pron. | the passengers | trod | | upon which no sooner |
| h. but they fell through them into the tide | Adv. sent. (time) to g. | but (= than) | they | fell | | through them into the tide |
| i. and [they] immediately disappeared | Adv. sent. (time) to g., co-ord. to b. | and | they | disappeared | | immediately |
| 3.(1) a. Through the hushed air a whitening shower descends At first thin, wavering | Prin. sent. | | a whitening shower, at first thin, wavering | descends | | through the hushed air |
| b. till at last the flakes fall broad, dimming the day with a continual flow | Adv. sent. (time) to a. | till | the flakes, dimming the day with a continual flow | fall | | broad |
| c. and [the flakes fall] wide, [dimming the day with a continual flow] | Adv. sent. (time) to a, co-ord. to b. | and | [the flakes, dimming the day with a continual flow] | [fall] | | wide |

264  KEY TO

| | | Sentence. | Kind of Sentence. | Connective. | Subject. | Predicate. | Object. | Extension. |
|---|---|---|---|---|---|---|---|---|
| (2) | d. | and [the flakes fall] fast [dimming the day with a continual flow]. | Adv. sent. (time) to a, co-ord. to b, c. | and | [the flakes, dimming the day with a continual flow] | [fall] | | fast |
| | a. | The cherished fields put on their winter robe of purest white | Prin. sent. | | The cherished fields | put | their winter robe of purest white | on |
| | b. | 'Tis brightness all | Prin. sent., co-ord. (cop.) to a. | | it all | is brightness | | |
| | c. | save [it be] | Adv. sent. (cause) to b. | save | [it] | [be] | | |
| | d. | where the new snow melts Along the mazy current. | Adv. sent. (place) to c. | where | the new snow | melts | | along the mazy current |
| 3. | a. | The night has been unruly | Prin. sent. | | The night | has been unruly | | |
| | b. | where we lay | Adv. sent. (place) to c. | where | we | lay | | |
| | c. | Our chimneys were blown down | Prin. sent., co-ord. (cop.) to a. | | Our chimneys | were blown | | down |
| | d. | and Lamentings [were] heard i' the air | Prin. sent., co-ord. (cop.) to a, c. | and | Lamentings | [were] heard | | in the air |
| | e. | as they say | Adv. sent. (manner) to d. | as | they | say | | |

ENGLISH GRAMMAR AND ANALYSIS.   265

| | Sentence. | Kind of Sentence. | Connective. | Subject. | Predicate. | Object. | Extension. |
|---|---|---|---|---|---|---|---|
| f. | strange screams of death [were heard i' the air] | Prin. sent., co-ord. (cop.) to a, c, d. | | strange screams of death | [were heard] | | [in the air] |
| g. | And prophesyings with accents terrible Of dire combustions [were heard i' the air] | Prin. sent., co-ord. (cop.) to a, c, d, f. | and | prophesyings with accents terrible of dire combustions | [were heard] | | [in the air] |
| h. | and [prophesyings with accents terrible of] confused events New hatch'd to the woful time [were heard i' the air] | Prin. sent., co-ord. (cop.) to a, c, d, f, g. | and | [prophesyings with accents terrible of] confused events new hatch'd to the woful time | [were heard] | | [in the air] |
| i. | the obscure bird clamour'd the livelong night | Prin. sent., co-ord. (cop.) to a, c, d, f, g, h. | | the obscure bird | clamour'd | | the livelong night |
| j. | some say | Prin. sent., co-ord. (cop.) to a, c, d, f, g, h, i. | | some | say | | |
| k. | the earth Was feverous | Noun sent., object to j. | | the earth | was feverous | | |
| l. | and [the earth] did shake. | Noun sent., object to j, co-ord. to k. | and | [the earth] | did shake | | |

| | Sentence. | Kind of Sentence. | Connective. | Subject. | Predicate. | Object. | Extension. |
|---|---|---|---|---|---|---|---|
| 10. | | | | | | | |
| a. | Part in the plains contend | Prin. sent. | | Part | contend | | in the plains |
| b. | or [they contend] in the air sublime upon the wing | Prin. sent., co-ord. (disjunc.) to a. | or | [they] | [contend] | | in the air sublime upon the wing |
| c. | or [they contend] in the swift race | Prin. sent., co-ord. (disjunc.) to a, b. | or | [they] | [contend] | | in the swift race |
| d. | as [men contended] at th' Olympian games | Adv. sent. (manner) to a, b, c. | as | [men] | [contended] | | at th' Olympian games |
| e. | or [as men contended in the] Pythian fields | Adv. sent. (manner) to a, b, c, co-ord. to d. | or [as] | [men] | [contended] | | [in the] Pythian fields |
| f. | Part curb their fiery steeds | Prin. sent., co-ord. (advers.) to a. | | Part | curb | their fiery steeds | |
| g. | or [they] shun the goal with rapid wheels | Prin. sent., co-ord. (disjunc.) to f. | or | [they] | shun | the goal | with rapid wheels |
| h. | or [they] fronted brigades form | Prin. sent., co-ord. (disjunc.) to f, g. | or | [they] | form | fronted brigades | |
| i. | As [fronted brigades are formed] | Adv. sent. (manner) to h. | as | [fronted brigades] | [are formed] | | |

| | Sentence. | Kind of Sentence. | Connective. | Subject. | Predicate. | Object. | Extension. |
|---|---|---|---|---|---|---|---|
| k. | when, to warn proud cities, war appears Wag'd in the troubled sky | Adv. sent. (time) to *l*. | when | war | appears | | wag'd in the troubled sky to warn proud cities |
| l. | and [to warn proud cities], armies rush To battle in the clouds | Adv. sent. (time) to *j*; co-ord. to *k*. | and | armies | rush | | to battle in the clouds [to warn proud cities] |
| m. | before each van Prick forth the airy knights | Prin. sent., co-ord. (cop.) to *o, f*. | | airy knights | prick | | forth before each van |
| n. | and [they] couch their spears | Prin. sent., co-ord. (cop.) to *o, f, m*. | and | [they] | couch | their spears | |
| o. | Till thickest legions close | Adv. sent. (time) to *n*. | Till | thickest legions | close | | |
| p. | with feats of arms From either end of Heav'n the welkin rings. | Prin. sent., co-ord. (cop.) to *o, f, m, n*. | | the welkin | rings | | with feats of arms from either end of Heav'n |

### Exercise 219.

1. It wás | a fríar | of ór | ders gráy     *Iambic tetrameter.*
   Walk'd fórth | to téll | his béads.     *Iambic trimeter.*
2. 'Tis níght, and | the lándscape | is lóvely |   *Amphibrachic tetra-*
   no móre ;     *meter catalectic.*
   I móurn, but, | ye wóodlands, | I móurn not | for yóu.   *Do.*
3. I've séen | the smíl | ing    *Iambic dimeter hypermetrical.*
   Of fórtune | beguíling.    *Amphibrachic dimeter.*
4. Bówers a | diéu ! where | lóve de | cóying,   *Trochaic tetrameter.*
   Fírst en | thráll'd this | héart o' | míne.   *Trochaic tetrameter catalectic.*
5. I sáw from | the béach, when | the mórning   *Amphibrachic tetra-*
   | was shíning     *meter.*
   A bárk o'er | the wáters | move glórious | ly   *Amphibrachic tetra-*
   ón.     *meter catalectic.*
6. Líke le | vía | tháns a | flóat    *Trochaic tetrameter catalectic.*
   Láy their | búlwarks | ón the | bríne.   *Do.*
7. Fást they come, | fást they come    *Dactylic dimeter.*
   Sée how they | gáther.    *Dactylic dimeter catalectic.*
8. I bríng | fresh shówers | for the thírst | ing   *Iambic tetrameter.*
   flówers
   From the séas | and the stréams.    *Anapœstic dimeter.*
9. I have bréath'd on | the Sóuth, and | the   *Amphibrachic trimeter*
   chéstnut | flówers     *hypermetrical.*
   By thóusands | have búrst from | the fórest | bówers.   *Do.*
10. Mérrily, | mérrily | sháll I live | nów   *Dactylic trimeter hypermetrical.*
    Under the | blóssom that | hángs on the | bóugh.   *Do.*

THE END.

CPSIA information can be obtained
at www.ICGtesting.com
Printed in the USA
LVOW13s0237100718
583230LV00009B/152/P